Mastering
Autodesk® Inventor® 2011
and Autodesk®Inventor LT™ 2011

Mastering

Autodesk® Inventor® 2011 and Autodesk® Inventor LT™ 2011

Autodesk®
Official Training Guide

Curtis Waguespack

Thom Tremblay

Wiley Publishing, Inc.

Senior Acquisitions Editor: Willem Knibbe

Development Editor: David Clark

Production Editor: Dassi Zeidel

Editorial Manager: Pete Gaughan

Production Manager: Tim Tate

Vice President and Executive Group Publisher: Richard Swadley

Vice President and Publisher: Neil Edde

Book Designers: Maureen Forys, Happenstance Type-O-Rama; Judy Fung

Compositors: Jeffrey Lytle and Craig Woods, Happenstance Type-O-Rama

Proofreader: Publication Services, Inc.

Indexer: Ted Laux

Project Coordinator, Cover: Lynsey Stanford

Cover Designer: Ryan Sneed

Cover Image: © Richard Kolker / Photodisc / GettyImages

Copyright © 2010 by Wiley Publishing, Inc., Indianapolis, Indiana

Published simultaneously in Canada

ISBN: 978-0-470-88287-0

For general information on our other products and services or to obtain technical support, please contact our Customer Care Department within the U.S. at (877) 762-2974, outside the U.S. at (317) 572-3993 or fax (317) 572-4002.

Wiley also publishes its books in a variety of electronic formats. Some content that appears in print may not be available in electronic books.

Library of Congress Cataloging-in-Publication Data

Waguespack, Curtis, 1974-

 Mastering Autodesk Inventor 2011 and Autodesk Inventor LT 2011 / Curtis Waguespack, Thom Tremblay. — 1st ed.

   p. cm.

 ISBN: 978-0-470-88287-0 (pbk.)

 ISBN: 978-0-470-92211-8 (ebk)

 ISBN: 978-0-470-92213-2 (ebk)

 ISBN: 978-0-470-92212-5 (ebk)

 1. Engineering graphics. 2. Engineering models--Data processing. 3. Autodesk Inventor (Electronic resource) I. Tremblay, Thom, 1967- II. Title.

 T353.W183 2010

 620.0042'028553--dc22

                        2010023301

10 9 8 7 6 5 4 3 2 1

Dear Reader,

Thank you for choosing *Mastering Autodesk Inventor 2011 and Autodesk Inventor LT 2011.* This book is part of a family of premium-quality Sybex books, all of which are written by outstanding authors who combine practical experience with a gift for teaching.

Sybex was founded in 1976. More than 30 years later, we're still committed to producing consistently exceptional books. With each of our titles, we're working hard to set a new standard for the industry. From the paper we print on, to the authors we work with, our goal is to bring you the best books available.

I hope you see all that reflected in these pages. I'd be very interested to hear your comments and get your feedback on how we're doing. Feel free to let me know what you think about this or any other Sybex book by sending me an email at nedde@wiley.com. If you think you've found a technical error in this book, please visit http://sybex.custhelp.com. Customer feedback is critical to our efforts at Sybex.

Best regards,

Neil Edde
Vice President and Publisher
Sybex, an Imprint of Wiley

Acknowledgments

This book is a collaborative effort involving far more people than listed on the cover. Personally, we would like to thank our families, whose patience and understanding made this, and all other pursuits, possible. Professionally, we would like to thank the co-workers, clients, customers, and friends whose input and ideas have helped build the knowledge and experience that each of us draws from in applying concept to practice.

A special thank you goes out to the *Mastering Inventor 2009* team: Sean Dotson, Bill Bogan, Andrew Faix, Seth Hindman, Dennis Jeffrey, Loren Jahraus, Shekar Subrahmanyam, and Bob Van der Donck, all of whom are true masters of Inventor.

Thank you to the team at Wiley: David Clark, Jenni Housh, Connor O'Brien, Willem Knibbe, and Pete Gaughan, for their patience, focus, and professionalism, without which there would be no book. Your hard work and support have eased our efforts in turning ideas into pages.

—*Curtis Waguespack and Thom Tremblay*

About the Authors

Expert authors Curtis Waguespack and Thom Tremblay worked to pack this detailed reference and tutorial with straightforward explanations, real-world examples, and practical tutorials that focus squarely on teaching Inventor tips, tricks, and techniques. The authors' extensive experience across industries and their Inventor expertise allow them to present the software in the context of real-world workflows and work environments. Here is a bit more about each of them.

Curtis Waguespack is an Inventor Certified Expert and an Autodesk Manufacturing Implementation Certified Expert. He has served as lead author on two previous Autodesk Inventor books: *Mastering Autodesk Inventor 2009* and *Mastering Autodesk Inventor 2010*. He has taught Inventor in the classroom and has consulted with and supported manufacturing and design firms in industries ranging from aerospace, to consumer products, to industrial machinery. Curtis uses Inventor daily in a real-world design environment and has used Inventor to design a wide range of manufactured products.

Thom Tremblay is a Subject Matter Expert on the Autodesk Strategic Universities team. He is the author of two previous books on Autodesk Inventor: *Introducing Autodesk Inventor 2009 and Autodesk Inventor LT 2009* and *Autodesk Inventor 2010: No Experience Required*. Thom is an Inventor Certified Professional who has been using Autodesk software for 20 years to design everything from cabinets and castings to ships and video monitors. He has close ties to the Inventor community, is a frequent speaker, and presents at Autodesk University every year.

Contents at a Glance

Contents

Introduction

Autodesk Inventor was introduced in 1999 as an ambitious 3D parametric modeler based not on the familiar AutoCAD programming architecture but instead on a separate foundation that would provide the room needed to grow into the fully featured modeler it is now, a decade later. Inventor 2011 continues the development of Inventor with improved modeling, drawing, assembly, and visualization tools.

The maturity and continued development of the Inventor tool set coincides with the advancement of the CAD market's adoption of 3D parametric modelers as a primary design tool. And although it is important to understand that 2D CAD will likely never completely disappear from the majority of manufacturing design departments, 3D design will increasingly become a requirement for most. With this in mind, we have set out to fill the following pages with detailed information on the specifics of the tools, while addressing the principles of sound parametric design techniques.

Who Should Read This Book

This book is written with a wide range of Inventor users in mind, varying from beginner to advanced users and Inventor instructors:

◆ Beginner Inventor users who are making the move from traditional 2D CAD design to Inventor 2011. These readers might have experience with AutoCAD and will possess an understanding of basic design and engineering concepts, as well as a desire to improve their skill set and stay competitive in the marketplace.

◆ Intermediate Inventor users who are self taught or have gone through formal Inventor training during their company's initial implementation of Inventor and are looking for more information on a specific module within Inventor. This book also targets users looking for a desktop reference to turn to when they come upon an area of Inventor they do not encounter on a day-to-day basis.

◆ Advanced Inventor users who have mastered the Inventor tools used over and over daily but want to conquer the parts of the program they do not utilize during their normal design tasks. This book also targets advanced users who want to add to their skill set to move up the ranks within their current company or want to expand their knowledge in pursuit of a new position with another employer.

◆ Inventors of any skill and experience level who are preparing for the Inventor Associate or Professional exam.

◆ CAD and Engineering instructors looking for text to use in instructor led classroom training.

Attempting to learn all the tools in Inventor can be an intimidating experience, because of the wide range of task-specific modules available. It is the goal of this book to separate these modules into easy-to-tackle chapters relating to real-world situations for which the tools were designed, while also including chapters on general Inventor tools, techniques, and design principles.

What you will learn. The following pages will explain the Inventor settings while teaching you how each tool functions. Just as importantly, though, these pages are filled with the tips and techniques learned by the authors while spending years using, researching, and discussing the tools that are Autodesk Inventor. You should come away from reading this book with a solid understanding of the capabilities of Inventor and a strong idea of how to tackle your design challenges in the future, as well as an abundance of timesaving tips and tricks.

What you will need. The files needed to complete the tutorial projects in this book can be downloaded from the Sybex Publishing website at:

www.sybex.com/go/masteringinventor2011

Download the collection of zip files, and extract all of the files to a folder on your computer, such as \My Documents\Mastering Inventor 2011. In this folder you will have a subdirectory for each of the 19 chapters, plus a file called Mastering Inventor 2011.ipj, as shown here:

Once the files are in place, set the Mastering Inventor 2011 project active:

1. From within Inventor, close any open files.

2. From the Get Started tab, select the Projects button.

3. From the Projects dialog box select the Browse button.

4. From the Choose Project File dialog box browse to the Mastering Inventor 2011 folder and select the Mastering Inventor 2011.ipj file and click Open.

5. Note that the Mastering Inventor 2011 project is denoted as being the active project with a check mark.

6. Click Done to close the Projects dialog box. Now you are ready to get started. You'll find a more detailed explanation of working with and setting up projects in Chapter 2, "Data and Projects."

To install and run Inventor, you should consult the system requirements information found on the installation media and ensure that you have a system capable of running Inventor competently. For basic educational purposes dealing with small tutorial-sized assemblies, Autodesk recommends a minimum of 2 GB of RAM and 16 GB of available hard disk space to accommodate the installation files and temporary files created during the installation. Note that these are the minimums to install and run the program, and you might see slow performance when executing operations that require heavy calculations.

We recommend a 64 bit operating system with a minimum of 6GB of RAM for doing production work on moderate-sized assemblies and encourage you to consider an appropriate workstation when considering large assembly design. You can find more information about workstations specs and large assemblies in Chapter 9.

The Mastering Series

The Mastering series from Sybex provides outstanding instruction for readers with intermediate and advanced skills in the form of top-notch training and development for those already working in their field as well as clear, serious education for those aspiring to become pros. Every Mastering book includes the following:

◆ Real-world scenarios, ranging from case studies to interviews, that show how the tool, technique, or knowledge presented is applied in actual practice

◆ Skill-based instruction, with chapters organized around real tasks rather than abstract concepts or subjects

◆ Self-review test questions, so you can be certain you're equipped to do the job right

What Is Covered in This Book

This is what the book covers:

◆ Chapter 1, "Inventor Design Philosophy," covers how to design the "Inventor way" when transitioning from other 2D or 3D design applications.

◆ Chapter 2, "Data and Projects," examines file structures and search paths and explains project file types and configurations.

◆ Chapter 3, "Sketch Techniques," explores the principles of creating parameter-driven sketches for use in modeling features and parts.

◆ Chapter 4, "Basic Modeling Techniques," conquers creating parametric features and building 3D parts models.

◆ Chapter 5, "Advanced Modeling Techniques," explores complex feature creation including sweeps, lofts, and more.

◆ Chapter 6, "Sheet Metal," covers how to create accurate sheet-metal models and flat patterns as well as how to create documentation and set up sheet metal styles and templates.

◆ Chapter 7, "Part and Feature Reuse," examines the different methods for reusing parts and features for maximum consistency and design efficiency.

◆ Chapter 8, "Assembly Design Workflows," covers a thorough understanding of this key concept of Inventor design, including the use of assembly constraints, subassemblies, and more.

- Chapter 9, "Large Assembly Strategies," explores the tips and techniques to getting the best performance out of your Inventor workstation and considers upgrade requirements for the future.

- Chapter 10, "Weldment Design," explores Inventor's weldment modeling environment and the weldment documentation tools.

- Chapter 11, "Functional Design," gives you a thorough look at this collection of Inventor design accelerators and considers the difference between standard modeling and functional design.

- Chapter 12, "Documentation," covers how to use the Drawing Manager and presentation files to create both traditional, 2D annotated drawings as well as animated assembly instructions.

- Chapter 13, "Inventor Tools Overview," examines this collection of Inventor utilities including AutoLimits, the Design Assistant, the Drawing Resource Transfer Wizard, style tools, and much more.

- Chapter 14, "Exchanging Data with Other Systems," shows the available options for importing and working with solid models from other CAD packages.

- Chapter 15, "Frame Generator," covers how to get the most out of this utility when creating structural frames from Inventor's library of common shapes.

- Chapter 16, "Inventor Studio," covers this powerful tool set to create photorealistic images and animations of all your Inventor models.

- Chapter 17, "Stress Analysis and Dynamic Simulation," explores the simulation tools used to analyze load stress and mechanism motion on your models.

- Chapter 18, "Routed Systems," covers the cable and wire harness and tube and pipe environments and their uses in creating routed design layouts.

- Chapter 19, "Plastics Design Features," explores the tools used specifically for plastics design as well as the general tools used in specific ways for plastics design. Also included is the Inventor Tooling module used to design mold tooling for plastic part design.

- Appendix A, "The Bottom Line," gathers together all the Master It problems from the chapters and provides a solution for each.

- Appendix B, "The Autodesk Certification Exams," points you to the chapters in this book that will help you master the objectives for each exam.

How to Contact the Authors

We welcome your feedback concerning *Mastering Autodesk Inventor 2011*. We want to hear what you liked, what you didn't, and what you think should be in the next edition. And if you catch us making a mistake, please tell us so that we can fix it on our errata page (available at www.sybex.com/go/masteringinventor2011) and in reprints. Please email us at inventormasters@gmail.com or contact Wiley customer service at http://support.wiley.com.

Thank you for purchasing *Mastering Autodesk Inventor 2011*; we hope it helps you on your way to happy and successful inventing, and we look forward to hearing your comments and questions.

Chapter 1

Inventor Design Philosophy

In this chapter, you will be introduced to the concept of parametric 3D design and the general tools and interface of Inventor. This chapter will focus on the concepts of parametric modeling and the work flow, tools and interface elements found in Inventor that are used to turn your ideas into a design.

In this chapter, you will learn how to:

◆ Create parametric designs

◆ Get the "feel" of Inventor

◆ Use the Inventor graphical interface

◆ Work with Inventor File Types

◆ Move from AutoCAD to Inventor

◆ Create 3D virtual prototypes

◆ Use functional design

Understanding Parametric Design

Autodesk Inventor is first and foremost 3D parametric modeling software. And although it has capabilities reaching far beyond the task of creating 3D models, it is important for you to understand the fundamentals of parametric 3D design. The term *parametric* refers to the use of design parameters to construct and control the 3D model you create.

Creating a Base Sketch

Most typically, the 3D model starts with a 2D sketch, which is assigned dimensions and *2D sketch constraints* to control the general size and shape. These dimensions and constraining geometries are the parameters, or input points, that you would then change to update or edit the sketch. For instance, Figure 1.1 shows a base sketch of a part being designed.

FIGURE 1.1
Creating a
parametric
model sketch

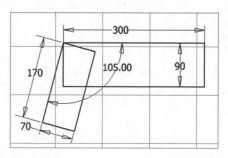

You can see four dimensions placed on the two rectangles defining the length and width of each, along with a fifth dimension controlling the angle at which the two rectangles relate. These dimensions are parameters, and if you were to change one of them, at any point during the design or revision of the part, the sketch would update and adjust to the change.

Creating a Base Feature

In addition to 2D sketch parameters, you add parameters to control the 3D properties of parts as well. This is done by using the sketch to create a feature, such as an extrusion, that gives a depth value to the sketch. The depth dimension is a parameter as well, and it can be updated at any time to adjust the part model as required. Figure 1.2 shows the previous sketch after it has been given a depth using the Extrude tool.

FIGURE 1.2
A basic part model created from the sketch

Adding More Features

Once the part is three dimensional, more sketches can be added to one surface or another of the 3D shape, and that new sketch can be used to create some feature that further defines the form and function of the design. The model is then enhanced with more features such as holes, fillets, chamfers, and so on, until it is complete. Each added feature is controlled by still more parameters defined by you, the designer. If a change is required, you simply update the parameter and the model updates accordingly. This type of parametric design allows you to build robust and intelligent models very quickly and update them even faster. Figure 1.3 illustrates the typical workflow of adding secondary features to a base feature to fully realize the part design, in this case a simple pivot link.

FIGURE 1.3
Adding features to complete the part model

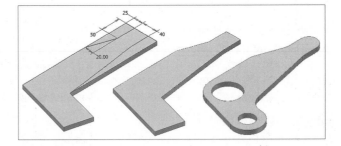

Using the Part in an Assembly

Once the part model is built up from the features you create, you can use it in an assembly of other parts created in the same manner. You can copy the part to create multiple instances of the same part, and you can copy the part file to create variations of the original part. In order to assemble parts, you create geometric relationships called *assembly constraints* defining how the parts go together. The constraints are parameters that can be defined and revised by you at any time in the design process as well. Part models can be arranged into small assemblies, and placed into larger assemblies, to create a fully realized subassembly structure that matches the way your design will be built on the shop floor. Figure 1.4 shows the part model from the previous illustrations placed multiple times in a subassembly and then that subassembly placed in a top-level assembly.

FIGURE 1.4
A subassembly and an assembly model using the part model

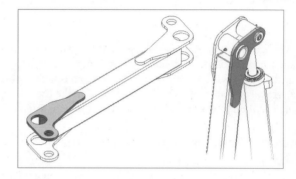

Making Changes

This process of creating parameter-based sketches, to define parameter-based features, to design a parameter-driven part, to then be used in parameter-driven assemblies, is essentially *parametric design*. Of course, as with building anything, there are general rules and best practices to be learned and followed in order to prevent your work from "falling apart." For instance, what if the pivot link used in the previous examples were to incur a design change that made one leg of the link longer? How would the holes be affected? Should they stay in the same place? Or should they stay at some defined distance from one end or the other?

Anticipating changes to the model is a large part of being successful with Inventor. Imagine, for instance, that a simple design change required that the pivot link become 50mm longer on one leg. This should be a simple revision that requires you only to locate the dimension controlling that leg length and change the parameter value. Unfortunately, if you did not follow the best-practices guidelines when creating the part originally, the change in the length might displace the secondary features such as holes and material cuts and require you to stop and fix each of those as well. This is one of the most frustrating parts of learning Inventor for any new user who has not taken the time to learn or follow the known best practices of parametric modeling. Fortunately for you, within the pages of this text you will learn how to create models that are easy to update and do not "fall apart" during design changes.

Understanding History-Based Modeling

Inventor is often referred to as a history-based modeler, meaning that as you create sketches and turn them into features, and then add more features and still more features, each addition is based on a previous feature, and so the model is said to have history. This history is recorded and tracked in the model browser. The model browser is a panel that displays on-screen and shows every feature you create during the design of your part. Figure 1.5 shows the model browser for the pivot link file.

FIGURE 1.5
The model browser showing the feature tree (history) of a part named Pivot_Link.ipt

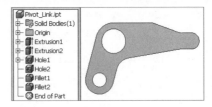

You can see that each feature is listed in the browser in the order it was created, forming a history tree. In order to create a part that handles changes predictably, you must create a solid foundation on which to build the rest of the model. In most cases, when you are designing a part model you will start off with a sketch, much like the one shown back in Figure 1.1. This base sketch will be your foundation, and therefore you must create it to be as stable as possible.

Looking Closer at Sketch Dimensions

A large part of creating a stable sketch is understanding the way Inventor's sketch dimensions work. To do so you might compare Inventor dimensions with AutoCAD's standard dimensions. When you created a design in AutoCAD, that design process was not much different from creating the same design on a drawing board. But in AutoCAD you can draw precise lines, arcs, circles, and other objects and place them precisely and with accurate dimensions reflecting your design, in a way that you cannot do by hand. When a design requires modification, you erase, move, copy, stretch, and otherwise manipulate the existing geometry more quickly than you can by hand as well. But other than those gains in speed and accuracy, the workflow is much the same as working on a drafting board. In short, AutoCAD automates drafting tasks but does less to speed up and enhance the design process.

DRIVEN DIMENSIONS

Standard dimensions in AutoCAD are called driven or reference dimensions. A *driven dimension* is controlled by the geometry, and it reflects the actual value of the geometry that is referenced by the dimension. If you stretch a line, for example, the dimension attached to the line will update to the new value. If you think about it, the only reason for a dimension on a typical AutoCAD drawing is to convey the value of a feature or part to the person who is going to build it. If you import that 2D file into a CAM package, no dimensions are needed because the line work contains all the information about the part.

PARAMETRIC AUTOCAD

Starting with AutoCAD 2010, you can create 2D parametric dimensions and constraints much like Inventor.

DRIVING DIMENSIONS

The workflow in Inventor sketching is substantially different from that of traditional AutoCAD, even beyond dimensions. In Inventor, you create sketches in 2D and then add geometric constraints such as horizontal, vertical, parallel, and so on to further define the sketch entities. Adding the geometric constraints allows line work to adjust in a predictable and desired manner and helps control the overall shape of the sketch. Once geometric constraints are in place, you add parametric *driving dimensions* to the sketch geometry. By changing the value of the dimension, you change or drive the size of the sketch object. As you can see, the Inventor dimension is far more powerful than the standard AutoCAD dimension because it not only conveys the value of a feature or part but also serves as a design parameter, allowing you to change the dimension to update the design. Figure 1.6 shows dimensions being edited in a sketch on the left and the result of changing three of the dimensions on the right.

FIGURE 1.6
Editing Inventor
sketch dimensions

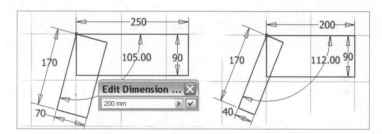

Part Modeling Best Practices

A solid sketch is the foundation on which stable parts are built. Many new users do not understand the importance of having fully constrained sketches, and they find it highly frustrating to have a model fail when a simple change is made, all because a sketch was not properly constructed.

KEEP SKETCHES SIMPLE

The most effective way to create a healthy sketch is to keep it simple. The purpose of keeping your base sketch simple is to get it fully defined, leaving no part of it up for interpretation. Undefined, sketch entities (lines without defined lengths, circles without defined diameters, and so on) will most likely not update properly and will cause your sketches to distort and break when you try to update them. And because you will base the rest of you model on the initial sketch, your entire feature tree comes crumbling down, requiring you to have to stop and spend time rebuilding it again. If the idea of simple sketches seems not to fit the type of design you do, understand that most any design will benefit from the simple sketch philosophy. More important, if you start out employing simple sketches, you will more quickly master the sketch tools and then be ready to create more complex sketches when a design absolutely requires it.

CREATE SIMPLE FEATURES FROM SIMPLE SKETCHES

Another aspect of creating simple sketches is that it allows you to create simple features. Parametric feature-based modeling relies on the creation of numerous simpler features within the model, to achieve a complex design in the end. By creating a number of features within the model, you are able to independently change or modify a feature without rebuilding the entire model. An example of editing a feature would be changing a hole size. If you create a base feature first and then create a hole feature in that base feature, you can makes changes to both independently.

PATTERN AND MIRROR AT THE FEATURE LEVEL

Although there are mirror and pattern (array) tools in the sketch environment, it is generally best to create a single instance of the item in the sketch, then create a feature from it, and create a mirror or pattern feature from that feature. The logic behind this is based on the previous two ideas. First, this approach keeps the sketch simple. Second, should the mirror or pattern feature need to be updated, it is much easier to do so as a separate feature.

CREATE SKETCH-BASED FEATURES AND THEN PLACED FEATURES

Part features can be broken into two categories: sketch based and placed. *Sketch-based features*, as you might guess, are created from sketches. *Placed features* are features such as fillets and chamfers that are placed on model edges or faces and have no underlying sketch. Issues arise when placed features are created too early in the development of the part, because you may then be required to dimension to the placed feature, which creates a weak dependency, for instance, if you place fillets along the edges of a part and then use the fillet edges to define the placement of a hole. But then if you realize that machining capabilities require a beveled chamfer edge rather than a rounded filleted one, the hole feature is sure to fail. Keep this in mind as you create placed features such as fillets and chamfers, and reserve placed features for the end stages of the part.

UNDERSTAND DEPENDENT AND INDEPENDENT FEATURES

Parametric model features are typically either dependent or independent of one another. A *dependent* feature is dependent on the existence or position of a previously created feature. If that previously created feature is deleted, then the dependent feature will either be deleted also or will become an independent feature. Each part file contains default origin geometry that defines the X, Y, and Z coordinates of the part. These origin features are used to create the first sketch in every part by default. An *independent* feature is normally based on an origin feature or is referenced off the base feature.

For instance, in order to create the base feature for the pivot link, you would create a sketch on a default origin plane, such as the XY plane. Because the XY origin plane is included in every part file and cannot be changed, your base feature is stable and independent of any other features that may follow. To create a hole in the base feature, you would typically select the face of the base feature to sketch on. Doing so would make the hole feature dependent on the base feature. The hole feature then, is inherently less stable than the base feature, because it relies on the base feature to define its place in 3D space.

Although the specifics of how sketches, features, and parts are created will be covered in the chapters to come, remember these principles concerning part file best practices, and you will find Inventor (and any other parametric modeler) much more accommodating.

Assembly Modeling Best Practices

Once you've created part files, you will put them together to build an assembly. And when you do, you want to build it to be as stable as possible, so that if you move, replace, or remove a part, the rest of the assembly will not fall apart. There are two parts to an assembly: links to the components it is made of and the geometric information about how those parts fit together. Basic assemblies are not much more than that, and understanding those two concepts will go a long way toward building stable assemblies.

UNDERSTAND FILE LINKING AND RELATIONSHIPS

The assembly file can be thought of as an empty container file to start. Once you place the first part in the assembly, the assembly file contains a link to that part file. When you place a second part and fit it to the first, the assembly then contains links to the two files and the information about how those files go together. If you decide to rename the first part file, and do so using Windows Explorer, the assembly file will still be looking for the file by the old name. When this happens, you will be prompted with a file resolution dialog box, asking you where the file went. You can then browse and manually point the assembly to that file, and it will record the new name in its internal link. If you decide to move the second part file to some other folder than its original, the assembly file might again prompt you to find it manually, depending on the folder structure. It should be your goal to never need to resolve file links manually, and understanding this part of how assemblies work is the first step in doing so. In the coming chapters you will learn how to set up Inventor properly so it can find your files without issue.

ALWAYS MAINTAIN AT LEAST ONE GROUNDED COMPONENT

To understand how grounded parts help you build stable assemblies, you should first understand a little about the assembly model browser. Figure 1.7 shows the model browser for an assembly model of a small hobby-type CNC router.

FIGURE 1.7
The model browser showing the model tree of an assembly named Router.iam

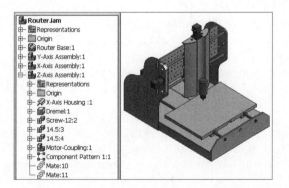

The model browser shows an assembly named Router Base at the top and under it three other assemblies named Y-Axis Assembly, X-Axis Assembly, and Z-Axis Assembly. The Z-Axis Assembly is expanded in the browser so you can see the parts it is made of as well. You should note that the

Router Base assembly is shown in the browser with a pushpin icon. This denotes that this assembly is grounded or pinned in place, and its coordinates cannot accidentally change. Keeping one grounded component in each assembly will allow you to fit other parts to it without it moving. You might imagine the old carnival game where you throw a ball at a pyramid stack of metal bottles. To win the game you had to knock down all of the bottles. However, if the bottle in the center on the bottom was nailed down, it was impossible to win the game, and as a matter of physics, it was more difficult to knock down the bottles next to it. Having a grounded component in your assemblies, one that is "nailed down," will likewise keep your assemblies from falling apart as you build on to it. You should note that by default the first component you place will automatically be grounded. You can unground it and ground another if need be, but you should always maintain at least one grounded component. You can also have more than one grounded component.

MAKE YOUR MODELS MIMIC THE MANUFACTURING PROCESS

The simplest advice that we can give to new users on the subject of assemblies is to structure them as you would in real life. If in the design you plan to assemble several parts into a transmission and then drop that transmission into a housing, then you should make the transmission a subassembly and insert it into the upper-level housing assembly. By making your models mimic the manufacturing process, you can also find possible flaws in your design, such as fasteners that cannot be accessed or areas where parts may interfere with each other during assembly.

In some instances a model will be developed in the research and development department and then handed to the manufacturing engineering department to be built. Although R&D may enjoy the freedom of "dreaming up" anything they can think of, an effective R&D designer will always have one eye on what can actually be built. Keep this in mind during the initial development cycle, and it will prevent those downstream of you from having to re-create much of your work. However, if restructuring the components into more or less subassemblies is required after the initial design, Inventor has demote and promote tools to assist with that. These tools will be covered in the chapters to come.

CONSTRAIN TO ORIGIN GEOMETRY

Each part file has default origin geometry built in. You should build parts around the origin geometry whenever possible. For instance, a transmission has gears, bearings, seals, and so on that are all concentric with the shaft. If you model all the parts so their x-axes will be aligned in the assembly, then it will be more stable. If you constrain the parts by selecting model features, you run the risk of constraints failing after a revision to a part that changes or removes the referenced geometry. In order to build a completely bulletproof assembly, you could constrain each part to the origin geometry of the assembly. In this way no matter how the geometry of the parts change, it will not cause issues with assembly constraints.

You will learn more about how to create assemblies, set up search paths to avoid manual file resolutions, and work with grounded components in the coming chapters, but you should remember these concepts and work to abide by them.

Understanding the "Feel" of Inventor

To the new user, Inventor's ever-changing interface may seem a bit disorienting. Taking a few minutes to understand why menus and tools change from one context to another will go a long way in getting comfortable with the "feel" of Inventor and anticipating the way it works.

Understanding the Intuitive Interface

The overall interface of Inventor might be called context intuitive, meaning that it changes menus depending on task and environment. Inventor works by grouping tools onto tabs that offer only the tools needed for the appropriate task at hand. If you are sketching a base feature, the tools you see are sketch tools. In Figure 1.8 the 2D Sketch tab is active, and displayed are tools you use to create and dimension sketches.

FIGURE 1.8
The Sketch tab and sketch tools

Upon the completion of a sketch, click the Finish Sketch button on the far right and you will exit the sketch. In doing so, the Model tab becomes active and the Sketch tab is hidden. This allows you to see the tools that are appropriate for the immediate task and only those tools, without having to hunt around for them. If you create a new sketch or edit an existing one, the Sketch tab is immediately brought back. Figure 1.9 shows the active Model tab.

FIGURE 1.9
The Model tab and model tools

When you work with assemblies, the tool tab changes to the Assemble tab (as shown in Figure 1.10), allowing you to place components, create new components, pattern them, copy them, and so on. There are also a number of other tabs shown that you can switch to at any time in order to use those tools.

FIGURE 1.10
The Assemble tab and assembly tools

When you create a 2D drawing of parts or assemblies, you are automatically presented with tools needed to create views and annotation. By default the Place Views tab is displayed because you need to create a view of a model before annotating it. However, you can manually switch to the Annotation tab by double-clicking it. Figure 1.11 shows the active Place Views tab and the inactive Annotate tab next to it.

FIGURE 1.11
The drawing tabs and drawing tools

As you can see, the collection of tabs (called the Ribbon menu) changes intuitively with every task or environment you switch to. With a task-based user interface, there is no need to display every possible tool all at once. In the next section you will explore more of the user interface.

Using General Tools vs. Specific Commands

In this section you'll compare the way Inventor tools are set up with those of AutoCAD. If you've never used AutoCAD, you can still gain some insight from this section, although you may have to use your imagination concerning the references to AutoCAD. A key difference between AutoCAD and Inventor is that in AutoCAD many commands are very specific. For example, there are different dimension commands for lines, angles, and circles. In contrast, Inventor has one General Dimension tool that creates the appropriate dimension based on what you select.

For instance, in AutoCAD you might select the horizontal dimension tool to place a dimension on a horizontal line, then select the diameter dimension tool to place a dimension on a hole, then select a radius dimension tool to place a dimension on a fillet, and so on. But in Inventor you select the General Dimension tool, select a horizontal line, and you get a horizontal dimension; then without exiting the dimension tool, you select a circle, and you automatically get a diameter dimension. And of course to dimension a fillet, you continue with the general dimension tool, and you will automatically get a radius dimension.

When in Doubt, Right-Click

Inventor is very right-click driven, meaning that many of the options are context specific and can be accessed by right-clicking the object in question. For instance, if you want to edit a sketch, you right-click the sketch in the browser and choose Edit Sketch. The same is true of a feature. If you wanted to change a hole feature from a countersink to a counterbore, you would right-click it in the browser and choose Edit Feature. You can right-click many objects in the graphics window, with no need to locate them in the browser.

Also worth mentioning are the options in the context menus. For instance, if you are editing a part in an assembly, and want to finish the edit and return to the assembly level, you could use the Return button on the Sketch tab menu, or you could just right-click (taking care not to click any sketch object) and choose Finish Edit from the context menu. Both options do the same thing.

DRAWING IN AUTOCAD BECOMES SKETCHING IN INVENTOR

The fundamental difference between traditional AutoCAD and Inventor is that in AutoCAD you draw and in Inventor you sketch. The difference sounds subtle but is very important. In AutoCAD you likely construct lines precisely to specific dimensions to form the geometry required. In Inventor you create lines and geometry that reflect the general form and function of the feature and then use constraints and dimensions to massage it into the desired shape. This is probably the single biggest stumbling block that experienced AutoCAD users face when starting to use Inventor.

Using the Inventor Graphic Interface

The Inventor graphic interface might be different from what you are accustomed to in other general software applications and even different from other design software. In Figure 1.12, you see the entire Inventor window, which shows an assembly file open for editing.

FIGURE 1.12
The complete Inventor screen in assembly mode

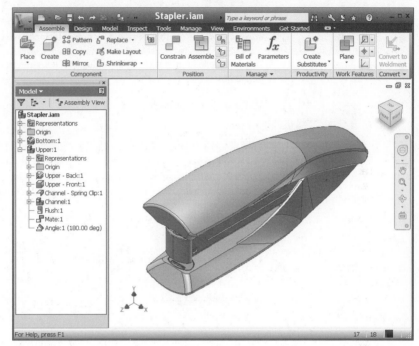

Inventor Title Bar

Starting at the upper left of the Inventor window, the Inventor button has a drop-down panel similar to the File menu in previous versions. The title bar includes two toolbars:

◆ The Quick Access toolbar has frequently used tools.

◆ The Help toolbar provides access to help files and Autodesk websites.

You can customize the Quick Access toolbar for each file type by selecting and deselecting icons from a list. The list of available tools can be accessed by clicking the drop-down arrow shown on the far right of Figure 1.13.

FIGURE 1.13
The Inventor button and Quick Access toolbar

Table 1.1 defines all the Quick Access toolbar icons available for the different file types.

TABLE 1.1: Quick Access toolbar icons

ICON	DEFINITION
	The New icon launches the New File dialog box. The drop-down list allows you to create a new part, assembly, drawing, or presentation file using the standard templates.
	The Open icon launches the Open dialog box. It displays a location defined in your active project.
	The Save icon saves the file.
	The Undo icon undoes the last action. The Undo list tracks changes for the current Inventor session, not just the current document. If you have two part files open, this icon will undo changes that are made in both files. Undo will also close files if your undo sequence takes you back past the point of a file being opened or created.
	The Redo icon restores a change that was removed with Undo. It will reopen a file that was closed with Undo.
	The Open From Vault icon opens a file in your Vault.
	The Print icon launches the Print dialog box. Drawings have a special Print Drawing dialog box with more controls.
	The iProperties icon launches an Inventor file properties dialog box.
	The Projects icon launches a dialog box to manage project files. Project files are used to help maintain references between files. You can have only one active project at a time, and you can't switch projects when a file is open.
	The Return icon switches from the current environment to the previous one. For example, if you are editing a part in an assembly, Return will take you back to the assembly environment.
	The Update icon updates the files. For example, if you edit a part in an assembly, other parts might need to be updated because of the changes. It is grayed out unless the file needs to be refreshed.
	The Select icon allows you to choose a filter for object selection.
As Material	The Color Override setting allows you to change the display color. This is a local override and does not change the component. For example, if you place a bolt in an assembly and change the color to Gold, the next bolt you place will still have the original color.

TABLE 1.1:   Quick Access toolbar icons   *(CONTINUED)*

ICON	DEFINITION
✚	The Design Doctor icon launches a dialog box that helps you diagnose and repair issues with a file. It is grayed out unless there is an issue.
▨	The Update All Sheets icon is used in the drawing environment to update all the sheets in a drawing at once.
f_x	The Parameter icon is used to access the parameters table where you can rename, change, and create equations in dimension and design parameters.
⊨	The Measure icon brings up the measure tool, allowing you to take distance, angle, loop, or area measurements from model edges, vertices, and faces.

The Help toolbar, shown in Figure 1.14, gives direct access to help files and Autodesk websites. Table 1.2 defines each Help toolbar icon.

FIGURE 1.14
The Help toolbar

TABLE 1.2:   Help toolbar icons

ICON	DEFINITION
🔍	The Search icon finds help topics that contain the keywords you enter in the field. You can click the down arrow next to the Search icon to select a specific section of Inventor Help.
🔑	The Subscription Center icon displays information from the Subscription Center site.
📡	The Communication Center icon displays information from the Communication Center site.
☆	The Favorites icon displays items that you have marked as favorites. This can include help topics and items from the Subscription Center and Communication Center.
?	The Help Topics icon launches Inventor Help. You can also press F1 to access Help at any time. Pressing F1 while in a command will activate Help for that specific command.

Inventor Graphics Window Tools

Inventor has two sets of tools for manipulating the graphics window:

◆ The *ViewCube* is used to change the view orientation.

◆ The *Navigation Bar* has tools such as Zoom and Pan.

EXPLORING THE VIEW CUBE

The ViewCube, shown in Figure 1.15, is a 3D tool that allows you to rotate the view. Here are some viewing options:

◆ If you click a face, edge, or corner of the cube, the view rotates so the selection is perpendicular to the screen.

◆ If you click and drag an edge, the view rotates around the parallel axis.

◆ If you click and drag a corner, you can rotate the model freely.

◆ If you click a face to have an orthogonal view, additional controls will display when your mouse pointer is near the cube.

◆ The four arrowheads pointed at the cube rotate the view to the next face.

◆ The arc arrows rotate the view by 90 degrees in the current plane.

FIGURE 1.15
The ViewCube

If you click the Home icon (looks like a house), the view rotates to the default isometric view. Clicking the drop-down arrow, or right-clicking the Home icon, reveals several options to change the default isometric view behavior. For instance, you can modify the home view to any view you like, and you can reset the front view in relation to your model so the named views of the cube match what you consider the front, top, right, and so on.

USING A WHEEL MOUSE AND 3D INPUT DEVICE

Using a wheel mouse with Inventor is recommended. Scrolling the wheel will perform a Zoom In/Out, while pressing the wheel will perform the Pan function. In Inventor, the wheel zoom is reversed from AutoCAD. You can change this setting by going to the Tools tab, clicking Application Options, selecting the Display tab, and selecting Reverse Direction in the 3D Navigation group.

Another useful tool for navigating in Inventor is a 3D controller device. A popular brand is the Space series made by 3Dconnexion. These devices are small "joysticks" or "pucks" that sit on your desk. The user grasps the puck, and by making very slight movements with the device, the model on the screen moves. Pulling, pushing, and twisting the puck allows you to zoom, pan, and orbit the model on-screen. Although you may find these devices awkward at first, most users say they could never work as efficiently without one after just a few days of use.

A Look at the Navigation Bar

Continuing with the interface tour, you'll see the navigation bar located on the right side of the graphics window. At the top of the bar is the steering wheel. Below the steering wheel are the other standard navigation tools: Pan, Zoom, Orbit, and Look At. Figure 1.16 shows the navigation bar.

FIGURE 1.16
The Navigation Bar

You can use the navigation bar's steering wheel to zoom, pan, walk, and look around the graphics area. Also available is the ability to rewind through previous steering wheel actions. The steering wheel has more functionality than can be explored in this book. You should review the help topics for more information (click the steering wheel and then click F1).

NAVIGATION TOOLS TUTORIAL

You can find a full tutorial exploring each of the navigation tools built right into Inventor, complete with tutorial files. To run through the Navigation Tools tutorial select the Get Started tab on the Ribbon menu and then click the Tutorials button. This will bring up the built-in Tutorial Learning Resource page. Select the New Users tab and choose the Navigation Tools selection below.

This will bring up a Tutorials help pane. You can advance through the tutorial by using the list on the left, or if you prefer to hide the list to gain more screen space, use the small arrows in top-right corner.

In order to follow the built-in tutorials, you'll need to point Inventor to the files by setting the project search path to tutorial_files. To do so follow these steps:

1. In Inventor, close any open files.

2. From the Get Started tab, click the Projects button.

3. In the Projects dialog box, select tutorial_files from the list.

4. Click the Apply button at the bottom of the Projects dialog box.

5. Note the check mark next to tutorial_files in the list, denoting that it is the active project, and then click Done to close the Projects dialog box.

Now you can return to the Tutorials help pane and follow along. More information about projects can be found in the next chapter.

The Ribbon Menu

The *Ribbon menu* is similar to the one introduced in Microsoft Office 2007 in that it is composed of tabs and panels. Each tab contains panels for a particular task, such as creating sketches, and each panel contains related buttons. As previously mentioned, the Ribbon will change to the proper tab based on the current task (for example, sketching brings up the Sketch tab), but you can select a different tab as needed.

You can customize the Ribbon menu by doing the following:

◆ Turning off tool button text, reducing icon size, or using a compact icon layout

◆ Turning off panels that you don't use

◆ Adding frequently used commands to a tab

◆ Minimizing the Ribbon

◆ Undocking the Ribbon so it becomes a floating tool palette

◆ Docking the Ribbon on the left, right, or top of the Inventor window

THE GET STARTED TAB

Most of the icons on the Get Started tab link to help topics. The Launch tools are used to access and create files. The *User Interface Overview* tools help you find your way around Ribbon menus. You can use the *What's New* button to read about the new features for the current release, as well as the last few releases. The *Learn About Inventor* tools contain a *Getting Started* guide, built in *tutorials,* (including files to use), and a collection of learning resources.

Of particular note is the *Show Me Animations* tool. It links to a comprehensive set of short videos that show you the "picks and clicks" of how to accomplish tasks in Inventor. For instance if you want to see how Inventor's Direct Manipulation tools work, you can click the Show Me Animations button on the Getting Started tab and select *Parts - Direct Manipulation* from the Show Me Animations topics list. You can use these to your benefit as quick reminders for tasks that you may not complete often and when you need a helpful reminder of how a particular tool works. Figure 1.17 shows the Get Started tab and its tools.

FIGURE 1.17
Tools found on the Get Started tab

THE VIEW TAB

The View tab, shown in Figure 1.18, has controls for object visibility and appearance, window control, and navigation. There are some variations in the icons, depending on the environment, but most of the icons are used in all of the modeling environments.

FIGURE 1.18

The View tab

The *Visibility* panel has tools for controlling which objects are visible. When you click Object Visibility, a large list is displayed so you can control the appearance of your graphics window.

The *Appearance* panel has tools for controlling the way models are displayed. You can switch between orthographic (parallel model lines appear parallel) and perspective (parallel model lines converge on a vanishing point) views. Additionally you can display the model in a number of visual styles, such as Realistic, Shaded, Shaded with Edges, Illustration, and many more.

Also on the Appearance panel you can set the model display to include shadows and reflections for an ultra realistic on-screen look. You should be aware that depending upon your hardware specifications, you may notice a performance lag when using some of these enhanced styles. For that reason you may want to use a basic set of settings during most of your work and then switch to the more realistic ones once a model is complete. Experiment with these settings to see what works best for you.

VISUAL STYLES AND WINDOWS XP

Inventor 2011 includes a number of enhanced visual styles, shadows, and reflection options not found in earlier versions. These enhancements are dependent upon the presence of DirectX 10. And because Windows XP does not support DirectX 10, the enhanced visual styles will not be available. If you are running XP you will want to go to the Tools tab, select the Application Options button, click the Hardware tab and then select the Compatibility option. No loss of visual styles found in previous versions of Inventor will be experienced, but you will not be able to use some of the newer visual styles.

Another important option found on the Appearance tab is the View Camera Projection setting, which allows you to choose between orthographic and perspective views. Setting the perspective options current displays the model with a vanishing point, as it would be in the real world. Using the orthographic option displays the model with points of the model projected along parallel lines to the screen.

Using a perspective view may be desirable when viewing the model in a 3D view but can be distracting when sketching on a flat face or viewing the model from a standard 2D ortho-graphic view, because you see what appears to be tapering faces and edges. However you can get the best of both projections by setting the ViewCube to Perspective With Ortho Faces so that the model is displayed in orthographic mode when one of the standard orthographic faces is active and is displayed in perspective mode in any other view. To do this, simply right-click the ViewCube and you will see the option. Note that this setting is per document rather than for the application itself. So you will typically need to do this for each model.

Most of the tools in the *Windows* panel are standard controls, such as switching tiling win-dows. If you click User Interface, a list of items such as the ViewCube and the status bar are dis-played. The Clean Screen icon hides most of the UI elements. Only the title bar and a minimized Ribbon bar are displayed. Although the Clean Screen setting certainly maximizes your screen real estate, it turns off one very critical interface object, the browser pane. In order to use the Clean Screen effectively you must turn it back on. To do so, use the User Interface drop-down and select the Browser option. You can click the small drop-down arrow to the right of the tabs to return the display of the tool panels.

Also on the View tab is a *Navigate* panel. The tools in the Navigate panel are the same as those found on the navigation bar, as discussed earlier in the chapter.

BEFORE YOU BEGIN...

In the next section you will be using the tutorial files that accompany the book. Before you begin, ensure that you have downloaded the tutorial files from www.sybex.com/go/masteringinventor2011. Place the files in a folder on your computer (such as \My Documents\Mastering Inventor 2011), and then be sure to set the Mastering Inventor 2011 project active:

1. From within Inventor, close any open files.

2. From the Get Started tab, select the Projects button.

3. From the Projects dialog select the Browse button.

4. From the Choose Project File dialog browse to the Mastering Inventor 2011 folder and select the Mastering Inventor 2011.ipj file and click Open.

5. Note that the Mastering Inventor 2011 project is denoted as being the active project with a check mark.

6. Click Done to close the Projects dialog box.

Now you are ready to get started. You'll find a more detailed explanation of working with and set-ting up projects in Chapter 2, "Data and Projects."

The Browser Pane

The *Browser Pane* (often called the model browser) is a listing of everything that makes up an Inventor file. The part browser shows all of the features, the assembly browser shows all of the components, and the drawing browser shows the sheets with the views. Because Inventor files are similar to actual parts and assemblies, the browser plays an important role in navigating the files.

USING THE BROWSER

In this section, you will explore the behavior of the browser pane when working in Inventor by opening an assembly and making an edit to one of its parts:

1. Go to the Get Started tab, and click Open.

2. To ensure that you are looking at all the files in the Mastering Inventor 2011 project (and only the files in this project), click Workspace in the Open dialog box, as shown in Figure 1.19.

FIGURE 1.19
Opening a file from the Tutorial Files folder

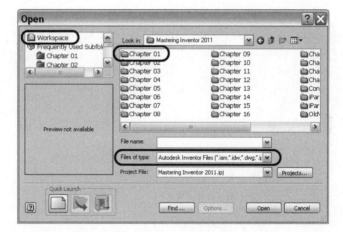

3. Check to see that the Files of Type box is set to Autodesk Inventor Files as shown in Figure 1.19 and then browse for and open the file called mi_1a_001.iam, in the Chapter 01 folder.

TURNING ON FILE EXTENSIONS

It's often helpful when working with Inventor files to be able to view the files extensions. By default Windows has the extensions for known files types turned hidden. To show file extensions follow the steps below for your operating system:

Windows XP: Open any folder, and then select "Folder Options…" from the Tools menu. Next select the View tab, and uncheck the Hide Extensions for Known File Types option.

Windows Vista: 1. Open Folder Options by clicking the Start button, then clicking Control Panel, then clicking Appearance and Personalization, and then clicking Folder Options. Uncheck the Hide Extensions for Known File Types option.

Windows 7: 1. Open Folder Options by clicking the Start button, then clicking Control Panel, then clicking Folder Options. Next select the View tab, and uncheck the Hide Extensions for Known File Types option. (If Folder Options is not available, change "View By" to "Large Icons" at the top right of the Control Panel.)

When opening an assembly file, the Assemble tab of the Ribbon bar is active. You'll notice that in the model browser (to the left of the screen) all items are shown in a white background, with no portion of the model browser grayed out. You are currently in the top level of the assembly, meaning that the uppermost level of the assembly is currently active and ready for edits.

4. Click the plus sign at the left of the Representations folder to expand the folder to show View, Position, and Level of Detail.

Figure 1.20 shows the contents of the assembly in the model browser with the representations folder expanded.

FIGURE 1.20
The Model browser contents

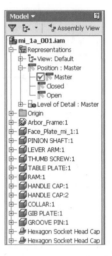

You can expand any portion of the Model browser by clicking the plus sign to the left of the item. In Figure 1.20, starting from the top, you can see a folder containing the representations categories, including view representations, position representations, and level of detail (LOD) representations. These representations allow the user to create various view states of the assembly. For example, Figure 1.20 shows that the Position folder contains a view called Open, which represents the press in a fully extended position, and another called Closed that shows the press with the ram all the way down.

5. Expand the Position node to see the various positional representations and then right-click on Open and choose Activate to see the position change.

You can switch back and forth between Open and Closed to see the model in both positions. In Chapter 8, "Assembly Design Workflows," you'll find more information about representations, including how to set up positional representations.

TURNING ON A MISSING MODEL BROWSER

Although it isn't common to need to turn the Model browser off, you can do so. More commonly, you may accidentally turn it off by clicking the X button on the right side of the browser title bar. To display it again, go to the View tab, and click the User Interface button found on the Windows panel. Most likely, you'll want to have all the items in this list selected.

EDIT A PART

Next you'll continue with the exploration of the browser by setting a part file active for edits, and making a change to a part feature.

6. In the browser double-click the part called Face_Plate_mi_1 to set it active for edits. If you hover for a moment over the icon the plus sign may automatically expand, you can disregard that and just double click the icon.

Note that it is best practice to get into the habit of double-clicking the icon next to the component name, rather than the name itself, because the latter may initialize an edit of just the name depending upon the speed of your clicks. Double-clicking the icon will activate the component for editing in place, within the assembly. Once a component is activated, all other portions within the Model browser will be grayed out. With the faceplate part activated, you will notice the Model tab becomes active in the Ribbon menu, and the model browser shows all the features of the faceplate. Both changes reflect that you are now editing a part file, and are therefore working at the part editing level of the model hierarchy, with part feature tools ready for selection.

Examining the features within the active part, you can see a folder named Solid Bodies, the standard Origin folder and then all of the features that were created to make the faceplate, such as extrusions, holes, fillets, and so on. You will also notice a red X at the bottom of the part signifying the end-of-part (EOP) marker.

CONTROLLING COMPONENT TRANSPARENCY

It is generally helpful to set the display settings so that as you activate one component in the context of an assembly, the other components become ghosted or transparent. This allows you to see which component you're actively editing and yet still reference other components in the assembly. You can toggle the Transparency setting on and off by going to the View tab and clicking the Component Transparency drop-down found on the Appearance panel.

---

7. Click and hold on the EOP marker and drag it up the model tree until you see a black bar above Extrusion1, and then drop it there.

You should see all of the features become grayed out in the browser and the faceplate disappear in the graphics area. Essentially you have rolled back the history of the faceplate to before it contained any features.

8. To bring the features back, click and hold on the EOP marker and drag it until you see a black bar under Extrusion1, and then drop it there. You'll see this base feature become visible again.

9. Do this for each feature in the tree, and you will step through the sequence of features and get an idea of how the faceplate was created. Note that some features are on the back side of the faceplate so you may not see them, depending upon your viewing angle. Ensure that you have the EOP back at the very end of the part (below Fillet3), before continuing to the next step.

FOUR WAYS TO USE EOP MARKERS

Since part features are listed sequentially in the order they were created, the EOP marker allows you to figure out how a part was constructed. Dragging the EOP marker to the top and then dragging it down one feature at a time recreates the part. This can be useful when working with parts designed by others and can be used as a powerful learning tool.

You can use the EOP marker to insert a feature anywhere in the model tree. For instance if you meant to create a hole before creating a rectangular cut, you could just use the EOP to suspend the rectangular cut feature, and then place the hole feature. Then to bring the rectangular cut back, you'd move the EOP back to the bottom.

Because part features are based hierarchically in that one is based on another, oftentimes a change to a primary feature will break a secondary one, which in turn breaks another, and another, and so on. The cascade of error down through the feature tree can be intimidating and appear to the new user as if every single feature will need to be rebuilt. In most cases though, if you move the EOP up to just below the first errant feature and then fix it, the following feature will be fixed as well. If not you would repair it and step down to the next one, and the next one, until all are healthy again. Using the EOP to fix features in the order they were created is the best way to approach the task.

In addition, dragging the EOP marker to the top of the part file and leaving it there reduces the overall part size significantly. This is a good way to reduce a file size if you need to email a part file to someone. When they receive it they can just drag the EOP down and then see the part as you designed it. Likewise, if you encounter a blank file in your modeling session, be sure to check the Model browser to make sure the EOP marker has been dragged to the bottom of the part file.

10. Next double-click the icon for Extrusion1 in the faceplate feature tree (or right-click Extrsuion1 and choose Edit Feature). This activates the feature for editing.

11. Replace the value of 0.5 in with **5mm**, taking care to enter the unit suffix mm in small case letters, then click OK and you'll see your edits take place.

12. To have a closer look at the change select the face on the View Cube marked Right. Then place your cursor over the faceplate in the graphics screen, and use your mouse wheel to zoom in to the faceplate. Note that you zoom to wherever your cursor is pointing on-screen.

You will see the change has created a gap between the faceplate and the end of the frame of the press, as shown in Figure 1.21.

FIGURE 1.21
Editing the
Faceplate

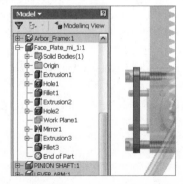

RETURN TO THE ASSEMBLY

Now that your part feature is edited, you will leave the part level and return to the assembly level where you started out.

13. On the Model tab click the Return button on the far right.

Notice that the faceplate is pulled back against the frame. This is the power of a parametric model. Because the arbor press assembly has parameters defining the mating constraints of the faceplate and frame, it automatically adjusts to the change you made by holding those parameter values.

You should also notice that in the model browser, you no longer see the feature tree of the faceplate that included the extrusions, holes and so on. Instead you see a list of Flush, Mate, and Insert constraints. These are constraint objects that exist and are accessed at the assembly level. In order to access the part features (extrusions, holes and so on) again you would simply edit the part as you did before.

As demonstrated in this quick tour of a typical assembly structure, the Inventor Ribbon tabs and model browser are unique and intuitive to the environment you are in at the time. You can close the model without saving changes to conclude this exercise. In the next example, you will explore the changes encountered in the Styles Editor located on the Format tab.

Task-Based Dialog Boxes

In addition to the tabs of the Ribbon menus updating based on the current environment as described in the previous section, some Inventor dialog boxes are also task-based. Instead of containing every control needed for every environment, most dialog boxes display only the controls necessary for the current task. Follow these steps to see an example of this:

1. To open an assembly, go to the Get Started tab, and click Open.

2. From the Chapter 01 folder select the file called mi_1a_002.iam, and then click Open.

3. Select the Manage tab from the Ribbon menu and then select Styles Editor, as shown in Figure 1.22.

FIGURE 1.22
The Inventor Manage tab

When the Style And Standard Editor dialog box opens, the styles collection relating to the assembly file will be shown, as in Figure 1.23. You will notice that while working with an assembly (or part), three style areas are available: Color, Lighting, and Material.

FIGURE 1.23
The Inventor Style
And Standard
Editor (assembly
mode)

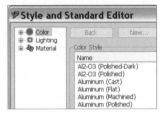

4. Close the Style and Standard Editor dialog box and then click the small X icon located just above the View Cube to close the assembly file. Note that there is an X at the very top right of the screen that closes Inventor completely; if you accidentally select that one simply restart Inventor and continue to the next step.

5. From the Get Started tab, click the New button.

6. In the New File dialog box, set the Default tab active and choose the Standard.idw icon, and then click OK. This creates a new Inventor drawing file.

7. With the new drawing file active, select the Manage tab from the Ribbon menu, and then click the Styles Editor button. You will see that the style area option reflects styles pertaining to drawings, as shown in Figure 1.13.

FIGURE 1.24
The Inventor Style
And Standard Edi-
tor (drawing mode)

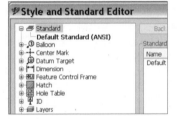

The drawing style collection contains various dimension styles, layers and layers names, line type settings, object defaults, text styles, and other settings related specifically to 2D drawing styles. If you compare Figure 1.23 and 1.24 you will see that the Styles Editor contains different styles collections depending upon the type of file you are working with. This is just one example of the way that Inventor uses task-based dialogs to present only the options that make sense. Figure 1.25 shows another, comparing two Extrude dialog boxes; one is for a solid feature and the other is for a surface feature.

FIGURE 1.25
Compare the avail-
able options for
these two extrude
dialog boxes

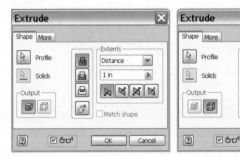

Because the task of creating a surface extrusion is different than creating a solid extrusion some options are simply grayed out and not available. You will notice this throughout Inventor as options are offered and suppressed depending upon the task at hand. You can close the drawing file you have open without saving changes and continue on to the next section.

Learning the File Types in Inventor

In AutoCAD, you might be used to having the `.dwg` file format as your main file format, in Microsoft Word you might use primarily just a `.doc` file, and in Microsoft Excel you might use the `.xls` file type for most of the work you do. All three of these commonly used programs use a single primary file type throughout. Inventor, on the other hand, follows the structure common to most other 3D modelers in the engineering field today, and uses different file types for different tasks.

Why So Many File Types?

The purpose of using multiple file types is so that the data load is distributed into many different files, instead of placing all information in one file. For instance, you use an `.ipt` file to create an Inventor part file, an `.iam` to assemble that part with other parts, and then you use an IDW to make a detail drawing of the parts and the assembly.

Placing the data in multiple files permits quicker load times, promotes file integrity, and vastly improves performance across the board on large designs. As an example, when you open an assembly made of 12 different part files, only the information concerning the file paths, the way the parts fit together in the assembly, and the information required to display the parts is loaded. Only when you decide to edit a part is the information about all of the parts features loaded. As you've already explored in the previous section, having different file types allows you to have environment-specific tools for working with each file type, as well.

Another payoff of multiple file types is exemplified in the comparison between the way that AutoCAD handles model space/paper space and the way that Inventor handles the same tasks. To put it simply, in Inventor the part and assembly files are the model (model space), and the drawing file is in effect paper space. Using multiple file types to handle the separate tasks required for modeling versus detailing simplifies the interaction between both tasks, and as a result, the headaches of managing model space and paper space that exists in AutoCAD are eliminated in Inventor.

Here are the primary file formats commonly used in Inventor:

◆ `.ipj`: Inventor project file - is used to manage file linking paths

◆ `.ipt`: Inventor single part file -is used to create individual parts

◆ `.iam`: Inventor assembly file - is used to assemble part together

◆ `.ipn`: Inventor presentation file - is used to create exploded views of assemblies

◆ `.idw`: Inventor 2D detail drawing file - is used to detail part, assembly and presentation files

◆ `.dwg` (Inventor): Inventor 2D detail drawing file - just like the IDW, DWG is used to detail part, assembly and presentation files

◆ .dwg (AutoCAD): AutoCAD nonassociative drawing file - is used to convert an Inventor drawing file to a standard AutoCAD file

◆ .xls: Excel files that drive iParts, threads, and other data - is used to manage tabled data, linked or embedded in a part, assembly or drawing file

Although this list may seem intimidating, once you become familiar with Inventor, having many different file types will be less of a concern. The benefit of using multiple file types to have fully associative, automatically updating designs is a cornerstone of most 3D parametric modelers. Performance and stability in the use of Inventor requires good data management principles, including storing the saved files in an efficient and organized manner. This subject will be introduced later in this chapter and expanded upon it in Chapter 2.

Drawing Files in Inventor

Originally Inventor had just one drawing file type, the .dwg. Then with the release of Inventor 2008, the Inventor .dwg was added. Inside of Inventor the two files are almost identical. However, the Inventor .dwg can be used outside of Inventor, in AutoCAD. This allows work to be shared between Inventor and AutoCAD users. Just like an .idw file, an Inventor .dwg file will update whenever parts or assemblies linked to the file are changed and updated.

Note too that if you have .idw files you want to turn into Inventor .dwg file or vice versa, you can do so by using the Save As option and then changing the Save As File Type option. This process can even be batched and scheduled to run overnight using the Task Scheduler, which you can open by selecting Start ➢ All Programs ➢ Autodesk ➢ Autodesk Inventor 2011 ➢ Tools ➢ Task Scheduler.

WORKING WITH DWGS

You can use .dwg files in a number of ways in Inventor. Although Inventor does not support the creation of AutoCAD entities, you can utilize AutoCAD geometry in Inventor sketches, Inventor drawings, title blocks, and symbol creation.

When creating a new part file in Inventor, you can copy geometry directly from an AutoCAD .dwg and paste it into an Inventor sketch. AutoCAD dimensions will even be converted into fully parametric Inventor dimensions. However, only minimal sketch constraints will be created when doing this. Using the Auto Dimension tool within the Inventor sketch environment, you can apply sketch constraints to the copied AutoCAD data quickly. It is important to remember that many AutoCAD drawings contain fundamental issues such as exploded or "fudged" dimensions and lines with endpoints that do not meet. Copying such drawings into an Inventor sketch will of course bring all of those issues along and will typically provide poor results.

Another way to use AutoCAD data in Inventor is in an Inventor .dwg file. Often you'll have symbols in AutoCAD in the form of blocks that you want to use on a drawing in Inventor, such as a directional flow arrow or a standard note block. Although you could re-create these symbols in Inventor, you can also simply copy the block from AutoCAD and paste it into the Inventor .dwg, or use the Import AutoCAD block option to import blocks without the need to open AutoCAD. This functionality exists only within an Inventor .dwg and is not supported in an Inventor .idw. In fact, it is one of the few differences you'll notice between an Inventor .dwg and an Inventor .idw from within Inventor.

You can open an Inventor .dwg file in AutoCAD and edit it, but with some limitation. The primary limitation is that the Inventor objects are protected from modification. AutoCAD dimensions and other entities can be added and will remain intact when the file is opened again in Inventor, but as a rule, objects must be edited in the application from which they were created.

Creating DWG Files from Inventor Drawings

Users of Inventor may often find that they are called upon to create native AutoCAD .dwg files from Inventor .idw files for use by customers or other people within the company. A user may create a .dwg file by simply performing a Save Copy As and saving it as an AutoCAD .dwg file. The newly created .dwg file will not be associative to the Inventor part or assembly or .idw file, and will not reflect any changes made to the part, assembly, or Inventor drawing file. It is common to use Save Copy As on an Inventor drawing and save it to an AutoCAD .dwg just before making revision changes, thereby preserving a copy of the drawing in a static state at that revision level. Once the static copy is saved, revision edits can begin, and the original Inventor drawing will update automatically.

DWG FILE SIZE

Although the benefits of using an Inventor DWG instead of an IDW may be favorable, you should be aware that the extra abilities of the DWG file do come at the expense of file size. Inventor DWG's are typically two to three times larger than identical IDW files. If you create large assemblies, it is advisable to use the IDW template as opposed to the DWG in order to keep files manageable. The extent at which the DWG in Inventor is employed will largely be determined by the amount of collaboration required between Inventor and AutoCAD users.

Another aspect of working with an Inventor .dwg in AutoCAD is that whereas the Inventor .dwg does not contain a model space by default, once it is opened in AutoCAD, you can access model space. From model space in an Inventor .dwg, you can use the Insert command to place the Inventor drawing views of the model as AutoCAD blocks. These blocks will update automatically so long as they are not exploded and remain in the current .dwg. However, you can explode the blocks and/or copy them into other .dwg files without worrying about having a negative impact on the Inventor .dwg. If objects such as these blocks are added to the .dwg's model space in AutoCAD, you will then be able to access model space for that file in Inventor. However, you will only be able to view, measure, and plot the model space objects.

If you are familiar with the X-Ref tools in AutoCAD, there are some interesting workflows that can be explored by inserting the block forms of the Inventor drawing views into the Inventor .dwg and then using X-Ref to insert them into other AutoCAD drawings. The result is that the drawing with the X-Ref will update when the Inventor file updates, allowing the Inventor user to make edits on parts and assemblies and the AutoCAD user to get those updates automatically in his or her layouts.

Moving from AutoCAD to Inventor

If you are moving from AutoCAD 2D to Inventor 3D modeling, you can have a great experience in the process if you put design concepts used in AutoCAD on the shelf while learning Inventor.

If your experience is like that of many others who made the transition from the drawing board to drawing lines in AutoCAD, it was difficult to say the least. At first you may have been frustrated with spending more time creating electronic drawings than it would have taken to produce the drawing with the board. However, a key reason for the acceptance of AutoCAD was the ability to make edits far more quickly than you could with eraser and paper. Once you master Inventor, you will find the same benefit of faster edits, as well as the many benefits that parameter-based design has to offer.

Making the move to Inventor successfully requires some evaluation of current methods of design in AutoCAD. The following are some of the evaluation steps in planning your successful move:

- Assess your current directory structure of AutoCAD drawings. How do you store, name, and reuse current AutoCAD files? Will the structure be compatible for storing Inventor documents, or is it time to take a deep look at your data management structure?

- Determine how you will manage Inventor files. Inventor utilizes projects to manage assemblies, drawings, and associated part files. What worked in AutoCAD will probably not be the ideal scenario in Inventor.

- Document your current design workflow when using AutoCAD. Is it time to reevaluate the design process in light of the efficiencies that may be gained when using Inventor? How are revisions, engineering change orders, and production currently being managed, and how can Inventor improve on the design-to-manufacturing processes?

- Determine whether your current computer hardware and network are up to the task of implementing and using Inventor. What gets by for using AutoCAD will seldom work for the demands of 3D modeling in Inventor.

- Set aside time for training and implementing Inventor. If you have multiple users, it might be best to consider phasing Inventor in over a period of time, allowing new users to acclimate themselves to a new way of design.

If you take the time to plan your leap into Inventor, your chances of success are greatly improved. The rewards of a successful transition can be a savings in time, money, and effort. There are many, many proficient AutoCAD users who today seldom ever open AutoCAD, as they have mastered the tools in Inventor and use it for all of their design work. On the other hand there are many industries that require both mechanical design and layout work. Because AutoCAD handles the layout tasks better than Inventor, and Inventor the design work better than AutoCAD, these users will probably always use both tools together.

3D models vs. 3D Virtual Prototypes

Starting out, you may simply be interested in learning how to create 3D models, but as you progress you should understand the concept of 3D Virtual Prototypes and how they differ from a simple 3D model.

What Is a 3D Virtual Prototype?

So, what is a 3D *virtual prototype*? Put simply, it's a prototype that functions (and malfunctions) just like the physical prototype that has not yet been built. It is far more than a just a 3D model. The virtual prototype consists of a main assembly, which contains many subassemblies that have individual parts. All these components are constrained in such a way that the fit and functionality of all parts and mechanisms can be visualized, tested, and proven before any parts are manufactured. Scrap and rework are minimized or eliminated if the design is fully completed and proven in Inventor before it ever reaches the shop floor.

Why a 3D Virtual Prototype?

Historically actual prototypes have been built to test or validate a design, and help discover weaknesses, limits of functionality, or areas that require a redesign due to an inability to manufacture cost effectively. Although the goal of prototyping is to perfect the design and save time and money associated with a failed design that reaches the market, the prototyping process itself can become costly and time consuming as well. In days past, prototyping was often the only way to know for certain if a design that was conceived and detailed on paper or in 2D CAD would really work. Even the best engineer or designer could not anticipate everything needed to create an accurate design the first time around. As mistakes were made, scrap was generated, and redesign and retooling was required.

FEWER PHYSICAL PROTOTYPES

Although you may never be able to go straight from Inventor to your first article design, you can use Inventor to reduce the number of physical prototypes needed to get there. More and more, creating physical prototype after physical prototype is becoming a part of "the old way" of doing things. It worked when you produced a small number of product units and had plenty of time and resources to lend to the project. It worked when material costs were relatively low. And it worked because it was the only method of testing and proving a design available.

In contrast, today's competitive marketplace is unlikely to afford you the luxuries of time and materials for repeatedly building physical prototypes, and you are expected to get a large portion of any design right the first time around. Clearly, anything that can be done to reduce or eliminate physical prototyping will greatly influence the financial health and competitive strengths of the company you work for. This is where creating a 3D virtual prototype becomes important.

USING ALL THE TOOLS

Making the virtual prototype allows the designer to explore the function of a mechanism before lengthy design and engineering time is expended on a design that just won't work. Developing the virtual prototype eliminates the part procurement and creation process, slashing the design time even further. The virtual prototype can be proven further with the use of stress analysis and dynamic motion simulation to find and correct weaknesses in the design, rather than just ensuring that everything is overbuilt and calling it a good design. Interference between components is also easily discovered while still in the design process. The use of functional design in the prototyping process allows engineers to properly determine loads, power, stresses, inertia, and other properties before a machine is built. Weights, center of gravity, and other physical characteristics are at your fingertips during any stage of the design.

MORE THAN JUST 3D

So now that you have Inventor you are guaranteed to cut time and money from the design process, right? Unfortunately that's not the case. Over the years, as design tools have evolved, so too have the ways we design. However, it is possible to use new design tools in the same manner we used the old tools if we are not careful. As companies moved from the drafting board to AutoCAD, many users continued to use AutoCAD in much the same way they used the board. Not reusing data in the form of blocks and block libraries and not employing block attributes to pack those blocks with intelligence are common examples of this.

In much the same way, it is possible to use Inventor as if it is AutoCAD. Creating 3D models simply for the sake of generating a 2D shop print is a common example of this. To ensure that you are getting the most out of Inventor, you want to make sure your designs are more than just 3D models. You want to use Inventor to create 3D virtual prototypes. You want to ensure that your 3D models are more than a collection of features and instead relate parameters from one feature to update based on the edits of another. You want your model to reflect the intent of the overall design accurately, anticipating change and revision and making it as robust and intelligent as you can. You want your model to be more than just 3D; you want it to be a 3D virtual prototype.

TOO BUSY GETTING DRAWINGS TO THE SHOP TO BUILD VIRTUAL PROTOTYPES?

You have deadlines to meet, you're trying to learn a new design tool (Inventor), and you are being told to spend more time building models? Deciding when to build a virtual prototype depends on your business and the complexity of the design. At some point, everyone has probably given rough sketches to the shop to get a part made, but no one wants to do that on a regular basis. In the beginning, the work you do with Inventor will probably lean more toward just a 3D model and less toward a 3D prototype, and that's okay.

As you continue to work, look for areas where you can improve your models and make them more intelligent. If you know a design is likely to change, build your model with those changes in mind. The better the model, the easier it is to verify that a replacement component will fit properly, and doing a major redesign on a product will go more smoothly if you have a solid base from which to work.

Keep in mind that Inventor has a large and deep tool set, but if you're like most people who use it in the real world, you'll probably not use many of these tools. If you create a lot of steel frames and weldments, it's likely that you will not have a big need for the plastic features tools. Take the time to understand and learn all of the tools available so that you know what Inventor has to offer, but then focus on the parts you need and use most often, and get the most out of those tools.

Understanding Functional Design

Part of creating a fully functioning, 3D Virtual Prototype is using the Functional Design tools. *Functional design* is an Autodesk term for a knowledge content tool that moves the user from creating geometrical descriptions (mere 3D modeling) to capturing knowledge. For instance, if you had the need to create a spring, what tools would you use? You could use the coil tool and develop a nice spring-shaped model. However, if the actual goal was to determine what size spring you needed for a particular set of load inputs, then you'd want to use the Compression Spring generator. You can use the functional design tools to analyze the function (load of a spring) and solve the design problems (what size spring is required), rather than spending time on modeling a solution needed to create 3D representations.

THE V-BELTS GENERATOR

An example of functional design and its benefit is the use of the Inventor's V-belts Generator. Traditionally, to design a pulley system, you would lay out the pulleys in positions as required by the design and then choose a belt that met the design requirements and came as close as possible to fitting the pulley spacing. The result oftentimes is that no common belt size fits the pulley spacing. The functional design approach to this task allows you to specify the belt from a standard catalog of belt sizes at the same time that you are creating the rest of the system. In this way, you know from the outset that the design is indeed functional and will work in the real world.

Functional design supports design through generators and wizards that add mechanical content and intelligence to the design. By using the components within Inventor functional design, you can create mechanically correct components automatically by entering simple or complex mechanical attributes inside the generator.

Using the functional design components within Inventor provides many advantages:

◆ You shorten the design and modification process through the use of intelligent components.

◆ You produce a higher level of design quality and accuracy.

◆ Functional design provides a more intuitive design environment, compared to creating complicated geometrical designs.

◆ Functional design can eliminate the need for physical prototypes for the purpose of analyzing stress and movement.

The following portions of Autodesk Inventor are part of the functional design system:

◆ Design Accelerator

◆ Frame Generator

◆ Inventor Studio

◆ AutoLimits

◆ Content Center

◆ Bolted Connection Generator

The Design Accelerator

The Design Accelerator is an important component of the functional design system, providing the user with engineering calculation and decision-making support to identify and place standard components or create standards-based geometry from the input provided by the user. Design Accelerator tools automate selecting standard parts and creating intelligent geometry. The initial design quality is improved by validating against design requirements. Standardization is simplified by selecting the same components for the same tasks.

The Design Accelerator provides a set of component generators and calculators that are able to create mechanically correct standard components automatically by entering simple or detailed information.

The Bolted Connection Generator

The Bolted Connection Generator is one example of a functional design tool. It can create and insert a complete bolted connection all at once by sizing the bolt diameter and length, by selecting the right parts and holes, and by assembling all the components together. You can create templates for common fastener stacks that you might use every day, as well.

The Frame Generator

The Frame Generator will create internal or external frame assemblies for machines. The Frame Generator functions by creating a skeleton part to define the frame within an assembly file. You then use the skeleton to place and size the frame members. You can then use multiple skeletal models within an assembly to create frame members, and you can create frame members between skeletal models. You can also create frame members from the vertices and edges of existing subassemblies. This ability allows you to build framing between other components within an assembly. Joining frame members together and adjusting the end treatments for connection between members is a simple matter when using the Frame Generator. Joining frame members with weld gaps and coped joints is supported.

The Inventor Studio

Inventor Studio is an environment within Autodesk Inventor with a complete set of tools for creating and editing renderings and animations. With Inventor Studio you will be able to create animated renderings and photorealistic still images of parts and assemblies to help visualize the appearance and motion of designs before they are built. Inventor Studio allows you to specify geometry and apply settings for background lights and cameras to create a scene for rendering or animation. You can create and save multiple animations within any one assembly file. You can use Inventor constraints and parameters to drive animations within the assembly file. In addition, any changes that are made in the part or assembly file will be transferred and reflected in the rendering and animation files.

AutoLimits

The AutoLimits tool monitors selected aspects of the design relative to boundaries that the user specifies. If results fall above or below the boundary limits, a warning indicator is displayed. AutoLimits can also be used to measure distance, length, volume, mass, and so on. Once AutoLimits are created, they constantly monitor to make sure the design still fits its requirements.

The Content Center

The Inventor Content Center libraries provide the designer with standard parts (fasteners, steel shapes, shaft parts, and so on) and part features. You can access the Content Center libraries from the Content Center in the Assembly tool panel, and you can share the libraries between users to provide a high level of standardization. The Content Center dialog box permits you to look up and insert standard parts and features into an assembly design. You can create custom Content Center folders to allow users to create custom parts for use within the Content Center. Content Center parts allow users to specify ANSI, DIN, ISO, and other international standard parts within the design environment.

The Bottom Line

Create Parametric Designs   The power of parameter-based design comes from the quick and easy edits, where changing a parameter value drives a change through the design. In order to make changes easily, though, you need follow certain general rules, so that the changes update predictably.

>**Master It**   You want to create a model of a base plate, a rectangular-shaped part with a series of holes, and rectangular cutouts. What would your initial sketch look like in Inventor?

Get the "Feel" of Inventor   Inventor's interface contains many elements that change and update to give you the tools you need to perform the task at hand. Getting comfortable with these automatic changes and learning to anticipate them will help you get the "feel" of Inventor.

>**Master It**   You create an extrude feature using the Extrude button, but cannot seem to find an Edit Extrude button. How can you edit the extruded feature to change the height?

Use the Inventor Graphical Interface   Inventor 2011 uses the Ribbon Menu interface first introduced in Inventor 2010. This Ribbon consists of grouped tools that make finding tools intuitive once you become familiar with the basic layout.

>**Master It**   You are trying to draw a line on the face of a part, but you cannot seem to find the sketch tab in the Ribbon. How do you get it back?

Use the Inventor File Types   Inventor supports many different file types in its native environment, separating tasks and files to improve performance and increase stability.

>**Master It**   You have trouble keeping the various file types straight because all of the file icons look rather similar to you. Is there a way you can see which file is what type?

Move from AutoCAD to Inventor   If you are making the move from AutoCAD to Inventor, you are not alone; most Inventor users have made that transition as well. You may find that over time you use AutoCAD less and less, or you might find that Inventor and AutoCAD both have a place in your design work. It is largely dependent upon the industry you work in.

>**Master It**   You find Inventor to be a bit foreign and wish it worked more like AutoCAD. How can this be overcome?

Create 3D Virtual Prototypes   It is important to understand that the full power of Inventor is realized when your models become more than just 3D, and become true prototypes of the object of your design.

>**Master It**   You want to make your models as intelligent and as close to real life as possible, so how do you get started?

Use Functional Design   Functional design includes a number of tools in Inventor. Most often, though, the design accelerators are what come to mind when one hears the term Functional Design.

>**Master It**   You need to fasten two assemblies together, but are not certain what size bolt to use; is there anything in Inventor that will assist with that?

Chapter 2

Data and Projects

In many design and manufacturing environments, teamwork is a way of life—an essential part of getting a product to market quickly. Concurrent design among multiple team members requires coordination, discipline, and organization. In other situations a designer might work primarily as a stand-alone user, collaborating with others but generally creating and accessing files as a single user. In either case, effort invested in setting up an efficient file management system saves time while designing parts and provides safeguards against rework and downstream errors for the designer. When working as part of a design team, the value increases exponentially.

In this chapter, you will learn how to:

- ◆ Understand how project search paths work

- ◆ Set up library and Content Center paths

- ◆ Create and configure a project file

- ◆ Determine the best project type for you

What Is an Inventor Project?

You can think of Project files in Inventor simply as configuration files which tell Inventor where to look for component files when working with assemblies and drawings. For instance, an Inventor assembly file is essentially an empty "bucket" into which parts (and subassemblies) are placed and assembled. Therefore, the assembly file contains only the file path references for the components it is composed of, and the information about how those components are assembled. As a result, the location of referenced files is a key issue. If, when opening an assembly, referenced files cannot be found at the search path recorded in the assembly file, a manual file resolution process is activated. This happens most often when component files are moved or renamed outside the cone of search established in the Project file.

Project Files and Search Paths

Project files are often referred to as IPJ files, as that is the project file extension. You can create a project file (.ipj) anywhere it makes sense to do so and Inventor will look at that location and lower in the directory structure for the files in your design. Take a moment and study the file structure shown in Figure 2.1.

Figure 2.1 shows a typical job based folder structure, where all files are located on the Engineering (I:) drive. Engineering contains three subfolders: CAD Files, Data Sheets, and Templates. In the CAD Files folder are three more folders: Content Center Files, Designs, and Library Files. The Designs folder contains a folder for each job number, and subfolders containing revisions. So where would you create an Inventor project file? There are two basic solutions: create multiple `.ipj` files for each new job or create a single all encompassing `.ipj` file for the entire engineering drive. Which method you should use depends largely on the way your engineering department operates.

FIGURE 2.1

A job based folder structure

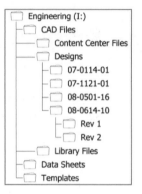

JOB BASED .IPJ SETUPS

You could create one project file for each of the four jobs. You would have a file named `07-0114-01.ipj` in the 07-0114-01 folder, one named `07-1121-01.ipj` in the 07-01121-01 folder and so on. This strategy can work fine if you typically work on one project at a time, and then "close" the project upon completion. In Inventor, you would simply switch to the specific project file that matches the job number you are working on (for example 07-0114-01) and because the `.ipj` file is stored in that folder, Inventor will only search for design files in its *Workspace*. The workspace is defined as the folder containing the `.ipj` folder and everything below it. It may help to think of a workspace as search cone, starting at the `.ipj` and spreading out from that point.

This job-based approach is fairly intuitive and is what people generally think of when they see the phrase project file; one `.ipj` file for each job/project. This is a common approach when jobs have long development cycles, and designs are very specific to that job.

But what happens if you want to use a part that was created for job 07-0114-01 in job 08-0614-10? You could place the part into the 08-0614-10 assembly, but the next time you opened that assembly, Inventor would not be able to find it, because it exists outside of the 08-0614-10 workspace. If you were to move a part file from the 07-0114-01 folder into the 08-0614-10, then Inventor would not find it while you were working on job 07-0114-01, because it would now be outside of its workspace. Likewise if you moved the file up to the Designs folder, or the CAD Files folder, or to (almost) any location that is not next to or below the `07-0114-01.ipj` file, Inventor would not find it, so long as you are working with that project file. If you copy the file to the 08-0614-10 folder then you have two versions of it and it becomes difficult to track changes, because you need to update both copies to keep everything up to date.

The solution would be to configure the `.ipj` file to include a *Library*. When a folder is configured to be a library in an `.ipj` file, Inventor sees all of the files in that folder (and its subfolder) as read-only. This protects commonly used files from being accidentally changed and upsetting all of the many designs that may be using them.

To solve the issue of the commonly used part in this example, you would configure each of your `.ipj` files to use the folder named Library Files as a library of approved, read-only parts, to be used across multiple jobs. Whenever you open an assembly, Inventor first looks in the library path for the parts, and then looks at the workspace. So to convert a part created as part of the 07-0114-01 job into a library part you would follow these steps:

1. Copy the file to the library folder.

2. If the original file has a job specific name, rename it according to a defined library nomenclature.

3. Open the assembly (or assemblies) that use the original part.

4. Use the replace components tool to replace the original part with the library part in the assembly(s).

5. Save and close the assembly(s).

6. Delete the original part, so that no duplicate is present.

SINGLE .IPJ SETUPS

Using the same folder structure as shown in Figure 2.1, you could use a single all-encompassing .ipj file and set it in the Designs folder. By doing so, you would be setting the workspace at that level. This configures Inventor's search paths to look for files in the Designs folder and every- thing below it. Essentially you have expanded the search cone by moving it up a level. Now if you need to use a part that resides in the 07-0114-01 folder in the 08-0614-10 assembly, you can do so and Inventor would be able to find it, without requiring it to be in a library folder.

Of course you can still use library folders when using the single .ipj file approach, and in fact it is generally recommended that you do convert common parts to library parts when they are being used in many different designs. Because folders configured as libraries in the .ipj file are handled as read-only, this protects them from accidental modifications.

One major caveat to using just a single .ipj file is that in order to prevent the possibility of the wrong part being loaded in an assembly, it is important for every part located in the search path to have a unique name. If Inventor finds two files named BasePlate01, it will either use the first one it finds or stop and make you decide which one to use. In either case, you should consider a nomenclature that references the job number, date, or other unique identifier in the name.

ITEM BASED SETUPS

If your company uses an item based file management setup, and tracks each part you create or purchase as an item, then you are probably not concerned with job numbers as much as you are about part numbers. Most likely you will want to employ a single .ipj file setup as described above, and again place the .ipj file in the Designs folder. Additionally your file structure may be a bit more flat and look like Figure 2.2, where the Designs folder has no subfolders.

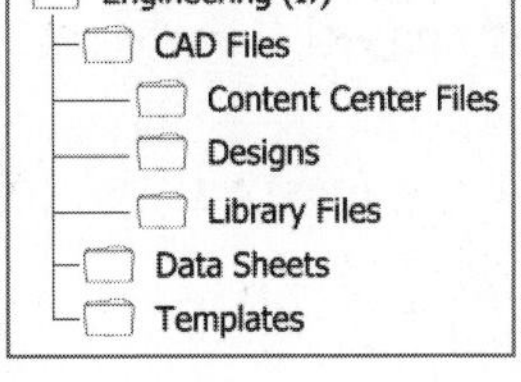

FIGURE 2.2
An item-based
folder structure

Engineering (I:)
- CAD Files
    - Content Center Files
    - Designs
    - Library Files
- Data Sheets
- Templates

In this flatter structure you can simplify the folder structure and drop all files into the Designs folder as shown in Figure 2.3.

FIGURE 2.3
A simplified folder structure

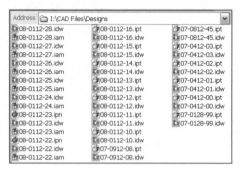

Of course, you could still populate the Designs folder with subfolders named by product line, top level item, or for each job just like in Figure 2.1, as well. Typically it is best to set up the .ipj file to accommodate your current file management system. However, if your current system is a mess or is simply no longer a good fit for your company, you might take the time to reorganize and plan out a good system, and set up Inventor accordingly.

Library Folders

As described previously, library folders contain existing, shared components. Library folders are useful repositories for purchased parts such as fasteners, clamps, motors, and connectors, as well as any other common, standard components. Library folders are defined in the .ipj file. Once the .ipj file is configured, all components stored in a folder designated as a library file are considered to be read-only by Inventor. This prevents the component from being unintentionally edited or from being revised without appropriate approvals. For example, before you modify a design that was completed as part of another job, it's important to determine where else that part was used. The goal is to ensure that the changes you plan will not render the part unusable for other designs.

Library folders should be located outside the main .ipj workspace path. In the job-based directory structure example shown in Figure 2.1, the Libraries folder is on the same directory level as the Designs folder and therefore outside the workspace search path. Library folders can be located anywhere outside the primary project data path, even on different drives or mapped servers. You should note that if you set up a library path in the .ipj file to a folder that does not exist, Inventor will create the folder as specified in the path. So a good way to set up libraries is to set the path, and let Inventor create the folder, so that you know it's in the right place, then populate the folder with the library files.

LIBRARY EDITOR .IPJ FILES

So if folders configured as library files are configured as read-only in the .ipj file, how are controlled, purposeful, revisions carried out on library files? The answer is to create a regular .ipj file that is configured to look at the Library file as a standard folder. For instance you might create an `.ipj` file in the Library Files folder and assign it no library path. You would then use this `.ipj` file only when doing library maintenance. Because this `.ipj` has no library path called out, the files are not handled as read only. Often- times in a large engineering department only a couple of people have access to the library editor project. When other team members see a need to change a library file, they would submit a change order and the designated person(s) would then make the change.

Content Center Files

In the previous illustrations you may have noticed a folder called *Content Center Files*. This is a special kind of library file that stores component files generated by the Content Center. This folder path is specified in the `.ipj` file, much like a library file is.

It is important to understand what Content Center is and how it works. The Content Center libraries are collections of table data containing the definitions for how to create 800,000-plus standard parts and features. This database is managed by the *Desktop Content* settings or the *Autodesk Data Management Server* (ADMS). Once you've installed the content libraries, you can use this content in your designs. To do this, choose a component from the database to place into your design, typically by using the Place From Content Center button in the assembly. Understand that it is at this point that the Content Center part file is created. Up until this point, the part existed only as a definition in the database table.

In your `.ipj`, you need to specify a Content Center file store location so that Inventor knows where to save the file, and where to find it next time. The file store folder will include additional subfolders where Content Center files will be stored once used in your designs. These additional folders are created automatically as parts are created. The next time a part is specified from the Content Center libraries, Inventor first searches the Content Center file store directories and then creates the part from the database only if the part file does not already exist in the file store location. It is required that the Content Center file store location be outside the main project data path. From this discussion of libraries, you can see that high importance is placed on planning the correct part locations and workflow.

How Search Paths and Project Files Are Used

Inventor's `.ipj` files are easy to create and use, provided you understand how Inventor uses them. An Inventor project file is a configuration file that lists the locations and functions of each search path. Inventor uses these definitions to resolve file links and locate the files needed for the parts and assemblies on which you want to work. Figure 2.4 shows how Inventor loads assemblies and parts inside an assembly file.

When opening an assembly file, Inventor resolves files by searching for the first file to be located within the assembly file. Inventor first looks in the library folders for that file. Next, Inventor searches in the local workspace for the file. When a file is not found in any of the referenced folders, Inventor launches a manual file resolution dialog box offering you the opportunity to browse and point to the file.

FIGURE 2.4
Inventor file reso-
lution protocol

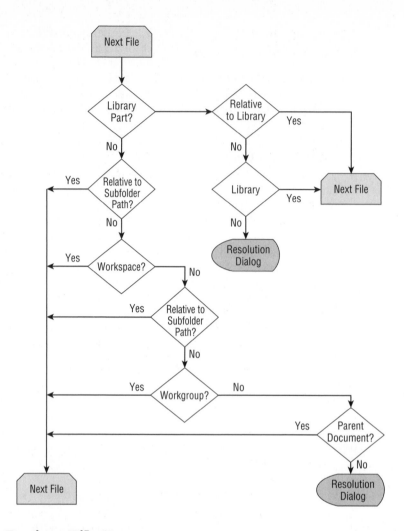

Exploring Project File Types

As mentioned previously, file management in Inventor is handled through the use of a project file (*.ipj). A *project file* is simply a configuration file set up and used to control how Inventor creates and resolves file links, where you edit files, how many old versions of the files to keep, and how Content Center files are stored and used. In the early days of Inventor, Autodesk offered two basic project types: single-user and multiuser projects. At this point, the Vault project has replaced the earlier multiuser project types.

Unless you have installed Vault, you have only one project type to choose from by default, the single-user project. The name *single-user* could be considered a misnomer, because this project is widely used by one-man shops and multi-seat design departments alike. The term *single-user* does not mean that only one user can access the files in that project as it might suggest, but instead it refers to the fact that there are no means of preventing files from being accessed for editing while another user is already editing the file. This can create a "last-man-to-save-wins" situation, if care is not taken.

Real World Scenario

SINGLE-USER PROJECTS AMONG MULTIPLE USERS

What happens when two users access the same file using a single-user project? Typically this is first noticed when one of the two tries to save the file. Inventor notifies the person trying to save that he or she is not working with the most current version, and gives the other user's name (depending upon network setup) so you know what is going on. Inventor instructs the user that he or she must save the file as a different name in order not to lose the changes made.

Typically, at this point a conversation takes place to determine how to proceed. If the first person is decided to be the one who needs to save changes, then the file they were working on is saved as another name, then the original file is deleted (or renamed as a reserve) and the other file is renamed to replace the original. In this way the changes have been preserved to the original files.

Although this may seem like a terrible hassle, there are many design departments that use single-user projects in a team setting effectively and only rarely run into this situation. More than likely you already have an idea of how often you and your colleagues handle the same files at the same time. But if try to use single-user projects and find this situation happens fairly often, then you should consider a true multiuser project.

Many design departments use single-user projects effectively in collaborative environments because of workflows that lend themselves to this type of project or by simply maintaining good communication among the design team. For collaborative environments that require some safeguard against situations where users could potentially save over one another's work, using a *multiuser* project (Vault project) is recommended.

Vault is a data management application that, as the name implies, locks down files for their protection. Once a file is in Vault, it is checked out by a user in order to be edited. Vault typically resides on a file server where the entire design team can access it. When the file is checked out of the Vault server, it is placed on the user's local machine for editing. The next user who comes along and attempts to access that file can access only a read-only version. Once the first user is finished editing, the file is checked back into Vault and automatically versioned.

It is also important to note that Inventor installs with a *default* project setup. The default project is typically not used for production work because it is not fully configurable and will almost always lead to file resolution issues, because it has no defined search path.

Creating the Project File

In Inventor, two project file configurations are available:

Single-user   A single-user project allows you to work in a file structure that is wholly contained on your system or on a network server location. This project file type is the simplest project file type to create and works well when users are not working on the same design concurrently.

Vault   Autodesk Vault is an easy-to-use data management tool that integrates work created with Inventor, Inventor Professional, AutoCAD Mechanical, and AutoCAD Electrical. It includes features that allow design teams to track work in progress and maintain version control in a multiuser environment. Design reuse is facilitated by consolidating product information and storing it in one place. Vault is a SQL database environment. A subset of the SQL environment exists in all current Windows operating systems (back to Windows 2000). Vault installs separately from Inventor. The Vault installation checks to make sure that your system is compatible and that auxiliary programs required for operation are installed. Vault is included with all versions of AutoCAD and Inventor.

Now, which type of project is best for you?

One or more designers can use projects using Vault. Single-user projects are most commonly used when there is a single seat of Inventor in the company or when only one designer works on a particular job more or less exclusively.

Multiuser Vault projects rely on a Microsoft SQL Server environment, which can be as simple as the Autodesk data management server, which supports up to 10 users with the default Microsoft SQL Server Express database. If you have a larger workgroup or require a higher capacity, a full version of Microsoft SQL Server is recommended. In addition, a workspace folder located on the individual user's system is required. Data servers should be on a separate server with rapid data access hard drives dedicated to the engineering department's use.

Inventor 9 and earlier allowed you to create shared and semi-isolated project file types. If you are currently using either legacy project type, then you should consider moving to Vault since Autodesk may not support the legacy types in future versions.

CREATING A GOOD DATA MANAGEMENT PLAN

A good data management plan is the key to using Inventor projects successfully. Using Vault will not resolve a poor project file or data management strategy.

One part of a successful Inventor deployment is the hardware and network on which the software will run. It is important that the engineering group has buy-in by the IT group. You will need to discuss several issues with this group, including hardware for servers and workstations, the network setup (100 Base-T or Gigabit), mapped network drives, and user permissions. A good server can be the difference between success and failure in your rollout.

Although you do need to think about your file structure, don't obsess over it. Most likely you will end up changing the structure at least a few times before you settle on a final structure. Keep an open mind, and realize that if you have five people in a room discussing file structures, you'll end up with five different ideas. Again, involve IT in your discussions.

Finally, you should designate one person in engineering to be the engineering administrator. This person needs to have administrative privileges on the engineering server or network share. IT may resist, but you need to keep pushing. This is important because you will need the ability to easily create, delete, and move files and folders without having to submit a help-desk ticket. Nothing will slow down a design process faster than having to wait for IT to make a simple change. Explain this need to your IT administrator, and most likely they will understand.

Creating Single-User Projects

Probably the best way to learn about projects is to create a "test" single-user project. Single-user projects allow you to open, edit, and save files without checking the files in or out. In the following sections, you will investigate the single-user file project mode. Once you gain an understanding of single-user projects, you will be ready to investigate the other project file types. To create a test project, you will use the Inventor Project Wizard.

THE INVENTOR PROJECT WIZARD

To get the most out of this exercise, open your version of Inventor, ensure that you have closed all the open files, and then access the Inventor Project Wizard by going to the Get Started tab and clicking the Projects button.

1. In the Projects dialog box, click the New button at the bottom.

2. You will see two options in the Inventor Project Wizard, as shown in Figure 2.5. Select New Single User Project, and then click Next.

FIGURE 2.5
Creating a single-user project

3. Enter **MI_Test_Project** in the Name input box.

4. Enter **C:\ MI_Test_Project** in the Project (Workspace) Folder input box.

Figure 2.6 shows a Project File page specifying the project.

FIGURE 2.6
The Project File page filled in

5. Click Next to advance to the next page of the wizard.

6. If you already created a folder for your library files and used those library folders in a previous project, those locations will appear on the Select Libraries page, shown in Figure 2.7. When creating a new project, you can choose to include some, all, or none of the defined library locations. Click the Finish button to include no libraries at this point.

FIGURE 2.7
Select Libraries
page

7. Click OK in the message box informing you that the project path entered does not yet exist.

8. Click Finish to create and save your new project file. The newly created project file link will appear in the list in the Projects dialog box.

SWITCHING AND EDITING PROJECTS

Only one project can be active at a time. To switch projects, you must first close all files that are open in Inventor. You cannot edit the file paths of the active project, but you can edit items such as Content Center libraries that are included. You can edit anything in a non-active project.

THE PROJECTS DIALOG BOX

Now that you have created your sample project file, you'll explore the options and settings available for your new project. To activate and use your new project, highlight the new project and click Apply. You can also activate or select a new project link by double-clicking the project link. Notice that MI_Test_Project has a check mark next to the project name indicating that the project is now active, as shown in Figure 2.8.

In the lower pane, you can view and access parameter settings for the following:

◆ The project type

◆ Optional included project file

◆ Style library options

◆ Libraries you want to use

◆ Frequently used subfolders

◆ Folder options

◆ Other project options

FIGURE 2.8
Projects dialog box

Right-click a parameter group to view the settings available within that group. Within the Project group, you can change the project type, view the project location, and include other project files. Project types were discussed earlier in this chapter. The project location is a read-only parameter. Included files deserve some additional discussion because the Included File parameter allows you to apply a master project to your current project; this setting, as well as the other project settings, are discussed in the coming pages.

Included Files

Although it's not required, you can include an existing project in the configuration of the current project by right-clicking Included File. The properties and settings in the project file that you attach override the settings in the current project file. This is useful for restricting and controlling a user's ability to change the project file. Also, if you frequently create new project files, you might consider creating a master project file that contains library locations and other settings you commonly use and then include the master project file in each new project file.

Workspace

For single-user projects, the workspace is defined by the location of the project file (*.ipj). For Vault projects, the workspace is defined on the workstation and is configured to match the Working Folder setting in the Vault settings. The workspace is the folder that files are copied to when they are checked out. The Workspace folder may include several subfolders containing various aspects of the design. Examples of subfolder types might be Parts, Assemblies, Drawings, or other subfolders as deemed necessary.

Workgroup

The workgroup search path specifies a location outside the current project file paths where Inventor can search for existing files that are not included in a library. A workgroup is specified when the project is created. Each single-user project should have no more than one workgroup.

Style Library

Inventor uses styles to specify dimensions, text, colors, materials, and other properties. This is similar to styles used in AutoCAD. However, Inventor allows you to store styles locally within the templates or in an external style library that may be used with any project file.

The Use Style Library function in projects specifies whether the project uses only local styles, local styles and the style library, or just local styles and a read-only version of the style library. The read-only style library is recommended for projects that have multiple users. With multiple users, changing or editing the style library on the fly can cause downstream problems. To change the Use Style Library parameter, right-click and select the new setting.

Remember that for your projects you can right-click to select another option when it is appropriate. Click Yes if you want to be able to edit styles in this project. Click Read-Only (the default) if you want to access style libraries and local styles without enabling style-editing capabilities. Click No if you want to restrict access to styles located within the current file and project template.

Library Options

Next on the list are libraries. Library folders are located outside the project file path. They may be located anywhere on your system or on your server. If you are sharing library files, it is recommended that you place them on your server in a commonly accessed location. The contents of directories specified as libraries in the project file are considered read-only by Inventor.

In your newly created project file, you have not added any library folders. If at any time you want to add library folders, you can do so by right-clicking Libraries and choosing Add Path, Add Paths From File, or Paste Path, as shown in Figure 2.9.

FIGURE 2.9
Adding library paths by right-clicking

You can manually add a path, either by browsing or by typing a new file location. Be sure to give the library a descriptive name that identifies the contents of that file location. Add Paths From File permits extracting library paths from another project file. Paste Path allows the user to copy and paste. Once you have specified library paths, the Delete Section Paths option becomes available, and you can remove paths not needed by the project. Deleting unused library paths reduces search and resolution time.

Shortcuts to Frequently Used Files

Frequently used subfolders are similar to the bookmarks you can set in Internet Explorer. The subfolders must already be nested within the current project workspace, workgroup, or library. Adding frequently used subfolders to your project provides navigation links in your open, save, and placed dialog boxes so you can quickly navigate to those locations. The Samples project is a good example of frequently used subfolders.

Folder Options

The Folder Options setting allows your project to access other file locations than are specified on the Files tab of the Application Options dialog box. Keep in mind that you may have to close and reopen Inventor in order to reinitialize the optional project file locations. You can use this option to specify different default locations for templates, design data, styles, and Content Center files. When the locations are set to the defaults, then the location/storage of the files is specified on the Files tab of the Application Options dialog box. Right-click any of the options to change the storage and access location.

Project Options

Expand the Options heading to show the global defaults for the selected project. The Options settings in a project determine file management functions; right-click an option to edit it.

Versioning and Backup

Use the Options setting to determine how many old versions or backup copies of each file to save. The Old Versions To Keep On Save option specifies the number of versions to store in the Old Versions folder for each file saved. The first time a file is saved in a project, an Old Versions folder for that file is created. When the file is saved, the prior version is moved automatically to the file's Old Versions folder. After the number of old versions reaches the maximum in the setting, the oldest version is deleted when a newer version is moved into the folder.

> ### INVENTOR OLD VERSIONS AND AUTOCAD .BAK FILES
>
> Inventor versioning is similar AutoCAD's backup scheme. AutoCAD creates a *.bak file saved in the same folder as the design. Inventor saves the backup files in a separate Old Versions directory.

All versions located in the Old Versions folder have the same name and extension, except that a number is appended after the name. The default setting of 1 creates one backup file in the Old Versions folder. If you are working with a very complex assembly or model, you can specify additional backup versions; however, remember that with each additional backup version you are creating additional files (and using additional space) on your hard drive. Setting Old Versions to –1 will cause Inventor to save all backup files.

File naming Conventions

The listing called Using Unique File Names in the Options is the setting that forces the user to create unique part names for all files in the project, including subfolders. Libraries are excluded in this option. The recommended setting for using unique file names is Yes. Proper design workflow demands that each unique part have a unique name, and that name will not be used for any other part. When parts are reused, you should ensure that any revision to that part be acceptable to all designs where that part is used. If that revised part cannot be used in all the designs, then you should use a new part name, because you have now created an additional unique part.

Setting the Using Unique File Names option to Yes forces unique file names for every file you create within the project. Duplicating file names results in resolution errors because the project search path is a relative path; it's relative to the location of the project file.

THE PROJECTS DIALOG BOX'S TOOL PANEL

The tool buttons along the right side of the lower pane of the Projects dialog box provide access to tools that allow you add, edit, and reorder project parameter settings and paths; check for duplicate file names; and configure the Content Center libraries used for the active project.

Use the magnifying glass icon located on the lower, right side of the Projects dialog box to check your project paths for duplicate filenames, as shown in Figure 2.10.

FIGURE 2.10
Using unique file names

Non-Unique Project File Names

The following files with non-unique names were found in the project:

Filename	Location	Relative Path
Part1.ipt	Workspace	760_JA\
Part1.ipt	Workspace	760_TE\
Part1.ipt	Workspace	760_TE\760_TE_001\

WHY RELATIVE PATHS?

An Inventor assembly file records relative paths when it links a subassembly or single parts to itself. The use of relative paths in assembly files allows the relocation of an assembly and its associated parts and subassemblies to other locations on servers or drives without requiring the resolution of a new location. Relative paths, however, introduce the danger of the assembly locating only the first of two parts that happen to have the same name. For instance if you've saved a file name Part1 in two different file folders, Inventor will resolve the link to the first one it finds and then stop searching.

To prevent the possibility of the wrong part being loaded in an assembly, it is important for every part located in the search path to have a unique name.

The Projects dialog box supports the configuration of one or more Content Center libraries. The Content Center provides multiple database libraries that can be used in assemblies or by the Design Accelerator (Functional Design System).

If you elected to install Content Center libraries while installing Inventor, you must configure the Content Center libraries in the project before you can access them. Click the Content Center icon in the lower right-hand corner of the project-editing dialog box. Then select the Content Center library or libraries you want to use, and click OK. Figure 2.11 shows the Configure Libraries dialog box.

Select the Content Center libraries you think you'll use. Installing all the Content Center libraries may slow your system down significantly when you are accessing Content Center because Inventor will need to index each library upon initialization.

When you finish editing the project file, click Save, and then make sure your desired project file is active before clicking Done to exit the Projects dialog box.

FIGURE 2.11
Configuring Content Center

Creating Multiuser Projects

Working as a team can increase productivity many times over. In a collaborative design environment, multiple users may be working on a project at the same time. When you create a multiuser project, you have the option to choose the Vault (if Vault is installed), shared, and semi-isolated project types. As stated earlier, Vault works in a similar fashion to a semi-isolated project. It prevents you from working on the original version of a file located inside Vault. Each user creates a local Vault project file that specifies a personal workspace located on the local drive and that includes search paths to one or more master projects.

To edit a "Vaulted" file, the user must check the file out of Vault. The process of checking the file out copies the file to the local workspace. Whenever the file is checked out for editing, the original stored in Vault is flagged as "checked out" to that particular user. Other users can view the checked-out files in read-only mode, but they can't edit the checked-out file.

The user who checked out the file can edit and save the file in his local workspace without checking the file back into Vault. When he saves the file, he will be prompted to choose whether he wants to check the file back into Vault. If he chooses to check the file into Vault, the file will be saved into Vault and is then available for editing by a different user. Optionally, he may save the file into Vault but keep it checked out to his local workspace, allowing other users to view the updated file without being able to edit it.

PROJECT SHORTCUTS

If you right-click in the project in the Project dialog box you can choose delete to remove it from the list. But if you browse out and look, you'll see the .ipj file is still there. What is going on?

When you create a new project file or point Inventor to an existing project file, Inventor will create a shortcut to that file. When you choose Delete and remove the project from the list, you are not actually deleting the .ipj file, but instead deleting the shortcut. When you choose browse and locate the .ipj file to add back to the list, the shortcut is recreated.

The shortcut path can be set by going to the Tools tab of the ribbon menu, then Application Options ➢ Files tab ➢ setting the Projects Folder path.

Collaborative design project files are created using the Inventor Project Wizard in much the same manner as a single-user project file. The file resolution process within a collaborative project file functions in the same way.

With Vault installed on your server or your own system, you can create and configure a Vault project. If Vault Explorer is not installed on your system, then you cannot install or create a Vault project on your system. Before you create your first Vault project, verify that Vault is correctly installed and that you can open and create a new Vault file store using the ADMS console. The new Vault file store must be accessible on your local system from Vault Explorer. If Vault functions correctly, you are now ready to create a Vault project file. As with a single-user project, use the Inventor Project Wizard to name the project, specify the workspace, assign libraries for use with the project, and configure project parameters.

Again, as in other project file types, you will need to edit the default settings in your project file and optionally configure your Content Center for use.

The Bottom Line

Understand how project search paths work   Knowing how Inventor resolves file paths when it opens linked files, such as assembly and drawings, goes a long way toward helping prevent broken links and repair links that do get broken.

> **Master It**   What type of file does Inventor use to point the assembly file to the parts that it contains?

Set up library and Content Center paths   Library and Content Center paths are read-only library configurations set up in the project file.

> **Master It**   When you set up a library or Content Center path to a folder that does not exist, what happens?

Create and configure a project file   Project files are a key component to working successfully in Inventor, however, for many people this is a one-time setup. Once the project is created for the most part you just use it as is.

> **Master It**   After creating a project file initially, you want to make one or more changes to the configuration, but you can't seem to do so. What could be the problem?

Determine the best project type for you   Although the Autodesk solution to a multiuse environment is Autodesk Vault, many people may not be able to use Vault. For instance, if you use another CAD application that links files together like Inventor, Vault will likely not know how to manage the internal links for those files.

> **Master It**   Because you generally do not work concurrently on the same files as your co-workers you think you might be best to set up a single-user project for now, while you continue to investigate the Vault solution, but you are not sure if that will work.

Chapter 3

Sketch Techniques

This chapter will cover the principles of creating parametric sketches used in part or assembly modeling. All the skills in this chapter are based primarily on creating a single part, whether in a single-part file or in the context of an assembly file.

Inventor utilizes two types of sketches, a 2D sketch and a 3D sketch. A 2D sketch is created on any geometry plane and is the more common of the two types. A 3D sketch is not limited to a sketch plane and can be comprised of geometry in any point in space. 3D sketches are often created from existing geometry. Both 2D and 3D sketches are controlled by two basic parameter types: dimensions and sketch constraints.

In Inventor, sketches are generally "roughed out" with basic geometry and sketch constraints first and then fully defined with dimensions that drive the geometry.

The dimensions dictate the length, size, and angle of the sketch geometry. For the dimensions to do this predictably, sketch objects must know how to interact with one another. This interaction is defined by the sketch constraints. This chapter will cover how to create a part and the features of basic 2D sketches, including the tools and settings that govern their creation. Also covered is how to use AutoCAD data to create sketches.

In this chapter, you'll learn to:

- ◆ Set up options and settings for the sketch environment
- ◆ Create a sketch from a part file template
- ◆ Use sketch constraints to control sketch geometry
- ◆ Master general sketch tools
- ◆ Create sketches from AutoCAD geometry
- ◆ Use 3D sketch tools

Exploring the Options and Settings for Sketches

Before you jump into creating a part sketch, take a look at the options and settings Inventor provides for sketches. Options and settings in part files are located in two different areas of Inventor depending upon whether the focus of these settings affects the application (Inventor) or the document (your part file). You'll look at both application options and document options in this section.

BEFORE YOU START...

Before you begin, ensure you have downloaded the tutorial files from www.sybex.com/go/ masteringinventor2011. Place the files in a folder on your computer (such as \My Documents\ Mastering Inventor 2011), and then be sure to set the Mastering Inventor 2011 project active:

1. From within Inventor, close any open files.

2. From the Get Started tab, select the Projects button.

3. From the Projects dialog, select the Browse button.

4. From the Choose Project File dialog, browse to the Mastering Inventor 2011 folder and select the Mastering Inventor 2011.ipj file and click Open.

5. Note that the Mastering Inventor 2011 project is denoted as being the active project with a check mark.

6. Click Done to close the Projects dialog box.

Now you are ready to get started.

Application Options

Application options change settings for your installation of Inventor. You can adjust the application settings as follows:

1. From the Tools tab, click the Application Options button.

2. Then choose the Sketch tab, as shown in Figure 3.1.

FIGURE 3.1
Sketch tab of Application Options dialog box

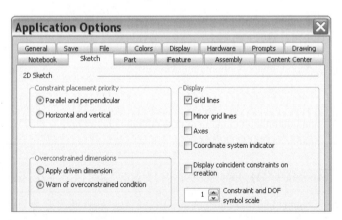

The application options on the Sketch tab are as follows:

The Constraint Placement Priority area   The options in this section determine the primary method of inferred constraint placement. In Inventor, your line work employs sketch constraints to tell lines, arcs, and circles how to interact with one another. Many of these constraints are

placed automatically while you sketch based upon the existing geometry. This automatic placement is called *constraint inference*. Parallel And Perpendicular, the default setting, will look
first for relationships between geometry, before looking at the coordinates of the sketch grid.
Horizontal And Vertical does just the opposite. Figure 3.2 shows constraint placement with parallel and perpendicular on the left and horizontal and vertical on the right.

FIGURE 3.2
Constraint place-
ment priority

The Overconstrained Dimensions area   This area controls the way redundant dimensions
are handled in sketches. As an example, if you sketch a rectangle of approximately 200 millimeters long and then place a dimension on one of the horizontal lines and set the dimension to be
precisely 200 millimeters, the rectangle will stretch horizontally to be exactly 200 millimeters.
But if you apply another dimension from the left vertical line to the right vertical line, Inventor
will either warn you of the overconstrained situation or automatically place the dimension
as a *driven dimension*. A driven dimension is one where the value is determined by the geometry, rather than a *driving dimension* that determines the value of the geometry it is placed on.
Figure 3.3 shows a driving dimension at the top and a driven dimension in parentheses.

FIGURE 3.3
A driving dimen-
sion and a driven
dimension

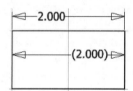

The Display area   Located in the upper-right portion of the Sketch tab, this area gives you
settings for grid lines, minor grid lines, axes, and a 2D coordinate system indicator. All of
these options set different visual references in the form of grid lines and coordinate indicators. You can experiment with these settings by deselecting the box next to each option and
clicking the Apply button while in sketch mode. To ensure that your screen matches the illustrations in this chapter, you can deselect all the options in this area except for the Grid Lines
box, as shown in Figure 3.1.

The Display Coincident Constraints On Creation check box   If selected, this option displays a yellow dot at all sketch points where coincident constraints are placed when sketching. Hovering your mouse pointer over the dots displays the coincident constraint symbol, as
shown on the left in Figure 3.4. If the check box is not selected, these coincident symbols are
not displayed initially, as shown on the right of Figure 3.4 but can still be displayed by pressing the F8 key (Show All Constraints) while in a sketch.

The Constraint And DOF Symbol Scale setting   This simply controls the size of the
icons present when viewing sketch constraints. You can see coincident symbols on the left
of Figure 3.4.

FIGURE 3.4
Display coincident
constraints on
creation

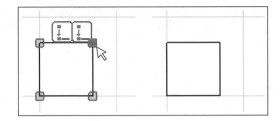

The Spline Fit Method area   This determines the initial type of transition for a spline between fit points. Figure 3.5 shows two splines drawn with the same input points. On the left, the standard spline solution is in bold with the AutoCAD solution dashed; on the right, the standard solution is dashed with the AutoCAD solution in bold.

FIGURE 3.5
Standard spline fit
(left) and AutoCAD
spline fit (right)

Standard   Creates a spline with a smooth continuity (G3 minimum) between points. This spline type tends to overshoot at sharp transitions. Use this for Class A surfaces such as automotive design.

AutoCAD   Creates a spline using the AutoCAD fit method (G2 minimum). This is not used for Class A surfaces.

Minimum Energy   Sets the fit method to create a spline with smooth continuity (G3 minimum) and good curvature distribution. Multiple internal points are used between fit points, resulting in a nice heavy curvature. This can also be used for Class A surfaces, but it takes the longest to calculate and creates the largest file size.

ABOUT CURVE CLASSIFICATION

Curves are classified by how smooth the continuity is where they connect to one another. This classification is as follows:

◆   G0 controls the position at which curves touch one another.

◆   G1 controls the tangent angle at which curves connect.

◆   G2 controls the radius at which curves connect.

◆   G3 controls the acceleration or rate of change of curves.

The Snap To Grid check box   This allows your mouse pointer to snap to a predefined grid spacing. The grid spacing is controlled per file in the *Document Settings,* as will be discussed in the coming pages.

The Edit Dimension When Created check box   This permits immediate input of a dimension value while applying sketch dimensions. This option can be toggled on and off by right-clicking while using the Dimension tool and selecting *Edit Dimension* from the context menu.

The Autoproject Edges During Curve Creation check box   This allows you to reference existing geometry from your sketch plane and have that geometry automatically included in your sketch. As an example, if you sketch on the top face of a part that has a hole on the bottom face, you might want to find the center of the hole to reference in your sketch, but since that hole exists on a different plane, it needs to be projected up into your current sketch before you can do so. Enabling this option allows you to "rub" your mouse over the hole and have it automatically projected into your sketch. Figure 3.6 shows a line being sketched from the middle of the cylinder to the center of a hole on the bottom face. With this option on, simply rubbing the edge of the hole will project it to the top face so that the line can be sketched to the center of the projected circle. This option can be toggled on and off by selecting *AutoProject* in the right-click menu of most of your sketch tools such as Line, Circle, Arc, and so on.

FIGURE 3.6
Autoprojecting a hole edge while sketching on the top face

The Autoproject Edges For Sketch Creation And Edit check box   This automatically projects the edges of the face when you create a sketch on it. Although this can be convenient in some cases, it can also become counterproductive because it places extra line work into your sketches. This can add a level of complexity to your sketches that is not required. Figure 3.7 shows the results of selecting this option.

FIGURE 3.7
Results of the Autoproject Edges For Sketch Creation And Edit check box being selected

The Look At Sketch Plane On Sketch Creation check box   This reorients the graphics window so that you are always looking perpendicular to the sketch plan while creating or editing a sketch.

The Autoproject Part Origin On Sketch Create check box   This automatically projects the part's origin center point whenever a new sketch is created. The origin center point is point 0 in the X, Y, and Z directions. Projection of this point makes it easy to constrain and anchor your sketch. If this option is not selected, you are required to manually project this point.

The Point Alignment On check box This allows endpoints and midpoints to be inferred by displaying temporary, dotted lines to assist in lining up sketch entities. Figure 3.8 shows an endpoint being located using the Point Alignment option.

FIGURE 3.8
Point alignment
inferring endpoint

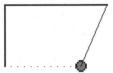

The Enable Heads-Up Display (HUD) check box This allows you to input numeric and angular values directly into input boxes when creating sketch entities. For instance, if you were to sketch a circle without HUD on, you'd rough in the approximate size and then use the Dimension tool to give the circle an exact diameter. With HUD, you can specify the diameter as you create the circle. Clicking the Settings button opens the Heads-Up Display Settings dialog box where you can adjust the HUD settings.

The Auto-bend With 3D Line Creation check box This allows corners to be automatically rounded when creating a 3D sketch. This feature can be turned on and off via the right-click menu when using the Line tool in a 3D sketch. Figure 3.9 shows two corners created without the auto-bend feature enabled and four corners created with it enabled through the right-click menu. The default auto-bend radius size is set per file via the document settings, but can be edited once the bends are created.

FIGURE 3.9
A 3D sketch line
with and without
Auto-bend With
3D Line Creation

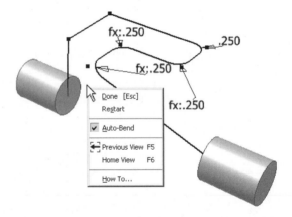

To set changes made to the application options, you can click the Apply button. You can save the changes you make to the application options for backup or distribution among other users by clicking the Export button at the bottom of the Application Options dialog box. In the resulting Save Copy As dialog box, simply specify the name of the .xml file, and click OK. You can import this .xml file at any time to restore your custom settings by using the Import button at the bottom of the Application Options dialog box.

Document Settings

In addition to the previous settings, which are set application-wide, there are also settings that control options per file. Document settings vary depending upon the file type you are in. For part files, you can modify the sketch settings by clicking the Document Settings icon on the Tools tab of the ribbon menu while you are in an open part file. Once open, click the Sketch tab to access the following settings:

Snap Spacing   This sets the spacing between snap points to control the snap precision when sketching in the active part or drawing. This is relevant only when using the Snap To Grid option on the Sketch tab of the Application Options dialog box. The settings for the x- and y-axes can be different.

Grid Display   This sets the spacing of lines in the grid display for the active file.

Line Weight Display Options   These set the options for line weight display in the sketch environment. This setting does not affect line weights in printed model sketches but merely the on-screen display.

Auto-bend Radius   This sets the default radius for 3D sketch line corners when the auto-bend feature is used.

You may want to configure the document settings in a template file and then save those settings back to that file so they are always set to your specification. To do so, click the Inventor button at the top left-hand corner of the screen, and select Save As ➤ Save Copy As Template. This will open the template file location and allow you to save the file as a template. Note that Inventor uses the template path to designate templates rather than a separate template file extension. Therefore, any .ipt file saved under the template path is considered a template.

CHANGING THE UNITS OF A PART FILE

If you start a part file using the wrong template (inches instead of millimeters or millimeters instead of inches), you can change the base units of the file by clicking the Document Settings icon on the Tools tab of the ribbon menu and going to the Units tab. Changing the base units will automatically convert parameters but will not override parameter inputs. For instance, if you entered a value of 3 inches for a dimension and then change the units of the file to millimeters, the dimension will show 76.2 mm; however, when you edit the dimension, you will see the original value of 3 inches.

Sketching Basics

Now that you've explored the sketch options and settings, you will explore the sketching tools by placing sketches on an existing 3D part. This will give you an introduction to creating 2D sketches in 3D space. The basic workflow for creating any 2D sketch is as follows:

◆   Establish the plane on which you want to sketch.

◆   Project geometry from existing feature in order to position new geometry.

- Create geometry such as lines, arcs, circles, and so on.

- Place sketch constraints on the geometry so the lines, arcs, and circles know how to relate to one another.

- Dimension the geometry so it is fully defined and there is no part of the sketch that can be accidentally adjusted.

Keep these basic steps in mind as you go through the following steps and explore the basics of sketch creation. To get started, you will open an existing file and use the faces of the part to sketch on.

1. Click the Inventor button, and choose Open (or press Ctrl+O on the keyboard).

2. Browse for the file named mi_3a_001.ipt located in the Chapter 3 directory of the Mastering Inventor 2011 folder, and click Open.

This file consists of a stepped block with one beige face, one face with two holes in it, and one face with a triangular feature on it. To start off, you will create a sketch on the top beige face. Before getting started, set your application options so you will not see any unexpected results as you follow these steps.

3. From the Tools tab, select the Application Options button.

4. In the Application Options dialog box, click the Sketch tab.

5. In the Sketch tab, ensure all of the check boxes shown in Figure 3.10 are set as shown.

FIGURE 3.10
Set your sketch
options as shown.

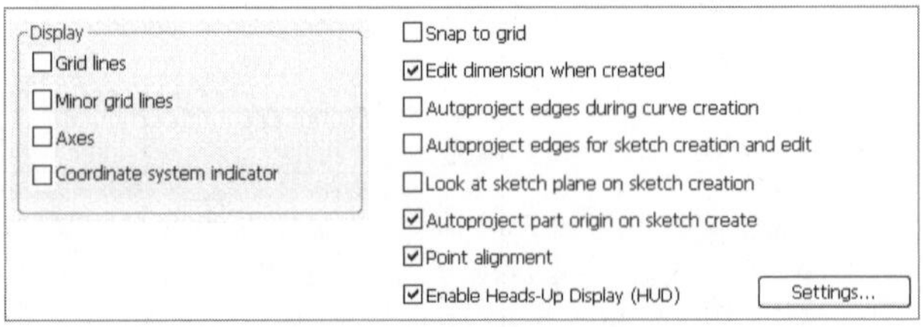

Display	
☐ Grid lines	☐ Snap to grid
☐ Minor grid lines	☑ Edit dimension when created
☐ Axes	☐ Autoproject edges during curve creation
☐ Coordinate system indicator	☐ Autoproject edges for sketch creation and edit
	☐ Look at sketch plane on sketch creation
	☑ Autoproject part origin on sketch create
	☑ Point alignment
	☑ Enable Heads-Up Display (HUD) Settings...

6. Click Apply and Close to set your sketch options, and close the Application Options Dialog box.

7. Hover your cursor over the ViewCube until you see the Home icon (looks like a house), and then click it to ensure you are looking at the model from the predefined home view.

8. From the Model tab, select the Create 2D Sketch button.

In order to create a 2D Sketch, you must select a plane to sketch on, as indicated by the glyph now present at your cursor (it looks like a pencil and paper). You should also note the input prompt found either at the bottom left of your screen or at your mouse pointer, depending upon the Dynamic Prompting settings you have active.

9. Click on the beige face to create the new sketch on it.

TURN ON DYNAMIC PROMPTING

As you use the various available tools, Inventor will prompt you with a short message concerning the input needed from you to complete the task. By default the prompts are displayed at the lower left of the screen. To help you notice them better, you can set them to display on-screen at your cursor. To do so, go to the Tools tab and click Application Options. Select the General tab, and select the Show Command Prompting (Dynamic Prompts) check box, and then click Apply and Close.

Once you've selected the face, you'll notice the change in the tools displayed on the ribbon menu and the activation of the Sketch tab. You should also notice the browser has grayed out all of the other features and only the new sketch (it should be named Sketch6) is active.

You'll also notice a sketch point (small dot in the center of the beige face) has been automatically created. This is the 0,0,0 origin point of the part. It has been automatically projected into your sketch due to the Autoproject Origin on Sketch Create setting, as shown in Figure 3.10. You will next project more geometry into your sketch.

10. Select the Project Geometry tool from the Sketch tab, and then click somewhere in the middle of the beige face. You will now see the rectangular edges of the beige face displayed as sketch lines.

11. Right-click and choose Done to exit the Project Geometry tool (or press the Escape key on the keyboard).

12. In the browser click the plus sign next to the Sketch6 browser node. You will see a projected loop listed under the sketch.

The projected loop was created by projecting the beige face into your sketch. These projected sketch lines are currently locked in place to always remain associative to the face from which they were created. In the next step you will break the associative link between the projected edges and the face.

13. Right-click on the projected loop in the browser and choose Break Link.

When you break the link, the projected loop node disappears in the browser and the projected lines around the beige face change color. The color change indicates that the sketch lines are no longer associated with the face.

Click and drag on any of the projected lines. You'll notice they can be dragged around anywhere in the sketch plane. Because the sketch plane extends out past the beige face, the lines can be dragged out even beyond the extents of the face. A 2D sketch stretches out infinitely in the two directions that make up the plane. Next you'll clean up the projected lines and project more lines.

14. Hold down the Ctrl key on the keyboard and select all four of the lines. Notice the color change indicating the selection status of the lines. If you want to remove a line from the current set of selected objects, you can click it again while holding the Ctrl key. To add it back, you would click it again, still holding the Ctrl key.

15. With all four lines selected, right-click and choose Delete.

16. Next select the Project Geometry tool again, and this time select just the circular edges of the two holes.

Watch the color coded selection closely to ensure you are getting just the hole edges and not the entire face the holes are on. If you choose the entire face, you will get the four rectangular edges and the two hole edges and a projected loop will be created under the sketch in the browser. If you do accidentally select the face, use the Undo arrow on the Quick Access toolbar and then repeat step 16.

Since you selected just the circular edges, there is no projected loop created. However, the circles are still created so that they are associative to the holes from which they were created. This means that if the original holes change locations or diameter, the projected circles will adjust accordingly.

Another point to note is that when you project the edges of the holes into your sketch, they are projected up onto the sketch plane, even though the holes are at a lower elevation. To see this clearly, you can use the ViewCube to adjust your viewing angle.

17. Click the face of the ViewCube labeled Front, and you will be able to see the projected edges are in the same plane as the beige face you created your sketch on.

18. Click the Home icon on the ViewCube to set your view back to the home view.

Next you will break the link with the projected circles and the holes they were created from. Since no projected loop was created when you projected just the edges, there is no projected loop node listed under the Sketch node in the browser. Instead you will break the link by selecting the circles in the graphics area.

19. Right-click on one of the circles and choose Break Link from the context menu. It will change colors indicting it is no longer associative to the hole and, therefore, no longer constrained in place.

20. Click on the non-associative circle and note you can resize it by clicking and dragging the circle itself, and you can move the circle by dragging the center point.

In the next steps, you will exit the current sketch and then delete the entire sketch. Then you will create a new sketch and create some geometry. Then you will use projected geometry to position and constrain the new geometry.

21. Click the Finish Sketch button on the Sketch tab (or right-click and choose Finish Sketch). Notice the Sketch node is no longer highlighted in the browser and that the Sketch tab has disappeared, leaving the Model tab active.

22. Right-click on the Sketch6 node in the browser and choose Delete. You will notice the sketch node is removed from the browser and, therefore, the projected circles are removed from the graphics area.

Next you'll create a sketch on the face that has the triangular cut in it. Rather than using the Create 2D Sketch button as you did before, you will create the sketch through the right-click context menu.

23. Right-click on the face that has the triangular cut in it, and then choose New Sketch. You will see the new Sketch node created in the browser, the Sketch tab appear in the ribbon menu, and the projected origin point appear in the sketch (the dot in the center of the triangle).

24. Click the face labeled Front on the ViewCube to look perpendicular to the sketch plane.

25. Select the Circle tool from the Draw panel of the Sketch tab.

26. Click to the left of the model as shown in Figure 3.11 to set the center of the circle. Then type **100** in the Heads Up Display input box, and press the Enter key on the keyboard to set the diameter. (If you do not see the Heads Up Display input check your settings with those shown in Figure 3.10).

FIGURE 3.11
Placing a circle
in the sketch

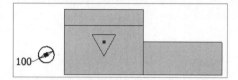

27. Select the Project Geometry tool from the Sketch tab and then select the face with the triangular cutout.

28. Select the Dimension tool from the Sketch tab and then click the projected bottom point of the triangle and the center point of the circle. Drag you cursor down until you see the dimension.

29. Click on-screen to set the dimension and then enter **150** into the input box, and click the green check mark to apply the input.

You will see the circle is repositioned to be 150 mm from the point of the triangle. This is what is meant by a *driving dimension*. The circle's position is driven by the dimension.

30. With the Dimension tool still active, select the center point of the circle and then the horizontal line of the triangle, and drag your cursor to the left until you see the dimension.

31. Click on-screen to set the dimension and then enter **150** into the input box, and click the green check mark to apply the input.

32. Right-click and choose Done to exit the Dimension tool.

At this point your sketch should be fully constrained as noted in the lower right of the screen, and it should resemble Figure 3.12.

FIGURE 3.12
Placing a circle in
the sketch

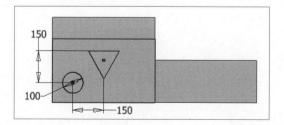

33. Use the Finish Sketch button to exit the sketch.

34. Click the Home icon on the ViewCube to set your view back to the home view.

This concludes the steps in this exercise. You can close the file without saving changes or experiment with this part and create more sketches just for fun. As you create 2D sketches in Inventor, you will often do so by selecting a face on the existing model, as you did in this exercise. If no plane exists, you can create what is called a work plane and sketch on it (work planes will be covered in the next chapter). When you create a new file, Inventor automatically creates a sketch and places it on one of the predetermined default origin planes. These planes include the YZ plane, the XZ plane, and the XY plane. In the next section, you will create a new part from a template file and create a base sketch.

Creating a Sketch in a New Part

When you create a new part file from a template, Inventor creates the first sketch for you. In the following steps, you will create a new part file and further explore the tools used to create sketch entities. To create a part model in Inventor, you will typically start with a 2D sketch and build a base feature from that sketch.

Creating a New Part File from a Template

You create new part files from an `.ipt` template. Once you open the `.ipt` template, you will automatically be in the sketch environment. In this exercise, you will use the `Standard(mm).ipt` file.

> **TURN OFF THE HEADS UP DISPLAY**
>
> In order to explore sketch fundamentals in the next exercise, you should disable the Heads Up Display (HUD) tools. The HUD tools allow you to place dimensions as you create sketch geometry, rather than having to go back and place dimensions later. Although the HUD tools are very helpful, and you will most likely want to turn them back on later, for the purpose of understanding sketch constraints and degrees of freedom, it is best to leave the dimensioning as a final step. To disable the HUD tools, go to the Tools tab and click Application Options. Select the Sketch tab, and uncheck the box labeled *Enable Heads-Up Display (HUD)*. You can turn this helpful feature back on later, but understand that the following steps assume it is disabled and your results may not match the exercise otherwise.

1. Click the Inventor button, and choose New ➢ New (to create a file from the list of templates), or just press Ctrl+N.

2. In the New File dialog box, click the Metric tab, and select the `Standard(mm).ipt` icon, as shown in Figure 3.13.

3. Click OK to create a new part file based on this template.

Creating Lines Using the Line Tool

Your screen should now show the Sketch tab set active on the Ribbon, and a sketch called Sketch1 has been created and set current in the Model browser. In the following steps, you will create simple geometry using the Line tool. These steps will focus on creation of 2D sketch constraints as well.

1. Pause your mouse pointer over the Line tool in the Sketch tab's Draw panel. (See Figure 3.14 for the location of the Line tool.)

FIGURE 3.13
Selecting
Standard(mm)
.ipt in the
Metric templates

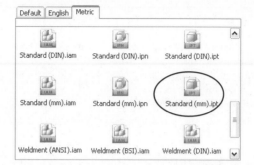

2. Note the tool tip that appears, providing the tool name, keyboard shortcut (in this case L), and a brief description of the tool. If you hover the pointer over long enough, a second stage of the tool tip appears with a more detailed description of the tool.

3. Click the Line button to start the Line tool.

4. Hover your mouse pointer over the dot in the center of the drawing area. This is the 0,0,0 origin point that has been automatically projected into Sketch1.

5. Note that when your mouse pointer moves over the dot, it changes to a green dot and shows a small glyph symbol. This green dot is a snap symbol indicating that a point, endpoint, or midpoint has been located. The glyph symbol indicates a sketch constraint is being placed. In this case, it is a coincident constraint, which ensures the endpoint of the line will stay coincident to the projected origin point. See Figure 3.15 for reference.

6. Start your line on this point by clicking the dot and releasing the mouse button.

7. Move your mouse pointer directly to the right, and you will see another glyph indicating that a horizontal sketch constraint is being placed. The horizontal constraint ensures the line will stay positioned horizontally. Note that if you move your mouse pointer so that the line is being drawn at an angle, the glyph disappears.

FIGURE 3.14
Locating the
Line tool on the
Sketch tab

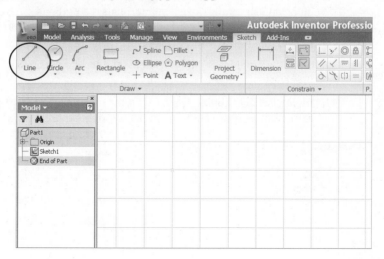

TURNING ON THE PROJECTED ORIGIN POINT

If you do not see a sketch center point in your file, close the file, and follow these steps to turn this option on:

1. From the Get Started tab, select the Application Options tab.

2. Then choose the Sketch tab.

3. Select the Autoproject Part Origin on Sketch Create check box.

4. Click OK.

5. Start a new file using the Standard(mm).ipt template.

FIGURE 3.15
Endpoint snap symbol and coincident glyph

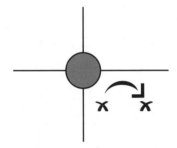

8. Notice the status bar at the bottom of the screen indicating the length and angle of the line as you move the mouse pointer. Click the graphics window while the horizontal glyph is displayed to create a line roughly 45 mm long (the length is shown at the bottom right of the screen). Don't worry about getting an exact length. You will set the precise length later; for now, you are just "roughing in" a general shape. Note the line continues when the first line segment is placed, and you can add more segments as required.

9. Move your mouse pointer straight up to add another line segment, and note another glyph appears at the mouse pointer. This is a perpendicular glyph indicating a sketch constraint is being placed that will hold the first and second line segments perpendicular (see Figure 3.16 for reference).

10. Click the graphics window to create the second segment at roughly 45 mm long and perpendicular to the first segment.

11. Right-click, and choose Done to exit the Line tool. Note that the Esc key will also exit the active tool, as indicated in the right-click menu.

FIGURE 3.16
Creating a vertical line with an automatic perpendicular constraint

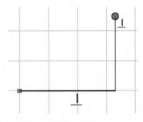

You should now have a single horizontal line and a single vertical line making a backward L shape. If you made a mistake, simply use the Undo icon at the top of the screen (or press Ctrl+Z) to undo and try again. Leave this file open for use in the next set of steps.

Understanding Sketch Constraints

The glyphs you were observing while creating the line segments were indicators that Inventor was placing sketch constraints automatically as you were sketching the lines. By default the sketch constraints have their visibility turned off. To see the sketch constraints that are present and how they work, continue with the following steps:

1. Right-click anywhere in the graphics window other than on the lines, and choose Show All Constraints (or press F8 on the keyboard). You will now see the sketch constraint icons for the constraints that were inferred as you created the line segments.

2. Hover your mouse pointer over the perpendicular constraint at the corner of the two line segments to see both lines highlighted, which indicates that these are the objects involved in this particular constraint definition.

3. Hover your mouse pointer over the yellow dot at the corner of the two line segments, and you will see two coincident constraints appear, as shown in Figure 3.17. Hovering your mouse pointer over each will highlight the line to which they belong. Coincident constraints are initially "rolled up" in this way because they are generally very numerous and tend to clutter the sketch when all constraints are shown.

WHEN IN DOUBT, RIGHT-CLICK

Inventor is very right-click driven, meaning that oftentimes you can find the option you are looking for by right-clicking the object you are dealing with.

In Inventor the right-click context menus are specific to the objects you have selected. If no objects are selected, right-clicking gives you the default right-click menu.

Unlike in some other applications, the Esc key does not clear selected on-screen entities in the graphics area. Instead, you can click any blank area in the graphics area to ensure you have nothing selected before right-clicking. This way you can be certain the right-click context menu you get is not specific to an accidentally selected object.

---

4. Click the X on any of the constraints to hide just that particular constraint.

FIGURE 3.17
Showing
constraints

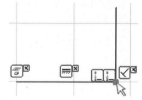

5. Next right-click anywhere in the graphics area other than on the lines, and choose Hide All Constraints (or press F9 on the keyboard). You can toggle the visibility of all sketch constraints on and off as needed in order to determine how sketch entities are constrained together.

6. Select the corner point of the two line segments, and hold down and drag around in a circle. You will notice the horizontal line will stretch as required but will always remain horizontal; the vertical line will always remain perpendicular.

7. Select the uppermost endpoint of the vertical line, and drag around in a circular motion. Note the two lines will adjust lengths as permitted but will always honor the sketch constraints they have placed on them.

8. Let up on the end of the line, and press F8 to show the constraints again.

9. Right-click the horizontal constraint.

10. Choose Delete to remove this constraint.

11. Press F9 to hide the constraints again.

12. Click the corner of the lines, and hold down and drag around in a circular motion. Note the lines will stretch and adjust orientation but will maintain their perpendicular and coincident relationships.

At this point, the constraints present in your sketch were all inferred (placed automatically). Letting Inventor infer sketch constraints is the quickest and often most desirable way to place sketch constraints; however, sometimes you'll need to constrain sketch elements manually. To do so, you can use the constraint tools found in the Constrain panel of the Ribbon.

To place the horizontal constraint back on the line from which you removed it, follow these steps:

1. Go to the Constrain panel of the Ribbon, and click the Horizontal Constraints icon, as shown in Figure 3.18.

FIGURE 3.18
Placing a horizontal constraint manually

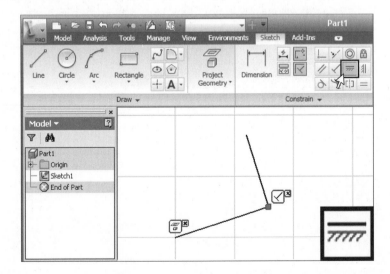

2. Click the first line segment you sketched to set it back to horizontal. Be careful to select the line itself and not the midpoint of the line (the midpoint shows as a green dot when selected).

Use the Line tool to add three more line segments to the sketch to complete the shape, as shown in Figure 3.19. Pay attention to the cursor glyphs as you sketch, and do not be concerned with the precise lengths of the lines or the angle of the diagonal line. You can keep this file open for use in the next set of steps or close it and use the file provided.

FIGURE 3.19
Completed sketch profile with all constraints shown

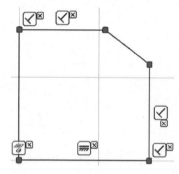

CONSTRAINT INFERENCE AND PERSISTENCE

You can suppress the automatic placement of sketch constraints (constraint inference) by holding down Ctrl on the keyboard as you sketch. You can also disable constraint inference and persistence using the Constraint Inference and Constraint Persistence buttons in the Sketch tab's Constrain panel.

If constraint persistence is disabled, you will still see the constraint glyph icon when sketching, and you will be able to place sketch entities in accordance with the displayed glyph; however, no actual constraint will be placed on the sketched object. For instance, sketching a line that is oriented perpendicular to an existing line without actually having a perpendicular constraint placed automatically is possible by toggling off the constraint persistence. Coincident constraints at the endpoints of the lines will still be placed.

Constraint persistence is automatically disabled if constraint inference is turned off, but inference can be on with persistence turned off. You can also control which constraints are inferred by right-clicking in a sketch and choosing Constraint Options.

Using Degrees of Freedom to View Under-Constrained Sketch Elements

Typically your goal is to create fully constrained sketches so that no aspect of the sketch can be changed without deliberate action. To examine your sketch for under-constrained elements, you can use the Degrees of Freedom (DOF) tool. To explore DOF, you can use the file you have been working with in the previous steps or open the file called mi_3a_002.ipt from the Chapter 3 directory of the Mastering Inventor 2011 folder. Ensure Sketch1 is active for edits by right-clicking it and choosing Edit Sketch.

1. To view the DOF arrows for your sketch entities, right-click anywhere in the graphics area that is not on a sketch object, and choose Show All Degrees Of Freedom. Your sketch should resemble Figure 3.20.

FIGURE 3.20
Showing the degrees of freedom in a sketch

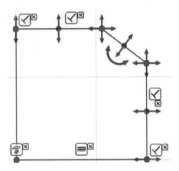

2. Notice the arrow indicators showing the DOF for each sketched line.

3. Drag a line endpoint, and you will see the sketch lines will drag only in a direction or orientation that follows the DOF arrows. If your sketch becomes distorted in an undesirable way, use the Undo icon at the top of the screen or press Ctrl+Z to set it back as it was.

> **DRAGGING TO REFINE YOUR SKETCH**
>
> Experienced Inventor users rely on the click-and-drag technique to fine-tune the general shape of a sketch rather than trying to get things precisely right from the beginning. Become familiar with this technique so you can use it to your advantage.

4. To toggle the DOF visibility back off, right-click again, and choose Hide All Degrees Of Freedom.

5. Note that you can right-click an individual sketch object or a selection set of sketch objects and choose Display Degrees Of Freedom to show the DOF for just those selected objects.

6. Right-click and choose Show All Degrees of Freedom again to have these displayed for reference in the next steps.

Using Dimensions to Fully Constrain a Sketch

To work toward your goal of a fully constrained sketch, you will now add dimensions to lock down lengths, angles, and so on. Adding dimensions will remove degrees of freedom from your sketch objects and help you define the intent of your design. You will use the General Dimension tool to place dimensions on your sketch. Note that although the tool is called General Dimension, the button simply reads Dimension. You can continue with the file you are working or open the file called mi_3a_002.ipt from the Chapter 3 directory of the Mastering Inventor 2011 folder. If opening the prepared file, ensure Sketch1 is active for edits by right-clicking it and choosing Edit Sketch, and then right-click and choose Show All Degrees of Freedom.

1. On the Sketch tab of the Ribbon, click the Dimension icon in the Constrain panel, as indicated in Figure 3.21.

FIGURE 3.21

Placing a dimension on the sketch

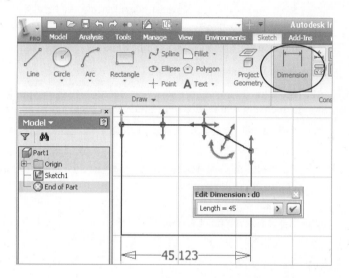

2. In the graphics area, click the bottom horizontal line, and drag down to display the dimension.

3. Click below the line to place the dimension, and you should see an Edit Dimension box, as shown in Figure 3.21. If you do not see the Edit Dimension box, you can right-click anywhere in the blank space of the graphics area and click Edit Dimension to ensure that this box shows up after placing each dimension. Then simply click the dimension to open this input box.

4. In the Edit dialog box, type **Length = 45**. Because you are working in a millimeter-based part file, the units are assumed to be 45 mm, and Inventor will add the mm automatically.

Notice the Edit Dimension box caption reads something such as d0. This indicates that this dimension parameter is named d0. Initially, Inventor names the first dimension used in the file d0, the next is named d1, and so on. By entering Length = 45, you are renaming the dimension from d0 to Length and changing this length value from the sketched value to a precise value of 45 mm. You are not required to rename your dimensions, but it is good practice to name any that you intend to reference later.

5. Click the green checkmark in the Edit Dimension box, or press the Enter key to set the dimension value. Take note that the dimension "drives" the sketch to be 45 mm long. Also notice that some of the DOF arrows have been removed.

6. Click the 45 mm dimension to edit it. Notice that the Edit Dimension box caption now reads Length and the value now reads 45 mm.

7. Change the value to **50 mm**, and click the green checkmark.

8. Next click the bottom horizontal line again and drag up, but do not click to place the dimension. You will see the same horizontal dimension displayed.

9. Click the top horizontal line, and drag down, and you will see the dimension change from the horizontal dimension evaluating the length of the bottom line to a vertical dimension evaluating the distance between the top and bottom lines.

10. Click in the graphics area to place the dimension.

11. Enter **Width =**

12. Click the 50 mm dimension you placed in the previous steps. Notice that clicking one dimension while editing another will create a reference between the two.

13. Complete the formula to read **Width = Length/2**, as shown in Figure 3.22.

14. Click the green checkmark or press the Enter key to set the dimension value. Observe that the Width dimension is evaluated at half the Length dimension and that it displays an fx: before the value to denote that there is a function used to evaluate this dimension. Also notice that more DOF arrows have been removed as you have further defined the sketch.

15. If your sketch has become a bit skewed, exit the Dimension tool by right-clicking and choosing Done (or by pressing the Esc key).

16. Click the top endpoint of the vertical line to the right, and drag it so that the general shape of the profile is restored.

17. On the Sketch tab of the Ribbon, click the Dimension icon in the Constrain panel, or just press D on the keyboard to start the Dimension tool again.

18. Click the vertical line to the right, and then click the diagonal line. Take care to click the lines and not the endpoints of the lines, because doing so will result in a different dimension type.

FIGURE 3.22
Referencing one
parameter to
another

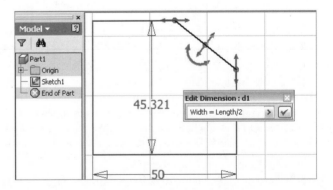

19. Click in the graphics area to place the dimension. You will be presented with an edit box for an angle dimension. Enter **Angle1 = 108**, and click the green checkmark.

20. Lastly, on the Sketch tab of the Ribbon, click the Equal button in the Constrain panel to place an equal constraint. Select the top horizontal line and the vertical line on the right to set those two lines equal.

Your sketch is now fully constrained and should resemble Figure 3.23.

FIGURE 3.23
A fully constrained
sketch

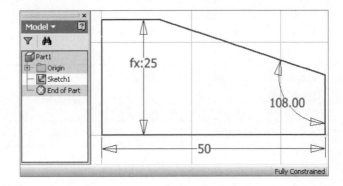

A fully constrained sketch is evident by taking note of the following:

◆   All the DOF arrows are now gone.

◆   You will see Fully Constrained in the status bar at the bottom right of the screen.

◆   Your sketch lines will have turned a different color than they were originally, before becoming constrained.

Understanding the Save Options

At this point, you may have seen a save reminder balloon in the top-right corner of the screen. It is always good practice to save often when working in any application. To save a part file, you must first exit the sketch and then save:

1. On the Ribbon's Sketch tab, click Finish Sketch in the Exit panel. Or right-click in the graphics area and choose Finish Sketch from the menu.

2. Click the Inventor button, and then select Save.

3. Select the Chapter3 folder, and name the file mi_001.

You should be aware of all the save options you have and how they differ. These can all be accessed by clicking the Inventor button and choosing Save or Save As from the Application menu. Here's a list:

Save   Choosing this option saves the active document contents to the file specified in the window title, and the file remains open.

Save All   Choosing this option saves all open document contents to the file specified in the window title, and the files remain open.

Save As   Choosing this option saves the active document contents to the file specified in the Save As dialog box. The original document is closed, and the newly saved file is opened. The contents of the original file are unchanged.

Save Copy As   Choosing this option saves a copy of the active file as specified in the Save Copy As dialog box, and the original file remains open.

Save Copy As Template   Choosing this option saves a copy of the active file as a template to the template folder, and the original file remains open.

ADJUSTING THE SAVE OPTIONS

Inventor does not have an automatic save function but instead has a save reminder utility that allows you to save by just clicking within the bubble to launch a standard save operation. To adjust the save timer settings, select the Application Options button and then select the Save Tab.

Making a Sketch Active for Edits

To save a file, you are required to exit the sketch. To continue making edits to the sketch once saved, you need to set the sketch active for edits. Here's how to activate the sketch:

1. Locate Sketch1 in the Model browser to the left of your screen, and either right-click and choose Edit Sketch or double-click the browser sketch icon.

2. Notice that the Sketch node listed in the browser consists of the sketch icon and the sketch name. Clicking the sketch name once and then again (don't double-click) allows you to rename the sketch. Therefore, you may want to develop a habit of double-clicking the sketch icon rather than the sketch name to set a sketch active for edits.

Look at the browser and notice that the rest of the browser nodes are grayed out and Sketch1 is highlighted, letting you know that the sketch is active for editing. You'll also notice that the sketch tools are available.

Using Construction Geometry

Now that the sketch is active, you will add more geometry and dimensions to further explore the sketch tools. You'll start by sketching a line and then converting that line to a construction line. Construction geometry is often used to help locate and constrain normal sketch geometry.

The primary difference between construction geometry and standard geometry is that construction geometry is filtered out of profile calculations. In other words, if you have a part profile consisting of a rectangle and you run a construction line down the middle of it, resulting in two halves of the original profile, Inventor will ignore the construction line and see only one profile when you go to create a solid part from the sketch. To create a construction line in your sketch, follow these steps:

1. Click the Line tool in the Sketch tab's Draw panel. (Recall you can access the Line tool by pressing the L key on the keyboard as well.)

2. Start the line at the bottom-left corner of the profile, keeping an eye on your mouse pointer to ensure that you see the green dot (indicating the endpoint) and the constraint glyph (indicating a coincident constraint is being inferred).

3. Set the second point of the line on the midpoint of the diagonal line. Again, you should see a green dot and a coincident glyph, as shown in Figure 3.24.

FIGURE 3.24
Placing a
construction line

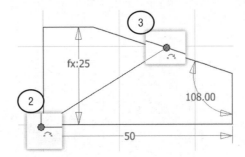

4. Right-click and choose Done to exit the Line tool.

5. Select the new diagonal line you just created.

6. On the Sketch tab (to the far right), click the Construction icon in the Format panel, as shown in Figure 3.25.

Notice the line has changed from a solid line to an orange dashed line, indicating it is now a construction line.

Using the Polygon Tool and Creating an Aligned Dimension

Next you will need to add a polygon to the midpoint of the construction line and manually place a constraint to position it in place. You will then need to place a dimension to size it:

1. In the Sketch tab's Draw panel, click the Polygon tool.

FIGURE 3.25
Converting to a
construction line

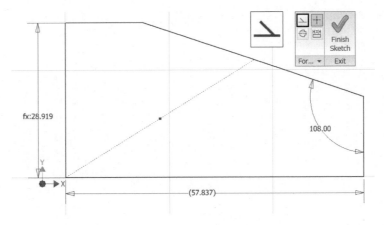

2. Select the midpoint of the diagonal construction line, keeping an eye on your mouse pointer for the green midpoint dot and the coincident glyph.

3. Leave the polygon settings at the defaults, and drag out the size and orientation to roughly match Figure 3.26.

FIGURE 3.26
Creating a polygon

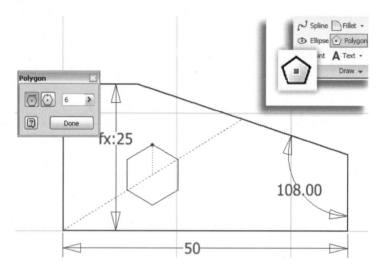

4. In the Sketch tab's Constrain panel, click the Parallel constraint icon.

5. Choose any of the flats on the polygon and the diagonal profile line, as shown in Figure 3.27, to make the two lines parallel.

6. In the Sketch tab's Constrain panel, click the Dimension tool.

7. On the polygon, click two opposing points, as shown in Figure 3.28, to create a dimension between the two points.

FIGURE 3.27
Setting the two
edges to be parallel

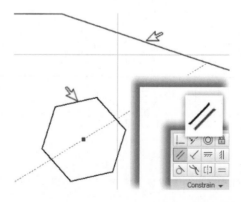

FIGURE 3.28
Creating a point
to point aligned
dimension

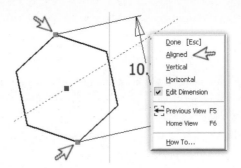

8. Pull your mouse pointer to the side to preview the dimension. Notice that the orientation wants to be horizontal or vertical depending upon the location of your mouse pointer.

9. Right-click and choose Aligned to force the aligned solution for this particular dimension.

10. Click the graphics window to place the dimension.

11. Enter **Hex_Size = 0.375 in**.

12. Click the green checkmark or press the Enter key to set the dimension value. Notice that although you entered an imperial unit of inches, Inventor converted the value automatically to the file default of millimeters. This is a powerful function that allows you to use dimension inputs to do conversion calculations on the fly.

USING AN UNDERSCORE IN PARAMETER NAMES

When specifying parameter names, keep in mind that spaces are not allowed, but you can use underscores.

CREATING MIXED-UNIT FORMULAS

You can mix any acceptable units in the same parameter formula and allow Inventor to do the conversion. For instance, entering the following into a dimension is perfectly acceptable:

3.25 ft – 1 m + 3 cm + 0.125 in

This would return a value of 23.775 mm in a millimeter part.

Using Offset and Creating a Three Point Rectangle

You will now use the Offset and Three Point Rectangle tools to create more sketch geometry:

1. In the Sketch tab's Modify panel, click the Offset tool.

2. Before selecting any geometry, right-click anywhere that is not on the sketch geometry.

3. Ensure that the Loop Select and Constrain Offset options are both selected.

   ◆ Selecting Loop Select means that all joined geometry will be selected as a loop. With this option toggled off, individual line or curve segments are selected.

   ◆ Selecting Constrain Offset means the new geometry is constrained to be equidistant to the original. If you turn this option off, the new geometry is created unconstrained to the original.

4. Click the polygon, and drag to the outside.

5. Click the graphics window to set the offset distance.

6. Right-click and choose Done (or press the Esc key) to exit the Offset tool.

7. In the Sketch tab's Constrain panel, click the Dimension tool (or press D on the keyboard)

8. To dimension the offset, select an edge of the original polygon, and then select the corresponding edge on the new offset polygon.

9. Drag the dimension out from the center of the polygon, and place it anywhere.

10. Enter **Hex_Offset = 1/16"**, and click the green checkmark. The result should appear similar to Figure 3.29.

11. In the Sketch tab's Draw panel, click the Rectangle flyout, and choose Rectangle Three Point, as shown in Figure 3.30.

12. Create the rectangle using the three points shown in Figure 3.3, click the top left point first, then the top right point, and then the bottom middle point. Make certain you are seeing the green snap dots and coincident constraint glyphs at each point.

13. Right-click, and choose Done. If your rectangle is not fully constrained, click the corner and drag it away from the line, and then back to the line, and set it on the line when you see the constrain glyph.

FIGURE 3.29
The offset polygon

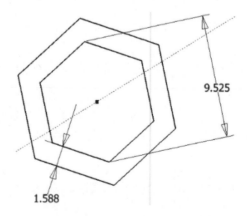

FIGURE 3.30
Accessing the
Rectangle Three
Point tool

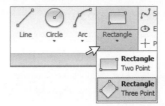

FIGURE 3.31
Placing a three
point rectangle

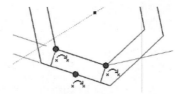

This completes the creation of most of your sketch objects in this exercise. Save your file and use it in the next set of steps. Your sketch should resemble Figure 3.32.

TO TRIM OR NOT TO TRIM

You can find the Trim tool in the Sketch tab's Modify panel. Although you might be tempted to use the Trim tool to tidy up the sketch, keep in mind that in Inventor you are creating solid models from these sketches, and therefore trimming "extra" lines from a sketch is not required.

More important, though, trimming these "extra" lines in a sketch often does more harm than good. This is because all the lines in the sketch have constraint relationships between them. When you use the Trim tool, you are inadvertently removing constraints that were holding your sketch objects together. As a rule, use the Trim tool only when necessary.

You might find the Split tool is actually what you want. Split will divide a line into separate segments without removing them. And it will also maintain sketch constraints. You can find the Split tool in the Sketch tab's Modify panel as well. Hover your mouse pointer over it for a moment and you will get a dynamic tool tip showing you how it works.

FIGURE 3.32
Your completed
sketch

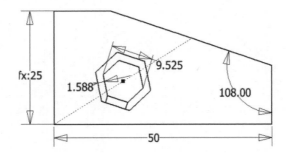

Creating Driven Dimensions

Now you'll take a look at creating driven dimensions and editing the parameters you just created through the Parameters dialog box. Because dimensions define the parameters of your design, you can use them to control the design intent. Other times you may want to place a dimension that does not drive the design but instead is driven by other parameters. In those cases, such dimensions are called driven dimensions.

Unlike Inventor's standard parametric dimensions, driven dimensions do not change the geometry but instead change when the geometry changes. Driven dimensions are created either by placing a dimension on already defined geometry or by explicitly making them driven.

You can use your current file or open the file called mi_3a_003.ipt from the Chapter 3 directory of the Mastering Inventor 2011 folder. If opening the prepared file, ensure Sketch1 is active for edits by right-clicking it and choosing Edit Sketch. Follow these steps to explore driven dimensions:

1. Double-click the 50 mm Length dimension.

2. Replace the value of 50 with **60**, and press the Enter key.

3. Take note that the vertical dimension retains the intent of your design and remains at half the Length value.

4. In the Sketch tab's Constrain panel, click the Dimension tool (or press D on the keyboard).

5. Select the vertical line on the right of the sketch, and click the graphics window to place the dimension.

6. You will be presented with a dialog box warning you that this dimension will overconstrain the sketch. Click Accept to place the dimension as a driven dimension.

Notice the dimension is created in parentheses, denoting it is driven by other parameters and, therefore, is considered a reference parameter. Driven dimensions are useful in capturing dimensions for use in the calculations of other features.

7. Next switch from the Sketch tab to the Manage tab on the Ribbon.

8. Click the Parameters tool. This will open the Parameter dialog box listing all the dimensions you've created in this part as parameters, as shown in Figure 3.33.

9. Enter **Vertical_Leg** for the Reference Parameter name. Be sure to use an underscore, rather than a space.

10. Change the Length value from **60 mm** to **65 mm**.

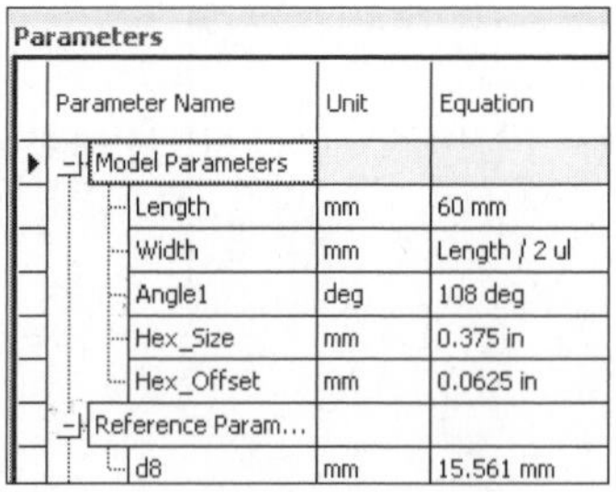

FIGURE 3.33
Parameters
dialog box

Parameters			
Parameter Name	Unit	Equation	
− Model Parameters			
Length	mm	60 mm	
Width	mm	Length / 2 ul	
Angle1	deg	108 deg	
Hex_Size	mm	0.375 in	
Hex_Offset	mm	0.0625 in	
− Reference Param...			
d8	mm	15.561 mm	

If you have the Immediate Update check box selected, the dimension is automatically updated in the sketch. If not, then you will need to manually update the dimension by go to the Quick Access bar at the top left of the screen, and click the Update button, as shown in Figure 3.34.

11. Ensure the Immediate Update check box is selected and then click Done to return to the sketch.

12. Right-click in the graphics area and choose Dimension Display ➤ Expression from the right-click menu.

13. Observe the dimension names and expression values and then right-click in the graphics area and choose Dimension Display ➤ Value from the right-click menu to set the dimension display back to display the calculated value.

You can leave this file open and use it in the next set of steps.

DIMENSION ARRANGEMENT

Although the arrangement of sketch dimensions is not all that important because these dimensions will ultimately be consumed by a solid model, it is still helpful to be able to read them in the sketch. You can rearrange jumbled sketch dimensions by clicking the text/numbers and dragging them as you like. Note too that this must be done once you've exited the Dimension tool, because clicking a dimension with the Dimension tool active edits that dimension.

You'll notice that because of the intelligence you've built into the sketch, when you modify and update the Length dimension (parameter) value, the dependant values change as well.

Next, you'll change a driving dimension to a driven dimension and a driven to a driving. By doing this, you can modify the intent of your design and change which parameter is a key input. You can use your current file or open the file called mi_3a_004.ipt from the Chapter 3 directory of the Mastering Inventor 2011 folder. If opening the prepared file, ensure Sketch1 is active for edits by right-clicking it and choosing Edit Sketch.

1. Click the 65 mm Length dimension.

2. In the Sketch tab's Format panel, click the Driven Dimension tool. Notice that the Length dimension is now set in parentheses, indicating that it is now driven rather than driving.

3. Double-click any blank area in the graphics window to unselect the previous dimension.

4. Select the vertical dimension that is in parentheses.

5. Click the Driven Dimension tool again to toggle this dimension from a driven to a driving dimension.

6. Double-click the vertical dimension to edit its value.

7. Enter **15 mm**, and click the green check mark. Notice that the Vertical_Leg parameter now drives the Length parameter, which drives the Width dimension. You should be beginning to see the power of parametric design.

8. You can close this file without saving changes.

Now that you've been introduced to the basics of creating a parametric sketch, take a more in-depth look at these tools in the next sections.

Taking a Closer Look at Sketch Constraints

In this section, you'll take a closer look at each of the available sketch constraints. As you proceed, it may occur to you that you could use some sketch constraints in place of the one suggested in the exercise steps. Be aware that as you create sketch constraints, there are often multiple solutions to get the same result.

In the following exercises, you will be opening a series of part files, setting the sketch within active for edits, and applying different sketch constraints. Each of these files demonstrates the function of a different type of sketch constraint. All of these files contain a sketch called <-- Double Click to Edit (Sketch 1). You will edit the sketch in each file and apply the appropriate sketch from the Constrain Panel of the Sketch tab, as shown in Figure 3.35.

FIGURE 3.35
Constrain tools

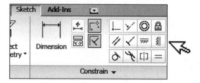

Tangent Constraint

The tangent constraint places one object or edge in a tangency to another object or edge. Objects can be tangent to another even if they do not share a physical point. Follow these steps to explore the tangent constraint:

1. Click the Inventor button, and choose Open (or press Ctrl+O on the keyboard).

2. Browse for the file named mi_3h_001.ipt located in the Chapter 3 directory of the Mastering Inventor 2011 folder, and click Open.

3. In the Model browser, double-click Sketch1 to edit it. Or, right-click it, and choose Edit Sketch.

4. Press the F8 key to show all the constraints. Note there is no tangent constraint between the large circle and the lines.

5. In the Sketch tab's Constrain panel, click the Tangent button. Click the line and circle, as shown in Figure 3.36.

6. Repeat to set a tangent constraint on the top line and the same circle.

7. Right-click, and choose Done.

FIGURE 3.36
Placing a tangent
constraint

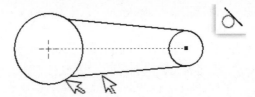

8. Press the F8 key to show all the constraints, and note the new tangent constraints.

9. You can exit the file without saving once you are finished.

Perpendicular Constraint

The perpendicular constraint constrains objects or edges to be always perpendicular. Follow these steps to explore the perpendicular constraint:

1. From the Get Started tab, select the Open button.

2. Browse for the file named mi_3h_002.ipt located in the Chapter 3 directory of the Mastering Inventor 2011 folder, and click Open.

3. In the Model browser, double-click Sketch1 to edit it. Or, right-click it, and choose Edit Sketch.

4. In the Sketch tab's Constrain panel, click the Perpendicular button.

5. Click the line, as shown in Figure 3.37, and then select either of the horizontal lines.

FIGURE 3.37
Placing a perpen-
dicular constraint

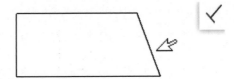

6. Right-click, and choose Done.

7. Press the F8 key to show all the constraints, noting the new perpendicular constraint.

8. You can exit the file without saving once you are finished.

Parallel Constraint

The parallel constraint constrains objects or edges to be always parallel. Follow these steps to explore the parallel constraint:

1. From the Get Started tab, select the Open button.

2. Browse for the file named mi_3h_003.ipt located in the Chapter 3 directory of the Mastering Inventor 2011 folder, and click Open.

3. In the Model browser, double-click Sketch1 to edit it. Or, right-click it, and choose Edit Sketch.

4. In the Sketch tab's Constrain panel, click the Parallel button.

5. Click the line as shown in Figure 3.38, and then select the lower horizontal line.

FIGURE 3.38
Placing a parallel constraint

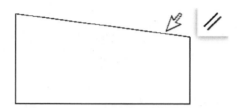

6. Right-click, and choose Done.

7. Press the F8 key to show all the constraints, and note the new parallel constraint.

8. You can exit the file without saving once you are finished.

Coincident Constraint

The coincident constraint places objects or points in contact with another object. Follow these steps to explore the coincident constraint:

1. From the Get Started tab, select the Open button.

2. Browse for the file named mi_3h_004.ipt located in the Chapter 3 directory of the Mastering Inventor 2011 folder, and click Open.

3. In the Model browser, double-click Sketch1 to edit it. Or, right-click it, and choose Edit Sketch.

4. In the Sketch tab's Constrain panel, click the Coincident button.

5. Click the center of the circle and then on the center point, as shown in Figure 3.39.

FIGURE 3.39
Placing a coincident constraint

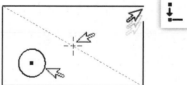

6. Right-click, and choose Done.

7. Next, click the endpoint of the vertical line at the top-right corner of the rectangular shape, and hold down as you drag to close the profile. Note that a coincident constraint is placed.

8. Press the F8 key to show all the constraints, and note the new coincident constraints, as shown by the yellow dots.

9. Hover your mouse pointer over the dots to see coincident constraint symbols.

10. You can exit the file without saving once you are finished.

Concentric Constraint

The concentric constraint places arcs and circles so that they share the same center point. Follow these steps to explore the concentric constraint:

1. From the Get Started tab, select the Open button.

2. Browse for the file named mi_3h_005.ipt located in the Chapter 3 directory of the Mastering Inventor 2011 folder, and click Open.

3. In the Model browser, double-click Sketch1 to edit it. Or, right-click it, and choose Edit Sketch.

4. In the Sketch tab's Constrain panel, click the Concentric button.

5. Click the edge of the circle and then the arc, as shown in Figure 3.40.

FIGURE 3.40
Placing a concen-
tric constraint

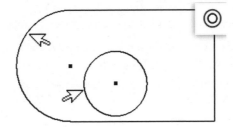

6. Right-click, and choose Done.

7. Press the F8 key to show all the constraints, and note the new concentric constraint.

8. You can exit the file without saving once you are finished.

Collinear Constraint

The collinear constraint lines up a line object or ellipse axis on the same line as another line object or ellipse axis. Follow these steps to explore the collinear constraint:

1. From the Get Started tab, select the Open button.

2. Browse for the file named mi_3h_006.ipt located in the Chapter 3 directory of the Mastering Inventor 2011 folder, and click Open.

3. In the Model browser, double-click Sketch1 to edit it. Or, right-click it, and choose Edit Sketch.

4. In the Sketch tab's Constrain panel, click the Collinear icon.

5. Click the lines as shown in Figure 3.41.

FIGURE 3.41
Placing a collinear
constraint

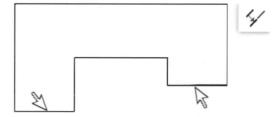

6. Right-click, and choose Done.

7. Press the F8 key to show all the constraints, and note the new collinear constraint.

8. You can exit the file without saving once you are finished.

Horizontal Constraint

The horizontal constraint makes an object line up parallel to the x-axis. Two points may also line up horizontally. Follow these steps to explore the horizontal constraint:

1. From the Get Started tab, select the Open button.

2. Browse for the file named mi_3h_007.ipt located in the Chapter 3 directory of the Mastering Inventor 2011 folder, and click Open.

3. In the Model browser, double-click Sketch1 to edit it. Or, right-click it, and choose Edit Sketch.

4. In the Sketch tab's Constrain panel, click the Horizontal button.

5. Click the line as shown in Figure 3.42, noting the new horizontal alignment.

FIGURE 3.42
Placing a horizon-
tal constraint

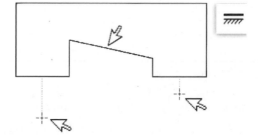

6. Next click both of the points, as indicated in Figure 3.42, noting that they will line up horizontally.

7. Right-click, and choose Done.

8. Press the F8 key to show all the constraints, and note the new horizontal constraints.

9. You can exit the file without saving once you are finished.

Vertical Constraint

The vertical constraint makes an object line up parallel to the y-axis. Two points may also line up vertically. Follow these steps to explore the vertical constraint:

1. From the Get Started tab, select the Open button.

2. Browse for the file named mi_3h_008.ipt located in the Chapter 3 directory of the Mastering Inventor 2011 folder, and click Open.

3. In the Model browser, double-click Sketch1 to edit it. Or, right-click it, and choose Edit Sketch.

4. In the Sketch tab's Constrain panel, click the Vertical button.

5. Click the line as shown in Figure 3.43, noting the new vertical alignment.

FIGURE 3.43
Placing a vertical constraint

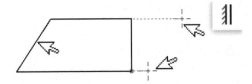

6. Next click both of the points as indicated in Figure 3.43, noting that they will line up vertically.

7. Right-click, and choose Done.

8. Press the F8 key to show all the constraints, and note the new vertical constraints.

9. You can exit the file without saving once you are finished.

Equal Constraint

The equal constraint makes two objects equal in length or radius. Follow these steps to explore the equal constraint:

1. From the Get Started tab, select the Open button.

2. Browse for the file named mi_3h_009.ipt located in the Chapter 3 directory of the Mastering Inventor 2011 folder, and click Open.

3. In the Model browser, double-click Sketch1 to edit it. Or, right-click it, and choose Edit Sketch.

4. In the Sketch tab's Constrain panel, click the Equal button.

5. Click the two circles as shown in Figure 3.44, and notice that they become equal.

FIGURE 3.44
Placing an equal
constraint

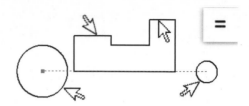

6. Click the lines, as indicated in Figure 3.44, noting that they too will become equal. You can make two of the vertical lines equal if you'd like as well.

7. Right-click, and choose Done.

8. Press the F8 key to show all the constraints, and note the new equal constraints.

9. You can exit the file without saving once you are finished.

Fix Constraint

CERT
OBJECTIVE

The fix constraint anchors any geometry or point in place within the part sketch. You should use this constraint sparingly. Follow these steps to explore the fix constraint:

1. From the Get Started tab, select the Open button.

2. Browse for the file named mi_3h_010.ipt located in the Chapter 3 directory of the Mastering Inventor 2011 folder, and click Open.

3. In the Model browser, double-click Sketch1 to edit it. Or, right-click it, and choose Edit Sketch.

4. Drag the corner as indicated in Figure 3.45, and notice that it may be repositioned freely.

FIGURE 3.45
Placing a fix
constraint

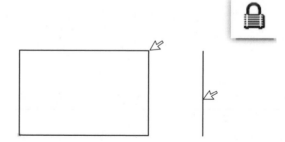

5. In the Sketch tab's Constrain panel, click the Fix button.

6. Click the same corner as before.

7. Right-click, and choose Done.

8. Drag the corner again, and notice that it is now fixed to that position.

9. Next apply another fixed constraint to the vertical line next to the rectangle, and be sure to click the line rather than the endpoint.

10. Right-click and choose Done to exit the constraint tool, and then drag either endpoint of the line. While the line position is fixed, the endpoints are still free to change.

11. Press the F8 key to show all the constraints, and note the new fix constraints.

12. You can exit the file without saving once you are finished.

Symmetric Constraint

The symmetric constraint creates a "mirror" constraint between two similar objects. This constraint relies upon a line to serve as a centerline about which objects are to be symmetrical. You need to specify the centerline only once during the command cycle. Follow these steps to explore the symmetric constraint:

1. From the Get Started tab, select the Open button.

2. Browse for the file named mi_3h_011.ipt located in the Chapter 3 directory of the Mastering Inventor 2011 folder, and click Open.

3. In the Model browser, double-click Sketch1 to edit it. Or, right-click it, and choose Edit Sketch.

4. In the Sketch tab's Constrain panel, click the Symmetric button, as indicated in Figure 3.46.

FIGURE 3.46
Placing a symmetric constraint

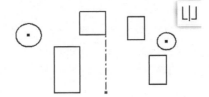

5. Click the circle on the left, and then click the circle on the right.

6. Next click the centerline, and observe that the circles become symmetric.

7. Continue by clicking a line on the square on the left side of the sketch.

8. Click the corresponding line on the rectangle on the right. Notice that this time you did not need to select the centerline. When using the symmetric constraint, you need only to establish the centerline once.

9. Continue making the sketch symmetric by selecting lines on the left of the sketch and then selecting the corresponding line on the right side.

10. Right-click and choose Done when the sketch is symmetric.

11. Press the F8 key to show all the constraints; note the new symmetric constraints.

12. You can exit the file without saving once you are finished.

Smooth Constraint

The smooth constraint creates a continuous curvature (G2) condition between a spline and another sketch object, such as a line, arc, or spline. The G2 condition brings the curve out past the tangency point to create a smooth transition from one curve into the next. Follow these steps to explore the smooth constraint:

1. From the Get Started tab, select the Open button.

2. Browse for the file named mi_3h_012.ipt located in the Chapter 3 directory of the Mastering Inventor 2011 folder, and click Open.

3. In the Model browser, double-click Sketch1 to edit it. Or, right-click it, and choose Edit Sketch.

4. In the Sketch tab's Constrain panel, click the Smooth button.

5. Click the spline and arc as indicated in Figure 3.47.

FIGURE 3.47
Placing a smooth
constraint

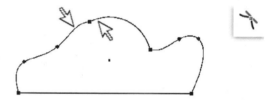

6. Right-click, and choose Done.

7. Press the F8 key to show all the constraints; note the new smooth constraint.

8. You can exit the file without saving once you are finished.

Gaining More Sketch Skills

There are many tools available in the sketch environment, each used to draw different types of geometry or modify geometry in a different way. Many of these are covered in the following pages, but as a reminder, if you hover your mouse pointer over the tool and then pause, you will see a tool tip appear; hover a bit longer, and a larger, more informative tool tip will appear. These progressive tool tips are a great help when attempting to use tools that you don't often use and need a helpful hint remembering what they do and how they do it.

Creating Arcs

You can create sketch arcs by using one of three arc tools available in Inventor's sketch environment. All three arc types are available in a drop-down menu in the Sketch tab's Draw panel. Once placed, the three arcs behave the same; it is simply the manner in which they are created that differentiates them.

A three-point arc is an arc defined by two endpoints and a point on the arc. The first click sets the first endpoint, the second sets the other endpoint, and the third point sets the direction and radius of the arc, as shown in Figure 3.48.

FIGURE 3.48
A three-point arc

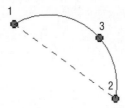

A center point arc is an arc defined by a center point and two endpoints. The first click sets the center point, the second sets the radius and start point, and the third point sets the endpoint and/or arc length, as shown in Figure 3.49.

FIGURE 3.49
A center arc

A tangent arc is an arc from the endpoint of an existing curve. The first click must be on the endpoint of an existing curve and sets a tangent constraint on the endpoint. The second point sets the end of the tangent arc, as shown in Figure 3.50.

FIGURE 3.50
A tangent arc

Additionally, you can create arc segments while using the Line tool, as illustrated in Figure 3.51.

FIGURE 3.51
Creating an arc
with the Line tool

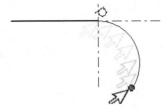

To do so, follow these steps:

1. From the Get Started tab, select the Open button.

2. Browse for the file named mi_3h_013.ipt located in the Chapter 3 directory of the Mastering Inventor 2011 folder, and click Open. The goal here is to re-create the oblong shape already present in the sketch.

3. In the Model browser, double-click Sketch1 to edit it. Or, right-click, and choose Edit Sketch.

4. In the Sketch tab's Draw panel, click the Line icon.

5. Click the projected origin point as the start point of the line, and then release the mouse button. This is the small dot located below the oblong and at 0,0 of the sketch.

6. Next pull your mouse pointer to the right, ensuring you see a horizontal or parallel glyph, indicating that your line is horizontal.

7. Click the screen to set the second point of the line, and then release the mouse button.

8. Now to sketch an arc without exiting the Line tool, click and hold the endpoint you just created, and then (still holding down on the mouse button) drag your mouse pointer out to preview the arc. If the arc previews in the wrong direction, simply return your mouse pointer to the endpoint and try again. It may be helpful to "trace" the guideline cross and exaggerate the arc size to get the direction established and then bring your mouse pointer back in to get the size you want.

9. Release the mouse button to end the arc and continue the Line tool.

10. Continue creating line/arc segments, or right-click and choose Done to exit the Line tool. Practice this a few times, and you'll have it mastered in a short time.

Creating Automatic Tangents with the Line Tool

When adding tangent line segments to a circle or arc, you can apply the tangent constraints automatically. To do so, start the Line tool, and click and hold on the circle or arc on which you intend to create the tangent line. You will see a tangent glyph. You can drag the line segment out to the length and direction desired. Figure 3.52 illustrates this technique.

FIGURE 3.52
Create automatic tangents with the Line tool by clicking and holding as you drag from an arc or circle.

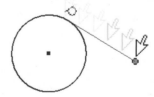

Understanding Point/Center Points

You can use the Point/Center Point tool, found in the Sketch tab's Draw panel, to create center marks for locating hole centers and specific coordinate points. Center points are used by the

Hole and Sheet Metal Punch tools in the modeling environment to automatically locate hole centers. Points, or sketch points as they are often called, are initially ignored by the Hole and Punch tools but can be manually selected for use. Another key difference between the two point types is that sketch points are deleted when the associated geometry is deleted. Center points are not.

You can change the center point to sketch points, or vice versa, by selecting the point and clicking the Center Point button on the Format menu of the Sketch tab, as shown in Figure 3.53.

FIGURE 3.53
Switch points from center points (left) to sketch points (middle) with the Center Point button (right).

Projecting Geometry

When creating a sketch on the face of existing geometry or a work plane, you can project existing points and edges into the sketch by using the Project Geometry tool found in the Sketch tab's Draw panel. To take a quick look at this functionality, follow these steps:

1. From the Get Started tab, select the Open button.

2. Browse for the file named mi_3h_014.ipt located in the Chapter 3 directory of the Mastering Inventor 2011 folder, and click Open.

3. In the Model browser, double-click Sketch3 to edit it. Or, right-click, and choose Edit Sketch.

4. In the Sketch tab's Draw panel, click the Project Geometry icon.

5. Click the edges of the red oval-shaped profile.

6. When you have the complete profile projected into the sketch as shown in Figure 3.54, click the Finish Sketch button.

7. Next, in the Model browser, double-click Sketch4 to edit it. Or, right-click, and choose Edit Sketch.

8. Once the sketch is active, right-click and choose Slice Graphics (or press F7 on the keyboard) to slice the part along the sketch plane.

FIGURE 3.54
Use the Project Geometry tool to project the profile into the active sketch.

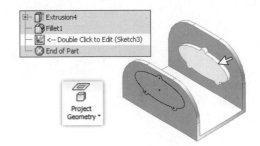

9. In the Sketch tab's Draw panel, click the drop-down for Project Geometry and choose Project Cut Edges. You'll see the sliced edges are now projected as sketch lines into the sketch. These lines can be used to dimension or constrain other sketch geometry too, and will remain associative to the sliced features. Oftentimes a work plane is used to create a sketch in the middle of a part such as this. Work planes are covered in Chapter 4, "Basic Modeling Techniques." For now you finish the sketch and close the file without saving changes.

Learning More About Dimensions

In this section, you'll take a look at more Dimension tools and settings to help you master this very important part of sketch creation.

USING ONE GENERAL DIMENSION TOOL TO DO IT ALL

It is important to understand that you get different results from the Dimension tool depending upon what geometry is selected or in what order it is selected. Here are the dimension types you can place with the General Dimension tool:

Linear dimension from one object.

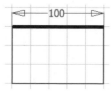

Linear dimension between two objects.

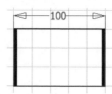

Aligned dimension between two objects: select the objects and right-click to choose the Aligned solution.

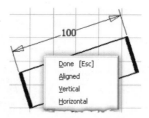

Angular dimension between two edges.

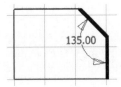

Angular dimension between three points.

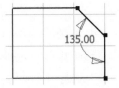

Dimensions to circles or arcs: select the object and then right-click to switch between diameter or radius solutions for either arcs or circles.

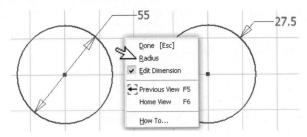

Dimension to the center of arcs and circles: select the first element of the dimension and then click anywhere on the arc or circle. Note the linear glyph indicating the linear solution you will get.

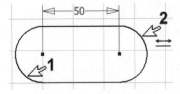

Dimension to the tangent of arcs and circles: select the first element of the dimension, and then click the tangent when you see the tangent glyph appear.

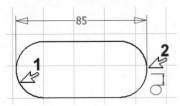

SETTING UP AUTOMATIC DIMENSIONS

In addition to the General Dimension tool, Inventor has an Automatic Dimension tool. It is generally poor practice to use the Automatic Dimension tool to apply all dimensions to your sketches because it will do so in an illogical way. However, you can benefit from this tool by placing the dimensions that define the intent of your design with the General Dimension tool and then allowing the Automatic Dimension tool to place the remaining dimensions to fully constrain the sketch.

To take a look at the Automatic Dimension tool in action, follow these steps:

1. From the Get Started tab, select the Open button.

2. Browse for the file named mi_3h_015.ipt located in the Chapter 3 directory of the Mastering Inventor 2011 folder, and click Open.

3. In the Model browser, locate Sketch1, and double-click to edit or right-click and choose Edit Sketch.

4. In the Sketch tab's Constrain panel, click the Automatic Dimension icon. Notice that the Auto Dimension dialog box shows the number of dimensions required to fully constrain the sketch.

5. Accept the default settings to add both dimensions and constraints.

6. With the Curves button enabled, select all of the geometry in the sketch (you can do this quickly with a selection window).

7. Click Apply to add dimensions to the selected geometry.

8. When finished, click Done.

9. You can close the file without saving changes.

Note that you can also use the Automatic Dimension tool to apply just sketch constraints by deselecting the Dimensions check box.

WORKING WITH SKETCH CENTERLINES

You can create centerlines in sketches by either creating a regular line and then changing it to a centerline or by changing the line type to centerline first and then creating the line. Dimensioning to a centerline gives you a diametric solution by default, but you can opt for a linear solution by right-clicking and deselecting Linear Diameter, as shown in Figure 3.55. In the following lists, you will find the steps for both methods of centerline creation, as well as how to change the solution when dimensioning to a centerline.

FIGURE 3.55
Dimensioning to a centerline

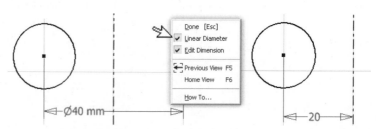

To change to centerline line type before creating sketch geometry, follow these steps:

1. Ensure the sketch is active for editing by double-clicking it or right-clicking and choosing Edit Sketch.

2. On the Sketch tab, click the Centerline icon in the Format panel.

3. Now use the Line tool to sketch lines as you would normally. Note that the Centerline icon stays pushed in (On) until you click it again.

To change an existing line to be a centerline, follow these steps:

1. Ensure the sketch is active for editing by double-clicking it or right-clicking and choosing Edit Sketch.

2. Select the sketch lines you intend to be centerlines.

3. On the Sketch tab, click the Centerline icon in the Format panel.

To create a dimension to a centerline, follow these steps:

1. Ensure the sketch is active for editing by double-clicking it or by right-clicking and choosing Edit Sketch.

2. On the Sketch tab, click the Dimension icon in the Draw panel.

3. Select an object to the side of the centerline.

4. Click the centerline. Note the diametric diameter.

5. Right-click, and note the Linear Diameter option.

6. Place the dimension on the screen.

Measuring Geometry

CERT OBJECTIVE

You can gather measurements from your model without placing a dimension by using the Measure tools. You can access these tools from the Tools tab or by right-clicking any empty place in the graphics area of the screen and choosing Measure from the context menu. When using the Tools tab, you can click the drop-down on the Measure panel to reveal the Region Measure tool. The measurement tools include the following:

Measure Distance   Measures the length lines and arcs, the distance between points, and the radius or diameter of a circle.

Measure Angle   Measures the angle between two lines or points.

Measure Loops   Measures the length of closed loops.

Measure Area   Measures the area of enclosed regions.

Measure Region   Measures the area, perimeter, and the Area Moment Of Inertia properties of sketch loop regions. This tool is available only while editing 2D sketches. Figure 3.56 shows the use of the Measure Region tool.

FIGURE 3.56
Measuring a region

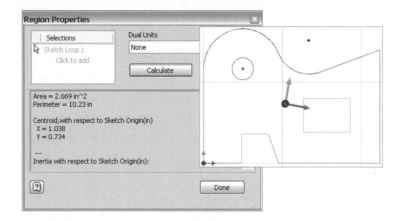

Creating Sketches from AutoCAD Geometry

Converting accurate, dimensioned 2D drawings eliminates redrawing all of the original geometry. Inventor allows selective importing of 2D drawings with associative geometry directly into a new part sketch. If you have an existing drawing library of 2D AutoCAD files, you may find it beneficial to use those file to create new 3D feature-based parametric parts in Inventor. Success in importing existing drawings depends on the following criteria:

◆ The AutoCAD file must contain accurate original geometry.

◆ Duplicate geometry must be deleted from the AutoCAD file.

◆ Proper AutoCAD drawing techniques must be employed in creating the AutoCAD file. For example, there must be only one line segment between any two points. Two shorter lines appearing as a single line will be imported exactly as drawn in the AutoCAD file.

◆ For dimensions to be converted to Inventor parametric dimensions, the existing AutoCAD dimensions must be associative to the geometry. Disconnected dimensions (AutoCAD Defpoints not snapped to the proper geometry location) will cause problems when converted to Inventor dimensions.

Importing Existing AutoCAD Designs

You begin the process of converting an AutoCAD drawing to Inventor parts by creating a new part file. When in active sketch mode, you can import AutoCAD sketch geometry by going to the Insert panel on the Sketch tab and clicking the Insert AutoCAD File icon. To see this process yourself, follow these steps:

1. From the Get Started tab, select the Open button.

2. In the New File dialog box, click the Metric tab, and select the Standard(mm).ipt icon.

3. Click OK to create a new part file based on this template.

4. On the Insert panel of the Sketch tab, click the Insert AutoCAD File icon.

5. In the resulting dialog box, select the file `Import1.dwg` from the Chapter 3 directory of the Mastering Inventor 2011 folder.

6. Click Open to start the conversion process. Once the AutoCAD file opens, you will move into a series of Import Destination Options pages. The first page is mostly grayed out except for specifying units, constraining endpoints, and optionally applying geometric constraints upon import under most conditions. Set your selections as shown in Figure 3.57.

7. Click Finish to complete the import.

CREATING SKETCHES FROM A GRAPHICS IMAGE

Occasionally you may need to create a part from a scanned image or napkin sketch. To do this, you can insert the image right into your sketch and sketch over the top of it. Although this is generally not a good approach for reproducing precise machined parts, it is a valid workflow when designing consumer products where the general shape and feel of parts needs to be captured. If you have a need for this type of design on a regular basis, you may want to investigate Autodesk AliasStudio as well. Here are the general steps for creating sketches from an image:

1. Place an image into a part sketch by clicking the Insert Image icon on the Sketch tab.

2. Browse for the image you want to place into the sketch, and choose Open when the image is located.

3. The mouse pointer is then attached to the upper-left corner of the image. Next click an insert point for the image.

4. Once the image is placed on the screen, the edges of the image can be dimensioned and constrained like any other sketch entity.

Now you can sketch on top of the image, tracing the edges to create the profile and then using general dimensions to tweak the sketch as required.

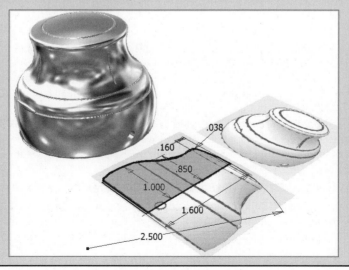

FIGURE 3.57
DWG import
options

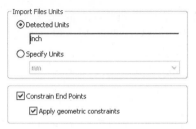

When an AutoCAD drawing is imported into a sketch, Inventor records the unit type of the AutoCAD file. By default, the unit type is displayed within the import dialog box but grayed out. If the unit type is not correct or the unit is of a different type than you require, you may input a different input unit type.

Selecting the Constrain End Points box allows insertion of coincident constraints between sketch objects found to have endpoints that occupy the same coordinates. When the Apply Geometric Constraints box is checked, Inventor will add minimal constraints to the imported AutoCAD geometry. Note too, that although some dimensions will not be imported, those that are will be parametric Inventor dimensions. Figure 3.58 shows the result of importing file, `Import1.dwg`.

FIGURE 3.58
Original DWG
(left) and finished
imported sketch
(right)

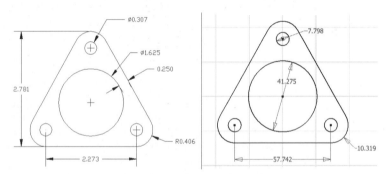

If the AutoCAD geometry was created at the 0,0 origin, then it should import into Inventor at the same location. If the AutoCAD geometry is not located at the origin of the sketch, then you can use the Move command, selecting both the geometry and any dimensions, to move the entire imported sketch into the proper location. You might also prefer to redefine the geometry origin in AutoCAD and then import or re-import it into Inventor.

You should note that this imported drawing might be further broken down into separate features. For instance, each hole could be a separate feature. Note too that having the round corners modeled as features separate from the base feature allows for easier edits in Inventor.

Copying and Pasting Existing AutoCAD Designs into Inventor

Although using the import wizard as described earlier works without having AutoCAD open or even installed, you can import AutoCAD geometry in an even more efficient manner by simple copying from an open AutoCAD file straight into an Inventor sketch, as described in these steps:

1. Open the existing file in AutoCAD.

2. From an open AutoCAD file, simply select the geometry you want to import, right-click, and choose Copy, thereby copying the selected objects to the Windows Clipboard.

3. Next, in Inventor and with a 2D sketch active for editing, simply right-click and choose Paste. You will be presented with a bounding box preview of the pasted entities.

4. At this point, you can right-click and choose Paste Options to ensure that the insert scale is correct or simply click the graphic window to place the pasted geometry.

Although importing geometry from AutoCAD can be an efficient way to reuse existing AutoCAD files, experienced Inventor users generally prefer to model parts from scratch rather than importing from AutoCAD. Importing from AutoCAD almost never provides results that are in line with the design intent of the part unless you just get lucky. Although you may find this to be helpful initially, you will learn that importing AutoCAD files has a place in Inventor but should not be used as a substitute for creating robust parametric Inventor models.

Creating and Using 3D Sketches

3D sketches permit the creation of nonplanar 3D features. 3D sketches are created in single-part files only and comprised of geometry located in various XYZ locations or points within the file. Although a 3D sketch may lie in a 2D plane, in most designs that will not be the case. 3D sketches should never be used for creating geometry that could be created within the 2D sketch environment. The 3D sketch tool is accessible only from within the part environment; however, you can project geometry from an assembly into the part to create the 3D sketch.

Creating a 3D Path

3D sketches are often used to define paths for modeling features such as sweeps and lofts and are generally created based on existing geometry. You can use a 3D sketch to create objects such as tubes, pipes, and wires, as well as negative features such as cam paths, recessed parting lines, and so on.

In this exercise, you will use the 3D Line and Spline tools to create a path along which a profile can be swept. This is a common use of 3D sketches. To start the exercise, follow these steps:

1. From the Get Started tab, select the Open button.

2. Browse for the file named mi_3h_016.ipt located in the Chapter 3 directory of the Mastering Inventor 2011 folder, and click Open.

3. On the Model tab, click the drop-down arrow on the Sketch panel below the Create 2D Sketch icon, and then click the Create 3D Sketch icon. Or right-click in an empty area of the graphics window, and choose New 3D Sketch.

Notice that although this is a part file, it has some reference surfaces in it already. These were included simply to emulate a situation where you might be creating a part within the context of an assembly. You will learn more about creating parts within an assembly in the chapters to come.

There is also a 2D Sketch called Profile1 already in the Model browser; you'll use this sketch at the end of this exercise. Your goal is to create a 3D sketch running from the center of the connection input of the box through each of the large holes in the flange brackets.

4. On the 3D Sketch tab, click the Spline tool icon.

You will see the Inventor Precise Input toolbar appear along with the 3D coordinate triad. The triad displays the X, Y, and Z planes and the corresponding axis in the form of three arrows. The red arrow indicates the x-axis, the green arrow indicates the y-axis, and the blue arrow indicates the z-axis. Notice that the triad is first positioned at 0,0,0.

5. Specify a start point for the spline by clicking the front, circular edge of the connection input.

6. Next click the center of the large hole of the first triangular flange bracket. It makes no difference if you choose the front or back edge of the hole.

7. Do the same for the other two flange brackets.

8. Right-click and choose Create to complete the spline.

9. Then right-click again, and choose Done to exit the Spline tool. Your screen should look similar to Figure 3.59.

FIGURE 3.59
3D sketch spline

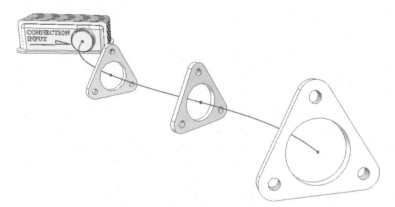

In the next section, you will add a 3D line to your 3D spline.

Using the 3D Coordinate Triad and Precise Redefine

CERT OBJECTIVE

Before continuing with the 3D sketch, take a moment to explore the 3D coordinate triad and its functionality. Each part of the triad is selectable for different tasks, as you'll see in the coming paragraphs. Figure 3.60 shows the anatomy of the triad.

1. Still in the 3D sketch, click the Line tool icon on the 3D Sketch tab.

2. Notice the return of the triad and Precise Input toolbar.

3. Click the endpoint of the spline to set the start of the line on this point.

You will see the triad move to the spline endpoint. Notice that the triad is not lined up with the bracket flange. To remedy this, you will use the Precise Redefine button found on the Precise Input toolbar.

4. Click the Precise Redefine button, as shown at the top of Figure 3.61.

FIGURE 3.60
Inventor's Precise
Input toolbar
and the 3D coordi-
nate triad

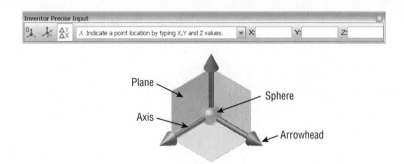

FIGURE 3.61
Precise Redefine
button

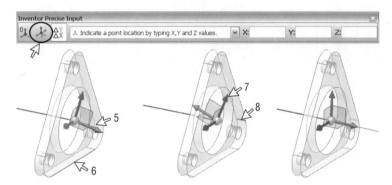

5. Then select the shaft of the red arrow.

6. Next click the bottom edge of the triangular flange bracket toolbar, as shown on the left of Figure 3.61.

7. Click the Precise Redefine button again, and this time click the green arrow shaft.

8. Then click the small edge indicated in the center of Figure 3.61. The triad orientation should now resemble the far right of Figure 3.61.

9. Next, click the triad plane between the blue and green arrows to isolate that plane to sketch on. It should highlight red and then stay shaded when selected, and you will see a 0 placed in the X cell of the Precise Input toolbar.

10. Fill out the rest of the input cells so that you have **X = 0, Y = 6, Z = 0.5**, and press Enter.

Note you can hit the Tab key to switch between the X, Y, and Z input cells. Values will be input as relative coordinates. Recall that with relative coordinates the new input coordinate point is based on the previous point rather than the absolute 0,0,0 origin point. You will now have a line running from the end of the spline out at 6 inches in the y-axis with a slight rise in the z-axis.

11. Still in the Line tool, right-click, and ensure that Auto-bend is selected in the right-click menu. Auto-bend will place a radius at the corners in your line route. The default radius size can be set by selecting Document Settings from the Tools tab and then going to the Sketch tab. Once bends are placed, they can be edited like any other dimension.

12. With the Line tool still active, click the plane between the green and red arrows on the triad to isolate the XY plane, and fill out the rest of the input cells so that you have **X = 4, Y = 4, Z = 0**. Press Enter on the keyboard to set this line. You will see a small dimensioned radius at the corner of your two line segments. This is a result of the Auto-bend option.

13. Right-click and choose Done to exit the Line tool. Your 3D sketch should resemble Figure 3.62.

FIGURE 3.62
3D sketch path

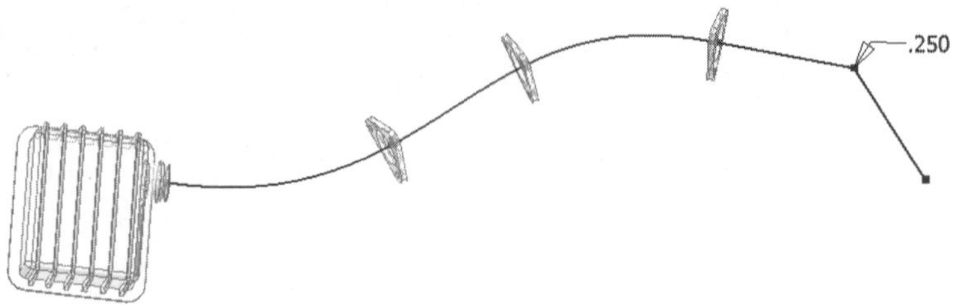

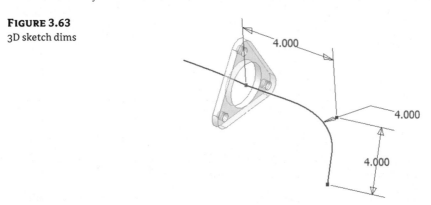

14. Click the Dimension icon in the 3D Sketch tab, and add dimensions, as shown in Figure 3.63. Notice you want to edit the bend radius that was created with the Line tool.

FIGURE 3.63
3D sketch dims

15. Right-click and choose Done to exit the Dimension tool.

16. Then right-click, and choose Finish 3D Sketch.

As a test to see whether you have successfully created your 3D sketch for its intended purpose, run a sweep along the path. Recall that there is a 2D sketch in the browser named Profile1. This will be your sweep profile, and the 3D sketch just created will be your path.

1. In the Model tab's Create panel, click the Sweep icon. Profile1 will be automatically selected as the sweep profile unless you have another unconsumed, closed profile sketch in your part, in which case you will need to select Profile1 manually.

2. Once the profile has been selected, ensure that the Path button in the Sweep dialog box is enabled, and then click the 3D sketch you just created. Your sweep should look like Figure 3.64.

FIGURE 3.64
Sweeping along a
3D sketch

You will look at the Sweep tool in more depth in Chapter 5, "Advanced Modeling Techniques." As a final note, the connection box and triangular bracket flanges have been derived into this part file as a reference feature. In the real world, once done with the part, you would locate that feature in the browser and turn off the visibility. To do this, expand the feature in the browser called DerivedPart1.ipt. Right-click the feature called Derived Work Body1, and uncheck the visibility box. If you'd like, you can save and close the part.

Exploring More 3D Sketch Tools

In addition to the Line and Spline tools used for sketching 3D geometry, several tools permit you to include and combine existing geometry to create 3D sketch elements.

INCLUDING 3D GEOMETRY

CERT
OBJECTIVE

You'll often need to use edges of parts as a path for another feature, in much the same way that you project geometry in a 2D sketch. In a 3D sketch, however, you are not really projecting the geometry onto a sketch plane but simply including it for use in your 3D sketch. To see how this works, follow these steps:

1. From the Get Started tab, select the Open button.

2. Browse for the file named mi_3h_017.ipt located in the Chapter 3 directory of the Mastering Inventor 2011 folder, and click Open.

This file has a 2D sketch named Lip Profile already created and ready to be used in a sweep feature. However, before you can do that, you must define a path along which to sweep the profile.

3. On the Model tab, click the drop-down arrow below the 2D Sketch icon in the Sketch panel, and then click the Create 3D Sketch icon. Or, right-click in an empty area of the graphics window, and choose New 3D Sketch.

4. On the 3D Sketch tab, click the Include Geometry icon. Next click each edge, as shown in Figure 3.65, to define the sweep path.

5. Once the edges are selected, right-click, and choose Finish Sketch.

The path created by including geometry could not have been created with a 2D sketch because it does not exist in a single plane. You can use this path to sweep the profile if you'd like.

FIGURE 3.65
Including geom-
etry in a 3D sketch

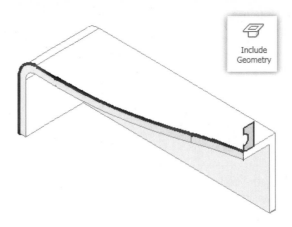

FIGURE 3.65
Including geom-
etry in a 3D sketch

USING AN INTERSECTION CURVE

**CERT
OBJECTIVE**

You can use a 3D sketch to find the intersection of two surfaces, sketch profiles, work planes, or some combination thereof. The resulting sketch is fully associative and will update automatically should the curves change. To see it in action, follow these steps:

1. From the Get Started tab, select the Open button.

2. Browse for the file named mi_3h_018.ipt located in the Chapter 3 directory of the Mastering Inventor 2011 folder, and click Open.

3. On the Model tab, click the drop-down arrow below the 2D Sketch icon in the Sketch panel, and then click the Create 3D Sketch icon. Or, right-click in an empty area of the graphics window, and choose New 3D Sketch.

4. On the 3D Sketch tab, click the Intersection Curve icon.

5. Next click the surface and the curved face, as shown in Figure 3.66.

FIGURE 3.66
3D intersection
curve

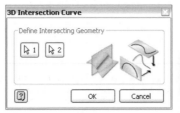
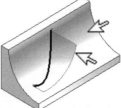

6. Right-click the surface and choose Visibility to toggle the visibility off. Note the resulting intersecting curve.

7. Click OK.

8. You can close the part without saving changes.

USING THE PROJECT CURVE TO SURFACE TOOL

CERT OBJECTIVE

You can find intersections of curves and faces using the Project Curve To Surface tool in a 3D sketch. This tool has three variations of output. Geometry created using these tools will adjust if the original geometry changes. Or, if desired, the link can be broken from the parent geometry to prevent it from adjusting automatically. To see it in action, follow these steps:

1. From the Get Started tab, select the Open button.

2. Browse for the file named mi_3h_019.ipt located in the Chapter 3 directory of the Mastering Inventor 2011 folder, and click Open.

3. On the Model tab, go to the Sketch panel, and click the drop-down arrow below the 2D sketch icon. Then click the Create 3D Sketch icon. Or, right-click in an empty area of the graphics window, and choose New 3D Sketch.

4. On the 3D Sketch tab, click the Project To Surface icon.

The first output, Project Along A Vector, requires a face, a curve, and a direction. Projecting to a continuous face such as a cylinder results in a 3D sketch entity that follows the surface as if the curve were slicing straight down through the face.

5. Click the face of the cylinder.

6. Then click the Curves button. Note the Direction button, which allows you to change the projection direction. In this case, the default direction will work, so you can leave this as is.

7. Click the line on the far left.

The second output is called Project To Closest Point and projects curves in the shortest possible path normal to the surface. The result of a 3-inch line to a convex surface would be a curve less than 3 inches, because the endpoints of the line would take the shortest path to the curve, rather than wrapping about it.

8. In the Output area of the Project Curve To Surface dialog box, click the middle button to choose the Project To Closest Point output.

9. Click the face of the cylinder.

10. Click the Curves button.

11. Click the line in the middle.

The third output is Wrap To Surface. This output creates a curve that will be the same overall dimension as the curve from which it was created. If you wrap a string around a cylinder, the string stays the same length.

12. In the Output area of the Project Curve To Surface dialog box, click the right button to choose the Wrap To Surface output.

13. Click the face of the cylinder.

14. Click the Curves button.

15. Click the line on the right.

16. Click OK.

17. You can close the part without saving changes.

Figure 3.67 shows all three outputs; note the different outputs created from three identical lines. You can break the link of the projected curves by locating the curves in 3D sketch from the Model browser, right-clicking them, and choosing Break Link. You must have the sketch active for edits to break the link. Doing this disallows the ability for the projected curves to update if the founding geometry is updated.

FIGURE 3.67
Project Curve To Surface tool

USING A HELICAL CURVE

You can create 3D helical curves such as thread paths and coils by using the Helical Curve tool within the 3D sketch tools. Helixes can be specified by pitch and revolution, pitch and height, revolution and height, or a true spiral. A helix can be combined with other 3D sketch objects to compose as complex a path as required.

1. From the Get Started tab, select the Open button.

2. Browse for the file named mi_3h_020.ipt located in the Chapter 3 directory of the Mastering Inventor 2011 folder, and click Open.

3. Notice the existing 2D sketch consisting of a single line.

4. On the Model tab, go to the Sketch panel, and click the drop-down arrow below the 2D sketch icon. Then click the Create 3D Sketch icon. Or, right-click in an empty area of the graphics window, and choose New 3D Sketch.

5. On the 3D Sketch tab, click the Helical Curve icon.

6. For the start point, select one end of the line.

7. Select the other end of the line for the endpoint of the helical curve.

8. Click in the graphics window to rough in the diameter.

9. Set the precise diameter value in the dialog box, as shown in Figure 3.68.

10. Enter **10 mm** for the pitch.

11. Enter **5** for the revolutions.

12. Click OK.

FIGURE 3.68
A helical curve

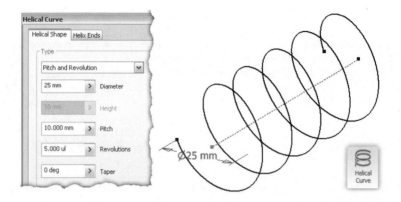

13. Examine the resulting helical curve, as shown in Figure 3.66.

14. Note you can change the inputs of the curve by right-clicking it and choosing Edit Helical Curve.

15. You can close the part without saving changes.

USING A SILHOUETTE CURVE

You can create an associative 3D curve along the outer boundary of a body as defined by a selected direction. Imagine a beam of light cast on an object from a single direction. The curve created where the shadow line begins would be the silhouette curve. You can use the Silhouette Curve tool to determine the parting line of organic shapes; just follow these steps:

1. From the Get Started tab, select the Open button.

2. Browse for the file named mi_3h_021.ipt located in the Chapter 3 directory of the Mastering Inventor 2011 folder, and click Open.

3. On the Model tab, go to the Sketch panel, and click the drop-down arrow below the 2D sketch icon. Then click the Create 3D Sketch icon. Or, right-click in an empty area of the graphics window, and choose New 3D Sketch.

4. On the 3D Sketch tab, click the Silhouette Curve icon.

5. For the Body selection, click anywhere on the part.

6. For the Direction selection, click the work axis.

7. Click OK.

Note the resulting curve, as shown in Figure 3.69.

You can exit the sketch and close the file when finished.

You can break the link of the projected curves by locating the curves in 3D sketch from the Model browser, right-clicking them, and choosing Break Link. Doing this disallows the projected curves to update if the founding geometry is updated.

FIGURE 3.69
A silhouette curve

REFINING AND CONSTRAINING A 3D SKETCH

You can anchor and constrain a 3D sketch in much the same fashion as you do with a 2D sketch using dimensions and constraints. Additionally, with 3D splines, you can add vertex points and control curve fit with handles. Further refining can take place because you can adjust the fit method and spline tension to create the exact curve shape desired.

Best Practices for Working with Sketches

Here is a list of points to keep in mind as you continue working with sketches in Inventor. Keep in mind that sketches are the foundation for good modeling, and therefore the importance of creating stable, fully constrained sketches cannot be overstated.

- ◆ Keep sketches simple.

- ◆ Your goal should always be to have a fully dimensioned and constrained sketch.

- ◆ Sketches that are not fully constrained tend to distort unpredictably when you make modifications and updates.

- ◆ Rough out size and shape before adding dimensions and constraints in order to avoid distorting the sketch when dimensions and constraints are added.

- ◆ Add dimensions to lock down shape, and then come back to change the size.

- ◆ Endpoint, midpoint, center, and intersection snap points can be helpful when creating sketch entities, but be aware of how they affect dimensions compared to selecting the line itself rather than the snap points.

- ◆ You can use backspace to clear last selected points; for instance, if you select a point for the corner of a line and then realize you should have selected another point instead, use backspace to clear the first selection and then start the line where it should have been.

- ◆ Use Centerlines to define revolution axes and diametric dimensions.

- ◆ Use Construction lines to further define sketches and create "helper" geometry.

◆ When you need to select multiple sketch entities, you can use a crossing selection or a window selection. A crossing selection is created from right to left and selects any object that is touched or contained by the window. A window selection is created from left to right and selects only objects that are completely contained in the window.

◆ Use the Delete key on the keyboard to quickly remove accidentally created geometry.

◆ Use the Split tool rather than the Trim tool when you can, as it does not break previously defined constraints.

◆ Turn off automatic edge projection, to avoid extra sketch geometry, and only project the edges you need. This will make sketches easier to edit.

◆ Reserve Fillets and Chamfers for feature level whenever possible. Although you can fillet and chamfer at the sketch level, it is generally best to keep your sketches simple and fillet and chamfer the solid features rather than the sketches.

◆ You can create pattern and mirrored geometry in the sketch, but it is generally best to make a simple sketch and then pattern or mirror the feature. The results are often the same, but the feature patterns are much easier to edit.

The Bottom Line

Set up options and settings for the sketch environment Understanding the settings and options that apply to the sketch environment is an essential first step in working with Inventor.

Master It You want to configure your own set of options and settings for your sketch environment and then back them up and/or distribute them to other workstations. How would you do this?

Create a sketch from a part file template Creating a sketch in a blank template file is the fundamental step in creating 3D parametric models. You will use this basic step to start most of your part designs.

Master It How would you capture the intent of your design when creating a base sketch for a new part?

Use sketch constraints to control sketch geometry Understanding what each sketch constraint does when applied will allow you to determine when to use each type. Recall that often more than one constraint will work in any given situation.

Master It How would you create a sketch that allows you to test "what if?" scenarios concerning the general shape and size of your part?

Master general sketch tools Learning the features and tricks of the sketch tools will allow you to master Inventor sketching.

Master It You are given a print of mixed units to work from and need to enter dimensions exactly as they are on the print. You understand that you can enter any dimensions in any unit simply by adding the correct suffix. But how would you create a radius dimension on a circle or a dimension from the tangents of a slot?

Create sketches from AutoCAD geometry   You can use existing AutoCAD files to create a base sketch for an Inventor model of the same part.

Master It   You have many existing 2D AutoCAD drawings detailing legacy parts. You want to reuse these designs as you convert to 3D modeling. How would you proceed?

Use 3D sketch tools   Much of working with a 3D parametric modeler can be done by sketching in a two-dimensional plane and then giving depth to the sketch to create 3D features. However, sometimes you need to create paths or curves that are not planar. In those cases, you use the 3D sketch tools.

Master It   You know the profile of a complex curve as viewed from the top and side views. How would you create a 3D sketch from this data?

Chapter 4

Basic Modeling Techniques

This chapter covers the principles of creating a 3D parametric part, which makes it one of the most important chapters in this book. You'll start by looking at the general options and settings associated with Inventor and part files and then move on to a basic exercise exploring the fundamentals of creating parametric models. Then you'll take a deeper look at the options and tools found in the primary feature tools.

All the skills in this chapter are primarily based around creating a single part, whether it be in a single-part file or in the context of an assembly file. Do yourself a favor and learn or review these basics before jumping into the more complex features.

In this chapter, you'll learn to:

- ◆ Set application options and settings for part modeling
- ◆ Create basic part features
- ◆ Use the Extrude tool
- ◆ Create revolve parts and thread features
- ◆ Create work features
- ◆ Use the Fillet tool
- ◆ Create intelligent hole features
- ◆ Bend parts

Exploring Application Options and Settings for Part Modeling

As in previous chapters, you should make sure that your settings in Application Options match the approach we're using in this book. This will ensure that the examples you work on will match the results you see here.

Specifying Global Settings

You maintain global settings for Autodesk Inventor within the Application Options dialog box. For this section of the chapter, we will be concentrating on the Part tab in Application Options, which allows you to maintain part-specific settings. You can adjust the application settings as follows:

1. On the Tools tab, click Application Options.

2. Then choose the Part tab, as shown in Figure 4.1.

FIGURE 4.1
The Part tab

Sketch On New Part Creation   This section allows you to predetermine in which origin plane the first sketch will be placed. If No New Sketch is selected, then Inventor will create a new part file without an initial sketch. You can then determine the origin plane for the first sketch.

Construction   This setting determines whether created surfaces will be translucent by default or opaque like parts are.

Auto-hide In-line Work Features   This option allows automatic hiding of a work feature when it is consumed by another work feature. For instance, if you create a work plane by clicking a work axis and a work point, the work axis and work point will be stacked under the work plane in the browser.

Auto-consume Work Features And Surface Features   This option allows Inventor to consume surfaces when converted to a solid, in addition to consuming work features.

3D Grips   These settings affect how 3D grips can modify a part file. In normal use, 3D grips allow you to modify part features by selecting and dragging a grip. If a dimension is controlling the feature, then the dimension will update to reflect the changes in the part.

If *Never Relax* is selected, then any features controlled by the dimension will not change.

When *Relax If No Equation* is selected, a dimension value will update unless that dimension value is determined by an equation. Selecting *Always Relax* will always allow the use of 3D grips, even when controlled by an equation. The *Prompt* setting will prompt you to accept any changes during drag operations.

The settings in the Geometric Constraints area control how constraints will be handled during drag operations. *Never Break* prevents grip editing when sketch constraints are controlling a sketch. *Always Break* allows constraints to be broken as required during grip edits. The *Prompt* setting asks you to make a decision on a case by case basis for each grip edit.

Edit Base Solids   These settings allow you to choose between the *Legacy Solid Edit Environment* and the *Inventor Fusion* preview tools, provided the fusion add-in has been loaded.

Specifying Document-Specific Settings

To change the options in a specific part file, you'll need to access the part's Document Settings dialog box by going to the Tools tab and clicking Document Settings while that part is open. The Document Settings dialog box that opens allows specific settings for an individual file in the following areas:

♦ Lighting styles

♦ Materials

♦ Units

♦ Modeling dimension display values

♦ Individual sketch settings

♦ Model values

♦ Bill of materials (BOM)

♦ Default tolerances

Any changes made in the part's Document Settings dialog box will be applied only to the current document. Current document settings will not affect the settings in other parts within an assembly.

Figure 4.2 shows the part's Document Settings dialog box with the Standard tab active. The Standard tab controls the active lighting style of the current graphics window. In addition, you can set the physical material properties of the current part here.

FIGURE 4.2
The Standard tab in the part's Document Settings dialog box

THE STANDARD TAB

The Standard tab allows you to set the *Active Lighting Style*, the *Physical Material* of the part, and the *Display Appearance*. The lighting style is selected from a preset list in the drop-down menu as is the physical material. The display appearance is configured by clicking the Settings button and adjusting the various settings in the resulting dialog box. In order to set part to use the display appearance settings configured in the part file, you must first go to the Display tab of the Application Options dialog box and select Use Document Settings.

THE UNITS TAB

The Units tab allows you to set the input, as shown in Figure 4.3. The settings on this tab allow you to change the unit specification values. As an example, you could open a metric (mm) part and change the input settings to inches.

FIGURE 4.3
Units tab in Document Settings

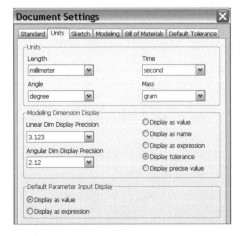

Modeling Dimension Display Precision   These settings allow you to define the model dimension's display precision by the number of decimal places and define how that dimension will be displayed. Many people prefer the *Display As Expression* setting because it shows the dimension name along with any expression that exists in the dimension; if no expression exists, then the dimension name and dimension value are displayed.

Default Parameter Input Display   This setting allows you to see the parameter name in the input box when editing a dimension or feature input. Figure 4.4 shows the difference between the two settings.

FIGURE 4.4
Default parameter input display

THE SKETCH TAB

On the Sketch tab, shown in Figure 4.5, you can adjust how the 2D sketch tools work and appear in an active sketch. In addition, you can change the preset value for Auto-Bend Radius in the 3D Sketch area.

Snap Spacing   This allows you to set the spacing between snap points to assist with precise layouts. For instance, if you are using Frame Generator to create a steel frame with uprights at 2000 mm on center, then you might set the snap spacing to 2000 mm and then go to the Sketch tab in the Application Options dialog box and set the sketch to Snap to Grid. Then when creating your skeletal base sketch, you can set line segments and spacing to 2000 mm with precision.

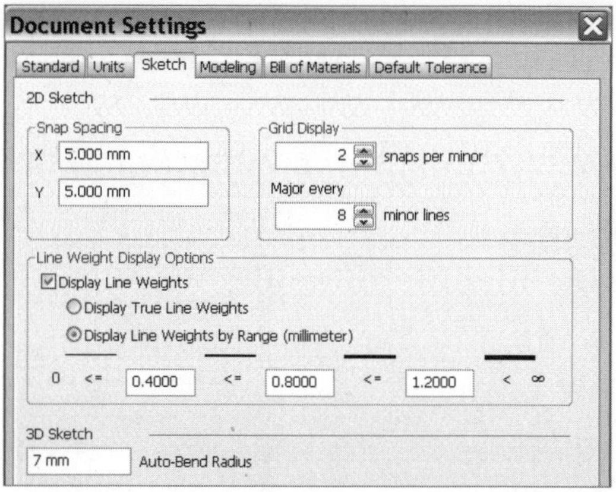

FIGURE 4.5

The Sketch tab in
Document Settings

Grid Display   These settings allow you to set the major and minor grid spacing. If the *Snaps Per Minor* were set to 2 with the 2000 mm snap spacing used in the example above, then the spacing between grid lines would be 4000 mm. If the *Major Every* setting were set to 5, then distance between the major grid lines would be 20,000 mm. In order to display grid lines, you would go to the Sketch tab in the Application Options dialog box.

Line Weight Display Options   These options allow the display of unique line weights in model sketches. Note that this does not influence line weights in printed model sketches. *True Line Weights* displays line weights on-screen as they would appear on paper regardless of the on-screen zoom level. *Display Line Weights by Range* displays line weight according to the entered values.

3D Sketch   This area involves only one setting, the *Auto-Bend Radius*. When creating a 3D line, you can turn on the Auto-Bend option and have intersecting line corners automatically rounded. This setting controls the default radius at which bends are created. Once they are made, the bends can be edited to a different value.

THE MODELING TAB

Figure 4.6 shows the Modeling tab, which allows changes to the behavior while modeling the current active part.

Here are the settings found on the Modeling tab of the Document Settings dialog box:

Adaptivity Used In Assembly   This is available only when a part is adaptive. When deselected, an adaptive part becomes static. This setting can be controlled by right-clicking an adaptive part in the assembly browser also.

Compact Model History   This allows Inventor to purge all rollback document history when you save the current file. Compacting the model history improves performance in large assembly files. You should select this option only when performance is affected in large assembly files or when existing disk space is limited.

Advanced Feature Validation   This permits Inventor to use a different algorithm to compute features. Using this option can produce more accurate feature results in rare cases such as

Shell, Draft, Thicken, and Offset features. However, this option is slower in calculation than the default option and should be used only on rare occasions where the accuracy of the model may be in question.

FIGURE 4.6
Modeling tab in
Document Settings

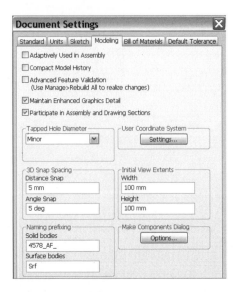

Maintain Enhanced Graphics Detail   This enables graphics information to be saved with the file on disk. This information is used in the graphics display if the display quality is set to Smoother in Application Options.

Participate In Assembly And Drawing Sections   When not selected, the part will default to None in the section participation settings of an assembly or drawing section view. However, you can adjust each instance of the part to section or not section as needed. For instance, if you created a part file for an O-ring and intended to use it in the design of several shaft assemblies, you could set deselect this option in the O-ring file to ensure the O-ring remained un-sectioned in the section drawing views of the shafts you used the O-ring on. If you needed to show a particular section view of the shaft assembly with all parts sectioned, you would do so by setting the section participation settings for the O-ring to section, in that one section view.

Tapped Hole Diameter   This determines how the size of tapped hole features are controlled. Thread representations in drawings are generated correctly only when Tapped Hole Diameter is set to Minor.

User Coordinate System   Click the Settings button to access the UCS Settings dialog box where the UCS naming prefix can be set, the default plane defined, and the visibility of UCS and its features determined.

3D Snap Spacing   This sets the spacing between snap points in 3D sketches. This setting also controls the snap precision when using the Move Bodies tool to free drag a solid body.

Initial View Extents   This sets the initial visible height and width of the graphics window when creating a model from a template. For instance, if you create a lot of steel frames, you may find it helpful to create a template with the setting adjusted so that your initial sketch is not always zoomed in to a very small area. Configure this setting in your template files to affect new files. You can set the initial height and width of the graphics window. This setting affects only the initial sketch when using a template. When creating a secondary sketch or opening an existing part, the view is controlled by the size of the part.

Naming Prefixing   This sets the default file naming for parts generated from multibody part designs. Again, these tools are covered in Chapter 5, "Advanced Modeling Techniques."

Make Components Dialog   Clicking Options in the Make Components Dialog area opens the Make Components Options dialog box. The Make Component settings shown in the options dialog box are specific to the active project. These options are employed when creating multibody parts, as described in Chapter 5.

THE BILL OF MATERIALS TAB

The Bill Of Materials tab determines the structure of the current file and how that structure relates to the bill of materials in an Inventor assembly. Figure 4.7 shows the default settings for structure and quantity.

FIGURE 4.7
Bill Of Materials
tab in Document
Settings

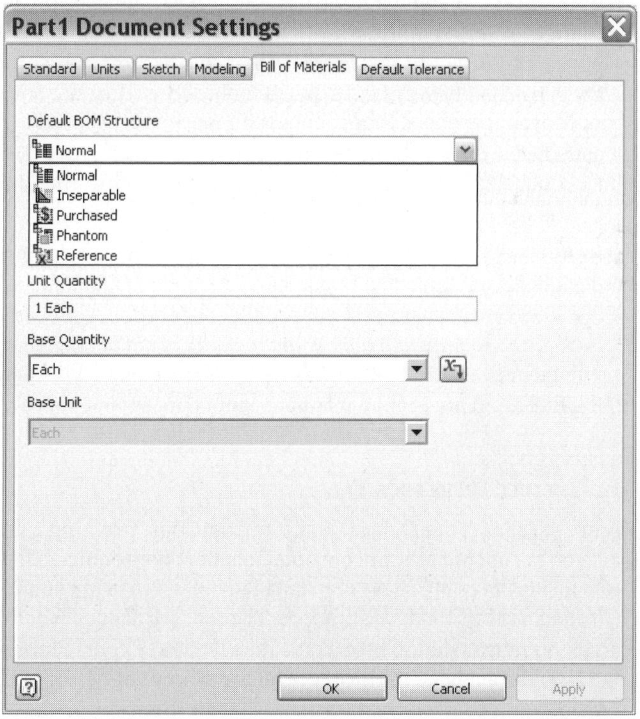

You can add BOM structure properties to individual parts in the Document Settings dialog box. Figure 4.7 shows the choices available in a model or assembly file for setting individual file properties. Here are the details:

Normal These components are given an item number and included in quantity calculations. The placement of normal parts in the bill of materials is determined by the parent assembly properties. A normal subassembly may be composed of any combination of inseparable, phantom, purchased, and reference parts without having any effect on how those parts are listed in the BOM. Normal is used for most components.

Inseparable These components are assemblies that allow the inclusion of press-fit, glued, welded, or riveted components that might be damaged if taken apart. A good example is a hinge that is fully assembled but should be listed in the BOM as a single part. Although the Inseparable structure is listed in the part's Document Settings dialog box, it is intended as an assembly property.

Purchased These components are parts that are not normally fabricated or manufactured by your company but instead purchased from vendors. Any purchased component, whether part or assembly, will be listed in a parts-only parts list. A purchased component assembly will not normally have the component parts listed in the BOM, since that component will be purchased as a single unit.

Phantom These components exist in the design but are not included as specific line items in the BOM. A construction assembly that exists as a container (subassembly) within a higher-level assembly, simply to hold a number of components together for assembly purposes, can be set to Phantom. When this assembly is set to Phantom, it will not appear in the parts list; however, the parts included within the construction assembly will be listed as individual parts. Phantom components are ignored by the BOM. No item number is assigned, and no quantity calculations are performed on the phantom assembly. However, the quantity of individual parts contained within the phantom assembly will be multiplied by the quantity of the phantom component included in the top-level assembly.

Reference These components are used to provide reference information within an assembly design. An example of a reference part might be a product container placed in a conveyor assembly. The conveyor components are the parts and assemblies you are designing, but the container is required to ensure the clearance and function of your design. In a drawing, reference parts will be indicated in the view as hidden line geometry. Reference components are excluded from the BOM and are excluded from quantity, mass, and value calculations.

THE DEFAULT TOLERANCE TAB

Figure 4.8 shows the Default Tolerance settings. Creating tolerance values affects sketches and parts only. Adding tolerance values to a part file requires that you select either *Use Standard Tolerancing Values or Export Standard Tolerance Values*, or you can select both options.

You can select the Use Standard Tolerancing Values box to use the precision and tolerance values set in this dialog box. You can select the Export Standard Tolerance Values box to export tolerance dimensions to the drawing environment.

Once you've selected an option, you can then add linear or angular tolerance values. You can add any number of tolerance values by precision to this part. When you have added your values to the part, click Apply to stay in the dialog box and apply the new settings to this tab, or click

OK to apply the settings and exit the dialog box. Chapter 5 covers the use and setup of part tolerances in more detail.

FIGURE 4.8
Default Tolerance
tab in Document
Settings

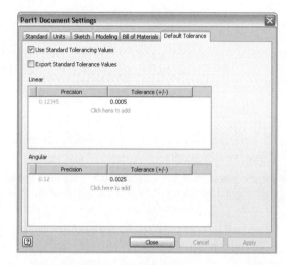

CREATE YOUR OWN TEMPLATE FILES

This may seem like a lot of settings, and it's true there are a lot, but you really need to set them only once. Open a template, make all your settings the way you want them for a particular type of part (for instance an inch unit part), and then use the Save Copy as Template option. It will then be available as a template when you create a new part. Make another template for metric parts. Make perhaps another for sheet-metal parts and so on. You can make as many as you'd like, each with its own set of document settings specific to the template.

A good idea is to make a folder in your template directory named Custom or Our Templates. Store all your templates in this directory. This folder (and any other folder in the template directory) will show up as a tab in the New File dialog box. This way, you will still have access to Inventor's standard templates as well as your company's custom templates.

You can set the template file location in two places:

◆ Go to the Tools tab of the Ribbon, click Application Options, and select the File tab in the dialog box that opens.

◆ Go to the Get Started tab of the Ribbon, click Projects, and select the Folder Options entry in the dialog box that opens.

Keep in mind that if these two settings are not the same, Inventor uses the Projects setting.

Creating Basic Part Features

Inventor 3D part modeling is based upon the principle of creating a base feature and then adding features to the base feature to build a more complex part. Figure 4.9 illustrates the basic workflow for creating a part composed of multiple features.

FIGURE 4.9
Part creation
workflow

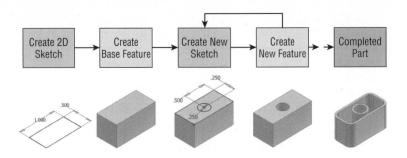

As you create parts in Inventor, you should keep in mind the following concepts because each will go a long way toward making your modeling endeavors more productive:

♦ Anchor and orient your base sketch to the 0,0,0 origins of the part file. This will make your parts much easier to manage as you go forward. The base feature will generally be the largest feature in the part, unless there is a specific reason for not making it so.

♦ Look for areas of your design that are likely to change, and create your part features to accommodate these future edits. As an example, the plate thickness of a support might likely change as loads are determined throughout the rest of the design. Creating the plate sketch from the end view and then extruding the length would make it easy to modify the length of the plate but not as easy to modify the thickness. Therefore, a better choice would be to create the base sketch of the top view and extrude the thickness.

♦ Identify relationships between design parameters. For instance, the distance from the edge of a part to the edge of a bolt hole might be required to be always 2× the diameter of that hole.

♦ Keep an eye out for patterned and symmetrical design features. It is much easier to create and modify the first instance of a pattern than it is to edit several identical features that were created separately.

♦ Build logical feature dependencies. Features are dependent upon other part geometry when you cannot delete or modify a portion of the part or feature without affecting another feature built later in the part. As an example, if you were to create a simple block and then create an additional feature on that block, then you could not delete the block without upsetting the new feature.

♦ Reserve fillets and chamfers for the end of the part as much as possible. Because these features often change, it is best to place them at the end of the design process. Placing them at the beginning of the design and then having to change them is likely to upset other features that you have created afterward that might depend on the filleted or chamfered edges.

♦ Create simple sketches to create simple features to create complex parts. Using numerous features within a 3D model allows simplified control over modifications of the model in the future. Separate features may be suppressed or modified to alter the design without having to make changes in a complicated sketch. Instead of attempting to create all the geometry in a single sketch, we'll analyze the proposed part first.

CONSIDER MODELING VS. MACHINING

Although the "design as you'd manufacture" paradigm is a great philosophy to follow when creating 3D parts, there is a major difference between modeling and machining. One major difference is that you have the ability to add material when modeling, whereas a machining operation only takes away material. Deciding which route to take depends on what resources are available in your shop and how much time you have.

Modeling and machining are important subjects to consider when designing parts. Inventor offers a lot of features that may make it easy to design a part that might be impossible or at least very expensive to make with the tooling equipment your shop has available. In some cases, although a part may be easier to model as one piece, it might be less expensive to machine as multiple pieces. Also, consider the size of the equipment and tooling, such as end mills and drills, when creating parts. For example, in Inventor you can create very small fillets or square corners in a design, but try to machine a 0.010' fillet in a cavity that is 3' deep, and you'll likely earn a scolding from the people on the shop floor who are required to turn your design into reality.

One example for how to make a realistic design for your shop is the fixture block, as shown here. If a CNC machine center is available, this simple part is easy to model in Inventor and not a problem to create in the shop.

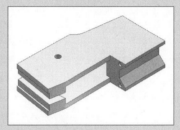

However, without a CNC approach, even this simple model might prove to be difficult and/or expensive to produce by more traditional machining techniques. Reconsidering the design to match the shop's abilities will be required. In this case, you might consider a sandwich block design of simple parts welded and fastened together to achieve the same end result, as shown here.

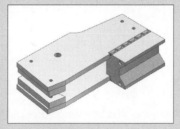

Although this might require more thought and planning on your part within Inventor, it will make the design achievable with the tools and technology at hand. Often the best resource for helping you determine what your shop's capabilities are will be the people who will actually be making the parts.

Simplifying Your Sketches

There is probably no concept that will help you master creating parts in Inventor that is more important than the idea of creating simple sketches from which to build simple features that will add up to create complex parts. Standard 2D drafting practice requires that you place all part details or components within a single view. However, it is not good practice to use the same 2D drafting workflow within any feature-based 3D modeler. Complicated sketches can drag down sketching performance and virtually eliminate easy changes to features. Consider the part shown in Figure 4.10. This illustration shows the base sketch which is then revolved to form the shaft.

FIGURE 4.10

A complex sketch for a revolved part

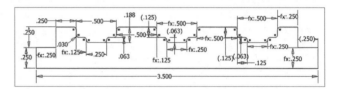

Now compare the same part modeled using the simple sketches approach shown in Figure 4.11.

FIGURE 4.11

A series of simple sketches create a revolved part.

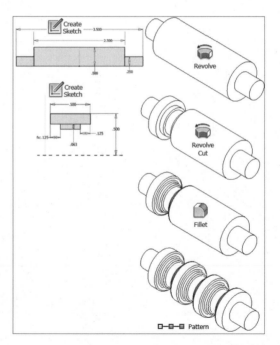

The version in Figure 4.10 would prove difficult to modify, due to the number of sketch constraints and dimensions required to create it. Most likely a seemingly simple change would result in the breaking of some part of the sketch. By comparison the version in Figure 4.11 would be easy to modify because each feature is broken out into its own sketch or placed feature.

Of course, sometimes creating a more complex sketch is required, but if you follow the simple sketch rule of thumb, you will find Inventor much more accommodating, and you will quickly master part creation and be ready to tackle complex sketches when they are needed.

Creating a Base Feature

In the pages to follow, you will create a part similar to the part shown in Figure 4.11. To do so, you'll begin by creating a new part file from the Standard(mm).ipt template:

1. On the Get Started tab, click the New button.

2. On the Metric tab of the New File dialog box, select the Standard(mm).ipt template.

3. On the Sketch tab, click the Rectangle button, and place the rectangle so that the origin point is to the inside.

PROJECTING THE ORIGIN POINT

If you do not see an origin point in your sketch, you may want to take this opportunity to turn on the option that will automatically project it into every new sketch. To do this, just follow these steps:

1. On the Tools tab, click Application Options.

2. Then choose the Sketch tab.

3. Ensure that the Autoproject Part Origin On Sketch Create option is selected, and click OK.

4. Start a new file from a template, and you will see that the origin point is now present.

---

4. On the Sketch tab, click the Line tool, and sketch a diagonal line from corner to corner of the rectangle.

5. Next select the diagonal line, and then click the Construction button in the Format panel on the Sketch tab (toward the far right). This converts the diagonal line from a standard line to a construction line so that Inventor will ignore it as a profile entity. Your line should now be dashed and will have changed colors.

6. In the Constrain panel of the Sketch tab, click the Coincident button, and place a coincident constraint between the midpoint of the diagonal line and the origin point.

7. Use the Dimension tool found on the Sketch tab to dimension the sketch at **150 mm** by **300 mm** as shown in Figure 4.12.

FIGURE 4.12
Initial sketch

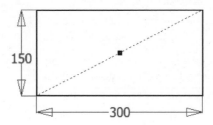

8. Right-click and choose Finish Sketch, and then click the Extrude button on the Model tab.

9. If needed, click the corner of the ViewCube to find an isometric view of the sketch so you can see the preview (if it's not displayed, go to the View tab, go to the Windows panel, click the User Interface button, and click the drop-down arrow).

10. Generally Inventor will select the profile for you if you have just one closed profile present to extrude. If the profile is not selected, click anywhere in the rectangle to select it. If you did not make the diagonal a construction line, you will need to select both triangular halves of the rectangle.

11. Enter **25 mm** in the Distance input box. Click the arrow buttons to change the extrude direction just to see how the preview updates. Then click the left arrow button, and click OK.

Creating a Second Feature

Now that you've created your base feature, you will continue by adding features to it. Before doing so, it is a good idea to save your part. To do so, click the Save icon from the Quick Access bar at the top of the screen, or click the Inventor button and then select Save. You can save the file in the Chapter 4 folder and name it anything you like.

Now that the part is saved, it's time to create a second feature:

1. On the Model tab, click the Create 2D Sketch button, and then click the large front face of the part (or right-click the face and select New Sketch). Sketch2 is now created and active.

2. Use the ViewCube to orient your view of the part so that you have a flat 2D view of your sketch plane with the rectangle running horizontally on your screen.

3. If you see sketch lines outlining the base feature, then you have the Autoproject Edges For Sketch Creation And Edit option turned on. If you do not see those sketch lines, select the Project Geometry tool on the Sketch tab, and select the face again to project the edges.

ENABLING PROJECT EDGES ON SKETCH CREATION

If you see the outline of the faces automatically projected into your new sketches, you may want to consider turning it off. In general, it is not recommended to use this. It may be helpful in the beginning, but be aware that your sketches can become cluttered with unneeded geometry. When all edges are projected, it is more difficult to determine the design intent and can make editing sketches difficult. Instead, consider disabling this option and developing a practice of projecting only necessary edges.

To do so, follow these steps:

1. Go to the Tools tab, and click Application Options.

2. Then choose the Sketch tab.

3. Ensure that the Autoproject Edges For Sketch Creation And Edit option is selected to enable it or deselected to disable it, and click OK.

---

4. Sketch a rectangle on the face selected for the sketch. Place this rectangle in the middle of the face, being careful not to accidentally constrain it to the origin point or the edge of the base feature (you will relocate it using a sketch constraint later).

5. Select the Circle tool on the Sketch tab, and sketch a circle at the end of the rectangle starting with the midpoint of the vertical line on the right and snapping to the endpoint of the top or bottom line. You don't need to trim the circle before converting this sketch into a feature, and in fact, unneeded trimming of sketch entities often works against you because it may remove sketch constraints.

6. Use the Dimension tool on the Sketch tab, and add a dimension to the circle. Rather than just entering a value, enter **Diameter = 40 mm**, thereby assigning the dimension a name and a value (be sure you have named this dimension, as you will be using it in the steps to come).

7. You'll next create an equation for the length of the rectangle based on the length of the diameter value. With the Dimension tool, select the edge of the rectangle, and enter **Slot_Length =**.

8. Then click the 40 mm diameter dimension you just created. This will link the two dimensions. Finish the equation with ***5** so that your end equation reads **Slot_Length = Diameter*5**. Note that you must use an underscore here because spaces are not allowed in parameter names. Your sketch should look similar to Figure 4.13.

FIGURE 4.13
Creating and dimensioning geometry in Sketch2

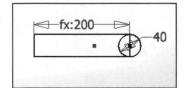

9. Create a coincident constraint between the midpoint of the left vertical line of the rectangle and the midpoint of the left, projected, vertical line of the base feature.

USE WORK FEATURES TO ANCHOR YOUR SKETCHES

Another way to anchor this sketch to the midplane of the rectangle is by using work features. Before starting a sketch, click the Plane icon found on the Work Features panel. Select one side of the rectangular feature and then the other. This will create a parametrically centered work plane.

Then you can create a sketch and use the Project Geometry tool and select the edge of the work plane. This will project the work plane as a line onto the sketch plane. You can then use this line as a centerline in your sketch creation sequence. If you were to ever change the size of the base feature, then the work plane, the projected line, and hence this sketch would all update and remain centered.

10. Select one (or all) of the projected lines of the base feature, and convert it to a construction line (this ensures that Inventor will not attempt to extrude the large projected profile in the next step).

11. Finish the sketch, and choose Extrude on the Model tab.

12. If needed, use the ViewCube to view the part from an isometric view.

13. Select the rectangle and the circle you just created for the profile.

14. Click the Cut button (the second button down in the list of operation buttons) so that the profiles will be cut out of the base feature. Your preview should be red when the Cut operation is selected. Check the direction arrow to ensure that the cut is going in the correct direction.

15. In the Extents drop-down, select All. The All option extrudes the profile through all the current features of the entire part in the specified direction or in both directions if you chose the Midplane option. If the size of the base part features change, then the cut extrusion feature will update accordingly. Click OK when your options look like Figure 4.14. And then save your file.

FIGURE 4.14
Extruding (cutting) the second feature

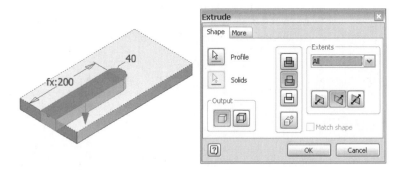

Creating a Sketch-Based Hole Feature

Hole features are very powerful components of Inventor. Many methods are available for creating Hole features. You can create holes in the following ways:

◆ By utilizing existing sketches containing sketch center points

◆ By distance from two planar edges

◆ On a face by referencing concentric edge

◆ By using a work point feature

You can continue with the file you are working on or open the file called mi_4a_002.ipt. Follow these steps to create another sketch, and then use that sketch to place a hole:

1. On the Model tab, click the Create 2D Sketch button, and then click the large front face of the part (or right-click the face and select New Sketch). Sketch3 is now created and active.

2. If needed, use the ViewCube to orient your view of the part so that you have a flat 2D view of your sketch plane with the rectangle running horizontally on your screen.

3. You might see the outline of the sketch plane face automatically projected into your sketch (if not, click the Project Geometry button, and select the sketch plane).

4. On the Sketch tab, select the Offset button found on the Modify panel.

5. Before selecting anything to offset, right-click and ensure that both the *Loop-Select* and *Constrain Offset* options are selected.

   ◆ Loop-Select - when selected this option selects lines/curves joined at their endpoints. Deselect to select one or more lines/curves individually.

   ◆ Constrain Offset - when selected this option constrains the distance between the new geometry and the original to be equidistant.

6. Click the radius, and then drag the offset profile so that it is created to the inside of the part. Then right-click and click Done.

7. Place a dimension between the offset profile and the outside edge of the part, and enter **Offset = 20 mm** in the input box (again, be sure to name this, because you will be using it in the steps to follow).

8. Window-select the entire part/sketch so that all of the lines are selected, and then click the Construction button and convert the lines to construction lines.

SELECT OBJECTS WITH A WINDOW SELECTION

You can create multiple entity selections using what is referred to as a Window Selection. Window selection sets include objects differently depending upon whether the window is created left to right or right to left:

◆ Position the pointer slightly above and to the left of the left-most entity to select, and then click and drag the pointer slightly below and to the right of the right-most entity that you want to select. All objects that are fully enclosed within the rectangle are selected and highlighted.

◆ Position the pointer slightly below and to the right of the right-most entity to select, and then click and drag the pointer slightly above and to the left of the left-most entity that you want to select. All objects that are enclosed by and/or intersected by the rectangle are selected and highlighted.

You can use the Ctrl and Shift keys to add and remove entities to the selection sets.

---

9. Select the Point tool on the Draw panel of the Sketch tab, and place a point on the corner of the offset loop, as shown in Figure 4.15.

10. Finish the sketch, and choose the Hole tool from the Model tab.

11. If needed, use the ViewCube to view the part from an isometric view.

12. The Hole tool should have automatically selected your sketch point; if not, ensure the Placement drop-down is set to From Sketch and the Centers button is selected, and then select the sketch point on-screen.

FIGURE 4.15
Placing a sketch
point for hole
placement

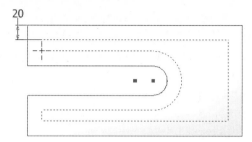

13. In the Termination drop-down, select Through All to ensure that the hole depth always cuts through the part. Then set Type to Tapped, set the Threads options to ISO Metric Profile M10x1.5 (as shown in Figure 4.16), and then click OK; finally, save your part.

FIGURE 4.16
Hole options

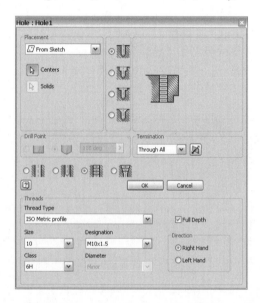

SELECTING SKETCHED HOLE CENTERS

The Hole tool will automatically select sketched center points as long as only one visible unconsumed sketch is available. If you find that the Hole tool is not picking up your center point automatically, check to see that you haven't accidentally created an extra sketch in the model tree. You can hover your mouse pointer over the sketch node in the browser to see the sketched entities highlight on the screen. If you determine that you have accidentally created an extra sketch, you can right-click it and click Delete.

Note too that only center points (small cross marks) are automatically selected by the Hole tool, and simple points are not. However, you can manually select simple points for hole placement. You can also convert center points to simple points, or vice versa, by using the Center Point button on the Sketch tab (you'll find it next to the Construction tool).

Creating a Rectangular Hole Pattern

So far, the features you've created have been based on a sketch. These types of features are, therefore, referred to as *sketched features*. Features not based on sketches are referred to as *placed features*. Placed features are solely dependent upon existing part geometry. Later in this section, we will discuss the steps necessary to create a placed feature in the form of a rectangular pattern.

When creating patterns, you have the choice of creating them at the feature level or at the sketch level. For instance, you could have patterned the sketch point using a sketch pattern and then have placed multiple holes at once using the Hole tool. It is generally best, though, to create patterns as features rather than sketch patterns. There are two reasons to consider feature patterns:

◆ A feature pattern saves time when creating spaced, multiple instances of a feature, and it makes editing the spacing easily accessible.

◆ Using a feature pattern in a part allows you to later use that pattern to create a component pattern in an assembly and follow the original part pattern. For instance, if you placed this part into an assembly, you could pattern a bolt to occupy every hole within the pattern by simply constraining one bolt into the original hole feature and then use the Component Pattern tool to automatically pick up the hole pattern count and spacing. The Component Pattern tool is available only within the assembly environment.

First you'll need to determine the pattern spacing. From the creation of the second feature, you know that the round end of the slot has a width of 40 mm. From the creation of the placed hole, you know that the offset from the slot edge is 20 mm. From this information, you will determine that the spacing of the two rows of holes are (2 × offset value) + 40 mm, therefore 80 mm. Assume the design specification requires eight holes in each row and that they need to be spaced at a distance of 25 mm apart. With this information, you are now ready to proceed with creating the hole pattern. You can continue on with the file from the previous section or open the file called `mi_4a_003.ipt`.

1. On the Model tab, click the Rectangular Pattern button found on the Pattern panel.

2. In the Rectangular Pattern dialog box, you are being asked to select the features to pattern. You can select the hole from the graphics area, but may find it easier to do so from the Model browser. No matter the method you use, check the Model browser to ensure that Hole1 and only Hole1 is highlighted (you can use Ctrl+click to deselect any accidentally selected features).

3. Next, click the arrow button under Direction 1, and select the edge of the slot cutout. Use a direction button to change the direction if required, and set the count and spacing to **8** and **25 mm**, respectively. You can confirm that your settings look similar to Figure 4.17.

4. Next, click the arrow button under Direction 2, and select one of the short ends of the part. Use a direction button to change the direction if required, and set the count to **2**.

Although you could just change the spacing value to 80 mm and complete the pattern, you might want to consider what would happen if the width of the slot feature were to change. If that were to happen, the hole pattern spacing would stay at 80 mm and no longer remain symmetric to the slot width. To avoid this, you will make the pattern spacing parametric by calling the dimensions of earlier features into your pattern spacing. In this way you are building a formula right into the pattern so that if those dimensions change, the spacing setting will follow.

FIGURE 4.17
List parameters from the Rectangular Pattern dialog box

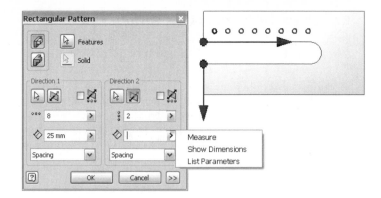

5. To do this, first clear the Direction 2 length input box.

6. Next click the arrow at the right of the length input box, and click List Parameters from the flyout shown in Figure 4.17.

7. Choose Diameter from the list, then choose List Parameters again, and finally choose Offset.

8. Edit the input to read **Diameter + 2* Offset**.

9. If the text shows in red, there is an error. When you have a valid formula, it will display in black. Check the preview, ensure that the pattern looks correct, and then click OK. Confirm that your part looks like Figure 4.18, and then you can save your file.

FIGURE 4.18
A rectangular hole pattern

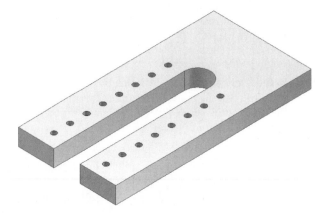

Editing Sketches and Features

You will often need to modify a sketch and/or feature after you have created it. Oftentimes you may find that because designs are similar, it is most efficient to copy an existing part and then make changes to the copy.

In the next steps, you'll edit some of the features you've just created, but before doing so, it will be helpful to understand the behaviors associated with the model tree and browser nodes. When a feature is sketch based, you can expand the plus sign next to it to reveal the sketch. Likewise, when a feature has multiple elements such as a pattern, you can expand it to view and control each element. If a feature is placed rather than sketch based, it may not have any elements and, therefore, will lack a plus sign. Figure 4.19 shows the anatomy of the three browser nodes.

FIGURE 4.19
Editing features
and sketches

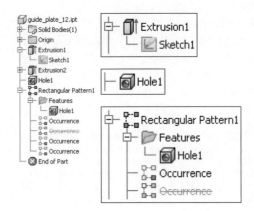

The extrusion is based on Sketch1, as you can see. However, the hole in Figure 4.19 is a placed feature based solely on the edges of other features and, therefore, contains no sketch (you'll place a hole of this type in the pages to come). The pattern, when expanded, shows the features that it contains and each occurrence of those features.

EDITING A SKETCH

To edit a feature or a sketch, you can right-click it and choose Edit Feature or Edit Sketch, or you can double-click the browser node icon for that feature/sketch. Be sure to double-click the node icon rather than the node text; otherwise, you set the text active for renaming. Follow these steps to explore the edit procedures of features and sketches:

1. On the Get Started tab, choose Open (or press Ctrl+O on the keyboard).

2. Browse for the file named mi_4a_004.ipt located in the Chapter 4 directory of the Mastering Inventor 2011 folder, and click Open.

3. In the Model browser, right-click Extrusion2, and choose Edit Sketch. You'll notice that the sketch becomes active for edits and the part displays in a rolled-back stage as it existed when the sketch was originally created.

4. You want to edit the diameter dimension and change it to an inch-based value. To do so, double-click the dimension, type **2 in** into the input box, and then press Enter.

You'll notice that Inventor converts the value to a millimeter equivalent for you. You can mix units as required, but know that any value that does not have a unit is assumed to be the part's base unit. This means if you were to enter **2** without the "in" suffix, the diameter would be set to 2 mm, because this part is mm based.

5. Click the Finish Sketch button on the Sketch tab (or right-click and click Finish Edit) to return to the feature level of the part.

You'll also notice that as a result of the sketch edit of the diameter, the length of the slot cutout adjusts automatically as well, because it contains a formula to ensure that it is always 5× the diameter of the circle.

EDITING A FEATURE

Note that the spacing for the rectangular pattern adjusted automatically on each side of the slot cutout but did not adjust for the length of the pattern. This is because the pattern contains a parametric formula that controls the width spacing but not the length. To fix this, you'll edit the rectangular pattern, as shown in these steps:

1. Double-click Rectangular Pattern1 in the browser to open the edit dialog box.

2. On the left side, clear the value of 25 mm, click the arrow button, choose List Parameters from the flyout, and select Slot_Length from the list.

3. The spacing is now adjusted so that the holes are patterned at the Slot_Length value. Looking at the preview, obviously this is not correct. To fix this, click the drop-down at the bottom left, and change it from Spacing to Distance. Click OK to accept these changes.

You may decide that the rectangular pattern needs to include features that were not originally present when the pattern was created, such as Extrusion3 and Chamfer1 found in this part. If you edit the pattern, you'll notice that the part rolls back to the state that existed at the time of the pattern; therefore, you cannot add the new features to the pattern. To resolve this, you will reorder the features and then edit the pattern.

4. In the Model browser, select Extrusion3 and Chamfer1, and drag them above the rectangular pattern.

You can reorder features in this way so long as they are not dependent upon one another. For instance, if you attempt to drag Chamfer1 above Extrusion3, you'll find that it can't be done. This is because the chamfer is based on the geometry of the extrusion.

5. Once the features have been reordered, double-click the rectangular pattern to edit it, or right-click and choose Edit Feature.

6. Ensure the Features button is pushed in, and select Extrusion3 and Chamfer1 from the Model browser so that they are added to the pattern. Your preview should update as well. Click OK to accept these changes.

You may decide that although the pattern provides the correct spacing of the elements, you need to exclude some of the middle instances to accommodate other features. You can do this easily by suppressing the instances you do not need and still maintaining the constant pattern spacing.

7. Expand the rectangular pattern feature in the browser, and note all the instances of the patterned features are listed as occurrences.

8. Roll your mouse pointer down over the list, and you will see the instances highlight on-screen indicating which occurrence they are.

9. Identify the fourth and fifth instances on each side of the pattern, right-click them, and choose Suppress. You can do this one at time or hold Ctrl as you select them and suppress

them all at once. Notice that these occurrences are no longer present on the part and are marked with strikethrough in the browser. Figure 4.20 shows the results of these edits. You can close the part without saving changes.

FIGURE 4.20
The edited part

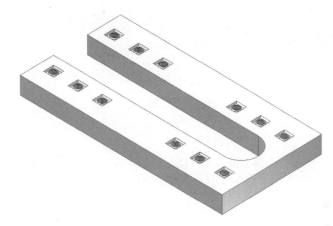

Repairing Features and Sketches

Ordinarily, you want to create chamfer and fillet features at the end of the overall part creation process. Creating chamfers and fillets at the end of the process reduces errors because of feature dependencies associated with these features. In the following exercise, however, you will create a chamfer before creating a hole and then make a change to illustrate both the folly of creating placed features too early in the design and the method of repairing a feature error:

1. On the Get Started tab, choose Open (or press Ctrl+O on the keyboard).

2. Browse for the file named mi_4a_007.ipt located in the Chapter 4 directory of the Mastering Inventor 2011 folder, and click Open.

3. Select the Chamfer tool on the Model tab, and select the corner indicated with the red arrow.

4. Set the distance to **30 mm**, and click OK.

5. Next, click the Create 2D Sketch button and create a sketch on the yellow face.

6. Use the Point tool to place a point near the chamfered corner, dimension it as shown in Figure 4.21, and then click Finish Sketch.

7. Select the Hole tool on the Model tab, and place a counterbore hole as shown in Figure 4.21.

8. Next it is decided that the chamfered corner will not work with this design and should have been a rounded corner. To make this change, right-click the chamfer feature in the Model browser, and choose Delete from the menu.

9. Because the counterbore hole is dependent upon the chamfer, you are prompted with the option to keep it or let it be deleted also. You will choose to keep it by deselecting the Dependent Sketches And Features box and clicking OK.

FIGURE 4.21
Dimensions from
the chamfered
corner

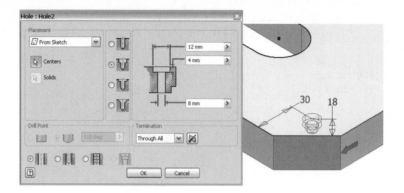

10. Notice the Hole feature in the browser now has a marker symbol next to it indicating this feature is "sick" and is in need of some repair. Expand the Hole2 feature node, and you will see the sketch is also marked as "sick." Right-click the sketch, and choose Recover, as shown in Figure 4.22.

FIGURE 4.22
Selecting Recover
to examine
sketches with
errors in them

11. In the Sketch Doctor dialog box, you will see a list of the issues present in the problematic sketch. Click Next to see the recommendations for resolving this problem. The recommendation is to edit the sketch.

12. Click Next again, and you will see there is only one treatment option in this case.

13. Click Finish and then click OK in the message box informing you that you are being taken to the sketch environment.

Depending upon the extent of the error, the Sketch Doctor may offer you the ability to delete objects, close open loops, and so on. Of course, you could have just edited the sketch originally and ended up with the same result, in this case. But in cases where you do not know the extent of the problems, the Recover option is often helpful in determining the issue.

14. In the sketch, you will see the unresolved sketch entities highlighted in a magenta color. Right-click the magenta line, and choose Break Link. This breaks the link with the missing chamfer edge but does not fully fix the problem.

15. Select the magenta endpoint(s), and use the Break Link option on it/them as well. This results in the diagonal line being underconstrained. You have two choices to resolve this:

◆ Use the coincident constraint along with the General Dimension tool to lock down the diagonal line.

◆ Delete the diagonal line and its referencing dimensions, and re-dimension the hole center point off the edge of the base part.

16. Once you have re-constrained the hole center by one of these methods, click Finish Sketch, and return to the feature level of the part. Notice that the hole and sketch are no longer "sick."

17. Choose Fillet from the Model tab, and select the same edge previously used by the chamfer to place a 30 mm fillet. Once done you can close the file without saving changes.

Although there is probably no way you will ever completely avoid having to repair features and sketches, using placed features such as chamfers and fillets as late in the design as possible will go a long way toward reducing these issues. You should also strive to avoid referencing these features with dimensions when they are present.

Exploring the Extrude Tool

Although you have explored the basics of creating extrude features, you have many options to understand before you can truly master this simple but powerful tool. In the next several pages, you will open a series of files that have been set up to demonstrate the various options to you. You can find all of these files in the Chapter 4 directory of the Mastering Inventor 2011 folder.

DIRECT MANIPULATION TOOLS

The Direct Manipulation tool set is a set of user interface tools introduced in Inventor 2011 that enable you to modify a model while viewing the changes in real time. The buttons on the In-Canvas Display correspond to the buttons and inputs found in dialog boxes and menus. You can choose to use the Direct Manipulation tools or use the traditional dialog boxes and menus to achieve the same result.

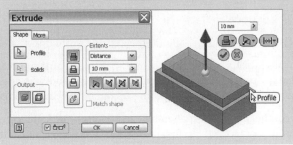

The Direct Manipulation In-Canvas Display consists of manipulator arrows, mini toolbars, selection tags, and value input boxes.

Once you become comfortable with the Direct Manipulation tools you can right-click on the dialog box of the each tool and choose Auto-hide in order to save screen space.

You should note that you cannot disable the Direct Manipulation tools when using the standard Inventor interface; however, if you are using the classic interface (no Ribbon Menu), the Direct Manipulation tools are disabled.

To learn more about Direct Manipulation go to the Get Started tab and click the Tutorials button. Select the Introduction to Direct Manipulation tutorial on the New Users tab of the Tutorial Learning Resource dialog box.

Extruding with Cut and Taper

You can use the Extrude tool's Cut option to remove material from your parts. Although you may think of this as a tool to create holes, keep in mind that Inventor's Hole tool is the better choice to create standard holes because of the advanced detailing functions that accompany the Hole tool. With that said, the Cut option in the Extrude tool will allow you to cut material using any sketched profile that you might come up with.

1. Open the file named mi_4a_010.ipt.

2. Click Extrude on the Model tab (or Type E on the keyboard).

3. Select the rectangle shape for the extrude profile, and set the distance to **20 mm**.

4. Choose the Cut option and just drag the manipulator arrow down into the part; notice that the preview turns red and the direction automatically switches. Change the direction so that the preview is going up out of the part, and then click OK.

5. Note that an error is generated, and it states the feature you specified did not change the number of faces. Keep this in mind as you use the Extrude tool. Inventor will generally

set the correct direction for you, but occasionally you might need to set the direction manually. Click Edit to return to the extrude options.

6. Change the direction again so that you are indeed cutting the part.

7. Click the sphere on the manipulator arrow or click the More tab as shown in Figure 4.23.

8. Enter **-12** in the Taper input box, and click OK. When finished, you can close the part without saving changes.

FIGURE 4.23
A tapered cut extrusion

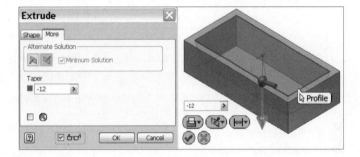

Extruding with Intersect

You can create complex shapes by sketching the two separate side profiles and then using the extrude Intersect option to keep the combined volume of the two, as shown here:

1. Open the file named mi_4a_012.ipt.

2. Click Extrude on the Model tab (or Type E on the keyboard).

3. Select the visible sketch for the extrude profile (if not automatically selected).

4. Change the Extents drop-down from Distance to All.

5. Click the Intersect button, and ensure the extrude direction is correct (or use the mid-plane option to extrude both directions).

6. Check your settings against Figure 4.24 and then click OK, and you will see that only the volume shared between the existing solid and the intersect profile is kept. When finished, you can close the part without saving changes.

FIGURE 4.24
An intersect extrusion

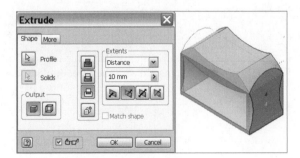

Extruding Surfaces from Open Profiles

In addition to creating solids with the Extrude tool, you can also create surfaces. If the profile is open and there is no other geometry to relate to, the surface solution is automatically selected. For closed profiles, you are required to switch the output from solid to surface manually, as shown here:

1. Open the file named mi_4a_014.ipt.

2. Select Extrude on the Model tab (or Type E on the keyboard).

3. The visible shape will automatically be selected because it is the only available profile. Because it is found to be an open profile, the Surface output is automatically selected as well.

4. Change the distance to **25 mm**, and set the direction arrow to the midplane option so that the surface is extruded out in both directions from the profile. And then click OK.

5. To explore how to create a surface extrusion from a closed profile, right-click Sketch2 in the browser, and turn on the visibility.

6. Select the Extrude tool, and notice that Inventor automatically selects the profile and sets the output to Solid.

7. Click the Surface button to change the output to an extruded surface, and then change the Extents option to To.

8. This allows you to specify a point or surface to extrude to. You might notice that the surface created in the previous step was created in two halves. Select the arc-shaped half (rather than the spline-shaped half), and notice the preview terminates as if the arc half wrapped around.

9. Deselect the check box next to the To selection arrow (the Terminate Feature On Extended Face check box) and you will notice the preview terminates at the furthest extent of the selected surface, matching the spline shape.

10. Click OK to create the extruded surface.

Figure 4.25 compares the two termination solutions when using the To option. Keep in mind that although this example used surface extrusions, the To option works the same for Solids. You can close the file without saving changes.

FIGURE 4.25
Extruded surfaces

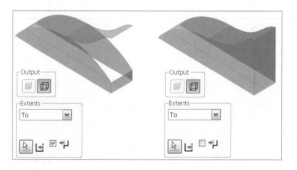

Extruding Solids from Open Profiles

In addition to extruding surfaces from open profiles, you can extrude solids, provided sufficient geometry is present to allow the open profile to solve correctly. This technique employs the Match Shape option and is the default solution when an open profile is selected in the Extrude tool while the solid output is selected. To do this, follow these steps:

1. Open the file named mi_4a_016.ipt.

2. Select Extrude on the Model tab (or Type E on the keyboard).

3. Click the arc profile, and notice that the Match Shape check box is automatically selected; in addition, the preview has extended the arc down toward the plate to provide a closed profile.

4. Click in the highlighted profile to select it.

5. Change the Extents drop-down to Distance and enter **60 mm.**

6. Set the Direction to go into the base plate feature, and click OK. Your result should look like Figure 4.26. You can close the file without saving changes.

FIGURE 4.26
Extruding an
open profile

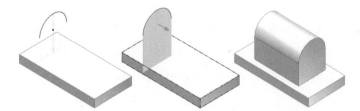

To take a look at the Match Shape option and how it can be used to change the output, you'll open a file that has two possible solutions for the final matched shape. One solution will match the shape of the existing geometry, and the other will not. Follow these steps to see how this works:

1. Open the file named mi_4a_018.ipt.

2. Select Extrude on the Model tab (or Type E on the keyboard).

3. Click the visible profile sketch in the center of the part.

4. You'll notice that Inventor attempts to create a closed profile from this open profile by extending the profile past the extents of the existing geometry. Select the profile on the side with the grid feature.

5. Change the Extents drop-down to Distance, enter **1 mm**, and click OK. Notice how the extrusion fills the shape of the part.

6. Next edit the extrusion you just created, and deselect the Match Shape box. And then click OK.

7. You'll notice that the extrusion runs through the grid feature ignoring the shape.

Figure 4.27 compares the results of an open profile extrusion with and without the Match Shape option selected. You can close the file without saving changes.

FIGURE 4.27
Match Shape
option for open
profile extrudes

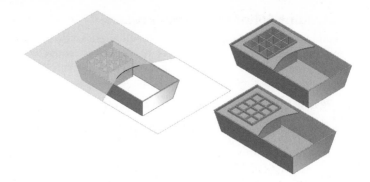

Extruding with To

It is often helpful to extrude to existing geometry rather than entering a distance value. In this way, if the existing feature changes, so too will your extrusion, and you can extrude to faces and vertices as well as work planes and work points, as shown here:

1. Open the file named mi_4a_020.ipt.

2. Select Extrude on the Model tab (or Type E on the keyboard).

3. For the profile, select one of the rectangular profiles.

4. Change the Extents drop-down from Distance to To.

5. Select the yellow face, and click OK. You will receive an error stating that the termination plane does not completely terminate the profile due to the way that the yellow face would wrap around in a circle if extended.

6. Click Edit in the error dialog box to return to the Extrude dialog box.

7. Uncheck the Terminate Feature On Extended Face check box in the Extents area, as shown in Figure 4.28, and then click OK.

FIGURE 4.28
Extruding to an
extended face

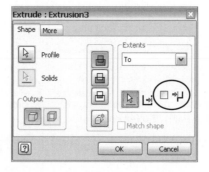

8. Next use the Extrude tool and select the remaining rectangle.

9. Change the Extents drop-down from Distance to To.

10. Select the red face, and you will see the preview terminates along the extended red face.

11. Uncheck the Terminate Feature On Extended Face check box in the Extents area, and you see the preview extend to the yellow face.

12. Click OK to create the extrusion. You can close the file without saving changes.

Follow these steps to take a look at some other Extrude To options:

1. Open the file named mi_4a_022.ipt.

2. Select Extrude on the Model tab (or Type E on the keyboard).

3. For the profile, select one of the ellipse-shaped profiles.

4. Change the Extents drop-down from Distance to To 5. Select the yellow face, and ensure that the Terminate Feature On Extended Face check box is checked. In this case, you would receive an error if this check box were not selected.

5. Click OK and you'll see that the ellipse face takes on the angle of the face to which you extruded.

6. Use the Extrude tool again, and select the other ellipse profile, and change the Extents drop-down from Distance to To, once again. This time select the work point for the terminating object, and click OK.

7. You'll see that the ellipse extrudes up to the work point height as shown in Figure 4.29. You can close the file without saving changes.

FIGURE 4.29
Extruding to a face
and a point

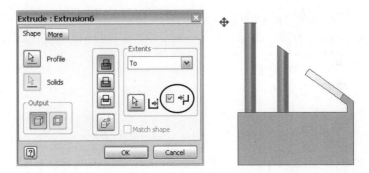

Oftentimes when extruding to a cylindrical face, you will need to set the extrude to solve for the minimum solution since the face is continuous all the way around. To do this, follow these steps:

1. Open the file named mi_4a_024.ipt.

2. Select Extrude on the Model tab (or Type E on the keyboard).

3. For the profile, select the hex-shaped profile.

4. Change the Extents drop-down from Distance to To, select the outside face of the pipe, and then click OK.

You will notice that the hex shape stops at the closest face of the pipe. This is because the Minimum Solution option was defaulted to. However, if the goal was to extend the profile to the furthest extent of the cylindrical face, you would need to adjust the settings to the farthest extent of the cylindrical face.

5. To fix this, edit the extrusion you just created, and click the More tab (or click the sphere on the on-screen manipulator arrow).

6. On the More tab, select the Minimum Solution uncheck box as shown in Figure 4.30, and then click OK.

You'll see that without the Minimum Solution option selected, the extrusion extends to the far side of the selected face. You can close the file without saving changes.

FIGURE 4.30
Extruding to the minimum solution

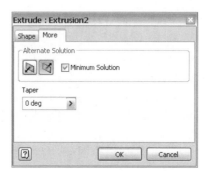

Extruding with To Next

Similar to extruding to a selected entity, you can use the To Next option and let Inventor automatically select the next available surface or face for you. It should be noted that solutions with through voids may not work with this option.

1. Open the file named mi_4a_026.ipt.

2. Select Extrude on the Model tab (or Type E on the keyboard).

3. For the profile, select the rectangular profile marked Profile1.

4. Change the Extents drop-down from Distance to To Next, and click OK.

5. Repeat the same steps for Profile2. You will receive an error because the extrusion cannot build to this solution.

6. In the error message dialog box, click Edit, and then set the extrude extents to To.

7. Select the back (yellow) face for the face to extrude to, and then click OK.

Oftentimes the geometry may require a bit of experimenting to get the solution you want. Just knowing the abilities and limitations of each option goes a long way toward knowing how to proceed. You can close the file without saving changes. Figure 4.31 shows the results of using the To Next extent option.

FIGURE 4.31
Extruding with
To Next

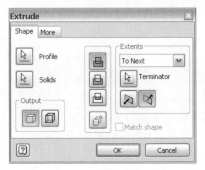

Extruding Between

You may need to define the beginning and the end of an extrusion that are not common to your sketch plane. To do this, you can use the Between option:

1. Open the file named mi_4a_028.ipt.

2. Select Extrude on the Model tab (or Type E on the keyboard).

3. For the profile, select Circle.

4. Change the Extents drop-down from Distance to Between.

5. Select both pipe-shaped pieces to define the from and to options.

6. Because you are extruding to hollow objects, you'll need to use the minimum solution option. Click the More tab, and ensure the Minimum Solution check box is selected.

7. Then flip the direction using a direction button next to the Minimum Solution check box. Click OK.

Figure 4.32 shows the results of using the Between extent option. You can close the file without saving changes.

FIGURE 4.32
Extruding with
Between

Extruding Multibodies

You may have noticed a couple of other buttons in the Extrude dialog box, one called Solids and the other called New Solid, as shown in Figure 4.33. These options allow you to create separate solid bodies within the part or choose which existing solid bodies to modify. To explore the multibody extrude options, follow these steps:

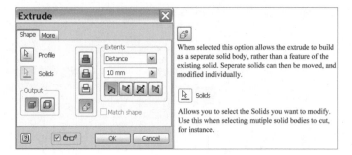

FIGURE 4.33
Multibody
solid options

Follow these steps:

1. Open the file named mi_4a_030.ipt.

2. Select Extrude on the Model tab (or Type E on the keyboard).

3. For the profile, select the visible rectangular sketch profile (if it is not automatically selected).

4. Change the Extents drop-down from Distance to To, and select the yellow face on the existing part.

5. Click the New Solid button, as shown in Figure 4.34, to set this extrusion as a separate solid body and then click OK.

Because you used the New Solid option, you now have a part file with two separate solid bodies. You can expand the Solid Bodies folder in the browser to identify each one. Currently, the second solid interferes with the first and needs to be dovetailed to fit.

6. From the Modify panel of the Model tab select the Combine button.

7. Choose the new solid for the Base selection and choose the original solid (the one with the yellow face) as the Toolbody selection.

8. Set the operation to Cut (middle button).

9. Select the Keep Toolbody check box and then click OK.

You should see the original solid disappear and the new solid result in a dovetail where it intersected with the first. Expand the Solid Bodies folder and ensure that you have two solid bodies still. If not, use the Undo button and repeat steps 6 through 9.

10. Right click either of the solids, and choose Show All to turn the visibility of the solid back on.

Next you'll use an existing sketch to cut a notched edge into both of the solid bodies at the same time.

11. Locate the sketch named Base Inset Sketch in the Model browser and right-click on it and select Visibility.

12. Use the Extrude tool, set to Cut, and then use the Solids button (found under the Profile button) to select both dovetailed bodies.

13. Set the distance value to **6 mm** and then click OK.

You can use the ViewCube to examine the resulting cut. You'll learn more about multibody parts in Chapter 5, including how to use the Make Components tool to write out each solid body as an individual part file. You can close the file without saving changes.

FIGURE 4.34
A multibody part

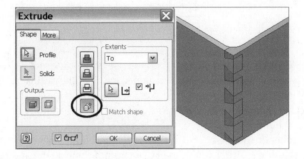

Creating Revolved Parts and Threads

Creating turned and revolved parts is a regular occurrence in many engineering departments because of the types of parts designed and manufactured. The parts consist of circular features around a common axis. There are actually two different workflows for creating circular parts, each with its own advantages and disadvantages. Creating threads on a part presents another challenge.

You can create circular parts using a single sketch and revolving it around a centerline axis. Alternatively, you can create multiple circular extrusions to produce the same part.

There are also two different workflows for creating thread features on a part. You can add threaded features to any circular component by means of the *thread* feature, which creates cosmetic threads on the part, or through the use of the *coil* feature, which creates physical threads. Typically, physical threads are created only when that geometry is required for the model. Generally, using cosmetic threads is sufficient because they are an intelligent feature that can be retrieved in the detail drawing of the part and called out as per the specifications of the feature.

Creating Revolved Cylindrical Parts

Revolved cylindrical parts utilize a sketch with a center axis. Figure 4.35 illustrates two ways to create the same sketch. The view on the left shows a sketch profile anchored at the origin and dimensioned from the origin. The view on the right illustrates the same sketch, anchored at the origin but dimensioned from a created centerline, which creates diametric dimensions. The two sketches will create the same revolved feature, the difference being that the centerline allows you to dimension the sketch using diameter dimensions to maintain the design intent of the part.

FIGURE 4.35
Dimension to
the sketch vs.
centerline

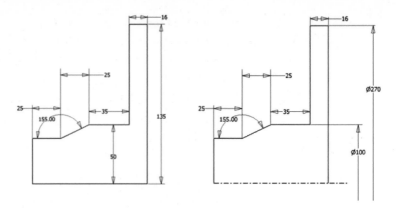

The centerline is created with the use of the Line tool with the Centerline tool toggled on. In this example, the centerline was created starting at the origin point and continuing to the right of the sketch, extending beyond the sketch for selection ease. When dimensions are created on the sketch and terminated at the centerline object, they will actually extend to the other side of the revolved part diameter.

The advantage of creating a revolved profile, rather than creating stacked circular extrusions, is that the relationship of every portion of the sketch can be easily visualized from the start. The disadvantage is that a contour sketch is not always easily edited to remove or change a portion of the feature. In addition, if the sketch is not fully dimensioned and constrained, it can create errors down the line with faces and edges. For this reason, you should always fully dimension and constrain your sketches. Figure 4.36 shows the finished revolved feature.

FIGURE 4.36
Revolved circular
features

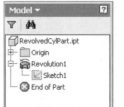 

Creating Extruded Cylindrical Parts

An alternate method, using extruded circular features, provides better control and can allow for editing of each individual portion of the cylindrical part. Essentially, this is the building-block approach of creating one feature after another until the entire cylindrical part is created. Figure 4.37 shows the finished extruded feature.

The advantage to this approach is that the same part design is comprised of four separate features, each one individually editable without affecting other portions of the part.

The disadvantage with this approach is that it takes a small amount of additional time to create the part and create features that are dependent upon the previously created feature. If any extrusion in the middle of the part is deleted, then, prior to deletion, the next feature down the model tree will need to be reassociated with a different face.

FIGURE 4.37
Extruded circular
features

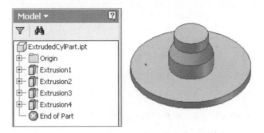

SHOULD YOU USE REVOLVED OR EXTRUDED CYLINDRICAL PARTS? IT DEPENDS!

Although neither revolved nor extruded cylindrical parts are inherently better, each has its place and its pros and cons. The extruded method is typically easier to edit and follow, but you may end up with many features to create a simple part. Also, editing one section of the cylinder may require editing several other features (for example, if you shorten one section by 30mm but want to keep the overall length unchanged, you will have to edit other features to add back this 30mm). The revolved method, on the other hand, allows you to control all the features in one place and more easily link the dimensions of the sketch so that changing one of the dimensions will change the others.

Revolves can be parts or features and solids or surfaces. Follow these steps to see how revolves are created:

1. Open the file named mi_4a_032.ipt.

2. Select Revolve on the Model tab.

3. For the profile, select the rectangular sketch profile and the small circle.

4. Click the Axis button in the Revolve dialog box, and then select the line indicated on the part for the axis.

5. Set the operation to Cut so that you are milling out the revolved profile.

6. By default the Extents drop-down is set to Full, giving you a 360-degree revolve. In this part, though, a full revolve cut would cut away part of the existing feature. So, you will set the Extents drop-down to Angle instead. Notice the other extents options available. They should all look familiar as options from the Extrude tool.

7. Set the angle to **180**, and then click OK. Figure 4.38 shows the revolve options.

FIGURE 4.38
Revolving a cut
feature

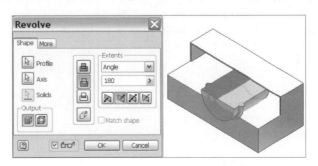

Next you'll use the Revolve tool on an open profile to create a revolved surface. You'll then use a tool called Thicken to turn the surface into a solid.

1. Open the file named `mi_4a_034.ipt`.

2. Before creating the revolve feature, you need to supply the sketch with some missing dimensions. To do so, right-click Sketch1 in the browser, and choose Edit Sketch.

3. Place dimensions from the points shown in Figure 4.39 to the centerline, and you'll notice that because the line is a centerline type, the dimensions are automatically diameter dimensions. Before placing the dimension, you can right-click and choose Linear Dimension if a diameter is not the correct choice.

FIGURE 4.39
Adding dimensions
to a centerline

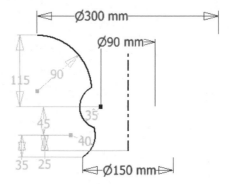

4. Once you've added the dimensions, click the Finish Sketch button, and click Revolve on the Model tab.

5. For the profile, select the sketch profile.

6. Click the Axis button, and then select the centerline.

7. Because the sketch was an open profile, the Surface output is automatically selected. Click OK to create the revolved surface.

8. Next you'll add some fillets. On the Model tab, click the Fillet button, and click the intersecting circular edges on the surface feature.

9. In the Fillet dialog box, change the radius to **12 mm**, and then click OK.

10. In the surface panel on the Model tab, click the Thicken/Offset button.

11. Click the Quilt option in the Thicken/Offset dialog box to allow you to select all the surface faces at once, and then click anywhere on the surface. Then click OK.

12. Rotate the part around or use the ViewCube, and you'll see that the surface is still visible. Locate it in the Model browser, and then right-click and turn its visibility off. Figure 4.40 shows the revolved shape.

FIGURE 4.40
A revolved and
thickened surface

Creating Threaded Features

Inventor offers the option of creating cosmetic threads that represent actual threads in the part, and it creates 2D geometry information for detailing those threads. Cosmetic threads are created with a threaded hole feature. Or you can use the Thread tool on the Feature panel bar to add threads to existing part features. The thread features are added to the Model browser as a separate feature.

COSMETIC THREADS

Creating cosmetic threads on a circular part is a relatively simple procedure. Cosmetic threads work by wrapping a scaled graphic around the feature to represent threads. This allows the model file size to stay smaller because it is not required to calculate all of the extra edges and faces of the threads. However, the cosmetic Thread tool does create fully intelligent thread features based on the specifications you choose, allowing you to detail the threads quickly and accurately in the drawing environment.

In the following steps, you will use the Split tool to divide a cylindrical surface into multiple faces and then apply cosmetic threads to them:

1. Open the file named mi_4a_036.ipt.

2. Select the Split tool in the Modify panel on the Model tab.

3. Select Work Plane1 for the Split tool, select the face of the cylinder it runs through, and then click OK.

4. Right-click the edge of the Work Plane1, and choose Visibility to turn the plane off. Recall that work planes are selectable only by their edges.

5. Now that the part is divided into two faces, click the Thread button in the Modify panel, and select the shortest face.

6. Click the Specifications tab, set the size to **17**, and the designation to **M17x1**, and then click Apply.

7. Switch back to the Location tab, and click the end of the middle cylinder.

8. Uncheck the Full Length check box, and enter **5 mm** for the Offset and **30 mm** for the Length. Click the direction button if you do not see the threads appear. Click Apply.

9. Run your mouse pointer over the third cylinder, and notice that as you get closer to one end or the other, the offset and direction switch.

10. Click the face, and apply another set of threads of any type you like; when you're done, click OK. Figure 4.41 shows the Thread tool options.

FIGURE 4.41
Placing cosmetic threads

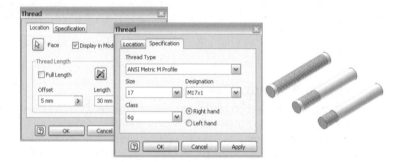

COSMETIC THREADS ARE USUALLY SUFFICIENT

Unless you are going to actually cut threads directly from your 3D model, cosmetic threads are usually sufficient. The advantage of these threads is that they contain all the thread information in the model that can later be extracted in a drawing without carrying the burden of complex modeling features.

Inventor pulls its thread specification information from the Thread.xls file found in the Design Data folder. You can edit this file to contain custom thread specifications and include proprietary threads or industry-specific threads not commonly listed.

PHYSICAL THREADS

You can create physical threads using the Coil tool. Physical threads create large file sizes compared to cosmetic threads and can seriously affect performance and assemblies. As a result, physical threads should be used only where absolutely necessary, such as the design of a bottle or jar top or other geometries such as a worm gear.

1. Open the file named mi_4a_038.ipt.

2. In the Model browser, select the sketch called Thread Cut Sketch, right-click, and select Edit Sketch.

3. Right-click and choose Slice Graphics (or press F7 on the keyboard) to temporarily slice away the material that hinders your view of the sketch. Recall that this option is available only while creating or editing a sketch that runs through a solid.

4. Zoom in on the sketch, change the depth dimension to **2 mm**, and then click the Finish Edit button to exit the sketch.

5. Zoom out (or double-click the mouse wheel to zoom all), and then click the Coil tool in the Create panel on the Model tab.

6. Select the sketch profile if it does not automatically select, and then select the work axis in the center of the cylinder for the axis.

7. Use a direction button to ensure the coil is running the correct way, and then click the Cut button.

8. Click the Coil Size tab, change the pitch to **4 mm** and the revolution to **12**, and then click OK.

Figure 4.42 shows the Coil Size tab. Be aware that you can create coils by specifying pitch and revolution, revolution and height, and pitch and height, or by defining a spiral. Also note the suffix of *ul* shown in the revolution dialog box. This suffix just means that the value is unitless. You do not have to specify this because Inventor will do so as needed.

FIGURE 4.42
Creating a physical thread with the Coil tool

Creating Work Features

Work features are construction geometry, used when part geometry is not present to create new features. There are three types of work features: work planes, work axes, and work points. In addition to work features that you might create, each part contains origin planes, axes, and an origin point. You can view these by expanding the Origin folder in the Model browser, right-clicking each feature, and selecting Visibility, as shown in Figure 4.43. Note that in this illustration the 3D indicator arrows have been drawn in for clarity. If it helps you, though, you can turn the indicator on and have it display in the lower left of your screen by going to the General tab of the Application Options dialog box.

Work Planes

A *work plane* is an infinite construction plane that is parametrically attached to a feature or features, typically to help you define other geometry. Work planes are created based on the geometry you select. Every work plane type is created by defining a location and an orientation. The following illustrations show the ways you can create work planes. You can open the corresponding part files and follow along. The part files are named `mi_4a_040.ipt` through `mi_4a_50.ipt`, as shown here.

FIGURE 4.43
Origin work features turn on

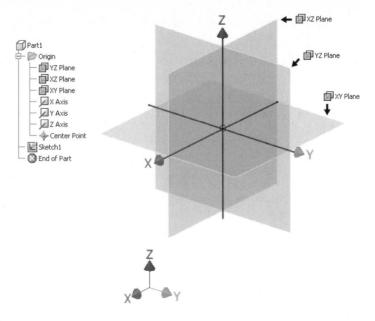

Midplane between two parallel planes   Two parallel planar faces or work planes (see `mi_4a_040.ipt`).

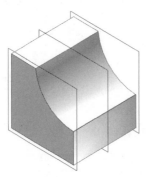

Three point   Any three endpoints, intersect points, midpoints, or work points (see `mi_4a_041.ipt`).

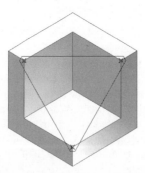

Normal to axis through point   A linear edge or axis and a point, in either order (see `mi_4a_042.ipt`).

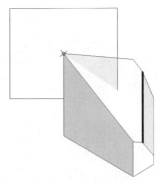

Parallel to plane through point   A planar face or work plane and any point, in either order (see `mi_4a_043.ipt`).

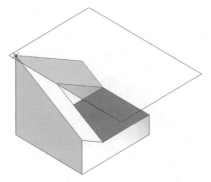

Two co-planer edges   Any two co-planar edges (see `mi_4a_044.ipt`).

Offset from plane Click a face, and drag in the direction of the offset. Enter the value of the offset (negative values are acceptable). (See mi_4a_045.ipt.)

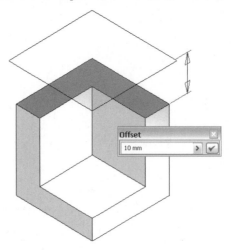

Angle to face around edge A part face or plane and any edge or line parallel to face (see mi_4a_046.ipt).

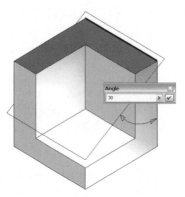

Tangent to surface and parallel to plane A curved face and a planar face or work plane, in either order (see mi_4a_047.ipt).

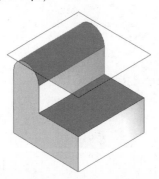

Tangent to surface through edge   A curved face and a linear edge, in either order (see `mi_4a_048.ipt`).

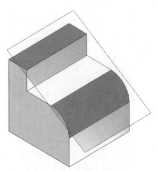

Tangent to surface through point   A line with ends coincident with the cylinder axis and edge and the tangent point on the cylinder edge (see `mi_4a_049.ipt`).

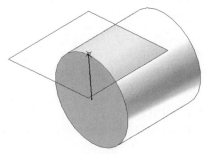

Normal to curve at point   An edge or sketch curve and a vertex, edge midpoint, sketch point, or work point on the curve (see `mi_4a_050.ipt`).

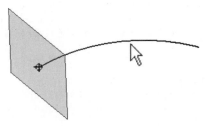

Midplane of a torus   A torus shape (see `mi_4a_051.ipt`).

Here are some other points to remember about work planes:

◆ You can right-click a work plane in the browser or the graphics window and then select Show Inputs to see how that work plane was created.

◆ You can move work planes by clicking an edge and dragging. This will slide the work plane in the plane of its definition only.

◆ When you place the mouse pointer on any corner of the work plane, a resize arrow appears, allowing you to drag the corner of the work plane to resize it.

◆ You can also right-click and set a work plane to Auto-resize, allowing it to resize off the extents of the part as it changes.

◆ Work planes have a positive and negative side to them. The Normal (positive) side has an orange tint, and the non-normal (negative) side has a blue tint. You can right-click a work plane and choose Flip Normal if needed.

◆ If you do not have the geometry you need present when creating work planes, you can right-click and choose Create Axis or Create Point in order to create an "in-line work feature." In-line features are stacked in the Model browser and automatically set not to display.

◆ When you start the Work Plane tool, you can right-click and choose Repeat Command to set the work feature tools to stay on until you right-click and choose Done. This helps when you are creating a lot of work features, because you do not have to keep clicking the button each time.

Work Axes and Work Points

CERT
OBJECTIVE

A *work axis* is a construction line of infinite length that is attached to a part based on the geometry used to create it. You can create a work axis on linear edges through circular faces and edges; through any combination of work points, midpoints, and vertex points; along 2D and 3D sketch lines; and at the intersection of work planes.

Work points may be created at the intersection of planes, surfaces, edges, work axes, 2D or 3D sketch lines, work points, and sketch points, in any combination. They can also be placed directly on sketch points, vertex corners, center points, edge midpoints, or grounded work points.

To see the practical application of the features, it's best to actually create them:

1. Open the part file named mi_4a_052.ipt.

2. Click the Plane button on the Work Features panel of the Model tab, click and hold down on the yellow face of the base plate feature, and drag out to create an offset plane. Enter **100 mm** for the offset value. You may need to use the ViewCube to change the view so you can see the yellow face.

3. In the browser, click the work plane node slowly twice, and rename it to **OP-1**.

4. Next expand the Origin folder in the model tree, right-click the z-axis, and choose Visibility.

5. Use the Work Plane tool again, and click the z-axis and the offset plane you just created (you can select these in any order). Enter **27.5**. Remember that work planes are selected by their edges.

6. In the browser, click the work plane node slowly twice, and rename it to **AP-1**.

7. Expand the browser node for AP-1, and note that it has "consumed" the OP-1. You can right-click AP-1 and deselect Consume Inputs if you'd like.

8. Now you find the intersection of the two planes with a work axis. Click the Work Axis tool, and simply select both work planes.

9. In the browser, click the work axis node twice slowly, and rename it **IA-1**.

RENAMING WORK FEATURES

Taking the time to rename work features can be helpful if you find that you must create and edit a lot of them. However, if you use just one or two here and there, it may not be that helpful. Using a consistent naming scheme will help you easily determine the work feature's use. Use OP for Offset Plane, IA for Intersect Axis, and so on.

Keep in mind that if you right-click a work feature and choose Redefine Feature, you can change the definition of a work feature and, therefore, might need to rename the feature if your naming scheme incorporates that information. For example, an offset plane may become an angle plane and, therefore, might be renamed from OP-4 to AP-6. Use what makes sense to you.

---

10. Double-click AP-1 to edit the angle value (double-click the browser node icon, not the text). Change the angle from 27.5 to **72.5**, and click the green check mark (or press Enter on the keyboard).

11. Notice the work plane did not update. Changes to work plane definitions must be manually updated. In the Quick Access toolbar (at the top of the screen), click the Update button (it looks like a lightning bolt). Figure 4.44 shows the intersection axis and the model tree at this stage.

FIGURE 4.44
A work axis at the intersection of two work planes

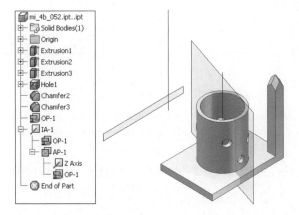

12. Next select the Work Axis tool, right-click, and ensure that Repeat Command is selected; this simply allows you to place multiple work features in succession without having to return to the menu to push the button each time.

13. Select the cylindrical face of each of the holes in the cylinder. This runs a work axis through the center of each hole. Rename these axes to **CA-1**, **CA-2**, and **CA-3**.

14. Select the Work Point tool, and then select OP-1 and CA-1, then OP-1 again and CA-2, and finally OP-1 a third time and CA-3. This places a work point at the intersection of the plane and axes.

15. Right-click the edge of OP-1, and choose New Sketch. This creates a new sketch on the work plane.

16. Right-click, and choose Slice Graphics (or press the F7 key) to temporarily clear the other geometry. Note that if you change your view to the opposite side of the sketch plane and then toggle the Slice Graphics option, you can change which side of the sketch is being sliced.

17. Select the Project Geometry tool on the Sketch tab, and select each of the work points and IA-1. This will create a sketch point at each work point and a line at the axis location. You could also get the same results by selecting only axes.

18. Create a sketch as shown in Figure 4.45. (All dimensions are 15 mm. Use project geometry to get the work points into your sketch.)

FIGURE 4.45
Sketch created
from projected
work features

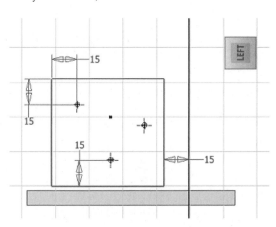

19. Finish the sketch, and extrude the profile 10mm away from the other features.

20. Create a work axis from the tip of the obelisk-shaped feature to the corner of the plate-shaped feature. The resulting axis should run through the cylinder. Name the work axis **PA-1**.

21. Create a work point by selecting the cylinder first and then PA-1. Be sure to select PA-1 on the side of the cylinder closest to the plate corner to ensure that the work point is created on the correct side of the cylinder.

22. Select the Hole tool on the Model tab, and set the placement drop-down to On Point. Select one of the work points you created for the Point input and its corresponding axis for the Direction input.

23. Set the diameter to **10 mm** and the Termination drop-down to Through All, and then click Apply. Repeat this for each work point.

24. Note that the hole running through the cylinder may not cut as you would expect. To resolve this, select the crescent-shaped face, and then choose Delete Face on the Model tab on the Surface panel. Ensure that the Heal option is selected as shown in Figure 4.46, and then click OK.

FIGURE 4.46
Using Delete Face
with the Heal
option to clean up
the Hole feature

25. Finally, right-click each work feature, and turn off its visibility. You can use the Ctrl key to select them all first as well. Work features should always have their visibility setting explicitly turned off at the part level so that their visibility can be controlled independently at the assembly level.

WORK FEATURE VISIBILITY VS. DISPLAY

Many Inventor users fight the control of visibility of work features (work planes, work axes, and work points) because of a lack of understanding of the tools available to control it. There are basically two methods of making work features not display on-screen:

◆ Right-click the work feature, and toggle off Visibility. (Always use this at the part level.)

◆ On the View tab, click Object Visibility, and then use one of the options listed. (Do not use this at the part level, only at the assembly level.)

These two methods both turn off the display, but only the first toggles the Visibility setting for each object. The second is a display override that suppresses the work feature display but does not change the Visibility setting.

The difference between the two methods becomes important at the assembly level. If you've used the Object Visibility tool to "override" the work feature visibility setting at the part level, you will find that all of the work features will display when you place the part into an assembly This requires you to toggle them all off again at the assembly level, and you will be required to do so for each instance of the part placed. You could use the Object Visibility tool in the assembly and suppress the display of all the work features for the entire assembly, but doing so doesn't allow you to access one or two work features at a time. As a result, you end up with all or none of the work features displaying.

In order to properly control work feature visibility, you should develop the habit of always right-clicking on the work features at the part level and explicitly toggling off the visibility setting, and never use the Object Visibility override in a part. If you do this, then when the part is used in an assembly, you can control the work features on an individual basis, per instance of the part. Then you can use the Object Visibility tool to toggle all of the visible work features on and off effectively.

Creating Fillets

The Fillet tool in Inventor may seem daunting at first because of the number of buttons and combination of options, but once you understand the layout of the dialog box and the intended use of the options, you'll be able to create fillets of all types. There are three basic types of fillets:

Edge fillets   These are fillets created based on selected edges.

Face fillets   These are fillets created between two faces or face sets.

Full round fillets   These are fillets that are tangent to three adjacent faces or face sets.

When you start the Fillet tool (on the Modify panel of the Model tab), it will default to edge fillets. You can switch the fillet type by using the buttons on the left of the dialog box.

Edge Fillets

Edge fillets are the most common type, and, therefore, naturally they have the most options. When Edge fillet is the active type, you'll see three tabs across the top of the dialog box, allowing you to set the following Edge fillet subtypes: Constant, Variable, and Setbacks.

CONSTANT FILLETS

Constant fillets have the same radius along the entire length of the edge. On the Constant tab, you can select a group of edges and then set the radius and type. You can create a new size group by clicking the Click To Add row in the selection pane and changing the radius size. Figure 4.47 shows two constant fillets groups being created. In this case, each group contains only one edge, but they vary in radius. Note the pencil icon indicating that the row is being edited. No edges can be selected at this time. To set the row ready to select edges, simply click the pencil icon so that it changes to an arrow.

FIGURE 4.47
Creating two
edge fillets of
different sizes

FILLET FAILURES

One of the most common issues with edge fillets arises when you select multiple edges that converge on a single corner vertex. Unfortunately, when this happens, the error message erroneously indicates an issue with the fillet size. However, you can generally resolve these issues by removing one or more of the competing edges from the selection, applying the fillet feature, and then applying another fillet feature using the removed edge(s). Keep this in mind as you place edge fillets, and remember that just because you can place multiple size edge fillets all in one feature, it isn't always the best solution.

Also on the Constant tab you can change the selection method from Edge to Loop or Feature. Figure 4.48 shows the selection method set to Feature and the results of selecting a hole. Note that all edges created by the hole feature are selected.

FIGURE 4.48
Fillet selection
by feature

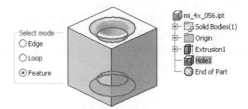

You can also select All Fillets (inside corners) or All Rounds (outside corners) to apply fillets to a part quickly, where it makes sense to do so. Figure 4.49 shows the same part with the two options applied to it for comparison. Keep in mind that you can select all rounds and fillets at once, as well.

FIGURE 4.49
All fillets vs.
all rounds

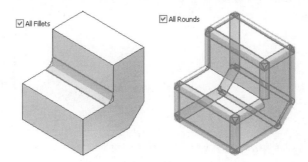

VARIABLE FILLETS

In contrast to constant-edge fillets are variable edge fillets. Variable edge fillets can have multiple radius sizes along the length of the edge. To create variable fillets, you click the Variable tab and then select an edge to make it variable. By default, the start and endpoints are added to the right pane. You can add points by simply clicking the edge in the place or places you want to transition to a different radius.

Once points are selected, you can change the radius and position of each point. The number listed in the Position column is a decimal percent of the edge length rather than the length. For instance, Figure 4.50 shows a point has been added at 60 percent of the edge length coming off the start end.

FIGURE 4.50
A variable-
edge fillet

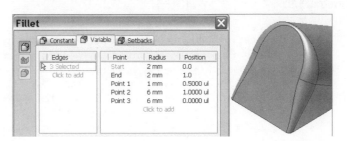

SETBACKS

Setbacks define the corner where multiple edge fillets come together. Once you select edges in the Constant tab, you can switch to the Setbacks tab and select corners to apply setbacks to. Setbacks are typically used for cast and molded parts where the corners cannot be too sharp.

On the Setback tab, select a corner using the Vertex pane first. Then enter a setback distance for each edge. Setback values should be no longer than the length of the edge they are placed on. You will typically get an error if you attempt to specify a value that is larger. If you click the Minimal check box, the setbacks will automatically adjust to the smallest length that can be built. Figure 4.51 shows a setback being created as well as the result.

FIGURE 4.51
A setback fillet

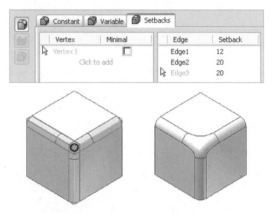

Face Fillets

Face fillets add fillets between two selected face sets. These faces or sets of faces do not need to share a common edge. You can adjust the radius once the fillet is previewed, but typically if you do not get a preview, it indicates an invalid selection set. You can add more faces, or you may need to use a different type of fillet solution.

Two options are selected by default:

Include Tangent Faces   Use this option to allow the fillet to continue over tangent, adjacent faces. Deselect this to ensure that the fillet is only between selected faces.

Optimized for Single Selection   Deselect this when making multiple selections per face set. When this is selected, the selection automatically changes from selection set 1 to selection set 2.

Figure 4.52 shows a face fillet created between the two dark faces.

FIGURE 4.52
Creating a
face fillet

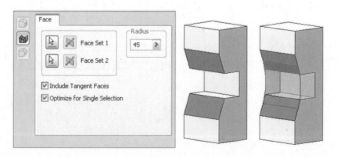

Full Round Fillets

Full round fillets can be used to quickly round over a feature without having to know the radius that would complete the full round. You can use this to create a full round on faces that are not parallel also. To create this type of fillet, simply select the faces in the order that they occur from side to center to other side, and the center face will be replaced with the radius face. Figure 4.53 shows a full round. The selection options are the same as described previously for the face fillet.

FIGURE 4.53
A full round fillet

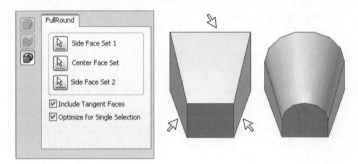

Creating Fillets

In this section you'll create the various types of fillets discussed in the previous pages. To do so open the file called mi_4a_053.ipt.

1. Select the Fillet tool from the Modify panel of the Model tab (or type F on the keyboard).

2. First, you'll create a simple edge fillet. Select the vertical edge where the yellow and blue faces intersect.

3. Set the fillet radius to **18 mm** and click Apply.

4. Next you'll create a variable fillet. Click the Variable tab in the Fillet dialog box.

5. Select the edge where the purple and red faces intersect.

6. Set the radius for the Start and End Points to **2 mm**.

7. Click on the word Start to set the dialog box from edit mode back to selection mode, and then click anywhere on the edge between the purple and red faces.

8. Change the radius to **6 mm** and then set the Position to **0.5** in order to set the new variable point to be half way between the start and end points. Note you could add another variable point to further define the variation of the fillet. In this case though, just click Apply to create the variable fillet.

9. Next you'll create a fillet setback. To do so switch back to the Constant tab and set the radius to **2 mm**.

10. Click the pencil icon in the current row to set it from edit mode to selection mode.

11. Select the edge between the yellow and pink face and then the edge between the yellow and green face. It may help to zoom in on the corner.

12. In the fillet dialog box, click the Click To Add text to add another row to the list.

13. Change the radius to **3 mm** and then click the pencil icon to set the row back to selection mode.

14. Select the edge between the pink and green face.

15. Select the Setbacks tab in the fillet dialog box.

16. Choose the corner where the yellow, pink and green faces intersect. You should see the vertex highlight as you locate it.

17. Enter **6 mm** for all of the setback values, and then click Apply to create the fillets with setback.

18. Next you'll create a face fillet. Click the Face Fillet button on the left of the fillet dialog box (the one in the middle).

19. For Face Set 1, choose one of the orange faces, for Face Set 2 choose the other. Then click Apply.

20. And finally, you will create a full round fillet. Click the Full Round Fillet button on the left of the fillet dialog box.

21. Select the tan faces on the protruding front feature in consecutive order (the right face for Side Face Set 1, the top face for Center Face Set, and the left face for Side Face Set 2, for example).

22. Click OK to create the fillet and close the fillet dialog box.

Have a look at the fillet features in the browser tree. You can right-click on any of them and choose Edit Feature to adjust the fillet as needed. In order to add or remove edges to any given fillet feature, you can use the Ctrl key and then click the edges on-screen. Figure 4.54 shows the part before and after fillets were applied. You can close the file without saving changes.

FIGURE 4.54
Before and
after fillets

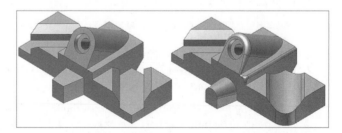

Note that if you try to place fillet along the edges where the pink and red faces intersect, you will receive an error due to the way the resulting fillet tapers. However, if you also choose the corresponding edges on the opposite of the rounded feature, the fillet will build without issue. Keep this in mind as you work with fillets that form sharp tapers. You can close the file without saving changes.

> ### COLOR OVERRIDES
>
> In order to change the color of any individual face on a model, you can right-click on the face and choose Properties from the context menu. You can do the same for entire features, by right-clicking them in the browser and choosing Properties.
>
> To remove color overrides, you can expand the Solid Bodies folder in the browser and right-click on a solid and choose Properties. In the Body Properties dialog box, you can set the Body Color Style to As Part, select the Strip Overrides check box, and then click OK. Be aware that parts translated from other file formats often come in with many color overrides and the Strip Overrides action can take a while to process.

Hole Features

CERT OBJECTIVE

Using Inventor's Hole tool, you can create counterbore, countersink, spotface, and drilled holes with user-defined variables such as thread designation and drill point angle. You can also specify a simple hole, a tapped hole, a tapped tapering hole, or a clearance hole.

Using the Thread and Clearance Spreadsheets

Two external files are related to the Hole tool. These are `Thread.xls` and `Clearance.xls`. Both files load at the time of installation to a `Design Data` folder in the install directory location, such as C:\Program Files\Autodesk\Inventor 2011\Design Data. If the Design Data folder has been relocated, you can determine its location by following these steps:

1. Go to the Get Started tab, and click Projects.

2. In the Project File editor, ensure that you are looking at the correct project, and locate and expand the Folder Options node in the lower pane.

3. Note the Design Data path listed.

4. If the Design Data path says = Default, then your project is reading the path from Inventor's options, so you should go to the Tools tab, click Application Options, and go to the File tab in the dialog box that opens. Note the Design Data path listed.

Once the path is determined, you can browse to the path and find the Thread and Clearance spreadsheets and make customizations as follows. To edit the thread spreadsheet, follow these steps:

1. Close Inventor.

2. Make a copy of the original spreadsheet, and store it in a safe location (this is just a precaution).

3. Open the `Thread.xls` file in Microsoft Excel.

4. To add or modify custom thread designations for an existing thread type, do the following:

   A. Choose the worksheet you want to customize.

    B. Edit the values in the Custom Thread Designation column to include your designations. These will then be available in the thread and Hole tool and can be recovered in hole notes in a drawing.

    C. Edit cell B1 to change the name Inventor displays in the Hole and Thread tools.

    D. Edit cell D1 to change the order that Inventor lists the thread types in the Hole and Thread tool dialog boxes.

5. To add a new thread type, complete these tasks:

    A. Copy an existing worksheet of the same type (parallel or taper).

    B. Rename the custom worksheet as required.

    C. Delete most or all of the rows below row 3. You may want to keep at least one row to use as a reference, at least temporarily.

    D. Add rows as required.

    E. Edit cell B1 to change the name Inventor displays in the Hole and Thread tools.

    F. Edit cell D1 to change the order that Inventor lists the thread types in the Hole and Thread dialog boxes.

    G. Hover your mouse pointer over cell A1 to see the tool tip containing the letter designations, and mark your sheet as appropriate.

6. Save the spreadsheet.

7. Restart Inventor. Changes are read when Inventor loads.

Modifying Clearance.xls is a very similar process.

Creating Holes in Parts

You have four options for placing holes with the Hole tool:

- From Sketch
- Linear
- Concentric
- On Point

To explore these placement options, open the file named mi_4a_053.ipt from the Chapter 4 folder of the Mastering Inventor directory, and follow these steps:

1. Select the Hole tool on the Model tab (or type H on the keyboard).

2. You'll notice the Placement option is set to From Sketch. This is because Inventor has detected that there are two sketches available for use. Click Cancel to exit the Hole tool.

3. Right-click Sketch5 in the Model browser, and choose Visibility to turn the visibility of this sketch off.

4. Start the Hole tool again. This time Inventor detects that there is a sketch available and automatically selects the center point found in that sketch.

5. Click the counterbore option, and set the counterbore, as shown in Figure 4.55, and then click OK.

FIGURE 4.55
Counterbore
settings

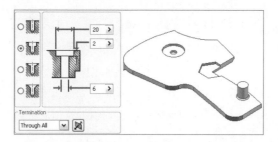

6. Right-click Sketch5, turn the visibility back on, and then click the Hole button again. Notice that it selects the center points automatically again. This is helpful; however, you do not want the hole in the hex-shaped cutout to be the same size as the others in this sketch. Hold down the Ctrl key, and click the center point at that location to remove it from the selection.

7. Choose the spotface option, and notice that it is essentially the same as the counterbore with the exception of the depth measurement. In the spotface, the depth is measured from the bottom of the bore. Set the spotface as shown in Figure 4.56, and click OK.

FIGURE 4.56
Spotface settings

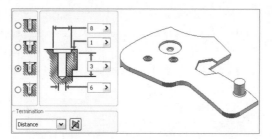

8. Since you removed the one center point before placing the spotface holes, you will reuse that sketch to place the next hole. To do so, that sketch must be visible. The Hole tool has toggled the visibility back off, so you need to locate Sketch5 again, and make it visible.

9. Place a simple drilled hole using the center point in the hex-shaped cutout. Set the termination to **Through All** and the diameter to **9 mm**, and click OK. Then turn the visibility of the sketch off one last time.

10. Start the Hole tool again. You'll note that because there are no longer any visible sketches, the From Sketch option is no longer the default placement option. Set the placement to Concentric, and select the top face of the part for the Plane input.

11. Next you need to specify a concentric reference. Select one of the yellow faces (or the circular edge of the yellow face).

12. Set the hole to the countersink option, and then set the inputs as shown in Figure 4.57. Click Apply (not OK just yet).

FIGURE 4.57
Countersink
settings

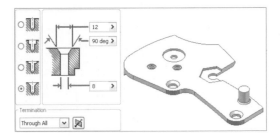

13. Set the plane, use the other yellow face to place another countersink of the same size, and then click OK.

14. Change your view so that you can see the work point at the work axis intersection of the green face.

15. Start the Hole tool again, and set the placement option to On Point.

16. Select the work point for the point input and then the work axis for the direction. Flip the direction if needed, using the button next to the Termination drop-down.

17. Leave the hole at the simple drilled option, and set the Termination drop-down to To.

18. For the To selection, click the bore face of the counterbore hole, and click the Terminate Feature check box.

19. Click the Clearance Hole option, set the options as shown in Figure 4.58, and click OK.

FIGURE 4.58
Clearance hole
settings

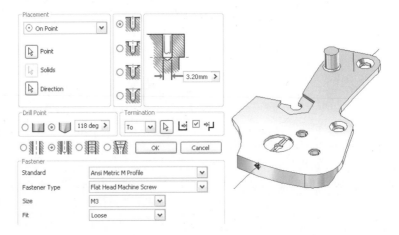

20. Rotate the part so that you can see the underside, and zoom in on the feature with the red face.

21. Start the Hole tool again, and select the red face for the Face input.

22. Next select one of the longer straight edges for Reference1, and set the dimension to **8 mm**. Select one of the shorter edges, and set the dimension to **12 mm**.

23. Set the termination to Through All and the hole type to Taper Tapped Hole.

24. Choose Din Taper from the Thread Type list, set the size to M5, and then click OK. You'll note that the hole is cut with the appropriate taper.

You can close the part without saving changes when you have created all of the holes.

As you can see, the Hole tool has an abundance of options allowing you to specify holes in a variety of ways. Keep in mind that features created with the Hole tool carry more intelligence with them than a simple circular extrude cut. This is particularly true when you begin to detail a part in the drawing environment.

Setting Tolerance Values in Holes

You can set tolerances for hole dimensions in the Hole dialog box. When setting a hole dimension, right-click a dimension edit box, and then select Tolerance, as shown in Figure 4.59.

FIGURE 4.59
Tolerance settings

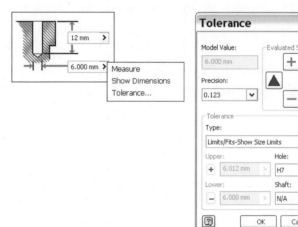

You can use these general steps to access the tolerance settings:

1. In the Tolerance dialog box, change the values as desired:

   ◆ In Precision, click the arrow to set the decimal precision of the dimension.

   ◆ In Evaluated Size, select Upper, Nominal, Median, or Lower to use when evaluating the dimension. This will set the size at which the hole is actually created.

   ◆ In Type, click the arrow, and select a tolerance type for the selected dimension.

2. Depending on your selection, enter values to set the upper and lower tolerance range and the tolerance for the hole and shaft dimensions (for Limits and Fits).

3. Click OK.

This will return you to the Hole dialog box. Keep in mind that although the value in the hole input will not change, the hole will be drawn to the tolerance you selected in the model. For instance, if the Upper option were selected in the hole shown in Figure 4.58, the hole would measure 6.012 mm rather than 6.000 mm. More about using tolerances is covered in Chapter 5.

Bend Parts

You can use the Bend Part tool to bend a part based on a sketched bend line. You can specify the end of the part to bend, the direction of the bend, the angle, the radius, or the arc length. You can find the Bend Part on the Modify tab of the Model tab. By default, it is hidden from view and must be accessed by using the flyout (the small black triangle on the Modify panel).

Here are some guidelines to be aware of when using the Bend Part tool:

◆ Sketches used for bend lines must be visible and unadaptive and should be located on a plane or surface that contacts the part.

◆ A sketched line on the top face of a part does not allow for the part to be bent down, only up, whereas a sketch that runs through the part allows the bend to be built up or down.

◆ Bend Part does not account for bend allowances in the way that sheet-metal features do and, therefore, should not be used with sheet-metal parts.

◆ You can specify the bend by Radius & Angle, Radius & Arc Length, or Arc Length & Angle.

Follow these steps to create a simple bend part:

1. Open the file named mi_4a_058.ipt.

2. Select the Bend Part tool from the flyout of the Modify panel.

3. Select one of the sketch lines as the bend line.

4. Adjust the arrow buttons so that just the end is bent up. Notice if you try to bend the end down, it will not work. This is because of the position of the sketch.

5. Set the radius to **100 mm**, and then click OK.

6. The bend will consume your sketch, so you will need to expand the Bend feature in the Model browser and then right-click the sketch and choose Share Sketch.

7. Create another bend to your specifications, experimenting with the other solutions.

Figure 4.60 shows the Bend Part tool in action. You can close the file without saving changes when finished.

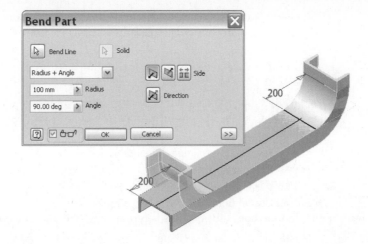

FIGURE 4.60
Bending a steel shape

The Bottom Line

Set application options and settings for part modeling   Understanding the settings and options that apply to the modeling environment is essential for getting the results you want from Inventor.

> **Master It**   You want to configure your options and settings for your sketch environment and then back them up and/or distribute them to other workstations. How would you go about doing this?

Create basic part features   In this chapter, you learned how to plan a workflow that allows you to create stable, editable parts that preserve the design intent.

> **Master It**   You need to create a fairly complex part consisting of many extrusions, revolves, sweeps, or lofts. In addition, you will need to create holes, fillets, chamfers, and other part modifiers. This part may need significant modification in the future by you or by other designers.

Use the Extrude tool   The Extrude tool is one of the most common feature tools in the Inventor modeling tool set. Understanding the options and solutions available in this tool will prove useful throughout your designs.

> **Master It**   Imagine you need to create an extruded feature but don't know the exact length; instead, you know the extrude will always terminate based on another feature. However, the location of that feature has not been fully determined just yet.

Create revolved parts and thread features   Creating revolved features and parts in Inventor can often resemble the creation of turned part and features in the real world. Applying thread features to a cylindrical face allows you to specify threads without having to actually model them.

> **Master It**   Let's say you have a part that you intend to fabricate on a lathe. Although you could create the part with a series of stepped circular extrusions, it occurs to you that the Revolve tool might work also.

Create work features   Using work features, work planes, work axes, and work points enable you to create virtually any part or feature. Work features are the building blocks for sketch creation and use.

> **Master It**   Your design will require creating features on spherical and cylindrical faces. You need to precisely control the location and angle of these features.

Use the Fillet tool   The Fillet tool has a great deal of functionality packed into it. Taking the time to explore all the options on a simple test model may be the best way to understand all the options.

> **Master It**   You are trying to create a series of fillets on a part. You create four sets of edge selections to have four different fillet sizes, but when you attempt to apply them, you receive an error stating that the feature cannot be built.

Create intelligent hole features   Although you can create a hole in a part by sketching a circle and extrude cutting it, this is typically not the recommended approach.

> **Master It**   You need to create a part with a series of various-sized holes on a plate. You would like to lay out the hole pattern in a single sketch and then use the Hole tool to cut the holes to the sizes required. However, when you select the From Sketch option in the Hole tool, it selects all of the holes, so you're thinking you must need to sketch out the hole pattern as circles and then use the Extrude tool to cut them out.

Bend parts   You can bend a portion of a part after you define a bend line using a 2D Sketch line. You can specify the side of the part to bend, the direction of the bend, and its angle, radius, or arc length.

> **Master It**   You need to create a model of a piece of rolled tube and would like to specify the bend direction, but when you use the direction arrow, you get a preview in only one direction.

Chapter 5

Advanced Modeling Techniques

Chapter 4, "Basic Modeling Techniques," introduced some of the basic modeling techniques required when creating a 3D parametric part. Modern parametric modeling utilizes numerous tools to create stable, editable parts. The basic workflow of creating a part is to create a base feature and then build upon that base. The tools used to build the additional features can vary depending upon your need and may range from simple extruded features to complex combinations of different feature types.

In this chapter, you will be exploring some of the more complex and curvy modeling techniques. Some of these features involve creating a base profile sketch along with support sketches used for defining paths and shape contours. Such features are based on the same rules used to create simpler features, such as extrudes and revolves, but they take it to the next level by using multiple sketches to define the feature. Other advanced features covered in this chapter depart from these concepts and move into new territory of feature creation. In either case, having a strong understanding of sketch creation and editing principles is assumed and recommended.

All the skills in this chapter are primarily based on creating a single part, whether in a part file or in the context of an assembly file.

In this chapter, you will learn how to:

◆ Create complex sweeps and lofts

◆ Work with multi-body and derived parts

◆ Utilize part tolerances

◆ Understand and use parameters and iProperties

◆ Troubleshoot modeling failures

Creating Complex Sweeps and Lofts

Now that you have moved on from creating simple features, you can explore the use of sweeps and lofts to create features of a bit more complexity. Both sweeps and lofts require one or more profiles to create a flowing shape. Sweeps require one sketch profile and a second sketched sweep path to create 3D geometry. Lofts typically require two or more sketch profiles and optional rails and/or points that assist in controlling the final geometry.

Creating and Using Sweeps

You can think of a sweep feature as an extrusion that follows a path defined by another sketch. 2D or 3D sketch paths can be used to create the sweep feature. As with most Inventor geometry, a sweep can be created as a solid or a surface. You should note that sweeps can add or remove material from a part, or you can use the Intersect option as you can with the Extrusion tool. If your intent is to create multi-body parts, then you can choose the New Solids option also.

CREATING 2D PATHS

When creating a sweep feature, you will typically want to first create the path sketch and then create a profile sketch that will contain the geometry to be swept along the path. To create the profile sketch, you will need to create a work plane at the end of your path. This work plane will be referenced to create a new sketch. It's not mandatory that you create the path and then the profile, but it is easier to define the profile sketch plane (that is, a work plane) by doing it this way. Normally, this geometry will be perpendicular to one end of the sweep path.

A basic rule of sweep features is that the volume occupied by the sweep profile may not intersect itself within the feature. Self-intersecting features are not currently supported. An example of a self-intersecting feature is a sweep path composed of straight-line segments with tight radius arcs between the segments. Assuming that the sweep profile is circular in nature with a radius value larger than the smallest arc within the sweep path, the feature will self-intersect, and the operation will fail. For a sweep to work, the minimum path radius must be larger than the profile radius. In the 2D sketch path example shown in Figure 5.1, the path radius is set at 12 mm. Knowing that the minimum path radius value is 12 mm, you can determine that the sketch profile radius must be less than or equal to this value.

FIGURE 5.1
2D sketch path

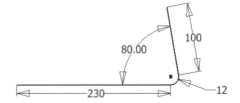

CREATING THE SWEEP PROFILE

Once a sketch path has been created, you can create a work plane on the path and then sketch the profile on that plane. To see this process in action, follow these steps starting with the creation of the path:

1. On the Get Started tab, click the New button.

2. On the Metric tab of the New File dialog box, select the Standard(mm).ipt template.

3. Create a 2D sketch as shown in Figure 5.1.

4. Once you've created the sketch path, right-click and choose Finish Sketch; then click the Plane button on the Model tab to create a work plane.

5. Select the endpoint of the 2D sketch path and then the path itself to create the plane. This creates a plane on the point normal to the selected line. Figure 5.2 shows the created work plane.

6. Once you've created the work plane, right-click the edge of it, and select New Sketch.

7. In the new sketch, use the Project Geometry tool to project the 230 mm line into this new sketch. It should come in as a projected point.

8. Next, create a circle anchored to the projected point, and give it a value of **20 mm** in diameter.

FIGURE 5.2
Creating a work
plane on which to
sketch

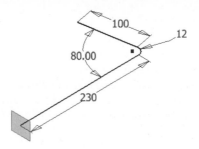

9. Finish the sketch, and select the Sweep tool. If you have a single sweep profile, then it should automatically select the profile and pause for you to select a path.

10. Select a line in the path sketch to set it as the path.

   Note that you can select either Solid or Surface for the feature. The sweep type will default to Path, and the orientation will default to Path also. The Sweep tool also has an option to taper the sweep feature, as shown in Figure 5.3.

FIGURE 5.3
Sweep dialog box
options

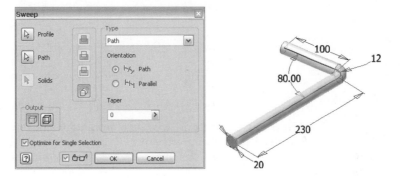

A number less than zero for the taper will diminish the cross section as the profile follows the path. A positive number will increase the cross section. If the taper increases the cross section at the radius of the path, to a value that exceeds the radius value, then the feature will fail because this will create a self-intersecting path.

11. Adjust the taper to a negative value to see the preview update. Note that if you enter a positive value that's 0.5 or more, the preview will fail, indicating a self-intersecting path. Set the taper back to **0**, and click OK to create the sweep.

You'll notice that this sweep feature consumes both sketches in the browser, just as an extruded feature consumes the sketch it is created from. To edit the sweep you can expand the browser node by clicking the plus sign and access both the profile and path sketches to make edits. You can also right-click on the sweep feature node and choose Edit Feature to change the options in the sweep dialog. Explore the ways to edit the sweep you just created and then you can close the file without saving changes. In the next section you will look at more sweep options.

Exploring Sweep Options

Although sweeping along a path is the default option, you can also utilize the Path & Guide Rail or Path & Guide Surface option to control the output of the Sweep tool. These options provide additional control for more complex results. Often these options are utilized on sweeps based upon a 3D sketch path, but this is not required.

PATH & GUIDE RAIL OPTION

The Path & Guide Rail option provides a means to control the orientation of a profile as it is swept along a path. In Figure 5.4, the rectangular sweep profile will be swept along the straight path but controlled by the 3D helical rail. This approach is useful for creating twisted or helical parts.

FIGURE 5.4
Sweep profile, Path & Guide Rail option

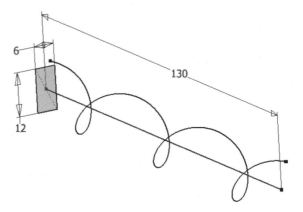

The 3D helical rail is guiding the rotation of the profile even though the sweep profile is fully constrained with horizontal and vertical constraints. Creating this part starts with creating the sweep path as the first sketch, followed by creating a second sketch perpendicular to the start point of the sweep path. The 3D helical rail is created using the Helical Curve tool in a 3D sketch.

1. Open the file mi_5a_004.ipt from the Chapter 5 directory of the Mastering Inventor 2011 folder.

2. Click the Sweep button on the Model tab.

3. Change the Type drop-down to Path & Guide Rail, choose the straight line as the path and the helix as the guide rail, and then click OK. Your result should resemble Figure 5.5.

FIGURE 5.5
Sweep with Path & Guide Rail option

Using guide rails to control the path and further define the shape of the sweep greatly expands the range of shapes you can create with the Sweep tool. You can close the current file without saving changes and take a look at the use of a guide surface in the next section.

PATH & GUIDE SURFACE OPTION

CERT OBJECTIVE

At times you will need to sweep a profile that will conform to a specific shape and contour. This is often necessary when working with complex surfaces, particularly when cutting a path along such a surface. In the following exercise, you will use some surface tools to manipulate a solid shape while exploring the sweep guide's Surface option.

1. On the Get Started tab, click Open, and open the file named mi_5a_006.ipt found in the Chapter 5 folder.

2. Click the small arrow on the Surface panel of the Model tab to see the Replace Face tool. Figure 5.6 shows the Surface panel expanded.

FIGURE 5.6
Surface tools

3. Click the Replace Face tool, select the red face as the existing face, then select the wavy surface for the new face, and finally click OK.

4. Right-click ExtrusionSrf1 in the browser, and select Visibility to turn it off.

5. Click the Plane button on the Model tab, click and hold down on the yellow surface, and then drag up to create an offset work plane at **85 mm**.

6. Right-click the edge of the work plane, and choose New Sketch.

7. Use the Project Geometry tool, and select the wavy face. This will result in a projected rectangle in your sketch.

8. Create a circle with the center point at the midpoint of the projected rectangle and tangent point on the corner of the rectangle so that your results look like the image on the left of Figure 5.7. Click the Finish Sketch button to exit the sketch.

FIGURE 5.7
Creating a
sweep path

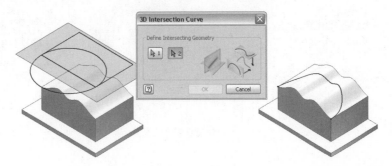

9. Click the Create 3D Sketch button on the Sketch panel, or right-click in the empty space of the graphics window and choose New 3D Sketch from the right-click context window.

10. Click the Intersection Curve tool from the 3D Sketch tab, and choose the circle and the wavy face. Finish the 3D sketch and turn the visibility of the 2D sketch and the work plane off. The result will be a curve as shown on the right of Figure 5.7.

11. Create a 2D sketch on the front face, as shown in Figure 5.8. Be sure to select the projected edges and make them construction lines so that Inventor won't pick up the entire front face as a sweep profile. The top two corners will be coincident to the curved construction line along the top. When the sketch is fully constrained and completed as shown in Figure 5.8, click Finish Sketch.

FIGURE 5.8
Creating a sweep profile

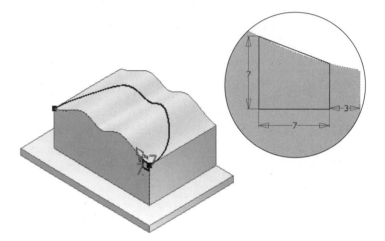

12. Next, select the Sweep tool, and choose the profile you just sketched for the profile input.

13. Select the 3D intersection curve for the path.

14. Click the Cut button to ensure that this sweep removes material from the part, and click OK.

15. The resulting cut sweep will be too shallow in some places, as shown on the left of Figure 5.9.

FIGURE 5.9
Path vs. Path & Guide Surface

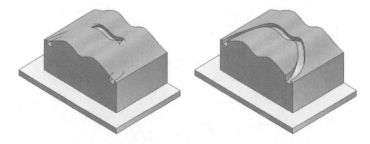

16. Edit the Sweep, and set the Type drop-down to Path & Guide Surface. Select the wavy surface as the guide surface, and then click OK. The result will look like the image on the right of Figure 5.9.

Using a guide surface to match the exact curvature of a complex shape is often the only way to achieve the type of features found on plastic parts and other consumer products of stylized form. You can close this file without saving changes and move on to the next section to explore lofted features.

Creating Loft Features

Whereas a sweep allows the creation of single profile extruded along a path, lofted features allow the creation of multiple cross-sectional profiles that are utilized to create a lofted shape. The Loft tool requires two or more profile sections in order to function. Rails and control points are additional options to help control the shape of a lofted feature. A good example of a lofted shape is a boat hull.

LOFT WITH RAILS

You could create a boat hull by defining just the section profiles, but you can gain more control over the end result by creating a loft with rails. Figure 5.10 shows the completed wireframe geometry to create a section of a boat hull. The geometry includes four section sketches, each composed of a 2D spline sketched onto a work plane. There are two rails: the top and bottom composed of 3D sketch splines.

FIGURE 5.10
Loft with rails
geometry

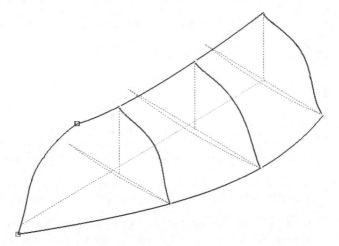

1. On the Get Started tab, click Open, and open the file named mi_5a_008.ipt found in the Chapter 5 folder.

2. Select the Loft tool in the Model browser.

3. Since the four section sketches are open profiles, the Loft tool will automatically set the output to Surface. Select the four cross section sketches in consecutive order, front to back or back to front.

4. Then click Click To Add in the Rails section of the dialog box, and select 3D sketches named Rail1 and Rail2.

5. If you have the Preview option selected at the bottom of the dialog box, you should see a preview of the surface indicating the general shape, as shown in Figure 5.11. Click OK, and the surface will be created.

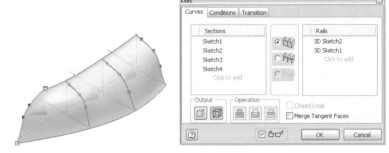

FIGURE 5.11
A surface loft
with rails

PATCH AND STITCH SURFACES

That concludes the lofting part of the boat hull, but if you'd like, you can continue with the following steps to learn a bit more about working with surfaces.

6. To finish the hull, select the Mirror tool on the Pattern panel of the Model tab.

7. Select the hull surface for the Features selection, and then click the Mirror Plane button.

8. Expand the Origin folder in the browser, click YZ to use as the mirror plane, and click OK.

9. Next you will create a 3D sketch to create a line for the top edge of the transom (back of the boat); right-click in the graphics window, and choose New 3D Sketch.

10. Click the Include Geometry button, and select the back edges of the hull.

11. On the 3D Sketch tab, click the Line tool, and draw a line across the back of the boat to form the top of the transom. Draw another line across the bottom of the transom where the two sides do not quite meet. Click Finish Sketch when the lines are drawn.

TURNING OFF THE TRANSLUCENCY OF SURFACES TO SEE BETTER

If you have difficulty seeing the end points when attempting to draw the 3D Sketch line, you can expand the mirror feature in the browser, locate the loft surfaces, and then right-click and deselect Translucent.

---

12. Select the Boundary Patch tool on the Surface panel, and select your 3D sketch lines and the projected geometry to create a surface for the transom. When creating boundaries, you need to select the lines in the order that they occur in the boundary. Click Apply, and then create another boundary patch across the top by selecting the two edges of the sides and the top edge of the transom.

13. You'll notice the gap in the base of the hull. Use the Boundary Patch tool to create a surface by clicking both edges of the gap and the small edge at the bottom of the transom.

14. Next, select the Stitch tool on the Surface panel, and select all five of the surfaces you created. It's easiest to window select them all at once.

15. Then click Apply and Done.

Using the Shell Tool

You should now have a solid boat. Of course, you would probably like to shell it out at this point. Before doing so, be sure to save your file. This is just good practice before running calculation-intensive operations like the Shell tool, particularly on free-form shapes like this boat hull.

16. Once your file has been saved, select the Shell tool on the Modify panel of the Model tab.

17. Click the top face for the Remove Faces selection, and set Thickness to **10 mm**.

If your system is a bit undersized, you might want to skip the next two steps and just click OK now to let the shell solve for just one thickness. Otherwise, you'll specify a unique thickness for the transom.

18. Click the >> button to reveal the Unique Face Thickness settings, click the Click To Add row, and then click the transom face.

19. Set the unique face thickness value to **30 mm**, and click OK to build the shell. Figure 5.12 shows the completed boat.

FIGURE 5.12
The completed boat

Although at this point you have gone far past the initial lofted surface to finish out the boat model, you started out by creating a loft from the 2D sketch profiles and then used the 3D sketches as rails to further define the shape. Of course, if you are a boat designer, you might see a few areas of the design that need improvement. But for now you can close the file without saving changes and move on to explore the Area Loft options in the next section.

Area Loft

Area loft is used in the design of components where the flow of a gas or liquid must be precisely controlled. Area loft is a different way of controlling the finer points of creating a loft shape. Figure 5.13 illustrates what might be considered a fairly typical loft setup, consisting of three section profiles and a centerline. The goal here is to create a loft from these profiles but to create a fourth profile to control the airflow through the resulting part cavity so that it can be choked down or opened up.

FIGURE 5.13
Area loft profiles

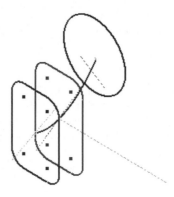

1. On the Get Started tab, click Open, and open the file named mi_5a_010.ipt found in the Chapter 5 folder.

2. Start the Loft tool, and select the three sections in order starting with the small rectangular shape.

3. Right-click, choose Select Center Line, and then click the centerline sketch line running down the middle of the profile sketches.

4. Right-click again, and choose Placed Sections; notice as you choose an option from the right-click menu that the dialog box updates to reflect your selections. You could have just as easily used the dialog box controls to do this, but oftentimes it is nice not to create the extra mouse travel.

5. Slide your mouse pointer over the centerline, and then click roughly halfway between the circular section and the middle section.

Once you click a location, the Section Dimensions dialog box appears, as shown in Figure 5.14, giving you control over the position and section area of the placed section. You can switch the position input from Proportional where you enter a percentage of the centerline length to Absolute, which allows you to enter an actual distance if you know it.

In the Section Size area, you specify the actual area or set a scale factor based on the area of the loft as calculated from the sections before and after the one you are creating. On the far left, you can switch the section from driving to driven, letting the area be calculated from the position. Any number of placed sections can be used to create precise control of the feature.

FIGURE 5.14
Section Dimensions dialog box

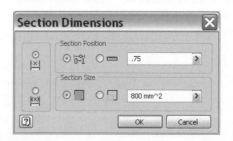

6. Leave Position set to Proportional Distance, change the position to **0.75**, set the area to **800** (as shown in Figure 5.14), and click OK. You can access the section again by double-clicking the leader information.

7. Double-click the End section leader text, and change it from driven to driving using the radio buttons on the left. Notice that you can set the area but not the position.

8. Change the area to **800**, and then click OK.

Figure 5.15 illustrates the placed loft section and the modified end section.

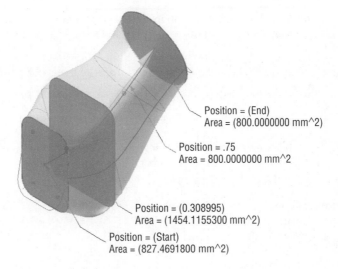

Position = (End)
Area = (800.0000000 mm^2)

Position = .75
Area = 800.0000000 mm^2

Position = (0.308995)
Area = (1454.1155300 mm^2)

Position = (Start)
Area = (827.4691800 mm^2)

You may have noticed that by changing the end section to an area of 800 square millimeters, you altered the size of the end profile from the original shape, in this case slightly reducing the diameter of the circle. Keep this in mind as you create area lofts and you can use the original sketch to just rough in the shape and not worry as much about getting the size exactly right, until you refine the area loft profile. Of course, as always, you should still fully constrain the sketch profile. You can close this file without saving changes and have a look at the centerline loft options in the next section.

CENTERLINE LOFT FEATURE

The centerline loft feature allows you to determine a centerline for the loft profile to follow, just like you did with the area loft. In the following steps, you'll create a wing feature using the centerline loft and look at some of the condition options available in lofted features as well:

1. On the Get Started tab, click Open, and open the file called mi_5a_012.ipt found in the Chapter 5 folder.

2. Click the Loft button, and select the yellow face of the wing stub feature and the sketch point at the end of the arc as sections.

3. Right-click, choose Select Center Line, and then click the arc. Notice how the lofted shape now holds the centerline, as shown in Figure 5.16.

FIGURE 5.16
A loft with and without centerline

4. Click the Conditions tab in the Loft dialog box so you can control the curve weight and transition type at the work point and wing stub profile.

5. Click the drop-down next to the Edges1 (Section) and set it to Tangent. Change the weight to **0.5** to adjust the blend from the wing stub feature.

6. Click the small drop-down to set Point Sketch2 to Tangent and then set the weight to **1.5**.

7. Currently, the loft is extending out past the work plane. Often this can be a problem because the work plane may have been established for the overall length of the part. To resolve this, set the drop-down to Tangent To Plane, and select the work plane on the screen. Notice the adjustment. Figure 5.17 shows the preview of the adjustments before and after the tangent plane is selected.

FIGURE 5.17
Adjusting curve weight and condition of the loft

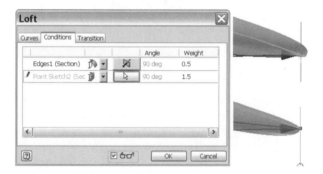

8. Click OK, and examine your lofted shape.

9. You can use the Mirror tool to mirror the loft you just created and the wing stub feature using the work plane in the tail area. Figure 5.18 shows the complete design.

Here is the full list of conditions available, depending upon the geometry type:

Free Condition   No boundary conditions exist for the object.

Tangent Condition   This condition is available when the section or rail is selected and is adjacent to a lateral surface, body, or face loop.

Smooth (G2) Condition   This option is available when the section or rail is adjacent to a lateral surface or body or when a face loop is selected. G2 continuity allows for curve continuity with an adjacent previously created surface.

Direction Condition   This option is available only when the curve is a 2D sketch. The angle direction is relative to the selected section plane.

Sharp Point   This option is available when the beginning or end section is a work point.

Tangent   This option is available when the beginning or end section is a work point. Tendency is applied to create a rounded or dome-shaped end on the loft.

Tangent To Plane   This is available on a point object, allowing the transition to a rounded dome shape. The planar face must be selected. This option is not available on centerline lofts.

FIGURE 5.18
The design with the wing loft mirrored

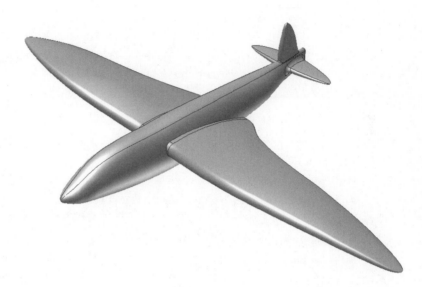

The angle and weight options on the Conditions tab allow for changes to the angle of lofting and the weight value for an end condition transition. In this example, if the endpoint condition is changed to Tangent on the work point, the weight is automatically set to 1 and can be adjusted. Click the weight, and change it to 3 to see how the end condition will change in the preview. Experiment with the weight to see the changed conditions. If a value is grayed out, then the condition at that point will not allow a change.

Creating a Part Using Loft and Sculpt

There are a couple of things to keep in mind when creating sketches to be used as lofts. First, you should always project the endpoints of rails into your profile sketches, or vice versa, so that the rail will map to the profile correctly. Second, it often helpful to create work surfaces or helper geometry to sketch on so that you know you are working in the right location and orientation as you sketch. In these steps, you'll create a lofted surface and use it to create a lofted solid:

1. On the Get Started tab, click Open, and open the file named mi_5a_014.ipt found in the Chapter 5 folder.

2. Extrude the rectangle up **30 mm**, making sure to do so as a surface rather than a solid (select the surface output in the Extrude dialog box).

3. You will now create a sketch on one of the larger side faces of the extruded rectangle. Create a **200 mm** arc and then dimension it **7 mm** from the corners of the referenced edges, as shown at the top of Figure 5.19.

FIGURE 5.19
Loft sketches

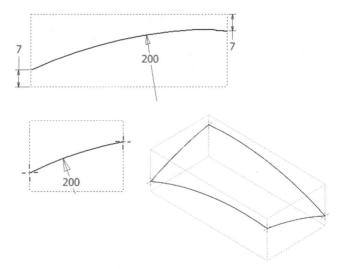

4. Create the same sketch on the opposite face of the extruded surface. The orientation of both sketches in relation to one another can be seen on the right of Figure 5.19.

5. Next, create a sketch on one of the ends of the extruded surface as well.

6. Project the ends of the arcs from the side sketches into this sketch for reference. The projected end points should show as center points. Use these projected points for the start and end of the arc. The sketch should look like the bottom left of Figure 5.19.

7. Create the same sketch on the final face of the extruded surface, as well following the same steps as in the previous step.

8. Select the Loft tool and set the Output option to Surface.

9. Choose the two end sketches as the sections and the two side sketches as rails then click OK. The result will be a twisted surface.

10. Select the Mirror tool and choose the lofted surface for the Features selection.

11. Next click the Mirror Plane button in the Mirror dialog box, and choose the XY origin plane (you may have to expand the Origin folder to see it), then click OK.

The result should put the mirrored surface below the extents of the extruded rectangular surface. In order to remedy this you next use the Extend Surface tool to bring the rectangular surface down to the mirrored surface.

12. On the Surface panel, select the Extend Surface tool (you may need to use the drop-down arrow on the Surface panel to reveal this tool).

13. Next select all the edges of the rectangular surface.

14. Set the Extents drop-down to the To option, and then select the mirrored surface. Then click OK.

Once the edges are extended down to the mirrored surface, you could use the Trim tool on the Surface panel to trim the rectangular surfaces down to the lofted surface, but in this case it is not actually necessary. Whether you decide to trim them or not the next step will be to use the Sculpt tool to fill in the enclosed volume of the surfaces.

15. Select the Sculpt tool on the Surfaces panel, select all three of the surfaces, and then click OK to create the solid. Figure 5.20 shows the results.

FIGURE 5.20
Using the
Sculpt tool to
create a solid

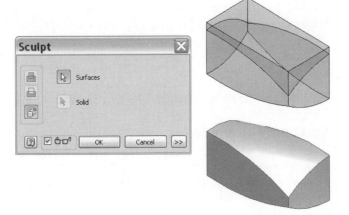

The Sculpt tool can use surfaces, work planes, and solid faces as 3D boundaries to "flood fill" any volume that exists. If there is not a "water-tight" volume, no solid can be created. You can use Sculpt to cut material from a solid as well. When cutting with Sculpt, the profile can be open. This tool differs from the Stitch tool in that surfaces do not need to be trimmed and in its ability to cut material. You can open the part named `mi_5a_016.ipt` found in the Chapter 5 folder, and experiment with using the Loft tool to cut material. Figure 5.21 shows the result of using the Sculpt tool to cut the combined volume of the two open profile extruded surfaces from the solid. Notice the >> button has been expanded to reveal the direction controls used to get the final result.

FIGURE 5.21
Using the Sculpt
tool to cut a solid

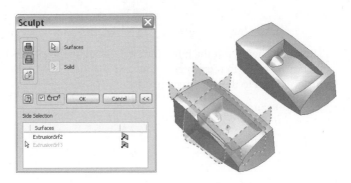

Creating Multi-body Parts

It is possible to create a multi-body part file with separate solids representing each part of an assembly and then save the solids as individual parts, even having them automatically placed into an assembly. Creating multiple solid bodies in a single part file offers some unique advantages compared to the traditional methods of creating parts in the context of an assembly file. For starters, you have one file location where all your design data is located. Second, it is often easier to fit parts together using this method, by simply sketching one part right on top of the other, and so on.

These two advantages are also the main two disadvantages. Placing large amounts of data (and time and effort) into a single file can be risky should that file be lost. And creating a part with an overabundance of interrelated sketches, features, and solid bodies can create a "house of cards" situation that makes changing an early sketch, feature, or solid a risky endeavor. Used wisely, though, multi-body parts are a powerful way to create tooling sets, molds, dies, and other interrelated parts.

If you do large machine design, you would be best off to create many smaller multi-body part files rather than attempting to build one large one. Or you might find that using multi-body parts will work well for certain interrelated components, while using traditional part/assembly techniques works for the rest of the design.

Creating Multiple Solids

In the following steps, you'll explore the creation of multi-body parts by building a simple trigger mechanism. The challenge here is to define the pawl feature on the trigger lever as it relates to the hammer bar. Figure 5.22 shows the trigger mechanism in its set position on the left and at rest on the right.

FIGURE 5.22
A simple trigger assembly

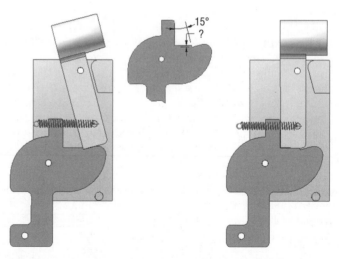

As the trigger lever is engaged, the hammer bar overcomes the pawl (lip), and the spring is allowed to force the hammer bar to swing. In the following steps you'll explore the multi-body solid options as you use one solid to determine the precise fit with the other.

1. On the Get Started tab, click Open, and open the part named `mi_5a_016.ipt` found in the Chapter 5 folder.

2. Create a sketch on the front face of the plate.

3. Create a rectangle, as shown in Figure 5.23, using the top hole as reference to anchor the rectangle.

FIGURE 5.23

The hammer bar sketch

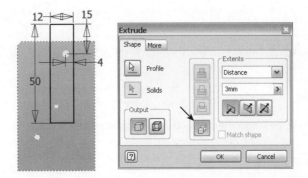

4. Extrude the rectangle **3 mm** away from the plate, and use the New Solid option in the Extrude dialog box (leave the circle unselected from your extrude profile so that you end up with a hole).

5. When you click OK, you'll see that the Solid Bodies folder in the model tree now shows two bodies present, one representing the base plate and another representing the hammer bar.

6. Create another sketch on the front of the plate, and create another rectangle toward the bottom, referencing the end of the hammer bar as shown in Figure 5.24.

FIGURE 5.24

The trigger-lever sketch

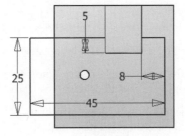

7. Extrude the rectangle **3 mm** away from the plate, use the New Solid option in the Extrude dialog box, and then click OK. This completes the base feature for the trigger lever.

8. Expand the Solid Bodies folder in the browser, and notice there are three solids listed (if you see fewer than three, edit your extrusions, and make sure you used the New Solid option).

9. Double-click the text that is your hammer bar, and rename it Hammer Bar, for reference later.

10. Right-click on the solid that is your trigger lever and choose Properties. In the resulting dialog set the name to Trigger Lever and change the color to blue, then click OK.

Here are several things to note at this point:

◆ If you expand the browser node for each solid listed in the Solid Bodies folder, you can see the features involved in each.

◆ You can right-click a solid or solids, choose Hide Others to isolate just the selected ones, and then use Show All to bring back any hidden solids.

◆ You can select the solid and then choose a color style from the Color Override drop-down on the Quick Access toolbar (at the very top of your screen).

◆ You can right-click each solid and choose Properties to set the name and color, view the mass properties, and strip previously, overridden values. For instance, if you'd set just the front face of one of the solids to be red and then decided you wanted the entire solid to be blue, you could use the strip overrides option to remove the red face and set the entire solid to blue. If you did not use the strip override option the red face would remain red and the other faces would become blue.

Using One Solid to Shape Another

Next you'll create the pawl notch in the trigger lever. To do so, however, you will first make a copy of the hammer bar and then turn that solid into a combined solid that represents the hammer bar in both the set and resting positions. After that, you'll cut that solid away from the trigger lever. You can continue on with the file from the previous steps or open the part named mi_5a_017.ipt found in the Chapter 5 folder.

1. Use the ViewCube to change the view so that you can see the cylindrical face of the hole in the hammer bar, and then choose the Circular Pattern tool on the Patterns panel.

2. Select the Pattern A Solid option, and click the hammer bar for the Solid selection.

3. Click the edge or face of the top hole for the rotation axis, and set the placement count and angle to **2** and **15** degrees, respectively.

4. Use the button at the top right corner of the dialog box to set the output to Create New Solid Bodies (the right-most button).

5. Ensure that the rotation direction is going counterclockwise, use the flip button if not, and then click OK.

If you expand the Solid Bodies folder in the browser you will see there are now four solids, the last being the patterned copy of the hammer bar. You will now turn the visibility of the original hammer bar off and use the copy to cut a pawl notch in the trigger plate.

6. Right-click on the solid named Hammer Bar in the Solid Bodies folder and choose Visibility, to hide that solid.

7. Select the Circular Pattern tool again, and choose the Pattern A Solid option, as you did before.

8. Click the edge or face of the top hole for the rotation axis, and set the placement count and angle to **2** and **15** degrees, respectively.

9. Set the rotation direction to go clockwise using the flip button. This should place the patterned copy in place of the original hammer bar.

10. This time use the button at the top right corner of the dialog box to set the output to Join, then click OK. This will merge the selected solid with the new patterned one.

11. Select the Combine tool on the Modify panel, and select the blue trigger lever for the Base selection.

12. Select the fused, rotated body for the Toolbody selection, and then set the operation type to Cut so that you are subtracting it from the trigger lever. Then click OK.

13. Select any solid in the Solid Bodies folder, and choose Show All to turn the visibility of all solids back on.

Now that you've solved the trigger pawl shape and size by using a multi-body part, you could finish the parts by adding features to each body. You'll note that if you create an extrusion, for instance, you can select which solid to add that extrusion to. If it is a cut extrusion, you can select multiple bodies and cut them all at once. The same is true of fillets, holes, and so on.

MOVE BODIES

You can also use the Move Bodies tool to reposition solids, once they are created. Try it on your trigger mechanism parts. Note that you have to click the edges or outlines of the preview object, rather than on the original object as you might suppose. You can also create a rotation using the Move Bodies tools, or you can move and rotate a body at the same time by creating a two-line action in the Move Bodies dialog box. Figure 5.25 shows the Move Bodies options.

FIGURE 5.25
Moving a solid body within a part file

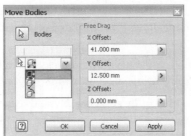
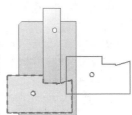

Free Drag.   Move via X, Y, or Z offsets, or better yet, just click the preview and drag it.

Move Along Ray.   Select an edge or axis to define the move direction, and then specify an offset value or just click and drag it in that direction.

Rotate.   Select an edge or axis to define the rotational pivot, and then specify an angle or click and drag it.

Click to Add.   Create as many move actions as you want and do them all at once.

SPLIT SOLIDS

Another tool that you may find useful when working with multi-body parts is the Split tool. For instance, if you create a simple solid block by sketching a rectangle on the XY plane and then extruding it 40 mm in both directions, you could then use the XY plane as a parting line to split the solid into two separate solids. You could also create a sketched curve and extrude it as a surface and use it to split the solid.

MAKE PART AND MAKE COMPONENTS

Once you have created your multi-body part, you can write out each solid as an individual part file. The resulting part files are what are known as *derived* parts. You can think of these derived parts as just linked copies of the solid bodies. If you make a change in the multi-body part, it will update the derived part. You can break the link or suppress the link in the derived part as well. Using the Make Part and Make Components tools allows you to detail each solid body individually in separate drawings. If you attempt to detail the multi-body part in the drawing you are will see all of the solids at once. There is no control to turn off individual solid bodies in a drawing view.

Additionally, you can choose to take your multi-body part and write the whole thing to an assembly. The assembly will consist of all the derived parts placed just as they exist in the multi-body part. These files will be grounded in place automatically so that no assembly constraints are required to hold them in place. If you decide you would like to apply constraints to all or some of the parts, you can unground them and do so, as well as organize them into subassemblies, and so on.

You should be aware, too, that any additional modeling that you do in the derived part or assembly will not push back to the multi-body part file. Although this may seem like a limitation, it can also be viewed as a good thing, allowing for the separation of design tasks that some design departments require. Here are the general steps for creating components from a multi-body part file:

1. Click the Make Components button on the Manage tab, and then select the solid bodies you want to create parts of.

2. Select additional solids to add to the list or select from the list, and click Remove From Selection to exclude any solids that you decide you do not want to create parts from.

3. Select Insert Components In Target Assembly, and then set the assembly name, the template from which to create it, and the save path, or clear this option to create the parts only. If the assembly already exits, use the Target Assembly Location's Browse button to select it.

4. Click Next to accept your selections, as shown in Figure 5.26.

FIGURE 5.26

The Make Components: Selection dialog box

5. The next dialog box allows you to name and set paths for the derived parts. Click the cells in the table to make changes for the parts as required:

◆ Click or right-click the cells to choose from the options for that cell type, if any.

◆ You can shift select multiple components and use the buttons above the Template and File Location columns to set those values for multiple parts at once.

6. Click Include Parameters to choose which layout model parameters to have present in the derived parts.

7. Click Apply or OK to make the components, as shown in Figure 5.27. If the component files are created in an assembly, the assembly file is created with the parts placed and left open in Inventor, but the assembly and parts are not saved until you choose to do so. If you choose to create the parts without an assembly, you are prompted to save the new files.

FIGURE 5.27

The Make Components: Bodies dialog box

You can set default behaviors of the Make Components dialog box in a multi-body part file (or a template file) by going to the Tools tab, clicking Document Settings, going to the Modeling tab in the dialog box that opens, and clicking the Options button. Figure 5.28 shows these options.

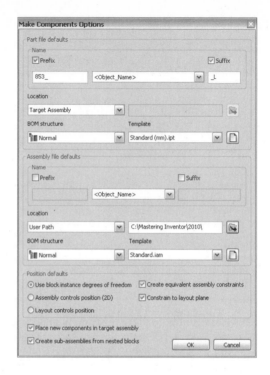

FIGURE 5.28
Setting the Make
Components
defaults

Creating Derived Parts and Assemblies

You can create parts derived from other components using the Derive tool. Common uses of the Derive tool are to create scaled and mirrored versions of existing parts, to cut one part from another part, and to consolidate an assembly into a single part file. Nonlinear scaling is accomplished using an add-in available in the Inventor installation directory.

Creating Derived Parts

Derived parts are base solids that are linked to the original feature-based part. Modifications are allowed to the derived part in the form of additional features. Original features are modified in the parent part, and changes to the parent part are moved to the derived part upon save and update. There is no reasonable limit to the number of times the parent part or succeeding derived parts can be derived again into more variations.

Deriving a Part File

CERT
OBJECTIVE

To derive a single part file, follow these steps:

1. From a new part file, select the Manage tab, and then click the Derive tab.

2. In the Open dialog box, browse to the part file, and then click the Open button.

3. Select from one of these derived styles:

   ♦ A single solid body with no seams between faces that exist in the same plane

   ♦ A single solid body with seams

◆ One or more solid bodies (if the source part contains multiple bodies)

◆ A single surface body

4. Use the status buttons at the top to change the status of all the selected objects at once, or click the status icon next to each individual object to set the include/exclude status.

5. Optionally, click the Select From Base button to open the base component in a window to select the components.

6. Specify scale factor and mirror plane if desired.

7. Click OK.

If the part being derived contains just one body, it is displayed on-screen. If the part being derived is a multi-body part with only a single body set as visible in the part, it is displayed on-screen. If the part being derived is a multi-body part with more than one visible body, none of the bodies is displayed on-screen. Select the bodies to include by expanding the Solid Bodies folder and toggling the status. To include all bodies, select the Solid Bodies folder, and then click the Include Status button. Figure 5.29 shows the Derived Part dialog box.

FIGURE 5.29
Derived part
options

Deriving an Assembly File

To derive an assembly file, follow these steps:

1. From a new part file, select the Manage tab, and then click the Derive tab.

2. In the Open dialog box, browse to the assembly file, and then click the Open button.

3. Select from one of these derived styles:

   ◆ A single solid body with no seams between faces that exist in the same plane

   ◆ A single solid body with seams

   ◆ One or more solid bodies (if the source part contains multiple bodies)

   ◆ A single surface body

4. Use the status buttons at the top to change the status of all the selected objects at once, or click the status icon next to each individual object to set the include/exclude status.

5. Optionally, click the Select From Base button to open the base component in a window to select the components.

6. Click the Other tab to select which component sketches, work features, parameters, iMates, and part surfaces to include in the derived assembly.

7. Click the Representations tab to use a design view, positional, and/or level of detail representation as the base for your derived part.

8. Click the Options tab to remove geometry, remove parts, fill holes, scale, and/or mirror the assembly.

9. Click OK. Figure 5.30 shows the Derived Assembly dialog box.

FIGURE 5.30
Derived Assembly
dialog box options

Modifying Derived Parts

Often you will need to modify a derived part source file after having derived it into new part. In order to do so, you can access the source part or assembly from the Model browser of the derived part by double-clicking it in the browser or by right-clicking it in the browser and choosing Open Base Component. The original file is opened in a new window where you can make changes as needed. To update the derived part to reflect changes to the source file, use the Update button found on the Quick Access toolbar (top of the screen).

You can edit a derived part or assembly by right-clicking it in the browser and choosing Edit Derived Part or Edit Derived Assembly. This will open the same dialog box used to create the derived part so that you can change the options and selections you set when the derived part was created. Updates will be reflected in the file when you click OK. The Edit Derived Part or Edit Derived Assembly options are unavailable if the derived part needs to be updated.

You can also break or suppress the link with the source file by right-clicking the derived component in the browser and choosing the appropriate option. Updates made to the source file will not be made to the derived part when the link is suppressed or broken. Suppressed links can be unsuppressed by right-clicking and choosing Unsuppressed Link From Base Component. Breaking the link is permanent and it cannot be restored.

Using the Component Derive Tool

Another way to derive components is to use the Derive Component tool on the Assembly Tools tab while in an assembly file. This tool allows you to select a part on-screen (or select a subassembly from the browser) and then specify a name for the new derived part file. You'll then be taken into the new derived part file. The resulting derived part or assembly uses the default derive options and the active assembly representations as they are saved in the source file. You can use the edit option in the derived part to change the settings if needed.

Using Nonlinear-Derived Part Scaling

You can accomplish nonlinear part scaling in Autodesk Inventor by using an add-in that you can find at C:\Program Files\Autodesk\Inventor 2011\SDK. The first time you access the SDK folder, you will need to unpack the user tools by double-clicking the UserTools.msi file.

Once the tools are unpacked, you can go to C:\Program Files\Autodesk\Inventor 2011\SDK\UserTools\DerivedPart_SP and run the Install.bat file. After installing the macro, a Derived Part (Scale/Position) button will be available on the Add-Ins tab. Selecting the Derived Part (Scale/Position) button will introduce a new dialog box, shown in Figure 5.31, permitting you to browse to the part file that will be scaled and allowing individual X, Y, and Z scale value inputs. You can use the same button to edit the derived component or right-click as you would any other derived component. Please note that this is not part of the Inventor software that is officially supported by Autodesk and is provided for your use as is.

FIGURE 5.31
Nonuniform scale settings

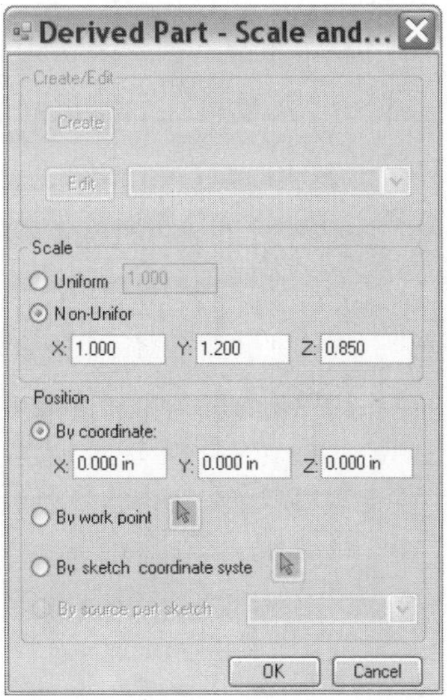

Working with Patterns

Inventor includes two tools to create patterns:

◆ Rectangular Pattern tool

◆ Circular Pattern tool

The Circular Pattern tool does just what you'd expect it to; it patterns a feature or set of features around an axis. The Rectangular Pattern tool also does what you'd expect, plus more. Using the Rectangular Pattern tool, you can create a pattern along any curve. If you select two perpendicular straight lines, edges, or axes, the result will be a rectangular pattern. However, if you select an entity that is not straight, the pattern will follow the curvature of the selected entity also.

Rectangular Patterns

Rectangular patterns use straight edges to establish the pattern directions. You can select a single feature or several features for use in the pattern. Be sure to check the Model browser to see that you have only the features that you intend to pattern select, because it is easy to accidentally select base features when attempting select negative cut features. Start your exploration of patterns by creating a simple rectangular pattern, as shown here:

1. On the Get Started tab, click Open.

2. Browse for the file named mi_5a_018.ipt located in the Chapter 5 directory of the Mastering Inventor 2011 folder, and click Open.

3. Select the Rectangular Pattern tool on the Pattern panel of the Model tab.

4. With the Features button enabled, select the three features whose names start with the word *switch* in the browser.

5. Right-click, choose Continue to set the selection focus from Features to Direction1, and then click the straight edge, as shown in Figure 5.32. Use the Flip Direction button to ensure that direction arrow is pointing toward the round end of the part.

6. Set the count to **4** and the spacing length to **10 mm**.

FIGURE 5.32
Creating a rectangular pattern

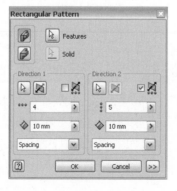
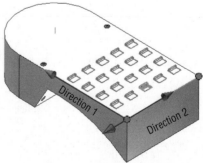

7. Click the red arrow button under Direction2 to set it active, and then click the straight edge along the bottom, as shown in Figure 5.32.

8. Set the count to **5** and the spacing length to **10 mm**.

9. Click the Midplane check box in the Direction2 settings to ensure that you get two instances of the pattern to each side of the original.

10. Click OK, and you will see the resulting pattern.

Circular Patterns

You can pattern features around an axis using the Circular Pattern tool. Angular spacing between patterned features can be set in two ways:

Incremental Positioning specifies the angular spacing between occurrences.

Fitted Positioning specifies the total area the pattern occupies.

FIGURE 5.33
Incremental vs.
Fitted positioning

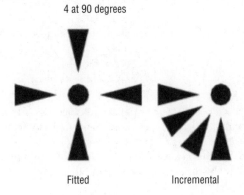

4 at 90 degrees

Fitted   Incremental

Figure 5.33 shows the same pattern of four occurrences at 90 degrees but set with different positioning methods. You can enter a negative value to create a pattern in the opposite direction, and you can use the Midplane check box to pattern in both directions from the original. Continue from the previous exercise with the open file, or open mi_5a_020.ipt to start where that exercise ended:

1. In the Model browser, select the end-of-part marker, and drag it down below the feature named Indicator Cut.

2. Select the Circular Pattern tool on the Pattern panel of the Model tab.

3. With the Features button enabled, select the feature named Indicator Cut.

4. Right-click and choose Continue to set the selection focus from features to axis.

5. Select the center face of the feature named Indicator Stud Hole.

6. Set the count to **4** and the angle to **90**; then click the >> button.

7. In the Positioning Method area, click the Incremental option so that the four occurrences of the pattern are set 90 degrees apart, rather than being fit into a 90-degree span. Alternatively, you could set the angle to 360 and leave the positioning method to Fitted and get the same result.

8. Click OK. Figure 5.34 shows the resulting circular pattern.

FIGURE 5.34
Creating a circular pattern

You'll note that your patterned objects require some adjustments. One of the occurrences of the Indicator Cut interferes with the switch feature, and the one opposite of that does not cut through the part correctly (use the ViewCube to look at the underneath of the part to see this clearly). To resolve this, you will first edit the circular pattern and change the way the occurrences solve, and then you'll suppress the occurrence of the switch feature in the rectangular pattern.

9. Right-click the circular pattern in the browser and choose Edit Pattern, or double-click it in the browser.

10. Click the >> button to reveal the Creation Method area, and then select the Adjust To Model option. This allows each instance of the pattern to solve uniquely based on the geometry of the model when the feature is using a Through or Through All termination solution.

11. Click OK, and examine the pattern again and you'll notice that the top instance of the Indicator Cut that was not cutting all the way through the part now is.

12. Expand the Rectangular Pattern in the browser to reveal the listing of each pattern occurrence.

13. Roll your mouse pointer over each occurrence node in the browser until you highlight the one that interferes with the circular pattern.

14. Right-click that occurrence, and choose Suppress.

Any occurrence other than the first can be suppressed to allow for pattern exceptions or to create unequal pattern spacing. Figure 5.35 shows the adjusted patterns.

FIGURE 5.35
The adjusted patterns

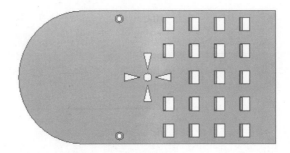

Patterns Along Curves

Although the Circular Pattern tool allows you to pattern objects around a center axis, it does not provide a way to keep the patterned objects in the same orientation as the original. To do so, you can use the rectangular pattern. Keep in mind that the term *rectangular pattern* is a bit of a misnomer; this tool might more accurately be described as a Curve Pattern tool, because it allows you to select any curve, straight or not, and use it to determine the pattern direction(s). Continue from the previous exercise with the open file, or open mi_5a_022.ipt to start where that exercise ended:

1. In the Model browser, select the end-of-part marker, and drag it down below the feature named Pin Insert Path Sketch.

2. Select the Rectangular Pattern tool on the Pattern panel of the Model tab.

3. With the Features button enabled, select the feature named Pin Insert Cut.

4. Right-click and choose Continue to set the selection focus from Features to Direction1.

5. Click the sketched curve (line or arc).

6. Set the count to **10**, and notice that the preview extends out into space.

7. Click the >> button to reveal more options.

8. Click the Start button in the Direction1 area, and then click the center of the Pin Insert Cut on-screen to set that center point as the start point of the pattern.

9. Change the solution drop-down from Spacing to Curve Length, and note that the length of the sketch curve is reported in the length box.

10. Change the solution drop-down from Curve Length to Distance, and then type **-14** at the end of the length value to compensate for the start and end point adjustments.

11. Toggle the Orientation option from Identical to Direction1 to see the difference in the two, and then set it back to Identical.

12. Click OK to set the pattern. Figure 5.36 shows the resulting pattern and the dialog box settings.

FIGURE 5.36

A pattern along a curve

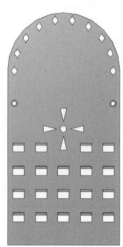

Spiral Patterns

In addition to creating patterns based on edges and sketches, you can use surfaces to define the pattern direction. In this exercise, you'll create a surface coil to use as a pattern direction. You can continue on from the previous exercise with the open file, or you can open mi_5a_024.ipt to start where that exercise ended.

1. In the Model browser, select the end-of-part marker, and drag it down below the feature named Coil Pattern Sketch.

2. Select the Coil tool on the Model tab.

3. In the Coil dialog box, set the output to Surface.

4. Next choose the line segment in the Coil Pattern Sketch at the base of the part for the Profile selection.

5. Select the visible work axis in the center of the part for the Axis selection.

6. Click the Coil Size tab, and set the type to Revolution and Height.

7. Set Height to **25 mm** and Revolutions to **4**.

8. Click OK to create the coiled surface.

   You'll now create two work points based on the coil location for use in placing holes. Once the holes are placed, you can pattern them using the surface coil.

9. Click the Point button on the Work Features panel of the Model tab, and select the vertical tangent edge and the surface coil to create work points at the intersections, as shown in Figure 5.37.

FIGURE 5.37
Work points at the
coils and tangent
edge intersections

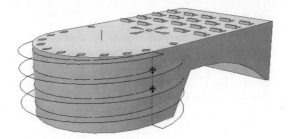

10. Click the Hole tool on the Model tab, and set the Placement drop-down to On Point.

11. Select one of the work points for the Point selection, and then select the flat side face of the part to establish the direction.

12. Set the termination drop-down to To, and then select the inside circular face of the part.

13. Set the diameter to **3 mm**, and then click Apply.

14. Repeat the previous three steps to place the second hole, and then click OK.

15. Click the Rectangular Pattern button on the Model tab.

16. Click the two holes for the features (it might be easiest to select them from the browser), and then right-click and choose Continue.

17. Select the surface coil for Direction1, and use the Flip button to change the direction so that you see the previewed pattern.

18. Set the count to **10** and the length to **10 mm**.

19. Click the >> button, and choose Direction1 for the orientation.

20. Set the Compute option to Adjust, and then click OK to create the pattern.

21. Right-click the coil and work points and turn off the visibility of these features to see the finished part clearly. Figure 5.38 shows the pattern.

FIGURE 5.38
A spiral pattern

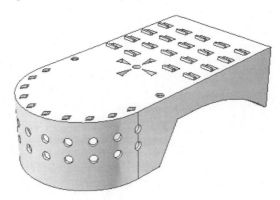

Pattern Solids

Oftentimes a part can be modeled as a base feature and then patterned as a whole in order to create the completed part. Once patterned, nonsymmetric features can be added, and/or patterned occurrences can be suppressed. You can also use the Pattern Entire Solid option to create separate solid bodies when creating multi-body part files is the goal. To take a look at patterning these options, open the part named mi_5a_028.ipt, and follow these steps:

1. Select the Rectangular Pattern tool on the Pattern panel of the Model tab.

2. Click the Pattern A Solid button so that the entire part is selected to be patterned. Notice the two buttons that appear in the top-right corner of the dialog box:

   Join   This option is used to pattern the solid as a single solid body.

   Create New Bodies   This option is used to the solid as separate solid bodies, for multi-body part creation.

3. Leave this option set to Join, and set Direction1 to pattern the solid in the direction of the part width four times at a spacing of **10 mm**.

4. Set Direction2 to pattern the solid in the direction of the part thickness two times at a spacing of **3 mm**, as shown in Figure 5.39.

FIGURE 5.39
Patterning a solid

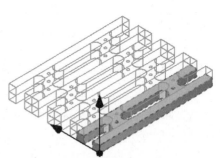

5. Next, expand the pattern in the Model browser, and right-click to suppress the two middle occurrences on the top level. Roll your mouse pointer over each occurrence to see it highlight on-screen to identify which occurrences are the correct ones. Figure 5.40 shows the results of suppressing the correct occurrences.

FIGURE 5.40
Suppressed
occurrences

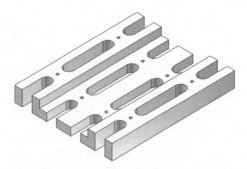

6. Now you'll pattern the entire solid again, select the Rectangular Pattern tool again, and click the Pattern A Solid button.

7. Set Direction1 to pattern the solid in the direction of the part length two times at a spacing of **50 mm**.

8. Set Direction2 to pattern the solid in the direction of the part width two times at a spacing of **40 mm**, as shown in Figure 5.41.

FIGURE 5.41
Patterning the
solid again

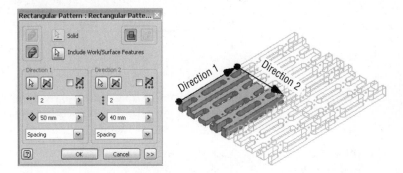

9. Create a new 2D sketch on one of the long narrow faces, and project the tangent edge of the slot cuts, or sketch a rectangle on the face. Do this for both ends of the face. Then use the Extrude tool, set the extents to To, and select the vertex as shown in Figure 5.42. The result will be the removal of all the partial slot features.

FIGURE 5.42
Filling the end
slots

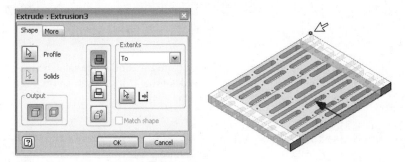

10. Create another sketch on the same face and sketch an arc from corner to corner, and set the radius to **400 mm**. Then use the Extrude tool to extrude just the arc as a surface (click the Surface Output button in the Extrude dialog box). Set the extents to To again, and select the same vertex as you did before.

11. Select the Replace Face tool from the Surface panel of the Model tab. You may have to expand the arrow on the Surface panel to expand the drop-down in order to find the Replace Face tool.

12. Select the two recessed faces for the Existing Faces selection, and then select the extruded surface for the New Faces selection, as shown in Figure 5.43.

FIGURE 5.43
Replacing faces

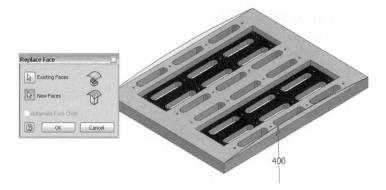

13. Next create a sketch on the top face, and create two rectangular profiles to use for creating an extrude cut, as shown in Figure 5.44. This cut removes the middle slots and holes resulting in two long slots down the middle.

FIGURE 5.44
Cutting the slots

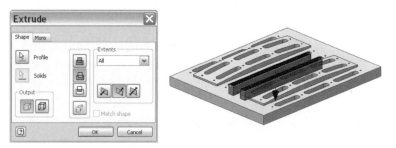

14. Finally, select the Shell tool from the Modify panel. Choose the bottom face as the Remove Faces selection, and set the Thickness to **1 mm**. Figure 5.45 shows the finished part from the top and bottom views.

FIGURE 5.45
The finished part

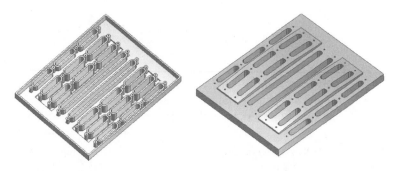

Dynamic Patterns

It is often desirable to have features such as holes set up in a standard spacing that will dynamically update based on changes to the overall length. You can do this by setting up your patterns with parameter formulas to calculate the spacing from the length parameter. Parts set up in this way can then be saved as template parts, allowing you to select them for new part creation and simply edit the length parameter. To set up a dynamic pattern, open the file named mi_5a_032.ipt, and follow these steps:

1. Click the Manage tab, and select the Parameters tool.

2. Notice that many of the dimensions in this part have been named. This is good practice when creating formulas. To create a formula to determine the spacing, click the Add button in the lower-left corner of the dialog box. This will create a new user-defined parameter. Enter **Adjust_Len** for the parameter name (recall that you are not allowed spaces in parameter names).

3. Click the unit cell, and set the Units to **ul**, meaning unitless.

4. Type **isolate(Length - End_Offset;ul;mm)** into the Equation column. There are two parts to this equation:

   Length – End_Offset   Subtracts the distance from the end of the part from the overall length of the part

   Isolate(expression; unit; unit)   Neutralizes the distance unit mm so that the Adjust_Len parameter can read it as unitless

5. Next click the cell for the Count equation, and enter **isolate(ceil(Adjust_Len / Spacing);ul;mm)** into the cell. There are three parts to this equation:

   Adjust_Len/Spacing   Divides the adjusted length distance by the value specified in the pattern spacing

   Ceil(expression)   Bumps the value up to the next highest whole number

   Isolate(expression; unit; unit)   Neutralizes the distance unit mm so that the Count parameter can read it as unitless

6. Next, click the Done button, and then use the Update button to update the part (you can find the Update button on the Quick Access bar at the top of the screen). Figure 5.46 shows the parameter dialog box.

FIGURE 5.46
Formulas to adjust the hole spacing

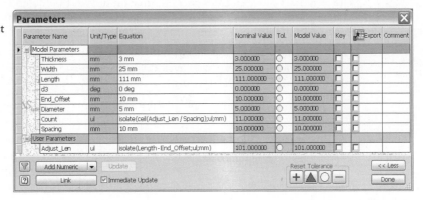

You may notice that because the length value is currently set to **111 mm** that the last hole is running off the part. Because the equation used the Ceil function to bump the calculated value to the next whole number, the count will always be on the high end. Depending upon the part length, this may leave you with an extra hole. You can suppress the occurrence of this hole in the Model browser quite easily. Another approach is to remove the Ceil function and allow Inventor to round the calculated value up or down automatically. Depending upon the length and spacing values, this might leave you with a missing hole at the end of the pattern, where a value gets rounded down. Both are valid options, and you can decide which works best for your situation.

Edit Extrusion1 to adjust the part length, and try different values to see how the count drops out. You can also open the files named mi_5a_033.ipt and mi_5a_034.ipt to examine similar hole patterns. In mi_5a_033.ipt, the pattern uses the Distance option in the pattern feature to evaluate the length of the part. It holds an end offset value and then spaces the holes evenly along that distance.

In mi_5a_034.ipt, the pattern is calculated from the center of the part rather than coming off one end. These are just a few examples of how to use user parameters to create dynamic patterns. There are other variations as well. In the next section, you'll take a more in-depth look at parameters.

Setting Parameters and iProperties

Parameters in part and assembly files can provide powerful control over individual parts and assemblies while also improving efficiency within designs. Part parameters enable the use of iParts, which are a form of table-driven part. Assembly parameters enable the use of table-driven assemblies and configurations. Parameters are accessed through the Tools menu and within the Part Features and Assembly tool panels.

iProperties

iProperties, generically known as *Windows file properties*, allow the input of information specific to the active file. The iProperties dialog box is accessed through the File drop-down in Inventor. iProperties are a powerful way to pass information from the model files to the drawing file, allowing you to fill out information in title blocks, standard notes, and parts list automatically. The dialog box contains several tabs for input of information:

The General tab   Contains information on the file type, size, and location. The creation date, last modified date, and last accessed date are preserved on this tab.

The Summary tab   Includes part information such as title, subject, author, manager, and company. Included on this tab are fields for information that will allow searching for similar files within Windows.

The Project tab   Stores file-specific information that, along with information from the Summary, Status, Custom, and Physical tabs, can be exported to other files and used in link information within the 2D drawing file.

The Status tab   Allows the input of information as well as the design state and dates of each design step.

The Custom tab   Allows the creation of custom parameters for use within the design. Parameters exported from the Parameters dialog box will also appear in the list. Formulas can be used within a custom parameter to populate values in preexisting fields within the Project and Status tabs.

The Save tab   Determines the behavior of the current file upon save.

The Physical tab   Allows for the changing of material type used in the current file and displays the calculated physical properties of the current part such as mass and moment of inertia, as determined by the material type.

Active use of iProperties will help the designer in improving overall productivity as well as the ability to link part and assembly information into 2D drawings. Adding search properties in the Summary tab will assist the user in locating similar files.

Custom iProperties are either created manually in the custom tab of iProperties or created automatically by exporting individual parameters from the parameter dialog. Custom iProperties may be linked to drawings and assemblies for additional functionality.

ACCESSING iPROPERTIES THROUGH WINDOWS EXPLORER

When you right-click an Inventor file in Windows Explorer and choose Properties, you can select the iProperties tab from the file properties dialog box. Clicking the iProperties button on the iProperties tab opens the Inventor iProperties dialog box just as you would see it in Inventor.

This can offer people in the office who do not have access to Inventor the ability to view and change iProperties when needed. For instance, someone in the Manufacturing department can use this to set the Mfg. Approved Date iProperty once a part has been successfully built on the shop floor based on a given drawing and/or part file.

You can also use the Details tab accessed in this way to quickly check the Inventor file version in order to confirm the Inventor version the file was created in and last saved under.

Part Parameters

CERT OBJECTIVE

Part parameters are composed of model parameters, user parameters, reference parameters, and custom parameters. Model parameters are automatically embedded as a part is dimensioned and features are created. Most are a mirror image of the sketch creation process. As each dimension is created on a sketch, a corresponding model parameter is created, starting with a parameter called d0 and continuing with the label value being incremented each time a new parameter is created. When you name a dimension, you are changing the automatically assigned parameter name. To access the list of parameters, click the Manage tab, and select the Parameters button. Figure 5.47 represents a typical parameter list.

FIGURE 5.47
Part parameter list

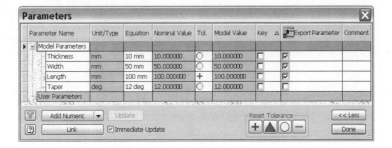

Looking at the columns across the top of the dialog box, you will see columns for the parameter name, unit type, equation, nominal value, tolerance type, model value, parameter export, and descriptive comments. Take a look at each of these columns:

Model Parameters   The values in this column correspond to the name of the parameters assigned as the part is built. Each parameter starts with a lowercase *d* followed by a numeric value. Each of these parameters can be renamed to something that is more familiar such as Length, Height, Base_Dia, or any other descriptive single word. Spaces are not allowed in the parameter name. Hovering your mouse pointer over a name will initiate a tool tip that will tell you where that variable is used or consumed.

Unit   The unit type defines the unit used in the calculation. Normally, the unit type will be set by the process that created it. When a user parameter is created, you will be presented with a Unit Type dialog box when clicking in the Unit column. This will allow you to select a particular unit type for the user parameter.

Equation   This either specifies a static value or allows you to create algebraic style equations using other variables or constants to modify numeric values.

Nominal Value   This column displays the result of the equation.

Tolerance   This column shows the current evaluated size setting for the parameter. Click the cell to select Upper, Lower, or Nominal tolerance values. This will change the size of tolerance features in the model.

Model Value   This column shows the actual calculated value of the parameter.

Key   A parameter can be made a key by selecting the key check box for the parameter row.

Export Parameters   These check boxes are activated to add specific parameters to the custom properties for the model. Downstream, custom properties can be added to parts lists and bills of materials by adding columns. Clearing the check box will remove that parameter as a custom property. After a parameter is added, other files will be able to link to or derive the exported parameter. Text and True/False parameters cannot be exported.

Comment   This column is a descriptive column used to help describe the use of that parameter. Linked parameters will include the description within the link.

User Parameters

User parameters are simply user-created parameters. They are parameters that are created by clicking the Add button in the lower-left portion of the Parameters dialog box. You can add numeric, text, and true/false parameters, however, only numeric parameters may be exported or contain expressions. Text and True/False parameters can be created for use in iLogic rules. User parameters can be used to store equations that drive features and dimensions in the model. The user-created parameter can utilize algebraic operators written in the proper syntax that will create an expression in a numerical value.

ARC LENGTHS AND PARAMETER FORMULAS

There is not a way to specify an arc length with the General Dimension tool when creating sketch entities or determine an arc length for use as dimension. However, you can use a parameter formula to either determine or specify the arc length, as shown here.

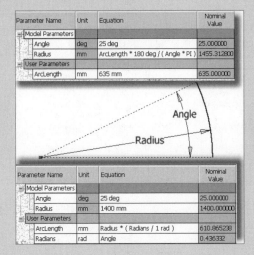

Parameter Name	Unit	Equation	Nominal Value
– Model Parameters			
– Angle	deg	25 deg	25.000000
– Radius	mm	ArcLength * 180 deg / (Angle * PI)	1455.312800
– User Parameters			
– ArcLength	mm	635 mm	635.000000

Parameter Name	Unit	Equation	Nominal Value
– Model Parameters			
– Angle	deg	25 deg	25.000000
– Radius	mm	1400 mm	1400.000000
– User Parameters			
– ArcLength	mm	Radius * (Radians / 1 rad)	610.865238
– Radians	rad	Angle	0.436332

At the top the ArcLength parameter is used to specify the arc length and determine the arc radius. At the bottom the Radius is specified and the ArcLength parameter is calculated from it.

REFERENCE PARAMETERS

Reference parameters are driven parameters that are created through the use of reference dimensions in sketches, the use of derived parts, attached via a linked spreadsheet, created by table-driven iFeatures or created through the use of the application programming interface (API). For instance, Inventor sheet-metal parts create flat pattern extents, which are stored as reference parameters.

FORMATTING PARAMETERS

You can right-click on a Parameter in the Parameter dialog box and choose Custom Property Format to access the Custom Property Format settings. There you can change Property Type, Units, Format and Precision, as well as control the display of Unit Strings, Leading Zeros, and Trailing Zeros. For instance if you have a part dimension on a part length of 100.00 mm and you want to call that length in part description, but do not want to see the units string (mm) or the zeros after the decimal point, then you would set a custom property format for that parameter and uncheck the Unit String and Leading Zeros options.

PARAMETER FUNCTIONS

One of the most important part of working with Parameters is the ability to create expressions using the available parameter functions. The functions in Table 5.1 can be used in user parameters or placed directly into edit boxes when creating dimensions and features.

TABLE 5.1:   Functions and Their Syntax for Edit Boxes

SYNTAX	UNIT TYPE	DESCRIPTION
cos(expression)	Unitless	Calculates the cosine of an angle.
sin(expression)	Unitless	Calculates the sine of an angle.
tan(expression)	Unitless	Calculates the tangent of an angle.
acos(expression)	Angularity	Calculates the inverse cosine of a value.
asin(expression)	Angularity	Calculates the inverse sine of a value.
atan(expression)	Angularity	Calculates the inverse tangent of a value.
cosh(expression)	Unitless	Calculates the hyperbolic cosine of an angle.
sinh(expression)	Unitless	Calculates the hyperbolic sine of an angle.
tanh(expression)	Unitless	Calculates the hyperbolic tangent of an angle.
acosh(expression)	Angularity	Calculates the inverse hyperbolic cosine of a value.
asinh(expression)	Angularity	Calculates the inverse hyperbolic sine of a value.
atanh(expression)	Angularity	Calculates the inverse hyperbolic tangent of a value.
sqrt(expression)	Unit^0.5	Calculates the square root of a value. The units within the sqrt function have to be square mm in order to return mm. For example, sqrt(144 mm^2) returns 12.
sign(expression)	Unitless	Returns 0 for a negative value, 1 if positive.
exp	Unitless	Returns an exponential power of a value. For example, exp(100) returns 2.688E43.
floor(expression)	Unitless	Returns the next lowest whole number. For example, floor(3.33) returns 3.

TABLE 5.1:   Functions and Their Syntax for Edit Boxes   *(CONTINUED)*

SYNTAX	UNIT TYPE	DESCRIPTION
ceil(expression)	Unitless	Returns the next highest whole number. For example, ceil(3.33) returns 4.
round(expression)	Unitless	Returns the closest whole number. For example, round(3.33) returns 3.
abs(expression)	Any	Returns the absolute value of an expression. For example, abs(3*-4) returns 12.
max(expression1; expression2)	Any	Returns the larger of two expressions. For example, max(3;4) returns 4.
min(expression1; expression2)	Any	Returns the smaller of two expressions. For example, min(3;4) returns 3.
ln(expression)	Unitless	Returns the natural logarithm of an expression.
log(expression)	Unitless	Returns the logarithm of an expression.
pow(expression1; expression2)	Unit^expr2	Raises the expression1 to the power of expression2. For example, pow(3 ul;2 ul) returns 9.
random()	Unitless	Returns a random number.
isolate(expression;unit;unit)	Any	Used to convert the units of an expression. For example, isolate(Length;mm;ul) where Length =100mm, returns 100 ul.
PI	Internal Parameter	Returns the constant equal to a circle's circumference divided by its diameter 3.14159265359 (depending upon precision). For example, PI*50 mm returns 157.079633.
E	Internal Parameter	Returns base of the natural logarithm 2.718281828459 (depending upon precision).
* 1 unit or / 1 unit	Any	Used to convert unit types of an expression much like isolate. For example, 100mm *10 ul returns an errant value for a unitless parameter. 100 mm / 1 mm * 10 ul returns 1000 ul. 100 mm * 10 ul / 1 mm also works.

Real World Scenario

SETTING UP USER PARAMETERS IN YOUR TEMPLATES

Although many times parameters are used to control design input on a per-design basis, you can often use pre-established parameters in template files so that the part file requires the change of only a couple of key parameters in order to create a new variant of standard part. User parameters are especially powerful when creating these types of template parts.

Consider, for example, a standard-type mounting bracket. The general shape is carried through in all iterations, but you can identify several key dimensions that are driven by the particulars of each new design situation. Dimensions such as length, width, height, or thickness are good examples of parameters that can be identified and set up in a template part.

Other things to consider for use as parameters would be critical dimensions such as hole locations from the edge of the part, hole sizes, hole counts, and hole spacing. If the hole offset is determined by the material thickness and hole size, then a formula can be established in the part template to calculate the minimum offset value.

Once the part parameters are created and tested for accuracy, the part can be turned into a template by using the Save Copy As Template option in the Save As menu. This will save the part file in the Template directory. Template parts can be as simple or complex as you need, but generally this works best for simple parts. For more complex parts, consider creating iParts, covered in Chapter 7, "Part and Feature Reuse."

When creating parameter-based template parts, you might want to consider creating user parameters with descriptive names for all the key parameters so that they are all grouped together. This way, you (or another user) can quickly identify key parameters used to drive the design later when creating parts in your real-world designs.

Assembly Parameters

Assembly parameters function in much the same way as part parameters, except that generally they will control constraint values such as offset and angle. When authoring an iAssembly, other parameters will be exposed for usage such as assembly features, work features, iMates, and component patterns, as well as other parameters that may exist within an assembly.

Adding Part Tolerances

Inventor allows you to analyze parts in a manner that ensures valid fit and function at dimensional extremes. When parts are assembled within an Inventor assembly file, you can check to ensure the parts can be assembled without interference, by setting each part to evaluate at the upper or lower tolerance value. By specifying dimensional tolerances within parts, you are capturing valuable design data that will assist in manufacturing and assembly. In addition to creating the parts separately, and then assembling them, you can use multi-body parts to create mated parts in one file, making it easy to design tolerances across multiple parts.

Tolerances are an important tool for communicating design intent to manufacturing. Large tolerances indicate that the dimensions aren't critical to the part's function, while tight tolerances indicate that manufacturing needs to pay extra attention to that machining operation. Loosening up tolerances can help manufacturing reduce the reject rate, while tightening up certain tolerances can reduce rework during the assembly process or in the field.

Tolerances in Sketches

You can add tolerances to any individual sketch dimension by right-clicking and choosing Dimension Properties to set precision and tolerance values for that individual dimension. You can also access the tolerance setting from within the dimension edit box in order to set the tolerance as you set the value. Altering the dimension to adjust for tolerance and precision using either method will not affect any other dimension within the part. However, a global file tolerance can be specified within a part using the Document Settings and will affect every dimension within the model.

In addition to the Dimension Properties and the dimension edit box option, you can access and modify tolerances in the Parameters dialog box. Using the Parameters controls, you can set parameter values for multiple dimensions to include the tolerance as needed. No matter how you access the tolerance setting there are four options you can use to evaluate the dimension/parameter:

+ Upper. The upper tolerance value in a stacked display. This value should Maximum Material Condition (MMC). For a hole, the smallest diameter is MMC, while for a shaft the largest diameter is MMC.

▲ Median The midway point between the upper and lower tolerances. This is commonly used when CNC machines are programmed from the solid model.

- Lower The lower tolerance in a stacked display. This value should be Least Material Condition (LMC). For a hole, the largest diameter is LMC, while for a shaft the smallest diameter is LMC.

○ Nominal This is the actual value of the dimension.

Figure 5.48 shows the access to the tolerance settings through the sketch dimension edit box, as well as the settings in the Tolerance Dialog box. In this case a deviation tolerance is placed on the 36 mm diameter, and the model is set to evaluate at the upper value (note the plus sign is selected). Since this document's settings are defaulted to three places, all sketch dimensions are in three places to start. In the illustration the precision has been set to just two decimal places, for just this dimension.

FIGURE 5.48

Sketch showing tolerances

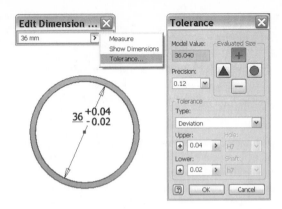

TOLERANCE VERSUS ALLOWANCE

Tolerance — Is the acceptable (but undesired) deviation from the intended (nominal) dimension.

Allowance — Is the intended (desired) difference of dimensions between two mating parts, depending upon the type of fit specified.

Setting Global File Tolerances

Adding tolerances during the design phase pays dividends down the road. There will be fewer errors creating drawings, and it provides clues to design decisions that are useful when updating an existing part. You might find that using standard tolerances makes the design process more efficient because the designer needs to focus only on the general tolerance for a dimension (two-place vs. three-place tolerance) and apply special tolerances where needed. You can create custom templates to store tolerance types and other settings for each standard. When the part is created using such a template, standard tolerance values can be overridden for specific dimensional values, or you can override all tolerances within a file or just a specific dimension.

An example of this type of tolerance would be a tolerance rule that states that all decimal dimensions held to two places shall be +/- 0.05, and all decimal dimensions held to three places shall be +/- 0.001, meaning a dimension of 0.50 would be held to an upper limit of 0.55 and a lower limit of 0.45, whereas a dimension of 0.500 would be held to an upper limit of 0.501 and a lower limit of 0.499.

You can create and modify global tolerance values within a single part by going to the Tools tab, clicking Document Settings, and then clicking the Default Tolerance tab within an active part file or template. By default, a file will not be using any tolerance standards. In Figure 5.49, the Use Standard Tolerancing Values box has been select to enable the addition of new standards for the file. In order to export the tolerance values to the drawing files, the Export Standard Tolerance Values check box has been selected as well.

Figure 5.49
Document settings
for tolerance

Once set, the dimension in the part will evaluate at the nominal value, meaning that if you entered a value of 36 for a part length then that is what the length would be. To evaluate the model at its upper limit at +/- 0.001, you would edit the dimension for the length and set the precision to three places, and the evaluated size to Upper (using the + button). The length would then change to 36.05, if using the earlier example. The default tolerances are set to +/- tolerances. To select another tolerance standard, simply override the existing tolerance values in the tolerance setting, and choose another tolerance type, such as deviation. You can see all of this in action in the following steps:

1. On the Get Started tab, click Open, and open the part named mi_5a_035.ipt found in the Chapter 5 folder.

2. Select the Tools tab and then click the Document Settings tab.

3. Select the Default Tolerance tab and notice there are two linear and one angular tolerance standards already set up. Note that there is a linear precision for one decimal and another for two decimals but there is not one for three decimals. Keep this in mind as you proceed.

4. Click the check box to use the standard tolerancing values, and then click Apply, and the Close.

Now that the part is set to use a global part tolerance, you will edit a dimension and change the precision setting to two decimals so that it will use one of the global, linear tolerance settings. It is important to note that the dimension precision for all of the dimensions in the part are currently set to three decimal places (the default setting).

5. Edit the 15 mm dimension by double-clicking on the text of the dimension.

6. Click the fly-out arrow in the dimension input box and select Tolerance.

7. Set the precision to just one decimal place, and then click the blue plus sign to evaluate the dimension at its upper value.

8. Click OK to exit the Tolerance dialog box, and then click the green check mark in the Dimension Edit box.

9. Although the sketch automatically updates to evaluate the dimension at its upper value, you'll need to update the model to see the solid update. Click the Update button on the Quick Access bar (at the top of the screen, it looks like a lightning bolt).

10. To evaluate the entire part at the lower value, go to the Manage tab and select the Parameters button.

11. In the Parameters dialog box, click the red minus sign in the Reset Tolerance area, and then click the Update button in the dialog box to see the Model Values column update.

Compare the nominal and model values in the parameter table to see that some of the dimensions are now reevaluated. Since the dimension default precision for the part is set to three places, the 25 mm and 3 mm dimensions are using that precision, for which no tolerance was set, and therefore have no lower value. Don't be confused by the precision being displayed in the Parameters table, as that precision is display only. You can click the Equation cell for each dimension, and then right click and choose Tolerance to access the tolerance and precision settings for each dimension, in order to see or change the actual precision for each dimension.

12. Click Done to exit the parameter dialog.

13. To change the global dimension precision go to the Tools tab and click Document Settings.

14. Select the Units tab and set the Modeling Dimension Display for Linear Dim Display Precision to two places, then click OK.

Now the 25 mm dimension is using the file default precision of two places, and since it is still set to evaluate at the lower value, it changes to 24.99. You can begin to see the power of using tolerances in your models to evaluate tolerance ranges as you design. You can close this file without saving changes. In the next section you'll look at using Limits and Fits tolerances.

PART TOLERANCES IN DRAWINGS

Keep in mind that when a part moves forward into the drawing environment, it will reflect the current evaluated model dimensions, and will only show the tolerance callout for retrieved dimensions.

Typically it is best to create multiple dimension styles with various precision and/or tolerance options in the drawing environment and handle tolerance dimensioning for the print using those tools. You must keep in mind that the tolerance settings in the part are designed to function with the assembly environment and allow calculating tolerances and stack-ups within the assembly. They are not meant to provide tolerancing in the drawing environment.

Limits Fits

A fit tolerance defines the way two components mate together. There are three basic categories of fits:

- Clearance - allows the mating components to slide together freely, allowing them to be assembled and disassembled easily.

- Transition - provides a fit close enough to securely hold the two components together, but still allowing them to be disassembled.

- Interference - often called a Press fit or Friction fit, provides a means to hold two components together by slightly oversizing one component that fits into the other. Some force is required to achieve the fitting of the two components together, and disassembly is not intended.

You can create parts according to fits by adding tolerance values to sketch dimensions and setting the tolerance type to one of the Limits/Fits options. Using a fits table as a reference you can then set the tolerance according to the desired fit type.

In the following exercise you will edit a part and set tolerances for the two mating solid bodies, using Table 5.2 as guide for the fits. To start off you will set the inside and outside diameters to use tolerances based off of a common diameter of 36 mm. The goal is have a loose fit that allows the insert to slip freely into the sleeve.

1. On the Get Started tab, click Open, and open the part named mi_5a_036.ipt found in the Chapter 5 folder.

2. Select the dimension called Sleeve_ID, and double-click on it to bring up the Dimension Edit box.

3. Click the fly-out arrow and choose Tolerance from the list.

4. Set the Type drop down to Limit/Fits-Show Size Limits.

5. Set the Hole drop down to H11, in order to create a loose running fit as listed in Table 5.2.

6. Click the red minus sign to evaluate the inside diameter at its lower limit.

7. Click OK to exit the Tolerance dialog box, and then click the green check mark in the Dimension Edit box.

8. Next, select the dimension called Insert_OD, and double-click on it to bring up the Dimension Edit box.

9. Click the fly-out arrow and choose Tolerance from the list.

10. Set the Type drop down to Limit/Fits-Show Size Limits.

11. Set the Shaft drop down to c11, in order to create the other half of the loose running fit.

12. Click the blue plus sign to evaluate the outside diameter at its upper limit.

13. Click OK to exit the Tolerance dialog box, and then click the green check mark in the Dimension Edit box.

14. Zoom in on the cutout in the sleeve and you'll see a green arrow on one corner. Zoom in closer on the green arrow and you will see the gap between the diameter sketches of the sleeve and insert reflecting your tolerance edits. However, the model itself currently displays no tolerance and needs to be updated to match the sketch.

15. Click the Update button on the quick access toolbar (looks like a lightning bolt at the top of the screen).

You should see a gap between the solids, providing a loose running fit. Because the current model is being evaluated at the extremes (the upper tolerance for the inside diameter and the lower for the outside diameter), you can determine whether the current design will provide the correct fit. In the real world you might determine that the outside diameter of the insert needs to be less than 36 mm for the nominal value so that you can ensure a better fit.

Continue with the following steps to explore more options when working with part tolerances.

16. Zoom back out and then click once on any blank area of the graphics screen (to clear any currently selected entities) and then right-click and choose Dimension Display, and choose Tolerance from the fly-out menu. This will show you the evaluated dimension values, as shown in Figure 5.50.

FIGURE 5.50
Dimensions showing limit/fits

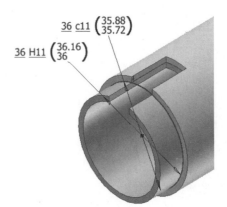

17. Right-click on either of the dimensions and choose Dimension Properties.

You'll notice that you can set and adjust the tolerance options in this menu as well. You can use the document settings tab to set up standard tolerances for the entire file and change the precision and dimension display. These are the same settings you accessed by editing the dimensions and parameters in the previous steps.

This concludes the formal steps of this exercise, but you can continue experimenting with the tolerances using Table 5.2 as a reference. For instance you might set up a press fit, and evaluate the inside diameter at the upper value and the outside at the lower, to check to see if there is indeed enough interference to provide a solid press fit when both dimensions are evaluated at their extremes.

TABLE 5.2:   Example of limits and fits using hole basis (note: this is not a complete fits list and is provided as reference for this exercise only)

TYPE	FIT	USE	HOLE	SHAFT
Clearance	Loose Running	General fits with smaller clearances.	H11	c11
Clearance	Sliding	Very small clearances for accurate guiding of shafts, with no noticeable clearance once assembled.	H7	g6
Transition	Locational	Snug fit with small clearance. Parts can be assembled and disassembled manually.	H7	jh
Transition	Keying	Small clearances or slight interferences. Parts can be assembled with little force, such as a rubber mallet.	H7	k6
Interference	Press	Guaranteed interference, using cold pressing.	H7	p6
Interference	Shrink	Medium interference, using hot pressing or large force cold pressing.	H7	s6

Troubleshooting Failures with the End-of-Part Marker

Once in a while, even the most skilled design engineer experiences a modeling or design failure. The part may be supplied by a customer or co-worker who has not practiced sound modeling techniques, or you may have to drastically modify a base feature in a part you designed. These edits change a base feature to the point that dependent features cannot solve, and a cascade of errors can occur. Knowing how to fix these errors can save you hours of work

One of the best ways to troubleshoot a part and determine exactly how the part was originally modeled is to use the end-of-part (EOP) marker to step through the creation process. In the Model browser, drag the end-of-part marker to a location immediately below the first feature. This will effectively eliminate all other features below the marker from the part calculation.

Often when making modifications to a part, you might change a feature that causes errors to cascade down through the part. Moving the end-of-part marker up to isolate the first troubled feature allows you to resolve errors one at a time. Oftentimes, resolving the topmost error will fix those that exist after it. Figure 5.51 shows a model tree with a series of errors. On the right, the end-of-part marker has been moved up.

FIGURE 5.51
Using the end-of-part marker to troubleshoot feature errors

Step 1: Editing the First Feature

Normally, the first feature will start with a sketch. Right-click the first feature, and select Edit Sketch. Examine the sketch for a location relative to the part origin point. Generally, the first sketch should be located and anchored at the origin and fully dimensioned and constrained. If the sketch is not fully constrained, then add dimensions and constraints to correct it.

If you see sketch entities highlighted in a magenta color, you probably have projected geometry that has lost its parent feature. To resolve errors of this type, it is often required to break the link between the missing geometry and allow the projected entities to stand on their own. To do so, right-click the objects in the graphics area or expand the sketch in the browser, and right-click any projected or reference geometry that are showing errors; then choose Break Link. This frees up the geometry so that it can be constrained and dimensioned on its own or simply deleted. Figure 5.52 shows the Break Link option being selected for a projected loop.

FIGURE 5.52
Breaking projected object links

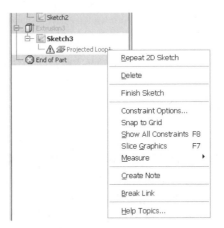

Once the sketch is free of errors, you can return to the feature level. Often you'll be greeted by an error message informing you that the feature is not healthy. Click Edit or Accept. Then edit the feature. Most often you will simply be required to reselect the profile or reference geometry. Once the feature is fixed, drag the end-of-part marker below the next feature, and repeat the step. Continue through the part until all sketches are properly constrained.

Occasionally, a base sketch may become "lost" and may need to be reassociated to a sketch plane. To do so, you can right-click and choose Redefine, as shown in Figure 5.53. Depending on how drastic the change in sketch plane is, this may be all that is required. Often, though, you will need to edit the sketch, clean up some stray geometry using the Break Link option, and then dimension and constrain it so that it is stable.

Step 2: Moving the EOP Marker Down One Feature at a Time

Step 2 might be called "learn from your mistakes" (or other people's mistakes). When you have part/feature failures, you should take advantage of them and analyze how the part was created to determine why the sketch or features became unstable. It's always good practice to create the major features first and then add secondary features such as holes, fillets, and chamfers at the end of the part. On occasion, loft and sweep features may fail or produce incorrect results because fillets and chamfers were created before the failed feature. To determine whether this is the case in your model, suppress any holes, fillets, chamfers, or any other feature that you might think is causing the failure.

FIGURE 5.53
Redefining a sketch

Once the failed feature is corrected, introduce one suppressed feature at a time until you encounter a failure. This will identify the cause. You may then attempt to move the offending feature below the failed feature and examine the result. If you are unable to move the offending feature, then reproduce the same feature below the failed feature, and leave the original suppressed. When the problems are corrected in a part, you can go back and delete the suppressed offending features.

Although it's not always a silver bullet, you might want to try the Rebuild All tool right after fixing the first broken sketch or feature. Very often if the fix was fairly minor, Rebuild All will save you from having to manually edit dependent features one at a time. You can access this tool by going to the Manage tab and selecting Rebuild All.

USING THE END-OF-PART MARKER TO TIME TRAVEL

The end-of-part marker is a powerful, yet often neglected, tool. With this tool, you can go "back to the future" and edit or add features to your model. A good example of using the EOP marker is to preserve design intent. Let's say you created a base feature, placed some holes down the center of the part (based on dimensions), and then altered the side faces of the part. The holes are linked to the unaltered edges of this part. You now want to tie the holes to the midplane of this part regardless of the feature size.

You could do this by placing a centered work plane down the part. However, you cannot do this now because when you go back to edit the hole sketch, the work plane would not be available for projection onto the sketch plane. You also cannot drag the work plane above the holes because it was created on the new, altered base feature faces. In this case, you'll want to drag the EOP marker above the hole feature. Now you can place the work plane centered on the two faces. Drag the EOP marker back down to the bottom of the tree. Now edit the hole feature and project the work plane so that the hole centers can be constrained to it.

You can also use the EOP to reduce file size when you email a model. If you drag the EOP to the top of the browser, only the feature tree (commonly called the *part DNA* or *part recipe*) is saved to disk. When the EOP marker is dragged down to the bottom again, all the feature data is recalculated.

The Bottom Line

Create complex sweeps and lofts   Complex geometry is created by using multiple work planes, sketches, and 3D sketch geometry. Honing your experience in creating work planes and 3D sketches is paramount to success in creating complex models.

Master It   How would you create a piece of twisted flat bar in Inventor?

Work with multi-body and derived parts   Multi-body parts can be used to create part files with features that require precise matching between two or more parts. Once the solid bodies are created, you can create a separate part file for each component.

Master It   What would be the best way to create an assembly of four parts that require features to mate together in different positions?

Utilize part tolerances   Dimensional tolerancing of sketches allows the checking of stack-up variations within assemblies. By adding tolerances to critical dimensions within sketches, parts may be adjusted to maximum, minimum, and nominal conditions.

Master It   You want to create a model feature with a deviation so that you can test the assembly fit at the extreme ends of the tolerances. How would this be done?

Understand and use parameters and iProperties   Using parameters within files assists in the creation of title blocks, parts lists, and annotation within 2D drawings. Using parameters in an assembly file allows the control of constraints and objects within the assembly. Exporting parameters allows the creation of custom properties. Proper usage of iProperties facilitates the creation of accurate 2D drawings that always reflect the current state of included parts and assemblies.

Master It   You want to create a formula to determine the spacing of a hole pattern based upon the length of the part. What tools would you use?

Troubleshoot modeling failures   Modeling failures are often caused by poor design practices. Poor sketching techniques, bad design workflow, and other factors can lead to the elimination of design intent within a model.

Master It   You want to modify a rather complex existing part file, but when you change the feature, errors cascade down through the entire part. How can this be done?

Chapter 6

Sheet Metal

The sheet-metal functionality in Inventor is extremely powerful, centered around productivity and capturing your manufacturing intent. When you first begin working in the sheet-metal environment, you may feel overwhelmed; however, a mastery of some basic fundamentals can make Inventor sheet metal straightforward and highly integrated with your manufacturing environment.

In this chapter, you'll learn to:

- ◆ Take advantage of the specific sheet-metal features available in Inventor

- ◆ Understand sheet-metal templates and rules

- ◆ Author and insert punch tooling

- ◆ Utilize the flat pattern information and options

- ◆ Understand the nuances of sheet-metal iPart factories

- ◆ Model sheet-metal components with non-sheet-metal features

- ◆ Work with imported sheet-metal parts

- ◆ Understand the tools available to annotate your sheet-metal design

- ◆ Harvest your legacy sheet-metal styles into sheet-metal rules

Understanding Sheet-Metal Parts

The sheet-metal environment was introduced in Inventor R2. Since sheet-metal parts have so many unique requirements, such as flat patterns and manufacturing-specific features, a modified part file is used. Sheet-metal parts use the same .ipt file extension, but extra sheet-metal capabilities and data are added.

Sheet-metal design is driven by manufacturing considerations. A basic sheet-metal part consists of flat faces joined by bends. For cost-effective manufacturing, all the bends and corner reliefs are generally the same radius. The sheet-metal environment captures sheet thickness, bend, and relief information in a rule and the rule is then used during modeling. This saves you considerable time during design because the features automatically use the settings in the rule. If you have to make a change, such as a different material thickness or bend radius, you can select a different rule, and the part automatically updates.

Many sheet-metal parts are brackets or enclosures that are made to fit a particular assembly. The sheet-metal tools were designed to simplify the process of creating and updating models. For example, you can change a bend to a corner seam simply by right-clicking the bend in the browser and selecting Change To Corner from the context menu.

Getting to Know the Features

The Inventor sheet-metal environment contains numerous specialized tools to help you design components that follow your sheet-metal manufacturing guidelines and process restrictions. The following sections describe general feature classifications and capabilities that will provide you with a quick road map to the features. Once you understand how the features work, you will be able to build models that capture your design intent.

Starting with a Base Feature

Out of all the sheet-metal features provided, only four of them create what are referred to as *base features*. Base features are simply the first features that appear in the feature history. The tools that can create base features are as follows:

- Face
- Contour Flange
- Contour Roll
- Lofted Flange

FACE

The Face tool is the simplest base feature; it utilizes a closed profile to produce a simple extrusion automatically set to the Thickness parameter value. The profile can be constructed out of any shape and can even contain interior profiles, as shown in Figure 6.1. Profiles for face features are often generated from the edge projections of planar faces or surfaces, and this capability enables numerous assembly-based and derived workflows.

FIGURE 6.1
Face base feature containing an internal profile

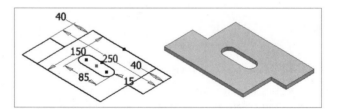

CONTOUR FLANGE

The Contour Flange tool is a sketch-based feature (using an open profile) that has the ability to create multiple planar faces and bends as the result of a single feature, as shown in Figure 6.2. Profile sketches should contain only arcs and lines; if sketch intersections are not separated by an arc, a bend will be automatically added at the intersection equal to the BendRadius parameter, as determined by the sheet-metal style. To create base features with a profile sketch, contour flanges have a width extent option called Distance, which allows a simple open profile to be utilized to create a sheet-metal condition extrusion of the thickened, filleted profile.

FIGURE 6.2

Contour Flange base feature

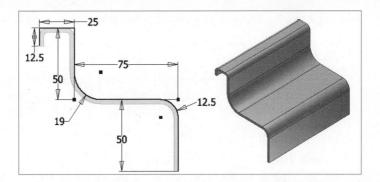

You can use the Contour Flange tool to create sheet-metal base features; in fact, it is often the fastest way to create them. Although you could create the part shown in Figure 6.2 using the Face tool and then adding flanges, it would be more time-consuming. Using the Contour Flange tool has one drawback, however: since you are combining many features, you lose some flexibility for revising the shape.

Follow these steps to explore the basics of creating a base feature with the Contour Flange tool:

1. Click the Get Started tab, and choose Open.

2. Browse for the file named mi_6a_001.ipt located in the Chapter 6 directory of the Mastering Inventor 2011 folder, and click Open.

3. Select the Contour Flange tool from the Create panel of the Sheet Metal tab.

4. For the Profile selection, click anywhere along the sketch profile.

Depending upon where you selected on the sketch, the preview will show to either the outside or inside of the sketch. Also notice that the corners at each end of the 25 mm leg are automatically rounded even though no radius was specified in the sketch. This is due to the predefined BendRadius parameter.

5. Use the Flip Side buttons (three arrow buttons) to change the preview so you can see how each changes the result. Then set the preview to look like Figure 6.2 so that the preview is to the inside of the sketch profile, and therefore holding the overall dimensions of the sketch.

6. Enter **6 mm** in the Bend Radius input box, and notice the corners at each end of the 25 mm leg are updated.

Entering a value in the Bend Radius input box overrides the predefined BendRadius parameter and sets this contour flange feature to always use 6 mm. If the part were set to use another predefined style, bends in this feature would not update to follow the style but would instead stay at 6 mm.

7. Click the >> button to expand the Contour Flange dialog box (if it isn't already expanded) and then set the Distance input box to **150 mm**.

8. Use View Cube to change the view so that you can see the direction of the contour.

9. Click the Distance Mid-plane button so that the part is created equally to both sided of the sketch.

10. Click OK to create the feature.

In the preceding steps you created a base feature using an open profile sketch and the Contour Flange tool. From this point you could begin adding secondary features as required. You can close this file without saving changes and you'll continue looking at other tools used to create base features.

CONTOUR ROLL

The Contour Roll tool is a variation on the Contour Flange tool. To create a Contour Roll you sketch an open profile, but you revolve it instead of extruding it. Sketch geometry is limited to lines and arcs, and the Contour Roll tool will automatically add a bend at line intersections. The rolled hat flange in Figure 6.3 was created using the simple sketch geometry shown.

FIGURE 6.3
Contour roll
base feature

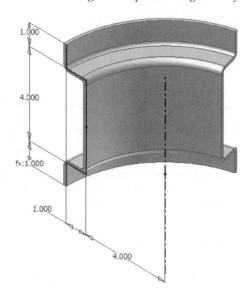

Follow these steps to explore the basics of creating a base feature with the Contour Flange tool:

1. Click the Get Started tab, and choose Open.

2. Browse for the file named mi_6a_002.ipt located in the Chapter 6 directory of the Mastering Inventor 2011 folder, and click Open.

3. Select the Contour Roll tool from the Create panel of the Sheet Metal tab.

4. Set the Unroll Method drop-down box to Centroid Cylinder if it is not already. For the Profile selection, click anywhere along the sketch profile.

5. Select the centerline for the Axis selection.

Note the options in the Unroll Method drop-down box.

◆ *Centroid Cylinder* - the neutral cylindrical surface is derived by the centroid location of the profile, based off of the selected axis. The Neutral Radius and Unrolled Length are displayed.

◆ *Custom Cylinder* - allows you to select a sketched line to define the cylindrical neutral surface. The Unrolled Length is displayed.

◆ *Developed Length* - allows you to enter the developed length, and displays the adjusted Neutral Radius.

◆ *Neutral Radius* - allows you to enter the Neutral Radius, and displays the adjusted Unrolled Length.

These options all derive the developed length by multiplying the rolled angle by a neutral radius, but differ from one another by the type of input specified.

6. Set the unroll method to Custom Cylinder, and select the sketch line denoted as Custom Neutral Axis for the Neutral Axis selection. Note the displayed Unrolled Length.

7. Set the unroll method to Neutral Radius and enter **60 mm** into the input box. You'll notice the displayed Unrolled Length adjusts based on the change.

8. Set the unroll method to Developed Length and enter **100 mm** into the input box. You'll notice the displayed Neutral Radius adjusts based on the change.

9. Click OK to create the feature.

10. Next click the Create Flat Pattern button on the Sheet Metal tab.

11. Right-click on the Flat Pattern node in the browser and choose Extents. You'll see the width of the flat pattern has been held to 100 mm.

12. Click the Close button in the Flat Pattern Extents dialog box.

13. Click the Go To Folded Part button on the Sheet Metal tab to return to the folded model.

In the preceding steps you created a base feature using an open profile sketch and the Contour Roll tool. You can close this file without saving changes and you'll continue looking at other tools used to create base features. Before continuing though, you can open the file called mi_6a_003.ipt to create a secondary contour roll feature based off of the first.

LOFTED FLANGE

The Lofted Flange tool creates sheet-metal shapes typically seen in HVAC transitions and material handling hoppers. Figure 6.4 shows a square-to-round transition. Basically, you create sketches of the beginning and end of the transition, and then use the Lofted Flange tool to transition between the two. The Lofted Flange tool gives you the option of a die form or a press brake transition. For press brake transitions, you can define the bends by chord tolerance, facet angle, or facet distance. The chord tolerance is the distance between the angled face and the theoretical curved surface. As the chord tolerance is decreased, more facets are added.

FIGURE 6.4
Square to round lofted flange

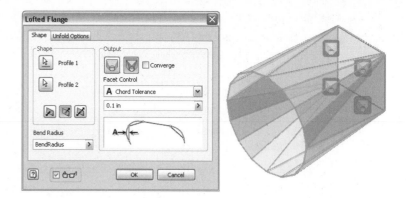

To create a lofted flange, follow these steps:

1. Click the Get Started tab, and choose Open.

2. Browse for the file named mi_6a_004.ipt located in the Chapter 6 directory of the Mastering Inventor 2011 folder, and click Open.

3. Click the Lofted Flange button in the Create panel.

4. Select the square and the circle for the profile selections.

5. In the output area of the dialog box, click the Die Formed button, and note that the preview changes to remove the press brake facets and that the facet controls in the dialog box are hidden.

6. Click the Press Brake icon and use the Facet Control drop-down to experiment with the Chord Tolerance, Facet Angle and Facet Distance options to familiarize yourself with their behavior.

   ◆ The *Chord Tolerance* value sets the maximum separation distance from the arc segment to the chord segment.

   ◆ The *Facet Angle* value sets the maximum angle to the chord segment at the facet face vertex.

   ◆ The *Facet Distance* value sets the maximum width of the length of the chord.

   ◆ The *Converge* check box sets the bends of the flattened faceted sections to converge near a singular point.

   Deciding which of these options to use, depends largely on the design inputs you know and the equipment to be used to create the part on the shop floor.

7. Ensure the Converge check box is not selected, and set the Facet Control drop-down to Facet Distance, and change the distance to **50 mm**.

Note that there is a glyph icon at each of the transition corners on the model preview. If you hover your cursor over them you can see them better. Clicking one of these *Bend Zone Edit Glyphs* displays a dialog box to change the facet control and also displays individual glyphs for each bend. The Bend Zone Edit dialog box enables you to change the facet control for that corner, as shown in Figure 6.5. Clicking one of the bend glyphs displays a Bend Edit dialog box that enables you to override the bend radius and Unfold Rule for an individual bend.

FIGURE 6.5
Bend Zone Edit
dialog box

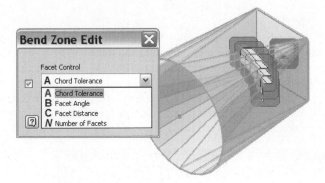

8. Click one of the Bend Zone Edit glyphs.

9. Click the check box in the Bend Zone Edit dialog box, and select Number Of Facets.

10. Enter **2** in the edit field, and note the preview updates.

11. Click one of the Bend Edit glyphs, and then click the Bend Radius check box in the resulting Bend Edit dialog box.

12. Change the bend radius to **BendRadius*10** and note the preview.

13. Click OK, and note that the Bend Edit glyph has changed. A pencil is added to indicate that it has been overridden.

14. Click OK in the Bend Zone Edit dialog box. Hover your mouse pointer over the glyph, and note that a pencil has been added to it as well.

15. Click OK in the Lofted Flange dialog box to create the feature.

16. Click the Create Flat Pattern button on the Sheet Metal tab. Note that the part isn't flattened because it is a continuous piece.

17. Click the Go To Folded Part button on the Sheet Metal tab to return to the folded model.

To get the lofted flange transition to flatten you'll need to create a rip feature in one of the faces. The Rip tool will be discussed in the Adding, Removing, or Deforming Material section in the pages to come. For now you can close the file without saving changes and continue to the next section to explore the creation of flanges.

Creating Secondary Flange Features

Once a base feature is created you can add secondary features in the form of flanges. Flanges are simply planar faces connected by a bend, and can be created using a number of different tools. The Flange tool automatically creates bends between the flanges and the selected faces. You can also use the Contour Flange tool to create several flanges at once. The Hem tool allows you to create specialized flanges to hem sharp edges or to create rolled flange features. Another tool commonly used along with these tools is the Face tool. Depending on the selected tool, you can either control flange options or allow Inventor to apply predefined relationships and values.

FLANGE

The Flange tool creates a single planar face and bend for each edge selected with controls for defining the flange height, bend position, and relief options at the edge intersections. For flanges referencing a single edge, width extent options are also available by clicking the >> button in the Flange dialog box. If multiple edges have been selected for flange locations, corner seams are automatically added, as shown in Figure 6.6. The bend and corner seam dimensions follow the sheet-metal rule unless a value is entered to override them per feature. The preview displays glyphs at each bend and corner seam. If you click a glyph, a dialog box displays so you can override the values.

FIGURE 6.6
A multiedge flange feature preview with bend and corner edit glyphs

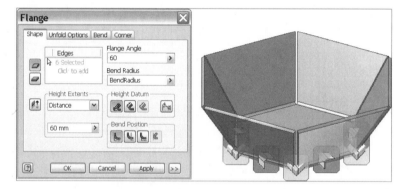

Creating Basic Flanges

To explore the Flange tool follow these steps:

1. Click the Get Started tab, and choose Open.

2. Browse for the file named mi_6a_005.ipt located in the Chapter 6 directory of the Mastering Inventor 2011 folder, and click Open.

3. Select the Flange tool from the Create panel of the Sheet Metal tab.

4. Click the Loop Select Mode button (on the left of the of the Edges selection box).

5. Place your cursor over the top face of the hexagonal shaped base feature. Click the edge when you see all 6 edges highlight. Note that if you chose the bottom edge rather than the top, you can use the Flip Direction button to change the direction.

6. Click the Edge Select Mode button and then hold the Ctrl key and de-select one of the selected edges. The Edges selection box will indicate that you now have only 5 selected.

7. Set the flange height to **100 mm**.

8. Set the flange angel to **60**.

9. Click the Corner tab, and uncheck the Apply Auto-Mitering check box to observe the preview change, then re-select the Apply Auto-Mitering check box to allow the flanges to flare out into the miters corners.

10. In the Miter Gap input box enter **1 mm**, in order to reduce the gap size from the current default value (the GapSize parameter is currently set at 3 mm.)

11. Click Apply to create the 5 flanges, and leave the Flange dialog box open (recall that OK creates the feature and closes the dialog box).

12. Click the Shape tab and ensure the Edge Select Mode is selected.

13. Click the edge that you removed from the previous selection set. Note that if you chose the bottom edge rather than the top, you can use the Flip Direction button to change the direction.

14. Set the Flange Angle to **90**.

15. Set the Height Extents drop-down box to To, and then click the top most corner vertex of any of the existing flanges. Figure 6.7 shows the To point being selected.

FIGURE 6.7
Setting a flange
height using the
To option

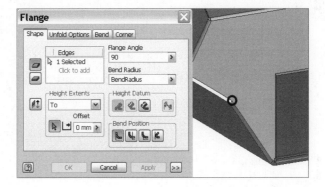

16. Click OK to create the flange.

If you click the Front plane on the view cube you can see all the flanges terminate in the same plane. Keep this in mind as you create flanges of varying angles. You explore the tools used to close the remaining gaps in this flange combination later in this chapter when looking at the Corner Seam tool, but for now you can close the file without saving changes, and continue to explore the Flange tool.

Control Flange Widths

In this next set of steps you'll create flanges of varying widths, by adjusting the extents options:

1. Click the Get Started tab, and choose Open.

2. Browse for the file named mi_6a_006.ipt located in the Chapter 6 directory of the Mastering Inventor 2011 folder, and click Open.

3. Select the Flange tool from the Create panel of the Sheet Metal tab.

4. Select the top edge of the yellow face to place a flange along the edge.

5. Set the flange height to **50 mm** and leave the angle at 90 degrees.

Note that currently the flange runs along the extents of the edge. If you imagine the flat pattern that would result from adding this flange, you'll understand that creating this flange would create a conflict at the inside corner. Although Inventor will not prevent you from creating the flange as is, it will issue an error to the flat pattern. To resolve this you will set the flange width and an offset to hold it back from the corner. There are four possible Width Extents settings:

◆ The *Edge* option runs the flange the length of the selected edge.

◆ The *Width* option allows you to specify the width of the flange, and position it with centered on the selected edge or offset from a selected reference.

◆ The *Offset* option allows you to specify offsets from both ends of the selected edge.

◆ The *From To* option allows you to specify a start and end reference to establish the flange width.

The option you use will depend on the result you are trying achieve and the available existing geometry.

6. Click the >> button to expand the Flange dialog box.

7. Change the Width Extents Type to Width.

8. Enter **96 mm** in the Width input box.

9. Switch the option from Centered to Offset.

10. Enter **0 mm** for the offset value.

11. Click the outside end of the selected edge to establish the offset point. Use the Flip Offset button to redirect the flange if needed.

12. Click OK to create the flange.

13. Click the Go To Folded Part button on the Sheet Metal tab to have a look at the resulting flat pattern.

Although the flange width options are easy to overlook because they are initially hidden in the more options area of the dialog box, you should keep these options in mind as you create flanges. For now, you can close this file without saving changes. Here are more options to be aware of when creating flanges:

Flange Height Datum   There are three Height Datum solutions available. These options control which faces are used to determine the height measurement. In Figure 6.8 each of the options is shown using a 40 mm flange.

◆ *Bend from the intersection of the two outer faces* measures the flange height from the intersection of the outer faces, as shown on the left of Figure 6.8.

◆ *Bend from the intersection of the two inner faces* measures the flange height from the intersection of the inner faces, as shown in the center of Figure 6.8.

◆ *Parallel to the flange termination detail face* measures the flange height parallel to the flange face and tangent to the bend, as shown on the right of Figure 6.8.

FIGURE 6.8
Flange height
datum solutions

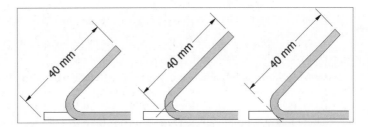

Orthogonal and Aligned Flanges   You can use the *Aligned VS Orthogonal* toggle button to determine whether the height measurement is aligned with the flange face or orthogonal to the base face. In Figure 6.9, the flange on the left is set to orthogonal while the measurement on the right is aligned.

FIGURE 6.9
Orthogonal and
aligned flanges

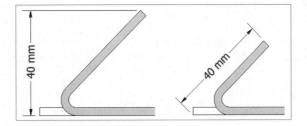

Bend Position   There are four options to select from to determine the bend position relative to the face of the selected edge. Figure 6.10 compares the four options, with the dashed line representing the selected edge of the base feature.

FIGURE 6.10
Bend positions
compared

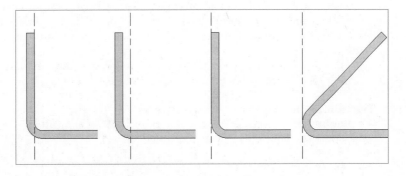

The *Inside of base face extents* option positions the flange so that it honors the overall dimension of the selected base part, as shown on the far left of Figure 6.10.

The *Bend from Adjacent Face* option holds the face of the selected edge as the start of the bend, as shown on the center left of Figure 6.10.

The *Outside of base face extents* option positions the inside face of the flange so that it remains outside of the face of the selected edge, as shown on the center right of Figure 6.10.

The *Bend tangent to side face* option holds the bend tangent to the face of the selected edge, as shown on the far right of Figure 6.10.

Old Method   When checked, this option disables the new functionality introduced in Inventor 2008. If you open a file created in an older version the features will likely have this option selected. You can uncheck the box to update the file to use all of the available options. There really is no reason to check this box on parts that you create with the current version of Inventor.

Bend and Corner Edit Glyphs   Although you will often create flanges along multiple edges as a single flange feature, you can still control the bend and corner options individually by using the edit glyphs displayed on the features in the graphics area. You can access the edit glyphs by expanding the Flange node in the browser and then right-clicking on the Bend or Corner and choosing Edit Bend or Edit Corner. Once displayed you can simply click on the edit glyph for the bend or corner you want to edit and make changes on an individual basis. You can also click the edit glyphs during the creation of flanges as well. Once bends or corners are edited, they can be reset to the defaults by expanding the Flange node in the browser and then right-clicking on the Bend or Corner and choosing Reset All Bends/Corners.

Contour Flange

In addition to creating base features as explored previously, the Contour Flange tool can also be used to add flanges to an existing feature. Since the Contour Flange tool uses open profile sketches, it is ideal for quickly creating complex shapes and enclosures designs. As discussed earlier, the Contour Flange tool can either automatically bend line intersections or use sketched arcs for bends. Contour flanges automatically create a bend between the contour flange and a selected edge on an existing face. The sketch profile for the Contour Flange tool does not need to be coincident with the edge; it simply needs to be sketched on a plane that is perpendicular to it. If the sketch profile is coincident with an edge, a bend will automatically be positioned to connect the sketch profile to the face. If the sketch is not coincident with a reference edge and the width extent option is changed to Distance, the result will be a contour flange that isn't attached to the part.

Just like in the Flange feature, automatic mitering of adjacent flanges and the placement of corner reliefs occur when multiple edges are selected, as shown in Figure 6.11.

FIGURE 6.11
A multi-edge Contour Flange feature with automatic mitering and large radius bends

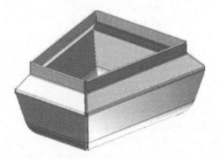

To explore the Contour Flange tool a bit more follow these steps:

1. Click the Get Started tab, and choose Open.

2. Browse for the file named mi_6a_007.ipt located in the Chapter 6 directory of the Mastering Inventor 2011 folder, and click Open.

3. Select the Contour Flange tool from the Create panel of the Sheet Metal tab.

4. Select the visible sketch profile as the Profile selection.

5. Select one of the edges (top or bottom) that have the two work planes running through it.

You'll note that you cannot add any more edges to the selection. This is because the sketch is disconnected from the base feature, and therefore can only be used to create a flange along the one edge. Next you'll use the work planes to define the width of the flange.

6. Click the >> button to expand the dialog box and reveal the Width Extents options.

7. Set the Type drop-down box to From To.

8. Select the two visible work planes as the From and To selections.

9. In the Bend Extensions area, click the left button (Extend Bend Aligned to Side Faces).

10. Click OK to create the Contour Flange.

You should notice the flange width starts and stops at the work planes selected for the width extents. You'll also notice the edge of the base feature extends out to meet the flange. This is due to the Bend Extension option. The Bend Extension options are as follows:

♦ *Extend Bend Aligned to Side Faces* will extend the base feature out to meet the flange.

♦ *Extend Bend Perpendicular to Side Faces* will extend the flange out to meet the base feature. This is the default.

You'll explore these options a bit more in the section covering how to use the Face tool to create flanges, but for now you'll edit the flange and toggle this option to compare the results.

11. Right-click on the Contour Flange feature in the browser and choose Edit Feature.

12. In the Bend Extensions area, click the right button (Extend Bend Perpendicular to Side Faces).

13. Click OK, and note that the flange has now extended to the base feature, as shown on the right of Figure 6.12.

FIGURE 6.12
Bend Extension options

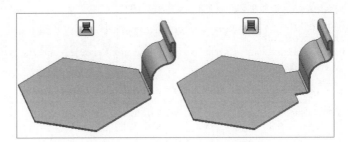

14. Next right-click on Sketch3 in the browser and turn the visibility on.

15. Select the Contour Flange tool from the Create panel of the Sheet Metal tab.

16. Select the sketch profile in Sketch3 as the Profile selection.

17. Select the five edges of the hex shaped face that were not used in the previous contour flange.

18. Notice the automatic mitering of the corners, then click OK to create the flanges.

As you can see the Contour Flange can be used to quickly create multiple bend flanges from a basic open profile sketch. This is often the quickest way to create even simple flanges when they are the same on all edges of a base feature, particularly when the flanges require a miter fit. You can close this file without saving changes, and continue on to the next section to explore Hems.

Hem

The Hem tool is like a contour flange because it has the ability to create multiple planar faces and bends for a selected edge, but it is restricted to predefined common hem profiles and geometric relationships.

To explore the different hem flange types and options follow these steps:

1. Click the Get Started tab, and choose Open.

2. Browse for the file named mi_6a_008.ipt located in the Chapter 6 directory of the Mastering Inventor 2011 folder, and click Open.

In this file each of the four hem types has been created on the left of the part. You can use the cutouts on the right to create a hem matching each of the ones on the left. Once you have experimented with the hem types using the cutouts. Continue on to create a hem on the edge of the yellow face.

3. Use the View Cube to find a view of the yellow interior face.

4. Select the Hem tool from the Create panel of the Sheet Metal tab.

5. Set the Type to Single.

6. Select the edge along the outside of the yellow face.

7. Set the Gap to **2 mm**.

8. Set the Length to **12 mm**.

9. Click the >> button to expand the dialog box.

10. Change the Width Extents Type to Offset.

11. Use the appropriate offset input box to set the end that will interfere with the existing hem to **5 mm**.

12. Set the other offset to **0 mm**, so that no offset is created.

13. Click OK to create the Hem flange.

Although the Hem tools are fairly straight forward, it is often the use of offsets that allow you to place hems as needed. You can close this file without saving changes and continue on to the next section.

FACE

The last feature capable of creating flanges is the Face tool. The Face tool uses a closed profile sketch, and it can automatically create an attaching bend to a selected edge. This automatic case is very powerful because it allows you to create a skeletal surface model of your design, project the planar surfaces into sketches, and create face features with attaching bends. The manual controls can be utilized to connect face features to preexisting geometry, create double bends (joggles), or even deselect edges that have been automatically inferred because they share a common edge.

You can also use the Face tool to create models from 2D flat patterns that had been created in another application such as AutoCAD. By importing the 2D flat pattern, the Face tool can be used to thicken it to the desired value. A flat pattern can be produced for a planar face (no unfolding needs to actually occur), which enables the use of special translation tools, Drawing Manager consumption, and a variety of other uses.

In the following steps you'll derive a frame into your sheet metal part and use it as a reference to create a face. You'll then create another face and use the built in Bend tools to connect them.

1. Click the Get Started tab, and choose Open.

2. Browse for the file named mi_6a_009.ipt located in the Chapter 6 directory of the Mastering Inventor 2011 folder, and click Open.

3. Select the Manage tab click the Derive button on the Insert panel.

4. Browse for the file named mi_6a_888.ipt located in the Chapter 6 directory of the Mastering Inventor 2011 folder, and click Open.

5. In the Derived Part dialog box select the Body As Work Surface button at the top. This brings the frame in as surface that can be turned off later.

6. Click OK to create the frame surface.

7. Expand the mi_6a_888 node in the browser and right-click on the Frame:mi_6a_888.ipt node.

8. From the right-click context menu, deselect the Translucent option. This will make the frame edges easier to see.

9. Next right-click on the face of the frame side with the triangular corner gussets and choose New Sketch to create a 2D sketch on the side of the frame.

10. Click the Project Geometry drop-down menu and select Project Cut Edges. This will project the face of the fame into the sketch. Alternatively, you can use the Project Geometry tool and select the four outer edges and the eight holes.

11. Once the projected edges are created, click the Finish Sketch button to return to the Sheet Metal tab.

12. From the Sheet Metal tab select the Face button.

13. Choose the sketch boundary(s) so that the entire side of the frame, minus the holes, is selected.

14. Ensure the face is not going into the frame, use the Offset button if the direction needs to be adjusted, and then click OK to create the face feature with holes. Figure 6.13 shows the fame and face.

FIGURE 6.13
Face from a
derived frame

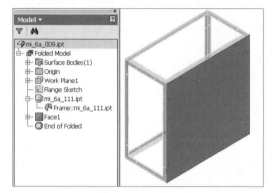

15. Next locate the sketch called Flange Sketch in the browser and then, right-click on it and choose visibility from the right-click context menu. This sketch was prepared in the sheet metal file ahead of time for this tutorial, but it the real world you would create it by referencing the frame as you did for the first face feature.

16. From the Sheet Metal tab select the Face tool again and choose the rectangular profile minus the slots, as the Profile selection.

17. Use the Offset button to ensure the face is coming out away from the frame.

18. Click the Edges button in the Bend area of the dialog box, and then select the left vertical edge of the first face feature. This will create a bend connecting to two faces.

19. Click OK to create the new face with bend feature.

If you examine the slotted flange face you might notice that it does not rest on the face of the frame. This is because the pre-made sketch that you made visible was created on a work plane at 302 mm from the center of the 600 mm wide frame. By using the offset work plane a 2 mm gap was created, allowing space for the bend radius, insert studs, and spacer hardware that might be required.

As a final note, be aware that when you are done with a derived work surface (the frame in this case) you can right-click on it in the browser and toggle off the visibility. This leaves only the sheet metal part showing. In order to create the next sheet metal part of the frame, such as the front or back covering, you would create a new sheet metal part and derive the frame in again. Once all of the parts are complete, you can place them into an assembly file knowing that they will all fit around the frame they were based on. For now though, you can close this file without saving changes and continue on to the next section.

Adding, Removing, or Deforming Material

Once the general shape of a sheet-metal component is roughed in, generally material will need to be either removed or. Several sheet-metal-specific features have been created to optimize the process of adding, removing and deforming sheet metal parts because most sheet-metal manufacturing operations (punch presses, for example) create features perpendicular to the surface. The current capabilities of Inventor assume that these manufacturing operations are done in the flat prior to folding and therefore should not interfere with unfolding (Inventor does not support post-folding manufacturing operations such as gussets, for example).

Cut

The Cut tool is a special sheet-metal extrude. It creates a hole based on a sketched profile. The Cut tool helps simplify the options of the regular Extrude tool because the distance parameter defaults to Thickness, and therefore cut features automatically update if the sheet metal part is changed to use a different material thickness. If a cut is not intended to be the full depth of the material thickness, you can enter an equation based off of the thickness value, such as Thickness/2 to create half thickness cuts.

The Cut tool can also wrap the sketch profile across planar faces and bends, as shown in Figure 6.14. This option is particularly helpful because it allows you to force a uniform cut across multiple planar faces and bends with a value greater than zero and equal to or less than Thickness.

USING CUTS

With sheet-metal parts it is often best to create your base features and flanges and then apply the cuts as required. You will find that this provides a more stable model when creating a flat pattern, and allows you to edit features individually. It is recommended you use the Cut tool whenever possible rather than creating voids in the base sketch. You should also use the Cut tool rather than using Extrude to cut, as general rule.

FIGURE 6.14
Cut feature utilizing Cut Across Bend option

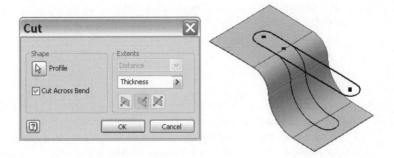

To explore the options of the Cut tool follow these steps:

1. Click the Get Started tab, and choose Open.

2. Browse for the file named mi_6a_010.ipt located in the Chapter 6 directory of the Mastering Inventor 2011 folder, and click Open.

3. Select the Cut tool from the Modify panel of the Sheet Metal tab.

4. Click OK to create the cut feature. Note how the cut remained only in top plane, and is not accurate for a slot that would be cut in the flat pattern.

5. Right-click on the cut feature in the browser and choose Edit Feature.

6. Select the Cut Across Bend check box, note the preview, and then click OK to see the cut through the part across the bends.

7. Edit the cut feature again, and enter **Thickness/2** in the extents distance input box, and then click OK.

As you can see the Cut tool allows you to create cutouts in the formed part that are accurate to the way the cutout is created in the flat pattern. To see the difference between a cut across bends and an extrude cut continue with the following steps.

8. Next locate the sketch called Sketch3 in the browser and then, right-click on it and choose visibility from the right-click context menu.

9. Click the Model tab and select the Extrude button.

10. Select the profile in Sketch3 as the profile selection.

11. Set the Extents drop-down box to All.

12. Click the Cut button in the Extrude dialog box, ensure the direction is correct, and then click OK.

13. Use the View Cube to look at the part from the Top view and note the difference in the extruded cut and the one using the Cut tool.

14. Click the Sheet Metal tab and select the Go To Flat Pattern button to examine the issues with the extruded cut.

If you measure the length of the two cuts you'll see the extruded cut exceeds the intended 150 mm length, even though the sketches for both sketches are set at 150 mm. When you are finished comparing the two cuts, you can close the file without saving changes, and continue to the next section.

PUNCH TOOL

You can use the Punch tool to either remove material or deform it by placing predefined Punch tool geometry, as shown in Figure 6.15. Punches are special versions of iFeatures; they can be predefined with additional manufacturing information and can be built using a variety of standard and sheet-metal features. The "Authoring and Reusing Punches" section discusses punch features in detail.

To explore the methods and options used to place punch features, follow these steps:

1. Click the Get Started tab, and choose Open.

2. Browse for the file named mi_6a_011.ipt located in the Chapter 6 directory of the Mastering Inventor 2011 folder, and click Open.

3. Select the Punch tool from the Modify panel of the Sheet Metal tab.

4. In the Punch Tool Directory dialog box, use the scroll bar in the left window to locate the Chapter 6 folder.

5. Locate and select the file called Knockout_73x.ide, and then click Open.

FIGURE 6.15
Multiple instance punch feature placing a footing dimple

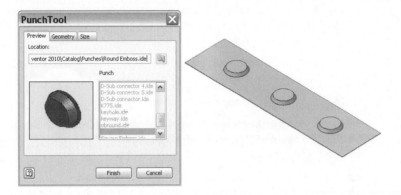

SETTING THE SHEET METAL PUNCH TOOL DEFAULT LOCATION

By default Inventor is set to look for the punch library in the install directory on your local drive. If working on a network share drive you will most likely want to point the Punch tool to automatically go to a path on the network. To do so go to the Tools tab, click the Application Options button, select the iFeature tab, and set the Sheet Metal Punches Root to the path of your choosing.

---

6. Because this part has two visible sketches no centers are automatically selected. Select any one of the center sketch points on the part.

7. Continue selecting center points and note that you can only select points that share the same sketch.

8. When you have added all of the center points you can (it will either be three or four depending upon which sketch the points are in), click the Size tab.

9. Enter **35 mm** for the diameter value, then click in the space below the Diameter row in the dialog box.

10. Click the Refresh button to see the diameter update on-screen. Note that if the diameter does not update, you probably did not click out of the Diameter row to set the edit. The refresh option is a bit "picky" in this way. Keep in mind, however, that the punch preview does not need to be refreshed to build correctly.

11. Next click the Finish button to create the punches.

12. Right-click and choose Repeat PunchTool, and then In the Punch Tool Directory dialog box, use the scroll bar in the left window to locate the Chapter 6 folder.

13. Locate and select the file called `Knockout_73x.ide`, and then click Open.

14. You'll notice that because you only have one visible sketch now, all of the center points in the sketch are automatically selected.

15. Click the Geometry tab and then select the Centers button.

16. Press and hold the Ctrl key on the keyboard and then deselect any one of the selected center points, by clicking the sketch center points. Note that it is often easier to do this when viewing the sketch from straight on.

17. With all but one of the available center points selected, change the Angle to **45** degrees. Note that all of the current punches are rotated.

18. Click Finish to create the punches.

19. Locate the sketch with the unused sketch point in the browser and then right-click on it and choose Visibility to turn it back on.

20. Right-click and choose Repeat PunchTool, and then In the Punch Tool Directory dialog box, use the scroll bar in the left window to locate the Chapter 6 folder.

21. Locate and select the file called `Knockout_73x.ide`, and then click Open.

22. The final center point should be automatically selected, if not select it and then click Finish to create it at the default size and orientation.

In the preceding steps you explored the options and methods used to place sheet-metal punches. Later in this chapter you will learn how to create sheet-metal punches of your own. For now, you can close this file without saving changes, and continue on to the next section.

CORNER ROUND AND CHAMFER

Corner Round and Corner Chamfer are special sheet-metal tools that allow you to remove or break sharp edges similar to filleting and chamfering. Edge selection has been optimized within the two tools, filtering out edges that are not normal to the sheet top and bottom faces for easy application. To explore the methods and options used to place round and chamfer features, follow these steps:

1. Click the Get Started tab, and choose Open.

2. Browse for the file named `mi_6a_012.ipt` located in the Chapter 6 directory of the Mastering Inventor 2011 folder, and click Open.

3. Select the Corner Round tool from the Modify panel of the Sheet Metal tab.

4. Set the Radius to **8 mm**, and then click the pencil icon in the Corner Round dialog box to change the focus from edit to select.

5. Select the two sharp corner edges on the green flange, and then click OK.

6. Right-click and choose Repeat Corner Round, and then set the Select Mode radio button to Feature.

7. Next, select any of the yellow flanges and you will see all of the sharp corners for the feature called Flange1 are automatically selected.

8. Change the Radius to **15 mm**, and then click OK to create the rounds.

9. Select the Corner Chamfer tool from the Modify panel of the Sheet Metal tab.

10. Select the remaining two sharp corners and set the Distance to **18 mm**, then click OK to create the corners.

As a final step you might want to right-click on Flange1 in the browser and choose Properties from the right-click context menu and set the Feature Color Style to As Part. You can do the same to Flange2 as well. When finished you can close the file without saving changes and continue to the next section.

CORNER SEAM

The Corner Seam tool allows you to extend (as shown in Figure 6.16) or trim flange faces in order to manage the seam between them and select corner relief options. The Corner Seam dialog box contains numerous options for specifying the seam and contains two fundamentally different distance definition methods: Maximum Gap and Face/Edge. In older versions of Inventor, only the Face/Edge method was available for the Corner Seam tool. The face/edge method works for many situations but also tends to suffer from an inability to maintain a constant seam gap between planar faces that do not have an identical input angle. The maximum gap method was developed from the perspective of a physical inspection gauge, where the nominal value of the seam is exactly the value entered at every point; but you just might need to twist the tool as you draw it through the seam.

FIGURE 6.16
Corner seam feature, applying the No Overlap seam type

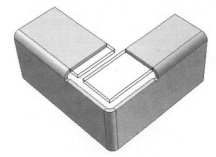

Creating a Basic Corner Seam

To explore the Corner Seam tools and its options follow these steps:

1. Click the Get Started tab, and choose Open.

2. Browse for the file named mi_6a_013.ipt located in the Chapter 6 directory of the Mastering Inventor 2011 folder, and click Open.

3. Select the Corner Seam tool from the Modify panel of the Sheet Metal tab.

4. Select the left edge of the yellow face, and either edge of the blue face next to it. In the preview the red edges represent the material to be removed and the green edges represent the material to be added.

5. In the Seam area of the Corner Seam dialog box, select the Symmetric Gap option, if not already selected

6. Set the Gap to **1 mm** and notice the change to the preview.

7. Click Apply to create the seam feature.

8. Select the right edge of the orange face, and either edge of the blue face next to it, and then click OK to create this seam and close the dialog box.

As you can see Corner Seams are useful when needing to close up a corner between two seams. You can close this file without saving changes and continue with the next set of steps to explore more of the settings in the Corner Seam tool.

Understanding Corner Seam Gap and Overlap Settings

In these steps you'll explore the gap and overlap settings found in the Corner Seam tool:

1. Click the Get Started tab, and choose Open.

2. Browse for the file named mi_6a_014.ipt located in the Chapter 6 directory of the Mastering Inventor 2011 folder, and click Open.

3. Select the Corner Seam tool from the Modify panel of the Sheet Metal tab.

4. Select the short edge of the orange flange nearest the yellow flange, and the short edge of the yellow flange nearest the orange flange.

5. You'll note that the preview show the two flanges come together in a 45 degree miter. Click the Overlap button to see the preview change to extend one of the flanges out so it overlaps the other.

6. Click the Reverse Overlap button to see the opposite overlap in the preview.

7. Click Apply to create the seam.

8. Next click a short edge of the yellow flange nearest the blue flange and a short edge of the blue flange nearest the yellow flange.

9. Set the Seam option to Maximum Gap Distance (if it is not already), and select the Symmetric Gap button.

10. Click OK to create the corner seam, and use the click the Top face on the View Cube to observe the corner of the yellow and blue flanges. Note it may be helpful to zoom up on the corner.

If you were to measure the gap distance at the inside vertices between the two flanges it will be 3 mm, which is what the GapSize parameter is set to, as shown on the left of Figure 6.17.

11. Edit the corner feature you just created and switch the radio button to Face/Edge Distance, and then click OK.

Now the GapSize parameter holds the distance between the face and edge of the two flanges as shown on the right of Figure 6.17.

FIGURE 6.17

Maximum Gap Distance compared to Face/Edge Distance

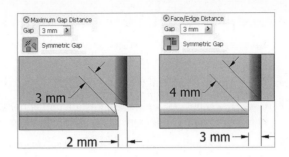

12. Edit the corner feature again and this time click the Overlap button.

13. Enter **0.5** in the Percent Overlap input box, and then click OK.

You will see that the yellow flange overlaps the edge of the blue flange exactly half way or fifty percent. You can specify the overlap as a percentage of the flange thickness using a decimal value ranging from 0.0 to 1.0. For instance, 1.0 equals 100 percent, 0.5 equals 50 percent, and so on.

14. Edit the corner feature once again and click the Reverse Overlap button.

15. Enter **1.0** in the Percent Overlap input box, and then click OK.

You will see that the blue flange now overlaps the yellow flange completely, or the full 100 percent. Figure 6.18 shows a comparison of overlap values with the same gap setting.

FIGURE 6.18

Overlap comparisons

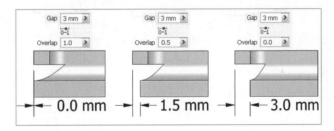

In the previous steps you explored the gap and overlap settings of the Corner Seam tool. You can close this file without saving changes and continue with the next set of steps to explore one more set of options in the Corner Seam tool.

Understanding Corner Seam Extend Options

In the following steps you will look at the options for controlling the way flanges are extended when their edges are not perpendicular:

1. Click the Get Started tab, and choose Open.

2. Browse for the file named `mi_6a_015.ipt` located in the Chapter 6 directory of the Mastering Inventor 2011 folder, and click Open.

3. Select the Corner Seam tool from the Modify panel of the Sheet Metal tab.

4. Select the shorter edge of the blue flange and the closest edge of the yellow flange.

5. Click the >> button in the Corner Seam dialog box and set the Extend Corner option to Perpendicular, then click Apply.

6. Select the taller edge of the blue flange and the closest edge of the orange flange.

7. Click the >> button in the Corner Seam dialog box again (if needed) and toggle the Extend Corner option between Perpendicular and Aligned to see the difference.

8. Then set the Extend Corner option to Perpendicular and click OK.

Figure 6.19 shows a comparison of the Perpendicular and Aligned extend options. In the image on the right the front most flange use the aligned solution and the other uses the Perpendicular solution.

FIGURE 6.19
Perpendicular and Aligned extend corner options

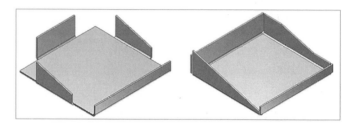

As you can see becoming familiar with all of the settings in the Corner Seam tool can offer a great number of combinations, and in the end provide the exact corner you are trying to achieve. You can close this file without saving changes and continue on to explore the Fold tool.

Fold

The Fold tool enables you to design a flange with a unique profile by allowing you to sketch the position of the bend centerline on a planar face, and then fold the part using the sketch line, as shown in Figure 6.20.

FIGURE 6.20
Fold tool being applied to a face with a spline contour

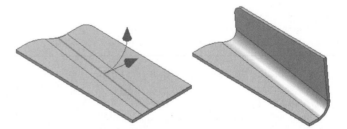

This tool is a sketch consumption feature and contains numerous controls for specifying exactly how a planar face should be manipulated into two planar faces connected by a bend. The sketch bend centerline must be coincident with the face extents, requiring you to project edges and constrain the sketch. When utilizing the Fold tool, remember that the feature works from the opposite design perspective of other sheet-metal features, where bend allowance is actually consumed, not added to the resulting folded feature. The Fold tool can be combined with the Face tool to help import preexisting 2D flat patterns and then deform them into their final shape.

To explore the Fold tool follow these brief steps:

1. Click the Get Started tab, and choose Open.

2. Browse for the file named mi_6a_016.ipt located in the Chapter 6 directory of the Mastering Inventor 2011 folder, and click Open.

3. Select the Fold tool from the Create panel of the Sheet Metal tab.

4. Select the visible sketch line on the circular feature for the Bend Line selection.

5. Use the Flip Side and Flip Direction buttons to set the preview arrows so that they are going up and out from the center of the part.

6. Set the Fold Angle to **45** degrees and the Bend Radius to **16 mm**.

7. Use the Fold Location buttons to set the fold so that it does not include the cutout.

8. Click OK to create the folded feature.

9. In order to reuse the sketch containing the bend lines you'll need to make it visible again. To do so, expand the Fold feature in the browser, right-click on the sketch and then choose Visibility from the right-click context menu.

10. Create a fold for each of the remaining lines, setting the Fold Angle to **90** degrees, the Bend Radius to **2 mm**, the Fold Location to *Centerline of Bend*, and use the flip controls to set the folds so they are all going up and out from the center of the part.

Although not the most commonly used of the sheet metal tools, the Fold tool can be very useful in some circumstances. If you happen to have a lot of flat pattern drawings done in AutoCAD for instance, you can use the Fold tool to convert them to folded models. You can close this file without saving changes and continue on to explore the Bend tool in the next section.

BEND

The Bend tool allows you to connect two planar faces by selecting a pair of parallel edges. Since Inventor supports the modeling of multiple lumps, the Bend tool can add either a single bend or a double bend (*joggle*) depending on the number of selections you make. For design situations in which multiple lumps have been produced, the Bend tool is often used to combine the lumps into a single body.

There are four possible double bend results, depending on the orientation of the edges and which option you choose. If the sheet-metal edges face the same direction, then either a full round bend, or two bends connected with a face is created. If the sheet-metal edges face in opposite directions, then a joggle is created with either two 45-degree bends and one edge fixed or both edges fixed and the angle calculated. In both cases, the faces will be extended or trimmed as necessary to create the bends.

Exploring Bend Options

The following example demonstrates the various ways in which double bends can be created:

1. Click the Get Started tab, and choose Open.

2. Browse for the file named mi_6a_017.ipt located in the Chapter 6 directory of the Mastering Inventor 2011 folder, and click Open.

3. Select the Bend tool from the Create panel of the Sheet Metal tab.

4. Select an edge along each of the yellow faces for the Edges selection. Note the *Full Radius* and *90 Degree* double bend controls are enabled.

5. Set the Double Bend option to Full Radius.

6. Toggle the *Flip Fixed Edge* button and note how the preview updates. Then set it so that the upper face is the fixed edge (the preview will display partially into the lower face).

7. Click Apply to create the Bend feature.

8. Select an edge along each of the orange faces for the Edges selection.

9. Set the Double Bend to use the 90 Degree option.

10. Set the Flip Fixed Edge button so that the lower face is the fixed edge, and the bend previews on the outermost edge.

11. Click OK to create the Bend feature, and note how lower face width is carried through to the upper face.

12. Right-click on the Bend feature you just created in the browser and choose Edit Feature.

13. Click the *Extend Bend Aligned to Side Faces* button in the Bend Extension area, and then click OK. Notice how the upper face width is now carried through to the bend.

14. Select the Bend tool again, and choose the edge of the blue face on the small feature with two holes, and then select the edge of the blue face on the large base feature (indicated with the arrow). Keep in mind the selection order is important for this step. When you have the correct order, the preview should show the upper feature being extended down into the lower base feature.

15. Set the Bend Radius to **18 mm**, and then click OK.

16. Right-click on the Bend feature you just created in the browser and choose Edit Feature.

17. Change the Double Bend option to use Fix Edges, and the click OK.

Although this file showcases the available options of the Bend tool, you would not typically create faces that just float in space above or below one another. Instead these tools are often used to created bends on faces that are modeled to fit around other existing parts. You can close this file without saving changes, and have a look at the next steps to see the Bend tool used in a more realistic manner.

Using the Bend tool to create an Enclosure

In the following steps you will mirror an existing side of an enclosure around the centerline of a derived frame, and then use the Bend tool to join the two halves:

1. Click the Get Started tab, and choose Open.

2. Browse for the file named mi_6a_018.ipt located in the Chapter 6 directory of the Mastering Inventor 2011 folder, and click Open.

3. Click the Mirror button on the Pattern panel of the Sheet Metal tab.

4. Select the features called Right_Side_Face, Front_Flange, and Back_Flange from the browser for the Features selection.

5. Click the Mirror Plane button in the Mirror dialog box, and then choose the visible YZ plane. Recall that you must select work planes by clicking their edges in the graphics area, or by selecting them from the browser.

6. Click OK to create the mirror feature.

7. Select the Bend tool from the Create panel of the Sheet Metal tab.

8. Select the top edges of the two sheet metal faces, leave the Double Bend option set to 90 Degree, and note the preview of the bend connecting the two faces.

9. Click OK to create the bend feature. Figure 6.21 shows the two sides being connected with the Bend tool.

FIGURE 6.21
Creating a bend to connect the sides of an enclosure

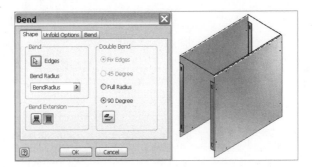

In the previous steps you have not only created bends, but have essentially defined the entire top face of the enclosure with the Bend tool. Using the bend tool to connect faces in this way can be a quick way to use geometry projected in from an assembly or a derived work surface. You can close this file without saving changes and continue on to the next section to explore the Rip tool.

RIP

The Rip tool creates a gap in a sheet-metal part. A common workflow is to create a transition with the Lofted Flange tool and then add a Rip feature so it can be flattened. The Rip tool creates a gap that is cut normal to the selected face. The rip tool interface is optimized to create a simple gap with minimal inputs.

Inventor has three options for creating a rip:

Single Point If the corner of a face is selected as the single point, the rip will follow the edge. If a sketch point located on an edge is selected, then the rip will be perpendicular to the edge.

Point To Point For Point To Point, a linear rip is created between the two points.

Face Extents For face selection, all edges of the face are ripped.

Follow these steps to create a simple Rip feature on a square to round transition:

1. Click the Get Started tab, and choose Open.

2. Browse for the file named mi_6a_019.ipt located in the Chapter 6 directory of the Mastering Inventor 2011 folder, and click Open.

3. Click the Rip button in the Modify panel on the Sheet Metal tab.

4. Set the Rip Type drop-down box to Point to Point.

5. Select the yellow face for the Rip Face selection.

6. Select the midpoint of the arc along the top of the yellow face, and the midpoint of the arc along the bottom of the yellow face for the Start and End point selections.

7. Then click OK to create the Rip feature. Figure 6.22 shows the Rip tool selections.

FIGURE 6.22
Ripping a crease on a square to round transition

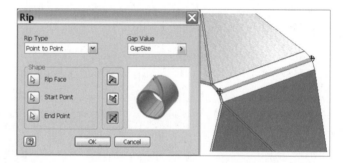

Creating Rip features allows you to open up a part for unfolding, in quick and easy manner. Keep in mind, however, that you can use an extruded cut to do this as well. In most cases though, the Rip tool will be the best tool to use. You can close this file without saving changes and continue on to the next section to explore the Unfold and Refold tools.

UNFOLD AND REFOLD

The Unfold and Refold tools are a powerful tool combination that allows you to unfold and then refold the model. There are several reasons to do this:

◆ To add features in the unfolded state

◆ To refold the model in bend order to see the manufacturing stages of the part

◆ To change the orientation of the folded model in space

One of the limitations in previous versions of Inventor was that you couldn't fold a deformation. Using Unfold or Refold, you can add a deformation that crosses the bend zone and then refold it. Since the deformation is simply calculated around the bend, there can be distortion issues when the deformation is large with respect to the bend radius. For best results, limit the deformation to the thickness. For larger deformations, make sure the final results match what would be created in the shop.

Many sheet-metal parts are complex, with several bend order possibilities. Using Unfold or Refold allows you to experiment with bend order so you can determine the best way to manufacture the part.

Changing the orientation of the folded model is an interesting workflow. When you unfold a model, you select a face that remains stationary. When you refold the model, you also have to select the stationary face. If you don't select the same face, the model will have a different orientation when you are done.

Unfolded vs. Flat Pattern

The flat pattern is a separate model object that shows the completely flattened part for documentation. The flat pattern also contains manufacturing information such as bend direction. Unfold and Refold features can't be directly accessed in the drawing, so you can't have views showing different states of the same model. To show intermediate fold states in a drawing, use derived parts or an iPart to create models with refold features suppressed, and then create views of those models.

Unfolding and Refolding Sheet Metal Parts

The Unfold/Refold process is straightforward. The selections have filters for the correct geometry, so you are not required to focus on a small target.

1. Click the Get Started tab, and choose Open.

2. Browse for the file named mi_6a_020.ipt located in the Chapter 6 directory of the Mastering Inventor 2011 folder, and click Open.

3. Click the Unfold button in the Modify panel.

4. Select the blue face on the part for the Stationary Reference selection.

5. Select all the bends on the folded model. Each bend will highlight when you hover your mouse pointer over it, so you know when you have a valid selection. The unfolded preview updates as you select each bend. Alternatively you can use the Add All Bends button.

6. Click the Sketches button, and select the visible sketch in the graphics window, so that it is unfolded to match the face it resides on.

7. Click OK. The model should look like Figure 6.23. Note that a copy of the sketch was placed on the unfolded model and that the original (Sketch12) is still displayed as a reference.

8. Right-click on Sketch12 in the browser and choose Visibility to toggle of its visibility, so that the copied sketch can be more easily viewed.

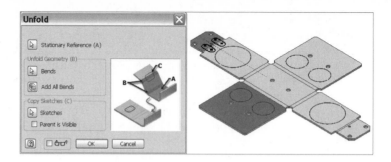

FIGURE 6.23
Unfolded model
with sketch

You may have noticed that there was an option to turn off the visibility of the parent sketch in the Unfold tool as well. Most likely that is the way you would handle copied sketches, but in this case you've been instructed to do this manually to observe the way the sketches are copied.

9. Next, click the Cut button in the Modify panel.

10. Select the two oblong profiles in the copied sketch, and click OK.

11. Select the Model tab, and click Extrude.

12. Select the two oblong profiles in the copied sketch.

13. Click the fly-out arrow in the Distance input box and choose List Parameters, and then select Thickness from the list.

14. Click the Symmetric button so that the extrusion will extend equally both directions from the sketch plane, and then click OK.

15. Expand the Unfold1 feature in the browser and right-click on `Sketch12:Copy` and choose Visibility to turn off the sketch.

16. Select the Sheet Metal tab, and click Refold in the Modify panel.

17. Select the yellow face on the part.

18. Click the Add All Bends button to automatically select all the bends. Then click OK.

Note that the model is in a different position than it was before the unfold action since the yellow face was kept stationary during the refold. If you drag the End-of-Folded marker above the Unfold feature, the model will be in its original position.

Unfolding and Refolding Contour Rolls Features

You can also Unfold or Refold a contour roll. If the tools detect that the part is a contour roll, work planes are displayed on each end face. Since a flat reference face is required, you can select one of the work planes and then unfold the contour roll, as shown in Figure 6.24.

PROJECT FLAT PATTERN

CERT OBJECTIVE

A well-hidden segment of sheet metal–specific functionality is a special version of sketch projection called Project Flat Pattern (nested at the end of the sketch projection fly-out). Project Flat Pattern is available from the folded model environment and is utilized to include the projected edges of the flattened sheet-metal component, oriented to the sketch plane that is active.

FIGURE 6.24

Unfolding a
contour roll

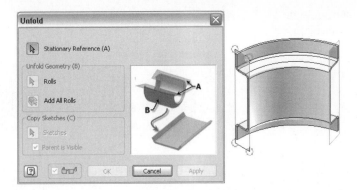

This option is very powerful when combined with the Cut Across Bend option because it allows you to create parametric dimensions and constrained relationships from the perspective of the flattened sheet. When utilizing the Project Flat Pattern option, it isn't necessary to select every face; just pick the ones at the extremities (ensuring that they're on the same flattened side of the part as your sketch), and all the connecting planar faces and bends will automatically be included.

In the following steps you'll use the Project Flat Pattern tool to place sketch entities as they would be on the flat pattern. You'll then use the Cut Across Bends option of the Cut tool to create the features in place on this rather extreme example of a bent sheet metal part:

1. Click the Get Started tab, and choose Open.

2. Browse for the file named mi_6a_021.ipt located in the Chapter 6 directory of the Mastering Inventor 2011 folder, and click Open.

3. Select the orange face and create a new 2D sketch on it.

4. Click the drop-down arrow next to the Project Geometry button and select Project Flat Pattern from the drop-down menu. See Figure 6.25 for reference.

5. Select one of the yellow faces to project the chain of faces between it and the orange face into the sketch, then select the other yellow face to complete both sides.

6. Next try and select the blue faces to project into the sketch, and you'll note that nothing happens.

This is because the blue faces are actually opposite the original orange face when this part is flattened out. You could select the underside of the blue faces to include them into the sketch, but in this case you can just use the green faces.

7. Select the green faces to project the remainder of the flat pattern into the sketch. Keep in mind that you really only need to project the faces you plan to use in the sketch, but for this example you've been instructed to select them all.

8. Next add three circles to the sketch. Two of the circles are to be placed at the center points of the projected yellow faces, and will be **50 mm** diameters, and the third circle will be **25 mm** in diameter and is to be placed in line with the center of the part and **375 mm** off the tip of the orange face. Figure 6.25 shows the completed sketch.

FIGURE 6.25
Adding geometry to a projected flat pattern sketch

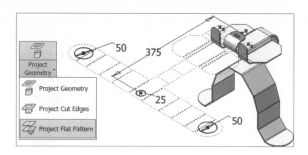

9. Click the Finish Sketch button when the sketch is complete, and then select the Cut tool from the Modify panel.

10. Select all three of the circles in for the Profile selection.

11. Select the Cut Across Bend check box, and then click OK.

The result is the circular cuts are placed on the folded model in accordance with their position in the flat pattern. This ability to layout features in the flat pattern and then cut them across existing bends is a subtle but very powerful tool. Keep in mind, too, that the projected flat pattern is fully associative and will update along with changes made to the features from which it was created. You can close this file without saving changes and continue on to the next section.

Using Sheet-Metal Templates and Rules

Inventor offers the ability to create sheet-metal rules that can be stored in the Inventor style library. The style library makes sheet-metal definition information more manageable, reusable, and ultimately more powerful than simply using a template file to manage sheet metal styles; however, using sheet-metal styles and templates to manage material and unfolding setups are both supported.

What Are Sheet-Metal Rules?

Sheet-metal parts of a certain material and thickness often share bend, corner, and gap parameters. The unfold, bend, and corner settings as well as representation of punch features in the flat pattern and the bending angle or open angle option when the part is shown in the flat pattern all make up a sheet-metal rule. For instance you might have a sheet-metal rule called 3 mm Galvanized Steel. In this rule the material would be set to galvanized steel, the thickness to 3 mm, and the bend, corner, punch representation, and flat pattern bend angle settings would be configured to output those features consistently.

When a new part is created you can select the predefined sheet-metal rule and the part will follow the settings outlined within it. When a new feature such as a flange is added, the bend and corner options defined in the rule are automatically used to define it. If a setting such as a corner relief needs to deviate from the rule, it can be modified in the feature as needed. If the part is changed to use a different sheet-metal rule, the overridden settings honor the overrides, and all others update to match the rule settings.

Creating a Sheet-Metal Rule

Sheet metal rules are created and accessed in one of two ways. You can go to the Manage tab and click the Styles Editor button, or you can click the Sheet Metal Defaults button found on the sheet-metal tab. The Sheet Metal Defaults dialog allows you to specify the sheet-metal rule, and whether to use the thickness, material style, and Unfold Rules defined in the sheet-metal rule or to override them. To create or edit a sheet-metal rule click the Edit Sheet Metal Rule button (looks like a pencil), and you will be taken to the Styles and Standards Editor. Figure 6.26 shows the sheet-metal rule options in the Styles and Standards Editor.

FIGURE 6.26
Style And Standard Editor dialog box, Sheet Metal Rule page displaying active rule

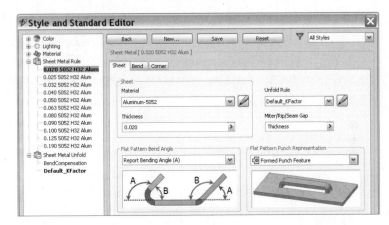

Follow these general rules to create a new rule:

1. Select an existing rule and click the New button at the top of the screen.

2. Enter a name for the new rule.

3. Set the Sheet Material and Thickness.

4. Set an Unfold Rule to use.

5. Set the Gap thickness to use. You can set this to Thickness so that it will update to match the sheet thickness, or set it to a fixed value.

6. Set the Bend Angle to either bending angle or opening angle.

7. Set the Flat Pattern Punch Representation style.

8. Click the Bend tab and set the bend options.

9. Click the Corner tab and set the corner options.

10. Click the Save button along the top of the Style and Standard Editor dialog box. The rule is now saved in the current part file.

11. Optionally right-click on the new Unfold Rule name in the left-hand list and choose Save to Style Library to write the new Unfold Rule to the external style library XML file.

12. Click Done to exit the Style and Standard Editor dialog box.

BEND AND CORNER QUICK REFERENCES IN THE HELP FILES

Autodesk has done a good job of hiding the help references for many of the sheet metal features. However once you find them they are very helpful in determining what these options adjust. Once found you can create a Favorites link so they are more accessible. Here are a couple you might want to add to your favorites:

Sheet Metal Bend Options: Press F1 to bring up the help pages. Go to the Contents tab of the help. Expand the tree to find Autodesk Inventor, Parts, Sheet Metal Parts, Sheet Metal Features, Faces, and then click the Quick Reference tab in the right-hand pane. Select Sheet Metal Bend Options.

Sheet Metal Corner Options: Press F1 to bring up the help pages. Go to the Contents tab of the help. Expand the tree to find Autodesk Inventor, Parts, Sheet Metal Parts, Sheet Metal Features, Corner Seams, and then click the Quick Reference tab in the right-hand pane. Select Sheet Metal Corner Options.

To add them to the favorites, click the Favorites tab and click Add in the left-hand pane, while viewing the page. Once added you can rename them via the right-click menu.

SHEET-METAL RULES VS. SHEET-METAL STYLES

Sheet-metal rules are set up using the Style and Standard Editor. Initially the rules are created in a part file as a local style, meaning they exist in that part file only. If you save the part file as a template file, then all of your new parts will contain the sheet-metal rule. In addition to using templates to mange sheet-metal rules you can add the rules to the Styles Library. Style Libraries are XML files that are stored externally to the part files, and therefore can be used by newly created parts or existing parts. You save a rule to a library by right-clicking on the rule in the Style and Standard Editor and selecting Save to Style Library (assuming your project (.ipj) file is set up to use a Style Library).

UNFOLD RULES

Whenever you fold a sheet-metal part on the shop floor, some material deformation occurs at the bend location. To the outside of the bend the material stretches and to the inside of the bend the material is compressed. In order to calculate this deformation for each bend Inventor uses *Sheet-Metal Unfold Rules*. Sheet metal Unfold Rules control the method of unfolding used to create the flat pattern for a folded sheet-metal part. You can create Unfold Rules using a *K-factor* or a *Bend Table*.

K-Factors

K-factors define the theoretical percentage of the material thickness where a folded part is neutral and neither expands or contracts. The reason that this surface is referred to as the *neutral* surface is that it defines a measurable position within the bend that has the same length value in the folded and unfolded states. For instance if your material is 10 mm thick and you use a K-factor of 0.44, bends and folds are calculated so that deformation of the bend takes place at 4.4 mm (or 44% of the material thickness). Unfolding with a K-factor is accomplished by determining the bend allowance (the amount of material required to produce a bend) for a given bend by using the sheet thickness, the bend angle, the inner bend radius, and a K-factor value. The

K-factor you use will depend on numerous factors, including material, thickness, and tooling. Most likely, you will need to perform a number of test bends on a specific press brake to determine the ideal K-factor for you.

Determining the developed flat pattern length using a K-factor uses the following equation:

Total Length = Leg 1 + Leg 2 + Bend Allowance

Where the bend allowance is calculated using:

BA= Pi (A / 180) (R+K × T)

- ◆ BA = bend allowance
- ◆ R = inside bend radius
- ◆ K = K-factor
- ◆ T = material thickness
- ◆ A = bend angle in degrees

Figure 6.27 shows a basic bend.

FIGURE 6.27
Basic bend
references

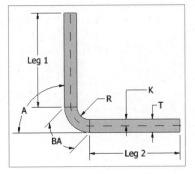

CUSTOM UNFOLD EQUATIONS

In addition to K-factors Bend Tables you can created custom unfold equations to use as an unfold method. You can find more information concerning custom unfold equations by going to the Index tab of the help file searching the keyword *Unfolding* and then selecting *Sheet metal equations* from the list.

To create an Unfold Rule to use a K-factor follow these general steps:

1. Click Manage tab and select the Styles Editor button to open the Style and Standard Editor dialog box.

2. Click the plus sign to the left of the Sheet Metal Unfold Rule node in the left-hand pane of the Style and Standard Editor dialog box to display the existing Unfold Rules.

3. Click the existing default rule to serve as the template for the new rule.

4. Click the New button along the top of the Style and Standard Editor dialog box.

5. Enter the name of the new sheet metal Unfold Rule, and click OK.

6. Ensure the unfold method is set to Linear.

7. Enter a new K-factor value.

8. Click the Save button along the top of the Style and Standard Editor dialog box. The rule is now saved in the current part file.

9. Optionally right-click on the new Unfold Rule name in the left-hand list and choose Save to Style Library to write the new Unfold Rule to the external style library XML file.

10. Click Done to exit the Style and Standard Editor dialog box.

Bend Tables

An alternative to using K-factors is to create a Bend Table. Bend Tables are the most accurate method of unfolding as they created by taking measurements of actual bent test parts of the exact material and thickness made on the shop floor. In order to create a Bend Table in Inventor you must first gather accurate bend information by creating bend tests. The granularity of the experimental values is up to you. It could be based upon 15-degree increments or perhaps 0.5-degree increments; it depends on how much experimental data you have.

Typically a number of test blanks are cut from a given material and thickness and then bent to the most common angles and radii used. By measuring the folded sample using virtual sharp locations, the values obtained will inherently be too large. The overmeasurement of the test fold sample needs to be compensated for by deducting an amount of length. By subtracting your combined measurements from the initial measurement of the sample taken prior to folding, you will be able to determine the value of excessive length (overmeasurement); this is what gets entered into the Bend Table and is where the method name *bend deduction* comes from. Bends are then calculated as:

Total Length = Leg 1 + Leg 2 – Bend Deduction

You can set up a test Bend Table as described in the following steps:

1. Click the Get Started tab, and choose Open.

2. Browse for the file named mi_6a_022.ipt located in the Chapter 6 directory of the Mastering Inventor 2011 folder, and click Open.

3. From the Sheet Metal tab select Sheet Metal Defaults.

4. Click the Edit button for Unfold Rule (looks like a pencil).

5. In the Styles and Standard Editor expand the Sheet Metal Unfold node from the list on the left (if not already), select Default_KFactor and then click the New button at the top. This creates a new Unfold Rule based from the existing one.

6. Enter **Mastering Bend Table** for the name and click OK.

7. Change the Unfold Method drop-down box to Bend Table.

8. Set the Linear Unit to millimeter (mm) to match the units of this part file.

9. Click the Click Here To Add row in the Thickness box, and enter **2.00**, for 2 millimeters.

10. Enter **30** into the left-most cell of the table to define the angle at 30 degrees.

11. Enter **1.0** into the top-most cell to define the bend radius at 1 mm.

12. Enter **0.5** into the cell to the right of the angle cell and just under the bend radius cell. This is the bend deduction (in this case 0.5 is a hypothetical value).

13. Next add another bend angle row by clicking on the cell containing 30 and choosing Insert Row.

14. Enter **45** for the angle and **0.6** for the bend deduction.

15. Next add another bend radius column by clicking on the cell containing 1.000000 and choosing Insert Column.

16. Enter **2.0** in the column header for the bend radius and then enter **0.55** for the 30 degree row and **0.65** for the 45 degree row.

17. Add a third row of **60** degrees with a **0.70** and a **0.75** bend deduction in the 1.000000 degree and 2.000000 degree columns, respectively.

18. Add a third column of **3.0** mm with **0.60**, **0.70**, and **0.80** for the 30, 45 and 60 degree rows, respectively.

19. Bends greater than 90 deg and bends less than 90 deg are handled differently, so in this case you want to set the Angle Reference radio button to use the Bending Angle Reference (A) option. This allows the table to match the existing part. If you wanted to use the Open Angle Reference (B) your table angles would need to be 150, 135, and 120.

20. Click Save and then Done to finish the Bend Table.

21. In the Sheet Metal Defaults dialog box choose **Mastering Bend Table** from the Unfold Rule drop-down box, to make it the active Unfold Rule for this part, and then click OK.

BENDING ANGLE AND OPEN ANGLE REFERENCES

Originally the Inventor Bend Table was designed to reference an "open angle" datum structure (which is still default) for measuring bends. However, Inventor's sheet-metal features all use a "bending angle" datum structure to create bent features. As a means to bridge this disparity in measurement convention, the Bend Angle option at the top of the Bend Table interface allows you to declare in which structure your values were measured; Inventor will use this option to convert the values internally if necessary. Keep in mind, the angular values are not altered within the table when this option is changed.

As you can see the process of creating a Bend Table in Inventor is a straightforward endeavor. Typically the real work is in creating the test blanks and bends to gather the information to put into the table.

Here are a few more things to know about creating Bend Tables:

♦ Note that you can reorder rows and columns by clicking on the header cell and dragging them into place.

♦ You can also right-click on the top left-most cell and choose Paste Table to paste in a table copied from an Excel spreadsheet. Likewise you can choose Copy Table to copy the table into Excel.

♦ You can add a Bend Table for each thickness required by clicking the Click To Add row in the Thickness box.

♦ If the bend deduction is outside of the values defined in the table, Inventor uses the Backup K-factor. You can imagine this like an insurance plan that allows you to obtain a flat pattern even if your Bend Table doesn't define what deduction to use for smaller or large combinations of bend angle and radius.

♦ For combinations that fall within the table boundaries but not exactly at angle/radius coordinate values, Inventor uses linear approximation to derive a value; depending on the change in bend compensation between steps in the table, you can achieve better results with smaller angle increments.

♦ You can specify a Table Tolerance to allow Inventor to include thicknesses, radii, and angles that are within the specified tolerance. For example if the angle tolerance is 0.004 and an bend angle measures 30.002, Inventor would use the 45 degree row in your table to calculate the deduction.

To test the Bend Table you can examine the flat pattern, where a sketch has been placed to display the flat pattern length. Because the part file has a current thickness of 2 mm, a bend angle of 60 degrees and a bend radius of 2 mm the bend deduction indexed from the Bend Table will be 0.75 mm, as shown in Figure 6.28.

FIGURE 6.28
The sample
Bend Table

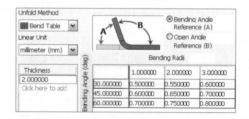

In this case then the bend deduction is calculated as follows:

Leg 1 + Leg 2 - Bend Deduction = Total Flat Patten Length

25mm + 25mm - 0.75 mm = 49.25 mm

If you were to change the angle to 45 degrees and check the flat pattern again, and you would expect to see:

25mm + 25mm - 0.65 mm = 49.35 mm

What would happen if you were to set the angle to 37.5 degrees which is halfway between 30 and 45 degrees? Because the Bend Table has no entry for 37.5 degrees Inventor uses a linear extrapolation of the bend deductions of 0.55 mm for 30 degrees and 0.65 mm for 45 degrees and arrives at the halfway point of 0.60 mm for 37.5 degrees. If you check the flat pattern you will expect to see:

25mm + 25mm − 0.60 mm = 49.4 mm

ABOUT K-FACTORS AND BEND TABLES

The most common question asked about flat patterns concerns the use of K-factors and Bend Tables. Which to use depends upon your manufacturing processes and the capabilities of your machines. These are the key questions to ask when determining which is right for you:

- Do you outsource your sheet-metal manufacturing?

- How accurate do your parts need to be?

Whether you build the parts in-house or you outsource them, you should be able to get the data from the shop. If your sheet-metal shop is unsophisticated, they may use rules of thumb to determine the bend allowance. In that case, you need to work with them to determine whether a K-factor or a Bend Table is the best solution. One of the advantages of using sheet-metal rules is that you can create rules for each shop. For example, if you generally use your shop but you outsource when you are busy, you can select the rule for the other shop, and the flat pattern will automatically update.

In general, K-factors are used for parts with large tolerances. Since the K-factor is an approximation, the actual value will vary depending on the machine. For parts with very tight tolerances, you need to know specific compensation values for the bend radius and angle for the machine, material type, and thickness. Depending on the material, you might need different values depending on the grain direction. For extremely tight tolerances, you might need different values for each shipment of material. The good news is that the use of sheet-metal rules pushes all of this work onto the manufacturing department. Since the flat pattern and drawings update automatically, the shop can simply select the proper rule, update the model and drawing, and have the correct information.

Bend Compensation

In addition to K-factors and Bend Tables you have the ability to enter an expression for a *Bend Compensation*. Instead of entering values for specific bend angles and using linear interpolation between the values, you can enter ranges of bend angles that use an expression to determine the proper compensation within that range. To access the Bend Compensation settings, go to the Manage tab, click the Style Editor button, and then expand the Sheet Metal Unfold node in the left pane. Finally, select BendCompensation. Figure 6.29 shows the BendCompensation settings.

Working with Styles and Templates

If your project location is set to use the style library, then it is important to understand what has been defined within your template and what has been stored within the style library. As an example, imagine if you were to have a sheet-metal rule named MyRule1 with the Thickness value equal to 0.2 mm stored only locally in your template file and a another sheet-metal rule also named MyRule1 but with the Thickness value equal to 0.5mm stored in your style library. Each time you start a new design from the template referencing MyRule1, you will see a Thickness value of 0.5mm being applied.

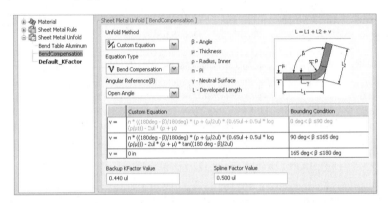

FIGURE 6.29
BendCompensation settings

The reason for this is that the style library is the "published" source of your standards; its definition will always win. After saving your design, if you want to make changes to the Thickness value of MyRule1, you can apply the changes without fear that they might be automatically overwritten, because this occurs only when creating a new document using the template. (As a side note, if you did want to overwrite the local/document definition with the style library's definition, right-clicking an existing rule will present a context menu from which you can select Update Style, which will manually refresh the rule's definition in the document.)

It is a good practice when using the style library to have perhaps a single sheet-metal rule embedded in your template file. Once you know what sheet-metal rule you want to apply to your model, selecting it either in the Style And Standard Editor dialog box or in the Sheet Metal Defaults dialog box will automatically draw the information into the active document. This process keeps extraneous information out of your document, providing a smaller footprint, and helps reduce the chance of style information mismatch. If you have a template file that has numerous sheet-metal rules stored within it, after publishing them to the style library, you can use the purge functionality with the Style Management Wizard to remove them.

Authoring and Reusing Punches

The most common method to cost effectively cut or deform sheet metal is by using a punch machine. Since this process is so fundamental to the sheet-metal manufacturing environment, Inventor sheet metal contains a special Punch tool feature. Inventor Punch tools are a specialized subtype of iFeatures that embody unique capabilities and a simplified placement process.

Exploring Punches and iFeatures

The process of creating a punch is almost identical to creating a standard iFeature, but you need to be aware of a few key differences. Different from regular iFeatures, punches require the inclusion of a sketch center point in the insertion sketch; this is the highest-level sketch consumed by a feature that you are including in the published punch feature. The iFeature extraction dialog box actually checks for the inclusion of this sketch point to ensure you don't go to the trouble of publishing punches that cannot be placed. After you have created your Punch tool geometry, go to the Manage tab, and click Extract iFeature to begin the publishing process. Located at the top of the Extract iFeature dialog box is a type group that contains a Standard iFeature option and a special subtype Sheet Metal Punch iFeature option. Select the Sheet Metal Punch option when creating a punch iFeature.

The vast majority of the options in the iFeature extraction dialog box are generic to standard iFeatures and punches, but once you have selected the punch subtype option, you will see that the Manufacturing and Depth fields become enabled. Punch tools have the ability to store additional manufacturing information that is introduced during the creation process. The Punch ID field is where you can store a string that represents the Punch tool number.

The simplified representation selection control allows you to select a 2D sketch representation or symbol that you want to display in the flat pattern instead of the actual formed shape. The sketch must also contain a center mark so that it can be oriented with the punch's insertion center mark. The Punch Depth field is where you can enter a value that reflects the intended throw depth of your tool into the sheet face. For example, when creating a dimple or a half shear, you need to specifically call out a Punch tool depth to ensure that the formed feature turns out exactly as you expect. The Punch Depth field allows you to enter a value or even a parametric expression that specifies this tooling depth.

REFERENCING PARAMETERS

If you want to create a parametric expression that references a parameter, that parameter must be consumed within the Punch tool's definition. A good example of such a parameter is Thickness.

Since published Punch tools are in fact just special versions of iFeatures, they are saved with `.ide` file extensions and can be opened within Inventor for edit. Once the Punch tool is opened, utilize the Edit iFeature tool to alter embedded information or add information that was not originally included. This capability could enable you to add Punch tool numbers as well as punch depth information to Punch tools that had been published prior to the availability of these data sources.

Creating Successful Punches

When deciding how to create the geometry and parametric relationships for your punch, you may want to follow a few guidelines to improve the potential for successful authoring, ease of placement, and the computational result. Creating successful punches (and iFeatures) takes a little longer than regular modeling since you're trying to anticipate conditions in which your tooling will be placed and establishing expectations of how it will react. The following sections touch on two areas that are commonly the root of punch problems.

AVOIDING WORK GEOMETRY

Although it's a common practice to use work geometry to model features, this practice is never a good idea when creating punches (or iFeatures). The most problematic type of work geometry is the work plane, which has a defined normal direction that cannot be robustly persisted or recovered within the authored punch. Work planes are often ideal when modeling your punch tooling because you require a midplane in order to sketch a uniform cross section that can be swept. Sometimes a careful progression of additional features can help you compensate for this work plane requirement.

For example, in the process of creating a dimple, you might need to cut out material and then sweep a deformed cross section in its place. Instead of cutting out the entire round, cut out only half of the profile so that a planar detail face is created in the center. You can sketch your dimple cross section upon the detail face before cutting away the remaining half round. The dimple can be finished by sweeping the profile around the original cut profile. During this process, it's critical to remember that any projections or sketch references must exclusively be made to the top face, or unintentional orientation references might be inferred. This solution didn't require a work plane but utilized the same references that you might have obtained by creating one. Since all the features were based on the geometry originally defined from the punch's insertion face, the computation is stable.

Setting the Parameters Within Your Punch

Punch features (and iFeatures) consume parameters that can be utilized to vary the size of the families of punches or help adapt your punch to different conditions. Sheet metal in particular has a number of reference parameters that are guaranteed to be in any sheet-metal document since the sheet-metal rule ensures their creation. These parameters can be either useful or detrimental, depending on how you utilize them. For example, when we made the round cut while creating the dimple, we utilized the parameter Thickness to define its cut depth. In that case, this was a good idea since you would want the cut depth to be able to accommodate a variety of sheet thicknesses for which it might be placed upon in the future.

Defining the various radii in the dimple cross-section sketch is a very different situation. If you reference a sheet-metal parameter when creating the cross section, it might change significantly when utilizing different sheet-metal rules with a variety of sheet thicknesses. The tool may fail, since the value might change in unexpected ways that cannot be computed. Although tooling generally has well-known radius values, sometimes it seems convenient to define these values as a proportion of a parameter. Resist this practice, and choose all parameter values carefully.

Using Alternate Representations

Punch tools have a unique ability to change between formed and 2D representations in the flat pattern; this capability is enabled by a technology called *alternate punch representations*. To enable the alternate representation functionality, during the punch-authoring process you are afforded the opportunity to select a 2D sketch that depicts a representation you desire. The sketch geometry can be something similar to the formed geometry; it can be constructed of the projected edges of the formed geometry (this representation can change if it interacts with other features), or it can be a simple sketch that represents the Punch tool symbolically. To orient the 2D representation sketch to the insertion sketch of the Punch tool, you must insert a single center mark. You can in fact use the same sketch for both inserting the Punch tool and defining the alternate representation.

Regardless of whether the Punch tool represents removed or deformed material, the 2D alternate representation (2D Sketch, 2D Sketch And Center Mark, and Center Mark Only) can be displayed on the flat pattern in place of the actual punch, as shown in Figure 6.30.

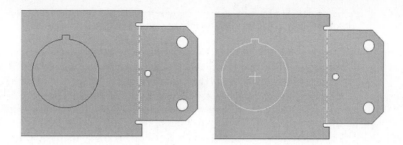

To change the punch representation in a flat pattern, first ensure that you have the flat pattern set active for edits (right-click the Flat Pattern node and select Edit Flat Pattern), and then right-click the Flat Pattern browser node and choose Edit Flat Pattern Definition. Click the Punch Representation tab, and then choose the representation type from the drop-down. You may need to use the ViewCube to view the opposite side of the flat to see the 2D representation depending upon the specifics of how your punch was placed relative to your default orientation.

You can replace the formed punch with the simplified representation as long as it does not interfere with the outer contour/profile of the flat pattern. If the punch does intersect the flat pattern outer contour and a 2D alternate representation is selected, you will be prompted with a notification that will alert you to the fact that these punches could not be replaced. The punch alternate representation is set within the active sheet-metal rule within the options on the Sheet tab. The punch representation can also be overridden from within the flat pattern environment using the Flat Pattern Definition dialog box's Punch Representation tab controls.

Placing Your Punch

The process of applying a published Punch tool to your sheet-metal design is fairly straightforward. In fact, the reason why Punch tools are special versions of iFeatures instead of standard iFeatures is to make the placement process faster and more reliable. As discussed in the previous section, when authoring a Punch tool, the first sketch-based feature referenced to create the Punch tool needs to contain a single sketched center mark. To place a Punch tool, another sketched center mark is all that is needed. To place a Punch tool, follow these general steps:

1. Create a 2D sketch containing a sketched center mark.

2. Launch the Punch tool from the Modify panel of the Sheet Metal tab.

3. Once the Punch Tool Directory dialog box appears, select a Punch tool file from the catalog list.

4. Once you've selected the tool, the interface will change to the Punch Tool dialog box and display options for changing the punch, geometry, and size (if available within the punch definition); select Geometry.

5. On the Geometry tab, enter an angle to rotate the Punch tool preview.

6. Click Finish to create the iFeature.

ADDITIONAL INPUTS WHEN PLACING A PUNCH

If you run into a situation in which your punch needs additional geometric inputs to orient properly, you should know that Punch tools can be authored with these additional inputs predefined. The inputs will be automatically captured during the authoring process, which may or may not be your intention, and displayed on the Geometry tab during placement.

Patterning Your Punch

You can use a few methods to pattern punches within a sheet-metal design. Since a sketched center mark (center point) is required for inserting the punch, you can create an array of center marks within a sketch to apply numerous punches at the same time. When you launch the Punch tool, it will attempt to automatically select all visible center marks in your sketch as long as only one sketch is visible. This method also allows you to utilize the Geometry tab, which "centers" selection control to either add center marks that were not participating or deselect center marks that you do not want a punch placed at, as shown in Figure 6.31. One powerful capability of patterned sketch center marks is the creation of irregular patterns that are produced by deselecting specific center marks in symmetric array. The sketched pattern method works, but it is limited to patterning within a single plane (2D sketch plane) and has some performance impacts when patterning large numbers of punches.

FIGURE 6.31
Sample back bracket folded model with irregular punch pattern created using center mark deselection of a symmetric sketch array

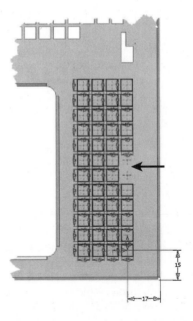

The second method for patterning punches is to insert a single punch feature and then use the rectangular or circular patterning features to create additional punch instances. Although the definition process is similar, you can create nonplanar arrays and achieve additional performance enhancements. When you click the >> button of the Rectangular Pattern and Circular Pattern dialog boxes, an option called Optimize is available. Whenever you are trying to pattern large numbers of punches, features, or iFeatures, this option should be enabled to improve performance. Irregular punch patterns can also be produced using this method but must be computed as a symmetric array first, and then individual child occurrences can be suppressed using the feature browser.

Working with the Flat Pattern

CERT OBJECTIVE

The flat pattern derived from the folded model ties the design to the manufacturing environment. Within Inventor, the flat pattern model is an actual flattened version of the folded model versus a sheet that has been pieced together and thickened. Numerous tools, utilities, and data sources have been provided to enable the flat pattern to suit your individual manufacturing and documentation needs.

The flat pattern contains a wealth of manufacturing information that is stored progressively during the design process. Punch and bend information is stored within the flat pattern model specifically so that customers working with drawings, customers working with the API, or those who want to translate the flat pattern to a different file version can control all their options in a common location; the flat pattern is commonly referred to as the *jump-off point* for all downstream consumers.

The following sections detail these capabilities and tools.

Exploring the Flat Pattern Edit Features

The flat pattern environment has its own panel bar containing a customized set of modeling tools drawn from the Part Features panel bar and the Sheet Metal Features panel bar. The flat pattern tools are referred to as *flat pattern edit features*, because they are intended to apply small alterations to the flat pattern model instead of large-scale modeling. Flat pattern edit features are applied only to the flat pattern, whereas folded model features are applied first to the folded model and then carried over to the flat pattern. The flat pattern can be imagined as a derivative of the folded model, establishing a parent-child relationship (flat pattern edit features are not reflected in the folded model). There are many situations in which the generated flat pattern is not exactly what you need for manufacturing; flat pattern edit features are ideal for making small associative tweaks that previously required exporting the flat pattern to an external (disassociated) file.

Adding Manufacturing Information to the Flat Pattern

There are two features specifically designed to allow you to add manufacturing information to the flat pattern. The Bend Order Annotation tool enables you to specify the order in which bends are created. The Cosmetic Centerlines tool marks bend locations, such as cross brakes, where there is mild deformation.

Bend Order Annotation   When you click the Bend Order Annotation icon in the Manage panel, the bends are automatically numbered. The context menu has two options for overriding the numbering: Directed Reorder and Sequential Reorder. Directed Reorder automatically renumbers any bends between two selected bend number glyphs. Sequential Reorder renumbers bends as you pick them. You can also renumber individual bends by double-clicking the number glyph. This allows you to renumber a few bends in a complex flat pattern. Inventor will automatically renumber the remaining bends in a flat pattern, but any bend numbers that are already overridden will not update. As a result, you need to renumber the largest series of bends first and then manually renumber any remaining bends.

Cosmetic Centerlines Cosmetic Centerlines capture bend information in the flat pattern without changing the model. After you create a sketch with the desired bend locations, click the Cosmetic Centerline icon in the Create panel. You can select the sketched lines and edit the bend information.

Using the Flat Pattern Definition Dialog Box

You can manipulate the flat pattern model by using a tool called Edit Flat Pattern Definition, which is available by right-clicking anywhere in the graphics area and selecting Edit Flat Pattern Definition. The Flat Pattern Definition dialog box allows you to control a number of aspects pertaining to the flat pattern's orientation and the information stored within it.

The first tab of the Flat Pattern Definition dialog box relates to the flat pattern orientation. The selection control allows you to select either an edge or two points to define the horizontal or vertical orientation. The orientation of the flat pattern is very important, because the implied x-axis is utilized to calculate the rotational angle of Punch tools that have been applied to the model. By orienting the flat pattern to your specific punch equipment, the required tool rotation angle should be directly available from your flat pattern.

Since the flat pattern base face is going to be either the face already selected or the backside, the control of the base face has been simplified to a "flip" option. Base face definition is critical because it establishes a directional reference for bends and punch tooling as well as an association with the Front navigation tool view and the default Drawing Manager view.

The second tab is the Punch Representation tab, which allows you to override the representation setting in the sheet-metal document without having to edit the active sheet-metal rule.

The third tab is the Bend Angle tab, which allows you to declare how bend angles should be reported to the API and Drawing Manager. As an example, this means that by changing the Bend Angle option to an open angle, Drawing Manager annotations of your flattened bends will recover the complementary angle of the bending angle.

Manufacturing Your Flat Pattern

There is a very close association between sheet-metal design and manufacturing, and the flat pattern solution within Inventor embraces this relationship. Inventor generically supports the ability to translate models to a variety of file formats, but Inventor sheet metal actually has its own utility to support the translation to .sat, .dwg, and .dxf formats. After selecting the Flat Pattern browser node, you can right-click and select Save Copy As; this launches the Flat Pattern Translation dialog box. For .sat files, a simple option defining the file version will be presented. For .dwg and .dxf file formats, an extensive list of options and file-processing capabilities are made available to you.

Within the Flat Pattern Translation dialog box, you will find standard options for file type, but there is also a Layer tab that supports layer naming and visibility control. The last tab is the Geometry tab, which allows you to decide whether you want to apply a variety of manufacturing-specific options to the translation. The first of these options is for spline simplification, because many CNC profile manufacturing centers cannot leverage splines and are restricted to arcs and lines.

This utility allows you to apply faceting rules to break the outer contour of flat patterns into linear segments. The second options group relates to the post-processing of the translated file, allowing you to force the 2D result into positive coordinate space and to merge interior and outer contours into polylines, which may be critical for a path-based tool. Sometimes you'll need additional tool path manufacturing information in your `.dxf`/`.dwg` output. For this, the flat pattern has the ability to export unconsumed sketches created on the flat pattern. Only visible sketches are exported, and a layer called IV_UNCONSUMED_SKETCHES was added to support the collection of these sketches.

Using Sheet-Metal iPart Factories

iParts are part configurations or part families that allow you to create a base part and then add a table to it. Once the table is added the part features can be suppressed or configured to create a family of parts based on the original. The configured part is referred to as an iPart factory, and the individual configurations are called members. Sheet metal iParts have a number of uses from creating variations of basic parts, to creating progressive die parts.

Consuming Sheet-Metal Rules

In the "Using Sheet-Metal Templates and Rules" section earlier in this chapter, we discussed a number of advantages related to the move from templates to the style library. An additional advantage that we didn't discuss was that this evolution also makes sheet-metal rules and Unfold Rules consumable by iPart factories. In a nutshell, this means configurations of sheet-metal parts can be differentiated exclusively by referencing different rules. So, from the perspective of the folded model, identical fit and function designs can be made with completely different manufacturing processes reflected per member file.

For example, a bracket could be designed and configured in basic mild steel or optionally in an upgraded stainless steel version. Sheet-metal configurations via iParts could be very beneficial and profitable to a company that deals in varieties of components that need to fit into the same space but utilize different materials and/or manufacturing processes. On the other front, the folded model might be identical for all members, but a different sheet-metal Unfold Rule could be used to accommodate different manufacturing locations of your component.

With the addition of flat pattern edit features and named flat pattern orientations being added to the iPart definition (the new Sheet Metal tab within an iPart author table), full support for sheet-metal manufacturing configurations can also be realized in Inventor. There has been a great deal of discussion about Autodesk's digital prototyping strategy within the CAD/CAE community, but the enhancements in Inventor with regard to sheet-metal configurations and manufacturing configurations really deliver on the promise of this concept.

Using Folded and Flat Members

We alluded to the next significant enhancement to sheet-metal iParts in the discussion of flat pattern edit features: flat pattern models are now included within member files. In the past, a single flat pattern was computed for the iPart factory, and changing the active folded member simply forced the flat pattern to be recomputed. Although this might not sound so bad from the perspective of the factory, once a folded member file is generated to disk, this limitation becomes apparent.

Before Inventor 2009, factory member files did not contain a flat pattern model, only the factory did. When you created a drawing of an iPart factory flat pattern, you were actually documenting the active factory member's flat pattern. This meant you would need to defer updates of your drawing so that you could ensure that when editing you had the correct folded member selected so as to not change the result of the flat pattern view. Since Inventor 2009, both the folded and flat pattern models are generated to disk, allowing you to create flat pattern documentation referencing the member file flat pattern instead of the factory.

For sheet-metal designers who already have iPart factories with sheet-metal member files on disk, a number of provisions have been added to help get the additional flat pattern body out to the instantiated member files. The first thing to remember is that Inventor migration has changed over the years to have minimal impact on files; this has been done to reduce the performance impact of opening a legacy file or files in a newer version of Inventor. This also means that aspects such as getting the newly available flat pattern information into an existing file will not be automatic.

There are a number of scenarios in which it is fundamentally detrimental to have these updates automatically push out, most notably for a situation in which Vault, Product Steam, or other PDM system is utilized for data management. The iPart factory member nodes support a context menu entry called Generate Files, as shown in Figure 6.32. This tool is intended to support the batch creation of member files on disk; it can also be used to force updates, such as the flat pattern, out to the member files already in existence. In addition, you can use a pull method versus a push method. If you open the iPart factory, execute the Rebuild All operation, and then save the rebuilt and migrated data, the member files when individually opened will see that they are out-of-date with the factory. Selecting the now-enabled Update button within the individual member file will then draw in the flat pattern information automatically.

FIGURE 6.32
Sheet-metal iPart factory example, displaying Generate Files for a selected member file

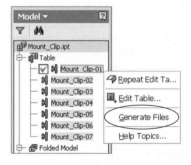

iParts for Fold Progression

If you have the need to show the order a part is created such as detailing progressive dies, you might want to explore the use of iParts and the unfold tool. Once a folded part is complete, you can convert it to an iPart and use the unfold tool to detail each step of the progression. In the iPart the unfold features can then be suppressed to show the part folding back up. Because each iPart member (in this case representing the same part in different stages) can be detailed on a drawing, you can quickly illustrate the progression of the blank flat to finished part.

Modeling with Non-Sheet-Metal Features

Although the sheet-metal feature set is extensive, sometimes using non-sheet-metal features can be helpful or possibly even required to accomplish your design. The challenge when using non-sheet-metal features is to honor the guiding principles of sheet-metal design so that the resulting component can be unfolded; in addition, you want to incorporate sheet-metal conditions so that the features are manufacturable and therefore cost effective.

Selecting Problematic Features

Although it's possible to design sheet-metal components using lofts, solid sweeps, and shells, these features can produce unpredictable and hard-to-control results. The Loft tool, unless highly restricted, produces doubly curved surfaces that cannot be unfolded properly. Although it's possible to utilize rails to control loft curvature, it's time-consuming and invariably frustrating. Solid sweeps are a measure better than lofts, but these too can create unintended doubly curved surfaces. The Shell tool can be used nine times out of ten to successfully create a legitimate sheet-metal feature, but the tenth time, if it doesn't work and it's not clear why, will be confounding. If you use the parameter Thickness to shell your component, you'll probably be in fairly good shape, but there are certain situations in which the Shell tool cannot assure uniform thickness after the shell. These situations are not always simple to predict.

Using Surface-Based Workflows

By far, the most successful non-sheet-metal feature workflows typically leverage a surface that is later thickened. The reason that these workflows are so successful is that it's often easier to ensure that the resulting model embodies sheet-metal conditions (the side faces are perpendicular to the top and bottom faces) since the part can be thickened normal to the surface. When constructing surfaces that will be thickened, the Extrude and Revolve tools are excellent choices because they have restricted directions in which features are created, which can help ensure that only cones, cylinders, and planes are created (these can be unfolded). The Sweep tool is possibly another good choice, but care needs to be taken to ensure that the profile and the sweep path do not contain any splines or ellipses that might prevent unfolding. For each of three previously mentioned features, the sketch profile geometry should ideally be limited to arcs and lines to help ensure the creation of unfoldable geometry. Another common surface-generating workflow is to use Derived Component, where you select the Body As Work Surface option when placing the derived component into the sheet-metal file. This workflow can be combined well with either a thicken feature or a sheet-metal face feature after creating projected sketches for each planar surface.

One of the biggest benefits of working with surfaces is that you can apply complicated alterations to the surface prior to thickening. Some of the most common features utilized to create cutting surfaces are Extrude, Revolve, and Sweep. The Split tool (and perhaps Delete Face) can be utilized to remove faces from the thickened surface selection. When using the Sweep tool, the Guide Surface Sweep option is ideal because the swept profile is rotated along the path to ensure that it remains normal to the guide surface. Sometimes a thickened sheet-metal component needs to be trimmed with a complicated profile. For these situations, a swept surface combined with the sculpt feature can result in a model that still has sheet-metal conditions.

Working with Imported Parts

The Inventor sheet-metal environment has been designed to work with imported geometry, because its solid unfolder is concerned with topology, not with features. This means that imported parts can be brought into Inventor and unfolded as well as modified with additional features. To be successful working with imported sheet-metal models, you must follow a few general guidelines.

Setting Yourself Up for Success

There are two main methods for importing parts into Inventor: the Open dialog box and the Import tool that's on the Insert panel of the Manage tab. If you are able to use Open (which is preferred), a standard part template is going to be utilized by default to embed initial styles and document options, so the first step will be to use the Convert To Sheet Metal tool to draw the sheet-metal subtype options and rules into the document. If you use the Import tool from within an empty sheet-metal document, the imported geometry will be in the form of a surface. To work with this geometry, you will need to thicken each surface, which can be a time-consuming process. It is recommended, when possible, to "open" imported parts so that a solid body can be recovered.

The next step you need to accomplish is the measurement of the sheet thickness of your imported model; once you have this value, you can match it with an appropriate sheet-metal rule (or create a new one). Matching the thickness can be as simple as taking a measurement from the sheet and overriding the Thickness value within the Sheet Metal Defaults dialog box with a simple copy and paste. Since the solid unfolder works with evaluated topology to facilitate the unfolding, the thickness of the actual part must match the thickness of the active sheet-metal rule exactly.

If the imported part contains portions that are not of uniform thickness, proper unfolding may not be possible; spend some time evaluating your imported model to ensure that it conforms to sheet-metal conditions. If your imported model contains faces defined by splines or ellipses, you are not going to be able to unfold your part. In these cases, removing these faces and replacing them with faces defined by tangent arcs may be an acceptable modification.

Converting Components

On the Environments tab is the Convert To Sheet Metal tool. The purpose of this tool is to take a component that has been designed with a regular part template and convert that document to a sheet-metal subtyped document. This means all the sheet-metal reference parameters and the default sheet-metal rule and Unfold Rule are automatically added to the document.

You can also convert a sheet-metal part back to a part document. Basically this deletes the flat pattern and disables the sheet-metal functionality, but the sheet-metal parameters are not deleted.

BE CAREFUL WHEN CONVERTING BACK TO A STANDARD PART

You should convert a sheet-metal part back to a standard part file only if the manufacturing process for a part has changed. Some people have gotten into the habit of using the convert tool to access the part-modeling tools. Using the convert tools to navigate back and forth can have undesirable effects. Most notably, it can delete your flat pattern and break associations with downstream documentation; therefore, use the convert tools sparingly.

Annotating Your Sheet Metal Design

The Drawing Manager environment contains several tools and functions specifically focused on helping you document your sheet-metal design. A quick overview of sheet-metal–specific tools might help you understand them a bit better.

Creating a View of Your Sheet-Metal Design

The first step in creating your documentation will be to choose which model file to reference, but sheet metal has the added requirement of deciding between a folded model and a flat pattern view, as shown in Figure 6.33. Once a sheet-metal model file is selected on the Component tab, a Sheet Metal View options group will appear immediately below the file's path information. The displayed options allow you to choose between creating a folded or flat pattern view and, in the case of a flat pattern, choose whether you want center marks to be recovered for any embedded Punch tools. The default view options will change based on your selection, because the flat pattern has a clear distinction between its top (default) face and its bottom (backside) face. The actual orientation of the 3D flat pattern defines what is a top and what is a bottom face. This also impacts bend orientation with respect to what is reported as up and what is reported as down. All punch angular information is based on the virtual x-axis previewed during flat pattern orientation.

FIGURE 6.33
Drawing Manager: Drawing View dialog box's Component tab with options displayed for sheet-metal view creation

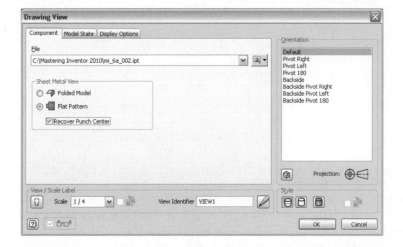

The Model State tab may also be of interest, because sheet-metal iPart members can be individually selected when a factory file is referenced, as shown in Figure 6.34. Choosing between a folded model and flat pattern is also necessary when creating a drawing view of the sheet-metal iPart member. If the member has not already been placed, selecting the member from the Drawing View dialog box will automatically create the file.

The last tab is the Display Options tab, which is important because it controls whether sheet-metal bend extents should be drawn in the view as well as controls other annotations such as work features and tangent edges, as shown in Figure 6.35.

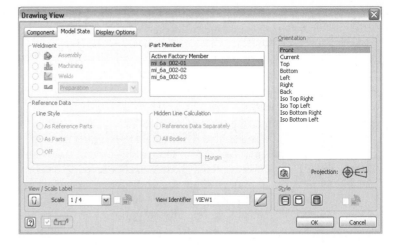

Adding Bend, Punch, and Flat Pattern Annotations

Once you've created the view of your sheet-metal component, you can switch to the drawing Annotate tab to complete the documentation of your design. The sheet-metal annotation tools within the Drawing Manager are specific to flat pattern views. You can add bend notes and punch notes, as shown in Figure 6.36. Bend notes allow you to recover bend angle, bend direction, bend radius, and K-factor (not on by default) for any bend centerline. The punch note allows you to select a formed punch, center mark, or 2D alternate punch representation in order to recover the punch angle, punch direction, punch ID, and punch depth (punch ID and depth need to be added to the Punch tool description when authored). When editing the punch note, you will also see a Quantity option that allows you to recover the number of instances of the same Punch tool in the view.

FIGURE 6.36
Drawing Annotate
tab with Punch
and Bend tools
displayed

You can utilize the General Table tool to create a Drawing Manager Bend Table (not to be confused with Bend Tables utilized for unfolding) that documents all the bends in a selected view. To create a Bend Table, follow these steps:

1. Select General from the Table panel of the Drawing Annotation tab.

2. Select an existing flat pattern view.

3. Decide whether the chosen columns are acceptable (bend direction, angle, and so on); if not, alter the selected columns.

4. Choose the Bend ID format, and enter a prefix if desired.

5. Click OK to create the Bend Table.

Punch table creation is a little different, because it has been incorporated within the preexisting Hole Table annotation tools. The reason that punch support was combined with hole tables is that you most likely used the Hole tool out of convenience, not necessarily to convey a manufacturing process. To make sure all of this tool-based information is consolidated together, an enhancement to hole tables was made. After invoking the Hole Table – View tool and selecting a flat pattern view, you will see that the standards in the toolbar have changed to reflect predefined hole table standards. Within this list (as shown in Figure 6.37) is an example standard for punch tables, which prevents you from having to first create a standard hole table and then editing it to add all the punch information columns.

FIGURE 6.37
Drawing Manager
active style toolbar
showing punch
table style preset

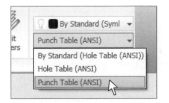

From within the Text tool, you can reference the sheet-metal flat pattern extent values by selecting a new Sheet Metal Properties option from the Type list, as shown in Figure 6.38. Once you've selected the Sheet Metal Properties type, the Property list will provide options for entering the flat pattern extents area, length, or width in the text box.

USE SHEET-METAL MANUFACTURING ANNOTATION EFFECTIVELY

You may have noticed that different toolmakers and machinists like to see different annotations. Although there are some definite right and wrong ways to annotate a part, there is a lot of gray area concerning this also, because there is no specific way to annotate the part "correctly." It is in these areas where you must talk to your fabricators and outside vendors to determine what information they'd like to see on the prints and to explain what type of annotation you plan to provide. Don't be afraid to ask the fabricators what information would make their job easier. As long as it does not impact your workflow dramatically, it might just save you some time and money on your parts.

FIGURE 6.38
Drawing Manager
Format Text dialog
box displaying
Sheet Metal Prop-
erties option for
flat pattern extents

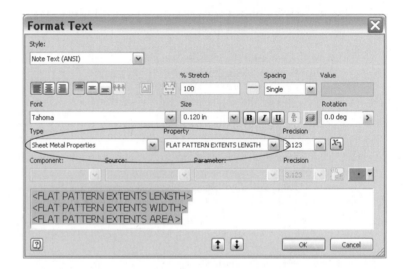

The last annotation tool that can interact with sheet-metal properties is the Parts List tool. To recover flat pattern length and width extents within the parts list, follow these steps:

1. From within your sheet-metal model, right-click on the file name node in the Model browser and choose iProperties.

2. Select the Custom tab and create a new custom iProperty named Length.

3. Ensure the type is set to Text.

4. Enter a value of = **<FLAT PATTERN LENGTH> cm**.

5. Repeat steps 2–4 for a custom iProperty named Width, entering a value of = **<FLAT PATTERN WIDTH> cm**.

6. Save the sheet-metal model file.

7. From within the Drawing Manager, launch the Parts List tool.

8. Using the Select View tool, select a flat pattern view of the sheet-metal model containing the custom iProperties, click OK, and place the parts list on your drawing.

9. Right-click your parts list, and select the Edit Parts List tool.

10. Right-click the table, and select Column Chooser.

11. Select the New Property tool, and enter **Length**.

12. Repeat step 11, creating an additional property named **Width**.

13. Once complete, click OK.

14. Select the new column named Length, right-click, and select the Format Column tool.

15. Change the formatting and precision of the length to match your needs.

16. Repeat step 15 for the Width column, clicking OK when complete.

SAVING TIME WITH CUSTOM IPROPERTIES

If this information is something you might routinely want to access, create the custom iProperty values in your sheet-metal template file so that they are always available.

Harvesting Legacy Sheet-Metal Templates

During the discussion concerning the move from a template-based style environment to a style library, you may have been wondering how to actually go about making the switch. Luckily, some tools ship with Inventor that can help extract your previously defined sheet-metal style information. To determine whether these tools can work for you, the following sections detail some challenges that you might run into while harvesting your styles as well as some information pertaining to the tools that can help you through the process.

Parameter Indirection

One aspect of legacy sheet-metal styles that has no precedence in the style library relates to parameter indirection. In versions of Inventor previous to 2009, sheet-metal users were able to build sheet-metal styles that were driven by referenced parameters that in turn referenced externalized data sources (in other words, an Excel file). Within the XML-based style library, there is no way to ensure that the externalized file containing the parameter information will be found, so parameter indirection has never been supported.

However, numerous sheet-metal designers use this capability quite successfully to construct sheet-metal configurators. With this in mind, Inventor continues to support the use of linked parameters within the sheet-metal rule definition; it simply doesn't allow sheet-metal rules containing parameter indirection to be published to the style XML library. Since sheet-metal rules exist as document-level objects as well as published style XML entries, there's no reason you can't use externalized parameters with the sheet-metal template.

The Hidden Tools of Harvesting

When discussing the sheet-metal transition to the style library, a common question is often asked: what happens to my data? The good news is that Inventor can preserve and migrate all the sheet-metal style information that is stored in each sheet-metal document, whether the style is active or not.

Once users see that the data is still all there, the next question generally is this: how do I move my sheet-metal template styles to the style library? As a means to sort through and publish your sheet-metal styles as sheet-metal rules, two additional tools have been provided: the Style Library Manager and the Style Management Wizard. These utilities work in conjunction with Inventor and are fundamentally intended to support the process of making the big change away from templates and toward the style library. This also means these tools are typically used infrequently since it's not every day that new style information is made ready for consumption in the style library. With this in mind, we'll walk through these tools to ensure that you understand how to successfully publish your data.

STYLE MANAGEMENT WIZARD

The Style Management Wizard, also known as the *harvester*, allows you to select specific target files that contain style information and either purge that style information or publish it to style library XMLs. Although the harvester supports that capability to search all the files in a given project, most sheet-metal customers use a single template that contains every bit of sheet-metal style information they've ever thought of. This consolidation of information is one of the main problems that influenced the move away from templates and toward the style library, because most customer sheet-metal files are packed with style information that has never and will never be used.

The harvester also allows individual files to be added, regardless of the project location in which they reside. For the majority of sheet-metal customers, a single targeted file might contain all the style data you want to harvest and publish into the sheet-metal rule style XML file. The harvester then needs to know what to do with the extracted information. You can either create a new style library destination or select an existing style library (for example, your Inventor design data folder), but be cautious because this will overwrite any styles or rules that have an identical name.

This is in fact an important aspect of the Style Management Wizard—the last imported style definition for a given style name wins. Once you initiate the harvesting of style information, you will have to wait about five minutes because Windows, Inventor, and the harvester all have to work through some processes; don't exit—it will succeed…just give it some time. When the harvesting is finished, you will see a log entry that reflects that the target file was successfully harvested.

BE CAREFUL WHEN HARVESTING

Different from the Style And Standard Editor dialog box within Inventor, the harvester will allow you to publish sheet-metal rules that contain parameter indirection (in other words, a linked Excel file or references to model parameters), but the published rule will fail when referenced. Be careful to preview the contents of files from which you intend to harvest style/rule information.

To successfully accomplish the harvesting of your sheet-metal style information, you will need to complete a few preparation tasks. First, the file or files that you intend to extract styles information from must be migrated to the current version of Inventor. The next step is that you should ensure the project file containing the referenced file(s) has its Use Style Library option set to Yes. Lastly, ensure that the location you will be writing style information to is not read-only. It is not uncommon for the `Design Data` folder (the default location is C:\Program Files\Autodesk\Inventor 2011) to be set to read-only; if you're going to edit the styles in this location, you might want to verify that they're editable. If you want to harvest the style information from a specific file, follow these steps:

1. Launch the Style Management Wizard from the following location: Start ➤ All Programs ➤ Autodesk ➤ Autodesk Inventor 2011 ➤ Tools ➤ Style Management Wizard.

2. Once you arrive at the welcome screen, click Next.

3. Select a project file location that contains a file that you want to harvest sheet-metal style information from, and then click Next.

4. Select the folder icon in the upper-left corner in order to add a specific file to the harvesting queue.

5. Once selected, you will see the filename and file path in the harvest queue; click Next.

6. The next page allows you to select between harvesting and purging styles information; we will use the default option, which is Harvest Styles Into A Target Style Library.

7. Next you must choose whether you want to create a new style library based on your target file or edit an existing style library. For this example, you will edit the Inventor 2011 Design Data library, but you may want to create a new library to verify the results. Click Next.

MY NEW LIBRARY IS MISSING STYLES

When you create a new library based upon a target file, only the styles located within that specific file will be used. Material, color, and various other styles may not be present within your target file and therefore will not be harvested.

8. The last step is to click Start to begin the process of extracting your sheet-metal style information.

9. When the harvesting log says it has finished and the Pause button changes to Finished, you have completed the harvesting process.

STYLE LIBRARY MANAGER

The Style Library Manager is a utility that allows you to manipulate styles that have already been published to a style XML file. Different from the Style Management Wizard, the Style Library Manager allows you to copy, rename, and delete styles. For the purposes of sheet-metal library management, you'll likely use the Delete function the most. An important key to remember when working with the Styles And Standard Editor dialog box is that style information can be added to the library only from within Inventor; there is no support within Inventor to delete items from the style XML files.

Although there is a tool named Purge Style within the right-click menu of a style (as shown in Figure 6.39), all of these tools are from the perspective of the document-level version of the style, the cached style. Update Style, for example, overwrites the cached style information with whatever is in the style file. If the style existed only in the cache, Update Style would never become enabled. The only entry in the Style right-click menu that adds information to the style XML file is Save To Style Library. For any editing of the style XML that requires renaming or deleting, you will need to utilize the Style Library Manager. To access the Style Library Manager, select Start ➤ All Programs ➤ Autodesk ➤ Autodesk Inventor 2011 ➤ Tools ➤ Style Library Manager.

FIGURE 6.39
Style And Standard Editor dialog box's right-click menu for managing document and library styles

The Bottom Line

Take advantage of the specific sheet-metal features available in Inventor   Knowing what features are available to help realize your design can make more efficient and productive use of your time.

Master It   Of the sheet-metal features discussed, how many require a sketch to produce their result?

Understand sheet-metal templates and rules   Templates can help get your design started on the right path, and sheet-metal rules and associated styles allow you to drive powerful and intelligent manufacturing variations into your design; combining the two can be very productive as long as you understand some basic principles.

Master It   Name two methods that can be used to publish a sheet-metal rule from a sheet-metal part file to the style library.

Author and insert punch tooling   Creating and managing Punch tools can streamline your design process and standardize tooling in your manufacturing environment.

Master It   Name two methods that can be utilized to produce irregular (nonsymmetric) patterns of punch features.

Utilize the flat pattern information and options   The sheet-metal folded model captures your manufacturing intent during the design process; understanding how to leverage this information and customize it for your needs can make you extremely productive.

Master It   How can you change the reported angle of all your Punch tools by 90 degrees?

Understand the nuances of sheet-metal iPart factories   Sheet-metal iPart factories enable you to create true manufacturing configurations with the inclusion of folded and flat pattern models in each member file.

Master It   If you created sheet-metal iPart factories prior to Inventor 2009, any instantiated files contain only a folded model. Name two methods that you could use to drive the flat pattern model into the instantiated file.

Model sheet-metal components with non-sheet-metal features   Inventor doesn't always allow you to restrict yourself to sheet-specific design tools; understanding how to utilize non-sheet-metal features will ensure that your creativity is limitless.

Master It   Name two non-sheet-metal features that can lead to unfolding problems if used to create your design.

Work with imported sheet-metal parts   Understanding the way in which Inventor accomplishes unfolding as well as how to associate an appropriate sheet-metal rule are keys to successfully working with imported parts.

Master It   Name the one measured value that is critical if you want to unfold an imported part.

Understand the tools available to annotate your sheet-metal design   Designing your component is essential, but it's equally important to understand the tools that are available to efficiently document your design and extract your embedded manufacturing intent.

Master It   What process is required to recover flat pattern width and height extents within your Drawing Manager parts list?

Harvest your legacy sheet-metal styles into sheet-metal rules   Using the harvesting utilities provided, you can extract your legacy sheet-metal styles and publish them into style library sheet-metal rules, pre-associated to material styles, sheet thickness values, and sheet-metal Unfold Rules.

Master It   How can you extract sheet-metal style information from legacy part files or template files for the purpose of publishing it with a Sheet-Metal Rule?

Chapter 7

Part and Feature Reuse

The ability to reuse parts and features in other designs is an important step to increasing productivity. Inventor provides this ability through several different workflows. This chapter introduces you to several methods that will assist you in achieving your goal.

Developing the proper workflow for your company will depend on several criteria. Depending on your involvement with the functional design aspect of Inventor, you may be converting some iParts to Content Center components. Additionally, you may decide to utilize iParts and iFeatures for design development if your design needs require them.

In this chapter, you will learn how to:

- ◆ Create and modify iParts
- ◆ Create and use iFeatures and punches
- ◆ Copy and clone features
- ◆ Link parameters between two files
- ◆ Configure, create, and access Content Center parts

Working with iParts

iParts differ from standard parts in that they are essentially table-driven part factories, allowing for many different variations to be generated from the same basic design. When an iPart is inserted into an assembly, a dialog box appears and allows you to specify a variation of the original part from the table.

Within the iPart factory, you can configure feature sizes by specifying different values for the same parametric dimension, you can choose to include or suppress entire features, and you can configure the iProperties of a part. In addition to these general configuration controls, you can configure thread features and work features such as work planes, axes, and points. There are two basic forms of iParts: table-driven and custom. Both types can be combined to create a table-driven part that allows custom input.

Each original iPart, often called a *factory part*, generates individual derived, noneditable member parts. Member parts placed within an assembly can be substituted with a different member of the factory. When a member part is replaced, generally all existing assembly constraints will be retained.

iParts bring several advantages within assemblies. They essentially function as completely different parts, allowing dimensional changes, feature suppression, transfer of iProperties, and other values.

Creating and Modifying iParts

iParts are created from an existing part. Existing parts already contain features and parameters. Although you can modify a standard part by changing the parameter values, this will affect the part wherever it is used. To create configurations of a standard part, you must first convert the part into an iPart.

You can publish iParts to a custom content folder for use as Content Center components or as additional content for functional design such as Frame Generator and Bolted Connections. Published iParts can also be used in other aspects of functional design where allowed.

MODIFYING THE PARAMETER LIST

Before converting a standard part into an iPart, you should first modify the parameter list and rename the parameters to something more meaningful than the default names, such as renaming d1 to Length. To explore these tools, follow these steps:

1. On the Get Started tab, click the Open button.

2. Browse for the file named `mi_7a_001.ipt` located in the Chapter 7 directory of the Mastering Inventor 2011 folder, and click Open.

3. Click the Parameters button on the Manage tab.

4. The Parameters dialog box opens, and you'll note that many of the parameters have been named already. Name the unnamed parameters d0, d1, and d2 to Length, Width, and Height, as shown in Figure 7.1, and then click Done to exit the Parameters dialog box.

FIGURE 7.1
Parameters
dialog box

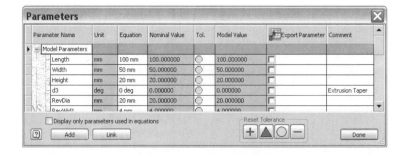

TIPS FOR WORKING WITH PARAMETERS

Recall that you cannot use spaces in parameter names; however, you can use an underscore or capital letters to help separate words in the parameters names, such as Base_length or BaseLength.

Be aware that modifying the parameter name after creating an iPart table will not automatically update the parameter name in the table; therefore, parameters should always be named before being included in the iPart table in order to maintain consistency.

Parameter names will be used as column header names in the iPart table. Parameters that have been renamed will automatically be pulled into the iPart table. You can manually add unnamed parameters to the iPart table; however, it is best practice to give all parameters to be used in the iPart meaningful names.

Selecting the Export Parameter column permits creation of custom iProperties within the part file. By exporting parameters as iProperties, you can easily access them in parts lists and BOMs.

CREATING THE IPART

After you've modified the parameter list, you then create the iPart table, configure it to include columns of features you want to modify, and add rows for each new configuration of the part you want to create.

1. On the Author panel of the Manage tab, click the Create iPart button. All the named parameters will automatically show up in the iPart table.

2. To remove columns that you do not want to include in the table, click the parameter in the right pane, and use the << button. You can also select column headers in the table and then right-click and choose Delete Column. Remove all the columns except Length, Width, and Height.

3. Add a row to the table so that you can create a variation of this part. Right-click anywhere in row 1, and choose Insert Row.

4. Set Height to 40 mm, and leave the other values as they are.

5. Create additional rows until you have eight rows with the Length, Width, and Height values as shown here:

Length	Width	Height
100 mm	50 mm	20 mm
100 mm	50 mm	40 mm
100 mm	75 mm	20 mm
100 mm	75 mm	40 mm
200 mm	50 mm	20 mm
200 mm	50 mm	40 mm
200 mm	75 mm	20 mm
200 mm	75 mm	40 mm

6. Once your table is complete, click OK.

7. Find the Table node in the browser, and click the + sign to expand the node. You will see each member (variation) of the iPart table listed, as shown in Figure 7.2.

FIGURE 7.2
iPart browser list

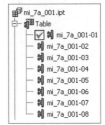

You can switch between each member of the iPart by double-clicking it or by right-clicking it and choosing Activate. Making changes to the features or sketches will change the active member but will not automatically update the table. If you make a change and then go to set another member active, you will be prompted to save the changes to the table or discard those changes. This is because the default edit mode is set to edit the entire iPart factory rather than the members individually. Changes made in the table will be carried through to the members either way. You'll learn more about adjusting the edit scope in the "Working with Sheet-Metal iParts" and "Changing Color in iParts" sections.

EDITING THE iPART TABLE

CERT OBJECTIVE

To edit an iPart, you can double-click the Table node in the Model browser, or you can right-click and choose Edit Table. You can also right-click and choose Edit Via Spreadsheet to edit the table with Microsoft Excel. Although some iPart table-editing tasks can be done in both Inventor and Excel, others should be done only in Inventor. Follow these steps to explore the process of editing an iPart table:

1. On the Get Started tab, click the Open button.

2. Browse for the file named `mi_7a_003.ipt` located in the Chapter 7 directory of the Mastering Inventor 2011 folder, and click Open.

3. Right-click the table in the browser, and choose Edit Table.

4. In the iPart Author dialog box, right-click the Length column header, and choose Key. Then click the arrow and select 1 to designate that this is the first parameter by which this part should be specified.

5. Set the width to be key 2 and the height to be key 3; then click OK to close the iPart Author dialog box.

6. Right-click the table in the browser, and choose List By Keys. This sets the members to be listed by parameter keys in descending order, creating a drill-down tree so that you can select the length, then the width, and then the thickness, as shown in Figure 7.3. Note that the active member is designated by a check mark next to the appropriate key.

FIGURE 7.3
iPart browser
listed by keys

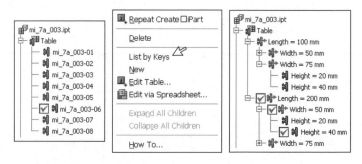

> ## KEY SELECTION IS IMPORTANT WHEN CREATING IPARTS
>
> You should take time to consider how your users will utilize the parts. For example, consider a socket head cap screw iPart. In the iPart, you might have diameter (¼", $5/16$", $3/8$"), pitch (UNC or UNF), length (2", 3", 4", 5"), and material (stainless steel, alloy steel). Each of these columns could be key 1, but you should consider what makes it easiest to navigate to the correct part. In many cases, you might want to make the material the primary key with the diameter, pitch, and length as the second, third, and fourth keys. This means that the user will first select the material and only then be presented with the remaining diameters, pitches, and lengths for that given material. It would be a poor choice (in most cases) to have the pitch as the primary key because this is usually not the first descriptive factor when choosing a fastener.

7. Next, right-click the table in the browser, and choose Edit Table again.

8. Click the Properties tab to see the list of iProperties that are available for this part.

9. Locate the Project category in the left pane, and expand it to reveal the Description property.

10. Select Descriptions, and use the >> button to include it in the iPart table.

11. Confirm that the Description column shows as a column in the table, and then click OK.

12. Right-click the table in the browser and choose Edit Table via Spreadsheet to open the table in Microsoft Excel.

13. Select cells F2 through F9, and then right-click and choose Format cells.

14. Set the cells to General, and click OK. This is necessary to allow Excel to evaluate the expression you will build in the next step.

15. In cell F2, enter = **C2 & " X " & D2 & " X " & E2**.

16. Right-click cell F2, and choose Copy.

17. Then select cells F3 through F9, and right-click and select Paste. Figure 7.4 shows the Excel table complete.

FIGURE 7.4
Excel table used to add descriptions

	A	B	C	D	E	F
	F2		f_x =C2 & " X " & D2 &" X " &E2			
1	Member<defau	Part Number [	Length<k	Width<	Height<k	Description [Project]
2	mi_7a_003-01	mi_7a_003-01	100 mm	50 mm	20 mm	100 mm X 50 mm X 20 mm
3	mi_7a_003-02	mi_7a_003-02	100 mm	50 mm	40 mm	100 mm X 50 mm X 40 mm
4	mi_7a_003-03	mi_7a_003-03	100 mm	75 mm	20 mm	100 mm X 75 mm X 20 mm
5	mi_7a_003-04	mi_7a_003-04	100 mm	75 mm	40 mm	100 mm X 75 mm X 40 mm
6	mi_7a_003-05	mi_7a_003-05	200 mm	50 mm	20 mm	200 mm X 50 mm X 20 mm
7	mi_7a_003-06	mi_7a_003-06	200 mm	50 mm	40 mm	200 mm X 50 mm X 40 mm
8	mi_7a_003-07	mi_7a_003-07	200 mm	75 mm	20 mm	200 mm X 75 mm X 20 mm
9	mi_7a_003-08	mi_7a_003-08	200 mm	75 mm	40 mm	200 mm X 75 mm X 40 mm

18. Save the spreadsheet and close Excel.

19. Because your table now contains data that is not in the part file, you will be prompted to update the file. Click Yes in the message dialog box.

20. Right-click the table in the browser, and choose Edit Table.

21. In the iPart Author dialog box, notice that the cells in the Description column are highlighted to inform you that there is a formula in those cells.

22. Click OK to exit the iPart Author dialog box.

CONVERTING AN IPART TO A STANDARD PART

You can convert an iPart to a standard part file by right-clicking the table in the Model browser and choosing Delete. The part will assume the active members' feature values and states.

INCLUDING AND EXCLUDING FEATURES

A common use of iParts is to create a configuration of a part family that might include features in some cases and not include them in others. You can add a column to the table to control feature suppression. To do this, follow these steps:

1. On the Get Started tab, click the Open button.

2. Browse for the file named mi_7a_005.ipt located in the Chapter 7 directory of the Mastering Inventor 2011 folder, and click Open.

3. Right-click the table in the browser, and choose Edit Table.

4. In the iPart Author dialog box, click the Suppression tab.

5. Select the feature called Round_Boss1, and click the >> button to add it as a column in the table.

6. Enter suppress for the all the 100 mm length rows.

SUPPRESSING VS. COMPUTING

You can enter **suppress** or **compute**, **S** or **C**, and **0** or **1** for the suppress/compute cells. You can mix these options as well, meaning you can change only some values from Compute to S, for instance.

---

7. Click the Verify button to ensure that you haven't entered a value that will not work, such as entering a spelling error. Errant cells will highlight in yellow, and you should fix them.

8. Click OK to return to the model.

9. Use the browser tree to activate different members, and notice that the boss features will be suppressed for all the 100 mm members. Figure 7.5 shows the iPart Author dialog box.

FIGURE 7.5
Suppressing
features

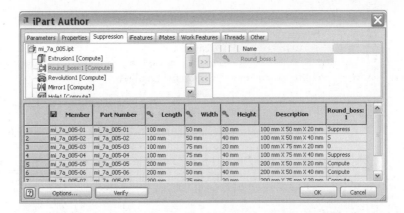

You'll notice that by suppressing the boss feature, both instances of the boss are suppressed. This is because the boss was mirrored. To suppress just one boss, you could suppress the mirror feature; however, doing so would suppress one of the revolved features as well, because it was included in the mirror. Keep this in mind when creating left and right configurations of the same part. Oftentimes you will need to create separate features so that they can be controlled independently.

CREATING STACKED, TOGGLED FEATURES

Often when creating part configurations, you might need to create two features at the same location so you can toggle between the two features depending upon the configuration. For instance, you might have an existing rectangular cut but then want to add an oblong cut in the same location so you can set the iPart to toggle between the two. When you attempt to place the oblong, Inventor warns that the feature did not change the number of unique faces and then results in an error. To correct this problem, simply accept the error and then right-click the oblong and choose Suppress Features. Then you can set up the iPart table to toggle between the two features.

INCLUDING OR EXCLUDING WORK FEATURES IN iPARTS

You can use the Work Features tab to indicate whether each work feature is included or excluded individually. A common use for this would be to create several work features in an iPart and then include only the one that is to be used for mating the specific iPart member in the assembly environment so as to control a specific offset value.

WORKING WITH THREADED iPART FEATURES

You can change the thread parameters of a tapped hole or external thread feature for each member of the iPart table independently. Just use the Thread tab to include any thread parameters, which will vary. You should include all parameters that will vary between any of the table members; otherwise, the hole/thread feature may generate errors when switching between members. Oftentimes these errors may not become apparent until you attempt to publish your iPart to Content Center.

An example of this would be if you neglected to add the Class parameter to the table, even though not all of the members in the table have the same thread class. The thread class would then be set to the original thread class and would not get changed when the iPart is switched to a thread that does not include the original thread class. The same would be true of course if the Class column was included but wasn't changed.

WORKING WITH SHEET-METAL IPARTS

You can specify the sheet-metal rule, the sheet-metal unfold, and a named flat pattern orientation for individual members in an iPart. To edit the bend order, you must edit the member scope as opposed to making the edits per the iPart factory. Once the iPart is set to Member Scope, bend order changes in the flat pattern are set to the active member. To do this, you need to first enable the iPart/iAssembly toolbar:

1. Go to the Tools tab, and click Customize on the Options panel.

2. In the Customize dialog box, select the Toolbars tab, and select the iPart/iAssembly toolbar from the list.

3. Click the Show button to turn the toolbar on.

4. Click Close, and then click and drag the toolbar to the desired position.

5. Click the drop-down, and click the Member Scope button, as shown in Figure 7.6.

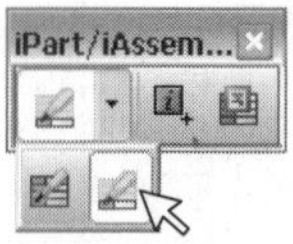

FIGURE 7.6
Setting the iPart edits to Member Scope

Once the scope is set to edit just members, you simply set the member you want to edit to be active and then make the bend order changes needed.

CHANGING COLOR IN IPARTS

To set iPart members to be different colors, you can create a custom iPart parameter on the Other tab and set it to the Display Style Column option. Then you can edit each member row of the iPart to be a different color. It is important that the name matches exactly, however, so be careful to match case. This means that entering **red** for Red will cause a mismatch. To avoid this, it is recommended that you use the Member Scope edit mode, as described in the previous section, to make color style edits to the part. This way, you can just set the member active, change its color, and have the color change recorded in the iPart table automatically. To set up a color column, follow these steps:

1. On the Get Started tab, click the Open button.

2. Browse for the file named mi_7a_012.ipt located in the Chapter 7 directory of the Mastering Inventor 2011 folder, and click Open.

3. Right-click the table in the browser, and choose Edit Table.

4. In the iPart Author dialog box, click the Other tab.

5. On the Other tab, click the Click Here To Add Value line.

6. Type **Color** for the value name.

7. Right-click the column header, and choose Display Style Column, as shown in Figure 7.7.

FIGURE 7.7
Creating a color
column

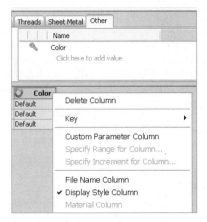

8. Type **Default** into the Color column for each of the three rows. Then click OK to exit the iPart Author dialog box.

SETTING COLORS

Note that if you do not enter Default or some other valid color style, you will receive a warning that states "Errors occurred while setting factory to specified member." You can click Accept and then edit the table again.

---

9. Ensure the iParts/iAssembly toolbar is active. To do this, follow these steps:

   A. Go to the Tools tab, and click Customize.

   B. Click the Toolbars tab.

   C. Select the iPart/iAssembly toolbar from the list.

   D. Click the Show button.

   E. Click the Close button.

   F. Click the drop-down, and click the Member Scope button.

10. From the Quick Access bar (located at the top of the screen), select the color style drop-down, and choose Blue.

11. Expand the iPart table, use the keys to set the 25 mm × 50 mm member active, and then set its color to Red.

12. Change the edit scope to Edit Factory Scope using the iParts/iAssembly toolbar.

13. Use the keys to set the 50 mm × 50 mm member active, and then set its color to Green.

14. Right-click the table in the browser, and choose Edit Table. You will receive a message asking whether you would like to set the table to match the document (that is, the part). This demonstrates that when you are making edits to the model with the edit scope set to Factory, the changes to members do not get written back to the table automatically. Using the Member Scope edit option is therefore recommended. You also get this message if you change the active member because the table is verified every time you switch members.

15. Click Yes, and then take a look at the Color column to ensure that the colors match what you have set them to.

Exploring the Authoring Options

The Options button located in the lower-left corner of the authoring dialog box allows you to create and edit part numbers and member names for iParts. You will typically want to set these naming options before you begin adding rows to the iPart table so that as rows are added, they are automatically named according to these options.

Notice the disk symbol located in the Member column header in Figure 7.8. This indicates that the Member column will be used as the filename for each iPart member. If you prefer to have the Part Number column used for the filenames, you can right-click that column header and select File Name Column.

FIGURE 7.8
Member column
used for filename

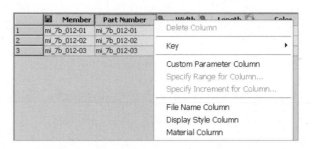

A Member Name value is automatically created for each member as rows are added based on the settings for part number and member name options. You can override these by editing the table in Excel, and you can even use a formula to create the names based on a concatenation of other column values in the table.

GENERATING MEMBER FILES

Once your iPart table is complete, you may want to generate the parts from the table. You can do this so that the parts are established ahead of time, or you can allow the files to be generated automatically as they are used. If you have an iPart table with two dozen rows, it might make sense to generate them ahead of time. However, if you have an iPart table of 200 member rows, then it might make sense to allow parts to be generated only when that particular size is used. To generate member part files, right-click the table, and choose Generate Members. Each member in the row will be created as a derived part based on the table values. Because these parts are often used over and over in many assemblies, it is often recommended that they be stored in a library folder. Recall that folders designated as libraries in your project file are handled as read-only by Inventor.

The library directory where you want to save the iPart members is set up by you, and it is required that you use the same name as the factory library but preceded with an underscore. As an example, if you place the iPart factory file in a library folder named Fasteners, Inventor will automatically place all iPart members generated from that factory part in a second library folder named _Fasteners.

However, you are not required to store iParts in libraries. If you do not use libraries and you place an iPart member into an assembly or use the Generate Members option, Inventor will create a folder of the same name, and at the same level as the iPart factory, and store the iPart members there. For example, if you have an iPart factory file named `ClipBracket.ipj` saved at `C:\Mastering Inventor\`, then when `ClipBracket.ipt` is used in an assembly, a subdirectory called ClipBracket is created (`C:\Mastering Inventor\ClipBracket`), and the iPart member file is created there. Custom iPart members are always stored in a location specified by the user.

CREATING CUSTOM IPARTS

A custom iPart is an iPart factory that has one or more columns designated as a custom parameter column. A custom parameter column allows input of any value and, in turn, generates a custom iPart with infinite variations. Custom iParts are valuable for creating tube and pipe lengths, structural steel members, and other parts that require unique size input at the time of insertion.

To designate a column as a custom parameter column, simply right-click the column, and select Custom Parameter Column. Columns that are set as keys are not permitted to be custom columns. Rather than setting an entire column to be custom, you may want to set just the column entry for a single member to be custom. To do this, you can right-click any cell in a nonkey column and choose Custom Parameter Cell. After that, you can right-click and set both columns and cells to restrict input to a specified range and increment.

Here is a common example of setting a range for a fastener part:

1. You set the Length column to be custom.

2. You set the range so the fastener can be placed only in lengths from 25 mm to 150 mm, as shown in Figure 7.9.

3. You set the increment to 5 mm so that the lengths are limited to standard sizes.

4. When you place the custom iPart into an assembly, you specify the increments.

5. Unlike standard iParts, you save custom iParts to a location of your choice at the time of placement.

FIGURE 7.9
Custom column
settings

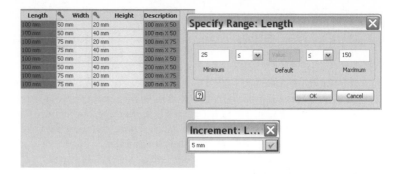

TESTING THE IPART

Before placing a completed iPart into production for others to use, test the accuracy and interface of your part by inserting the iPart using Place Component within a blank assembly file. Using Place Component, insert every member in the table, and inspect and/or measure the placed component.

Moving the test forward, create an IDW file with a base view of your assembly. You will also need to generate a parts list with the desired columns and verify the accuracy of each cell. Once you are assured of having accurate member components, you can then place this iPart into a project library folder. If you will be using this iPart in conjunction with the functional design features of Inventor, you will need to publish the factory iPart to a custom Content Center library.

NO ZERO-VALUE DIMENSIONS

You should not attempt to create a zero-value dimension as a method of suppressing features, because they will cause errors within iPart generation. It is better to create a column to suppress individual features, rather than attempt to do so through dimensions.

EDITING THE IPART FACTORY

Editing an original iPart factory follows the same workflow as creating an iPart. If you've placed the original iPart factory into a project library folder, then within that same project, it will not be able to be edited. Instead, create a new project file for the purpose of editing library parts. When creating a new project file, define the workspace for the project file by locating the project file in the main libraries subfolder. Any subfolder within the library path will now be editable with this specific project file.

With the new Library Edit project file active, open the iPart you want to edit. Locate the table in the Model browser, and either double-click or right-click to activate the iPart Author dialog box. At this point, you can edit any part of the table. When you have completed your editing, you can save the part to its original location.

You can convert an iPart factory component into a standard parametric part by deleting the table attached to the iPart. Simply right-click the table in the Model browser, and select Delete. The part will revert to a parametric part with no history of the iPart functionality in the part.

Using iParts in Designs

Using an iPart in an assembly design is a little bit different from creating parts within an assembly. With standard parts, you can edit any feature by activating the part. An iPart member or child cannot be edited since it is a derived component created by the factory or parent part.

To change between iPart members, follow these steps:

1. Locate and expand the iPart in the assembly browser tree.

2. Right-click the table.

3. Choose Change Component.

This opens the iPart placement dialog box, which allows you to specify a new member to be used in place of the existing one. Figure 7.10 shows the specific selection path for changing the component. This replacement procedure will replace only the selected component instance.

FIGURE 7.10
Changing the component

If you want to replace all exact duplicate members of the iPart within this assembly, follow these steps:

1. Right-click the part within the graphics window or the Model browser.

2. Select Component.

3. Choose Replace All. A dialog box will appear allowing you to select the same iPart factory.

4. Once the original iPart factory is selected, you will be prompted with the iPart placement dialog box to allow you to select the specific member to be used as the replacement.

When a component is replaced with a different member of the same family, as with iParts, normally all assembly constraints will be retained. If the replaced component is of a different family, then the assembly constraints might be broken. The same is true of parts in the same family if the original part used a certain feature to constrain to and the replacement part has that feature suppressed.

> **iPart Factories in Assemblies**
>
> You should be aware that Inventor does not allow you to place an iPart factory file into an assembly. Attempting to do so results in a member of the factory being placed. However, be aware that if you create a part file, place it into an assembly, and then turn it into an iPart factory, that changing the factory table does not place a member file, but simply updates the factory. Using factory files in assemblies is not the intended workflow for iParts.

Working with iFeatures

CERT OBJECTIVE

iFeatures are features that have been extracted from an existing part file and configured for reuse in other parts. If you are familiar with AutoCAD, you might relate iFeatures to blocks, in that you can write out blocks for reuse in other drawings. Any feature based upon a sketch can be used as an iFeature. Once extracted, the iFeature is stored in a catalog and can be placed into any other part file. Inventor is supplied with a number of standard iFeature parts. iFeatures cannot currently be published to Content Center.

Using iFeatures in your designs can greatly simplify your workflow and accelerate productivity, especially if your designs contain repetitive features. Figure 7.11 shows an example of a sheet-metal part that could be created in less than 10 minutes using iFeatures.

FIGURE 7.11
Sheet-metal part
with iFeatures

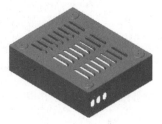

iFeatures support sheet-metal features as well as normal part features. iFeatures are stored in the `Catalog` subfolder of the Inventor program in four subfolders. You can create additional subfolders as required. iFeatures are also available online from such locations as `http://cbliss.com`, `www.sdotson.com`, and others.

The following are some tips for working with iFeatures:

◆ Keep your iFeatures clean, and do not include projected geometry or reference geometry unless required.

◆ If dependent geometry is required, have it dependent only on geometry within the iFeature.

◆ You should avoid the use of origin work planes, axes, and the origin center point for work features.

◆ Use parallel and perpendicular constraints to other geometry in the iFeature, rather than horizontal and vertical constraints.

◆ Know that updates to table-driven iFeatures do not update existing instances of the iFeature.

◆ Save iFeatures before placing in other parts.

Creating iFeatures

Once you have a part that consists of a feature or features that you want to reuse during the design of other parts, you can easily extract those features and place them into the catalog. The chief advantage of using iFeatures is that the original part does not need to be open in order to copy the feature. In addition, you can alter any of the parameters at will when inserting the feature into a new part.

To reuse a part feature, select the Extract iFeature option on the Tools drop-down menu. Select the feature to be reused from the Model browser or the graphics window. If additional features exist that are dependent upon the selected feature, they will be added to the iFeature as well but can be deleted during iFeature creation if not needed. Figure 7.12 illustrates how to remove a dependent feature while creating an iFeature.

FIGURE 7.12
Removing a dependent feature

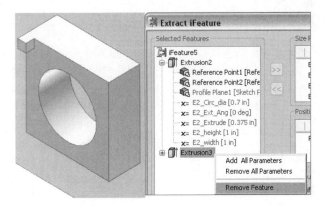

A standard iFeature similar to this will require a profile plane only in order to position the geometry onto a new part. In this example, you will notice that the named parameters and values are transferred from the existing part into the new iFeature. In Figure 7.13, you will notice that prompts will be added for each of the named parameters. When inserting this iFeature into a different part, you will be prompted to enter new values for these parameters if desired.

FIGURE 7.13
Parameters and prompts

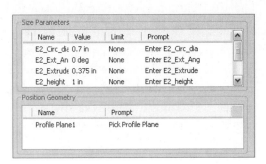

PLACING AN IFEATURE

To place an iFeature in a standard part (not sheet metal), you simply browse to the stored iFeature and then select the face you want to use for placement. During the placement, you can adjust the rotation angle and size parameters. To see a simple example of how iFeatures are extracted and placed, follow these steps:

1. On the Get Started tab, click the Open button.

2. Browse for the file named mi_7a_017.ipt located in the Chapter 7 directory of the Mastering Inventor 2011 folder, and click Open.

3. On the Manage tab, click the Extract iFeature button.

4. In the Model browser, click Extrusion2 as the selected feature, and the dialog box will be populated with the parameter information found in that feature.

5. Click the parameter named E2_Ext_Ang, and use the << button to remove it from the parameter list.

ADJUSTING EXTRACTED FEATURES

In this case, the parameters have been renamed previously using the Parameters dialog box. However, you can adjust parameter names and the corresponding prompts at this point if needed.

You can also adjust the default values for the parameters without adjusting the current model. Add lists and ranges to each parameter using the Limits column.

---

6. For this example, accept the default for the rest of the parameters, and click Save.

7. Notice that Inventor takes you straight to the Catalog folder. This location is specified in the Application Options dialog box and can be changed if needed. Choose a location under Catalog or create your own subdirectory, and name this iFeature SquareSocket .ide. If warned about saving outside of the project path, click Yes.

8. Place the iFeature back into the model as a test. On the Manage tab, select the Insert iFeature tool.

9. Click the Browse button to go to the Catalog folder automatically.

10. Locate the SquareSocket feature you just created, and click Open.

11. Select the top face of Extrusion1 to use as the profile plane.

12. Once the plane is selected, set the angle to 45 degrees, use the flip arrow to ensure that the feature placed in the correct direction, and then click Next.

13. Enter 0.5 for the E2_Circ_Dia parameter and then click the Refresh button to see the diameter of the feature adjust. Once the size parameter has been adjusted, as shown in Figure 7.14, click Next.

FIGURE 7.14
Inserting a simple
iFeature

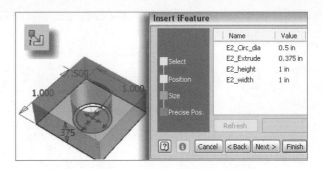

14. You will be presented with two options for placing the iFeature; choose Activate Sketch Edit Immediately, and click Finish.

15. You will see that the iFeature sketch is set and ready to be edited.

16. Finish the sketch, and close the file.

TAKING THE TIME TO CONSTRAIN THE SKETCH

You should also notice that the sketch is currently underconstrained. In particular, it has no dimensions or constraints holding it in position. You can place general dimensions into the sketch to anchor it in place. Also present are some relic geometry that originated from the sketch from which the iFeature was extracted. It is poor practice to extract iFeatures without cleaning them up first, so eliminate this stray geometry.

It is also good practice to create a separate part file from which to generate an iFeature rather than attempting to use a part file designed for production. You can copy the part features from a production part into your iFeature test part using one of the copy or cloning methods discussed in the upcoming pages.

EDITING AN IFEATURE FILE

Once iFeature files (.ide) have been extracted and tested, you can open them in Inventor and edit them much like iParts. Follow these steps to explore the options involved in editing an iFeature:

1. On the Manage tab, click the Place iFeature drop-down, and click the View iFeature Catalog button, as shown in Figure 7.15. This will take you directly to the Catalog folder in the Inventor program files where all iFeatures are stored.

2. Locate and open the file named SquareSocket.ide that you created in the previous exercise. If you did not complete that exercise, you can open the file named mi_7a_025.ide from the Chapter 7 directory of the Mastering Inventor 2011 folder.

Use the Edit iFeature icon to refine parameter names, sizes, and instructional prompts for the placement of iFeatures. If the iFeature has dependent features, you can edit them as well. You can also rename the iFeature if you want to configure it in a more in-depth manner by using the iFeature Author Table dialog box.

FIGURE 7.15
Accessing the
iFeature catalog

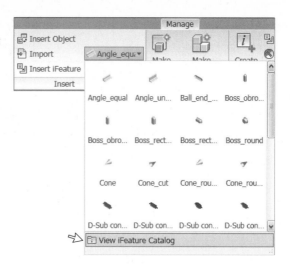

The iFeature Author Table dialog box allows a table to be added to the iFeature so that rows and columns can be added to configure the iFeature in the same way that you configured a part file using the iPart Author dialog box. Once you've added the table to the iFeature, you can further edit it by clicking the Edit Using Spread Sheet icon to open the table in Microsoft Excel.

When creating iFeatures, it is usually a good idea to keep the original IPT file that you used to create the IDE file. This is often useful in case you want to totally redesign the iFeature or make a similar iFeature.

INCLUDING PLACEMENT INSTRUCTIONS

You can embed an instructional document detailing the placement selection requirements for more complex shapes that require faces to be selected in a certain order or need more information about size and settings. Here are the steps for including placement instructions:

1. On the Tools tab, click Insert Object.

2. Select Create From File, browse for the pre-created instruction file, and then click OK.

3. The file will show in the 3rd Party browser node, as shown here.

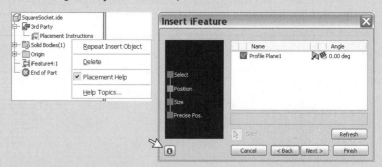

4. Right-click the embedded object and select Placement Help to allow this file to be accessed from the feature dialog box during placement.

Creating Punch Features

Punch features are really just iFeatures with extended functions that behave slightly differently than standard iFeatures. Punch features require a single sketch center point during iFeature creation. The sketch center point will be used to locate the punch feature upon insertion. The destination part will require an active sketch containing sketch center points for the location of the punch feature.

CREATING PUNCH FEATURES

When creating a punch feature, consider that in normal use most features extend through the thickness of the sheet metal. Therefore, it is important to use the Thickness parameter when creating the iFeature. Constructed properly, the punch feature will adjust to the thickness of any sheet-metal part to which it is applied.

The part used in the following steps is a simple sheet-metal part with one cut feature. Figure 7.16 shows the sketch underlying the cut feature. The sketch was created utilizing a single center point, which will be used for placement when inserting the punch feature. There was no need to anchor the sketch, since it was created for the sole purpose of extracting a punch iFeature.

FIGURE 7.16
A sheet-metal sketch

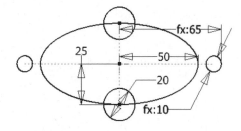

1. On the Get Started tab, click the Open button.

2. Browse for the file named mi_7a_027.ipt located in the Chapter 7 directory of the Mastering Inventor 2011 folder, and click Open.

3. On the Manage tab, select the Extract iFeature tool.

4. Select Cut1 in the Model browser.

5. Click the radio button at the top of the dialog box to toggle the iFeature type to Sheet Metal Punch Feature.

PUNCHES AND CENTERPOINTS

If you have created multiple center point locations within your sketch, you will receive an error message when trying to create the punch feature. Recall that you can switch extra center points in your sketch to standard points so that they will not interfere, by using the Center Point icon next to the Construction icon. In this example, you have only one center point within the sketch, even though there are other points locating the various circles.

6. Under the Manufacturing area, specify the punch ID as K775. Although not required, if it's included, this punch ID can be retrieved and placed onto a drawing in the form of a punch note or punch table so the shop floor will know which punch to use.

7. Click the Select Sketch button for Simplified Representation, and then click Sketch3 in the Model browser. Simplified sketches are optional but may help represent complex sketches more cleanly in the detail drawing.

8. When your dialog box resembles Figure 7.17, click Save, and select the Punches folder in the Catalog directory.

9. Name the punch feature K775.ide. If warned about saving outside the project path, click Yes.

FIGURE 7.17
Extracting a sheet-metal iFeature

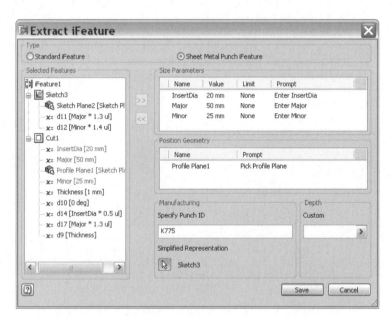

---

iFEATURES ARE POWERFUL TOOLS

These tools allow you to quickly create standard features in your models. Examples include o-ring grooves, louvers, bosses, ribs, electrical connector punches, patterns of holes, and an infinite number of other features. Another major advantage of iFeatures is that they enforce standards. Since the iFeature can be designed to allow the user to select predefined sizes only, the possibility of error is greatly reduced. Take a few moments to examine your designs, and you'll likely see many opportunities for iFeatures.

PLACING A SHEET-METAL PUNCH FEATURE

When working on a sheet-metal part, you can access iFeatures through the Punch tool or the Insert iFeature options in the Sheet Metal Features tool panel. The Punch tool is optimized for sheet-metal parts, so unless you are placing a regular iFeature, you should always use the Punch tool. Prior to placing a feature, you must have an unconsumed, visible sketch containing one or more center points from which the punch will position itself. Follow these steps to place a sheet-metal punch:

1. On the Get Started tab, click the Open button.

2. Browse for the file named mi_7a_029.ipt located in the Chapter 7 directory of the Mastering Inventor 2011 folder, and click Open.

3. Sketch3 has been prepared for you so that you can use it to place your new punch.

4. Next, locate and select the Punch tool on the Sheet Metal tab.

5. Select K775.ide from the Punches folder, and click Open. For ease of use, the Punch tool takes you directly to the Punches folder and, upon selection of the folder, displays a list of punches. You will notice that every unconsumed center point within the sketch will be populated with the selected punch.

CENTER POINTS

If you want to reserve a sketch center point for some other feature, click the Geometry tab in the Punch Tool dialog box, and hold down the Ctrl key while selecting the center point to be removed. If you want to place only one center point, hold down the Ctrl key, click the sketch away from a center point, and then click the center point where you want the punch. If you have more than one visible, unconsumed sketch, the center points will not be automatically selected because you will need to tell Inventor which sketch to use.

---

6. Click the Geometry tab, and set the angle to 90.

7. Click the Size tab, and set InsertDia to 10 mm, Major to 40 mm, and Minor to 20 mm.

8. Click the Refresh button to preview the results. Figure 7.18 shows the punch parameters.

FIGURE 7.18
Placing a punch

9. Then click the Finish button to complete the punch action.

10. Double-click Flat Pattern in the Model browser to view the flat pattern.

11. Right-click the Flat Pattern node in the Model browser, and choose Edit Flat Pattern Definition.

12. Click the Punch Representation tab, set the drop-down to 2D Sketch Rep And Center Mark, and then click OK. Note the simplified version of the punches. This can be useful for placing grouped punches or helping to simplify drawings that have many punches on them.

Note that you could use the Insert iFeature option to place this punch but you would not be offered the same placement options. Instead, it would behave similar to a standard iFeature, requiring constraining of the placed punch by anchoring it to the base feature. In general, it is best to use the Punch tool for sheet-metal parts, rather than placing punches as a standard iFeature. Note that whereas the iFeature tool is available in the standard and sheet metal environments, the Punch tool is available only in the sheet metal environment.

Reusing Existing Geometry

Geometry reuse is a productive technique in Inventor. You can reuse existing features and sketch geometry to create additional features within the same part or even on other open parts. You don't need to create additional new sketches to utilize this technique. The following sections will cover how to copy sketches and features while developing dependent and independent relationships between the features.

Copying Features

Copying features in Inventor is a relatively simple procedure using the Model browser. In an existing model, simply right-click a feature within the browser, and select Copy. Next, select a different face within the model, right-click, and select Paste. Figure 7.19 shows a preview of the placement and the Paste Features dialog box.

FIGURE 7.19
Copied features

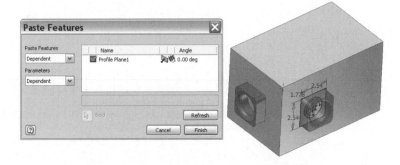

There are two questions to consider when copying a feature:

◆ What should Inventor do with features that are built based on the feature you are copying?

◆ What should Inventor do with the dimensions for your new feature?

We'll explore the features first:

1. On the Get Started tab, click the Open button.

2. Browse for the file named `mi_7a_031.ipt` located in the Chapter 7 directory of the Mastering Inventor 2011 folder, and click Open.

3. Right-click Extrusion2 in the Model browser, and choose Copy.

4. Next, right-click anywhere, and choose Paste.

5. Drag your cursor over any face of the part, and you will see a preview of the copied feature.

6. In the Paste Features dialog box, set the Paste Features drop-down to Dependent, and you will notice that the fillets are now in the preview as well, because they are dependents of Extrusion2.

7. Click the front face of the part to position the new feature as shown in Figure 7.19.

8. Use the +-shaped arrows to move the feature around the selected face.

9. Use the C-shaped arrow to rotate the new feature, and notice the rotation angle is reflected in the dialog box and can be adjusted there as well.

   By default, the dimensions of the new feature will be independent, meaning that because the original feature has a width of 1 inch, the new feature will have the same value, but the two will not be linked. However, if you set the parameter drop-down to Dependent, the dimensions of the new feature will reference the original feature so that if the original width changes from 1 inch to 2 inches, the new feature follows.

10. Set the parameter drop-down to Dependent, and click Finish.

11. Locate and edit Sketch2 in Extrusion2, and set the diameter dimension to 0.25 inch.

12. Finish the sketch, and notice that the new feature follows the edits of the original.

Once you've copied the feature, you should edit the copied feature sketch to properly anchor the sketch on the destination face. When editing a dependent sketch, notice that the dimensions indicate that they are being driven by a parameter from the original feature. If you change the dimensions from a parameter value to numeric value, you will break the dependency with the original sketch.

Cloning

Cloning is the process of copying feature geometry from one open part to another. The cloning process creates independent features, meaning that the new feature in the new part will have no relationship to the original feature in the original part unless set up manually.

To clone a feature from one part to another, you must first have both parts open in Inventor. Here are the general steps:

1. From the source part, right-click the feature to be copied in the Model browser, and choose Copy.

2. Next, switch to the destination part, right-click anywhere, and choose Paste.

3. Drag your cursor over the face of the part you want to paste onto, and you will see a preview of the copied feature.

4. Click the face, and then click Finish when the part has positioned to your liking.

The primary difference between copying features within the same part and cloning features between two parts is that parameters can be set to be independent only during the cloning process.

It will be necessary to fully constrain and anchor the feature sketch to the new part once the feature has been copied. To accomplish this, simply edit the new feature sketch and project construction geometry from the new part base feature to serve as anchor points.

Linking Parameters Between Two Files

You can establish a relationship between two parts, between two assemblies, or between a part and an assembly by linking the files' parameters. This can allow you to place all the design information in one file and link other files to it so that design intent is maintained. Here are the steps to do this:

1. On the Get Started tab, click the Open button.

2. Browse for the file named `mi_7a_034.ipt` located in the Chapter 7 directory of the Mastering Inventor 2011 folder, and click Open.

3. This is a simple pin, and you want to link the shaft diameter to a hole diameter in another part. To do this, click the Parameters button on the Manage tab.

4. At the bottom of the Parameters dialog box, click the Link button, as shown on the left of Figure 7.20.

FIGURE 7.20
Linking
parameters

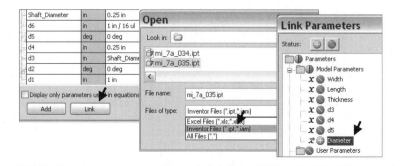

5. Adjust the Files Of Type drop-down to show Inventor Files, and then select the file called `mi_7a_035.ipt` from the Mastering Inventor 2011 folder.

6. This opens the Link Parameter dialog box, allowing you to choose which parameters to link to this part. Click the button next to the parameter named Diameter, and then click OK.

7. This will add the selected parameter to the user parameters in the pin part. Locate Shaft_Diameter in the list, activate the cell in the Equation column, and clear the existing value.

8. Click the arrow as shown in Figure 7.21, and choose List Parameters from the flyout.

9. Select Diameter from the Parameters lists, and choose Done at the bottom of the dialog box.

10. Lastly, click the Update button from the Quick Access bar (at the top of the graphics area) to see the model update.

FIGURE 7.21
Setting a param-
eter to reference a
linked parameter

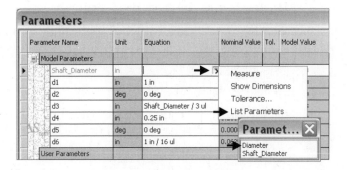

Now the shaft diameter is linked to the hole diameter in the part called mi_7a_035.ipt. You can open this part and change the diameter value to see the change carry through to the shaft of the pin. Linking parameters in this way allows you to place design information in one location and pull it into many other parts for automatic updates.

You can see this concept carried through to the assembly level by opening the file called mi_7a_033.iam, where the pin is linked to the hole diameter, so that the pin updates when the hole is changed.

Copying Sketches

Quite often it is desirable to copy existing part sketches to another location within the same part or a different part. A good example of this would be creating a loft feature where each profile sketch may simply change size.

In the example shown in Figure 7.22, the part contains one unconsumed sketch and multiple work planes parallel to the XY origin plane. To copy an existing sketch, simply right-click the target sketch, and select Copy. Then, select the destination work plane, right-click, and select Paste. Pasted sketches are always independent of the original sketch and will create additional parameters for each copy. The following exercise will explore copying sketches.

FIGURE 7.22
Copying a sketch

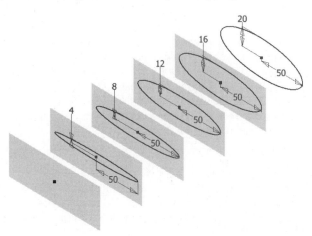

1. On the Get Started tab, click the Open button.

2. Browse for the file named `mi_7a_039.ipt` located in the Chapter 7 directory of the Mastering Inventor 2011 folder, and click Open.

3. Right-click Sketch1 in the Model browser, and choose Copy.

4. Next, click any edge of the work plane closest to the sketch, and then right-click and choose Paste.

5. Repeat this for each of the remaining work planes.

6. Edit each sketch and adjust the minor axis on each of the sketches, decreasing the dimension value by 4 mm on each subsequent sketch.

7. Edit Rectangular Pattern1 and change the pattern count to 6.

8. Right-click any edge of the new work plane, and choose New Sketch.

9. If not done automatically, project the origin center point to the sketch. You can use the Project Geometry tool on the Sketch tab and select the center point of the ellipse in any of the other sketches.

As you can see, copying sketches can be a quick way to duplicate repetitive geometry. To carry this thought through, you can create a loft utilizing all the sketches including the projected origin point. Apply a tangent condition to the projected point to achieve the result, as shown in Figure 7.23.

FIGURE 7.23
A loft created from copied sketches

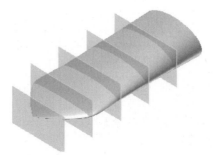

In this example, you copied a sketch within the same part. The procedure to copy an existing sketch to another part requires that both parts be open at the same time. Right-click the original sketch, and select Copy. Then, after selecting the destination part work plane or part face in the second file, right-click and select Paste.

Once the sketches are pasted, they can be edited at any time by adding additional geometry, changing dimensions, or simply using the pasted geometry for reference.

USING FLIP NORMAL

At times you may find that your sketch "flips" when pasting it onto a work plane. In many cases, you can easily fix this by right-clicking the work plane and selecting Flip Normal. This flips the positive axis of the work plane. Then, when you paste the sketch onto the work plane, it will no longer be flipped.

Introducing Content Center

Beginning with Inventor 2011, Content Center is available in two forms: Desktop Content and the traditional ADMS-based Content Center. The ADMS-based Content Center is a set of database libraries based in Microsoft SQL, generally used when sharing a central customized Content Center over a network. The other is a stand-alone install of Content Center that resides on your local machine. The stand-alone install is the default form of Content Center. No matter how you choose to install Content Center, you can choose which libraries to use. These libraries provide standard content in several common international standards, such as ANSI, ISO, and DIN, just to name a few. Figure 7.24 shows the complete list. Once properly configured and populated, Content Center provides an organized method for part and feature reuse.

FIGURE 7.24
Content Center
libraries

You can think of these libraries simply as recipes for creating parts, because no actual part files exist in the Content Center file store. Instead, Content Center is a table of part parameters stored in the Content Center database. Once these library databases are installed, you can access them from Inventor and place common parts into your designs.

Understand that it is at this point the Content Center part file is created. Up until this point, the part existed only as a definition in the database table. If you work in a shared environment, the Content Center part files might typically be stored on a network server so that as users collaborate on designs, they have access to the same part files used within the assemblies. Because the Content Center library database files are just definitions of the files, they can be installed on the user's local machines or on a network server, or both.

Content Center provides support for functional design using the Design Accelerator, Frame Generator, and other features within Inventor. When using these tools, the parts generated are pulled from the Content Center libraries. You can use Content Center in conjunction with standard iParts and iFeatures organized within libraries in the project.

Configuring Content Center

Inventor's Content Center, loaded with all the standard libraries, provides in excess of 800,000 variations in parts. To optimize loading, you will want to configure only the appropriate standards for your use. Installing all libraries will cause Inventor to take more time to search and index the data. There are two installation strategies for Content Center. Depending upon how you work, you may want to install the desktop Content Center or the ADMS version.

INSTALLING THE CONTENT CENTER FOR A STAND-ALONE USER

If you work as a stand-alone user, it is recommended you use the Desktop Content method. No server setup or login is required because the Content Center libraries are installed in the Desktop Content folder on your local hard drive. This is the default installation option. You can insert the install media and install or reinstall the Content Center libraries at any point by following the installation steps. Once the libraries are installed, you simply use the Place From Content Center tool or the Open From Content Center tool to access the Content Center libraries.

INSTALLING CONTENT CENTER FOR A COLLABORATIVE ENVIRONMENT

If working in a shared group, you will likely want to install Content Center on a server location instead of, or in addition to, the Desktop Content. When installing on a server, you will install the libraries on the Autodesk Data Management Server (ADMS). The ADMS is essentially just the interface with which you interact with the SQL database program. Once the ADMS is installed and the required Content Center libraries are loaded, users log into ADMS through Inventor.

When deciding between installing Content Center libraries on a network server or installing them locally, you should consider whether you plan to create and use a custom library. If not, then there may not be a need to install Content Center on a server, and you can choose to install the libraries on all the local machines only. Because the standard Content Center libraries are all read-only databases, they cannot become out of sync; therefore, two users can access two different instances of the standard libraries and work without issue. If you plan to create custom Content Center libraries, however, it is recommended that you install on a network server so that as the library is updated over time, all users are pulling from the same source. You can consult the installation media for more information on installing ADMS and the Content Center libraries.

MANAGING YOUR MEMORY FOOTPRINT

Installing all libraries into ADMS will increase your overall memory usage substantially. As mentioned earlier, installing only the libraries you use will keep Content Center efficient. As we will discuss in the coming pages, you can create a custom Content Center library based on the standard libraries and include only what you require. Once the custom library is created, standard libraries can be removed from ADMS. You can add them back at any time by reinstalling them from the Inventor installation disks.

CONFIGURING CONTENT CENTER LIBRARIES IN THE PROJECT FILES

Once you've installed ADMS and the required libraries, you will need to configure the project file to ensure that all required libraries are included in the project. To do this, you will want to close all files in Inventor so that the project file can be edited. Then follow these steps:

1. In Inventor, go to the Get Started tab, and click the Projects button.

2. In the Projects Editor dialog box, ensure your project is set active, and click the Configure Content Center Libraries button at the lower right of the Projects dialog box to open the Configure Libraries dialog box, as shown in Figure 7.25.

FIGURE 7.25
Configuring
Content Center
libraries

3. Use the buttons at the bottom of the dialog box to update, import, add, or remove libraries for the project. Removing libraries from a project will speed up the interaction between Inventor and Content Center when placing a part because fewer library tables are required to be read, searched, and indexed. Once a library is removed, you can add it to the project again at any time.

If you only occasionally access a certain library because you typically do not work with that standard, you might install it but remove it from your Inventor project. When you do need to access this library, simply use the Configure Libraries dialog box to load it for use and then unload it once you are finished. Although the suggestion to add and remove libraries may seem like a hassle, it will pay off in time savings because you will not find yourself waiting for the libraries to load every time you access Content Center.

Using Content Center

Content Center is used in many areas of Inventor. Components from Content Center are used in functional design tools, such as the Shaft Generator or Frame Generator, as well as in the use of individual, reusable components in general assembly design. Content Center is also available for use within the part environment using the Place Feature tool.

PLACING COMPONENTS INTO AN ASSEMBLY

Let's take a closer look at placing components into an assembly from Content Center:

1. Make sure you have either Desktop Content or the ADMS installed and the ANSI Content Library loaded to continue with this example.

2. If you are running Content Center through ADMS, ensure you are logged in to ADMS by clicking the Inventor icon and selecting Vault Server ➤ Content Center Log In.

3. If you are already logged in or logged into vault, Log In will be grayed out and will not be an option in your menu.

4. Enter your login information, if known. By default ADMS installs with a user account called Administrator with no password set. You can also select the Content Center library's Read-Only check box to access content without logging in.

5. Specify the name of the server on which you installed ADMS. If you have installed ADMS on your local machine, enter **localhost**. In the Database text box, enter the name of the ADMS database; the default is Vault.

PLACING PARTS FROM CONTENT CENTER

Once logged in to the ADMS, or if you have installed Desktop Content (there is no login required), you are ready to place parts from Content Center. To do this, follow these steps:

1. From the Get Started tab, click Open.

2. Browse for the file named mi_7a_044.iam located in the Chapter 7 directory of the Mastering Inventor 2011 folder, and click Open.

3. On the Assemble tab, click the Place From Content Center icon. Check to see that the three buttons as indicated in Figure 7.26 are selected. From left to right these buttons are Filters, AutoDrop, and Tree View.

FIGURE 7.26
Place From
Content Center
settings

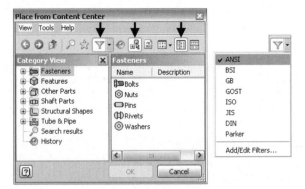

Filters button   Select ANSI to filter out all other standards. To turn the filter off after this exercise, simply click the Filters button again and deselect ANSI.

The AutoDrop button   This turns on the ability to automatically size components based on geometry in the model.

The Tree View button   This simply splits the screen so that the Category View pane is accessible on the left of the dialog box.

4. Select the Fasteners category in the left pane, browse to Bolts and then Round Head, select Cross Recessed Binding Head Machine Screw – Type I, and click OK.

5. In the model, zoom in to one of the castor wheel assemblies, and take note of the empty holes.

6. Pause your mouse pointer over one of the holes on the castor plate.

You will see the AutoDrop icon activate and flicker as Inventor indexes the database for an appropriate size. If no matching size can be found in the database, a cursor note will appear saying so. If an appropriate size is found, a cursor note will display it, and a preview of the part will be shown.

7. Once the size appears, click the edge of the hole to set the screw in place. The AutoDrop toolbar will appear along with the red grip arrow.

8. Drag the grip arrow up or down to specify the length of the screw. Note that only lengths found in the database are available.

9. Click the Apply button, and continue placing screws as you see fit. Experiment with placing the mouse pointer over one of the large diameters in the castor assembly to watch AutoDrop attempt to find an appropriate size. Figure 7.27 shows the AutoDrop toolbar.

FIGURE 7.27
Placing a screw
with AutoDrop

Here is a brief description of each of the tool icons shown in the AutoDrop toolbar in Figure 7.27:

Insert Multiple The first icon is available when Inventor identifies multiple targets that are like the selected target. In this case, the other holes in the plate are picked up and previewed. If you apply the screw now, four screws will be placed at once. If you do not want the multiples to be placed, you can click the Insert Multiple icon to turn it off.

Change Size The second icon is grayed out while Insert Multiple is on. It inserts the part and opens the Part Family dialog box, which allows you to edit the component.

Bolted Connection The next icon opens the Bolted Connection Component Generator and allows you to place bolts, nuts, and washers sets as a group.

Apply The fourth icon sets the previewed component(s) and allows you to continue placing more components of the same family.

Done The last icon sets the component(s) and exits the AutoDrop mode.

The AutoDrop toolbar is context sensitive, meaning that the icons may vary depending upon the component to be placed and the selected geometry. If you press F1 on the keyboard while the AutoDrop toolbar is displayed, Inventor will open the help file and list all the icons and their descriptions.

Now that you've placed Content Center components, let's examine where Inventor is filing the newly generated Content Center files. Go to the Tools tab, and click Application Options; then click the File tab. Look for the file path indicating the default Content Center files, as shown at the top of Figure 7.28.

FIGURE 7.28
Content Center
files storage path

This is where Inventor will place all standard parts placed from Content Center by default. Typically you should change this path to a path that is on the network server, particularly if you're working in a multiuser environment. If you work only on your local hard drive, you will still likely want to change the path to be similar to the path where you save your Inventor designs.

If this path is left at the default, Content Center part files will be saved on your local machine. This causes a problem when a co-worker opens an assembly you created. There is one more place where you can set this path, and that is in the project file under Folder Options, as shown at the bottom of Figure 7.28. It is important to note that a path set in the project file takes precedence over a path set in Application Options. If the project file is set as Content Center Files = [Default], then the files are stored at the Application Options path.

Only standard Content Center files are stored at this location. Custom-sized Content Center part files, such as standard steel shapes, pipes, and so on, are stored at a path chosen by you at the time of their creation.

CONTENT CENTER APPLICATION OPTIONS TAB

You can access the Content Center tab from Application Options to configure the following settings:

Refresh Out-Of-Date Standard Parts During Placement   When selected, existing standard part files are automatically replaced with newer versions. For instance, if you update a standard part with your part number in the Content Center library tables, but that part has already been placed in other assemblies and therefore already exists in the Content Center parts file folder, having this option selected will update the Content Center file folder and place the new version in the assemblies.

Custom Family Default   Set this option to place a custom Content Center part as a standard part. When you place a custom part as standard, the part file is saved in the Content Center files folder and is considered a standard part.

Access Options   This sets the source of the Content Center libraries. You can choose between Desktop Content and the ADMS/Vault Server.

Customizing Content Center Libraries

Standard Content Center libraries supplied with Inventor are designated as read-only and cannot be modified. If you need to create custom part libraries or modify standard content such as adding part numbers or material types, you can do this by creating a custom Content Center library. Custom libraries are initially set as read-write libraries so that you can add and modify content.

DO YOU NEED TO USE CONTENT CENTER?

Many people find the file structure of Content Center-generated files to be at odds with the way that they store purchased and standard parts. If you find this is the case with your setup, you might want to use Content Center to generate parts, but then save them under your own file structure as needed.

CREATING CUSTOM LIBRARIES FOR ADMS INSTALLS

You add libraries from the Autodesk Data Management Server Console when using Content Center with the ADMS. You can access the ADMS by selecting Start ➤ All Programs ➤ Autodesk ➤ Autodesk Data Management ➤ Autodesk Data Management Server Console. Typically this would be done on the server machine. Figure 7.29 shows how to create a custom library.

FIGURE 7.29
Creating a custom library in ADMS

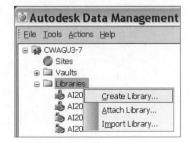

Once logged into the ADMS Console, expand the folder in the top of the left pane, right-click the Libraries subfolder, and select Create Library. Create a new library called **Mastering Inventor**. Once the library is created, follow these steps:

1. Go to the Get Started tab.

2. Click the Projects button.

3. Click the Configure Content Center Libraries button at the bottom-right corner of the Project Editor dialog box.

4. Ensure that the In Use check box for this new library is selected so that the project is configured to include it.

CREATING CUSTOM LIBRARIES FOR DESKTOP CONTENT

You can create a custom Content Center library for Desktop Content through the Content Center configuration of the Projects editor. To do this, follow these steps:

1. Go to the Get Started tab.

2. Click the Projects button.

3. Click the Configure Content Center Libraries button at the bottom-right corner of the Project Editor dialog box.

4. Click the Create Library button, and enter **Mastering Inventor** into the input box, as shown in Figure 7.30.

5. Click OK.

6. Ensure that the In Use check box for this new library is selected so that the project is configured to include it.

FIGURE 7.30
Creating a custom library with Desktop Content

COPYING EXISTING LIBRARIES INTO CUSTOM LIBRARIES

After creating a custom library, you can copy entire or partial contents of existing standard libraries into your custom library. You might use this process when you want to simplify one of the standard libraries, remove portions of the library that are not needed in your work environment, or edit component properties such as part numbers. Here are the steps to copy families to a custom library:

1. Access the Content Center Editor from within Inventor by going to the Tools tab and clicking the Editor button on the Content Center panel. This editor looks similar to the Content Center dialog box.

2. Locate the library or the part family within a library that you want to copy, right-click, and choose Copy To ➤ Mastering Inventor, as shown in Figure 7.31.

The library must be included in the project file configuration list in order to be visible within the editor. If you copy an entire library to your custom library, then the entire folder structure and contents will be replicated in your custom library. If you copy an individual part to your custom library, then only the affected category structure will be replicated in the custom library along with the copied part.

To copy only a portion of the category structure, browse to the last hierarchical portion of the structure that you want to replicate. Otherwise, starting from the top and copying the structure will replicate the entire structure.

FIGURE 7.31
Copying a Content
Center family

Real World Scenario

CREATING MULTIPLE MATERIAL TYPES FOR CONTENT CENTER FAMILIES

It's pretty easy for your design department to have the Content Center parts reflect their own internal part numbers so that bills of materials and parts lists will extract this information automatically. Doing this is as simple as copying the appropriate standard Content Center categories to a custom read/write library and editing the tables to include the new part numbers.

However, if multiple material types are used for the same component type, then multiple copies of the family can be made to accommodate this. For instance, if you use stainless steel fasteners of a given type for certain design instances and also use galvanized fasteners of the same type in other design instances, you would most likely need these to have separate part numbers.

You can use the Material Guide to add materials in one of three ways:

◆ You can edit a family table and select the members to add new materials to. Then click the Material Guide button or right-click and choose Material Guide to copy the selected members, add them to the family table, and assign the new materials to them.

◆ You can use the Material Guide for an entire family, copying all members with a new material and adding them to the existing family. Select the family in the Content Center Editor and click the Material Guide button, or right-click and choose Material Guide. Then choose the option called Add Materials As New Family Members, thereby copying all members into the same family table and setting a new material at the same time.

◆ You can create new families of a different material as well. Select the family in the Content Center Editor and click the Material Guide button, or right-click and choose Material Guide. Then choose the option to Create New Family For Each Material, thereby copying the entire existing family and setting a new material for this new family at the same time.

SETTING CATEGORY PROPERTIES

Each category within Content Center contains category properties. Within the category properties is general information regarding the category itself. The General information tab contains the category name, category image, and source library.

The Parameters tab contains parameters used within the category to assist in the description of parts located within that category. Figure 7.32 illustrates the parameter list in the ANSI Socket Head category.

FIGURE 7.32
Socket head parameters

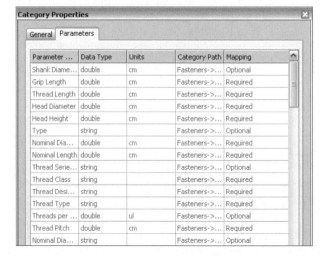

Parameter ...	Data Type	Units	Category Path	Mapping
Shank Diame...	double	cm	Fasteners->...	Optional
Grip Length	double	cm	Fasteners->...	Required
Thread Length	double	cm	Fasteners->...	Required
Head Diameter	double	cm	Fasteners->...	Required
Head Height	double	cm	Fasteners->...	Required
Type	string		Fasteners->...	Optional
Nominal Dia...	double	cm	Fasteners->...	Required
Nominal Length	double	cm	Fasteners->...	Required
Thread Serie...	string		Fasteners->...	Optional
Thread Class	string		Fasteners->...	Required
Thread Desi...	string		Fasteners->...	Required
Thread Type	string		Fasteners->...	Required
Threads per ...	double	ul	Fasteners->...	Optional
Thread Pitch	double	cm	Fasteners->...	Required
Nominal Dia...	string		Fasteners->...	Optional

Within the parameters shown earlier, some are optional and some are required. If you are placing a part within this category, you must map your part properties to all required fields for proper operation. Optional fields do not require mapping.

What this means is if you are planning on publishing a large number of your own parts to Content Center, then your part parameters must match the category parameters. If you are unable to match the parameters, then consider creating a new category.

EXPECT SOME INCONSISTENCY

The mapping required for Content Center is not consistent for all types of parts because of the evolution of these tools over time. Some of the categories require authoring before you can publish a part. Other categories are open for publishing without authoring. The requirements for restricted categories are driven by tools such as the Design Accelerator, Bolted Connection, and AutoDrop, which require certain parameters so they can intelligently place components. One inconsistency is Frame Generator. Since Content Center steel shapes predate Frame Generator, which originally had its own shape library, there weren't any authoring requirements. Just be aware of the inconsistencies.

Right-clicking an individual Content Center part will allow you to view the family properties and mapping of that part. Compare the category parameters of the part with the parameters of the intended category. Matching the two parameter lists ensures that the part will map easily into that category.

EDITING A CUSTOM CONTENT CENTER FAMILY

A Content Center family is an individual part, similar to an iPart. The part consists of a standard factory part with a family table attached that generates any of the optional table values.

You can edit any individual part by first switching the library view to your custom library designation, as shown in Figure 7.33.

FIGURE 7.33
Editing a Content
Center part

In the previous example, we switched the library view to the Mastering Inventor custom library. Right-click a part located within the custom library, and select Family Table. This launches a dialog box that allows the user to modify values, copy/paste, add/delete rows, or suppress existing rows within the table. The dialog box also allows the addition, deletion, and modification of columns and properties.

Publishing Parts to Content Center

Developing a process for reusing parts within your company's design environment is essential for standardization and improved productivity. Part of this process may include publishing existing Inventor parts stored in project libraries. Both normal parts and iParts can be published to a custom Content Center library.

The act of publishing a standard part into the custom library adds a family table to the published part. Exported Part parameters will be converted to table parameters when published to the Custom Content Center. iPart tables are converted to family tables when published.

PREPARING THE PART FOR PUBLISHING

If the part you intend to publish will be included in an existing Content Center family category (that is, fasteners, shaft parts, and so on), you can use the Component Authoring tool to prepare components with the necessary properties for use as "smart" content in the Content Center Library. You can do this by following these steps:

1. On the Get Started tab, click the Open button.

2. Browse for the file named `mi_7a_064.ipt` located in the Chapter 7 directory of the Mastering Inventor 2011 folder, and click Open.

3. Go to the Manage tab, and click the Component Authoring button on the Author panel.

4. From the drop-down list, select Fasteners ➢ Bolts, and select Other. Note the graphics and selection prompts change depending on the category of component selected.

5. Select the geometry for each row in the dialog box that corresponds to the dialog box graphic in order to map iMate placement to this part (iMates are preprogrammed assembly constraints).

6. Click the Parameter Mapping tab. Note that the parameters listed in the light yellow/orange rows are required, whereas the others are optional. Click the … button for the Grip Length row.

7. In the Part Template Parameters dialog box, expand the browser to find Parameters ➢ User, and select GripLength. This maps the part parameter to the corresponding family table parameter. Click OK.

8. Map the Nominal Diameter and the Nominal Length to the NomDiameter and NomLength model parameters, respectively (you can find these at Parameters ➢ Model rather than Parameters ➢ User).

9. Click the OK button to write the mapped parameters and iMates to the part file. You could also click the Publish Now button to start the publishing process.

You can author parts ahead of time and use the Batch Publish tool to publish one or more unopened parts at once. Or you can publish one part at a time as covered in the next section. Figure 7.34 shows the Component Authoring dialog box tabs.

FIGURE 7.34
Component
Authoring tabs

PUBLISHING THE PART

To publish a part to Content Center, you must have a custom library with read/write capability created, and your current project file must be configured to include this custom library. In this example, you will publish a simple part that has already been authored to the custom read/write Content Center library called Mastering Inventor. If you haven't already created this library, review the steps in the "Creating Custom Libraries" for desktop content of ADMS, depending on which method applies to your setup.

1. On the Get Started tab, click the Open button.

2. Browse for the file named mi_7a_068.ipt located in the Chapter 7 directory of the Mastering Inventor 2011 folder, and click Open.

3. Go to the Manage tab, and click the Publish Part button on the Content Center panel.

4. Select the Mastering Inventor library, and set the language as required; then click Next.

5. Ensure the Category To Publish To is set to Fasteners ➢ Bolts ➢ Other; then click Next.

6. Notice most of the parameters are already mapped, because this part has previously been authored per the steps in the "Preparing the Part for Publishing" section. Recall that all parameters in the light yellow/orange rows are required. Click the ellipsis button (the three dots) for the Thread Type row.

7. In the Part Template Parameters dialog box, expand the browser to find Threads ➢ Thread1, select Type, and then click OK.

8. Click Next in the Publish Guide dialog box.

9. Select Nominal Diameter, Nominal Length, and Part Number in the left pane, and use the arrow button to include them in the right pane. This defines keys that are available for selection upon placement of the Content Center part once published. At least one Key column must be defined. Click Next to continue.

10. Enter **EyeBolt** for the family name, and set the Standard Organization option to ANSI. Only the family name is required; however, designating the Standard Organization option allows the part to be listed when filtering per standard. You can also type a custom standard into the field, such as your company name. This allows you to create a filter for the parts you published.

11. Click Next, and notice the preview thumbnail. You can use the Browse icon to select a different graphic file for use as a thumbnail, if one exists.

12. Click Publish to complete the task and add this part to your custom Content Center library. Click OK in the successful publish confirmation box.

This creates the part family table in the Content Center library, but at this point there is only one row in the table. Typically you will want to add a row for each size or different type of the component. You can do this by using the Content Center Editor (found on the Manage tab). Figure 7.35 shows the family key and properties steps of the Publish Guide.

FIGURE 7.35
Publishing a part
to Content Center

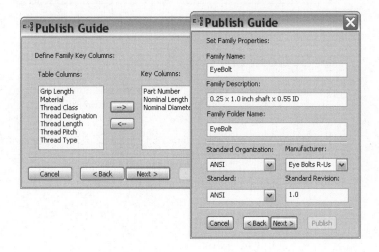

You can also convert a part to a table-driven iPart before publishing and include the rows for each size and type of the part configuration in the iPart table. Once you have a workable iPart that behaves correctly, you can then open the original factory iPart and publish the part. The iPart may be a custom iPart or a fully table-driven factory. iParts containing multiple row definitions in the table will convert to a fully table-driven Content Center part. You can find more information on iParts in the "Working with iParts" section at the beginning of this chapter.

Before using a newly published Content Center component in production, test the part in a blank assembly for proper function.

ADDING A NEW CATEGORY TO CONTENT CENTER

If you need a unique category for your own specific parts, you can simply add a new family of parts instead of using an existing category. You can do this from the Content Center Editor (accessed from the Manage tab). Make sure the library view is set to view only the read/write library you intend to create the new category in and that the tree view is enabled. Then right-click in the blank space in the Category View pane, and choose New Category. You can also create a subcategory by right-clicking an existing category and selecting New Category.

The Bottom Line

Create and modify iParts   iParts are the solution to creating parts that allow for an infinite number of variations without affecting other members of the same part family already used within your designs.

Master It   You use a purchased specialty part in your designs and would like to create the many size configurations this part comes in ahead of time for use within assembly design. How would this be done?

Create and use iFeatures and punches   Creating a library of often-used features is essential to standardization and improved productivity within your design workflow.

> **Master It**   You want to be able to place common punches, slots, and milled features quickly, rather than having to generate the feature every time. What is the best way to approach this?

Copy and clone features   You do not have to create iFeatures in order to reuse various part features in your designs. If a part feature will have limited use in other designs, it is often better to simply copy it from part to part or from face to face on the same part.

> **Master It**   You need to reuse features within a part or among parts. You consider iFeatures, but realize that this feature is not used often enough to justify setting up an iFeature. How would you proceed?

Link parameters between two files   Linking design parameters between two or more files allows you to control design changes from a single source, making it easy to update an entire design from one file.

> **Master It**   You want to specify the overall length and width of a layout design in a base part and then have other components update as changes are made to this part. What are the methods to do this?

Configure, create, and access Content Center parts   Content Center provides a great opportunity to reuse database-created geometry within assemblies and within functional design modules. The Content Center Editor provides the means to add custom content into Content Center. You can create and add custom libraries to your current project file.

> **Master It**   You would like to change the part numbers in some Content Center components to match the part numbers your company uses. You would also like to add proprietary components to Content Center. How do you customize the Content Center?

Chapter 8

Assembly Design Workflows

A typical assembly file is composed of links to the included *components* and *assembly constraints*. The components are parts or subassemblies that exist as separate files. When these components are placed into an assembly file, links to those individual files are created in the assembly file. Initially a component is free floating and can be moved and rotated in any direction, unless grounded in place or constrained to other components.

For example, if you were to create an assembly of a simple drilled base plate and a bolt to be inserted in the hole you would have three files:

- The assembly file (.iam)
- The base plate part file (.ipt)
- The bolt part file (.ipt)

When the part files are placed into the assembly file, links are created to the locations of those files. If the hole in the base plate part is made larger, the assembly is automatically updated to reflect that change since it is linked to the part file. In order to assemble the plate and bolt at least one assembly constraint would be placed by selecting the shaft of the bolt and the hole in the plate. Constraints have two functions:

- Constraints define how two or more components relate to one another.
- Constraints limit the degrees of freedom any one component has in the assembly.

Developing a good assembly design workflow is paramount to achieving performance, flexibility, and stability in your designs. In this chapter, you'll explore several types of workflows to achieve that goal. Included in this chapter is a discussion on how to use subassemblies to enhance performance. Using subassemblies within your design can substantially improve performance and ease of constraining. Component count can be in the hundreds of thousands of parts, as long as you have sufficient memory on your system.

In this chapter, you will learn how to:

- Assemble components using assembly constraints
- Organize designs using structured subassemblies
- Work with adaptive components
- Create assembly level features
- Manage bills of materials

- Use positional reps and flexible assemblies together

- Copy assembly designs for reuse and configuration

Assembly Constraints

Mastering the use of assembly constraints is an important part of learning to create assemblies in Inventor. Constraints are the glue and nails of construction when it comes to building your assemblies. Properly using assembly constraints will permit the construction of stable assemblies, assist in developing stack-up tolerances, and allow parts to be driven to show the animation of a process.

Improperly using assembly constraints can create a nightmare of broken and/or redundant constraints, preventing assemblies from functioning properly, destroying assembly performance, and creating rework. Understanding how assembly constraints function in an assembly will help assure success in building and editing your design.

How Constraints Work

In Inventor, assembly constraints are used to attach parts or subassemblies together, creating assembly relationships between the components, and therefore defining the way they fit together based on the selection of faces, edges, or vertices and user defined parameters. In general practice, constraint function follows real-world assembly techniques where fasteners, adhesives, and welds attach one component to another.

There are six basic types of constraints in Inventor. Most of the constraint types have multiple solution types that can be used to achieve the result you are looking for. Here is a list of the constraint types and their solutions:

- *Mate constraints* position components face to face or adjacent to one another.

    - The *Mate solution* positions selected faces normal to one another, with faces coincident; imagine two plates butted together.

    - The *Flush solution* aligns components adjacent to one another with faces flush; imagine two plates flushed along an outside corner.

- *Angle constraints* position two components at a specified angle to define a pivot point.

    - The *Directed Angle solution* always applies the right-hand rule to selected faces or edges.

    - The *Undirected Angle solution* allows either orientation and is used in situations where component orientation flips.

    - The *Explicit Reference Vector solution* defines the direction of rotation axis.

- *Tangent constraints* position two components to contact at a point of tangency.

    - The *Inside solution* positions the first selected component inside the second selected component at the tangent point.

    - The *Outside solution* positions the first selected component outside the second selected component at the tangent point.

◆ *Insert constraints* is a combination of a face-to-face mate constraint between planar faces and a mate constraint between the axes of the two components.

   ◆ The *Opposed solution* reverses the mate direction of the first selected component.

   ◆ The *Aligned solution* reverses the mate direction of the second selected component.

◆ *Rotation constraints* allow one component to rotate based on the selection of a second component.

   ◆ The *Rotation solution* allows the first selected component to rotate in relation to another component using a specified ratio; imagine two gears.

   ◆ The *Rotation-Translation solution* allows the first selected component to rotate as it translates the face of another component; imagine a rack and pinion.

◆ *Translational constraints* specifies the relationship between a cylindrical component and a contiguous set of faces on another component, such as a cam in a slot.

When using constraints, a minimum of two and a maximum of three constraints are required to fully constrain two components together so that their relationship is fully defined. Undercontrained components allow a motion in the unconstrained axis or plane. Components fully contained within a subassembly will not figure into the constraint analysis when the top-level assembly is opened or modified.

Degrees of Freedom

Each unconstrained component existing within an assembly file possesses six degrees of freedom initially. The degrees of freedom (DOF) are bidirectional and consist of three axial degrees of freedom along the X, Y, and Z origin axes, as well as full rotational freedom around the same axes.

For ease of use when learning and applying constraints, it might help to make the degrees of freedom visible through the View tab by clicking the Degrees of Freedom button. As constraints are applied to your component, the DOF triad will change to only show the remaining DOF. When the component is fully constrained, the triad will disappear. Figure 8.1 illustrates the activation process.

FIGURE 8.1
Activating Degrees
of Freedom view

 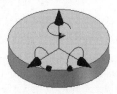

You can also analyze the degrees of freedom for the complete assembly. The Degree of Freedom Analysis button is located in the Productivity panel drop-down list found on the Assembly tab. A dialog box displays each component (part or subassembly) at the active level of the assembly. The number of translation and rotation DOF are listed.

If you select Animate Freedom at the bottom of the dialog box, and then select a component in the list, it will move to show the DOF, assuming it is not already fully constrained. Figure 8.2 shows the Degree of Freedom Analysis dialog box.

FIGURE 8.2
Animating an underconstrained component from the Degree of Freedom Analysis dialog box

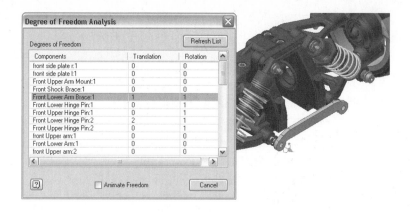

Follow these steps to animate the underconstrained component:

1. Click the Get Started tab and choose Open.

2. Browse for the file named `mi_8a_001.iam` located in the Chapter 8 directory of the Mastering Inventor 2011 folder and click Open.

3. Click the View tab and then select the Degrees of Freedom button to turn on the degrees of freedom triad for each part.

You'll notice that each part has a triad denoting the axes the part is able to translate along, or rotate around. There are only three triads shown because the part called 8-001 is grounded and cannot move at all.

4. Click the Assemble tab, then select the drop-down on the Productivity panel and select Degree of Freedom Analysis.

5. Select Animate Freedom at the bottom of the dialog box.

6. Click 8_002 in the list. Watch it rotate in the free axis, demonstrating its DOF.

7. Click 8_003 in the list. Watch it rotate and move up and down, demonstrating its DOF.

8. Click 8_004 in the list. Watch it rotate and slide along the face of the plate in two directions, demonstrating its DOF.

These tools can be very helpful when trying to determine how parts are constrained or not constrained in an assembly. You may find that leaving the DOF triads turned on will help you as you learn how constraints work. You can close the current file without saving changes and continue on to the next section.

Grounded Components

When you place a component into a new assembly it is automatically given a *grounded* state. A grounded component is fully constrained and has 0 degrees of freedom. You can ground or un-ground any component in an assembly by right-clicking on and selecting Grounded from the right-click context menu. Every assembly should have at least one grounded component. If components are not grounded the assembly can become misaligned from the X, Y, and Z axes and will cause problems when you try to detail the assembly in the drawing environment.

> ### PLACING COMPONENTS IN AN ASSEMBLY
>
> In order to place components in an assembly, you can use the Place button found on the assembly tab and then browse to locate the component. Additionally you can drag part and assembly files from Windows Explorer and drop them into the assembly.
>
> To place additional instances of components already in the assembly, you can copy and paste components from the graphic area or simply click and drag components from the browser.

In certain workflows where parts are placed into the assembly in the correct position and orientation to begin with, all components can be grounded. This is done automatically when an assembly is created from a multi-body part using the Make Components tool. If a particular component needs to be adjusted, it can be un-grounded and then constrained using assembly constraints.

The ground all strategy can also be used to rebuild assemblies that have a great many errant assembly constraints due to major uncontrolled changes. For instance if you opened an assembly that has fifty constraints and of those forty-two of them have errors, you might be better off to select all of the components and ground them in place. Next you would set the browser from Assembly View to Model View using the toggle at the top of the browser, and then select all of the constraints with errors from the Constraint folder, and delete them. You could then leave everything grounded or un-ground and re-constrain them one at a time.

Working with Constraints

As mentioned there are several types of constraints available for use in an assembly. In order to know which one to use and when, you should be familiar with each. Keep in mind, however, certain constraint types are used more often than others. In the following pages you will explore the creation of the various constraint types.

MATE CONSTRAINT

The Mate constraint type is made up of two solutions: Mate and Flush. Figure 8.3 compares the two solutions. On the far left the selections are shown, in the middle the Mate solution is shown, and on the right the Flush solution is shown.

FIGURE 8.3
Mate and Flush
solutions

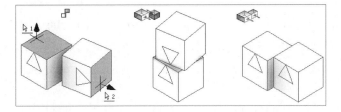

To explore the Mate constraint options you will open a simple fixture assembly and assemble two plates to match the completed assembly next to it.

1. Click the Get Started tab, and choose Open.

2. Browse for the file named `mi_8a_002.iam` located in the Chapter 8 directory of the Mastering Inventor 2011 folder, and click Open.

3. Click the View tab, and select the Degrees of Freedom button to turn on the DOF triad for each underconstrained part.

4. From the Assemble tab, click the Constrain button (or type C on the keyboard).

5. In the Place Constraint dialog box, ensure the Assembly tab is active and the Mate button is selected for the Type. Make sure the Preview check box is selected and the Predict Offset and Orientation check box is cleared.

Within the Place Constraint dialog box, you have three check boxes:

Pick Part First   This check box, indicated by the small red cube, is useful when parts are partially obscured or are positioned in such a way that clicking a face or edge is difficult. This option requires you to first select the component and then filters the selectable geometry to that single component.

Predict Offset and Orientation   This button measures the distance between the selected faces, allowing you to eyeball a part placement and then retrieve the distance. If the check box is not selected, a default of 0 is entered for the offset.

Preview   This check box, denoted by the eyeglasses icon, controls whether the selected components will adjust position or orientation in order to review the constraint before clicking Apply or OK to actually create the constraint.

6. For Selection 1, click the orange face on the part with the triangular feature. Watch the on-screen highlights to be careful to select the face and not an edge. It may be helpful to zoom in.

7. For Selection 2, click the circular face on the base part.

You should see the part "snap" into place based upon your selection points. This is just a preview of the constraint and is controlled by the Preview check box. Notice the first and second geometry selection buttons are color coded in the Place Constraint dialog box. Also notice that as you select faces, they are shaded to match the first and second geometry selections.

8. In order to adjust the constraint selection, press the Selection 2 button in the Place Constraint dialog box. This removes the previous selection (the circular face) and allows you to re-select the mating face.

9. For the re-selection, click the orange face on the base plate.

10. Click Apply to place the Mate constraint on the two parts.

11. Next, select the yellow face of the base plate and the yellow face of the side plate for Selection 1 and 2.

12. You should see the two yellow faces mate together in a way that is not what you want. Click the Flush button in the Solutions area of the dialog box and you should see the preview update to give a more desirable result.

13. Click OK to place the flush constraint and close the dialog box.

At this point the DOF triad should only have one remaining arrow, indicating that all of the other DOF have been removed as the constraints were added.

14. Click and drag on the part with the triangular feature and note that it will slide in the direction indicated by the DOF symbol, and only in that direction.

Using Rotate and Move

Next you will place the final constraint required to fully assemble the two parts. But before placing the remaining constraint it may be helpful to rotate the part so that you can easily select the required faces. To do so you will use the Rotate tool. The Rotate tool allows you to rotate a selected component and rotate just it in the assembly. The Rotate tool suspends any constraints currently involving the selected component to allow it to be rotated. The constraints are activated again when the Update button is clicked or when some other action, such as placing another constraint forces an update. The Move tool works the same as the Rotate tool regarding constraints. Continue on from the previous step to see how this works.

15. From the Assemble tab, click the Rotate button.

16. Select the part with the triangular feature and you will see the Rotate "globe" appear.

17. Spin the part so that you can see the purple face.

- For free rotation, click inside the rotate "globe" and drag in short strokes.

- To rotate about the horizontal axis, click the top or bottom handle of the rotate "globe" and drag vertically.

- To rotate about the vertical axis, click the left or right handle of the 3D rotate symbol and drag horizontally.

- To rotate flat to the screen, place your cursor over the edge of the "globe" until the symbol changes to a circle, and then click and drag around the "globe."

18. Right-click and choose Done to exit the Rotate tool.

19. From the Assemble tab, click the Constrain button.

20. Select the purple face on each part and then click OK.

This will fully constrain the part and remove the final DOF arrow from display. You can close this file without saving changes and continue to the next section to explore more constraint options.

Editing and Deleting Constraints

Each of the constraints you placed in the previous steps was added to the browser under the parts involved. You can access these constraints in order to make changes or delete them by expanding the browser node for one of the components. In the following steps you will edit and delete a constraint.

1. Click the Get Started tab, and choose Open.

2. Browse for the file named mi_8a_003.iam located in the Chapter 8 directory of the Mastering Inventor 2011 folder, and click Open.

3. Expand the plus icon next to both of the parts in the browser to reveal the constraints listed below them. There are two mates and one flush constraining these two parts.

4. Right-click on the Flush constraint and select Edit.

You'll notice that the options are much like those used to create the constraint. You can re-select selection inputs 1 and 2, modify the solution from Flush to Mate, or even change the type. In this case you will add an offset value.

5. Enter **-10 mm** in the Offset input box. If the preview button is selected, you should see the part adjust to preview the flush offset.

6. Click OK to accept the edit.

7. Click on the Flush constraint in the browser again. Notice that it now displays the offset value.

8. At the bottom of the browser is an input box where you can adjust the offset without needing to bring up the edit dialog box. Enter **12 mm** and press the Enter key on the keyboard. The part will adjust to the new offset.

9. Next, double click on the icon next to the Flush in the browser.

10. An Edit Dimension box will appear, offering another way to edit the offset parameter for this flush constraint.

11. It is often helpful to name constraint offset parameters for use later on. Type **Block_Offset = 40 mm** into the box and then click the green checkmark button (or press the Enter key on the keyboard).

12. Go to the Manage tab and click the Parameters button.

13. In the resulting dialog box, you'll see the Block_Offset parameter in the list. Note the other two parameters are for the Mate constraints. Click Done to exit the Parameters dialog box.

14. Click the View tab and the select the Degrees of Freedom button to turn on the DOF triad for each underconstrained part. In this case, no triads appear because the assembly is currently fully constrained.

15. Right-click on the Flush constraint in the browser and choose Delete. You'll now see a DOF arrow showing you that the part is now free to slide along one axis.

16. Click and drag the part to see it move in its free axis.

17. From the Assemble tab, click the Constrain button.

18. In the Place Constraint dialog box, click the Predict Offset and Orientation check box (find it next to the preview check box).

19. Set the solution to Flush and then select the yellow faces of the two parts.

20. Note the offset value reports the current distance between the two yellow faces. Enter **Block_Offset = 20 mm**, and then click OK.

Editing and creating Mate and Flush constraints will likely make up a majority of the constraint types you create. Take the time to master these constraints and you will find the other constraint types much easier to learn as well. You can close this file without saving changes. If you'd like more practice with Mate and Flush constraints, you can open the files called mi_8a_004.iam, mi_8a_005.iam, and mi_8a_006.iam and assemble them using the concepts you just learned. Use the assembled parts as an example to put together the unassembled parts in each of these files.

Mate to Edges, Centerlines, and Vertices

In addition to selecting faces for creating Mate constraints, you can also use edges, centerlines, and vertices as selections. When using edges or centerlines, keep in mind that you are defining a different number of degrees of freedom than when using faces, therefore the results can be quite different. It is also important to understand that edges and centerlines have no negative or positive value, and therefore edge-to-edge type constraints are not a good choice for creating mate offsets. Instead use a face-to-edge mate in those cases.

Depending on the available geometry, you will often need to use the Select Other tool to cycle through the available selections in order to select an edge or vertex. To use the Select Other tool, hover over a selection and wait for the Select Other toolbar to appear. Then slide your cursor to the left or right arrow on the toolbar and click. When the geometry you want is highlighted, slide your cursor back to the green button in the center of the toolbar and click. This will select the geometry. Figure 8.4 shows the Select Other tool being used to select a centerline on the left, a cylindrical face in the center, and the back face on the right.

FIGURE 8.4
Using the Select
Other tool

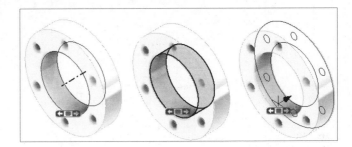

ANGLE CONSTRAINT

The Angle constraint permits three solutions within this constraint type. The solutions are Directed Angle, Undirected Angle, and Explicit Reference Vector. The Directed Angle solution always applies the right-hand rule, meaning that the angle rotation will function in a counterclockwise direction.

The Undirected Angle allows either counterclockwise or clockwise direction, resolving situations where a component orientation will flip during a constraint drive or drag operation.

The Explicit Reference Vector solution allows for the definition of a z-axis vector by adding a third click to the selection. This option will reduce the tendency of an Angle constraint to flip to an alternate solution during a constraint drive or drag. Figure 8.5 illustrates the selections required for this solution.

1. Click the Get Started tab, and choose Open.

2. Browse for the file named mi_8a_007.iam located in the Chapter 8 directory of the Mastering Inventor 2011 folder, and click Open.

3. From the Assemble tab, click the Constrain button (or type C on the keyboard).

4. In the Type area of the Place Constraint dialog box, select the Angle button.

5. In the Solution area, click the Directed Angle button.

6. For Selection 1, click the large face of the painted board that the hinges are mounted on.

7. For Selection 2, click the large face of the unpainted board that the hinges are mounted on.

8. Enter **90** into the Angle input box, and note the preview displays as expected.

9. Click the Selection 1 and 2 buttons to clear them and then select the unpainted board for Selection 1 and the painted board for Selection 2. Pay attention to which selection button is pushed in as you select to ensure that you get this right.

FIGURE 8.5
Explicit reference vector

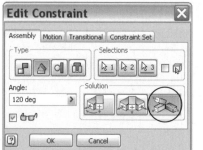 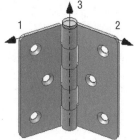

PLACE ASSEMBLY CONSTRAINTS USING ALT-DRAG

Rather than using the Place Constraint dialog box, you can press and hold the Alt key and then drag a component into position. Constraints are inferred based on the type of geometry selected. The constraint is previewed in the graphics area as you drag over the components involved. To set a specific constraint, release the Alt key and enter one of the following shortcut keys. You can press the space bar to flip the constraint solution, from mate to flush, for example.

M or 1 Changes to a mate constraint.

A or 2 Changes to an angle constraint.

T or 3 Changes to a tangent constraint.

I or 4 Changes to an insert constraint.

R or 5 Changes to a rotation motion constraint.

S or 6 Changes to a translation motion (slide) constraint.

X or 8 Changes to a transitional constraint.

To see the Alt-drag method in action, go to the Get Started tab, and click the Show Me Animations button. Click the Assemblies – Constraints link in the list and then choose Alt-drag Shortcut Animation from the next list.

You will see from the result that the 90 degree angle is dependent upon the selection order. In this case you could enter **–90** to flip the angles also, but had you selected edges rather than faces entering **–90** would not work. Next continue on to explore the Undirected Angle solution.

10. Click Cancel to exit the Place Constraint dialog and then click the Constrain button to bring it back up (this ensures that your selections and input are cleared before continuing).

11. In the Type area of the Place Constraint dialog box, select the Angle button, and then in the Solution area, click the Undirected Angle button.

12. Select the two faces and enter **90** degrees again. You'll note the preview updates as expected.

13. Click the Selection 1 and 2 buttons to clear them and then select the unpainted board for Selection 1 and the painted board for Selection 2. Pay attention to which selection button is pushed in as you select to ensure that you get this right.

You will notice that the angle is not dependent on the selection order. And if you try entering **–90** for the angle input, you'll see that the negative value does not change the angle. This option can be more stable for use in setting up angles that will be changed in configurations, animations, and so on, but it is still largely dependent upon the other constraints in the assembly. If the constraints holding the hinge to the boards were modified, the undirected angle constraint may need to be adjusted. Next, continue on to explore the Explicit Reference Vector solution.

14. Click Cancel to exit the Place Constraint dialog and then click the Constrain button to bring it back up.

15. In the Type area of the Place Constraint dialog box, select the Angle button, and then in the Solution area, ensure the Explicit Reference Vector button is selected.

16. For Selection 1, click on the large face of the painted board that the hinges are mounted on.

17. For Selection 2, click on the large face of the unpainted board that the hinges are mounted on.

18. Next run your cursor over the cylindrical faces in the center of either hinge. You should see the direction arrow flip back and forth depending upon which face is highlighted.

19. When you find a face that points the arrow in toward the center of the assembly, click it. This selects the center axis of the hinge pivot, and therefore defines the entire angle constraint without relying on other existing constraints to establish the vector reference.

20. Enter **90** degrees.

You'll note the preview updates incorrectly, flipping the assembly down and causing an interference situation. To correct this, you can enter a negative angle or you can simply reselect Selection 3 so that it points the other way.

21. Click the Selection 3 button again to clear it, and then find a face that makes the arrow point out from the center of the assembly and select it. You'll notice the preview updates to flip the assembly up, as desired.

You may be wondering why there are so many angle options at this point. Originally, Inventor did not include all three of these angle solutions, and options were added to improve the predictability of angle constraint updates. At this point though, if you use the default Explicit Reference Vector solution, your angle constraints will update predictably.

As a final note on angle constraints, you will probably find that using edges rather than faces for angle constraints will provide more predictable results, particularly when setting up constraints to be used in creating positional variations for animation or documentation purposes. You can close this file without saving changes, and continue on to the next section.

USING THE RIGHT-HAND RULE

A good way to visualize the Explicit Reference Vector command is to use the right-hand rule. Take your right hand and make a "gun" shape with your index finger pointing out and your thumb pointing up. Now point your middle finger to the left, 90 degrees to the index finger. Your hand will then be making the three major axes. You can then use the thumb to determine the positive axes of the cross product of the x- and y-axes (the index and middle finger).

TANGENT CONSTRAINT

A Tangent constraint results in faces, planes, cylinders, spheres, and cones coming in contact at a point of tangency. Tangency can exist inside or outside of a curve depending on the direction of the selected surface normal. The number of degrees of freedom a Tangent constraint removes depends on the geometry. When a Tangent constraint is applied between a cylinder and a planar face, the constraint will remove one degree of linear freedom as well as one degree of rotational freedom from the set.

1. Click the Get Started tab, and choose Open.

2. Browse for the file named mi_8a_008.iam located in the Chapter 8 directory of the Mastering Inventor 2011 folder, and click Open.

3. From the Assemble tab, click the Constrain button (or type C on the keyboard).

4. In the Type area of the Place Constraint dialog box, select the Tangent button.

5. For Selection 1, click the face of one of the sphere-shaped ball bearings.

6. For Selection 2, click the face of one of the half-sphere cutouts in the block.

7. Note that the preview sets the bearing to the outside. In the Solution area, click the Inside button.

8. Click Apply and create an identical tangent constraint for the second ball bearing.

9. Create another tangent constraint, but this time use the Outside solution and select the cylinder of the shaft and the spherical face of one of the ball bearings.

10. Before creating the last tangent constraint, click OK to exit the Place Constraint dialog box and click on the shaft and pull it up toward the top of the ball bearing it is tangent with. This is just so that the next tangent constraint will not solve to the lower hemisphere and run the shaft into the block.

11. Create another tangent constraint, again using the Outside solution and select the cylinder of the shaft and the spherical face of one of the ball bearings.

Tangent constraints are fairly straightforward, and although they are not the most common constraint type to use, they are often the only one that will allow you to get the result you need when working with cylinders, spheres, and curved faces. You can test the function of the shaft and bearing constraint set by clicking and dragging on the shaft to see it rotate, and then you can close the file without saving changes. Figure 8.6 shows the placement of a Tangent constraint.

FIGURE 8.6
Tangent
constraints

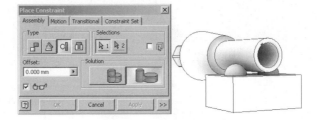

INSERT CONSTRAINT

The Insert constraint is probably the best choice for inserting fasteners and other cylindrical objects into holes or for constraining any parts where circular or cylindrical geometry is to be constrained to one another. A single Insert constraint will replace two Mate constraints (one along the edge and one through the centerline), retaining one rotational degree of freedom. Options for the Insert constraint are Opposed and Aligned. The Insert constraint also allows for specifying offset values between components. Figure 8.7 shows common uses of Insert constraints.

1. Click the Get Started tab, and choose Open.

2. Browse for the file named mi_8a_009.iam located in the Chapter 8 directory of the Mastering Inventor 2011 folder, and click Open.

3. From the Assemble tab, click the Constrain button (or type C on the keyboard).

4. In the Type area of the Place Constraint dialog box select the Insert button.

5. Select the bottom edge of one of the screw heads for Selection 1. Notice the highlight shows the edge and the centerline are selected.

6. Select the top edge of one of the eight holes on the plate for Selection 2.

7. Toggle the solution button to see the difference in the two solutions and then set the solution to Opposed.

8. Enter **2 mm** in the Offset input box, and then click Apply.

9. Select the edge of one of the washers and then the bottom edge of the screw head to place and apply another insert constraint.

10. Next, set another insert constraint using the edge of the yellow face of one of the boss features and one of the nuts. Use the Aligned solution to flip the nut so it is set down inside the boss feature.

11. Use insert constraints to place the blue cover on the base part by selecting the rounded corners.

FIGURE 8.7
Insert constraints

You can continue to practice with the remaining hardware. Use copy and paste to add more instances if you'd like. When you're done, you can close the file without saving changes.

MINIMUM DISTANCE USING THE MEASURE TOOL

You can find the minimum distance between two assembly components by using the Measure tool. To access the Measure tool, go to the Tools tab and select Measure Distance from the Measure panel. Click the priority drop-down box in the Measure Distance tool and set it to Part Priority. Next, select the first part and then select the second part. The returned value is the minimum distance between the two parts.

Motion Constraints

Within the Place Constraint dialog box are the Motion tab and the Translational tab. From the Motion tab, you can add *Rotation* constraints and *Rotation-Translation* constraints. A rotation constraint is typically placed between two components, such as gears, simulating a ratio-based rotation. Rotation-Translation constraints allow a linear distance and revolution ratio to be applied, for component pairs such as rack and pinion sets. From the Translational tab, you create constraints between a rotating and nonlinear translating face, such as cams and followers.

ROTATION CONSTRAINT

To create a simple Rotation constraint, first place two components constrained around their axes. Neither component should be grounded; instead, they should be constrained to allow rotation around the axes. The Rotational constraint applies a forward or reverse solution to the two components, along with a ratio that will determine rotation speeds, as shown in Figure 8.8.

FIGURE 8.8
Rotation constraint options

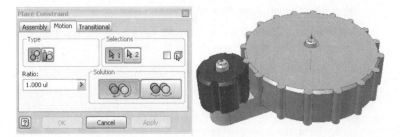

In the following steps you will create a reverse rotation constraint on a small cog set.

1. Click the Get Started tab, and choose Open.

2. Browse for the file named mi_8a_010.iam located in the Chapter 8 directory of the Mastering Inventor 2011 folder, and click Open.

3. From the Assemble tab, click the Constrain button (or type C on the keyboard).

4. Click the Motion tab in the Place Constraint dialog box.

5. In the Type area of the Place Constraint dialog box, select the Rotation button.

6. For Selection 1, click the yellow face on the large cog and for Selection 2, click the yellow face on the small cog.

7. In the Solution area, click the Reverse button.

8. Note the Ratio is automatically set to 3 ul (ul means unitless). Based on the selected geometry, you could enter any value you want, but in this case you'll leave it at 3. You should be aware had you selected the cogs in the opposite order, the ratio would be 0.333, the reciprocal of its current value. Click OK to create the rotation constraint.

Currently, the assembly is fully constrained and will not rotate. This is because of the Mate constraint named Alignment Mate, which has been placed on the XZ origin planes of each cog. The purpose of this Mate constraint is simply to line the cogs up in their start position. In order to let the rotation constraint work, the mate must be suppressed or deleted.

9. Locate the Alignment Mate constraint in the browser. You can do so by expanding either of the cogs in the browser.

10. Right-click on the Alignment Mate and choose Suppress. The constraint will now be grayed out and will not calculate against the assembly.

11. Click and drag on either of the cogs to rotate them.

If you start the rotation with both yellow faces showing and count the number of times the small cog rotates before the yellow face on the large cog comes back around, you will see it make three revolutions to every one of the large cog, as specified by the ratio in the constraint input. You can close the file without saving changes, and continue to the next set of steps where you will create a Rotation-Translation constraint.

ROTATION-TRANSLATION CONSTRAINT

CERT OBJECTIVE

In the following steps you will create a Rotation-Translation constraint as would be used to constrain a rack and pinion gear set.

1. Click the Get Started tab, and choose Open.

2. Browse for the file named mi_8a_011.iam located in the Chapter 8 directory of the Mastering Inventor 2011 folder, and click Open.

3. From the Assemble tab, click the Constrain button (or type C on the keyboard).

4. Click the Motion tab in the Place Constraint dialog box.

5. In the Type area of the Place Constraint dialog box select the Rotation-Translation button.

6. For Selection 1, click the yellow face on the cog. Notice the selection glyph displays a rotation arrow, indicating it is looking for the rotational selection. Selection order is important in this case.

7. For Selection 2, in the Solution area, click along the bottom edge of the rack. Be certain to select the edge, not the face. Although there is nothing preventing you from selecting the face or indicating that it is not the correct selection, the constraint will simply not work if the face is selected.

8. Note the value added to the Distance input box. This is the total travel of the rack for one revolution of the cog. This value is initially calculated from the selections, but you can enter your own value as required. In this case, the number it is not an even number due to the mix of imperial and metric dimensions used in this model. Click OK to create the constraint.

Figure 8.9 shows the constraint selections.

FIGURE 8.9
Rotation-Translation constraint options

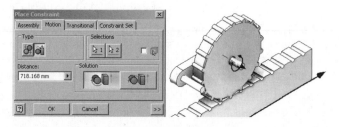

Currently, the assembly is fully constrained and will not rotate. This is because of the Mate constraint named Start Point Mate, which has been placed on the rack and cog. In order to let the Rotation-Translation constraint work, the mate must be suppressed or deleted.

9. Locate the Start Point Mate constraint in the browser. You can do so by expanding the rack in the browser.

10. Right-click on the Start Point Mate and choose Suppress. The constraint will now be grayed out and will not calculate against the assembly.

11. Click and drag on the rack to see the rotation and translation take place.

Although motion constraints are easy to place, be aware that the real work is in the calculations of creating components with the correct geometry beforehand. If you have a need to create a lot of gears, you'll want to explore the gear generator design accelerator. For now, you can close the file without saving changes and continue to the next section.

TRANSITIONAL CONSTRAINTS

CERT
OBJECTIVE

Transitional constraints allow the movement of an underconstrained component along a path in a separate part. To create a Transitional constraint, you first select a moving face on the underconstrained component. Then you select a transitional face or edge on a fully constrained or grounded part.

Figure 8.10 illustrates a cam and follower with a Translational constraint applied.

1. Click the Get Started tab, and choose Open.

2. Browse for the file named `mi_8a_012.iam` located in the Chapter 8 directory of the Mastering Inventor 2011 folder, and click Open.

3. From the Assemble tab, click the Constrain button (or type C on the keyboard).

4. Click the Translational tab in the Place Constraint dialog box.

5. For Selection 1, click the yellow face on the follower wheel. Note the first selection must be the moving face.

6. For Selection 2, click the orange face on the cam. Note this selection must be the translational face.

7. Click OK to create the constraint.

8. Click and drag on the cam and rotate it around the axis to see the assembly in action.

FIGURE 8.10
A Transitional
Constraint

Components used in Translational constraints must always be in contact for them to work, therefore no offsets are permitted. The translational face (in this case the cam) can be any combination of flat, arced or splined defined faces, however it is generally best to avoid sharp corners. When finished examining the Translational constraint functionality, you can close the file without saving changes.

Additional Constrain Tools and Options

In addition to the basic constraint types and options, there are a number of other tools and options to be aware of. These tools and options are covered in the following pages.

USING THE ASSEMBLE TOOL TO PLACE CONSTRAINTS

The Assemble tool allows you to move a component into place and place a constraint based on the selected geometry. This tool is designed to select a component and then fully constrain it. When using the Assemble tool, you select the component you want to move into place first and then the component you want to constrain to. Because of this, you can constrain only one component at a time with this tool. To constrain a second component, you must click OK to exit the Assemble tool and then select the Assemble button again or right-click and select Repeat Assemble.

As constraints are placed, the geometry involved is left highlighted on-screen. These new constraints are not created until the Assemble tool is exited by clicking the OK button. If any conflicts with existing constraints are created, you are presented with the Assemble Constraint Management dialog box. You can find options in this dialog box to resolve the conflicts.

You can open the file called mi_8a_013.iam to explore the Assemble tool, following these general steps:

1. From the Assemble tab, click Assemble button.

2. Select some geometry on the component to be moved into place.

3. Select some geometry on the component that is intended to stay in place.

4. Enter values such as offsets or angle values if needed.

5. If necessary change the solution type (from mate to flush, for example).

6. From this point you can do any of the following:

   ♦ Click Apply and continue to define other constraints for the selected component.

   ♦ Click OK to create the constraints based on the previous selections and exit the Assemble tool.

   ♦ Click Undo to delete current selections and then continue defining constraints.

CONSTRAINT AUDIO NOTIFICATION

When you place a constraint in an assembly, Inventor makes a sound at the time of the preview or at the time of the constraint creation, depending upon the preview option at the time. You can disable this sound by going to the Tools tab, selecting Application Options, and then clicking the Assembly tab. Uncheck the Constraint Audio Notification check box to disable the sound.

You can change the sound by replacing the default sound file with one of your choice. The sound file is called `Connect.wav` and can be found in the `C:\Program Files\Autodesk\Inventor 2011\Bin` folder (assuming that is the install path).

CONSTRAINT SETS

Constraint Sets allow you to constrain two components together using their User Coordinate Systems (UCS). You define the UCS in the part or subassembly file first and then place constraints on the coordinate system planes and axes rather than the component geometry.

You can open the file called `mi_8a_014.iam` to explore constraint sets, following these general steps:

1. From the Assemble tab, click the Constrain button.

2. In the Place Constraint dialog box, click the Constraint Set tab.

3. Expand the browser nodes for both components so you can see the UCS features listed.

4. Select each UCS for Selections 1 and 2.

5. Click OK to create a set of constraints between the two UCS triads.

CONSTRAINT LIMITS

Constraint Limits allow you to define minimum and maximum constraint values so components can move freely within the limits but not beyond them. You can imagine a model of a door hinge. You might want the hinge to swing from 0 to 270 degrees, but not outside of that range, or the hinge might interfere with itself.

You can open the file called `mi_8a_015.iam` to explore constraint limits. In this assembly there are four parts. These would be four subassemblies in reality, but for the sake of simplicity they have been condensed into part files. The router base is grounded in place and the Y- and Z- axis Assemblies have been fully constrained with constraint limits, so they are free to slide within the bounds of the bearing rods and gantry uprights. You can click and drag on the Z-Axis Assembly to see how it behaves in a realistic manner due to the existing constraint limits. But if you click on the X-Axis Assembly, you will see it does travel along the bearing rods realistically, but it can continue sliding through the Router Base and beyond. To fix this, you will add a constraint set to the X-Axis Assembly, limiting its travel to a more realistic result.

1. From the Assemble tab, click the Constrain button (or type C on the keyboard).

2. Set the solution to Flush.

3. Select the two yellow faces for Selection 1 and 2.

4. Click the >> button to expand the dialog box.

5. Click the Maximum and Minimum check boxes.

6. Enter **-10 mm** for the maximum value.

7. Enter **-395 mm** for the minimum value.

8. Click the Use Offset As Resting Position check box.

9. Enter **-150** for the offset value (located back toward the top of the dialog box).

10. Enter **X Travel** in the Name input box, and then click OK to create the constraint.

11. Click on the X-Axis Assembly, and you will see it now stops before running through the other components.

Figure 8.11 shows the constraint limit being created.

FIGURE 8.11
Transitional
constraint

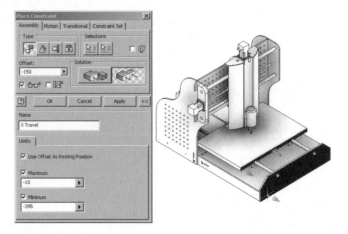

You can drag the X-Axis Assembly to its minimum and maximum limits, but when you let go it returns to the resting value you set in the dialog box. Keep in mind, you are not required to use the resting position option. If no resting value is used, the assembly will stay where it was last placed, which is the behavior exhibited by the Z-Axis Assembly.

Constraint Limits are a great tool to use in the setup of free moving components to get them to behave predictably. However, you should be aware there may be a small performance hit when using too many of these at once. So keep that in mind as you use them. You can close the assembly without saving changes.

DRIVING CONSTRAINTS

It is often desirable to simulate motion by driving a constraint through a beginning position and an ending position to confirm the intent of the design. In general, Offset and Angle constraints may be selected to drive components within an assembly. To accomplish this, simply right-click the desired constraint, and select Drive Constraint (as shown in Figure 8.12).

You can open the file called mi_8a_016.iam to explore the drive constraint options. If you expand the Z-Axis Assembly node, you will find two constraints labeled Drive Me. When you right-click on a constraint and choose Drive Constraint, the Drive Constraint dialog box will appear, allowing you to alter the constraint by specifying steps between the start position and the end position. When a constraint is driven, any components constrained to the driven component will move in accordance to their particular shared constraints. The motion may be set to forward or reverse, stopped at any time, and even recorded by clicking the Record button prior to activating the move. If any of the affected components are constrained to a grounded component, or if the movement will violate any existing constraint, then the drive constraint will fail.

FIGURE 8.12
Driving a
constraint

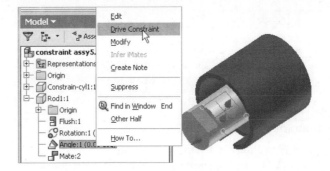

Expanding the dialog box as shown in Figure 8.13 by pressing the >> button will reveal additional controls over the drive constraint. The increment of movement can be controlled by a value or by a total number of steps from beginning to end. The length of a particular driven constraint can be controlled by the number of allowable repetitions from Start to End or can be reversed by using the Start/End/Start option. For a continuous revolution by degrees, you may exceed 360° by specifying the total number of degrees of revolution or by including an equation such as 360 deg *3.

FIGURE 8.13
Drive Constraint
dialog box options

Other parts properly constrained within the driven assembly that are adaptive will adjust to changes if the Drive Adaptivity option is selected. This particular option allows determination of a maximum or minimum condition for the adaptive part.

Checking the Collision Detection option allows for determination of an exact collision distance or angle between the driven parts. Using the Collision Detection option will help you determine interferences between moving parts so that those parts can be modified before manufacturing.

> ### USING THE CONTACT SOLVER FOR COLLISION DETECTION
>
> If you have parts that interfere (such as a dowel pin in a hole) and have the Collision Detection option selected, the Drive Constraint command will stop immediately because it will have detected this interference. If you really need to test the collision of parts, look into using the Contact Solver.

CONTACT SOLVER

Another method for driving components within an assembly involves the Contact Solver option. With this option, only minimal constraints are required to drive a number of components. Components are not required to be constrained to one another for the Contact Solver to work.

The Contact Solver works in much the same way as parts interact within the real world. Without the Contact Solver applied, moving parts can be run through one another, creating interference. With the Contact Solver applied, parts will stop when they contact one another. A simple example of this is the slide arm pictured in Figure 8.14. On the left, you can see that the arm segments have been extended past the point that they could be in reality, allowing the slide stops to run through the slide slot. On the right, the parts have been added to a contact set, and the Contact Solver has been turned on, preventing the slide stops from running through the slots.

FIGURE 8.14
With and without
Contact Solver

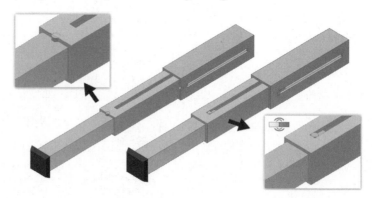

To add parts to a contact set, simply right-click the part, and click Contact Set in the context menu. An icon will appear before each component showing when a component has been added to the contact set. In addition to adding parts to a contact set, you must also ensure that the Contact Solver is turned on by going to the Tools menu and clicking Activate Contact Solver. Once all active participants within the contact set are selected and the Contact Solver is activated, then a single driven constraint can provide a real-life simulation. Note that it is best practice to turn the Contact Solver off when performance is a consideration.

To explore the contact sets, open the file called `mi_8a_017.iam` and follow these basic steps:

1. Select any components you want to be added in the contact analysis.

2. Right-click on the selected components and select Contact Set from the context menu.

3. Select the Inspect tab and click the Activate Contact Solver button.

4. Drag the part with the black end cap in and out to see the assembly extend and contract based on the contact points.

Redundant Constraints and Constraint Failures

Excessive constraints are considered redundant when you have overconstrained components. Redundant constraints will interfere with the proper operation of your assemblies and can cause constraint failures and performance issues.

Two toggles will assist in flagging bad constraints; you can find them by selecting Tools ➢ Application Options and going to the Assembly tab. Enabling Constraint Redundancy Analysis allows Inventor to perform a secondary analysis of assembly constraints and notifies you when redundant constraints exist.

Enabling Related Constraint Failure Analysis allows Inventor to perform an analysis to identify all affected constraints and components, if a particular constraint fails. Once analysis is performed, you will be able to isolate the components that use the broken constraint(s) and select a form of treatment for individual components.

Because analysis requires a separate process, performance can be affected if these two check boxes are active. Because of this, it is advisable to activate the analysis only when problems exist.

Understanding Subassemblies

You create assemblies by placing constraints between parts in order to position and hold those parts together. When working with small assemblies, you can often assemble all the parts together at one level. Working with larger assemblies, however, often requires the use of multiple levels of assemblies for the sake of organization and performance. Lower-level assemblies are referred to as *subassemblies*.

Making Assemblies Work for You

There are many ways to use assemblies, including using them as a model of your machine, capturing information for manufacturing, or maximizing the performance of your system. Most of us focus on the first aspect, but the other aspects are also important. When one of us worked at a large multinational company, the BOM drove our designs. Before we did any modeling, we roughed in the BOM structure and used that to set up our assemblies. Manufacturing efficiency was so important to the business that it drove the engineering processes.

Other companies we have worked for were primarily concerned with getting designs done in a timely fashion. Semi-custom design reused 95 percent of an existing machine with detail redesign. Models had to be structured to simplify reuse and modification. When we did "clean sheet" design, models started out simple and grew in complexity, requiring restructuring as the design took shape. Although we knew some basic parameters—such as interface geometry and some of the purchased components—up front, being able to explore alternatives and quickly change the model required discipline in the early stages. If we didn't structure the model correctly, it would fall apart when we made changes.

Inventor was designed to support these and other workflows. There are a lot of tools to help optimize your assembly design process. Since every company has different requirements, you will have to experiment with the various tools to determine which ones work best for you.

The Power of Subassemblies

Imagine a common caster wheel assembly. Although it may seem like a simple component, it is, of course, made up of many small parts. If you needed to use this caster in an assembly multiple times, you wouldn't place all the small parts into an assembly individually over and over. Instead, you would package them as a subassembly and place multiple instances of the subassembly throughout the top-level assembly. Figure 8.15 shows a caster wheel assembly ready to be placed as a subassembly.

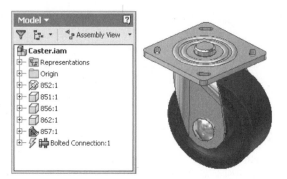

Most things that you design and build are typically made from subassemblies of some sort. In manufacturing it makes sense to create subassemblies of common parts to make the assembly process easier. It makes sense to design in exactly the same fashion. In the caster example, it saves you from having to duplicate the work of assembling the caster parts repeatedly for each instance of the caster that exists in the top-level assembly.

A second benefit to using subassemblies is the flexibility that they add to the bill of materials. Using the caster as a subassembly rather than as loose parts provides the ability to count the caster as a single item, to count the total of all the caster parts, or to do both.

KNOWING WHEN TO USE ASSEMBLIES

Although it is often necessary to create parts as assemblies (to have a correct bill of materials or to provide the correct motion), it is not always the best choice. For example, in the caster example, unless you need the casters to swivel in your assembly, consider modeling the caster as a single part or deriving the assembly into a single part. This will lower the overhead of your models as well as reduce the number of parts to track throughout your design.

There is a third and very important concept to consider when working with subassemblies. This is model performance. Imagine that you decided to place four instances of the caster into an assembly as loose parts rather than as a subassembly. For the sake of simplicity, say it takes 28 constraints among the caster parts and 2 constraints between the caster and the top-level assembly, for a total of 30 constraints. You do this for all 4 casters, for a total of 120 constraints in the top-level assembly. Had you assembled the caster as a subassembly and then placed that subassembly into the top-level assembly, you would have used just 28 in the caster subassembly and 2 per caster, for a total of only 36 constraints, as shown in Figure 8.16.

FIGURE 8.16
Reduced assembly
constraints

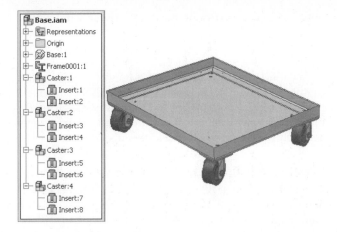

If you consider assembly constraints to be nothing more than calculations that Inventor must make to hold the assemblies together, then by using subassemblies you have required Inventor to create and maintain 86 fewer calculations overall. This reduction in constraints can have a significant impact on the assembly's performance and make the task of editing the assembly much easier.

Top-Down Design

Inventor allows you to approach the creation of parts and assemblies in three basic ways. Figure 8.17 shows these three distinctive workflows for assembly design.

FIGURE 8.17
Design workflows

Top Down	**Middle Out**	**Bottom Up**
Design Within Assembly	Design Within Assembly	Create Single Parts
Utilize Subassemblies	Utilize Subassemblies	Create iParts & Features
Share Part Geometry	Share Part Geometry	Develop Library Items
Most Efficient Workflow	Insert Parts and Assemblies	Repair Imported Parts
Facilitates Middle Out Design	Most Commonly Used	Least Efficient

The first of these methods is called *top-down* design. In the purest sense, top-down design is performed completely within the top-level assembly of a machine or device. Parts and subassemblies are created from within the uppermost assembly, as opposed to creating components outside the top-level assembly and then placing these components later. Using this approach, you can reference and project geometry from other parts within the assembly into new parts, thereby ensuring the fit of the new parts. Another benefit to top-down design is that the designer can better visualize how each part relates to others within the assembly. When properly utilized, you minimize the number of overall assembly constraints required and allow for a stable design.

The second method works by creating parts independently and then placing and constraining them into the assembly. This method is called *bottom-up* design. Bottom-up design is common when creating parts from existing drawings and new pencil sketches. This workflow is ideal for repairing imported geometry, creating standard parts for your library, and converting standard parts into iParts and iFeatures. Working in the single-part environment does not easily allow you to create or reference other parts that will be utilized within your assembly design. As a result, this is probably the least efficient workflow for 3D design but is often the one employed by new users.

The third method is some combination of top-down and bottom-up design and is the most common. This approach might be called *middle-out*. This is top-down design with the ability to add existing subassemblies and parts as needed. Utilizing various functions such as Parts Libraries, Frame Generator, Bolted Connections, and Content Center components within an assembly file are examples of middle-out design.

Developing an Efficient Assembly Workflow

CERT OBJECTIVE

Consider an example of a top-down workflow to better understand the benefits and efficiency of this type of design. Within this workflow, you will first create the top-level assembly file and then create the part files:

1. On the Get Started tab, click the New button, and select the Standard.iam template.

2. Click Create on the Assemble tab, or right-click in the browser or graphics area and select Create Component. The default option in the Create In-Place Component dialog box is to create a new component as a standard single-part file. Instead, click the drop-down arrow in the Template area, and select Standard.iam.

> **AVAILABLE TEMPLATES**
>
> The choices available in the drop-down are the templates from the default tab. If you want to use a template from a different tab, click the Browse Templates button instead. Once you click the Browse Templates button, you will be presented with the Open Template dialog box, which gives you a choice of standards and templates.

3. Name this assembly **2nd Level Assembly**.

If known at the time of creating the subassembly file, determine the BOM structure for this subassembly. Note that you can change this later using the BOM editor as needed. Figure 8.18 illustrates the selection choices for the BOM structure.

FIGURE 8.18
BOM structure options

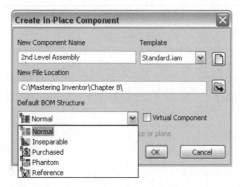

The choices for BOM structure are listed here with a brief description. You'll take a more in-depth look at BOM structure settings later in this chapter.

Virtual Components These components require no geometry, such as paint, grease, and so on.

Normal This is the default structure for all parts that are intended to be fabricated.

Purchased These are parts or assemblies that are not fabricated in-house.

Inseparable Generally, these are assemblies that cannot be disassembled without damage, such as weldments, riveted assemblies, and so on.

Phantom Typically, this is a subassembly created to simplify the design process by reducing assembly constraints and to roll parts up into the next highest assembly level.

Reference This is used for construction geometry or to add detail and references to the top-level assembly.

4. In this top-down design example, you will be using Normal components. Confirm the Default BOM Structure is set to Normal, and click OK.

5. You will then be prompted to select a sketch plane for the base component of this assembly. In the Model browser, expand the assembly origin folder, and select the XY Plane option.

This will place and anchor the new assembly to the top-level assembly origin. The origin planes of the new assembly will be anchored to the selected top-level assembly origin plane upon creation and will be grounded to the top-level origin plane. This new, second-level assembly will be activated within the Model browser, ready for editing, as shown in Figure 8.19.

FIGURE 8.19
Second-level
assembly active

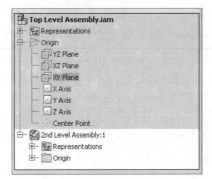

6. With the second-level assembly active, select Create Component once again, and this time use the `Standard.ipt` template to create a new part. Name this component **Rotary Hub**, and set it to be saved in a subdirectory called Parts within your workspace, as shown in Figure 8.20. If the subdirectory does not exist, you will be prompted to create it. Use the Normal BOM structure for all parts in this example.

7. To place the part, select the XZ plane from the origin folder in `2nd Level Assembly.iam`, and click the XZ plane.

FIGURE 8.20
Creating Rotary
Hub.ipt in the
Parts subdirectory

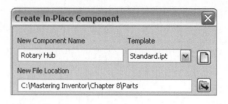

8. Because the XZ plane is perpendicular to the screen, you might need to realign the view to the current sketch plane. Click the View Face button on the Navigation bar, and click Sketch1 in the Model browser. When clicking this icon, you will notice that Sketch1 is active and everything else within your assembly is grayed out. You should now be properly oriented to view Sketch1.

9. Create and dimension the sketch, as shown in Figure 8.21.

FIGURE 8.21
Rotary Hub sketch

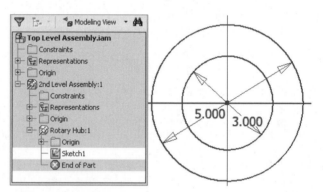

10. Press E to display the Extrude dialog box, and extrude the outer ring to a length of **1 inch**.

11. Create a sketch on the top face of the ring. Sketch a concentric circle offset **0.5 inch** to the inside of the overall diameter. Place a center point on the offset circle.

12. Start the Hole tool. The center point will be automatically selected. Set the diameter to **0.375 inch**, and set Termination to Through All.

13. Create a circular pattern of the hole feature with six instances, as shown in Figure 8.22.

14. Click the Save icon. Since the part is active, it is saved, but the top- and second-level assemblies are not. Click the Return button twice to return to the top-level assembly.

15. Click Save again, and you will be prompted to name the top-level assembly file. Name the file **Top Level Assembly**, and click OK.

16. The Save dialog displays the state of all the assembly files. Both of the assembly files are marked Initial Save. This means that they exist only in memory and haven't been saved to disc yet. If you were to click in the Save column to change it to No, the files would be closed without saving, and you would just have the part file on the disc drive. Confirm that the both files are marked Yes, and click OK.

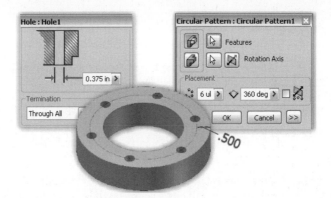

These steps illustrate the method of creating a true top-down design, starting with the assembly, then defining the subassembly and then creating a part to reside in the assembly structure. If this seems like a purely academic exercise because it is not the way you typically work, you might find that the concepts can still be useful to you every now and again. Often the top-down, middle-out, or bottom-up approach is dictated by the need to assign part numbers and create assembly structure to match. Keep these things in mind as you work with Inventor assemblies and you will more than likely find an opportunity to use them somewhere along the way.

Layout Sketches

Another top-down (and/or middle-out) design workflow is the use of layout sketches. Layout sketches are created in a part file, using sketch blocks to represent individual parts as basic 2D symbols. The 2D blocks are "assembled" in the part sketch and can be dimensioned and constrained to simulate simple assembly mechanisms in order to test function, and to some extent fit. The first step in creating a layout sketch is to create a part file and a sketch. Next, 2D sketch geometry is created and turned into sketch blocks, with a single block representing each component within the mechanism. Nested blocks (blocks made of other blocks) can be used to represent subassemblies and can even be set as flexible to allow them to pivot around or translate motion along an axis. Once the basic 2D layout design is complete, you can use the Make Part and Make Component tools to write out the blocks as individual part models from the sketch blocks. From there, a 3D assembly can be created based on, and linked to, the sketch blocks. In this way, if you update the sketch layout, the parts and assemblies will automatically update.

The following example will introduce layout and sketch block functionality:

1. Click the Get Started tab, and click Open.

2. Browse for the file named `mi_8a_019.ipt` located in the Chapter 8 directory of the Mastering Inventor 2011 folder, and click Open.

3. Locate the sketch called Layout Assembly in the browser and click the plus sign to expand it.

4. Notice the sketch contains a block called Base Mount. Right-click on the sketch and choose Edit Sketch.

5. Select the Create Block button from the Layout panel.

6. Select all of the geometry on the left of the sketch with the visible dimensions.

7. Click the Insert Point button in the Create Block dialog box and then select the lower left corner of the rectangle as the Insert Point.

8. Enter **Base Plate** for the block name, and then click OK to create the block.

9. Expand the Blocks folder in the browser and notice the Base Plate has been added to the block definitions. The geometry you selected has been converted to a block as well and now behaves as a single entity.

10. Place a Concentric constraint on each of the half circle shapes on the base plate and the corresponding half circle shape on the base mount. Exit the Constraint tool by right-clicking and choosing Done.

11. Next, select the Arm Assembly block from the block folder and drag it into the graphics area to place an instance of it.

12. Place a Concentric constraint on the right circle of the Base Mount and the large dashed circle on the bottom link of the Arm Assembly. Exit the Constraint tool by right-clicking and choosing Done.

13. Select the Cylinder Assembly block from the block folder and drag it into the graphics area to place an instance of it.

14. Place a Concentric constraint on the left circle of the Base Mount and the larger circle on the Cylinder Assembly. Exit the Constraint tool by right-clicking and choosing Done.

15. Right-click on the Cylinder Assembly and choose Flexible. This allows the underconstrained geometry to solve independently at the top level block.

16. Click and drag on the free end of the Cylinder Assembly to see the plunger slide in the cylinder.

17. Place a Concentric constraint on the free end of the Arm Assembly and the free end of the Cylinder Assembly.

18. Click Finish Sketch to return to the feature level. Figure 8.23 shows the layout sketch.

FIGURE 8.23
Blocks folder and
blocks in the sketch

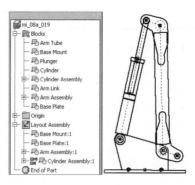

Notice you can continue to drag the sketch assembly to see the adjustment of the cylinder and the angle for the arm assembly. As you can see, creating layout sketches in this fashion allows you to solve linear and pivot motion layouts in 2D. Once the sketch layout has been completed you can use the Make Components tool to write each block out to an individual part and/or assembly file. You can close the current file without saving changes or use it to explore the Make Components workflow using these general steps:

1. Click the Make Components button on the Manage tab, and then select the sketch blocks you want to create components for.

2. Select additional blocks to add to the list or select from the list, and click Remove From Selection to exclude any blocks you decide you do not want to create components for.

3. Select Insert Components In Target Assembly, and then set the assembly name, the template from which to create it, and the save path, or clear this option to create the parts only. If the assembly already exits, use the Target Assembly Location's Browse button to select it.

4. Click Next to accept your selections.

5. The next dialog box allows you to name and set paths for the files to be created. Click the cells in the table to make changes for the components as required:

   ◆ Click or right-click the cells to choose from the options for that cell type, if any.

   ◆ You can Shift-select multiple components and use the buttons above the Template and File Location columns to set those values for multiple components at once.

6. Click Include Parameters to choose which layout model parameters to have present in the created parts.

7. Click Apply or OK to make the components. If the component files are created in an assembly, the assembly file is created with the parts (and subassemblies) placed and left open in Inventor, but the assembly and parts are not saved until you choose to do so. If you choose to create the components without an assembly, you are prompted to save the new files as they are created.

8. You can then open each part file and create 3D geometry based off of the sketch block. Changes to the original layout sketch push through to the 3D part and assembly.

Layout sketches can boost your productivity. During the initial stage of design, there are frequent changes as you nail down the details. When you initially create the layout sketch, you can easily investigate "what if?" scenarios. You can add as much or as little detail as you need to define the function and form. If you do need to make a change in the relationship of components, you can do that in the layout sketch, and then the update will get pushed to all the components. Once components are generated from the blocks, you can edit them and build the model parts based on the basic blocks. You can open the assembly called mi_8a_020.iam to examine a simple assembly created from the layout sketch used in the completed version of the previous exercise.

Flexibility

When multiple instances of the same subassembly are used within a design, each instance can be made flexible, allowing underconstrained components in the subassembly to be solved at the top-level assembly. The caster assemblies in Figure 8.24 have been made flexible so they can be swiveled and positioned independently as they would in the real world.

FIGURE 8.24
Flexible subassemblies

A subassembly instance is made flexible by right-clicking the instance within the browser and selecting Flexible. Flexible subassemblies are displayed with an icon next to the instance name in the browser so that you can easily determine which instances are flexible.

Flexible assemblies can be nested into other flexible subassemblies and will still update whenever the original assembly is changed. Common usages of flexible assemblies are hydraulic cylinders requiring different length extensions when used in multiple locations within a top-level assembly. When each instance of the assembly is made flexible, then each cylinder can move accordingly within the top-level assembly.

If a subassembly with nested flexible subassemblies is to be placed into a top-level assembly, then you simply right-click that subassembly to bring forward the flexibility of the nested flexible assemblies. Consider the example of the hydraulic cylinder. Multiple instances of the cylinder might be placed into an extension arm assembly and each instance made flexible so that they can be allowed to adjust as they are constrained to the extension arm parts.

If two instances of the extension arm are then placed into a top-level assembly, those instances of the extension arm need to be made flexible as well in order to allow the cylinders to demonstrate flexibility. You can use the file called mi_08a_030.iam to explore flexible subassemblies.

Adaptivity

Cross-part adaptivity is a powerful feature of Autodesk Inventor, and it can be turned on or off at will. Although adaptivity is a powerful tool when properly used, it can also cause performance problems when used indiscriminately in large assemblies or when an adaptive part is utilized in another assembly without its related part. But you can fix both situations with very simple methods.

Because active adaptive parts can cause performance issues in large assemblies, you should turn off adaptivity after use. If a related part is edited, adaptivity on the associated part should be turned on, and the assembly should be updated to reflect the changes on the related part. Once this is done, that adaptivity should be turned off once again.

TRACKING ADAPTIVITY

It is a good idea to turn off adaptivity when not in use; however, Inventor does not have a good method to tell you what parts *were* adaptive. One way is to rename the browser nodes so that you can tell what parts were adaptive. A simple way to do this is to append -A on the browser node. Now you'll know which parts were adaptive even where they are not currently adaptive.

If an adaptive part is to be used in other designs, then it is suggested that you save the part as a different filename and remove the adaptivity from the new part. Otherwise, the adaptive relationships will carry over into the other design, preventing the ability of shared parts to be edited.

Creating Adaptivity

This example creates an adaptive relationship between two parts and demonstrates how they are linked together:

1. On the Get Started tab, click Open.

2. Browse to Chapter 8 in the Mastering Inventor 2011 directory, and open `mi_08a_021.iam`.

3. Click the Create button on the Assemble tab, or right-click in the browser or graphics area and select Create Component.

4. Name the new part file **Gasket**. For the New File Location, browse to the Chapter 8 folder. Confirm that "Constrain sketch plane to selected face or plane" is selected, and click OK.

5. Select the top face of the rotary hub part for the new part sketch. When this face is selected, a Flush constraint is created between the two parts and a new sketch is created.

Sketch1 in the new part is automatically activated, and the existing part becomes transparent. The Component Opacity setting on the Application Options dialog box's Assembly tab controls this behavior.

6. Click Project Geometry on the Sketch tab, and select the top face of the existing part. The geometry is projected into the sketch. Note that adaptive glyphs have been added to the browser to indicate that the part and sketch are adaptive. Also, there is a Reference1 node nested under the sketch. This node contains the information linking the two parts, as shown in Figure 8.25.

FIGURE 8.25
Part marked with
Adaptive icon in
the browser

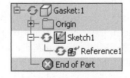

The adaptive glyph is displayed when adaptivity is turned on. You can turn adaptivity on and off by right-clicking the node in the browser. You can toggle the feature or sketch adaptivity while editing the part, but you have to return to the assembly level to toggle adaptivity on the part. Additionally, you can disable the creation of adaptive loops when projecting geometry altogether, by going to the Tools tab, clicking Application Options, selecting the Assembly tab, and then un-checking the Cross Part Geometry Projection option.

7. Finish the sketch by selecting Finish Sketch from the right-click menu, as shown in Figure 8.26. Do not click Finish Edit, otherwise Inventor will not only finish the sketch, but will also exit the part and return you to the assembly.

FIGURE 8.26
Selecting Finish
Sketch, not
Finish Edit

8. Extrude the Gasket part to a thickness of **2 mm**, click the Return button to return to the assembly, and then click Save.

9. To see how adaptivity works, double-click the rotary hub component to activate that part for editing. You can double-click the part in the graphics area or the icon next to the part name in the Model browser to activate any part for editing.

10. In the Model browser, right-click Extrusion1, and select Edit Sketch. Change the overall diameter from **130 mm** to **160 mm**, and click OK.

11. You will notice that the overall diameter and the diameter of the hole pattern of the rotary hub component have changed, but the corresponding gasket part remains unchanged.

12. Click Return to move up to the second-level assembly design state once again. Both parts are active at the subassembly level, so the gasket part updates to match the rotary hub component.

As you can see the ability to adapt one part to another can make updates across parts very easy. You can close this assembly without saving changes and continue on.

Removing Adaptivity from Parts

Once a design has been approved and released for production, you should completely remove adaptivity from all parts within your assembly. Removing the adaptivity ensures that the part can be reused within other designs without conflict, and will not be updated accidently.

If you decide to retain adaptivity within your original assembly but plan on using the adaptive part in other assemblies, the adaptive icon will not display on those instances of the part. This is because only one occurrence of a part can define its adaptive features. However, all occurrences reflect changes and adaptive updates, including occurrence in other assemblies. It is for this reason that you must use adaptivity carefully.

To completely remove adaptivity from a part, either activate or open the adaptive part, and activate the adaptive sketch. Expand the sketch and right-click Reference to select Break Link, as shown in Figure 8.27.

When the adaptive link is broken, the reference geometry is converted to normal sketch geometry. This geometry will need to be fully dimensioned and constrained. Once the geometry has been converted to normal sketch geometry, the part will no longer be able to be adaptive.

FIGURE 8.27
Breaking the
adaptive link

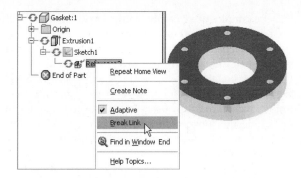

> **MAKING TEMPORARY USE OF ADAPTIVITY**
>
> Use adaptivity to find mounting holes for positioning hardware components on a base part. For example, consider a mounting clip and a base plate.
>
> Constrain the clip to the base plate; then make the base plate active for editing, and create a sketch on the plate surface. With the sketch active, project the mounting holes, locating holes, and other needed geometry from the mounting clip to the base plate. This creates adaptive relationships in the base plate to the mounting clip.
>
> Once the design is finalized and all the mounting clips are properly located, simply turn adaptivity off on the base plate. When the design is released for production, or at any other desired time, convert the reference geometry created when you projected the geometry to normal sketch geometry. Then dimension and constrain the mounting holes as you would any other feature.

Assembly Features

An *assembly feature* is a feature created and utilized purely within the active assembly file and environment. Because this feature was created within the assembly file, it does not exist at the single part or subassembly level. A good example of an assembly feature in use is the technique of creating drilled holes through a standard tabletop within an assembly. Common practice is to place brackets on the tabletop in order to find the mounting hole locations. This allows the holes to be drilled at the same time, ensuring an exact match and placement. Assembly features in Inventor mimic this approach.

Examining the individual tabletop file reveals that the part file does not contain the drilled holes, simply because the drill operation was performed at the assembly level rather than the part level. To understand the reasoning behind this, you might consider that the tabletop is a common part stocked in the shop and then machined as required for each assembly in which it is used. Although the stock part might exist as a cataloged item with no holes, it may exist in many different assemblies with holes of various sizes and locations. Using assembly features allow you to work in this manner.

Other examples of assembly features are contained within the weldment environment, where preparations used to facilitate welding components together are at the assembly level. Preparation features allow trimming of soon-to-be-welded components to eliminate interferences between welds and other parts of the weldment.

Care must be taken when creating geometry within the context of the assembly, because it is easy to create an assembly feature when intending to create a part feature. Although this is a common mistake that new users will make, it is one that anyone can experience. In a multilevel top-down design, always make sure you are working in the proper assembly or component by double-clicking the assembly or component in the Model browser for the purposes of opening that component for editing.

To explore the creation of assembly features follow these steps:

1. On the Get Started tab, click Open.

2. Browse to Chapter 8 in the Mastering Inventor 2011 directory, and open mi_08a_022.iam.

This assembly is made up of three parts, two of which are instances of the same part, Part_100_8. The other component, Part_200_8, currently interferes with the other two parts. Your goal is to cut a key hole in both instances of Part_100_8, so that the keyed bar will fit into them. Part_100_8 is a stock bracket used in many assemblies; therefore you must take care not to create a feature in it that will have a negative impact on its use in all of the assemblies that consume it. To start, you will explore a keyway created by another user at the part level.

3. Double-click on the front instance of Part_100_8 to set it active for edits.

4. Locate the feature called Keyway Cut in the browser, right-click on it, and choose Unsuppress Features.

5. Right-click and choose Finish Edit to return to the assembly level.

Notice how the keyway cuts the part in the same location on each instance of the part, missing the location on the second instance due to the orientation of the two instances of Part_100_8. Another important aspect of the keyway is that it impacts every instance of the part, in every assembly it was used in. To fix this, continue on.

6. Double-click on the front instance of Part_100_8 to set it active for edits again.

7. Locate the feature called Keyway Cut in the browser, right-click on it, and choose Delete. Click OK in the delete confirmation dialog box.

8. Right-click and choose Finish Edit to return to the assembly level.

9. From the Model tab, click the Create 2D Sketch button, and choose the large front face of the front instance of Part_100_8 to create the sketch on.

10. From the Sketch tab, click the Project Geometry button.

11. Select the circular edge and the three flat edges of the keyed bar's end profile, projecting the complete key profile into the sketch.

12. Click the Finish Sketch button. Notice the sketch location in the browser.

13. From the Model tab, click the Extrude button. Notice that the only operation available in the Extrude dialog box is cut. You cannot add material at the assembly level.

14. Set the Extents drop-down box to All, ensure the cut is going the right direction, and then click OK.

15. You should see the keyhole cut through both instances of Part_100_8 and the keyed bar (Part_200_8) disappear.

16. Expand the Extrusion1 feature in the browser and you will see the listing of all components involved in the extrusion cut.

17. Right-click on Part_200_8 and choose Remove Participant, so that the keyway cut does not cut the keyed bar.

18. Finally, right-click on either instance of Part_100_8 and choose Open. Notice that the keyhole is not present in the part file, as it only exists as an assembly level feature.

You can close this file without saving changes. You should know that in addition to removing participating components from an assembly level feature, components can be added to an assembly feature by right-clicking the feature, choosing Add Participant from the menu, and then choosing the component from the browser. On the left of Figure 8.28, a component named 1247 is being removed from the Hole feature so that the hole does not go through the part. On the right, the same component is being added to the feature.

FIGURE 8.28
Adding/removing participants from assembly features

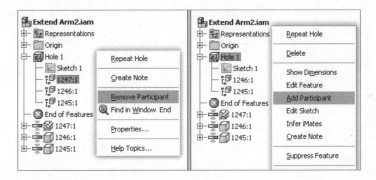

Assembly features can be made with the Extrude, Revolve, Hole, Sweep, Fillet, Chamfer, and Move Face tools. Keep in mind that all assembly features are allowed only to cut or remove material and cannot add material to a part. Other commonly used assembly feature commands within the Assembly panel environment include the Mirror and Patterns commands.

Managing the Bill of Materials

CERT OBJECTIVE

In Inventor, the BOM is the internal, real-time database that exists within every assembly. *Real-time* means that as components are added to the assembly, they are automatically added and counted in the BOM. Although you might be accustomed to referring to the tabled list of parts on the 2D drawing as a bill of materials, in Inventor such a table is called a *parts list*. Part lists pull directly from the assembly BOM.

The BOM is controlled at two different levels: the part level and the assembly level. Both levels factor in certain aspects of how the bill of materials is generated, how components are represented, and ultimately how the parts list is generated within the drawing environment.

Parts-Level BOM Control

In the part environment, the designer has the ability to define the BOM structure of just that part. At this level, the structure can be defined as Normal, Inseparable, Purchased, Phantom, or Reference. Determining the default setting at the part level allows control of how the part is identified within the overall assembly (or assemblies) BOM. By setting the structure at the part level, you can control the assembly BOM display according to the part settings. Any structure settings at the part level can be overridden and changed to Reference at the assembly level.

Another important structure setting at the part level is the Base Quantity property. This setting controls how the part is listed in the BOM. If the Base Quantity is set to Each, the part is tallied by count. This is the default for most standard parts. The Base Quantity can also be set to reflect the value of any given model parameter. This is most often set to a length parameter so that the Base Quantity property will tally the total length of a part used in an assembly. Parts pulled from the Content Center and the Frame Generator have their Base Quantity property set to pull a length parameter by default. The Base Quantity property is set by selecting Tools ➢ Document Settings and going to the Bill Of Materials tab.

Assembly-Level BOM Control

BOM control accelerates at the assembly level. You can access the Bill Of Materials dialog box by selecting the Bill Of Materials icon from the Manage panel of the Assemble tab. In the drawing environment, the BOM Editor dialog box is accessible by right-clicking the parts list and selecting Bill Of Materials.

The Bill Of Materials dialog box allows you to edit iProperties, BOM properties, and the BOM structure; override quantities for components; and sort and create a consistent item order for generating parts lists. Figure 8.29 shows the Bill Of Materials dialog box.

FIGURE 8.29
Bill Of Materials
dialog box

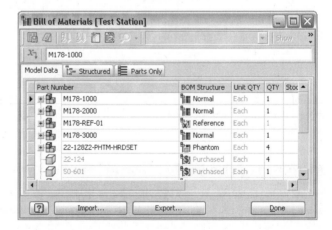

Exporting a bill of materials is a straightforward process, with icons across the top of the dialog box allowing the export of the BOM data in a structured or parts-only view in formats such as MDB, dBase, or various Excel formats. The Engineer's Notebook icon permits the export of database information as a note.

ADDING AND REMOVING COLUMNS

You can add columns to the model in any of the three tabs in the Bill Of Materials dialog box by clicking the Choose Columns icon, which will display a dialog box list in which you can drag a desired column to a specified location, as shown in Figure 8.30. To remove a desired column, simply drag the column to be removed back to the dialog box list.

FIGURE 8.30
Choose Column
dialog box

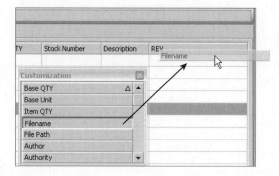

The next icon at the top of the Bill Of Materials dialog box allows you to add custom iProperty columns. The drop-down list shown in Figure 8.31 within the Add Custom iProperty Columns dialog box will display a combined list of all the available custom iProperties contained within the assembly.

FIGURE 8.31
Custom
iProperty list

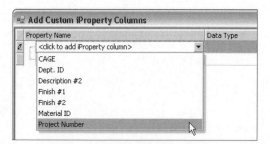

If a desired custom iProperty does not exist within the list of components, you can add it manually by selecting the <Click To Add iProperty Column> option displayed in the list box. Be sure to set the data type to the correct format when manually adding a custom iProperty to the assembly file. Manually added iProperties will be stored in the assembly file. Figure 8.32 shows the addition of a custom iProperty column called Assembly Station.

FIGURE 8.32
Creating a new
custom iProperty

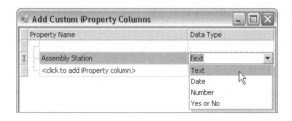

Once custom iProperty columns have been added to the assembly bill of materials, individual parts can be populated with custom iProperties as needed. Individual parts that already contain those iProperties will show the values within the respective row and column. iProperties that are edited or added to a respective part row will be pushed down to the part level; therefore, filling out iProperties at the assembly level is often the most efficient way to populate part iProperties.

The Create Expression icon located at the beginning of the Formula toolbar launches the Property Expression dialog box so you can create an iProperty expression. The newly created expression can contain a combination of custom text and iProperty names in brackets. The iProperty expression will be substituted for the field in which the expression was created, once the expression is evaluated. In Figure 8.33, the expression is created in the Description field.

FIGURE 8.33
Creating property
expressions

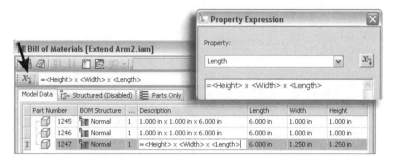

Looking across the top of the Bill Of Materials dialog box, the two icons to the far right are Part Number Merge Settings and Update Mass Properties Of All Rows. The Update Mass Properties Of All Rows icon recalculates the total mass for all components within the assembly.

Clicking the Part Number Merge Settings icon will allow different components possessing the same part number to be treated as the same component. For instance, say six base plates of the same size are used in an assembly. Four of these plates have holes drilled upon installation, and two have holes placed during fabrication. As far as the shop is concerned, all six are the same part, but in the design both plate types exist as separate part files.

To have the BOM count the total number of plates, you set the Part Number property to match on both items and then use the Part Number Merge Settings to have these files counted as a single item.

BOM Structure Designations

CERT OBJECTIVE

You can choose from five designations when assigning BOM structure to components: Normal, Inseparable, Purchased, Phantom, and Reference. Any part or assembly file can be assigned one of these designations within the BOM. That designation is then stored in the file, meaning that if a part is marked as Purchased in one assembly, it will be designated as Purchased in all assemblies. The structure designations are as follows:

Normal   This is the default structure for most components. The placement and participation in the assembly bill of materials are determined by the parent assembly. In the previous example, you are creating an assembly file rather than a single part. As a result, you will be determining the characteristics of how this assembly file will behave in the top-level assembly bill of materials. With a Normal BOM structure, this assembly will be numbered and included in quantity calculations within the top-level assembly.

Inseparable   These are generally assemblies that cannot be disassembled without damage. Examples of inseparable assemblies might include weldments, glued constructions, and riveted assemblies. In a parts-only parts list, these assemblies will be treated as a single part. Another example is a purchased part such as a motor.

Purchased   This designation is typically for parts or assemblies that are not fabricated in-house. Examples of purchased components are motors, brake calipers, programmable controllers, hinges, and the like. A purchased component is considered as a single BOM item, regardless of whether it is a part or a subassembly. Within a purchased assembly, all child parts are excluded from the BOM and quantity calculations.

Phantom   Use Phantom components to simplify the design process. A Phantom component exists within the design but is not shown as a line item in the BOM. A common use for a Phantom component would be a subassembly of parts that are grouped for ease of design. Setting the subassembly to be a Phantom component allows the parts to be listed in the BOM individually. Other examples of Phantom components could include hardware sets, screws, nuts, bolts, washers, pins, and various fastener-type components. A good example of a Phantom assembly would be a collection of parts that are normally assembled onto the machine one at a time. However, in the interest of reducing the overall number of assembly constraints within the design, the engineer might choose to preassemble the various components within a Phantom assembly. That assembly could then be constrained as one component instead of multiple parts.

Reference   Mark components as Reference when they are used for construction geometry or to add detail and references to the top-level assembly. A good example of a Reference component is a car body and frame that represents the outer shell for placement of a power train. In the 2D documentation, the car body and frame would be shown as hidden lines illustrating the overall design while highlighting the power train as the principal component within a view. Reference geometry is excluded from quantity, mass, or volume calculations regardless of their own internal BOM structure. As a result, they are not included within the parts list. They are placed only within the overall assembly to show design intent and position.

In addition to these five BOM structure designations for component files, you also have the ability to create a virtual component, which has no geometry and does not exist as an external file. A virtual component can have a complete set of properties that are similar to real components but are primarily used to represent bulk items such as fasteners, assembly kits, paint, grease, adhesive, plating, or other items that do not require creating an actual model. A virtual component can be designated as any of the previous BOM structure types and can contain custom properties, descriptions, and other aspects of the BOM data like any other component.

A virtual component will be shown in the Model browser as if it were a real part. Virtual components can be created by selecting the check box next to the BOM Structure drop-down in the Create In-Place Component dialog box, as shown in Figure 8.34.

FIGURE 8.34
Creating a virtual
component

VIRTUAL COMPONENTS IN TEMPLATES

If you use the same virtual components in most of your assemblies, you might want to create them in a blank assembly, fill out their BOM properties using the BOM editor, and then save the assembly as a template file. Then when you create a new assembly, the virtual components will already be present. Any of them not required can simply be deleted.

BOM VIEW TABS

Each tab in the Bill Of Materials dialog box represents a different BOM view. All tabs permit ascending or descending sorting of the rows in the BOM by clicking the respective column header. You can also reorder rows by simply clicking and dragging a component's icon.

With the Model Data tab active, you see the components listed just as they exist in the Model browser. You can add or remove columns to populate the Model Data tab independently of the other BOM view tabs. On this tab all components are listed in the BOM, regardless of BOM structure designation. Item numbers are not assigned on the Model Data tab. The model data is not exportable or available for placement as a parts list. Instead, this tab is typically used for organizing the BOM and assigning the BOM structure designation.

Figure 8.35 shows a bill of materials on the Model Data tab. Notice that there are no item numbers listed and that all component structure types are displayed, including Reference and Phantom components. Notice too that the last two parts listed are virtual parts and have been given different BOM structure designations.

FIGURE 8.35
BOM Model
Data tab

FIGURE 8.35
BOM Model
Data tab

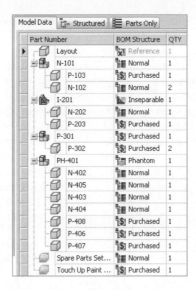

In addition to the Model Data tab are the Structured and Parts Only tabs. These tabs are disabled by default. To enable them, right-click the tab, and choose Enable BOM View; alternatively, click the View Options button along the top of the Bill Of Materials dialog box.

The Structured tab can display all components of the assembly, including subassemblies and the parts of the subassemblies. When in structured view, additional icons will be active on the toolbar, allowing you to sort by item and renumber items within the assembly BOM. The order of the BOM item numbers is stored in the assembly file.

The View Options icon allows you to enable or disable the BOM view and set the view properties from the drop-down. Choose View Properties to modify the Structured view. The resulting Structured Properties dialog box contains two drop-down lists defining the level, the minimum number of digits, and the assembly part delimiter value. If the level is set to First Level, subassemblies are listed without listing the components contained within. If set to All Levels, each part is listed in an indented manner under the subassembly, as shown in Figure 8.36.

FIGURE 8.36
Structured Properties dialog box

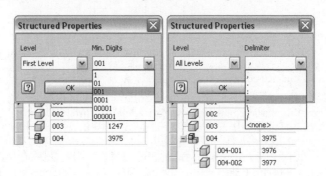

The Parts Only tab lists all components in a flat list. In this BOM view, subassemblies designated as Normal are not listed as an item, but all their child components are displayed. By contrast, Inseparable and Purchased subassemblies are displayed as items, but their child components are not displayed.

Bill of materials settings that are modified by the Bill Of Materials dialog box will carry forward into the drawing parts lists contained in the assembly. Note that if both the Structured and Parts Only views of the BOM are enabled, the same part may have a different item number in each view.

Figure 8.37 shows a bill of materials in the Structured view compared to the same assembly in the Model Data view. The first thing to note is that all the components have been assigned item numbers in the Structured view. You might also notice that the Reference and Phantom components that are listed in the Model Data view are filtered out of the Structured view. Closer inspection reveals that although the Phantom subassembly named PH-401 is not included in the Structured view, all of its child parts (N-402 through P-407) are listed, each with an arrow next to the icon to denote that they are part of a subassembly. Recall that Phantom subassemblies are used to group parts for design organization and to reduce assembly constraints while allowing the parts to be listed individually.

FIGURE 8.37
BOM structured view

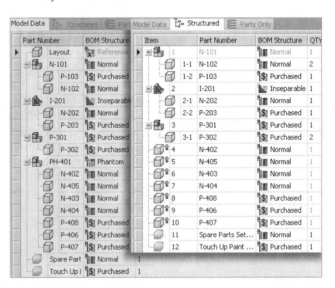

Figure 8.38 shows a bill of materials in the Parts Only view. This Parts Only view filters out Reference and Phantom components just as the Structured view does. Notice too that although the subassemblies are not listed as items, their child parts are. The exceptions to this are Purchased and Inseparable assemblies. In the figure, the Purchased subassembly lists as a single item, since it is a Purchased component comprised of two Purchased parts, and is assumed to be purchased as one item. Note that if you had the need to list the parts as items rather than the subassembly, you would designate the subassembly as Phantom rather than Purchased.

Take a look also at the Inseparable subassembly named I-201. It lists as an item along with one of its child parts named P-203. This child part lists because it is a Purchased item and needs to be ordered. Had both children of the Inseparable subassembly been Normal parts, neither would list in the Parts Only view.

FIGURE 8.38
BOM Parts
Only tab

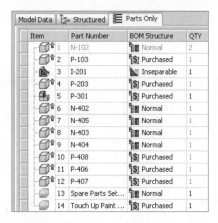

Item		Part Number	BOM Structure	QTY
1		N-102	Normal	2
2		P-103	Purchased	1
3		I-201	Inseparable	1
4		P-203	Purchased	1
5		P-301	Purchased	1
6		N-402	Normal	1
7		N-405	Normal	1
8		N-403	Normal	1
9		N-404	Normal	1
10		P-408	Purchased	1
11		P-406	Purchased	1
12		P-407	Purchased	1
13		Spare Parts Set...	Normal	1
14		Touch Up Paint ...	Purchased	1

HOW TO ADD TWO PARTS WITH THE SAME PART NUMBER

You may occasionally have the need to add two separate part files to an assembly, but have them listed as the same part number. For instance, when using the Frame Generator utility, each member is created as a separate part even though they might be identical in profile and length. This is done so you can modify each part individually as needed. However, if the parts remain identical once the design is complete, you can use the BOM editor and set each identical part file to use the same part number, even though the part files have different names. This allows the BOM to count the parts as a single item.

Assembly Reuse and Configurations

Quite frequently, existing assemblies are used in other designs or are used in multiple locations within the top-level assembly. There are three basic workflows for reusing and configuring assemblies in a design:

- Copying designs
- Using View, positional, and level of detail representations
- Using iAssemblies (table-driven assemblies)

Copying Designs

Quite often you'll need to copy a previous design in order to create a similar design based on the original. Part of the challenge of doing this with Inventor is creating copies of only the parts that will be modified in the new design while reusing parts that do not incur changes, all while maintaining healthy file links. To do this effectively, you can employ the Copy Components tool from within the assembly to be copied.

iCopy

Depending on the design, you might be called upon to create subassemblies containing similar geometry, but having different size and/or positions in the top-level assembly. Rather than manually creating each of these subassemblies you can use the iCopy tool. iCopy combines skeletal modeling (using a part file as the "skeleton" on which to arrange other components) and adaptivity. If you design curtain walls, trusses, bridge type frames, or any design where subassemblies are basically the same but vary in size and position, you may want to explore the iCopy tool. There are four general steps to using iCopy:

1. Create a *target assembly*, using the skeletal *target layout part*.

2. Create the subassembly to be patterned, using the *template layout part*.

3. Use the *iCopy Author* tool in the subassembly to make it useable as an iCopy template.

4. Use the iCopy tool to copy/pattern the subassembly.

You can find a full tutorial for the iCopy tool by going to the Get Started tab, clicking the Tutorials button, selecting the Experienced Users tab, and choosing the iCopy panel toward the bottom of the screen.

To begin this process, first select the top-level assembly from the browser tree, and then click the Copy Components button in the tool panel. You will be presented with the Copy Components: Status dialog box, which lists the top-level assembly and the components within, as shown in Figure 8.39. Use the Status buttons next to each component to set the component to be copied, reused, or excluded from the copy operation.

FIGURE 8.39
Copy Components:
Status dialog box

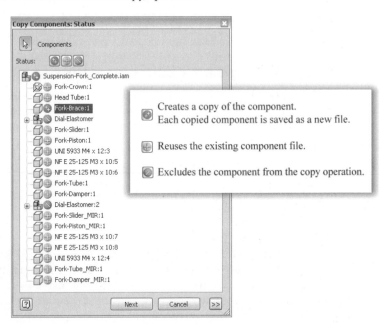

In the example in Figure 8.39, the Fork-Brace is the only part that needs to be redesigned for the new assembly; therefore, it is the only part set to be copied. In the original design, there are two instances of a subassembly called Dial-Elastomer. You can see that both instances have been excluded in this copy operation because they will be swapped out for another dial assembly that you have on file already. You will notice that all other components except the top-level assembly are set to be reused. Once the copy status of each part is set, click the Next button to move to the Copy Components: File Names dialog box, as shown in Figure 8.40.

FIGURE 8.40
Copy Components:
File Names
dialog box

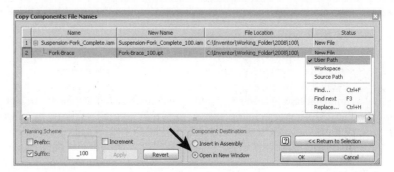

In the Copy Components File Names dialog box, you want to set the destination button to Open In New Window in order to create a new, separate assembly file. You can then use the Prefix and/or Suffix controls to modify the existing filenames, or you can type in new names as required. By default, the File Location is set to Source Path, meaning that the new files will land right next to the existing ones. If that is not desirable, you can right-click each File Location cell and choose User Path or Workspace. Care should be taken to ensure that file location paths are not set outside the project search path. When the filename and paths are set, click OK.

ROLLING REVISIONS

A large part of any engineering department's time and energy is focused on revision control. You can think of a revision roll as just a copy of an existing design with improvements. Here is a general procedure for rolling the revision of an approved design, where Rev1 is complete and Rev2 is being created:

1. Open the Rev1 assembly and start the Copy Components tool.

2. Configure the Copy Components list to include, exclude, and reuse components as required for Rev2.

3. Set the destination button to Open In New Window, and click OK, to create the Rev2 assembly.

4. Rename and set the file location for all copied components, as well as for the Rev2 assembly file.

5. Add additional components to the Rev2 assembly as needed and make any other modifications required.

6. Open the Rev1 drawing file, and use Save As to create a Rev2 copy.

7. In the Rev2 drawing, click the Manage tab and use the Replace Model Reference button to exchange all of the Rev1 views, parts lists, and other references with Rev2.

The new assembly file will open in a separate window. Interrogation of the Model browser should reveal that the components set to be reused are listed just as they were in the original assembly, the components set to be copied are listed as specified, and the components set to be excluded are not present at all.

Using Representations

CERT OBJECTIVE

Inventor provides the ability to create and store three basic types of representations within an assembly file. *Representations* allow you to manage assemblies by setting up varying views, positions, and levels of detail for your models. Each of these allows for the creation of user-defined representations, and each has a master representation. Note that although user-defined representations can be renamed and deleted as required, master representations cannot. Using representations enhances productivity and improves performance in large assembly design.

Once representations are created in an assembly, that assembly file can be opened in any combination of those representation states by clicking the Options button in the Open File or Place Component dialog box, as shown in Figure 8.41. Keep in mind that although you can open or place a file by typing the filename rather than scrolling and clicking the icon, you cannot access the Options button without explicitly scrolling and selecting the file in the dialog box.

FIGURE 8.41
Opening a file in a representation

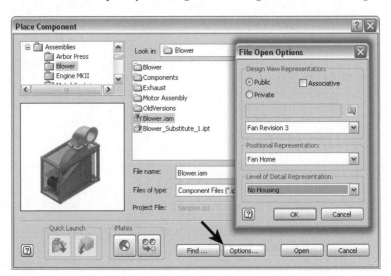

VIEW REPRESENTATIONS

CERT OBJECTIVE

View representations, also known as *design views* and *ViewReps*, are used to configure the display of an assembly and save that display for later use. View representations control:

◆ The visibility state of components, sketch features, and work features.

◆ Component color and styles applied at the assembly level.

◆ The enabled/not enabled status of components.

◆ The "camera view," meaning the on-screen zoom magnification and orientation.

◆ The browser tree state.

In effect, view representations allow "snapshot views" of portions of an assembly file. Each view representation is saved within the assembly file and has no effect on individual parts or subassemblies. View representations are relatively simple to create and use. To create a view representation, follow these general steps:

- While in the assembly, simply zoom and rotate your model until you have the desired view showing in the current graphics window.

- Then expand the Representations folder, and right-click View to select New, as shown in Figure 8.42.

- Now, turn off the visibility of a few parts; these visibility changes will take place only within this view representation.

- After creating the new view representation, click Save to preserve the newly created representation.

FIGURE 8.42
Creating
a new view
representation

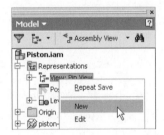

You can protect the view representation you create from accidental edits by right-clicking it and choosing Lock. View representations can be accessed either by double-clicking the desired representation or by right-clicking the desired representation and selecting Activate. Private view representations are views created in early releases of Inventor and are not associative.

ACTIVATING A NEW VIEW REPRESENTATION TO PREVENT ERRORS

Probably one of the most misunderstood "errors" in Inventor is the "The current Design View Representation is locked" message. This tells you that changes will not be saved and alarms a lot of new users. What this means is that you have turned off the visibility (or enabled status or any number of other things) while in the master view representation. Since the master is locked, these changes will not be saved, and the next time you open the file, the model will be back at the previous state. To circumvent this issue, be sure to activate a new ViewRep or use the one called Default, make your changes, and then save. This way, your visibility, color overrides, and other settings will be saved in the ViewRep.

POSITIONAL REPRESENTATIONS

**CERT
OBJECTIVE**

Positional representations, often referred to as *PosReps* for short, can be employed to set up and store components in various arrangements and are used to help test and analyze assembly motion. Positional representations work by overriding assembly constraints, assembly patterns, or component properties.

To create a new positional representation, expand the Representations heading in the browser, right-click the Positional Representations heading, and then choose New. Continue by right-clicking the component, pattern, or constraint in the Model browser that you want to change. Choose Override from the right-click menu. The override dialog box will open to the tab that is appropriate to the entity on which you right-clicked. You can rename the new representation from the default name to something more meaningful; however, you cannot rename the master representation.

In the following exercise, you will create positional representations to control the movement for the components of a hobby-type CNC router. Note, there are four components in this assembly. In the real world, these four components would be modeled as subassemblies; however, they have been created as simple part files in order to simplify the model. Follow these steps to explore the options involved in creating simple positional representations:

1. On the Get Started tab, click Open, and then select the file called mi_08a_023.iam from the Chapter 8 folder of the Mastering Inventor 2011 directory.

2. Click and drag on the component named Z-Axis Assembly_08, and notice how it can be dragged to cause interference and into an unrealistic location.

Currently this assembly has two sets of constraints defined. One set defines the X, Y, and Z travel limits and the other set defines the home position for each of the assembly components. In the current state, all of these constraints have been suppressed. In the next steps you will create a positional representation and unsuppress the home position constraints.

3. Click the plus sign to expand each component in the browser and notice the suppressed constraints.

4. Locate and expand the Representations folder in the browser. Click the plus sign next to the icon to expand it.

5. Right-click on Position and choose New to create a new positional representation, as shown in Figure 8.43.

FIGURE 8.43
Creating a new positional representation

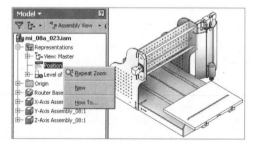

6. Expand the Position node, if needed, and notice a positional representation called Position1 has been created and is currently active as denoted by the checkmark.

7. Select Position1, then click on it and rename it **Home Position**.

8. Right-click on the Z Home constraint listed under the z-axis assembly component and choose Override as shown on the left of Figure 8.44.

FIGURE 8.44
Overriding a
constraint value

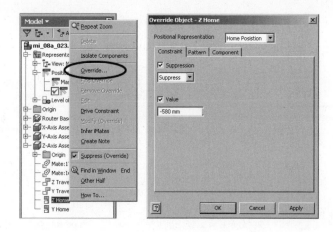

9. In the Override Object dialog box, click the Suppression check box and set the drop-down box to Enable.

10. Click the Value check box and set the value to **-580 mm**, then click OK. This sets the z-axis assembly to a static up and down position. You can click and drag on the component to see this.

11. Right-click on the Y Home constraint and choose Override.

12. In the Override Object dialog box, click the Suppression check box and set the drop-down box to Enable.

13. Click the Value check box and set the value to **-28 mm**, then click OK. This sets the y-axis assembly to a static left and right position. If you click and drag on the z-axis assembly, you will see it is now locked in place.

14. Right-click on the X Home constraint and choose Override.

15. In the Override Object dialog box, click the Suppression check box and set the drop-down box to Enable.

16. Click the Value check box and set the value to **395 mm**, then click OK. This sets the x-axis assembly to a static forward and backward position.

17. Right-click on the Master positional representation and choose Activate. Click and drag on the z-axis assembly and notice it is free to drag again.

18. Right-click on the Home Position representation and choose Activate to set the assembly back to its defined home position; notice it is constrained in place.

In the next set of steps you will create another positional representation and unsuppress the set of constraints that will control the X, Y, and Z travel limits.

19. Right-click on Position at the top level of the positional representation node and choose New to create a new positional representation.

20. Expand the Position node, if needed, and notice a new positional representation has been created and is currently active as denoted by the checkmark.

21. Rename the new positional representation to **Set to Range**.

22. Right-click on the Z Travel constraint and choose Suppress (Override) as shown in Figure 8.45.

FIGURE 8.45
Enabling a suppressed constraint

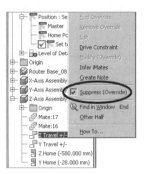

This toggles the suppression value of the Z Travel constraint and enables it so the travel is limited in the z-axis to hold it to a realistic range of motion. Next you will do the same for the Y and X Travel constraints.

23. Right-click on the Y Travel constraint and choose Suppress (Override).

24. Right-click on the X Travel constraint and choose Suppress (Override). Note you may need to expand the x-axis assembly component in the browser to find this constraint.

25. Right-click on the Home Position representation and choose Activate. Click and drag on the z-axis assembly to set the assembly back to its home position.

26. Right-click on the Set to Range representation and choose Activate to set the assembly so it can be dragged within its defined range of travel.

As you can see from the previous steps, positional representations are a powerful way to show components in multiple positions as required during the operation of a mechanism. You can close the current file without saving changes and continue on to explore the use of positional representations in subassemblies. Follow these steps to discover the tools used for handling positional representations in subassemblies:

1. On the Get Started tab, click Open, and then select the file called mi_08a_024.iam from the Chapter 8 folder of the Mastering Inventor 2011 directory.

2. Expand the Representations folder for the top-level assembly (located at the top of the browser tree).

3. Right-click on Position and choose New to create a new positional representation.

4. Expand the Position node, if needed, and notice a positional representation called Position1 has been created and is currently active as denoted by the checkmark.

5. Select Position1, then click on it and rename it **Range of Travel**.

6. Expand the component called CNC Hobby Router and then expand the Representations folder for this subassembly.

7. Next, expand the Position node to reveal the positional representations already created in this subassembly.

8. Right-click the Set to Range positional representation and choose Activate.

At this point, you have created a positional representation for the top-level assembly and then set that positional representation to use the Set to Range positional representation in the subassembly.

9. Click and drag on the router assembly and notice the parts will not move. To fix this, you need to set the subassembly to be flexible within the positional representation.

10. Right-click on the CNC Hobby Router (either in the browser or in the graphics area) and choose Override from the right-click context menu. In the Override Object dialog box, you will notice Set to Range is the active positional representation as defined previously.

11. Click the Flexible Status check box and set the drop-down box to Flexible, then click OK.

12. Click and drag on the router assembly and notice the parts will now move according to the Set to Range positional representation that is defined in the subassembly.

Once you've explored the nested positional representations you can close this file without saving changes. Positional representations also allow the reuse of identical subassemblies within a top-level assembly file. When using positional representations in conjunction with flexible assemblies, you can demonstrate a subassembly in different positions. Figure 8.46 shows an assembly containing three instances of a cylinder subassembly, each at a different extension length. This could be done by setting up positional representations in the cylinder subassembly defining each extension value or by leaving the cylinder subassembly underconstrained and then setting each subassembly to flexible.

FIGURE 8.46
Multiple instances
of a cylinder
subassembly

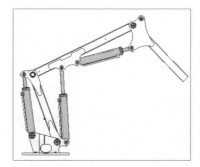

To help manage positional representations, you can set up the browser to display only the overrides present in each positional representation, as shown in Figure 8.47. The buttons along the top of the Representations browser allow you to create a new positional representation, validate the overrides ensuring that no errors are created in the representations, and manage the overrides via Microsoft Excel.

FIGURE 8.47
Representations
browser

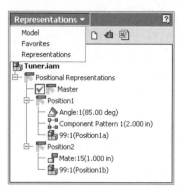

Because the positional representation properties of an assembly are stored separately, multiple views can be created in the drawing environment representing different positions of the same assembly. Figure 8.48 shows an example of an overlay view showing both available positions of this arm.

FIGURE 8.48
Overlay view
of a positional
representation

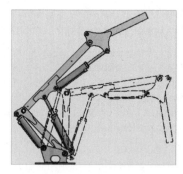

LEVEL OF DETAIL REPRESENTATIONS

Proper use of level of detail (LOD) improves speed and reduces the memory required to load and navigate large assemblies. When working with a large assembly, you suppress components that are not required for a certain aspect of working with the design and then save that suppression state as a level of detail representation. For instance, if you are designing a large material-handling unit, you might open the unit in the LOD representation with everything suppressed except the frame while you work on the frame skins, thereby significantly reducing the number of parts loaded into memory.

SUPPRESS VS. VISIBILITY

It is a common misconception that making components invisible reduces the overhead of your assemblies. However, when a component's visibility is toggled off, it is still loaded into memory. To unload it from memory, you must utilize LOD Reps. If you work with large assemblies, you can set the All Components Suppressed as the default LOD. The assembly will open more quickly, and then you can select a previously defined LOD or unsuppress just the parts you want to work with. This method consumes less RAM than opening the complete assembly and then suppressing components.

Another common example of LOD representations might be to suppress external components while working on internal components simply for convenience. In addition to this standard method of suppressing components to create LOD, you can employ substitute LOD representations to trade out a large multipart assembly with a single part derived from that assembly.

Just as view and positional representations have master representations, so too does the LOD. However, there are three additional default LOD representations: All Components Suppressed, All Parts Suppressed, and All Content Center Suppressed. These system-defined LODs cannot be removed or modified.

All Components Suppressed Suppresses everything within the assembly, allowing you to quickly open the assembly and then unsuppress components as required.

All Parts Suppressed Suppresses all parts at all levels of the assembly; however, subassemblies are loaded, allowing you to examine the assembly structure without loading all the part files.

All Content Center Suppressed Suppresses any component in the assembly that is stored in the Content Center Files directory as designated by the IPJ (project) file.

Although Chapter 9, "Large Assembly Strategies," covers the specific steps to create LODs, here are the general procedures.

To create a user-defined LOD, follow these steps:

1. Expand the Representations heading in the browser, right-click the Level Of Detail heading, and then choose New Level Of Detail.

2. Continue by right-clicking the component or components you want to suppress and choose Suppress from the menu.

3. Once this is done, you must save the assembly while still in the LOD.

4. After saving the assembly, you can create more LOD representations or flip from one to another to compare the results.

To create a substitute LOD, follow these steps:

1. Expand the Representations heading in the browser, right-click the Level Of Detail heading and then choose New Substitute.

2. There are two methods for creating substitutes. The first method simply prompts you to select any existing part file to swap out for the assembly file in the LOD, and the second creates a derived part from the source assembly.

3. When using the Derive Assembly method, you are asked to specify a part template to use and then are brought right into the derive assembly process.

4. The derived part is automatically marked as a substitute during the derive process and placed into the LOD.

On the left, Figure 8.49 shows an assembly in its master LOD with 304 component occurrences in the assembly and 81 unique files open in the Inventor session. On the right, the same assembly is set to a substitute LOD and reduced to a single component in the assembly and only two unique files open in the Inventor session. As you can imagine, you can achieve a significant savings in memory by placing an assembly with a substitute LOD active into a top-level assembly.

FIGURE 8.49

Substitute LOD representation

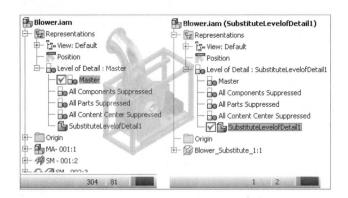

It is important to understand that substitute LODs are intended to be used by either excluding components during the derive process or in combination with user-defined LODs to exclude components. Simply making a substitute LOD of an assembly with all components included may not give you the performance gain you anticipated unless you have made the substitute from another LOD that has parts suppressed or you have excluded parts while creating the substitute LOD.

LOD states are created automatically when you suppress components while in the master LOD. To save suppressions to a new LOD representation, click Save, and you will be prompted to click Yes or No to save the LOD. If you choose Yes, you can specify a name for the LOD. If you choose No, the suppression states of the component are discarded, and the assembly is saved in master LOD.

Temporary LOD representations are created in subassemblies when a subassembly component is suppressed from a top-level assembly. A tilde and index number are listed after the subassembly name to denote a temporary LOD state. Note that the subassembly is not modified. You can open the subassembly on its own and save the suppression states as a named LOD if desired.

It is important to understand the difference between LOD representations and iAssembly configurations with respect to how they affect the bill of materials. Although you can suppress features at will and substitute part files for assemblies with the use of LOD representations, Inventor still understands that all the parts in the master LOD will be included in the bill of materials. When you suppress a component in an LOD representation used in a drawing view, the view updates and any balloons attached to that component are deleted. However, the parts list will still list the component because it always refers to the master bill of materials.

If your intent is to create an assembly configuration where some parts are to be listed in the bill of materials and others excluded, an iAssembly is the correct tool.

LODs and Parts Lists

New Inventor users often attempt to use LODs to create a parts lists in the drawing environment that only shows the unsuppressed components. However, this is not allowed outright. In order to use an existing LOD for parts list purposes, you should right-click on it in the browser and choose Copy to View Rep. Once the View Rep is created, it can be used in the parts list by editing the part list, clicking the Filter Settings button in the Parts List edit dialog box, and then selecting Assembly View Representation from the list.

Using iAssemblies

An iAssembly is a table-driven assembly file that allows the use of component part configurations to build variations of a design. Some of the strengths of assembly configurations of this type are the abilities to swap out one component for another, to include or exclude components all together, and to adjust assembly constraint offset values to create various configurations of the original assembly.

It is important to understand that when you create an iAssembly, you create what is called an iAssembly *factory*. The configurations that will be output from this factory are called the iAssembly members. It may help to think of the factory as the parent file and the members as children.

To create an iAssembly, most often you start with an assembly composed of iParts. First, the iParts are created for all parts that will vary in size or configuration of features. Next, create the assembly using iPart members where required. Once the basic assembly is created, you add the configuration table, turning the assembly into an iAssembly.

The assembly used in the next exercise represents a simplified push button panel. Your goal is to create an assembly configuration with variations in the number and type of buttons used, as shown in Figure 8.50.

1. On the Get Started tab, click Open.

2. Browse to Chapter 8 in the Mastering Inventor 2011 directory and open `mi_08a_025.iam`.

3. Switch to the Manage tab and click Create iAssembly on the Author panel. This will open the iAssembly Author dialog box, as shown in Figure 8.51.

4. The first thing you should do is consider the naming conventions for the iAssembly members. Click the Options button at the bottom of the dialog box to bring up the naming options. Here you would typically configure the name for the member part number and member names, so that as you add rows to the iAssembly table, the naming drops out automatically. In this case, you will simply click OK to choose the defaults.

FIGURE 8.50
Four configurations of a push button panel

Either column can be set to be the filename column from which member part numbers are generated. This can be done by right-clicking the Member or Part Number column headers and choosing File Name Column from the menu. The filename column is indicated by the save or disk symbol.

FIGURE 8.51

iAssembly Author
dialog box

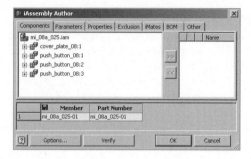

5. Next, examine the Components tab and expand the tree next to the part called cover_plate_08:1. In the tree of each part are four different nodes that you can use to add a column to the table. Select Table Replace from the tree, and use the >> button to add it as a column in the table.

6. Now that you have added a column to the table, you will add a row. Right-click anywhere on row 1 in the lower pane of the dialog box, and choose Insert Row. Your table should now resemble Figure 8.52.

FIGURE 8.52

Configuring an
iAssembly table

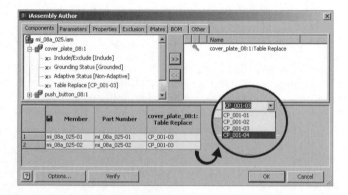

The Table Replace column allows you to replace an iPart member for another iPart member within the assembly. In this case, the part named CP_001-03 is the sheet-metal cover plate. This plate is an iPart that has four different sizes within the iPart table.

7. Click the cell in row 2 in the cover_plate_08:1 Table Replace column to activate a drop-down menu.

8. From the drop-down menu, select CP_001-04, as shown in the inset of Figure 8.52. Click OK to exit the dialog box.

9. Examine the Model browser, and you will notice that a table has been added to the browser. Expand the table, and you will find a listing of the iAssembly members, mi_08a_025-01 and mi_08a_025-02.

10. mi_08a_025-01 will have a check mark next to it informing you that this is the active member of the iAssembly. To set mi_08a_025-02 as active, right-click it and choose Activate, or simply double-click it.

WORKING WITH IASSEMBLIES

Many iAssemblies require only a few size variables and a few components that can be interchanged. Although in this example both the plate and buttons are iParts, often an iAssembly requires only a few components to be iParts for configuration.

It is typically best to tackle iAssemblies in a very structured manner, configuring only one part of the table at a time and then returning to the model to test that change. Making many changes in the table at once may make it difficult to determine how changes affect the model.

Once a couple of rows are added using the iAssembly Author interface, you can edit the table with Microsoft Excel to add many rows at once and quickly make changes to the column entries. Also in Excel, you can create formulas to concatenate column entries, calculate entries, or use if/thens to determine entries.

11. Now that you have used a different size plate, you will need to add another button to the assembly. To do this, select the existing black button, and use Copy and Paste to add a new instance to the assembly.

12. Next, place an Insert constraint between the new instance of the button and the empty hole on the plate, as shown in Figure 8.53.

FIGURE 8.53
Adding an Insert
constraint

13. Once the new button is constrained, set mi_08a_025-01 active again in the table tree, and notice that you are presented with an error message warning you that the new constraint is looking at geometry that is no longer present. Click Accept in the error dialog box.

Notice the new button remains, even though the hole it was constrained to is gone. To address this, you need to edit the table further and configure the iAssembly to suppress the extra button when not needed.

14. Right-click the Table icon in the Model browser, and choose Edit Table.

15. Locate part push_button_08:4 in the tree as shown, and use the >> button to place Include/Exclude in the table as a column.

16. Next, set the value for this column to be Exclude for row 1, as shown in Figure 8.54. Click OK to return to the model, and activate both members to see that no constraint errors occur.

FIGURE 8.54

Exclude/include components in an iAssembly

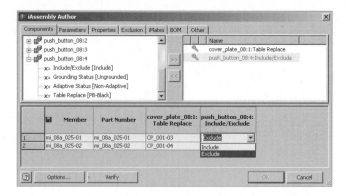

17. Next, you will change out the black buttons in member mi_08a_025-02 to use a second green and a second red button. Edit the table, and choose the last two instances of part push_button_08 from the tree in the top-left pane. Locate the Table Replace parameter for each, and use the >> button to include them in the table.

18. Set the Table Replace values in row 2 to Red and Green, as shown in Figure 8.55.

You do not need to change the values in row 1 because one of the buttons is already set to Black as required and the other, as you recall, you excluded so that it does not show in the row 1 configuration.

19. Click OK to exit the table authoring dialog box, and then activate mi_08a_025-02 from the table. Note the changes to the four button configuration. You should now have two red and two green buttons in an alternating pattern.

FIGURE 8.55

Table Replace in the iAssembly Author dialog box

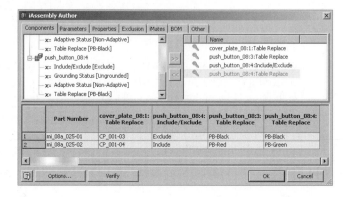

20. Last, you will set one of the buttons to be in a different position. Edit the table to return to the iAssembly Author dialog box again, and activate the Parameters tab.

21. Expand the Constraints folder, select Insert:1, and use the >> button to add it as a column in the table.

22. Set the value of this column to **7 mm** for row 2 of the configurations.

23. Click OK to exit the dialog box, and notice one of the buttons is now pushed in because you have modified the constraint offset value.

You can close this assembly file without saving changes. iAssemblies allow you to create configurations of your assemblies by including and excluding components, configuring constraints values, setting iProperties, and much more. When creating drawing files for iAssemblies, you often need a drawing for each member. The members have the same annotations and tables, with only some values differing.

The Bottom Line

Assemble components using assembly constraints   Assembly constraints are an important part of working with Inventor assembly files. Assembly constraints determine how assembly components fit together. As constraints are applied between components, degrees of freedom are removed.

> **Master It**   You are new to 3D and find the concept of assembly constraints a bit challenging. Where can you find a simple overview of constraints?

Organize designs using structured subassemblies.   Subassemblies add organization, facilitate the bill of materials, and reduce assembly constraints; all this results in better performance and easier edits. One of the habits of all Inventor experts is their effective use and understanding of subassemblies.

> **Master It**   You need to hand off an accurate BOM for finished designs to the purchasing department at the end of each design project.

Work with adaptive components   Geometry can be set to be adaptive so that it can be sized and positioned in the context of where it is used in the assembly. You can set underconstrained geometry to be adaptive by specifying the elements allowed to adapt.

> **Master It**   You want to set a feature of a part to be adaptive so that it can adapt to another part in an assembly. However, the feature is based on a fully constrained sketch. How would this be done?

Create assembly level features   An assembly feature is a feature created and utilized within the active assembly file. Because the feature is created within the assembly file, it does not exist at the single part or subassembly level.

> **Master It**   You want to make a notch in a standard part that will not affect its use in every other assembly it is used in. Can this be done?

Manage Bills of Materials   Managing a bill of materials can be a large part of any assembly design task. Understanding the BOM structure goes a long way toward successfully configuring your bill of materials.

> **Master It**   You need to mark a component as a reference component in just one assembly file. However, when you attempt to do so using the BOM editor, it is designated as reference in every assembly. How can you set just a single instance of a component to be a reference component?

Use positional reps and flexible assemblies together.   Often you may need to show a design in various stages of motion to test interference and/or proof of concept. Copying assemblies so that you can change the assembly constraints to show different assembly positions can become a file management nightmare. Instead, use flexible subassemblies and positional representations.

> **Master It**   You need to show your assembly in variations dependent upon the position of the moving parts and the task the machine is accomplishing at given stages of its operation.

Copy assembly designs for reuse and configuration   Because of the live linked data that exists in Inventor assemblies, using Windows Explorer to copy designs and rename parts is difficult and often delivers poor results. Using the tool provided in Inventor will allow you to copy designs and maintain the links between files.

> **Master It**   You need to duplicate an existing design in order to create a similar design.

Substitute a single part for entire subassemblies   Working with large assemblies, particularly where large, complex assemblies are used over and over as subassemblies within a top-level design, can tax almost any workstation if not approached in the correct manner.

> **Master It**   You would like to swap out a complex assembly for a simplified version for use in layout designs or to use in large assemblies in an attempt to improve performance.

Chapter 9

Large Assembly Strategies

Working with large assemblies is more manageable than ever before with fully native 64-bit support, removing the memory limitations related to the Windows XP 32-bit platform. Large assembly design on 32-bit systems is improved in Inventor with the use of tools such as shrink-wrap and substitution level of detail (LOD) representations. These LODs allow you to swap out complex subassemblies with single substitute parts of less detail, all while maintaining model properties and an accurate bill of materials.

Although every design department may have a different view on what a large assembly is, everyone can benefit from the large assembly tools and strategies discussed in this chapter. You can create fully functional digital prototypes ranging from 10 to 100,000 components if you approach the task with an eye to the topics covered here.

In this chapter, you will learn how to:

- ◆ Select a workstation
- ◆ Adjust your performance settings
- ◆ Use best practices for large assembly
- ◆ Manage assembly detail
- ◆ Simplify parts

Selecting a Workstation

Ensuring that you have an adequate system to accomplish the type of design work you intend to do is an important, but often overlooked, step in achieving successful large assembly design with any parametric modeler. Understanding the capabilities and limitations of your computer and then budgeting for upgrades is an important part of working in today's design world.

If you consider the time you spend waiting and the loss of work experienced when working on an undersized computer, you will likely determine that a workstation upgrade will pay for itself within a year. If you budget for upgrades every two years, then you could argue that the upgrade is actually paying for itself in the second year of use. Although this scenario might not fit your actual situation, it demonstrates the idea that operating costs (hardware and software alike) should be budgeted and planned for and always measured against lost work and downtime.

Physical Memory vs. Virtual Memory

When your system runs low on physical memory (RAM) and requires more to complete an operation, Windows begins writing to the system hard drive in order to continue. This is known as virtual memory and is often referred to as a page file.

When considering a workstation for doing large assembly design, it should be your goal to always work in RAM as much as possible, because when Windows begins to write to virtual memory, you will notice a considerable drop in performance. One of the weakest links in terms of speed on even the most adequate workstation is the hard drive. Accessing data from RAM can be thousands of times faster than accessing data from the hard drive. Therefore, one of the best ways to beef up a workstation is to simply add more RAM.

If you are running an older computer or skimped on RAM when you upgraded, you will notice that as you attempt to load large assemblies or drawing files of large assemblies in Inventor, you quickly use up available RAM. You will find yourself waiting for Windows to write and then read data to the hard drive. Although the unknowing user might think that Inventor has suddenly become slow, you should understand that no application can overcome the hardware and operating system limitations upon which it is installed.

If you run out of RAM on a 32-bit system, you have a limit of 4GB of virtual address space. Windows reserves 2GB of that space for the operating system by default, thereby leaving just 2GB for all the other running applications. If you work on extremely large assemblies, you might exceed the available 2GB of address space.

To resolve this, it is possible to configure Windows to reserve only 1GB of address space for the operating system and leave 3GB for the applications to use. This is referred to as "flipping the /3GB switch." Depending upon the size of the assemblies you work on, the configuration settings you adjust in Inventor, and the techniques you employ within Inventor, the extra 1GB of virtual memory might be adequate for your needs for those instances when you need a bit more memory. However, as stated earlier, it should be your goal not to be working in virtual memory but instead to always be working in RAM.

Please note that the /3GB switch was developed for server operating systems and therefore is considered a workaround when being used on a workstation. Although you may be able to employ this startup modification to your system, understand that it is an unsupported workaround and has been known to cause stability issues. Also note that some workstations may not permit this modification at all.

If you do utilize the /3GB switch, be aware that, although this does allow you to extend your system's capabilities, it may effectively create more "rope to hang yourself," meaning that it will allow you to build large assemblies that you can load but then cannot save or modify. Often this results in a crash of the application and the generation of errors and file corruptions. Therefore, consider this an option at your own risk, and use it to supplement your workstation capacity for the short term, but be careful of overextending the use of virtual memory. You can find instructional information on the /3GB switch on the Microsoft support website (`http://support.microsoft.com/`).

64-bit Systems vs. 32-bit Systems

The maximum amount of RAM that is supported on a Windows XP Professional 32-bit system is 4GB. If you determine that your needs currently exceed or will soon exceed the limits of a 32-bit system, you should consider a 64-bit workstation; 64-bit systems like Windows XP Professional 64,

Windows Vista Business, Enterprise, and Professional can handle up to 128GB of RAM and therefore do not have to slow down to write data to the virtual memory. Windows 7 Professional, Enterprise, and Ultimate 64-bit editions can address 192GB of RAM.

If your version of Windows XP, Vista, or Windows 7 includes the word Home in the title you should verify that it is supported for use with Inventor and be aware that it will not address the memory capacities listed above.

Most processors purchased by the time this book was published will be 64-bit. Understand that you must also run a 64-bit operating system, such as Windows XP Professional 64 or Windows Vista Business, Enterprise, and Professional, in order to gain the performance and memory increases attributed to a 64-bit system. Although Inventor 2008 was compiled to run on a 64-bit operating system, Inventor 2009 was the first fully native 64-bit version. All versions since Inventor 2009 take full advantage of a 64-bit system.

Hardware

Hardware upgrades are an important part of any design department. Budgeting properly and knowing what components to allocate more money to can make these upgrades more manageable. Dollar for dollar, you should give priority to the following components in the order listed.

RAM

Although the minimum system requirement for Inventor 2011 is 2GB, you should always consider adding as much RAM as you can afford to your workstation. If making the move to a 64-bit system, you will require a minimum of 2GB of RAM, and you should consider at least 8GB.

GRAPHICS CARDS

To ensure that your graphics card is set at the optimal settings, select the Tools tab, click Application Options, and go to the Hardware tab in the dialog box that opens. Direct3D graphics hardware is the default setting for Windows XP Professional 32-bit and 64-bit versions as well as Windows Vista 32-bit and 64-bit versions.

Inventor 2011 will use either OpenGL or the default DirectX 9 hardware acceleration modes when running Windows XP. Windows XP 64 uses DirectX 9 only. Windows Vista and Windows 7 support DirectX 9, 10, and 11. Inventor will automatically detect the appropriate level for your card. All configurations have OpenGL software emulation.

It is recommended that you consider a midrange graphics card for an Inventor workstation and save the money for frequent upgrades rather than investing in a high-end card, because of the rapid changes in video card technology. For recommendations on graphics cards and other hardware, refer to the following websites:

- Autodesk Inventor hardware: `www.inventor-certified.com/graphics/`

- Certified workstations: `www.inventor-certified.com/graphics/cert_ws.php`

- Autodesk Inventor hardware graphics database: `www.inventor-certified.com/graphics/registries.php`

- Autodesk Inventor 2011 Enhanced Visualization System and Graphics Requirements: `http://www.inventor-certified.com/graphics/graphics_hw_guidelines.php`

HARD DRIVES

Inventor files are segmented, meaning that the graphics are separate from the feature information. When an assembly is first opened, only the graphics segments are loaded. When you edit a file, the additional data is loaded at that time. This makes a fast hard drive important for performance.

Another aspect of hard drive performance stems from file storage and workspace setup. In Inventor, working from your local drive is the preferred method, and Autodesk recommends you avoid working on Inventor files across a network. The reason for this is simply because of the numbers of files that you might be editing at one time. For instance, a change to a large assembly could potentially modify hundreds of part files, requiring all those files to be saved at once. Doing this across a network, particularly one with latency issues, may result in file corruptions if the files are not saved correctly. Autodesk Vault is set up to store files on a server and copy those files locally when checked out for editing. When working in this manner, Inventor has a higher-performance requirement than standard office applications, and the hard drive workload is very heavy. Therefore, upgrading your hard drive to a higher-speed SATA or serial attached SCSI (SAS) drive may be worth considering.

PROCESSORS

When considering processors for an Inventor 2011 workstation, the chief question should concern multicore processors. As a minimum, you should consider a dual-core processor even though Inventor is not truly a multithreaded application. (Multithreaded means that the operating system or the application will spread the processing load across the processor.) If you opt for a dual-core processor, you can still take advantage of it, because Inventor will run on one core and other applications will run on the other.

There are parts of Inventor, such as Inventor Studio's rendering engine and its modeling kernel, that are multithreaded, so if you plan to do a lot of image and animation rendering in Inventor, you may want to opt for a quad-core processor. Otherwise, if you are trying to decide between a dual-core and quad-core processor, it will probably be more cost effective to go with a faster dual-core processor rather than a quad-core processor. This will likely change as the rapid pace of technology continues.

Working with Performance Settings

Whether or not upgrading workstations is an option, you should ensure that your system is set up for optimal performance when working with large assemblies. A number of options in Inventor will facilitate better performance when working with large assemblies.

Working with Drawing Settings

Generating and hiding lines when creating and editing drawing views in Inventor can be some of the most processor-intensive tasks in Inventor. To help ease the demand on the system, you should be aware of several settings when working with large assembly drawings. You can find these settings by selecting the Tools tab, clicking Application Options, and going to the Drawing tab in the dialog box that opens, as shown in Figure 9.1.

FIGURE 9.1
Drawing applica-
tion options

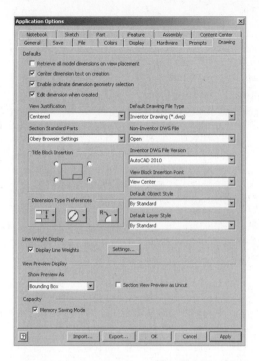

CALCULATING THE ROI OF NEW HARDWARE

It's often hard to convince management (especially nontechnical managers) that you really do need that new computer to get your job done. After all, you're currently getting your work done, right? So why do you need the faster computer? This is where a return on investment (ROI) calculation will come in handy.

Let's say you routinely have to open, modify, and print large assembly drawings. Do the following:

1. Measure how long it takes to do this process on your old machine.

2. Look at some benchmarks (see the certified workstations link mentioned previously) or talk to others who have faster machines, and make a conservative estimate of how long it would take you to do the same operations on the faster machine.

3. Subtract the two. You now have your time savings per operation.

4. Multiply this time by the number of times in a day or week you perform these tasks.

5. Multiply it by an hourly rate for your industry (you can always use your hourly salary) to get the dollar savings per time period (per week, month, and so on).

6. Now you can take the cost of the new system, and divide it by this cost savings per unit of time. This gives you the amount of time it will take to pay off that new computer.

Furthermore, once this time period has passed, you are actually making money because you are saving the company money once the investment has been paid off. Once you can show that the hardware will pay for itself relatively quickly, you should have fewer problems convincing management to upgrade your equipment.

Another consideration for the ROI is who will inherit your old system. Generally, some person in the office will also benefit from a faster system, even if they run general office applications. For instance, if the receptionist is required to access many documents quickly across a network while he or she assists customers and other office staff, there is a good chance that your old CAD station will improve the ability to do so. Because this key person is the through point of information for so many people who are currently required to wait on a slow computer, the ROI is exponential. Passing old workstations to the shop floor to allow shop staff to access digitally stored files quickly is another place to look for these ROI savings.

DISPLAY LINE WEIGHTS

The Display Line Weights check box enables or disables the display of unique line weights in drawings. Deselect the box to show lines without weight differences. Line weights will still print correctly even with this box selected. Deselecting this box will speed up the performance of your drawing during edits and annotation work.

VIEW PREVIEW DISPLAY

The options in the Show Preview As drop-down box set the type of preview you get when creating a view. All Components is the default, but you will find that selecting the Partial or Bounding Box option will improve performance because Inventor will not be required to create and update the preview as you drag your mouse pointer around the screen. The preview setting does not affect the drawing view result. Bounding Box previews a simple rectangle during the view creation, and Partial previews a simplified representation of the view. Bounding Box is the most efficient.

When using this option, you can still preview the assembly if you'd like by simply selecting the Preview check box in the Drawing View creation dialog box, but the default will be a simple bounding box. Using the Bounding Box option is suggested if you find yourself waiting for the preview to generate during drawing view creation.

The Section View Preview As Uncut check box will also provide some performance improvements when selected. This option will allow Inventor to display the section view preview as unsectioned in order to be more efficient. The section view will still be generated as normal.

MEMORY SAVING MODE

Memory Saving Mode sets the way that Inventor loads components into memory during view creation. When this option is selected, Inventor loads components into memory before and during view creation and then unloads them from memory once the view is created.

Although memory is conserved using this mode, view creation and editing operations cannot be undone while this option is enabled. You'll notice the Undo/Redo buttons will be grayed out after a view creation or edit. This option will also have a negative impact on performance when editing and creating views because the components must be loaded into memory each time. Because of this, you should consider setting this option as an application setting only if you always work with very large assemblies.

It is generally preferred to set this option per document by selecting the Tools tab, clicking Documents Settings, going to the Drawing tab in the dialog box that opens, and then setting the Memory Saving Mode drop-down list to Always, as shown in Figure 9.2.

FIGURE 9.2
Drawing document settings

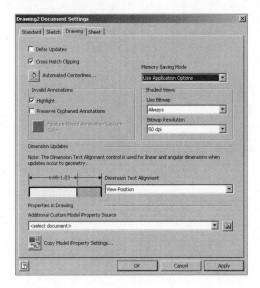

SHADED VIEWS

Also in the document settings, you can adjust the way that shaded views are displayed. Setting the Use Bitmap drop-down list to Always, as shown in Figure 9.2, improves performance by applying raster shading as opposed to a vector style. The difference impacts the display but typically does not affect printing.

You can also adjust the bitmap resolution; setting it lower conserves memory and speeds up performance. The default is 100 dpi. Setting the dpi to 200 or higher will invoke a prompt, warning you that increasing this setting for large assemblies may not be possible.

Working with Model Display Settings

When working within the modeling environment, you can adjust several settings to have a positive impact on performance. You can access these settings by selecting the Tools tab, clicking Application Options, and going to the Display tab in the dialog box that opens, as shown in Figure 9.3.

APPEARANCE

All of the various options for the Display options can be controlled as an Application setting or a Document setting. Using the application settings allows consistency across all of the documents that you work with. Document settings will adopt the settings that were used with the document that was saved.

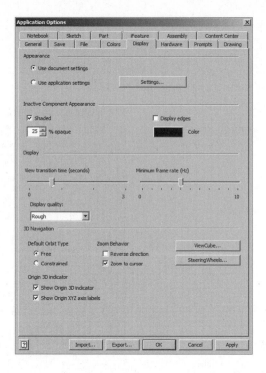

Not all settings are controlled by this option but very useful settings such as displaying the model in Orthographic or Perspective view and what Visual Style you want active can be defined.

Edge Display

Deselecting the Edges check box for Enabled components in the Shaded Display Modes area of the Display tab will lighten the amount of graphics rendering required to display and update the display of your large assemblies.

Display Quality

Setting the Display Quality drop-down list to Rough, as shown in Figure 9.3, will speed up performance by simplifying details. Navigation commands such as zooming, panning, and orbiting are particularly affected by this setting. If you find that the rough display is not to your liking, you can toggle back and forth according to the size of the assembly model you are working with.

View Transition Time (Seconds)

The View Transition Time (Seconds) setting controls the time required to smoothly transition between views when using zooming and viewing commands. A zero transition time takes you from the beginning view to the end view instantaneously. For instance, if you were zoomed in on a small component and wanted to zoom all while this slider was set to zero, you would not see the gradual zooming out that may provide a gain in performance but can make changes in position and orientation less clear.

Minimum Frame Rate (Hz)

You can use the Minimum Frame Rate (Hz) setting to specify how slowly the display updates during zooming and orbiting commands. It may be hard to see the effects of this option on a normal-sized part or assembly, because the views will typically update more quickly than the rate of this setting. Here is a quick description of the how the slider setting corresponds to the frame rate:

- 0 always draws everything in the view, no matter the time required.

- 1 tries to draw the view at least one frame per second. (Inventor will simplify or discard parts of the view if needed but will restore them when movement ends.)

- 5 draws at least five frames per second.

The settings in Display tab can not only affect the performance of the system, they can greatly affect the user's comfort when working in Inventor.

Working with General Settings

The following are a few general settings that you can adjust to help large assembly performance. You can access these settings by selecting the Tools tab, clicking Application Options, and going to the General tab in the dialog box that opens, as shown in Figure 9.4.

FIGURE 9.4
Default application options

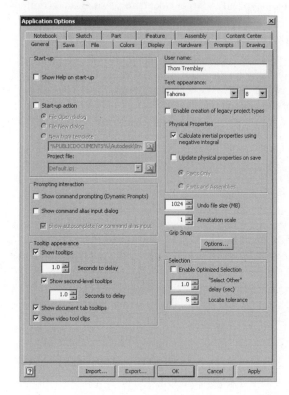

ENABLE OPTIMIZED SELECTION

The Enable Optimized Selection setting, located on the lower-right corner of the dialog box, improves the performance of graphics during prehighlighting in large assemblies. When activated, the algorithm for the Select Other function filters for only the group of objects closest to the screen. If you click through this first group of objects, the next group is considered for highlighting.

UPDATE PHYSICAL PROPERTIES ON SAVE

When checked, the Update Physical Properties On Save setting, located in the Physical Properties area on the right side of the dialog box, recalculates the mass properties of the model when you save the file. This ensures that mass properties are up-to-date. Setting this to Parts Only will ensure that the parts are all up-to-date without requiring you to wait on the recalculation for large assemblies. Note that this setting is disabled altogether by default but is recommended to be set to Parts Only if you find it helpful. Note too that the same function can be performed manually from the Bill Of Materials Editor and the Manage tab.

UNDO FILE SIZE

The Undo File Size option, on the lower-right side of the dialog box, sets the maximum size of the temporary file that records changes to a file so that actions can be undone. It's typically required to increase the size of this setting when working with large models and drawings, because each undo action is typically a larger calculation. Autodesk recommends adjusting this in 4MB increments.

CAPACITY METER

The Capacity Meter is displayed at the bottom-right corner of the Inventor screen, as shown in Figure 9.5. The meter has three memory use indicators. The number to the left is the total number of occurrences in the active document. The next number is the total number of files open in the Inventor session. The last indicator is a colored bar graph that displays the amount of memory used by the session. When hovering your mouse pointer over the Capacity Meter, a tool tip will display the details of used and available memory. In 32-bit systems, you can use the meter in two modes: Inventor Only and Physical Memory. Due to the extended memory accessibility of 64-bit operating systems no Capacity Meter is shown in the Status bar.

On 32-bit systems, the Capacity Meter display is set to look at just the Autodesk Inventor process. The bar color will change from the normal green to yellow when more than 60 percent of the allotted address space has been used. It will then turn red at 80 percent, and a warning dialog box will prompt you to close documents in an attempt to free up memory, as shown in Figure 9.6.

As a rule, you should not habitually work when the meter indicates that you have passed the 60 percent mark. When you do see the bar turn yellow, you should stop and create an LOD representation or close some files. LOD representations are covered later in this chapter. Working in limited memory can lead to memory corruptions in the file and result in a loss of work.

Typically what happens when a user continues to work past the 60 percent range is that some memory-intensive calculation is performed that will cause the virtual memory to fill and then have to "swap" out a large amount of data. During this time, your system may become unresponsive and any well-intentioned attempt to help may cause file corruptions.

FIGURE 9.5
Capacity Meter
in Inventor
Only mode

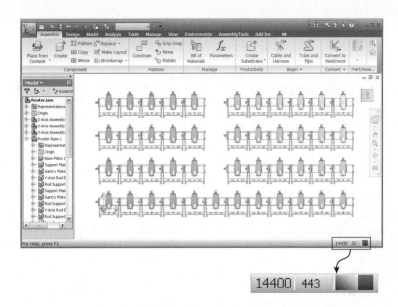

FIGURE 9.6
Warning received
at 80 percent
capacity

Other common results of working past the 60 percent marker occur when saving or creating a drawing view. When working in this manner, it is possible to reach a point at which you will not have enough memory available to save the files. The same can happen when attempting to create drawing views of an assembly when you have reached this marker.

Therefore, you should not work past the 60 percent marker, other than to create LODs and/or to take other actions to reduce the amount of memory your file is requiring.

Working with System Settings

You can adjust several settings in the operating system to help with performance. Setting the page file to twice the amount of RAM is common among Inventor users in order to gain performance. There are also many visual effects that you may have grown accustomed to that actually cost you resources. If you are serious about turning your workstation into a large assembly workhorse, it is advisable to disable these features.

ADJUSTING THE VIRTUAL MEMORY PAGING FILE SIZE

To change the size of the virtual memory paging file in Windows XP Professional, right-click the My Computer icon, and choose Properties. On the System Properties tab, click the Advanced tab, then click Performance Options, and finally, under Virtual Memory, click Change.

In Windows Vista and Windows 7, right-click the Computer icon, and choose Properties. On the System Properties tab, click the Advanced System Settings tab, then click Performance Options, and finally, under Virtual Memory, deselect Automatically Manage Paging File Size For All Drives. Then click Change.

Windows Vista and Windows 7 are set to an Automatic or System Managed paging file size. These setting work much better than the defaults in Windows XP. If you choose to set a Custom paging file size you should refer to the recommended size that the dialog offers and set the minimum and maximum to the same value to minimize fragmentation of the paging file if it needs to expand.

For Windows XP select Custom Size, set the Initial Size and Maximum Size settings to twice the available RAM, and click Set, as shown in Figure 9.7.

FIGURE 9.7
Setting the
page file size in
Windows XP

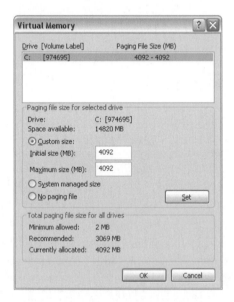

SETTING VIRTUAL MEMORY

Search the Internet, and you will find hundreds of incorrect theories as to how to set the values for your virtual memory. One of the major myths is that you should set the initial and maximum to different values. If you are dedicating a portion of your hard drive for a page file, why start it small and then let it grow? Just provide the maximum amount of space you can and let it be.

DISABLING COMMON VISUAL EFFECTS

Windows provides many options to set the visual effects of your computer. Many of them have a surprisingly high impact on performance when memory is scarce. Here are a few you might consider disabling in order to conserve resources:

Screen saver   Select Control Panel ➢ Display, and go to the Screen Saver tab. Set the Screen Saver drop-down to None. While you are working, screen savers are just another running process. You may want to set the Power Saving Mode option to turn off the monitor after a certain amount of time. If you use an LCD monitor, understand that screen savers do nothing to save an LCD screen.

Visual settings   Right-click the My Computer icon, and select Properties. Go to the Advanced tab and click the Settings button under Performance. Select Adjust For Best Performance. Windows will set back to a classic look and run much faster overall.

Appearance effects   Select Control Panel ➤ Display, and then go to the Appearance tab. Click the Effects button. You can deselect everything in this box and probably never miss any of it.

Screen resolution   If you're fortunate enough to have a nice, large-screen monitor, you probably have set the screen resolution up to maximize your space. However, this may be working against your large assembly pursuits. Experiment with setting the screen resolution to a lower setting such as 1024×768 to see whether you gain any performance when working with large assemblies.

Large Assembly Best Practices

Oftentimes Inventor users don't think about large assembly performance until it has already become an issue with the model on which they are working. It is possible for two Inventor users working on two identical workstations to create two seemingly identical models, and yet those two models might perform in dramatically different ways.

If the first user has been mindful of large assembly management all along, his model and drawings will be much easier to open and work with. If the second user concentrated only on her design and gave no thought to the memory demands of the files she was creating, her model will be slow to open and work with and ultimately more likely to cause application crashes and data corruption. When the next job comes along, user 1 can reuse his model to create a similar design, while user 2 will likely re-create the assembly model because she does not trust the integrity of the first model she created.

Understanding where performance savings can be gained as you create the model will help pay off once the large assembly is created and will make it much more manageable to work with along the way. And of course, a large assembly model can be revisited and cleaned up according to best practices to make it more manageable as well. Either way, having a model that is manageable and can be reused for similar work in the future should always be your goal.

You should be considering large assembly performance at three stages:

◆   Creating and editing the model

◆   Opening the model

◆   Detailing and annotating the model

Working with the Model

You can use several methods to ensure that your large assembly will not become unmanageable. It is important to remember that the words *large assembly* are subjective. To you, a large assembly may be 200 components, whereas to someone else it may be 20,000. Either way, following best practices ensures that you are developing good procedural habits and are prepared for the day when you are asked to design a much larger assembly than you typically do today.

As was discussed earlier in this chapter, hardware limitations might be an obstacle that you cannot overcome even if you follow every best practice, but you'll need to follow these practices to know that for certain. Conversely, even if you have a workstation that is extremely capable, you will still benefit by developing good work habits and making your models easier to handle on less capable workstations of others you collaborate with.

Improving File Open Time

It is a good practice to shut down Inventor and other Windows applications if you will be leaving them for an extended period of time. Closing these applications can allow the system to free up memory that is "leaked" by drivers and subroutines that take up memory when executed but do not release it when finished even if you don't use that function again.

When working with large datasets shutting down the application and reloading the model can be time consuming. With Inventor 2011 there is a default setting on the File tab of the Application Options that saves the last opened assembly and its component files in cache. You can also define a specific file to be kept so that you can work with others and maintain the benefits of the Quick File Open setting for a specific assembly.

Reducing Assembly Constraints

Using subassemblies within upper-level assemblies can reduce assembly constraints. The importance of this concept cannot be overstated. Reducing assembly constraints can eliminate the number of redundant calculations Inventor must make to solve your model, and therefore it pays off immediately in that respect. The increased organization and ability to reuse components already organized into subassemblies is a benefit that may be realized in the future.

To reorganize an assembly that has not been created using subassemblies, you can use the Demote option. To explore this concept, let's make some changes to an assembly.

1. Open the file named mi_9a_001.iam, located in the Chapter 9 directory of the Mastering Inventor 2011 folder.

Although not a large assembly by anyone's standard, this assembly has been created without using subassemblies to demonstrate the ability to demote components into subassemblies from the top down. Your goal is to restructure this assembly into three subassemblies so that you can reduce constraints and create subassemblies that can be used in other stapler designs. To do this, follow these steps:

2. In the Model Browser, select all the components with a prefix of 100.

3. Once you've selected those components, right-click and choose Component ➢ Demote, as shown in Figure 9.8.

4. You will be presented with a Create In-Place Component dialog box, where you can specify the name of the new subassembly, the template file, the file location, and the default BOM structure. Enter 100 for the name, and click OK.

5. Click Yes in the warning stating that assembly constraints will be moved with the demoted components, as shown in Figure 9.9.

This warning simply states that any constraints between the 100 series parts and the 200 and 300 series parts will now be redefined to be between subassembly 100 and the 200 and 300 series parts. The constraints between the 100 series parts and other 100 series parts are maintained in subassembly 100.

FIGURE 9.8
Demoting components to a subassembly

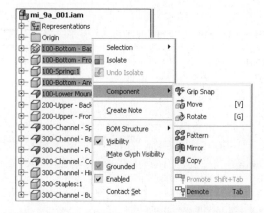

FIGURE 9.9
Restructuring components warning

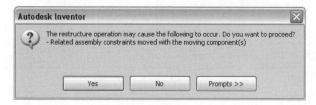

This is important in large assemblies because it can significantly reduce the number of constraints used. Consider the five components you selected to demote in the stapler. If these components all had just one assembly constraint each relating it to some part that will not be in the new subassembly, then those five constraints will be discarded.

Continuing with the example, you should now see the subassembly named 100.iam in the Model Browser. Because of the restructure, you will need to ground the assembly so that it cannot be accidentally moved. Then you can continue and demote components into another subassembly:

1. Right-click 100.iam, and click Grounded to set it in place.

2. In the Model Browser, select all the components with a prefix of 200.

3. Right-click, and choose Component ➤ Demote.

4. Enter **200** for the name, and click OK. Click Yes in the warning dialog box.

5. Repeat the steps for demoting for all the components with a prefix of 300 until your browser looks like Figure 9.10.

FIGURE 9.10
Subassemblies
created by
demoting

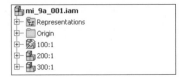

You can restructure components by dragging a component within the assembly browser from in and out of a subassembly. Moving components up out of a subassembly is called promoting rather than demoting. It is also important to understand that when you demote and promote components, you may need to edit the subassembly and ensure that components are constrained properly within that subassembly.

ASSEMBLY CONSTRAINT AND ADAPTIVITY OPTIONS

There are three Application Option settings to be aware of that can impact assembly performance. When working with large assemblies, you might want to have all three of these options deselected. You can find these by going to the Get Started tab and selecting the Application Options button, then clicking the Assembly tab:

◆ Enable Constraint Redundancy Analysis

◆ Enable Related Constraint Failure Analysis

◆ Features Are Initially Adaptive

ADAPTIVITY

Too many cross-part adaptive features can cripple the performance of even a modest-sized assembly if used without discretion. As discussed in Chapter 8, "Assembly Design Workflows," adaptivity should generally be turned off once the adaptive feature or part is created.

Often features and parts are made adaptive during the early design stages of a model, when changes are made quickly and you want many parts to follow these changes. Turning off the adaptive status in the part ensures that your assembly performance will not be affected. If the adaptive part needs to be edited, you can turn on its adaptive status so that you can make adjustments.

Many times parts become adaptive by default when creating a new part or feature in an assembly because a reference sketch is projected from one part to another. You can disable this by going to the Tools tab, clicking Application Options, going to the Assembly tab in the dialog box that opens, and then deselecting the Enable Associative Edge/Loop Geometry Projection During In-place Modeling option under Cross Part Geometry Projection.

You can also hold the Ctrl key while selecting individual edges for projection into your sketch. This only works selecting individual edges. Selecting a face will build an adaptive relationship. Either technique will create fewer accidental adaptive parts but may require more manual effort in projecting geometry across parts.

SELECTION TOOLS

When working with a large assembly, combing through all the many parts within that assembly that you want to select for a given task can be time-consuming and difficult if you attempt to locate them using the standard Pan, Zoom, and Orbit methods. Instead, make yourself familiar with the options in the assembly selection tool.

You can use selection tools to suppress sets of components based on such factors as size or on internal components that are not visible because of the presence of external housings, and so on. For instance, to maintain performance, you may not want to load all the internal components into memory when they are not important to your current design task. Once you've selected the internal components, you can suppress them and create an external part-only LOD representation.

Another use of assembly selection tools is to create view representations in the assembly to aid in the creation of views in the drawing file. As an example, when you place a view in the drawing using a design view that was created using the All In Camera tool, only the components in the screen view plane are calculated. This increases performance and memory capacity. Figure 9.11 shows the available selection tools.

FIGURE 9.11
Available
selection tools

The following are the selection tools:

Component Priority   Sets the selection to pick up the topmost structure level of components. If set, this will pick up subassemblies and not their children.

Part Priority   Sets the tool to select parts no matter their subassembly structure.

Feature Priority   Selects individual features rather than the parts that contain them.

Faces And Edges   Allows you to highlight and select faces or the curves that define those faces.

Sketch Features   Allows you to highlight and select sketches or the curves that define those sketches.

Visible Only   Selects only visible components in a selection set.

Enable Prehighlight   Displays prehighlighting when your cursor moves over an object. This does not affect the Select Other tool, which always shows prehighlighting.

Select All Occurrences   Selects all instances in the current file of the selected component.

Constrained To   Selects all components constrained to a preselected component or components.

Component Size   Selects components by the percent set in the Select By Size box. Size is determined by the diagonal of the bounding box of the components. Click the arrow to select a component and measure its size to use as a scale. Figure 9.12 shows the Select By Size box.

FIGURE 9.12
Select By Size box

Component Offset   Selects components fully or partially contained within the bounding box of a selected component plus a specified offset distance.

Sphere Offset   Selects components fully or partially contained within the bounding sphere of a selected component plus a specified offset distance.

Select By Plane   Selects components fully or partially intersected by a specified face or plane.

External Components   Selects external components based on a percentage of the component's viewable surface.

Internal Components   Selects internal components based on a percentage of the component's viewable surface.

All In Camera   Selects all components in the current view screen based upon a percentage of the component's viewable surface.

USING THE FEATURE SELECTION FILTER TO SELECT WORK PLANES

It can be a major pain to try to select a work plane while in a busy assembly file. To make it easier, use the Feature Selection filter as explained. Your cursor will no longer select parts but only features, making it easy to select even the most obscured work planes.

VIEW REPRESENTATIONS

View representations are often used in large assemblies to navigate to a predefined viewing angle so that you do not have to tax your system with heavy graphics regeneration. For instance, if you have an assembly that contains an entire production line of material-handling equipment, you may find it difficult to orbit around to the backside of the assembly in order to complete a simple task such as selecting a face or just looking at the assembly. If you set a design view before orbiting and then set another once you have orbited to the desired view, you can then easily toggle between the two views of this assembly, thereby increasing performance during navigation between these predefined views.

View representations have other large assembly benefits as well. When creating a drawing view of a large assembly, you can specify a preset view representation and reduce the time it takes to create the drawing view. If you have turned the visibility of some components off in the assembly view representation, the drawing view can generate even faster and provide you with a clearer and more concise view. Of course, if you already have the assembly open when creating the drawing view, the components are likely already loaded into memory.

Another way that the experienced Inventor user may use view representation is to navigate the Model Browser. For instance, if you set up a view representation to zoom in on a particular subassembly so that you can navigate to that component quickly, you can save that view representation while the entire model tree is rolled up and only the subassembly of interest is expanded. This browser state will be saved within the view representation.

Once a view representation is created, you can right-click it and choose Copy To Level Of Detail to copy the view representation to an LOD representation. This allows you to transfer the visibility settings from the view representation to the LOD where they will be suppressed. In this way, you do not have to duplicate the process of turning parts off.

FIND

Navigating a large assembly Model Browser can be a chore. To help with this, you can employ the Find tool to define search criteria for constraints, components, features, sketches, and welds. Searches can be saved for future use and recalled as needed using the Open Search button, as shown in Figure 9.13.

FIGURE 9.13
The Find tool in an assembly file

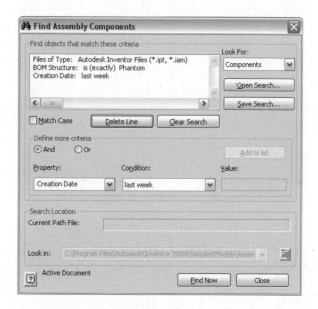

You can access the Find tool in the following ways:

♦ From within a file, click the binoculars icon in the Model Browser.

♦ In the Inventor Open dialog box, click the Find button.

Opening the Model

One of the most important aspects of working on a large assembly file is being able to open the file. Although this seems an obvious statement, many Inventor users seem to approach opening a model as an afterthought. Consider it in this way—if you were tasked with carrying a pile of stones up a flight of stairs, you would probably be unlikely to attempt to carry them all up the stairs at once. But this is exactly the kind of heavy lifting you are asking your workstation to do when opening a large assembly.

To allow your workstation to make multiple trips when opening an assembly file, you will use LOD representations. You create LOD representations by suppressing components in an assembly. Once the LOD is created, you can access it the next time you begin to open the file by using the Options button, as shown in Figure 9.14. Once the assembly file is open, you can unsuppress components as required, and those components will then be loaded into memory. You can also specify a default LOD so that the assembly opens to it without having to use the options dialog box every time. This is done from Application Options on the Assembly tab. You'll learn more about creating LODs later in this chapter.

If you need to open a large assembly that has not been properly managed you may find yourself having to locate or skip a number of parts and subassemblies. This can be a tedious task but the *Skip all unresolved files* option in the File Open dialog will bypass locating missing components and load the members of the assembly that can be located automatically.

FIGURE 9.14

Opening LODs

CERT OBJECTIVE

> ## LOD IN SUBASSEMBLIES
>
> Often you might create a complex assembly model as a stand-alone design because you need to insert that model into an upper-level assembly as part of a larger system. Because the original design was required to generate production drawings and an accurate BOM, it includes all the components in the design.
>
> However, because you will be placing multiple instances of this subassembly, you want to avoid placing it at the full level of detail. You might create an LOD in the subassembly where all internal components, all external hardware, and all internal and external fasteners are suppressed, leaving only the external housing and frame components.
>
> LOD representations of subassemblies can be accessed from the Options button in the Place Component dialog box when placing them into upper-level assemblies. By placing a subassembly at a reduced level of detail, you have created a much smaller top-level assembly file and yet still have the ability to pull an accurate BOM even from the top-level assembly.

Working with Large Assembly Drawings

Not only do large assembly files require some forethought and management, but so do the drawing files of these large assemblies. Because Inventor generates the line work from the models that you create views from automatically, it is easy to take the large number of calculations required to do this for granted. Stop for a moment and consider all the hidden lines, sectioned parts, and so on, which Inventor has to consider in order to render your drawing views accurately.

It is for this reason that you will want to adopt slightly different techniques than those you use to make part or small assembly drawings.

CREATING LARGE ASSEMBLY DRAWING VIEWS

When creating drawing of large assemblies, it is advised that you do so from an LOD representation already created in the model. Doing so reduces the number of files Inventor is required to access to create and update the line work in the view. To create views from assembly representations, you simply specify the representation(s) you want to use in the Drawing View dialog box, as shown in Figure 9.15. Keep in mind that when browsing for the file to create a view of, if you use the Options button in the Open dialog box to specify the representation, you will reduce the time it takes to create the view.

FIGURE 9.15
Creating a drawing view from an LOD

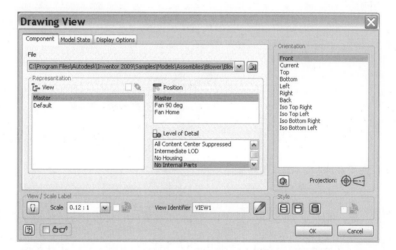

REDUCING HIDDEN LINES

Hidden line generation can be one of the most memory-intensive aspects of creating a drawing view. Generally, with large assemblies, it is not desirable to show the hidden lines of all components. Instead, you typically will want to enable hidden lines for just those components where hidden lines add clarity.

Rather than selecting the Hidden Line style in the Drawing View dialog box, first create the view with no hidden lines. Next locate and expand the view you just created in the browser, and select the components you intend to be shown with hidden lines. Right-click the components, and choose Hidden Lines.

You will be prompted with a message box informing you that you are changing the view style to show hidden lines and that any children of this view will be granted an independent view style based upon their current setting, as shown in Figure 9.16. The result will be that only the components you chose will be displayed with hidden lines.

FIGURE 9.16
Managing
hidden lines

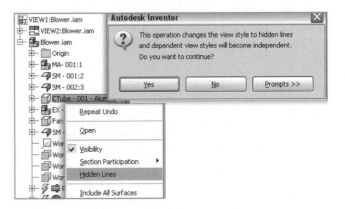

CREATING TITLE BLOCK LOGOS

A sure way to slow down your drawing's performance is to create an unnecessarily complex title block. If you have included a bitmap of your company logo in your title bock, ensure that the bitmap file is reduced in resolution and file size as much as possible. You can use any photo editor to do this.

Once you've reduced the bitmap file as much as possible, consider embedding the file into the title block rather than linking it. Although linking the bitmap does give you greater flexibility in updating the logo independent of the title block, Inventor will be required to locate the bitmap each time the drawing is loaded. To embed rather than link the logo bitmap, simply deselect the Link check box when inserting the bitmap.

If you have pasted the logo in from AutoCAD, ensure that the logo is as clean as possible. You may be better off removing the hatches from the logo in AutoCAD and then adding them using the Fill/Hatch Sketch Region tool in Inventor.

REDUCING THE NUMBER OF SHEETS AND VIEWS PER DRAWING FILE

Although it is possible to create a large number of sheets in a single drawing file, it is generally accepted that this is not good practice. Instead, you should consider making a new file for each drawing sheet when possible. Or at the very least, keep the number of sheets per file as low as possible. There are two primary reasons for doing this.

The first reason is simply to keep the file size down. If you have a drawing of a large assembly file that includes four sheets and has a file size of 80MB, you could spilt this into two files, each with two sheets and a file size of approximately 40MB. In this way, you do not have to load the extra 40MB in sheets 3 and 4 just to make an edit to sheet 1.

The second reason to minimize drawing sheets is so you are not guilty of placing "all your eggs in one basket." Creating multiple tab or sheet files in any application can be risky. Imagine you created a load calculation spreadsheet and you developed the habit of adding a tab for each new calculation you do, rather than creating a new file for each calculation. If the file becomes corrupt, you've lost all your calculations rather than just one set of calculations. The same thing could happen with your Inventor drawing if you habitually create new sheets instead of new files.

Managing Assembly Detail

In Chapter 8, you learned about creating LOD representations within your assemblies in order to reduce the memory requirements of working with large assemblies. Here you will consider how you can use these LOD representations to make you more successful in your large assembly pursuits.

LOD Strategies

All Inventor assemblies have four default LODs predefined and ready for you to use. Learning to use these and creating your own LODs is an important part of working with large assemblies. The default LODs are as follows:

Master   This shows your assembly with no parts suppressed. You can think of this as the highest level of detail for any assembly.

All Components Suppressed   This suppresses everything within the assembly. You can think of it as the lowest level of detail for any assembly.

All Parts Suppressed   This suppresses all parts at all levels of the assembly, but subassemblies are loaded.

All Content Center Suppressed   This suppresses any component in the assembly that is stored in the Content Center Files directory as designated by the IPJ (project) file or the Application Options settings.

When opening a large assembly, you can use the All Components Suppressed LOD to quickly open the file and then manually unsuppress components as required. However, it is more practical to create your own LODs and use them to efficiently open your assemblies. Consider creating intermediate LODs based upon your design process.

For a closer look at LODs in action, follow these steps:

1. From the Get Started tab choose Open.

2. Browse for the file named mi_9a_002.iam, located in the Chapter 9 directory of the Mastering Inventor 2011 folder, and click Open.

3. Expand the Representations folder and the Level Of Detail node in the Model Browser if not already done.

4. Right-click the Level Of Detail header, and choose New Level Of Detail. Rename LevelofDetail1 to MediumLOD.

5. In the Quick Access toolbar, click the selection tool drop-down list (see Figure 9.17), and set your selection focus to Component Priority if it is not already.

6. Using the same drop-down list, now choose Internal Components, as shown in Figure 9.17.

7. Set the slider to 85 percent, and click the green check mark.

FIGURE 9.17
Selecting internal components

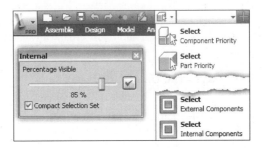

8. Right-click anywhere on the screen, and choose Isolate to get a better view of the components you selected. Your screen should look similar to Figure 9.18.

FIGURE 9.18
Isolated internal components

9. Now bring back one component to add to your selection set. Select the component called MA- 001:1 in the browser, right-click, and choose Visibility. You should see the motor sub-assembly become visible.

10. Select all the components on the screen. You can use a crossing window to do this quickly.

11. Right-click, and choose Suppress.

12. Right-click anywhere, and choose Undo Isolate to bring back the visibility of the remaining components.

13. Save the assembly to ensure that the changes to your newly created level of detail are recorded.

14. Switch back and forth between the master LOD and your MediumLOD to observe the differences.

15. To modify the MediumLOD, activate it and suppress any component you'd like; then save the assembly.

Substitute LODs

You can use substitute LOD representations to trade out a large multipart assembly with a single part derived from that assembly. Substitute LODs improve efficiency by reducing the number of files Inventor is referencing and, if created from other LODs, can also reduce the amount of geometry required.

For example, in the blower assembly, you could create a substitute LOD from the entire assembly and then place that substitute into a top-level assembly as needed. You would certainly gain some efficiency by doing this because the top-level assembly is referencing only one file. However, if you created a substitute from the MediumLOD, you would be maintaining an even higher level of performance in the top-level assembly because all the internal geometry that was suppressed in the creation of that LOD would be omitted.

To create a substitute LOD, follow these steps:

1. From the Get Started tab choose Open.

2. Browse for the file named mi_9a_003.iam, located in the Chapter 9 directory of the Mastering Inventor 2011 folder, and click Open.

3. Expand the Representations folder and the Level of Detail node in the model browser if not already done.

4. Double-click the MediumLOD to set it as the active LOD if not already done.

5. Right-click the Level Of Detail header in the browser, and choose New Substitute and then Shrinkwrap. Notice that Inventor is asking you to specify a filename, a file template, and a location to create this file.

6. Enter mi_9a_003_Substitute_100 for the name in the New Derived Substitute Part dialog box, and leave the template and file location at the defaults.

7. Click OK. Inventor opens a new part file and takes you directly into the shrink-wrap process, bringing up the Assembly Shrinkwrap Options dialog box.

8. In the Style area at the top, ensure that the Single Composite Feature option is selected. The following are the descriptions of each of the three available options:

   Single Solid Body Merging Out Seams Between Planar Faces Produces a single solid body without seams. Merged faces become a single color, where required.

   Solid Body Keep Seams Between Planar Faces Produces a single solid body with seams. Colors are retained.

   Maintain each Solid as a Solid Body Produces a single part file with multiple bodies. This is the closest approximation to an assembly.

   Single Composite Feature Produces a single surface composite feature and the smallest file. Colors and seams of the original components are maintained. The mass properties of the original assembly are stored in the file for reference.

9. Ensure that the Remove Geometry By Visibility check box is selected.

10. Select Whole Parts Only.

11. Play around with the slider, clicking the Preview button to see what is removed.

12. Set the slider to 78 percent.

13. Under Hole Patching, select All.

14. Ensure that Reduced Memory Mode is selected at the bottom of the dialog box. When selected, this option allows the derived part to be created using less memory by not including the source bodies of the assembly parts.

15. Refer to Figure 9.19 to check the settings, and then click OK.

16. Click Yes when asked about the mass properties. Note that Inventor closes the derived part file and returns to the assembly, and an LOD named SubstituteLevelofDetail1 has been created. You can rename this if you like by clicking it once and then a second time.

17. Save the assembly.

18. Double-click the MediumLOD to set it active, and compare the substitute LOD by clicking back and forth on them.

19. To see that the substitute shrink-wrap is a surface model, click the View tab, and choose the Half Section View icon from the drop-down list on the Appearance panel.

20. Click Workplane2 in the Model Browser.

21. Right-click, and choose Done.

22. Choose End Section View from the drop-down list on the Appearance panel to turn off the section view.

Figure 9.20 shows the Substitute LOD as it appears in the browser.

Recall that all LODs maintain an accurate BOM listing. To confirm this, select the Assemble tab, click Bill Of Materials, and interrogate the BOM to see that even though the substitute LOD consists of a single part, Inventor still maintains the BOM information for the entire assembly.

FIGURE 9.19

Deriving a shrink-wrap LOD

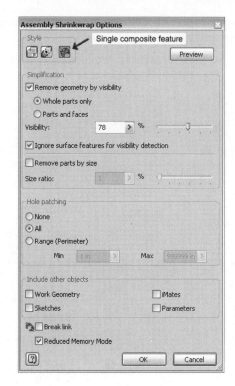

FIGURE 9.20

Substitute LOD

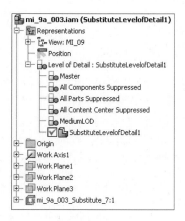

Subassembly LODs

Subassembly use is where LOD representations really begin to pay off in terms of performance. Once LOD representations have been created in your assembly, you can switch the LOD in the subassemblies to match in three ways:

◆ Place the subassemblies into a top-level assembly with the matching LOD by using the Options button.

◆ Switch the LOD manually in the subassembly in the Model Browser.

◆ Use the Link Levels Of Detail tool at the top-level assembly to automatically set the subassemblies to the matching LOD.

In Figure 9.21, all the subassemblies have LODs named High, Moderate, and Low set up within them. Then the LODs were linked. The LOD name is set in parentheses next to the assembly name.

FIGURE 9.21
Nested LODs with a consistent naming scheme

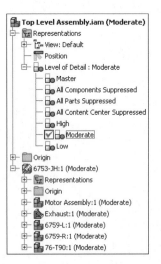

You might take this concept one step further and edit your assembly templates to automatically have High, Moderate, and Low LODs already in them. This way you do not have to create the LODs, but instead you can simply activate them and then suppress parts as required to "fill them out."

Recall that Inventor specifies your template location on the File tab of the Application Options dialog box. Note that this can be overridden in your project file. Check this by selecting the Get Started tab and then clicking the Projects button, and look in the Folder Options section of the Project File Editor that opens. If a path is specified there, that is where your templates are located. If it shows = Default, then the path found in Application Options is where your templates are located.

In the following exercise, the subassemblies all have LODs created in them. These are called Bolts, Washers, Nuts, and Galvanized. Each subassembly was configured with these LODs set up as described in the previous exercise. The top-level assembly has three LODs created called Bolts, Washers, and Nuts. Although these LODs have been created, they have not been configured and currently do not differ from the master LOD. The following steps take you through the linking of the Bolt LOD at the top-level assembly to the Bolt LODs in the subassemblies:

1. From the Get Started tab choose Open.

2. Browse for the file named `mi_9a_004.iam`, located in the Chapter 9 directory of the Mastering Inventor 2011 folder, and click Open.

3. Expand the Representations folder and the Level Of Detail node in the Model Browser if it is not already expanded.

4. Double-click the LOD named Bolts to set it active, or right-click it and choose Activate.

5. Click the Assemble tab, expand the drop-down list for the Productivity panel, and choose Link Levels Of Detail.

6. Click Bolts within the Link Levels Of Detail dialog box.

7. Click OK in the Link Levels Of Detail dialog box, and click OK to accept the warning that the assembly will be saved.

Note the subassemblies have all been set so that the Bolts LOD is active in them. If one of the subassemblies did not have an LOD called Bolts, it would be left at its current LOD. You can continue this exercise by repeating these steps for the Washers and Nuts LODs if you'd like. Note too that each of the subassemblies has an LOD called Galvanized in which all parts that are not galvanized steel have been suppressed. You can create an LOD in the top-level assembly called Galvanized and then use the Link LODs tool to suppress all the parts not made of galvanized steel. You can also set different instances of a subassembly to display differing LOD representations.

USING LOD NAMING CONVENTIONS

There are an infinite number of naming conventions for LODs, including the one suggested here (High, Moderate, and Low). Making LODS that have certain parts of the design turned on can be useful as well, for example: Frame Only, Frame & Transmission, Transmission Only, Conveyors Off, No Robots, and so on. By giving them descriptive names, other users can select the appropriate LOD for the work they need to complete.

Simplifying Parts

Albert Einstein once suggested that things be made as simple as possible but not simpler. This is a good concept to keep in mind when creating models in Inventor. Adding extraneous details to common parts can have a negative impact on large assembly performance. Of course, if the part file is to be used for fabrication, then a certain level of detail is required. Oftentimes, though, we create models of common parts to be used in an assembly for the end goal of getting an accurate bill of materials. Your assembly performance could most likely be improved by reducing the amount of detail in those types of parts.

Removing or Suppressing Unneeded Features

Reducing the number of edges and faces in a part is a sure way to minimize the size of the part file. Removing fillet and chamfers for purchased parts is a good way to eliminate extra faces. If you have common parts that are used in large numbers throughout your assemblies, you might consider creating two versions of these parts: one version for use in large assemblies and another from which you create production drawings and Inventor Studio renderings. In Figure 9.22, you can see two versions of the same part. The file on the left is right at 600KB, whereas the one the right is less than 175KB.

FIGURE 9.22
A simplified part

In the following steps, you will derive a simplified version of a part and set the part numbers to match so that the two files report the same in the BOM and parts lists. To create a simplified part, follow these steps:

1. From the Get Started tab choose Open.

2. Browse for the file named mi_9a_010.ipt, located in the Chapter 9 directory of the Mastering Inventor 2011 folder, and click Open.

3. Click the end-of-part (EOP) marker in the Model Browser, and drag it to right under Revolution1.

4. Change the color to As Material (at the top of the screen in the Quick Access toolbar, click the color drop-down arrow, and scroll to the top).

5. Do not save the part.

Figure 9.23 shows the end-of-part marker being placed above the existing features.

6. From the Get Started tab choose New.

7. Choose the Standard.ipt template to create the new file, and click OK.

8. In the new part, right-click and choose Finish Sketch.

9. On the Manage tab, click the Derive icon on the Insert panel.

10. In the resulting Open dialog box, browse for the file named mi_9a_010.ipt, located in the Chapter 9 directory of the Mastering Inventor 2011 folder, and click Open.

11. Choose Maintain Each Solid As A Solid Body as the derive style.

FIGURE 9.23
Using the EOP marker to simplify the original part

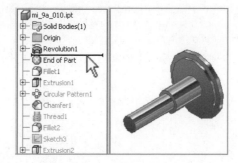

12. Click OK.

13. In the Model Browser, right-click the part name, and choose Suppress Link With Base Component. This ensures that the derived part will stay at the simplified state.

14. Click the filename at the top of the Model Browser, and choose iProperties.

15. Choose the Project tab of the iProperties dialog box, and enter mi_9a_010 as the part number. This ensures that as you use the simplified part in an assembly it will have the same part number as the original part and report an accurate BOM.

16. Save the file as mi_9a_010_simple.ipt.

17. Return to the original part (mi_9a_010.ipt).

18. Either close the file and click No when asked to save changes, or drag the EOP marker back to the bottom of the Model Browser, reset the part color, and then save the file.

The result is two files representing the same part. Both will list at the same component in the BOM, but the derived component will add far less overhead when used over and over in an assembly.

Working with Colors

Adding a reflective color to a part can increase the file size as well; therefore, you should consider using a flat color for simplified parts you intend to use over and over again in large assemblies. It is good practice to purge all unused color style definitions for common parts as well. Each time you change a material or color in a part file, the style definitions are cached in the file. If the file is used many times in an assembly, the unused definitions can have an impact on memory. To purge unused style definitions, select the Manage tab and click the Purge button found on the Styles and Standards panel.

USING STYLE LIBRARIES

If you have not looked at using style libraries to manage your material, color, and lighting style definitions, then you should take the time to do so. Style libraries are not always the right choice for every design office, but if you determine that they are right for you, you can speed up the processing of your files considerably. To determine whether this is the right choice for you, go to the help files as shown here.

The Bottom Line

Select a workstation Having the right tool for the job is the key to success in anything you do. This is true of selecting a large assembly workstation. You have learned that for optimal performance you should strive to keep your system working in physical memory (RAM).

Master It You notice that your computer runs slowly when working with large assemblies and want to know whether you should consider a 64-bit system.

Adjust your performance settings You have learned that there are many settings in Inventor and in Windows that you can use to configure the application to work more efficiently with large assemblies.

Master It You want to make your current workstation run as efficiently as possible for large assembly design.

Use best practices for large assembly Knowing the tools for general assembly design is only half of the battle when it comes to conquering large assemblies. Understanding the methods of large assembly design and how they differ from a general assembly design is a key to success.

Master It You want to create adaptive parts so that you can make changes during the initial design stage and have several parts update automatically as you work through the details. But you are concerned about how this will adversely affect your assembly performance.

Manage assembly detail   Inventor includes several tools to help manage assembly detail so that you can accomplish your large assembly design goals.

> **Master It**   You want to reduce the number of files your large assembly is required to reference while you are working on it and yet maintain an accurate bill of materials.

Simplify parts   Creating highly detailed parts may be required for generating production drawings or Inventor Studio renderings, but using those high-detail parts in large assemblies may have an adverse affect.

> **Master It**   You want to create a lower level-of-detail part file for common parts to be reused many times over in your large assemblies but are concerned about managing two versions of a part.

Chapter 10

Weldment Design

This chapter assumes you have a good understanding of parts, assemblies, and drawings. In this chapter, we will cover the various aspects of weldment design. Starting from weldment workflows and design methodologies, we will cover preparations, weld beads, machining features, and weld symbols, as well as how to document the weldment design. You will also learn some tips and tricks along the way.

Weldments are available in the assembly environment as a subtype of the assembly document. Most of the topics in this chapter require an assembly to be open. Therefore, this chapter is not applicable if you have only Inventor LT installed.

In this chapter, you will learn how to:

◆ Select and use the right weldment design methodology

◆ Create and edit weld preparations and machining features

◆ Create and edit different kinds of weld beads such as cosmetic, fillet, and groove

◆ Document weldment stages in drawings

◆ Generate and maintain a consistent set of BOMs across welded assemblies, drawings, and presentations

Exploring Weldment Design Methodologies

One of the basic questions in weldment design is what design methodology should be used to create weldments. Unfortunately, there is no "one-size-fits-all" strategy. The design methodology you use depends on your individual needs and requirements. We will start by defining the different design methodologies:

◆ *As-assembled* means a view of the assembly with no weld preparations, beads, or machining features. This represents a stage in the weldment design.

◆ *As-welded* means a view of the assembly with weld preparations and weld beads but no machining features.

◆ *As-machined* means a view of the final welded assembly with the machining features that goes through the weld beads.

All these represent the various stages in weldment design. Once the weldment design is done, it helps to document the various stages of weldment design in the drawing.

Depending on the need for documentation, interference analysis, mass properties, and other design criteria, you can group the weldment design methodologies into the following four broad categories:

Part files and part features.   You can create a weldment design using part features in part files. With this approach, you use the rich modeling features of the part (sweeps, chamfers, fillets, and lofts) to create a wide variety of weld bead shapes. However, this will be one big mess of a design that has no logical partitions. The main difficulty is creating drawings with different stages—for example, as-assembled, as-welded, and so on—from a single design. You will not be able to see certain edges separating weld beads and components in drawings because they will not even exist (be merged out) in the part design. In addition, the bill of materials will not list all the individual components needed to assemble the welded structures. Still, this might be an acceptable strategy for small weldment designs that have minor design changes over a period of time. Besides, the assumption is that the designer does not need to create the different stages in design documentation from a single weldment assembly. You could place the part weldment into an assembly and then create presentations and drawings of that assembly. (However, in drawings, you will not be able to create the different stages of weldment design.) Figure 10.1 shows this methodology.

FIGURE 10.1
Part files and part
features

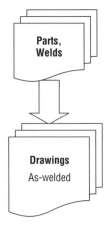

Weldment assembly and derived technology.   With this approach, you can derive the weldment assembly (.iam) into a single-part file (.ipt) and model the welds in the derived assembly file using part features. Optionally, you can derive the part file into another part file to show machining on welded assemblies. Similar disadvantages exist as mentioned in the first method; however, you can modify assembly constraints to create variants of weldment assemblies with this approach. The preparations, welds, and machining features will all exist in the derived component files. This might be a good strategy for weldments where a BOM listing is needed and there is no need to document different stages of weldment design from a single weldment assembly. Figure 10.2 shows the document layout of this methodology.

Weldment assembly.   With this approach, you use a mixture of cosmetic, fillet, and groove welds with preparations, machining features, and weld symbols at the assembly level. The main advantage is that the weldment can be documented as-assembled, as-welded, and so on. The BOM outlines the different part components. It does not preclude Finite Element analysis since the weldment assembly can be derived into a part. You might find this approach difficult initially, but you can see large gains in productivity later while documenting the weldment. This is the recommended approach for large weldments that need mass properties, interference analysis, and complete documentation. (Examples are structural frames, piping, industrial gates, fences, and steel furniture.) You can use a combined approach of all four methods if that's what works best for your needs. However, when new enhancements are made to weldments, this approach lends itself to easily leverage the new functionality. Figure 10.3 shows the document layout of this design methodology. (The figure doesn't show the various subassemblies that the weldment assembly might contain by breaking it into logical pieces.) Good planning helps in generating a well-built design that can be understood and easily maintained by designers. All in all, you should use this design methodology if you cannot decide on one of the other three methods.

FIGURE 10.2
Weldment assembly and derived technology

FIGURE 10.3
Weldment assembly design methodology

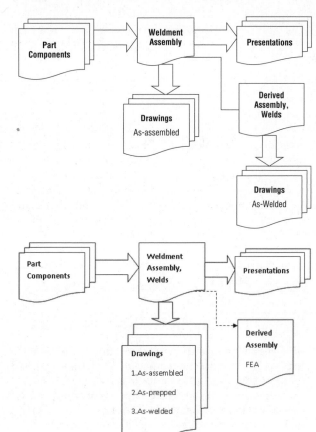

Using multi-body part files.   Since a completed weldment exists in a larger assembly as a single component, an interesting way of defining the weldment can be done by using multi-body parts. To use this approach you create separate bodies within the single part file by using the *New Solid* option in the Extrude, Revolve, and other sketched feature dialogs. This creates a virtual assembly made up of multiple features in a single file. Once the component is defined it can then be divided into an assembly using the *Make Components* tool as described in Chapter 5. From that point on you can treat your weldment assembly as though you created it from separate part files from the beginning, with one notable exception. You can then update the assembly and the weldment based by editing the multi-body part you created initially. Figure 10.4 shows the layout of the multi-body method.

FIGURE 10.4
Using multi-body
part files

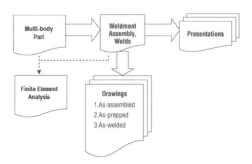

You can create a weldment assembly in two ways. For the first method, you create a new weldment assembly by selecting any of the weldment templates provided by Inventor. To do this, just select the Get Started tab, then click the New button and then select an assembly template designated as a weldment template. Or you can convert an existing assembly document into a weldment assembly by going to the Assemble tab and clicking Convert To Weldment.

Once you convert an assembly into a weldment, it is not possible to convert it into a regular assembly. Also note that in a weldment document, you cannot create new positional representations or use flexible assembly functionality, because a weldment is meant to be an assembly of parts fixed in place. Once you've created a weldment assembly, you can then go to the next logical step of modeling preparations.

COMMUNICATION IS THE KEY TO DEALING WITH WELDMENTS

Depending on your needs, weldments can be as simple as a single part or as complex as assembly weldments with preparations, welds, and machining. Talk to the group that is going to be manufacturing your parts (whether the job is farmed out or in-house), and find out what level of detail the group requires when making the parts to your prints. Often you will find that what is important to the designer is not as important to the welder (and vice versa). By speaking with these groups, you'll get a better understanding of what path you should take for your weldment models and drawings.

Modeling Preparations

Imagine that you've created the weldment assembly for a boxed container and want to add weld beads. Before adding the weld beads, the assembly needs weld preparations to create space for the weld bead to be placed. You can model a variety of preparation features to mill or remove material. Note that preparations are assembly features only, meaning that these features exist only in the assembly and not at the part level. Here are the most common preparation features:

♦ Extrude

♦ Revolve

♦ Hole

♦ Sweep

♦ Chamfer

♦ Move Face

Figure 10.5 shows the preparations environment and the relevant tools. To create the features in the previous list, you use the same set of steps that you used in part (Chapter 4) or assembly modeling (Chapter 8). The Move Face functionality is primarily intended for weld preparation in the assembly environment and is available in both the part and assembly environments.

FIGURE 10.5
Weldment features

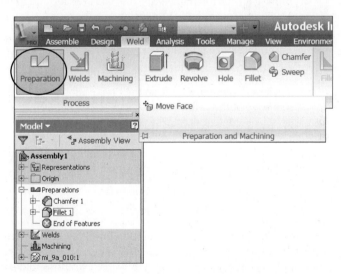

Groove welds are classified by the different kinds of weld preparations. Figure 10.6 shows some commonly used weld preparations. In the left column, from top to bottom, you can see the Square Groove Weld, Bevel Groove, and U-Groove types. In the right column, from top to bottom of the figure, you can see the Double Bevel Groove, V-Groove, and Double-U types. Observe that these preparations might be referred to by slightly different names in the welding industry. Although most groove welds require nothing more than a simple chamfer, in most cases groove welds require some sort of material removal preparation.

FIGURE 10.6
Types of weld preparations

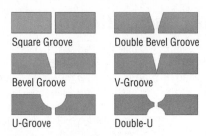

The alternative to weld preparation is to build the shape of the preparation using the sketch and then a swept volume (Extrude, Revolve, and Sweep) cut using that sketch to create the feature shape in the part file. However, it is recommended that you use the weld preparation feature, which helps show the manufacturing process. In addition, it aids in documenting the weldment in a drawing with just the components and preparations. Another advantage is that the designer, weld fabricator, or manufacturing instruction–generating program can easily find these features in one place—in other words, in the Preparations folder. This might be useful for generating the desired manufacturing information.

To create a preparation feature, follow these steps:

1. From the Get Started tab click the Open button.

2. Browse for the file named `mi_10a_045.iam` located in the Chapter 10 directory of the Mastering Inventor 2011 folder, and click Open.

3. You have three choices for this step: double-click the Preparations folder in the Model browser to activate the weld bead features, right-click the Welds folder and select Edit, or click the Preparation button on the Process panel of the Weld tab.

4. Click the Chamfer button on the Preparation And Machining panel, and select the bottom edge of the yellow face.

5. Set the chamfer size to **7 mm**, and click OK.

6. Next, exit the preparations environment either by clicking the Return To Parent button or by right-clicking and choosing Finish Edit.

You can double-click the Preparations folder and edit the individual preparation features as needed. Think of the Preparations folder as a separate environment with its own set of tools. The End Of Features (EOF) node in the browser works differently than in the End Of Part (EOP) part modeling browser. In the part modeling browser, when the EOP is moved around, it sticks at that location even after an update. In the preparations environment, the EOF can be moved to above or below any feature location in the Preparations folder just like in part modeling.

However, when you leave the preparations environment—either by double-clicking the top-level assembly node in the weldment assembly or by right-clicking and selecting Finish Edit in the graphics window—the EOF is rolled all the way to the end in the Preparations folder. It might be thought of as a browser node that does not stick in its dragged browser location, unlike parts. The EOF has similar behavior whether you are in the preparations, welds, or machining environment.

Once you've placed the weld preparations, you are ready to place welds. Keep in mind that you do not have to create preparations. Also, you can return to the preparations environment even after having placed welds.

Exploring Cosmetic Welds

To create or edit a weld feature, click the Welds icon on the Process panel, or right-click the Welds folder in the Model browser and select Edit. You can also double-click the Welds folder and edit the individual features. Figure 10.7 shows the available features in the welds environment.

FIGURE 10.7
Weld Features panel

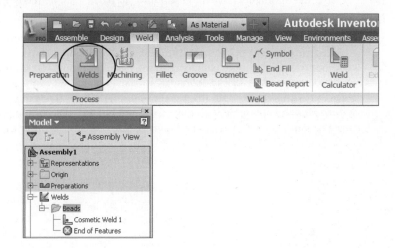

The *cosmetic weld* feature is available by clicking the Cosmetic icon in the Weld panel. Figure 10.8 shows the Cosmetic Weld dialog box. When using the cosmetic weld feature, you simply select edges of the model. These edges can belong to part components or other weld beads.

FIGURE 10.8
Cosmetic Weld dialog box

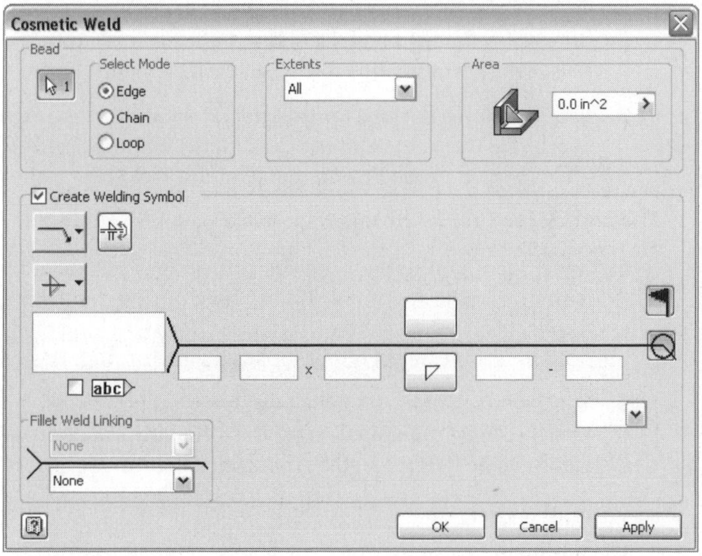

Cosmetic welds are recommended for use when you have the following:

◆ A need for lightweight representation.

◆ No requirement for interference analysis.

◆ No need for the estimated total mass of the assembly with solid weld beads. However, you could optionally have the cosmetic weld participate in mass property calculations.

Note that the bead (the upper portion of the weld dialog boxes) and the weld symbol (the lower portion of the weld dialog boxes) are decoupled; in other words, optionally you can create a weld symbol. This applies to all types of weld beads. In addition, you can use a single weld symbol to denote multiple welds involving cosmetic, fillet, and groove welds. Cosmetic welds can represent a wide variety of welds. You can create them using edges (the Edge option), tangent continuous set of edges (the Chain option), or loops (the Loop option).

Selecting the option of applying a weld symbol will place a symbol on the screen without being prompted for its placement. You can move the symbol after the weld has been added.

To create a cosmetic weld feature as shown in Figure 10.9, follow these steps:

FIGURE 10.9
Creating a cosmetic weld

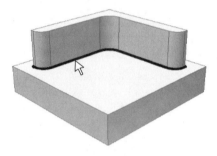

CERT
OBJECTIVE

1. From the Get Started tab click the Open button.

2. Browse for the file named mi_10a_001.iam located in the Chapter 10 directory of the Mastering Inventor 2011 folder, and click Open.

3. You have three options for this step: double-click the Welds folder in the Model browser to activate the weld bead features, right-click the Welds folder and select Edit, or click the Welds button in the Process panel of the Weld tab.

4. Click the Cosmetic icon on the Weld panel.

5. Select the Chain option, and select the edges as shown in Figure 10.8. The Chain option is similar to the Automatic Edge Chain option in the Fillet dialog box in part modeling. It collects all the tangent continuous edges in a loop on a single face. Note that you may need to use the Select Other tool to toggle through the available loops.

6. You can now enter a suitable bead cross section based on the leg lengths. The bead cross section can be calculated using the following equation, and the bead cross section area value can be entered in the Area control:

Bead cross section = ($\frac{1}{2}$ × Leg Length 1 × Length 2)

The bead cross section area value is critical in determining the mass of cosmetic welds. Later in the "Bead Property Report and Mass Properties" section, you'll see how to use this for mass properties calculations.

In certain cases when there is no edge to click as input, you can split the faces of the components in the part file (.ipt) at the location where it is welded and use the split edges as input to the cosmetic weld feature. On the left of Figure 10.10, for example, there are no explicit edges to click at the intersection of the planar face on the hollow tube and the cylindrical face on the cylinder. Therefore, you can edit the cylindrical part and use the split feature to split the cylindrical face of the cylindrical part so that you can use those split edges to create the cosmetic weld feature. The right side of Figure 10.10 shows the split edge. Work points cannot be clicked as part of the cosmetic weld feature. The edges need to have finite length in order to be clickable for the cosmetic weld feature.

FIGURE 10.10
Cosmetic welds
using split edges

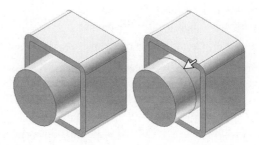

You can specify extents with parallel planes or planar faces. The extent trims the cosmetic weld bead between the From and To termination planes or planar faces. To generate the From-To cosmetic weld in Figure 10.11, follow these steps:

CERT OBJECTIVE

1. From the Get Started tab click the Open button.

2. Browse for the file named mi_10a_002.iam located in the Chapter 10 directory of the Mastering Inventor 2011 folder, and click Open.

3. You have three options for this step: double-click the Welds folder in the Model browser to activate the weld bead features, right-click the Welds folder and select Edit, or click the Welds button in the Process panel of the Weld tab.

4. Click the Cosmetic weld tool on the Weld panel. Select the edge shown in Figure 10.11.

5. In the Extents drop-down menu in the Cosmetic Weld dialog box, select From-To.

6. Click the From button, and select one of the assembly work planes.

7. Click the To button, and select the other assembly work plane.

8. Click OK in the Cosmetic Weld dialog box.

FIGURE 10.11
Cosmetic welds
with extents

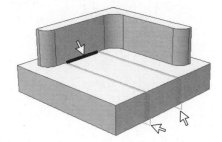

Creating Weld Beads

A *weld bead* feature is a parametric, solid representation of the real-world weld bead. It can be generated from input faces of a single component or from input faces of multiple components including bead faces in a weldment assembly. In other words, you can select faces from weld beads too as input faces to generate new weld beads. You can also create a weld on a single part that is placed in a weldment assembly. Some examples are as follows:

Example 1 Place a single sheet-metal part in a weldment assembly, and create fillet welds at flange corners to create a container.

Example 2 Create a fillet or groove weld between two plates (two parts or one part that has two extrusion features for the plates).

Example 3 Create a fillet or groove weld between two plates and another weld bead.

Weld beads automatically contribute to mass property calculations and can take part in interference analyses. All weld bead features create an independent body that does not take part in boolean operations with the assembly components. Other machining features can cut into weld beads. There are two major weld features to create physical 3D welds:

Fillet weld feature A fillet weld builds up corners by adding weld material between faces. Fillet welds are the most commonly used type of weld in industrial machinery. You should use this feature when there is no gap between the components. A specialized kind of fillet weld with a gap is supported.

Groove weld feature A groove weld feature predominantly fills gaps between components. However, you can also use it when the components are touching each other. There are many opportunities to combine cosmetic, fillet, and groove welds to generate the desired weld beads.

WELD CALCULATORS

The weldment environment also has several weld calculators (only if the Design Accelerator add-in is loaded). Weld calculators assist you in the design of weld joints. You can check typical welds with different types of loading. You can use these calculators to check static weld loading and to check butt and fillet weld joints for both static and fatigue loading.

Creating Fillet Welds

The basic idea behind a *fillet weld* is that you are joining two sets of faces. You can control the weld bead definition parametrically by using the parameters shown in Figure 10.12. This is known as *leg length measurement*. You can enter the two leg lengths used to generate the bead and also specify the throat measurement. You just enter the throat length, and Inventor calculates the rest of the size of the weld bead. The offset value has relevance only when you declare the weld to be concave or convex. Figure 10.12 shows the two leg lengths and the two types of measurement.

FIGURE 10.12
Fillet weld definition

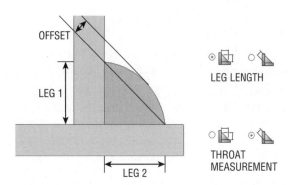

The top shape of a fillet weld can be flat, convex, or concave, as shown in Figure 10.13 (from left to right). For flat, the offset is 0.0. For concave or convex based on the offset, Inventor calculates the necessary bump or depression shape.

FIGURE 10.13
Flat, convex, and concave shape for fillet welds

To create a simple fillet weld, follow these steps:

CERT OBJECTIVE

1. From the Get Started tab click the Open button.

2. Browse for the file named mi_10a_003.iam located in the Chapter 10 directory of the Mastering Inventor 2011 folder, and click Open.

3. You have three choices here: double-click the Welds folder in the Model browser to activate the weld bead features, right-click the Welds folder and select Edit, or click the Welds button in the Process panel of the Weld tab.

4. Click the Fillet weld tool on the Weld panel. You will get the dialog box shown in Figure 10.14.

FIGURE 10.14
Fillet Weld dialog box with start and end offsets

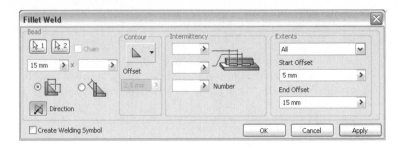

5. Enter the leg length value for the Leg1 control, as **15 mm**. Leg2 is assumed to be same as Leg1 if left blank.

6. Ensure that the first Select Faces button (the red arrow) is selected, and then click the yellow face.

7. Click the second Select Faces button (or right-click and select Continue), and then click the red face. Note the lightweight weld bead preview, as shown in Figure 10.15.

FIGURE 10.14
Fillet weld preview and fillet weld

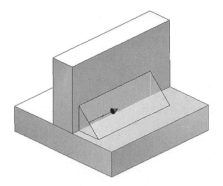

8. In the Extents area of the dialog, enter **5 mm** in the Start Offset box.

9. Click the Direction button on the left of the dialog box to change the start position of the weld bead.

10. Enter **15 mm** in the End Offset box, and click OK.

11. Locate the Welds folder in the Model browser, and expand it to find the Beads folder.

12. Expand the Beads folder, right-click the weld bead found within, and then click Edit Feature.

13. In the Extents area of the Fillet Weld dialog, click the top drop-down list, and change the extents solution from All to Start-Length.

14. Notice that Start Offset remains the same, but End Offset is replaced with a length input. You can use this option to specify a known weld length when required.

15. Set the length to **50 mm**, and click OK.

Figure 10.16 shows a hole gap through which a cylinder is passing. You can use a fillet weld to bridge the gap, but it will not fill the gap. The fillet weld will work even if the two components are separated by a gap at some places and touch at other places.

FIGURE 10.16
Shaft through plate

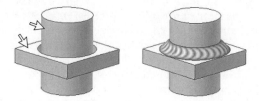

To create these fillet welds, you still click the two facesets, as shown in Figure 10.16. Inventor infers the gap and generates the fillet weld bead. To fill the gap between the two mating faces of components, you should use groove welds.

Figure 10.17 shows another variant of two components that are separated by a gap. Here the solution is dependent upon the size of the weld and the amount of face available. On the left, a 10 mm weld comes up short on the corners. On the right, an 18 mm weld runs past the flat edges of the tube and therefore will not build as selected. The weld adjusts to fit as required. If the weld size is too small to bridge the gap at all or is too large for the selected face, the weld will not be built.

FIGURE 10.17
Shaft through hollow tube

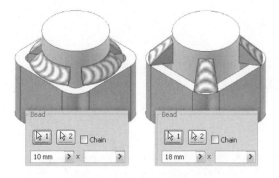

Figure 10.18 shows a simple gap being bridged with two fillet welds.

FIGURE 10.18
Fillet welds across a gap

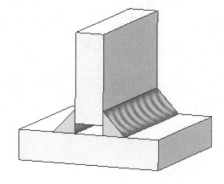

DON'T FORGET TO SPEAK WITH THOSE MANUFACTURING THE PARTS

Inventor provides just about every possible option that you could want as a designer with regard to weld sizes, shapes, and contours. However, you should always speak with those who will be manufacturing the parts to determine whether what you have designed can be built efficiently. It would be unfortunate to spend a lot of time with specific contours, sizes, and finishes if the weld shop is just going to give you a standard fillet weld regardless of the details you call out. You'll need to decide whether it's time to find a new welder or whether you are putting too much information into the part. More than one designer has found this out the hard way when that $10 bracket suddenly ends up costing $100 because of the demanding weld callouts placed on the print.

Creating Intermittent Fillet Welds

Intermittent fillet welds essentially produce patterns of the weld bead along a set of edges. Figure 10.19 shows an example of an intermittent fillet weld using the Start-Length extents solution to adjust the orientation so as to avoid interference with the existing holes.

FIGURE 10.19
Intermittent ISO
fillet weld

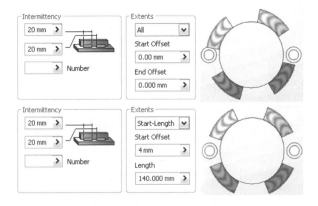

For the ANSI standard, you specify bead length and the distance between bead centers. For ISO/BSI/DIN/GB, you specify the bead length, the spacing between beads, and the number of beads. For JIS, you specify the bead length, the distance between bead centers, and the number of beads. Figure 10.20 shows these parameters.

FIGURE 10.20
Intermittent fillet
weld parameters

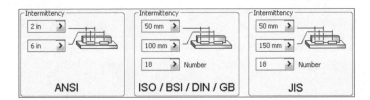

The Extents control allows you to select the beginning and ending planar faces or planes between which the weld bead will be created. The steps to produce a From-To fillet weld bead are similar to the steps outlined for extents and cosmetic welds. When welding a long piece of metal, often intermittent welds are both cost-effective and reduce warping in the part.

Creating Groove Welds

A *groove weld* is primarily used to fill gaps between two sets of faces. Once such gaps are filled, you might top the groove weld with a fillet weld. Figure 10.21 shows some examples.

FIGURE 10.21
Groove weld
examples

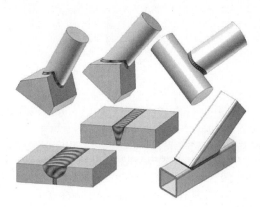

Like fillet welds, a groove weld needs two sets of faces. The Full Face Weld option when selected specifies whether to use the full face to generate the weld. The Full Face Weld option when not selected specifies to use only a portion of the face. Inventor calculates the specific portion of the face by projecting the smaller face set to the larger faceset (if the two facesets are the same size, Inventor picks one of them to project). Figure 10.22 shows the resulting weld bead. Since on the left of Figure 10.22 the Full Face Weld option is disabled for Part1, only part of the face of Part1 is used for the weld bead. On the right of Figure 10.22, the Full Face Weld option is enabled for Part1. This implies that the full face of Part1 be used to generate the weld bead.

FIGURE 10.22
Full Face Weld
option

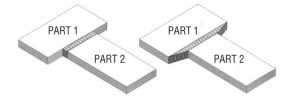

The Ignore Internal Loops option controls whether to ignore or consider the internal loop to generate the weld bead. When selected, it results in a "hollow" (Figure 10.23, left) groove weld; selecting the option results in a "solid" weld bead (Figure 10.23, right).

FIGURE 10.23
Ignore Internal
Loops option

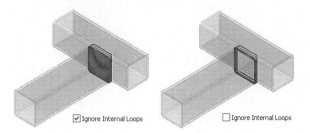

The fill direction is used to project one set of faces to another to generate the groove weld bead. In Figure 10.24, you can see the difference between the resulting weld bead shapes.

FIGURE 10.24
Fill direction

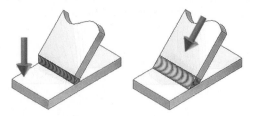

Be aware that the Fill Direction option is not available when you use the Full Face Weld option for both faceset 1 and faceset 2 or when using the Radial Fill option. When you are using the Fill Direction option, you might observe that Inventor can create welds that are not manufacturable, depending upon the direction you choose.

You can select the following for the fill direction:

◆ Planar faces and work planes (specifies the direction normal to chosen face/plane)

◆ Cylindrical, conical, or toroidal faces (specifies the direction of the surface's axis)

◆ Work axes

◆ Linear part edges

One of the questions that comes up frequently is, What direction should be selected for the fill? One guideline you can use is to imagine the average geometric center of faceset1 and the average geometric center of faceset2. The line connecting the two geometric centers will be the fill direction to generate the groove weld bead. You are not required to calculate the geometric centers of the facesets. It is advisable to try different fill directions to get the desired weld bead shape.

You can use the Radial Fill option to project the weld bead around a curve. When using the Radial Fill option, the Fill Direction option is not available. Figure 10.25 shows a radial-filled groove weld.

FIGURE 10.25
Radial Fill option

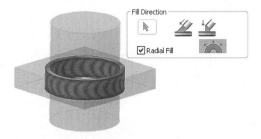

To create a simple groove weld, follow these steps:

CERT OBJECTIVE

1. From the Get Started tab click the Open button.

2. Browse for the file named mi_10a_004.iam located in the Chapter 10 directory of the Mastering Inventor 2011 folder, and click Open.

3. You have three options for this step: double-click the Welds folder in the Model browser to activate the weld bead features, right-click the Welds folder and select Edit, or click the Welds button in the Process panel of the Weld tab.

4. Click the Groove weld tool on the Weld panel.

5. Select the yellow face for faceset 1 and the red face for faceset 2. Note you may need to rotate the view to see the red face.

6. Click the Fill Direction button, and click the visible work axis or any edge or face that establishes the direction to be the same as the work axis.

7. Select the Full Face Weld option for faceset1 to extend the weld to cover the entire yellow face. Note that selecting Full Face Weld for faceset 2 does not change the weld since the weld bead already covers the entire face.

8. Click OK; your result should resemble Figure 10.26.

FIGURE 10.26
Groove weld
results

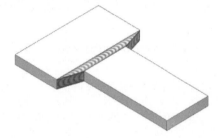

As a general rule of thumb, if the preview comes up, it is almost certain that the bead will succeed.

Performing Machining Operations

Once you've created the preparations and welds, you can create machine features. The features available for machining are similar to the preparations environment. In terms of operations, they are performed after the generation of weld beads. One of the main advantages of providing the machining operations in a separate environment is that in drawings you can document them in the as-machined state. Holes and extrude cuts are typical post-weld machining features.

Figure 10.27 shows a welded assembly with machining operations performed on it.

FIGURE 10.27
Machining features on a weldment assembly

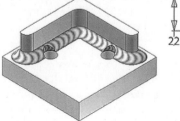
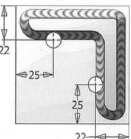

To create the machining features, follow these steps:

1. From the Get Started tab click the Open button.

2. Browse for the file named mi_10a_005.iam located in the Chapter 10 directory of the Mastering Inventor 2011 folder, and click Open.

3. Double-click the Machining folder in the Model browser to activate the machining folder for editing, right-click the Welds folder and select Edit, or click the Machining button in the Process panel of the Weld tab.

4. From the Weld tab, click the 2D Sketch button to create a new sketch.

5. Choose the yellow face to place the sketch, and place two hole centers corresponding to the two holes shown in Figure 10.27.

6. Right-click and choose Finish Sketch, and select the Hole feature from the Preparation And Machining panel.

7. Set the hole size to **10 mm** and the termination to Through All, and click OK.

8. Right-click and choose Finish Edit (or double-click the top-level assembly in the browser) to exit from the machining environment.

Holes that are important to the location of welds should be placed into the parts that are being welded together. Because the machined view of the weldment is a subset of the welded view, you cannot refer to "machined" holes when detailing an as-welded model.

Machining features include, but are not limited to, the following:

- Extrude
- Revolve
- Hole
- Sweep
- Chamfer
- Move Face

Exploring Weld Properties and Combinations

The following sections cover the additional aspects of weldments. Specifically, we will cover setting weld properties, replicating welds, combining fillet and groove weld beads to produce the desired weld bead shape, and using the split technique.

Weld Properties

To turn off the visibility of all weld beads in an open assembly, select the View tab, and select Object Visibility ➤ Welds. You can also expand the Welds folder in the Model browser, right-click the Beads folder, and then deselect Visibility to turn off the weld beads of a particular assembly or subassembly. You can suppress individual weld bead features in the Model browser; the suppress feature is similar to part feature suppression.

You can choose the weld material during the initial conversion of an assembly to a weldment or change it after the fact. Welded Aluminium-6061 is the default material. Note that not all materials are available to use as a weld bead material by default. To add another material so it appears in the Weld Bead Material drop-down list, follow these steps:

CERT OBJECTIVE

1. From the Manage tab, select Styles Editor.

2. Expand the Material node in the left pane of the Style And Standard Editor, and select a material such as Aluminium-6061 AHC.

3. On the right side of the Style And Standard Editor dialog box, select Use As Weldment Material. It is recommended that you save these changes to the style library.

4. Once done, Aluminium-6061 AHC should appear in the Weld Bead Material drop-down list in the Convert To Weldment dialog box, as shown in Figure 10.28, and in the Physical tab of the iProperties for weld beads, found by right-clicking the Welds folder and selecting Properties.

FIGURE 10.28
Convert To Weldment dialog box

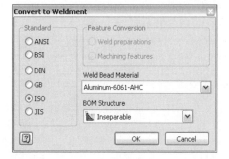

In existing weldments, you can change the weld color styles using the weld properties. In the Model browser, right-click the item Welds, select iProperties, go to the Weld Bead tab, and choose the weld bead color style or the end fill color style. You can use the weld bead color style to assign different color styles to the weld bead. Similarly, the end caps (faces) that you selected in the weldment assembly can be assigned an end fill color style.

Replication

Welds (cosmetic, fillet, and groove beads) can be copied or mirrored in assemblies through the Copy Components and Mirror Components tools. Both sets of components that support the weld need to be copied or mirrored for the welds to be copied or mirrored. For example, if a cosmetic weld exists only on component C1 and if C1 is copied or mirrored, the cosmetic weld is also copied or mirrored. You cannot copy or mirror the weld beads without its components being copied or mirrored. Weld beads can be derived from the assembly into another part document using the Derived Component tool in parts.

Groove and Fillet Weld Combinations

Most welds can be generated using a combination of groove and fillet welds. Figure 10.29 shows an example of welding two hollow tubes with a groove weld. The horizontal tube is welded with a vertical tube. Faceset1 is comprised of the two fillet faces, as shown in Figure 10.29. Faceset 2 is comprised of a single mating face on the bottom of the vertical tube. The fill direction (shown as a downward arrow) will be the face normal of faceset2—in other words, the vertical direction going down.

FIGURE 10.29
Generating the
groove weld bead

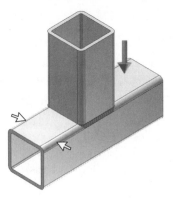

In Figure 10.30, a fillet weld is applied. Faceset1 is composed of three faces, the top horizontal face and the two corresponding fillet faces, as indicated by the light arrows. Faceset2 is composed of the three corresponding component faces on the vertical tube, as shown by the dark arrows in Figure 10.30. A second fillet weld would then be generated in the same way on the other side.

FIGURE 10.30
Generating the
fillet weld bead

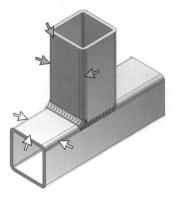

Split Technique

Since welds work on input faces (the two facesets that you select to do the weld), it is sometimes required and at other times desired to split the input faces in order to have the weld bead only on a certain portion of the face or to have better control of the resulting weld. Essentially, you are helping Inventor use the partial face that is generated from the split.

In certain situations, using fillet welds that involve multiple possibilities might make it difficult to control the placement of welds. One instance of this is when controlling the offset of welds around a cylindrical face. Figure 10.30 shows the difference between using a cylinder with a split face and one without. If the cylindrical face is split, you can place the weld in two parts and control the start and end offsets so that holes are given proper clearance. If the face is not split, Inventor automatically breaks the weld where it encounters the holes, but you can adjust the offsets for the first hole only.

1. From the Get Started tab click the Open button.

2. Browse for the file named `mi_10a_006.iam` located in the Chapter 10 directory of the Mastering Inventor 2011 folder, and click Open.

Take a look at the existing fillet weld around the blue cylinder. Notice that the offset on the one hole is not adequate. You will create a similar weld on the yellow cylinder but use the Split tool to ensure you have full control of the offsets.

3. Locate the part called mi_10a_014 in the Model browser, and double-click it to set it active for edits (or right-click and choose Edit).

4. Click the Split icon on the Modify panel of the Model tab.

5. Select WorkPlane1 from the Model browser for the Split tool.

6. Select the cylindrical face for the Faces selection.

7. Click OK. Note that the cylindrical face is now split into two halves. Figure 10.32 shows the Split selections.

8. Return to the weldment assembly by right-clicking in the graphics screen, and choose Finish Edit.

9. You have three options for this step: double-click the Welds folder in the Model browser to activate the weld bead features, right-click the Welds folder and select Edit, or click the Welds button in the Process panel of the Weld tab.

10. Click the Fillet weld icon to bring up the input dialog.

11. Click one of the cylindrical halves for faceset1.

12. Click the top (red) face of the mating plate for faceset2.

13. Enter **10 mm** for the size.

14. Enter **4 mm** in the Start Offset and Stop Offset boxes, as shown in Figure 10.33.

15. Click Apply, repeat steps 11–14 to create the other half of the weld, and click OK.

16. Right-click and choose Finish Edit (or double-click the top-level assembly in the browser) to exit from the weld environment.

17. Compare the welds you created to the existing weld.

FIGURE 10.31
Using a split to create multiple fillet welds

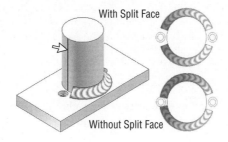
With Split Face

Without Split Face

FIGURE 10.32
Creating a split
face in the part

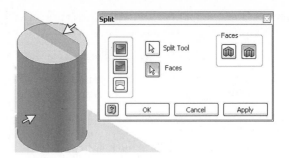

FIGURE 10.33
Creating a fillet
weld with start
and end offsets

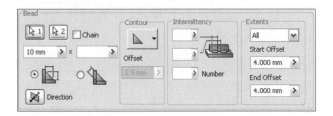

If you do not want to see the split edges in the weldment drawing, you can turn those edges off individually by right-clicking them in the drawing view and deselecting Visibility, as shown in Figure 10.34.

FIGURE 10.34
Turning off split
edges in a drawing

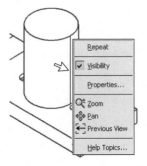

Using the Weld Symbol

You can create a weld symbol in assemblies by clicking the Welds folder and using the Weld Symbol tool. In drawings, you can find this tool in the Annotate tab. You have to make a decision to create them in the right place (assemblies or assemblies and drawings) based on your communication with the welding and other departments that are involved in producing the weldment. The weld symbol, which is optional in the assembly environment, has certain key characteristics:

◆ It cannot be created without a weld bead consuming it.

◆ The primary bead is the weld bead to which the welding symbol is attached.

◆ You're allowed to activate the weld symbol grips and reattach the weld symbol to any other visible bead edge from that symbol's group.

- Multiple weld beads (including cosmetic weld beads) can be grouped under a single weld symbol.

- The weld symbols are listed in a separate folder below the Weld Beads folder.

- A bead can be consumed by only one welding symbol object at any given time.

- A linked bead that is moved out of its welding symbol group causes the parent welding symbol to become unassociated.

- Cross-highlighting is supported for both the bead objects and the welding symbol object. If you select a welding symbol node in the Model browser, the welding symbol and all the beads consumed by that welding symbol will be cross-highlighted in the graphics window. Alternatively, if you select a bead node from either the welding symbols portion of the browser or the Beads folder portion of the browser, the bead will be cross-highlighted in the graphics window.

- A new welding symbol can be created for an already created weld feature.

- Welding symbols have visibility control.

- If a weld symbol references a weld feature, then it is consumed. Otherwise, the bead is unconsumed by any weld symbols. Therefore, three browser filtering options are available from the Beads folder context menu: Show All, Show Consumed Only, and Show Unconsumed Only.

Figure 10.35 shows a single weld symbol for the five welds (Fillet Weld 3 and Groove Welds 2 through Groove Weld 5) created for the single all-around weld. To add multiple welds beads to the same symbol, follow these steps:

CERT OBJECTIVE

1. Right-click the desired weld symbol.

2. Choose Edit Welding Symbol.

3. Add weld beads by selecting them in either the model window or the Model browser.

Only unconsumed weld beads should appear highlighted in the model window. Right-clicking the browser or model window lets you select weld beads and quickly see which weld beads have been unconsumed. To disassociate a weld bead from its corresponding symbol, right-click the bead in the Model browser, and choose the Unconsumed Bead tool from the context menu.

FIGURE 10.35
Single weld symbol
for five welds

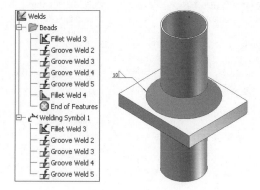

Understanding Bead Property Report and Mass Properties

To estimate accurate weld rod usage, fabrication time, and bead weights, the weld property reporting tool is available in assemblies. This can be used to help estimate costs. This tool allows you to query the mass, volume, length, type, and name of individual beads in the assembly. Through an option (available after you select Bead Report from the Weld Panel of the Weld tab), you can retrieve this data for the current assembly and all of its children weldment assemblies. This information will be exported to a standard Microsoft Excel spreadsheet, as shown in Figure 10.36. In the weldment workflow, you can generate a weld bead report for the core packaging unit that contains the three subassemblies.

FIGURE 10.36
Weld bead property reporting in assemblies

Document	ID	Type	Length	UoM	Mass	UoM	Area	UoM	Volume	UoM
c:\bead_report1.xls										
	Fillet Weld 3	Fillet	59	mm	0.001	kg	1.32E+03	mm^2	390.921	mm^3
	Groove Weld 2	Groove	N/A		0.008	kg	2.30E+03	mm^2	2.79E+03	mm^3
	Groove Weld 3	Groove	N/A		0.008	kg	2.30E+03	mm^2	2.79E+03	mm^3
	Groove Weld 4	Groove	N/A		1.597	kg	4.76E+04	mm^2	5.89E+05	mm^3
	Groove Weld 5	Groove	N/A		0.029	kg	6.07E+03	mm^2	1.07E+04	mm^3
	Fillet Weld 4	Fillet	150	mm	0.02	kg	794.955	mm^2	7.50E+03	mm^3

To calculate the total length of weld beads, you can sum up the total length using the Microsoft Excel Sum functions. Length and area values are not reported for groove welds. The default "save to" location is the parent assembly's directory location, but you can change this location. Weld properties are, at best, estimates. Many factors can change the weight of a weld bead. If the weight of a part is critical, consider machining the part to meet the criteria after welding.

The cross section entered in the Cosmetic Weld dialog box is multiplied by the length of the cosmetic weld bead and is optionally considered in the mass properties to calculate volume. When the Include Cosmetic Welds option is checked in the Physical tab of the iProperties dialog box, this volume is included in the calculations. The mass is determined by the selected weld material. This option is useful where you need only lightweight representation but at the same time need the welds to participate in mass properties.

Creating Drawing Documentation

The Weld Symbol dialog box, being the same in assemblies and drawings, is specific to the engineering standard you're using. Figure 10.37 shows an example of Welding Symbol (ANSI) dialog box in drawings, and when you hover your mouse pointer over each one, a tool tip will show the title of that input control. Table 10.1 describes what the various controls do.

FIGURE 10.37
Welding Symbol dialog box in an ISO drawing; see the definitions of the controls in Table 10.1

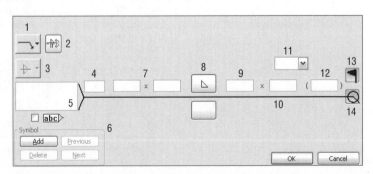

TABLE 10.1:   Welding Symbol Dialog Box Controls

CONTROL (REFERENCED BY NUMBER IN FIGURE 10.37)	DEFINITION
1	Select this option to have the identification line above or below the symbol or to omit it.
2	Toggle this to switch the values and options from above the reference line to below the reference line, and vice versa.
3	Select this option for fillet weld symbols when they are set on both sides of the reference line. Options include the following: No Stagger Weld Stagger – Move (ANSI) Weld Stagger – Move (ISO) Weld Stagger – Mirror
4	Enter a prefix for the symbol, such as depth of bevel, size, and strength, depending upon the weld.
5	Select this option to specify text to be associated to the welding symbol such as specification, process, or reference text. The Enclose Text option will enclose the note in a box at the tail of the symbol.
6	Use these controls to specify multiple welding symbols attached to a single leader. Add: Adds a symbol to the current symbol Delete: Removes the current symbol Previous: Cycles to the last symbol Next: Cycles to the next symbol
7	Enter the leg lengths for fillet weld. Other weld types may specify size, depth diameter, and so on, in this area, depending upon the type of weld.
8	The Weld Symbol drop-down menu lets you select different types of welds such as VGroove Weld, Flare-Bevel Weld, Seam Weld, Spot Weld, and so on. If using a drafting standard based on ANSI, a secondary fillet-type button can be used.
9	Specifies the number of welds, if applicable to the standard.
10	Specifies the length of the weld.
11	This specifies the contour finish of the weld. Choose from Flush or Flat finish, Convex finish, or Concave finish, or if using the DIN standard, you can choose Toes Blended Smooth.

TABLE 10.1: Welding Symbol Dialog Box Controls *(CONTINUED)*

CONTROL (REFERENCED BY NUMBER IN FIGURE 10.37)	DEFINITION
12	This specifies the space between welds.
13	Use this option to add the field weld flag to the welding symbol.
14	The All Around Symbol toggle allows you to add an all-around symbol to the welding symbol. Note that the GB standard includes a third symbol; all other standards will present a dual-state toggle.

BE EXPLICIT WITH SYMBOLS

Although you can refer to any textbook on welding for the correct use of the symbols listed in Table 10.1, keep in mind that many shops have their own "shorthand" versions of weld symbols. It is imperative that you communicate with the welders to make sure you agree on the symbols. Many weld shops do not know the "standard" yet still produce excellent parts.

A perfect example is the "all-around" symbol. Some shops take this to mean only opposite sides of the indicated line, while others interpret this symbol to mean you want all contiguous surfaces welded. When in doubt, you should be explicit with your symbols.

Weldment Design Stages

Now that you've explored the tools available in the weldment environment, we'll explore how to document the four major stages of weldment design in the drawing. You can create a weldment drawing in the following stages:

◆ Assembly: As-assembled with no assembly features

◆ Preparation: As-prepped

◆ Welds: As-welded

◆ Machining: As-machined

Figure 10.38 shows a weldment in the four stages during its creation.
Figure 10.39 shows drawing views of the same weldment detailed at the various stages.

FIGURE 10.38
Four stages of
the weldment
assembly

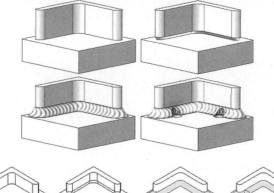

FIGURE 10.39
Four stages of the
weldment assem-
bly as drawing
views

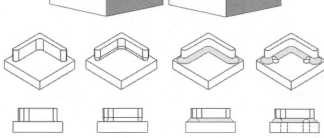

To create a model state view as shown in Figure 10.39, follow these steps:

1. Create a new drawing from an IDW or DWG template of your choosing.

2. Right-click and select Base View, browse for the file named mi_10a_007.iam located in the Chapter 10 directory of the Mastering Inventor 2011 folder, and click Open.

3. Back in the Drawing View dialog box, set Orientation to Top.

4. Click the Model State tab, and select Assembly, Machining, Welds, and Preparation while watching your view preview. Notice that the view changes for each weldment stage as you select it.

5. Select Preparation, and click the drop-down list to explore the options. Note that you can detail the part files individually, showing their preparations clearly without having to hide other parts in the assembly.

6. Once you've explored the different model states, click the Display Options tab.

7. Choose Weld Annotations and Model Welding Symbols.

8. Click the screen to set the view.

9. Check to see that your view resembles Figure 10.40.

You can also retrieve associative weld symbols from the model by right-clicking the drawing view and selecting Get Model Annotations ➤ Get Welding Symbols. You can retrieve associative weld end fills in the model by right-clicking the view and selecting Get Model Annotations ➤ Get Weld Annotations. You can also add nonassociative weld annotations to your drawing. You can create cosmetic weld symbols or weld beads through the Annotate tab by clicking the Welding or Caterpillar tool on the Symbols panel. Figure 10.41 shows the annotation retrieval tools in drawings.

FIGURE 10.40
A weldment view created with weld annotations and welding symbols turned on

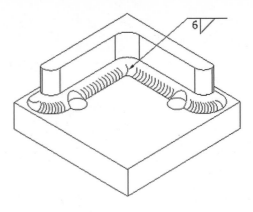

FIGURE 10.41
Retrieving weld symbols

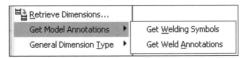

End Fill

In the Symbols panel, you will see the End Fill tool, which is used to represent seam weld end fills and the gap/groove process shape (concave and convex). Clicking the End Fill tool brings up the End Fill dialog box, as shown in Figure 10.42. Note that you can create any weld process shape that is desired in drawings without generating the specified weld in the model.

FIGURE 10.42
End Fill dialog box

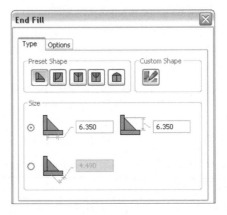

To create a seam weld process shape, follow these steps:

1. Click the End Fill icon on the Symbols panel of the Annotate tab.

2. Select the preset shape, for example, Seam Weld.

3. Select two points that represent the shape's arc chord length to create an arc. You can drag above or below the chord line to have the arc above or below.

4. Select the Options tab, and select Check Solid Fill.

5. Select a color, such as orange.

In the End Fill dialog box, the fillet process shape has Leg1 and Leg2 as parameters. J-Type, V-Type, and U-Type Preset Shape have controls for the width and depth.

Drawing Weld Symbol

Many times you may need to just create the weld symbol in the drawing without having to create any weld beads in the assembly. Although this may suffice for your needs much of them time, remember that you cannot perform any interference analysis or mass properties calculations the way that you can with modeled welds.

To create a welding symbol in the drawing, follow these steps:

1. Select the Welding symbol icon on the Symbols panel of the Annotate tab.

2. This activates the selection. The command message string displays the text "Click on a location."

3. Select an entity or location in the graphics area to define the location of the welding symbol.

When placing a symbol in the drawing you can create a complex leader by selecting more than one point as you are placing the symbol. If you would like to add more later you can do so by performing a right-click on the existing leader and selecting Add Vertex/Leader in the context menu.

4. Right-click within the graphics area, and select Continue from the context menu.

The Welding Symbol dialog box appears.

5. Specify the desired welding symbol.

6. The welding symbol preview dynamically updates.

7. Click OK, and the specified welding symbol appears at the specified location.

Caterpillar

You can create and use *caterpillars* (2D weld representations) in drawings when you want to use a lightweight representation for solid weld beads. As long as the welder is comfortable with this representation, you can use caterpillars. Figure 10.43 shows the dialog box for the Weld Caterpillars tool in drawings. You can create weld caterpillars using the boundary (extent) edges of the welds. This drawing annotation is not associated with weldments in the assembly model. In other words, you can create the caterpillar on any edge without the presence of any corresponding weld bead in the assembly. This is useful when you want to quickly document weld beads in drawings. The caterpillar could be used in addition to the weld symbol to make the documentation better.

FIGURE 10.43
Weld Caterpillars
dialog box

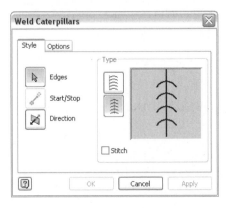

To create a caterpillar, follow these steps:

**CERT
OBJECTIVE**

1. Select the Caterpillar tool from the Symbols panel found on the Annotate tab.

2. Click Edges, and select one of the long edges (the lateral edge) of the groove weld.

3. Click Options, and enter the width parameter. Adjust other parameters such as Angle, Arc %, and Spacing.

4. Click the direction to change the shape to concave or convex.

5. The Start/Stop options in the dialog box, which are specified by points, are useful to terminate the caterpillar between the From and To locations. The caterpillar preview shows the effect of changing options.

Figure 10.44 shows the resulting caterpillar for a groove weld.

FIGURE 10.44
Weld caterpillar

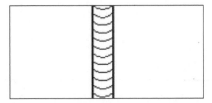

Caterpillars can be useful when you want to represent a weldment using a single-part file and create a drawing from it. You can then indicate the position and detail of the welds along the edge. Use the Split tool, which will allow you to create edges where none may exist.

WELDMENT WORKFLOWS

You are a designer working for a company in the packaging industry. The entire packaging system consists of several functional units that form its structure. You are interested in the high-level core packaging unit that consists of three subassemblies: A, B, and C. Let's say it contains parts consisting of a boxed container (A), a lift-arm mechanism (B) for the boxed container, and railings (C) on which the container moves from one station to another. Each subassembly is comprised of structural steel shapes and/or tubes that are bent and plates that are welded together.

You want to analyze subassembly A, which forms the container in the context of the top-level assembly, to check for interferences. For this, you need accurate solid weld beads to analyze the interference. You want to pattern these solid weld beads and their components and create a drawing of this subassembly. To accomplish this, you would place modeled fillet and groove weld beads.

On subassembly B, which forms the lift-arm mechanism, the weld beads are not very complex, so you don't require a modeled weld for each bead, but you do need mass analysis of welds. So in this case, you'll place lightweight, cosmetic welds and document them in the drawing.

On weld subassembly C, which forms the railings on which the container moves, you are interested neither in interference analysis nor in mass properties in assemblies. For C, you are interested only in quickly documenting the weldments in drawings. You need a streamlined interface to document the welds in drawings, and you want to generate any weld bead or symbol regardless of the weld standard. To do this, you will use just the Weld Symbol tool in the drawing environment.

By using the various weld tools in conjunction with one another, you can design and document weldments in a way that makes sense to the task at hand. You can take advantage of the flexibility that comes with using each of these tools together, to make weldment design accommodate your specific needs, even though they fulfill different design and documentation requirements.

Generating a Bill of Materials and Parts List

Once a weldment design is done, you typically need to generate a bill of materials (BOM) and a parts list. Also, you'll want to customize the BOM to represent a weldment.

You can automatically generate and maintain a consistent bill of materials across welded assemblies, drawings, and presentations. Components that are deemed "inseparable" are assemblies that cannot be taken apart without doing damage to one or more of their components, typically weldments. Manufacturing processes treat inseparable assemblies like purchased components and are represented as a single line item.

Inseparable components also have the following two characteristics:

◆ Some child components are considered part of the parent. Hence, they don't need to be tracked or revised separately.

◆ An inseparable assembly is a purchased assembly in a parts-only parts list.

When documented in its own context, an inseparable assembly is treated as a standard one, in that all of the parts are listed. Figure 10.45 shows the BOM for an assembly that is made up of a weldment assembly and single-piece part. On the left, the weldment is shown in a structured BOM view, listing the weldment and the parts within. On the right, the BOM is shown as Parts Only; note that the weldments are listed as a single component.

FIGURE 10.45
Inseparable components as handled by the BOM

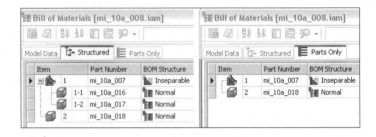

To modify the BOM structure, follow these steps:

1. Open the weldment assembly.

2. Click the Bill of Materials icon on the Manage panel of the Assemble tab.

3. On the Model Data tab, double-click in the BOM Structure column, select the drop-down for each component, and select Inseparable.

4. Click Done in the Bill Of Materials dialog box.

You can change the BOM structure of several components at once by right-clicking the BOM Structure cell of a component marked as inseparable, right-clicking and choosing Copy, Shift-selecting multiple components, and then right-clicking and choosing Paste.

The Bottom Line

Select and use the right weldment design methodology   We have shown you three weldment design methodologies. Before starting on any weldment design, it is imperative to keep the documentation, interference analysis, mass properties, and other design criteria in perspective and select the right design methodology.

Master It   What is the right weldment strategy for you? If you don't need to document the weldment design stages, you could consider the part files and part features methodology or the weldment assembly and derived methodology. With the weldment assembly methodology, you get to document the different stages of weldment design and reap the benefits of any new enhancements.

Create and edit weld preparations and machining features   Following the weldment methodology, you need to plan on creating the gaps needed (weld preparations) to deposit the weld beads. You need to create post weldment machining features that go through the weld beads.

> **Master It**   Where can you find preparation and machining features, and when do you use them? Weld preparations and machining features are similar to part modeling features. Based on the weld bead shape needed, you need to plan for creating the preparations in advance. Once the welds are done, you need to create the features for the machining processes.

Create and edit different kinds of weld beads such as cosmetic, fillet, and groove   We have described the relative advantages and disadvantages of cosmetic and solid weld beads. Weldment design involves the optimal mix of these weld beads based on needs and requirements.

> **Master It**   You need to create the weld annotations only in drawings, without any need to create them in the model. You have weld subassemblies that need only lightweight representation in both the model and drawings. In situations involving accurate interference and mass properties, you need accurate weld beads. The question is: What type of weld beads should you use?

Document weldment stages in drawings   Welds need to be documented in assemblies or drawings. It is important to show the different stages of weldment design in drawings to get a good idea of how to manufacture the weldment. You can use the drawing tools effectively to annotate the welds in drawings. This will help the welder understand the design intent better.

> **Master It**   What are the different tools used for weld documentation? You can annotate the welds in assemblies. If you prefer to document the welds in drawings, you could document the four stages of weldment design: as-assembled, as-prepped, as-welded, and as-machined stages in drawings. Besides, you could use other drawing manager tools to customize weld documentation.

Generate and maintain a consistent BOM across welded assemblies, drawings, and presentations   You have been shown how to generate and maintain a consistent bill of materials for weldment assemblies and a parts list in drawings. Mark parts or assemblies as inseparable to designate them as weldments.

> **Master It**   How do you generate the BOM and parts list for your weldment? You can generate the bill of materials and mark the components as Inseparable. In the drawing, you generate the parts list for the weldment assembly.

Chapter 11

Functional Design

In this chapter, you will be introduced to the concept of functional design in Inventor. The functional design tools enable you to create complex geometry by entering size data. Before any geometry is created, you can verify whether the design meets the requirements by performing calculations. The formulas used for the calculations are based on international standards, and they are fully documented in the Engineer's Handbook. This allows you to override or ignore certain calculations when experience dictates.

In this chapter, you will learn how to:

◆ Use Inventor's Design Accelerators

◆ Use Inventor's Design Calculators

◆ Understand the interaction of these tools with Content Center

◆ Develop best practices for using these tools

Geometric Modeling vs. Functional Design

In most industries, product requirements and design criteria drive the engineering process. As its name implies, *functional design* favors function over geometry. Rather than modeling geometry first and then hoping that the form satisfies all the design criteria, in the functional design method the designer or engineer makes sure the product operates correctly given the design criteria *prior* to finalizing the product's shape. If functional design is done well, the geometry will be the result of the design process rather than the input to it.

This chapter will concentrate on the Design Accelerator tools that Inventor offers to mechanical and electrical engineers so they can concentrate on the product requirements rather than spending most of their time creating geometry.

Most of the topics in this chapter require an assembly to be opened. Therefore, this chapter is not applicable if you have only Inventor LT installed.

You've probably been confronted with several of the design criteria listed here. They are typical requirements that a design engineer will have to satisfy (in no particular order):

◆ Strength (material, size, weight, load conditions, mechanical behavior, safety factors)

◆ Power (speed, torque, momentum, power transmission, lubrication, safety)

◆ Temperature (cooling, heat dissipation)

- ◆ Vibration and motion (frequency response/Eigen values/damping)

- ◆ Wear resistance (surface treatments, plating, tolerances/life cycle/wear/durability/ lubrication)

- ◆ Sound restrictions/considerations (insulation/packaging)

- ◆ Optical characteristics (color, surface characteristics, refraction, transparency, chromatic aberration, aesthetics)

- ◆ Electrical and magnetic characteristics

- ◆ Cost (materials, packaging, eco-sustainability, spare parts, stock parts, standard sizes versus custom made, maintenance, manufacturing and assembly methods, time restrictions)

A 15-TON HOIST MACHINE

Many of the examples in this chapter are taken from the 15-ton hoist depicted here. The hoist has a full gearbox and brake system, which is situated in the front-left side of the machine. The different components of the machine were generated through classic part and assembly modeling. However, for the dynamic study of the different components and the analysis of the forces and the power transmission, Inventor's Gear Generator was extensively used.

Often these requirements will conflict with one another; for example, improving strength or durability often will increase cost, and so on.

As a design engineer, you often use tools that help make the right trade-off by attempting to verify and optimize the design by using lab tests, calculations, stress analysis, rendering, and animations.

In this chapter, you will use the built-in calculation rules of the Design Accelerators in combination with animations and the Engineer's Handbook to satisfy the strength, power, wear, and temperature requirements of a particular design. While doing so, we will show some real-world examples to illustrate functional design concepts. To underline the diversity of the tool, we will show examples spanning various industries, such as engine design (springs and cams) and power transmission design (gearbox).

A General Introduction to Design Accelerators

CERT OBJECTIVE

Inventor's Design Accelerators can be overwhelming at first because of the sheer number of accelerators and because the user interface is slightly different from the rest of Inventor. Therefore, we'll look at the dialog boxes, the browser structure, and the user interface for these tools.

Design Accelerators Input

Inventor's Design Accelerators are available only in the assembly environment. Design Accelerator dialog boxes are tabbed dialog boxes, as shown in Figure 11.1. The Design and Calculation tabs appear in most of the dialog boxes. Two particular areas in these dialog boxes are worth pointing out. The Results pane displays the calculated values for a particular design. The Summary pane indicates whether a design is acceptable with the given parameters. These panes are hidden by default and can be displayed by double-clicking on the double line on the right and bottom edges of the dialog box or by clicking the chevron/arrows along the borders. The border of the Design Accelerator window turns red to indicate a design failure or to flag a more general error.

FIGURE 11.1
A typical Design Accelerator dialog box

The calculation is not an automatic operation; for example, if a calculation fails and the values turn red, you typically change the parameters to correct the problem. You will not see the result of your change unless you explicitly click the Calculate button. Many calculators offer different types of calculations. Choosing a particular calculation method will disable certain fields (driven values) and enable some other fields (input values).

REMEMBER TO CALCULATE

One common mistake is not clicking the Calculate button. The Design Accelerators will not update when you simply change values. You *must* click the Calculate button.

Figure 11.2 and Figure 11.3 show an example dialog box (belt) that shows how its fields will look like if you are calculating the power from the torque and speed (Figure 11.2) versus calculating the torque with the power and speed as inputs (Figure 11.3).

FIGURE 11.2
Calculating Power
using Torque
and Speed

FIGURE 11.3
Calculating Torque
using Power
and Speed

USING DEFAULT VALUES

The values used in the last calculation of a Design Accelerator component will be reused when you create a new Design Accelerator component with the same generator. If you want to use the default values of a Design Accelerator, hold down the Ctrl key when starting the Design Accelerator tool.

Table 11.1 shows the icons and buttons that appear in all the Design Accelerator dialog boxes. It will help if you familiarize yourself with them before diving into the rest of this chapter.

TABLE 11.1: Common Design Accelerator Dialog Box Elements

ICON	FUNCTION
	Export to a template
	Import a template
	File naming

TABLE 11.1:   Common Design Accelerator Dialog Box Elements *(CONTINUED)*

ICON	FUNCTION
$f_\oplus$	Disable/enable calculation
	Reset calculation data
	Display results in HTML format
	Expand/collapse the summary window
	Expand/collapse the result window
>>	More options
...	Select a different size or different properties
▾	Select a different type
☒	Delete a selection

Design Accelerators Output

There are two sorts of functional design tools: generators and calculators. It is important to understand the difference between these two categories. The output generated by Design *Generators* consists of subassemblies with actual geometry in them. The output generated by the Design *Calculators* (that is, the weld or plate calculators) consists only of a subassembly browser node. The calculators don't generate any geometry, but the result of the calculation can be edited and repeated with different values. The solve state of the subassemblies is indicated by an icon in the browser. Manual Solve is the default mode, but you can change it to Automatic Solve by right-clicking on the Design Accelerator component and selecting Component and then the solve mode you want to use. Figure 11.4 shows the Manual Solve icon on the left and Automatic Solve on the right.

There are three solve states that can be changed in the Component context menu, as described in Table 11.2.

FIGURE 11.4
Synchronous
belt in Manual
Solve mode

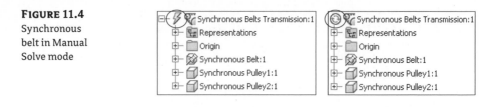

TABLE 11.2: Solve States of Design Accelerator Components

STATE	EXPLANATION
Solve Off	Changes to Design Accelerator input conditions have no effect on the Design Accelerator component.
Manual Solve	Changes to Design Accelerator input conditions only have an effect after editing the Design Accelerator component.
Automatic Solve	Changes to Design Accelerator input conditions immediately affect the Design Accelerator component.

The Solve Off, Manual Solve, and Automatic Solve options are mutually exclusive, meaning that when you select one option it turns the current one off. The Solve Off menu does exactly what its name suggests: it turns off the solver completely so that the Design Accelerator component is frozen until the next edit. The possible solve states are reflected in the context menu, as shown in Figure 11.5.

FIGURE 11.5
Possible
solve states

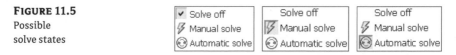

The difference between Manual Solve and Automatic Solve is simple. Let's take the example of a V-belt. When the distance between the axes changes, a V-belt will automatically readjust the pulley positions if Automatic Solve is on. If Manual Solve is on, the user will have to update the pulley position by clicking the Manual Solve menu. A red lightning bolt will appear in the browser, as shown in Figure 11.6. Manual Solve is used as the default for performance reasons and to prevent interactions with the assembly solver.

BE CAREFUL WITH AUTOMATIC

Although it might be tempting to set all your accelerators to Automatic Solve, keep in mind that these tools can be very taxing on your system, especially if you are using multiple accelerators or if you are working in a large assembly. Also, the Design Accelerator solver runs separately from the assembly constraint solver. If the Design Accelerator solver is set to Automatic, the two solvers can conflict. If you are going to be tweaking the position of a feature that affects the accelerator, you can set it to Automatic. However, set it to Manual Solve as soon as you have that part of the design firmed up. It's the same advice we give for adaptivity and the Contact Solver.

The Calculate option on the context menu is a toggle between two states; clicking it once turns it on, and clicking it again turns it off. You can do this by using the Calculate button at the top right of each Design Accelerator dialog box as well. When calculation is turned off, the performance of the generator is faster.

FIGURE 11.6
Out-of-date manually solved V-belt after moving one of its axes

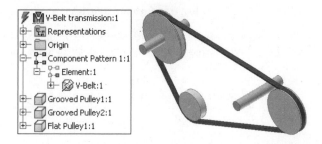

Because Design Accelerator assemblies typically consist of multiple parts that are constrained together, Inventor offers specific edit, delete, promote, and demote tools to handle these more complex entities. Figure 11.7 shows the edit and delete tools.

FIGURE 11.7
The special edit and delete tools

Figure 11.8 shows the promote and demote tools that are available on some generators only: gears, belts, cams, and shafts. Use these tools to demote Design Accelerator components out of their original Design Accelerator subassembly. This allows the grouping of components of different Design Accelerator assemblies into a single subassembly. You can edit a demoted component on the original Design Accelerator assembly by using the Edit Using Design Accelerator tool.

FIGURE 11.8
The special promote and demote tools in the Component context menu

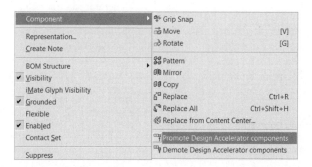

Be sure to set the Inventor selection priority to Components before you select Design Accelerator components; otherwise, you won't see the special tools.

Although you should generally avoid editing the subassembly itself using the traditional edit method and instead use the Edit Using Design Accelerator tools, components in the subassembly can be edited under certain circumstances. Copying or patterning Design Accelerator assemblies will maintain the geometry, but you will lose the ability to edit the copied assembly with the Edit Using Design Accelerator tool, which basically means you lose the Design Accelerator intelligence on the copy.

WHY DO THE GENERATORS CREATE A SUBASSEMBLY?

The subassembly is a container for the generator components. This does a couple of things. It isolates the components from the assembly solver and provides a way to provide special behavior for the Design Accelerators. For example, the context menu tools for the solve state and promote/demote are added by the subassembly. By default these subassemblies are set as phantom in the bill of materials (BOM) structure so that they are not counted as items.

Design Generators and Content Center

Most design generators use Content Center parts, but not all. Consult Table 11.3 when you don't have access to Content Center and still want to use some of the Design Accelerators.

TABLE 11.3:   Design Accelerators' Use of Content Center Database

GENERATOR/ACCELERATOR	NEEDS CONTENT CENTER
Bolted Connections	Yes
Weld Calc	No
Tolerance Stack Up Calc	No
Limits and Fits Calc	No
Beam Calc	No (but recognizes section properties of Content Center and Frame Generator parts; see Chapter 15, "Frame Generator")
Column Calc	No (but recognizes section properties of Content Center and Frame Generator parts; see Chapter 15)
Plate Calc	No
Shaft Generator	No
Cam Generator	No
Gear Generator	No
Bearing Generator	Yes
Key Connection Generator	Yes
Spline Generator	No
Belt Generator	No

TABLE 11.3: Design Accelerators' Use of Content Center Database *(CONTINUED)*

GENERATOR/ACCELERATOR	NEEDS CONTENT CENTER
Sprocket and Chain Generator	Yes
Spring Generator	Yes (but only for Belleville springs)
Pins Generator	Yes
Seals and O-rings Generator	Yes
Engineer's Handbook	No

PREREQUISITES FOR THIS CHAPTER

To follow the steps and exercises in this chapter, you will need to have Inventor's Content Center libraries installed and configured for many of the Design Accelerator tools used in this chapter. If you did not install the Content Center libraries originally, you can do so at any time using the Inventor installation media. You can learn more about installing and configuring Content Center in Chapter 7, "Part and Feature Reuse." Be certain to install the ANSI, ISO, and DIN libraries.

To access the Design Accelerator functionality, open any assembly document and select the Design tab of the Ribbon bar.

Bolted Connections

This generator is the most popular Design Accelerator tool because it is able to make an entire set of bolts, washers, nuts, and the necessary holes in the supporting geometry as an all-in-one operation. Figure 11.9 shows placement options for the Bolted Connections tool; you might notice the similarity between these options and the Hole tool placement options.

FIGURE 11.9
Placement options in a bolted connection

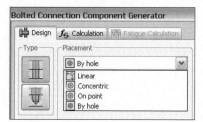

There are four placement options:

◆ Linear allows the creation of a bolted connection without any preexisting sketch by selecting a distance to two different linear edges.

- Concentric uses any circular edge (the edge does not have to be part of a hole feature; the edge can be part of a cylindrical extrusion) to make a bolted connection with a larger or smaller hole size.

- By Hole requires an existing hole, and the bolted connection will incorporate the existing hole.

- On Point requires an existing work point or vertex as input.

Although the Bolted Connections tool will create holes for you, it is often best to create the holes first with the regular Hole tool and then use the By Hole option rather than using the Linear or Concentric option. The disadvantage of the latter two options is that it creates only a point in a sketch, but the point is not dimensioned and could easily move. When the sketch point moves, the bolted connection will *not* follow the new position of the hole. When you use By Hole, the bolted connection will automatically follow any *positional change* of the preexisting holes but will not follow *diameter changes* automatically. Keeping the diameter of the holes generated by the bolted connection in sync with the diameter changes in the preexisting hole requires manually selecting a different diameter in the Diameter field of the bolted connection. The reason this was done is to give you a choice because you don't necessarily want all your bolts to increase in diameter when the underlying hole diameter increases.

Enough theory—now let's concentrate on an actual example; open the assembly called mi_11a_001.iam from the Chapter 11 folder. You need to connect the brown cap with the blue plate. The cap has three holes drilled in it, and they form a circular pattern. The plate has no holes yet, and this can be verified by activating the view representation called Section. The design problem you are trying to solve is the following: considering an axial force of 750 N and a tangential force of 300 N, will three bolts be sufficient to hold the cap on the plate?

As mentioned, to respect the existing hole pattern in the cap and create the necessary holes in the plate, you start the Bolted Connection tool first and follow these steps:

1. On the Get Started tab, click Open and browse to mi_11a_001.iam in the Chapter 11 folder.

2. Select the Design tab and then click the Bolted Connection button.

3. In the Placement area, confirm that By Hole is selected in the drop-down list.

4. Select the top face of the cap as the Start Plane.

5. Select one of the holes. Since there is a hole pattern, the preview will display at the original instance of the hole no matter which hole you select. Note too that the Follow Pattern option is displayed in the Bolted Connection dialog box. Check the box so all of the holes will get fasteners.

6. Click the Termination button and select the back side of the plate. The Bolted Connections Generator is smart enough to know which side of the plate is valid for termination. When you hover over the plate, the back side highlights and you can click to accept.

7. In the Thread area, set the Diameter to **8 mm** to match the holes in the cap. In Figure 11.10, you can see that holes have been added to the dialog browser pane.

Note that there are three drilled holes automatically added to the blue plate. You could click the Drilled Hole bar in the right pane and then click the down arrow to select a different hole type (for example, counterbore). The Bolted Connections Generator is clever enough to filter out countersink hole types for holes on faces that are not exposed.

FIGURE 11.10
Following the holes of an existing pattern

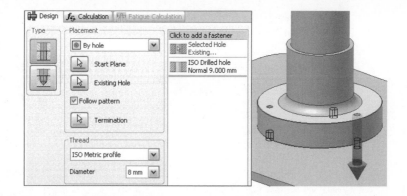

At this point, you can add all necessary hardware to finish the connection. It is important to note that the order of the icons in the pane on the right represents the stacking order of the bolted connection beginning from the start plane down. If you want to place a bolt on the start plane, you just click the area marked with Click To Add A Fastener.

8. Click the area marked Click To Add A Fastener above the holes. The bolt is long enough to go through the components. If you want to change the bolt length, drag the arrows at the end. Only valid lengths from Content Center can be selected. Figure 11.11 shows the bolt preview and the length adjustment arrow.

FIGURE 11.11
Adding a bolt and adjusting the bolt length via an arrow glyph

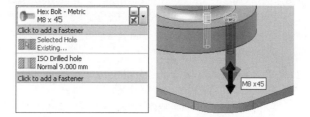

9. To finish the bolted connection by adding a nut and washer, click the area marked Click To Add A Fastener below the holes and select a DIN 988 washer. Click again and select a DIN EN 24033 nut. The completed bolted connection is shown in Figure 11.12.

FIGURE 11.12
Adding the washer and bolt

If you wanted to thread the plate to avoid adding a nut and washer, you could do so by clicking the… (ellipsis) icon in the ISO Drilled hole section of the pane, as shown in Figure 11.13.

FIGURE 11.13
Adding a
hole thread

The Calculation tab provides four strength calculation options:

♦ Bolt Diameter Design

♦ Number Of Bolts Design

♦ Bolt Material Design

♦ Check Calculation

Do you meet the design criteria with just three bolts? It all depends on the material you choose for the bolts.

10. Switch to the Calculation tab and confirm that Number Of Bolts Design is selected in the Type Of Strength Calculation area.

11. In the Loads area, enter **750 N** for Maximal Axial Force and **300 N** for Maximal Tangent Force.

12. This application requires fasteners with high thermal conductivity. In the Bolt Material area, check the box next to the field and select Copper-Nickel C96200. To narrow down the material choices, type **Copper** in the text field below the Material column header. Note that the text filter is case sensitive.

13. Click Calculate to analyze the fasteners. You can see in Figure 11.14 that you need four fasteners for these load and fastener materials.

14. Click OK to set the bolted connection to the current hole pattern of three holes.

To comply with the calculation, you need to update the hole pattern in the cap from three to four members, and the bolted connection pattern follows accordingly, as shown in Figure 11.15 (if Automatic Solve is on) *or* after expanding the pattern, right-clicking on the bolted connection, and then clicking Component ➤ Manual Solve (if Manual Solve is on).

Like many Design Accelerator assemblies, the bolted connection subassembly shown in Figure 11.16 is a phantom subassembly, which means that only its subcomponents are shown at the parent level in the BOM.

If you edit the plate, the holes in the plate have a lock symbol next to their icon in the browser, indicating that they are generated by a Design Accelerator and can be modified only by that same Design Accelerator. Proof of this is that the Edit Feature tool or the "double-click to edit" behavior is absent for these type of holes. If you want the holes in the plate to be independent from the Design Accelerator they were generated by, use the Explode context menu on the hole.

As explained earlier, the bolted connection makes the holes automatically for you. In a similar fashion, if you remove a bolted connection, you can choose to remove the associated holes if you want, as shown in Figure 11.17.

FIGURE 11.14
The calculator recommends four bolts.

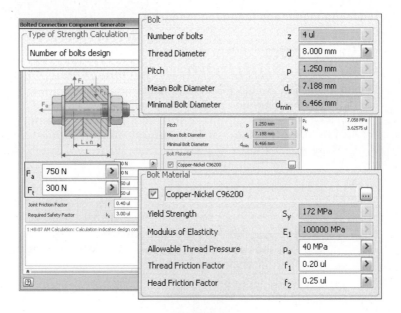

FIGURE 11.15
The final result with four bolted connections

FIGURE 11.16
The bolted connection assembly does not participate in the BOM.

Part Number	BOM Structure	Unit QTY	QTY
4184	Normal	Each	1
4187	Normal	Each	1
plate	Normal	Each	1
Bolted Connection	Phantom	Each	4
DIN 6921 - M6 x 45	Purchased	Each	1
DIN 988 - S8 x 14	Purchased	Each	1
ISO 4033 - M6	Purchased	Each	1

FIGURE 11.17
Deleting the
holes of a bolted
connection

Calculators

Inventor has several Design Calculators that perform a specific calculation without generating any geometry. The dialog box for calculators is also restricted to one tab, the Calculation tab. Calculators do generate a node in the assembly browser, which allows you to repeat the calculation with different input values. We'll cover the weld calculator in more detail than the others because all the calculators (weld, solder and hub joints, power screw, tolerance) are very similar.

There are a few interesting things to note about the weld calculator:

◆ There is no automatic link between the weld assembly and the weld calculator. To obtain the beam height, beam width, and weld height, use the Measure drop-down menu under the right arrow of the real value edit controls *inside* the calculator window, and proceed with measuring the weld bead in the model. Do not use the Measure tools in the Tools menu because this will exit the Design Accelerator dialog box. An alternative is to measure and copy these distances to the clipboard prior to entering the calculator and then paste them into the calculator.

◆ The actual weld results are stored as a subassembly without any geometry in the main assembly.

◆ Weld loads can be combined. The example in Figure 11.18 shows a combination of axial force, bending force, and torque.

◆ Weld results can be edited or can be exported to HTML files for viewing in a web browser.

◆ Fatigue calculation is not on by default; you have to explicitly turn it on by clicking the second icon at the top right of the dialog box.

FIGURE 11.18
Weld load types

Here is the functional design problem that you can solve with the weld calculator: what combination of weld bead material and weld height should you use for a given safety factor so that the weld withstands a lateral point force (3000 N) at a distance of 50 mm from the weld plane? To calculate the weld requirements, follow these steps:

1. On the Get Started tab, click Open and browse to `mi_11a_003.iam` in the Chapter 11 folder.

2. On the Weld tab, click the Weld Calculator drop-down and select Fillet Weld Calculator (Spatial).

3. In the Weld Form area, select the rectangle from the drop-down list.

4. In the Weld Loads area, select Bending Force Parallel With The Weld Plane and deselect the default, Axial Force Perpendicular To The Weld Plane. Note that at least one calculation type must be active, so you have to select the new type before deselecting the default one.

5. In the Loads area, enter a Bending Force value of **3000 N** and a Force Arm value of **50 mm**.

6. In the Dimensions area, enter **5.0 mm** for Weld Height, **20 mm** for Beam Height, and **10 mm** for Beam Width. See Figure 11.19 for the dialog box entries.

FIGURE 11.19
Fillet Weld calculator

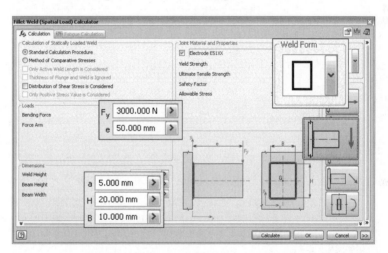

7. In the Joint Material and Properties area, check the box next to the User Material field to specify a material. Type **W** in the field under the Type column header to filter for weld materials, as shown in Figure 11.20. The filter is case sensitive. Select E51XX as the material and click OK.

FIGURE 11.20
Choosing a weld material in the weld calculator

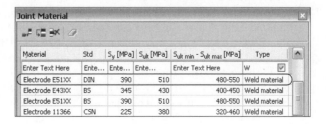

Material	Std	S_y [MPa]	S_{ult} [MPa]	$S_{ult\,min}$ - $S_{ult\,max}$ [MPa]	Type	
Enter Text Here	Ente...	Ente...	Ente...	Enter Text Here	W	☑
Electrode E51XX	DIN	390	510	480-550	Weld material	
Electrode E43XX	BS	345	430	400-450	Weld material	
Electrode E51XX	BS	390	510	480-550	Weld material	
Electrode 11366	CSN	225	380	320-460	Weld material	

You can now finally click the Calculate button, and all values will be displayed in black (not red) in the Results window, as shown in Figure 11.21. At the same time, the message "Calculation indicates design compliance!" will appear in the Summary window.

FIGURE 11.21
Weld calculator indicating a satisfactory design

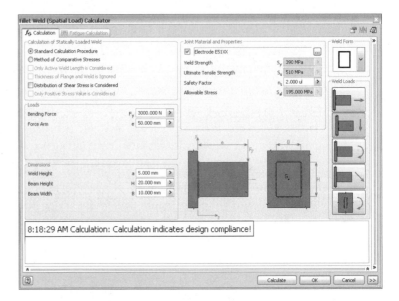

You will now explore an additional what-if scenario. What will happen if the anticipated force of 3000 is higher and you have a force of 8500 N? You will most likely have to increase the weld height or the weld material to avoid breakage if you pursue the same safety factor of 2x.

Follow these steps to calculate the new weld bead requirements.

8. Edit the Fillet Weld calculation and enter **8500 N** as the Bending Force.

9. Click Calculate. When one or more results values are marked in red, as shown in Figure 11.22, an error message displays in the Results window. The calculator has determined that the minimum weld height, amin, is **6.658 mm**.

10. Set Weld Height to **7 mm**, and click Calculate. The calculation results show that the weld meets the required factor. If you wanted to maintain the same weld height, you could select a weld material that has a higher yield strength.

11. Close the Dialog box when finished.

It is interesting to note that there is no relationship between materials as defined in the Design Accelerator dialog boxes and materials as defined in the Inventor style library.

To complete the exercise and to keep the calculator in sync with the actual assembly, two things need to happen. First, it would be good to also create the material E51xx in the Style And Standard Editor, as shown in Figure 11.23; mark it as a weldment material; and assign this material to the weld bead properties. If you are planning on using this material on a regular basis, it would be even a better idea to add this material to the style library so you can use it in every weldment assembly via a template file.

FIGURE 11.22
Weld calculator
flagging a
bad design

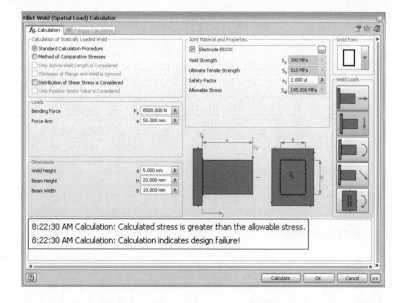

FIGURE 11.23
Definition of
Electrode E51xx as
weldment material

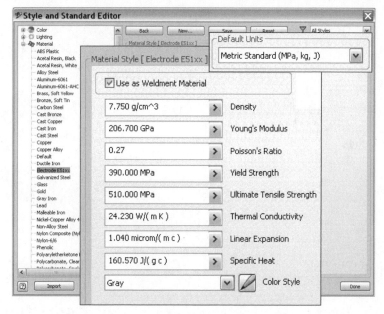

Second, if you plan to use the original material Electrode E51xx, you need to change the weld height to 7.5 mm in the weld beads of the assembly.

You used only one type of weld calculator. In Inventor there are different weld calculators for each weld type (fillet weld, butt weld, plug and groove weld, spot weld, bevel joint, lap joint, tube joint), but all use methods similar to the one explained earlier. So, it should be pretty straightforward to find your way around in the other weld calculators.

SAVE CALCULATIONS AND RESULTS

Once you click OK, you will be prompted to save an assembly (IAM) file. Once you save this file in your project directory, an assembly node is created in the browser. This assembly node has no geometry but contains all the information you used in your calculations. You should also click the Results icon in the upper-right corner of the dialog box to generate an HTML page with the inputs, calculations, and results. You can save this page to your project directory.

This approach helps you keep track of the calculations you have performed and allows others to see how you arrived at the current design. In some cases, this information might even be useful for legal purposes if the safety of your design is ever called into question.

Generators

The majority of the modules in the Design Accelerator add-in are generators. Generators not only perform calculations, but they also automatically generate the underlying geometry. This can be a real time-saver especially when you are talking about complex geometry such as helical gears or chains or synchronous belts. You will take an in-depth look at several of these generators.

Gear Generator

There are three gear families in Inventor: Spur Gears, Bevel Gears, and Worm Gears. The use of spur gears in the design of the gearbox, shown in Figure 11.24, will be explained here.

FIGURE 11.24
Gearbox assembly

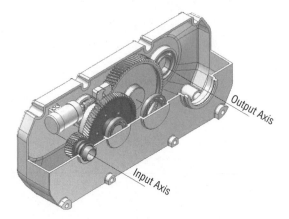

The output axis depicts the driving or motor side, and the input axis depicts the driven or load side. The design challenge in this gearbox is to add the remaining gear pair to connect to the output axis while fulfilling the power requirements on that axis (7.5 kW) and the speed requirements (260 rpm) and to select a gear material that guarantees a minimum life cycle of 15,000 hr.

To complete this exercise correctly and to get the same values as shown in the figures, be sure to choose the same options as explained in this section.

In this example, you will add a gear pair between the output axis and the middle axis closest to the output axis, as shown in Figure 11.24. The gear on the input axis (Gear 2) will be the larger gear. The gear on the middle axis (Gear 1) will be the smaller gear.

Follow these steps to create the gears:

1. On the Get Started tab, click the Open button.

2. Browse for the file named mi_11a_005.iam located in the Chapter 11 directory of the Mastering Inventor 2011 folder, and click Open.

3. Activate the View Representation called Mastering Inventor.

4. On the Design tab, click the Spur Gear button found on the Power Transmission panel. Note that if you've used the Worm or Bevel Gear tools last, you may need to use the drop-down to locate the Spur Gear button.

5. Expand the More options by clicking the >> button and set Input Type to Gear Ratio.

6. In the Common section, change Design Guide to Module. Enter **3.6** in the Desired Gear Ratio field. Enter **8 degrees** in the Helix Angle field.

7. For Gear 1, select the cylindrical face of the bearing (or any of the green faces) and the Red face of Gear 4. Set the number of teeth to **19**.

8. For Gear 2, select the cylindrical face of the bearing (or any of the yellow faces). Confirm that Facewidth for both gears is 20 mm.

9. When you click Calculate, the preview will update, as shown in Figure 11.25. If an error is displayed, check all of the inputs.

FIGURE 11.25
Smaller Gear 1
on the left, larger
Gear 2 on the right

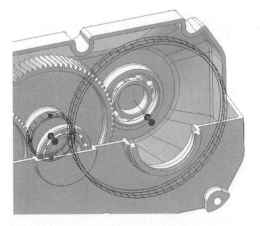

By choosing the Module Design Guide, you also determined the module value (this value is read-only in this method, which is indicated by its field being grayed out).

After satisfying the space and position requirements, you'll now concentrate on selecting the right material for the gears to satisfy the power and speed requirements.

10. Activate the Calculation tab, and set Method Of Strength Calculation to ISO 6336:1996.

11. Expand the More options by clicking the >> button and confirm Type Of Load Calculation is set to Power, Speed → Torque because power and speed are known inputs.

12. In the Material Values area, check the boxes to enable material selection for Gear 1 and Gear 2. Choose 37Cr4 with a face-hardened heat treatment for Gear 1 and 30CrMoV6 4 for Gear 2.

13. In the Loads area, enter **7.5 kW** for the power and **260 rpm** for the speed.

14. Set Required Life to **15000 hr**.

15. Click the Factors button to change load and lubrication parameters. The only modification you will make in this dialog box is to the Kinematic diagram of your gear. Use the slider to select the diagram, as shown in Figure 11.26. This diagram corresponds best with the gearbox situation.

FIGURE 11.26
Kinematic diagram of the gear set

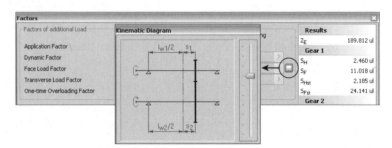

16. Click OK in the Kinematic Diagram dialog box and again in the Factors dialog box to return to the Spur Gears Component Generator dialog box. Then click Calculate.

You will notice that you exceed the safety factors for pitting and tooth breakage, as shown in Figure 11.27. To avoid breakage, you can make your gears stronger by making them wider.

17. On the Design tab, change the facewidth of Gear 1 to **60 mm** and the facewidth of Gear 2 to **58 mm**.

18. In the Advanced Options of the Calculation tab (click the >> button to access these options), change the Contact Safety Factor value of 1.2 to a less cautious factor of 1.0 and click the Calculation button to see if this design complies, as indicated in Figure 11.28. You can then click OK to build the gears.

Optionally, you can finish off the Gear 1 by adding a couple of cylindrical extrusions and chamfers to the Spur Gear 1 part so that it fits nicely between the two ball bearings. You can also make a 60 mm hole in Gear 4 so that it can slide over the shaft of Gear 1. Figure 11.29 shows the smaller Gear 1, while Gear 4 has been made invisible.

Gear design in Inventor is limited to one pair of gears at a time. When designing a gear train of five helical gears, you will have to perform three different gear set calculations and make sure you use the same units in each set.

FIGURE 11.27

The gear calculator indicates there's a risk of pitting or breakage for this design.

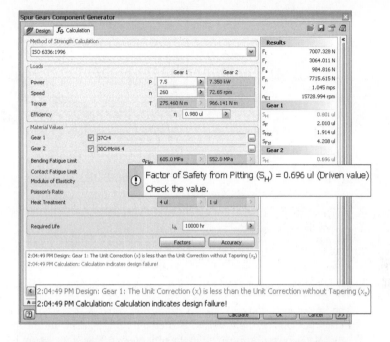

FIGURE 11.28

Gear calculation indicating compliance after changing the width and safety factor

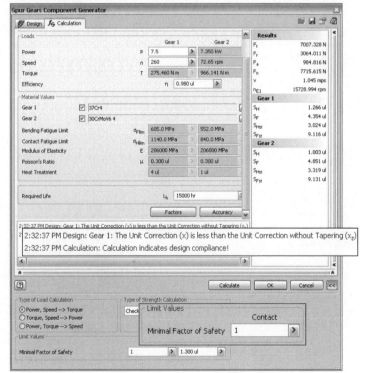

FIGURE 11.29
Finished Gear 1

Flexibility is turned on by default if you specify the Cylindrical Faces when the gear sub-assembly is designed. If you create the gears before you design the shafts or housing, then the gears are not marked flexible when you place them. If you want the gears to rotate, you can right-click on the subassembly in the browser and select Flexible.

Key Connections

The Key Connection and Spline Connection generators are typically used to fasten gears on shafts. In the previous example, you constructed a spur gear set, but the movement of the spur gear set is not yet driven or connected to the other gears. Therefore, you will use keys to make a rigid connection between Spur Gear 1 and Gear 4 of Gear Set 2 while trying to solve your design challenge. To do this, connect the gear on the shaft with a key connection, and make sure that the connection does not break for a given speed (260 rpm) and given power transmission (7.5 kW).

Follow these steps using the Key Connection Generator:

1. On the Get Started tab, click the Open button.

2. Browse for the file named mi_11a_007.iam located in the Chapter 11 directory of the Mastering Inventor 2011 folder, and click Open.

3. Activate the view representation called Gears. Make Gear Set:2 and Spur Gear:1 flexible by right-clicking on them in the browser and selecting Flexible. Verify that you can freely rotate Gear 1 around the axis of the bore hole in Gear 4. Figure 11.30 shows Gear 1 and Gear 4.

FIGURE 11.30
Gear 4 on the
left and Gear 1
on the right

4. Start the Key Connection Generator from the Power Transmission panel on the Design tab. In the Key area, confirm that the default key type is ISO 2491A. If another key type is selected, click in the field to display the list of keys from Content Center. Change No. Of Keys from 1 to **3**.

5. In the Shaft Groove area, confirm that the Groove With Rounded Ends type is selected. Select the Red cylindrical face of Gear 1 as Reference 1 and the Green end face of Gear 1 as Reference 2. A preview of the keys displays on the model.

6. In the Hub Groove area, select the Blue face of Gear 4 as Reference 1 and any circular edge of Gear 4 as Reference 2.

7. Based on these selections, the Key Connection Generator updates with an 18 mm × 7 mm × 50 mm key. You need a 63 mm long key, which can be selected from the drop-down list in the Key area. Only valid lengths from Content Center are displayed.

8. In the Select Objects To Generate area, confirm that the Key, Shaft Groove, and Hub Groove buttons are selected. Depending on your parts, the shaft or the gear may already have a groove.

9. Click OK to generate the Key and modify the Gears.

The Key Connection Generator selects an orientation based on the shaft. If you want a specific orientation, select a work plane on the shaft or gear. You can only select planes in the components or in their parent assemblies. No other planes can be selected.

You can change the angle of the first key relative to the orientation plane by dragging the red single-sided arrow or by double-clicking on it and entering a value, as shown in Figure 11.31.

FIGURE 11.31
Using single-sided arrow to set the angular orientation

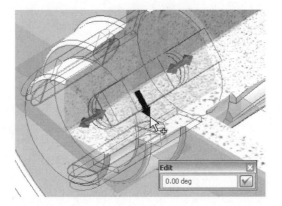

USE THE ARROWS TO CHANGE THE KEY

The key generator preview has three sets of arrows to control the size and location of the key. The single arrow controls the angular orientation, one pair of arrows controls the linear offset, and the other pair controls the length. You can manually drag the arrows or double-click on them to display an edit field.

Your design dialog box should now look like in Figure 11.32.

Before you click OK to generate the keys, you want to make sure that your design withstands the speed (260 rpm) and power (7.5 kW) you set forth. Enter the speed and power in their respective fields, and select surface-hardened steel for the key material. Leave the loading conditions at their default values in the Joint Properties panel. When you run the calculation, your design is considered to be safe, according to Figure 11.33.

Figure 11.34 shows a cross section of the completed key connection.

FIGURE 11.32
Defining three keys
on a gear shaft

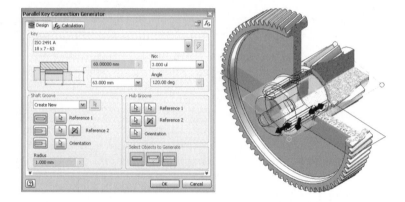

FIGURE 11.33
Key calculation on
a gear shaft

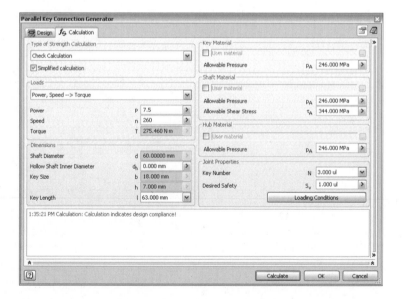

FIGURE 11.34
Completed key
connection

Shaft Generator

The Shaft Generator has a different workflow than other generators. A shaft is designed by adding sections together to come up with the final shaft. You can build a shaft independently, or you can select references in the model to help define the sizes of the sections. This workflow parallels shaft functionality. Each section of a shaft serves a purpose, whether it is locating a bearing or supporting a load.

The design challenge here is to design a shaft that holds the output gear so that it withstands the forces and bending moments generated by the driving gear while lifting a load of 2 tons (20 kN).

Follow these steps to design the shaft:

1. On the Get Started tab, click the Open button.

2. Browse for the file named mi_11a_009.iam located in the Chapter 11 directory of the Mastering Inventor 2011 folder, and click Open.

3. Start the Shaft Generator from the Power Transmission panel of the Design tab, and click in the graphics window to temporarily place the shaft.

4. The four buttons in the Placement section specify the exact location of the shaft. If the shaft is the first component, you can skip the precise placement. For this example, click the first button and select a cylindrical surface (such as one of the yellow ones) to define the axis. The next button is automatically enabled, and you select an inside surface to define the start of the shaft (such as the Green face).

5. Next, select the work plane to define the orientation. If the shaft preview extends outside the housing, click the Flip Side button.

6. The default shaft consists of four sections. Delete the first three sections by clicking on the section, either in the list or in the graphics window, and clicking the X icon on the right side of the segment. Your assembly should look like Figure 11.35.

Two sets of arrows are now visible on the shaft. The thin RGB arrows on the shaft depict the X, Y, and Z directions as usual and cannot be dragged. The thicker arrows, however, can be dragged.

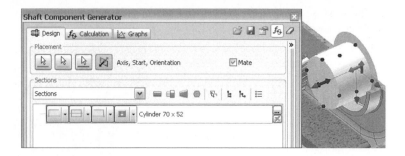

Dragging the thick double-sided red arrow changes the length of the active shaft segment, and dragging the red dots allows you to change the diameter (in Figure 11.35, above, the first segment is active). You can also enter the diameter and length values manually by clicking the… (ellipsis) icon (or double-clicking the segment row in the dialog box) and collect the dimensions by measuring the surrounding geometry.

Dragging the thick blue arrow allows you to change the orientation of the shaft. Dragging the thick green arrow offsets the end of the shaft from the housing. Note that by default the Mate icon is checked, indicating that the shaft will be constrained to the housing.

Every segment has four sets of drop-down icons. The second set defines the overall shape of the segment, and the other icons add detail such as chamfers, fillets, grooves, reliefs, wrench flats, threads, and keyways. Figure 11.36 shows the fourth drop-down set.

FIGURE 11.36
The four icon sets
that define the
geometry of a
segment

In these steps, you will create the shaft segments:

7. Double-click the green arrow at the end of the shaft and set the offset to **0.5 mm**.

8. Change the size of the first segment to **60 mm × 78.5 mm**, as shown in Figure 11.37. You can double-click the segment field to display a dialog box, or you can use the controls in the graphics window. Add a **0.5 mm** chamfer to the segment by using the first set of drop-down icons.

9. Add four more cylindrical segments to the shaft to accommodate the future bearings and the output gear. Right-click below the section and select Sections ➢ Insert Cylinder from the context menu. Change the size of each segment by measuring the distance in the housing and diameters of the openings. Here are the dimensions of the four extra segments, as shown in Figure 11.38:

68 mm × 64 mm

75 mm × 36.5 mm

80 mm × 20 mm

78 mm × 46 mm

FIGURE 11.37
Changing the size
of the first segment

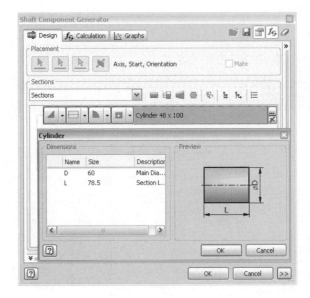

FIGURE 11.38
Geometry of shaft
with five segments

You have now created the geometry of the shaft so that it fits nicely within the confines of the gearbox, but does it also satisfy the load requirements?

10. To find out the forces and moments that are at play on the output gear, click OK in the Shaft Generator and create the shaft.

11. Right-click on the Spur Gears subassembly and choose Edit Using Design Accelerator. Click the Enables/Disables Calculation button (in the top-right corner of the dialog box) to enable the Calculation tab on the Spur Gears component.

12. Click the Calculate button and consult the calculation results by clicking the Results button on the Calculation tab. From the results (shown in Figure 11.39), you learn that the radial force on the shaft on the output gear location is 3064 N, the tangential force is 7007 N, and the axial force is 984 N.

13. Click Cancel to close the dialog box.

FIGURE 11.39
Load results of the output gear

☐ **Loads**

		Gear 1	Gear 2
Power	P	7.500 kW	7.350 kW
Speed	n	260.00 rpm	72.65 rpm
Torque	T	275.460 N m	966.141 N m
Efficiency	η	0.980 ul	
Radial Force	F_r	3064.011 N	
Tangential Force	F_t	7007.328 N	
Axial Force	F_a	984.816 N	
Normal Force	F_n	7715.615 N	
Circumferential Speed	v	1.045 mps	
Resonance Speed	n_{E1}	15728.994 rpm	

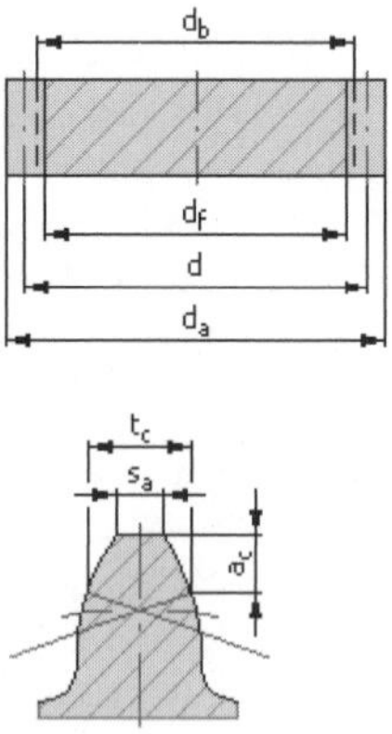

Now that you know the forces, you can start the shaft calculation:

1. Right click on the shaft in the browser or graphics window and select Edit Using Design Accelerator. Click the Calculation tab and select the green dot in the middle of section 2 in the 2D preview or in the graphics window.

2. Select Loads from the Loads/Support drop-down list. The available load types are shown in Figure 11.40; they are radial force, axial force, continuous load, bending moment, torque, and common load. Select the down arrow, which is the first load icon.

FIGURE 11.40
The six different load types

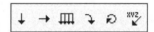

The radial force on the gear translates into a force in the X direction on the shaft. Likewise, the tangential force on the gear will result in a force in the Y direction on the shaft situated in the center of segment 2, which is the segment on which the output gear will sit. By clicking the … button on the force in the dialog box or by double-clicking the force arrow in the graphics window, you can change the Forces option to Forces in X and Y Axes.

3. Enter the Force in X axis = **3064 N** and the Force in Y axis = **7007 N**. See also Figure 11.41. You can now delete the default radial force on segment 1.

FIGURE 11.41
Entering the radial and tangential forces and positioning supports for the shaft

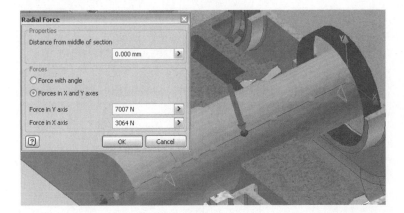

Here are a couple of tips for navigating around the shaft preview. The force arrow can be dragged along the shaft so that it snaps to one of the green hotspots. The green hotspots depict the center and the extremities of the segments and are associative to any shaft geometry change. The blue hotspot depicts the active hotspot (any load or support that is added will be added to the *active* hotspot). So, it is extremely important to position your blue dot in the right location prior to adding loads or supports!

The force arrows can be reconnected to the green hotspots by double-clicking the arrow and entering a zero distance. When you hold down the Ctrl key, you can rotate the force vector to change its angle.

Next, you add the rest of the forces.

4. Add a **−94 8 N** axial force to the center of section 2.

5. Add a torque of **966 Nm** to section 2 and a torque of **−966 Nm** to section 5. The torques must be equal and opposite, so the torque value for section 5 is preset to −966 Nm. Torque is shown with two circular arrow glyphs that are pointing in opposite directions, as illustrated in Figure 11.42.

The shaft will also undergo some bending because of the axial force on the output gear. Determining the value of the bending moment is relatively simple:

$$Bending\ moment = axial\ force\ on\ output\ gear \times \frac{pitch\ diameter\ of\ output\ gear}{2}$$

FIGURE 11.42
Adding torque
and axial force
to the shaft

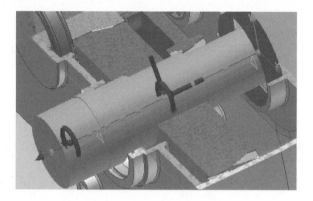

The value of the pitch diameter can be found once again in the gear calculation results table (274.673 mm) of Figure 11.40.

6. Enter a bending moment value along the x-axis of **948 N*274.673 mm/2** on segment 2, as shown in Figure 11.43.

FIGURE 11.43
Adding a bending
moment to
the shaft

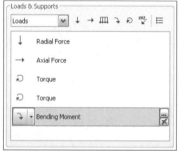

7. Finally, you add to segment 5 the actual load that the shaft will have to provide (**20 kN**). The load is shown as the arrow on the left pointing down in Figure 11.44.

FIGURE 11.44
Adding a 2-ton
load completes
the load
conditions.

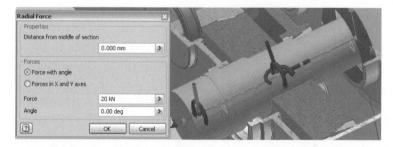

8. Select Supports from the Loads/Support drop-down list. Double-click the Free support and change the offset to **10 mm**. Select the hotspot in the middle of section 4 and add a Fixed support. Delete the default Fixed support.

To complete this exercise, inspect several types of graphs on the Graphs tab to see whether stresses remain within reasonable limits. With a 29.2 MPa total stress, as shown in Figure 11.45, this design is considered to be safe.

9. Click OK after reviewing the graphs to close the dialog box.

FIGURE 11.45
Reduced stress
graph of the shaft

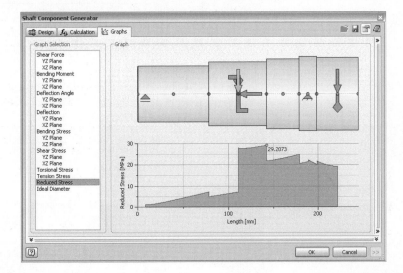

Cam Generator

Inventor has a Linear Cam Generator, a Disc Cam Generator, and a Cylindrical Cam Generator. For the benefit of this exercise, you will use the Disc Cam Generator only.

The challenge in this exercise is to design the camshaft of a four-stroke gas engine: design a camshaft that opens the inlet (and outlet valve) over a distance of 0.7 mm during ¼ of the full-cycle period. The engine runs at 1000 rpm.

Before you dive into the cam design, we'll point out several important things you need to know about the cam generator:

◆ The updates in the Design tab window are not automatic. You will have to click the Calculate button to update the graph after a change has been made.

◆ When hovering over the graph, the tool tip will give intermediate values.

◆ By default, there are two segments in the cam graph. You can add segments by clicking the Add Before or Add After button. Click the Delete button to delete segments. You are not editing all segments all the time. The segment number that is shown in the Actual Segment drop-down is the active segment. All edits will affect only the active or actual segment.

◆ The YZ origin plane of the Disc Cam component corresponds with the 0-degree angle of the graph. This is important to know when you later in the design add Angular constraints to this YZ plane to correctly orient the cam on the shaft.

◆ The start plane of the cam is the plane in which the cam profile sketch is created. The generator extrudes the sketch perpendicular to this start plane to obtain the cam.

◆ In the cam dialog box, you can superpose multiple graphs (torque, pressure, and so on). Figure 11.46 shows the icons for the different graph types. Each graph has its own color. For a disc cam, the x-axis of the graph goes from 0 to 360 degrees. For a linear cam, the x-axis represents the length. The vertical axis has no units because all the different cam parameters can be displayed simultaneously on the same graph. This would otherwise result in a ton of different units on the same axis.

FIGURE 11.46
Icons for different graph types

Now let's return to our exercise. To work correctly during the four phases of the Otto cycle, ideally our valves would have to work according to the diagram in Figure 11.47.

FIGURE 11.47
Lift vs. camshaft angle

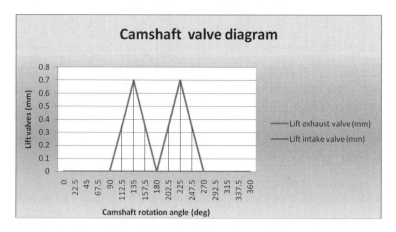

The question is how to follow this ideal diagram as closely as possible within the laws of physics. That is where the Inventor's Disc Cam Generator comes in handy.

1. On the Get Started tab, click Open.

2. Browse for the file named mi_11a_011.iam in the Chapter 11 folder.

SECTIONING OF SHAFT PARTS

You will note that the bearings and the shaft are not sectioned in this view representation. Shafts and fasteners typically do not get sectioned in technical drawings. If you still want to section the shaft in the assembly, you can do this by checking the Participate In Assembly And Drawing Sections check box in the Modeling tab of the document settings of the shaft part inside the shaft assembly.

---

3. Start the Disc Cam Generator from the Power Transmission panel of the Design tab.

4. Click the Cylindrical Face button and select the (red) camshaft.

5. Click the Start Plane button and select the side of the first raised section on the shaft. Note that because the assembly is sectioned you need to select the face on the un-sectioned side. In this case you can also select the Yellow face of the engine case, as both are in the same plane.

6. In the Cam area, enter **2.15 mm** for Basic Radius and **2 mm** for Cam Width.

7. In the Follower area, enter **0.5 mm** for Roller Radius and **0.4 mm** for Roller Width.

The cam angle versus lift data is entered in the Actual Segment area. You select the particular segment from the drop-down list at the top of the area, and enter the data.

8. Confirm that the Actual Segment drop-down is set to segment 1. This segment is part of the base radius, so you are going to set Lift At End to **0.00 mm**.

9. Change the drop-down list to segment 2. This segment continues the base radius, so you are going to leave the end height at **0.00 mm**.

10. Click Add After to create a new segment 3. This segment will transition from zero to maximum lift. Instead of using the linear transition shown in Figure 11.48, you are going to set Motion Function to **Harmonic (sinusoidal)**. Set Motion End Position to **225 degrees** and Lift At End to **0.7 mm**.

11. Click Add After to create a new segment 4. This segment will transition from maximum to zero lift. Confirm Motion Function is set to Harmonic Sinusoidal. Set Motion End Position to **270 degrees**, and Lift At End to **0.00 mm**.

12. Change the drop-down to segment 5. Confirm that Motion End is **360 degrees** and Lift At End is **0.00 mm**.

CONSIDER THE ORIENTATION OF CAMS

Because the XY plane is the 0-degree point in the generation of the cam, you may want to take this into consideration if you are going to need to make detail drawings of the cam. If the cam is symmetrical, it might be easier to document if you place the point of symmetry at the zero-degree angle.

You can also overlay other graphs like acceleration and torque over the inlet cam shape graph, as shown in Figure 11.49.

A full overview of all calculations and all graphs can be obtained by exporting the results into an HTML-formatted report by clicking the Results icon in the top-right corner.

13. Click the Calculation tab.

14. The camshaft rotates at half the crankshaft speed, so 1000/2 = 500 rpm. In the Cycle Data area, confirm that Speed is selected and enter **500 rpm**.

FIGURE 11.48
Inlet cam shape

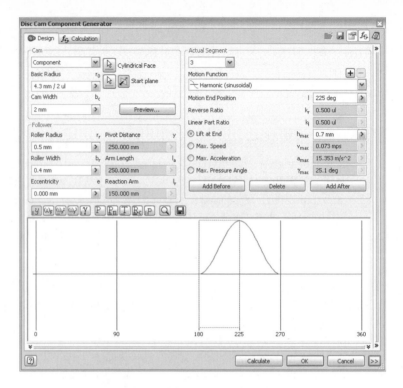

FIGURE 11.49
Inlet cam shape
with acceleration
and speed overlays

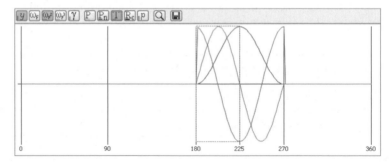

15. In the Follower Loads area, enter **1 N** as the Force On Roller. Confirm that the Accelerated Weight is 0.01 kg. Enter **0.544 N/mm** for Spring Rating, or spring constant k. Both the spring force and spring constant will be calculated in the next section of the chapter.

16. Set Cam Material and Follower Material to **Steel SAE 5130**. This material has an allowable pressure of **900 MPa**, which is 50% higher than the calculated maximum pressure.

17. Click OK to generate the Cam.

Figure 11.50 shows the calculation values and results.

FIGURE 11.50

Cam material chosen to meet maximum pressure

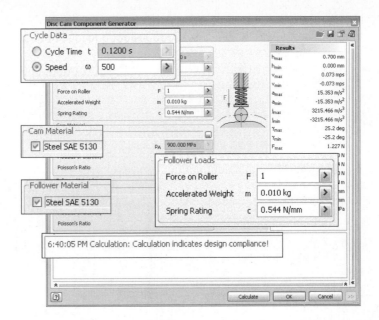

You could easily copy the Inlet cam and rename the copy to Exhaust Cam, but you would not have any Design Accelerator edit capability on the copy. An alternative and far better method is to use Design Accelerator templates. Most Design Accelerators have a Save icon at the top of the dialog box, and this allows you to create a template file. This is a small file in XML format that allows the reuse of all design and calculation parameters of a previous calculation in subsequent calculations.

You export the Inlet cam parameters in a file called harmonic.xml and start a new Cam Component Generator dialog box. In this dialog box, you import the harmonic.xml template (use the icon that looks like an open folder), remove the first segment, and reduce the angles of the remaining segments by 90 degrees. Figure 11.51 shows the completed lift graph of the exhaust cam.

FIGURE 11.51

Exhaust cam lift

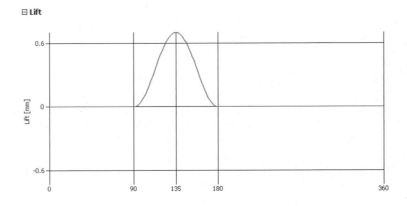

When the piston is placed at its top position (ignition), the two cams are mounted and oriented on the shaft in the position, as shown in Figure 11.52. Use Angular Mate constraints between the origin planes of the two cams and then between the origin plane of one of the cams and the origin plane of the shaft to accomplish the correct 90-degree angular shift between the inlet cam and exhaust cam so that the intake phase correctly follows the exhaust phase. This might require some experimentation. You can simulate the entire Otto cycle by opening the file called mi_11a_077.iam and driving the constraint called Drive Me found by expanding the Origin folder of the top-level assembly. If you have problems finding the right constraints, use the Modeling view mode in the assembly browser to group them.

FIGURE 11.52
Position of cams at
the ignition point

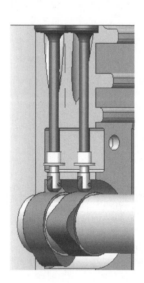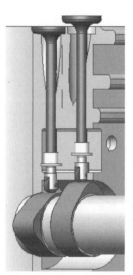

Spring Generator

Inventor can generate four spring types:

- Compression springs

- Extension springs

- Torsion springs

- Belleville springs

The following steps will illustrate how to use compression springs to generate the springs that allow you to keep the valves closed. For this exercise, you will use a single cylinder four-stroke engine assembly similar to the previous exercise.

1. Click Open on the Get Started tab.

2. Browse to the file called mi_11a_012.iam in the Chapter 11 folder.

3. The browser is set to Modeling view, so all of the constraints are in a folder at the top of the browser instead of being nested under the components. Find the Drive Me constraint and confirm that the value is 0.0 degrees.

4. Measure the distance between the Red face on the valve bushing and the Blue face on the crankcase. The result, shown in Figure 11.53, is the minimum working load length of the spring.

FIGURE 11.53
Determining the minimum load spring length

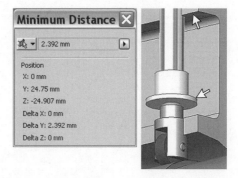

5. Start the Compression Spring Generator from the Spring panel on the Design tab.

6. In the Placement area, click the Axis button and select the valve stem. The Start Plane button is automatically enabled, so select the Red face of the valve bushing. A preview is displayed, but the default spring values are much too large for this application.

7. Confirm that Installed Length is set to **Min. Load**.

8. In the Spring Wire area, set Wire Diameter to **0.15 mm**.

9. In the Spring Start and Spring End areas, set Closed End Coils to **1**, Transition Coils to **1**, and Ground Coils to **0.5**.

10. In the Spring Length area, confirm that Length Inputs is set to L0, n → t. Enter **3.5 mm** for Loose Spring Length, which is considerably larger than the Minimum Working Load Length value of 2.392 mm, so the spring preload will keep the valve seated. Enter **6** for the number of active coils.

11. In the Spring Diameter area, set Diameter to Inner and enter **1 mm**. The geometric inputs are shown in Figure 11.54.

If you clicked Calculate, you would get impossible values for the minimum load length or pitch. This is because you did not define all load conditions yet, and so far, you have no idea if the spring you are designing meets the requirements for forces and stresses. To determine this, you will enter the working conditions for the spring on the Calculation tab.

12. Click the Calculation tab. In the Spring Strength Calculation area, select Work Forces Calculation from the drop-down list.

13. The spring dimensions are carried over from the Design tab, so you just need to enter the working dimensions for the spring. In the Assembly Dimensions area, select H, $L_1 \rightarrow L_8$ from the drop-down list. The Min. Load Length is carried over from the Design tab. Enter **0.7 mm**, the cam lift, for the Working Stroke value. Enter a nominal value of **2.39 mm** for the Working Load Length value.

FIGURE 11.54
Working load state of the compression string

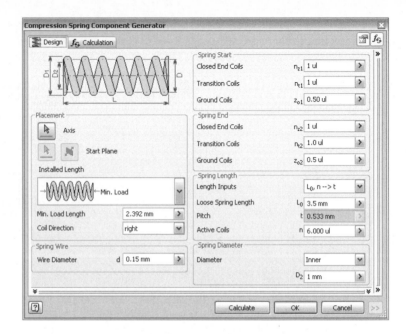

14. In the Spring Material area, select Heat Treated Wire Carbon Steel.

15. Click Calculate. If you look at the calculation results in Figure 11.55, you will see that the Max. Load is 0.984 N, which is satisfactory for this design, and the maximum torsional stress of 854 MPa is less than the material limit of 972 MPa.

16. Click OK to create the spring.

FIGURE 11.55
Compression spring force calculation with load lengths as input

The Spring Generator automatically adds a Mate constraint between the spring axis and the inlet valve axis. You can now view the spring as it will be when the valve is open and closed by editing the spring and changing the Installed Length setting from Min. Load to Max. Load. You finally make a copy of the spring so that you can put the copy around the outlet valve. This concludes the compression spring design. Figure 11.56 shows both valve springs, one set at the minimum load and the other at the maximum load.

FIGURE 11.56
Springs in minimum and maximum load positions

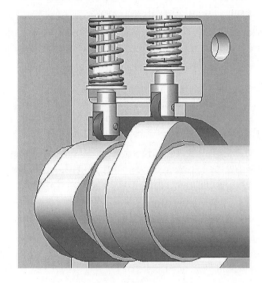

SPRING ANIMATION

It is convenient to use the Spring Generators because they simplify and speed up the design process. However, they remain a fixed length when the mechanism moves, which causes a problem in animations. If you need to create an animation, you can manually create a second spring and make it adaptive. If you want to see an animated version of the springs, open the file named mi_11a_079.iam. In this assembly there is a LOD representation called Simplified Springs that you can activate. This LOD has the more complex Design Accelerator–generated springs suppressed and has a set of simpler adaptive springs unsuppressed. The simpler springs are made with the Coil tool. You can drive the Drive Me constraint, and the simplified springs will compress during the animation. The second spring is set to Phantom so it doesn't impact the BOM. Although generally not required for standard design work, this approach can be useful when creating animations in Inventor Studio.

The Bottom Line

Use Inventor's Design Accelerators   Design Accelerators and Design Generators allow you to rapidly create complex geometry and the associated calculations that verify the viability of your design.

> **Master It**   Your design needs a bolted connection, but you are not certain about the number of bolts to use to ensure a proper connection.

Use Inventor's Design Calculators   Design Calculators do not create any geometry, but they permit you to store the calculations in the assembly and repeat the calculation with different input values at a later time.

> **Master It**   You need to calculate the size of a weld between two plates to withstand a certain lateral force.

Understand the interaction of these tools with Content Center   Some of the generators use content center, while others create custom geometry.

> **Master It**   You receive an error when you try to specify fasteners for a Bolted Connection.

Develop best practices for using these tools   In this chapter, you learned how to use Design Accelerators in the best possible way by providing best practices and tips and tricks concerning the use of templates, exploring the benefits of using a particular type of calculation or connection method for a given scenario, and showing how to select the right material to do the job.

> **Master It**   You need to design a camshaft to activate an inlet valve that needs to respect a specific lift-over-time graph. You also want to reuse the design and slightly modify it for other similar cams like the exhaust valve.

> **Master It**   You want to design a compression spring that operates within very strict dimensional limitations and find a spring material that also satisfies the load requirements.

> **Master It**   Your design needs a gear transmission between two shafts with a predefined position, and you want the gears to be separate components that need to be connected to the shaft.

Chapter 12

Documentation

At any point in your design process, you could choose to begin documenting your design. Although creating drawings, exploded views, and animations traditionally was something that had to wait until the design was fully complete, there are no such restrictions in Inventor. You can start to develop an annotated 2D drawing or a presentation file at any point in your process. It is recommended, however, that you start documenting as late in the design as possible for more predictable results in the documentation environments.

The ultimate goal of this chapter is to illustrate how you can use the Drawing Manager and presentation environments in Inventor to generate both traditional 2D annotated drawings and animated assembly instructions. Once complete, you can output your documentation in a variety of file formats, including DWF and PDF.

In this chapter, you will learn how to:

◆ Create an exploded assembly view by creating a presentation

◆ Create and maintain drawing templates, standards, and styles

◆ Generate 2D drawing views of parts, assemblies, and presentations

◆ Annotate drawing views of your model

Working in the Presentation Environment

Presentations are generally used to document how an assembly model is put together. Your end result could be as simple as a static explosion that you'll use to generate a 2D view in a drawing or a dynamic video where a design is assembled or disassembled through animation.

When you first create a new presentation file, you'll find the environment looks similar to the other part and assembly modeling environments, but it has a significantly reduced set of tools. The 3D navigation tools detailed earlier in this book (Orbit and ViewCube), as well as the browser, are used in presentations as well as in the 3D modeling environments. In the following pages, you will create a basic exploded assembly and explore how to create tweaks, animations, and assembly instructions.

Creating a Basic Explosion

In the following sections, you will take a look at the basics of creating a presentation from an assembly file. This includes accessing an IPN template file, creating an IPN view (explosion), and creating linear tweaks. You'll start with creating a presentation file from a template and then choosing an assembly to explode. Before you begin, ensure that you have loaded the tutorial files.

Also, be sure to set the Mastering Inventor 2011 project active if it is not already. From within Inventor, close any open files and then proceed as follows:

1. On the Get Started tab, click Projects.

2. In the Projects dialog box, click the Browse button.

3. In the Choose Project File dialog box, browse to the Mastering Inventor 2011 folder, select the Mastering Inventor 2011.ipj file, and click Open.

4. Note that the Mastering Inventor 2011 project is denoted as being the active project with a check mark.

ACCESSING AN IPN TEMPLATE

You create presentation files by using an .ipn template and then referencing an existing assembly. To create this presentation, start with the Standard (mm) .ipn template:

1. On the Get Started tab, click the New button.

2. In the New File dialog box, select the Metric tab, and choose the Standard (mm) .ipn template.

3. Click OK.

CREATING AN IPN VIEW

The first step in creating an assembly explosion is referencing an assembly. A presentation file can reference only one assembly file at a time, but the assembly can be used to generate as many explosions as you might need to properly document your design. For example, you may create one explosion to be used as a 2D drawing view and another explosion to be used as an animation. You may also choose to explode each subassembly in its own explosion. Walk through the following steps to create an assembly explosion:

1. On the Presentation tab, click the Create View button.

2. In the Select Assembly dialog box, shown in Figure 12.1, browse for the file named mi_12a_001.iam located in the Chapter 12 directory of the Mastering Inventor 2011folder, and click Open.

FIGURE 12.1
Select Assembly
dialog box

3. Click the Options button to specify which view, position, or LOD representation of the selected assembly you want loaded into the presentation environment.

4. Set the view representation to Default, and leave the positional and LOD representations set to Master.

5. Click the Associative check box to ensure that the presentation view will update if the assembly view representation is updated.

6. Click OK.

If you have a relatively small assembly and it was modeled with a full and robust set of assembly constraints, you may choose to create an automatic explosion in the Select Assembly dialog box and then make minor modifications to meet your needs. Otherwise, use the manual method.

7. Ensure that the Manual option is selected.

8. Click OK.

9. Locate Explosion1 in the Model browser, and click the plus sign to expand it so you can see a list of all the components in the assembly.

CREATING LINEAR TWEAKS

You'll now see the selected assembly in your presentation graphics area. It's time to start adding tweaks to explode the assembly. A *tweak* is simply a stored movement vector for a selected set of one or more components. You can define both linear and rotational tweaks. In the next steps, you'll create a linear tweak by first establishing a move direction, then choosing a component to move, and finally setting the move distance:

1. Click the Tweak Components button on the Presentation tab.

2. In the resulting dialog box (shown in Figure 12.2), ensure the Direction button is enabled.

3. Select the yellow face of the faceplate to define the direction of the tweak.

FIGURE 12.2
Tweak Component
dialog box

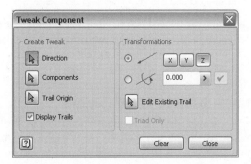

Note that the Components button in the dialog box is now enabled and ready for you to select the component(s) to be moved.

4. Select the component with the yellow face (FACE PLATE) and all four of the components named CAP SCREW. Do this either in the graphics area or in the browser.

MORE ON SELECTING COMPONENTS

If you select extra components by accident, simply hold down the Ctrl key and click them again to remove them from your selection set. Subassemblies must be selected from the Model browser rather than the graphics area, unless you change your selection filter.

---

5. Next, specify the tweak vector by choosing the Z button in the Transformations area of the dialog box.

6. Click somewhere in an empty space of the graphics area, and drag your mouse pointer in the positive Z direction (pull toward the lower left of the screen).

8. Note the tweak distance reported in the dialog box as you drag. Enter **100 mm** in the dialog box.

9. Click the green check mark to set the distance.

10. Hold down the Ctrl key and click the FACE PLATE component to deselect it. Check the browser to ensure it is deselected.

11. You'll create a tweak for just the cap screws. This time, rather than clicking in the graphics window, click the triad to select the Z vector, and drag the triad to approximately 75 mm. This simply demonstrates that the triad can be used to tweak components, allowing you to switch directions easily, as opposed to using the dialog box to do this.

12. Enter **30mm** in the dialog box, and click the green check mark to set the distance. By doing this you have set the tweak to 30 mm even though the initial drag value was approximately 75 mm. Clicking the check mark sets the final tweak value.

13. Click Close.

14. On the Model browser, click the filter button ▼ and choose Tweak View from the list.

15. You should see the two tweaks just created, listed in the browser.

Once you create a tweak or tweaks based on one set of inputs, you can continue to tweak additional components with new inputs by first clicking the Clear button without dismissing the dialog box. Now that you have created a basic linear tweak, you'll explore how to create more advanced tweaks in the next section.

Creating Advanced Presentations

In the following sections, you will look at some of the more advanced functions associated with creating presentations, particularly for use as 3D animations. You will explore how to create rotational tweaks, how to modify tweak trails, and how to group, reorder, and animate tweaks. You'll also discover how to create assembly instructions and publish animations and assembly instructions to a lightweight DWF file that can be easily shared.

CREATING ROTATIONAL TWEAKS

You can add rotational tweaks in much the same way as you created the linear tweaks, though rather than indicating the x-, y-, or z-axis for linear direction, the x-, y-, or z-axis is used as an axis of rotation, and the tweak value is entered as degrees of rotation rather than a linear distance.

1. Continuing where you left off in the previous section, click the Tweak Components button on the Presentation tab.

2. In the resulting dialog box, ensure the Direction button is enabled.

3. Select the shaft of one of the cap screws.

4. With the Components button enabled, select the same cap screw.

5. In the Transformations area of the dialog box, ensure the Z axis button is selected.

6. Switch the radio button to select the rotational option rather than the linear one.

7. Enter **6.25*360** in the input box (for six and a quarter revolutions).

8. Click the green check mark to set the rotation.

9. Note the tweak listed in the browser.

10. Click Clear.

11. Repeat steps 3 through 7 for each cap screw.

12. This completes a basic rotational tweak, so click Close to continue.

If you're tweaking only one component at a time and you're comfortable with the selection, orientation, and direction behavior, you can establish direction, choose your component, and input the tweak distance all with one mouse click. You can try this with the cyan-colored gib plate.

1. Start the Tweak Component tool.

2. Click the front face of the gib plate, and continue holding the left mouse button while dragging the plate away from the main assembly, and then release the mouse button when you've moved it out approximately 45 mm.

Your presentation should look similar to Figure 12.3. You can close this file without saving changes, as you will open another IPN file to continue in the flowing sections.

UNDERSTANDING TWEAK TRAILS

Trails are added by default. A *trail* is a line (or an arc in the case of a rotation tweak) that is displayed in the graphics area showing the start and endpoints of a particular tweak. By default, the start and endpoints are defined by the three-dimensional geometric center of all the components that are chosen for a tweak. However, an optional fourth step in the tweak creation process is to manually select the tweak points by selecting one or more points on each of your selected components. Here are a few more points to know about trails:

◆ By default, one trail is added per selected component in your tweak.

◆ Deselecting the Show Trails check box when creating tweaks will set the visibility of the tweak trails off.

- You can control the visibility of each tweak trail by expanding the tweak in the Model browser, right-clicking the component name, and choosing Visibility (assuming Tweak View is being used).

- You can control the visibility of trails for each component by right-clicking a component and choosing Hide Trails.

- You can edit a tweak by right-clicking the trail and choosing Edit or by clicking and dragging the endpoint of a tweak trail.

- You can delete a tweak or delete a component from a multiple component tweak by right-clicking the trail and choosing Delete.

- These trails are also visible in drawing views of presentations.

FIGURE 12.3
Creating tweaks

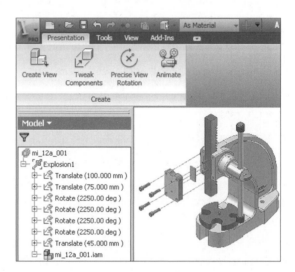

MORE ABOUT TWEAKS

Don't forget that the browser filter controls the way tweaks are listed in the browser. When in the Assembly View, as you create tweaks, a browser node representing that tweak is generated in your browser and nested under the selected components that are part of that tweak. When in the Tweak View, tweaks are listed as line items and the components are nested below them. By selecting the tweak in the browser, you can enter a new movement value.

Create Multiple Views/Explosions

If your assembly is large or complex, consider making several explosions and tweaking only a few components per explosion. You can add explosions by clicking the Create View tool. Each subsequent time the Select Assembly dialog box is shown, a new assembly file *cannot* be specified. You can, however, choose a different view, positional, or LOD representation than your previous explosions.

If the end goal of your presentation is to simply create an explosion that looks good in one or more 2D drawing views, then you already know just about everything you need to know, and you never have to use more than two tools inside the presentation environment. Simply continue adding tweaks as needed.

Save Camera

Before you save your file and move on to creating your drawing, make sure to set your camera view up exactly as you'd like to see it on the page. Use Zoom, Orbit, and the ViewCube in conjunction with the Precise View Rotation feature to get a view that makes things as clear as possible. Then right-click in the graphics area and choose Save Camera. You can use this saved camera to create a view in the 2D drawing. You can also right-click and choose Restore Camera any time you have changed the camera view.

UNDERSTANDING GROUP, REORDER, AND ANIMATE TWEAKS

CERT OBJECTIVE

You can group and reorder tweaks for the purpose of animating components in a presentation. For instance, in the steps in the "Creating a Basic Explosion" section earlier in this chapter, you pulled the cap screws out all at once and then rotated them one at a time. You may want to have these actions separated, reordered, or grouped in order for them to behave correctly when animated. To see how this works, follow these steps:

1. On the Get Started tab, click the Open button.

2. Browse for the file named mi_12a_002.ipn located in the Chapter 12 directory of the Mastering Inventor 20112011 folder, and click Open.

3. If you have zoomed or orbited the assembly, right-click and choose Restore Camera.

4. On the Presentation tab, click the Animate button.

5. In the Animation dialog box, click the >> button (at the bottom right corner) to expand the dialog box so you can view the animation sequence.

6. Click the Play Forward button to animate the tweaks; note how the rotation tweaks just spin in place, and the gibs plate moves out of order.

7. Click the Reset button.

8. In the Animation Sequence area, hold down Ctrl on the keyboard, and select all the rotation tweaks (2250 deg) and all of the 75 mm tweaks.

9. Click the Group button to group these tweaks into a single sequence step. They should all be set as Sequence 2 in the list; if not, select any of the tweaks in the group and use the Move Up or Move Down buttons to reorder.

10. Click the gibs plate and use the Move Up button to change it to sequence step 1.

11. Click the Apply button.

12. Click the Play Forward button to animate the tweaks, and note that the cap screws now rotate and move at the same time.

13. Click Reset and Cancel to exit the Animation dialog box. Note the Cancel button does not undo the changes you just made and should really be labeled Done rather than Cancel.

Although the rotation of the cap screws is still not true to life, you should be able to see that you can create tweaks in any order you choose and then group and reorder them as required later.

CREATING ASSEMBLY INSTRUCTIONS

You can create assembly instructions for a presentation animation to share with a customer, present to a group, or be used by the people on the shop floor. The animations and instructions can be published to a DWF file and viewed with the free Autodesk Design Review application. Follow these steps to explore how to create assembly instructions. You can skip the first two steps if you have the file from the previous exercise open still.

1. On the Get Started tab, click the Open button.

2. Browse for the file named mi_12a_003.ipn located in the Chapter 12 directory of the Mastering Inventor 2011 folder, and click Open.

3. In the Model browser, click the Filter button and choose Sequence View from the list.

4. Locate Explosion2 in the browser, and double-click it to activate it.

CREATING MULTIPLE EXPLOSIONS

Recall that you can create multiple explosions of the same assembly by using the Create View button. Each "view" becomes a separate explosion. You might show the assembly of external housing components in Explosion1 and then use Create View to create a second explosion. In Explosion2, you can turn the visibility of the housing components off and concentrate on just the internal components. Remember, too, that if you have created view or LOD representations to control the visibility of internal and external parts, you can use them when creating the explosion by clicking the Options button.

You can also copy existing explosions by right-clicking on an explosion in the browser and choosing Copy. Then right-click in the IPN file name node (the topmost node) in the browser and choose Paste from the right-click context menu.

---

5. Expand Explosion2 to see that there are two tasks within it.

6. Double-click Task2a to activate it.

7. In the resulting Edit Task And Sequences dialog box, click the Play button at the top.

8. Click Reset when it is done playing.

9. Click the Play button in the middle to play just Sequence1.

10. Click Reset when it is done playing.

11. Enter the following into the Description area for Task2a: **Assemble collar as shown**.

12. Enter **10** in the interval input to speed up the playback of this sequence.

13. Click Apply.

14. Click the Sequence1 Play button to view the faster playback, and click Reset when done.

15. Switch the sequence drop-down from Sequence1 to Sequence2.

16. Note the instructions have been filled out already.

17. Use the ViewCube, the Orbit tool, or your 3D controller to change the camera view so that you can see the ram and the shaft without obstruction. Zoom in as you see fit.

18. Click the Set Camera button.

19. Click the Apply button.

20. Click the Play button at the top to see the entire Task2a play back again. Note the changes in speed and to the camera view you made.

21. Click OK.

Here are a couple of other actions you can take to organize tasks:

Create tasks   When you create tweaks within an explosion, they are initially all created in a single task. To create multiple tasks, use the filter to set the view to Sequence View, and then right-click an explosion and choose Create Task. Then just drag the sequences into the task as needed.

Hide components   You can hide components per sequence by expanding the sequence while in Sequence View and revealing the Hidden folder. Then just select the component from the model tree and drag it up into the Hidden folder. If it lists in the hidden folder of a sequence, that component will not be visible for that particular sequence.

Publishing IPNs to DWF

If you need to share assembly animations and instructions with someone who does not use Inventor, such as the people on the shop floor, you can publish the presentations to a .dwf file:

1. On the Get Started tab, click the Open button.

2. Browse for the file named mi_12a_004.ipn located in the Chapter 12 directory of the Mastering Inventor 2011 folder, and click Open.

3. Click the Inventor button and choose Export ➢ Export to DWF.

4. In the Publish Presentation dialog box, select one of the following:

Express   Static exploded views are published. Bill of materials data, design views, and positional representations are not published.

Complete   The DWF file contains all presentation views, including animations, assembly instructions, and the associated assembly, as well as its design views, positional representations, and BOM.

Custom   You have full control over which animations and assembly instructions are included or excluded, as well as whether to include the assembly, the BOM, and so on.

5. Configure the general options for markup, measure, printing, and password protection.

6. Click Publish.

7. Set the filename and location as you see fit, and choose between DWF and DWFx for the file type.

8. Click Publish.

The key differences between the two DWF file types is that the 2D DWFx can be read by Windows Vista and XP (with Internet Explorer 7 installed) without the need for an extra viewer such as Autodesk Design Review. 3D DWFx and DWF files still require Design Review. Note too that the DWFx file is generally on the order of twice as large.

You can invite vendors and clients as well as the shop floor to download Design Review for free from the Autodesk website.

DISPLAY PUBLISHED FILE IN VIEWER FOR DWF AND PDF

At the bottom of the Publish Presentation dialog box, there is a check box allowing you to choose whether or not the published file will automatically be displayed in the designated viewer application (typically Design Review for DWF files). Be aware that this option also controls whether or not PDF that are generated using Export to PDF are automatically displayed in the designated PDF application. If you'd rather not have Design Review or Adobe Reader open each time you save a DWF or PDF, uncheck this option.

Using the Drawing Manager

Once you have created your 3D design, you can choose to document it with conventional 2D orthographic drawing views and traditional drafting tools. Creating this kind of documentation is done in Inventor's Drawing Manager environment.

These high-level Drawing Manager tasks are discussed in the following sections:

◆ Creating templates and styles

◆ Utilizing drawing resources

◆ Editing styles and standards

◆ Creating drawing views

◆ Annotating part drawings

◆ Creating assembly drawings

◆ Working with sheet-metal drawings

◆ Working with weldment views

◆ Working with iParts and iAssembly drawings

◆ Sharing your drawings outside your workgroup

Creating Templates and Styles

Although several drawing templates are installed with Inventor, it's recommended that before you begin to document your own designs and models, you create your own custom template or templates to best meet your needs. This is because most users need to adhere to a specific set of drafting standards dictated by their company, customer, or vendor specifications. These standards are typically derivatives of one of several international drafting standards such as ANSI, ISO, or DIN. Therefore, Inventor installs with a set of templates and drafting styles configured for the following international standards:

- ANSI (both English and metric units)
- BSI
- DIN
- GB
- GOST
- ISO
- JIS

When creating your own custom template, it is best to start with a standard template that closely meets your requirements and modify it accordingly. Creating templates in the Drawing Manager is not unlike creating templates in other applications. The primary difference being that many applications use a special file format for template files, whereas Inventor uses the same file format, but uses a folder location to designate all files within the template location as templates. As a result, you can use any `.idw` or `.dwg` file as a drawing template; you just need to save it in the template location.

UNDERSTANDING TEMPLATE LOCATIONS

By default, Inventor templates are stored in and accessed from `Program Files\Autodesk\ Inventor 2011\Templates`. The default location is initially set from the Tools tab by clicking the Application Options button and then selecting the File tab and entering a folder location in the Default Templates box. For stand-alone users, consider using this same location for your design projects. If you're part of a networked workgroup, you should create a template folder on a shared network drive and change the default templates path accordingly.

The default template location can be overridden on a per-project basis as well by setting the templates' location in the project file configuration. Keep in mind, if you have a template location set in Application Options and another set in the project file, the project file always takes precedence.

CHOOSING A FILE FORMAT

Prior to Inventor 2008, the `.idw` file format was the only native 2D file type recognized by Inventor. DWG TrueConnect, introduced with Inventor 2008, enables you to use both `.dwg` and `.idw` as valid file formats in Inventor's Drawing Manager.

Using `.dwg` as your file format enables you to open Inventor DWG files in AutoCAD (or an AutoCAD vertical product such as AutoCAD Mechanical) without going through a translation process. Although the data you create natively in Inventor cannot be manipulated directly in AutoCAD, all of the Inventor data can be viewed, measured, and printed using conventional AutoCAD commands.

Choosing .dwg as your default file format allows downstream users of your designs to view the 2D drawing documents in AutoCAD without having to purchase or install Inventor or download the Inventor file viewer. Vendors, customers, or other internal personnel can open the native Inventor DWG file and view, measure, and print the Inventor data, or they can even add AutoCAD data to the file to create a hybrid document that can be viewed quickly and efficiently in either application.

BE AWARE OF FILE SIZE

Although many design departments find the convenience of having their Inventor drawings in .dwg format well worth it, understand that Inventor DWG files will be larger than Inventor IDW files. The difference in size may vary depending upon the content, but differences of up to 3× as large can be common. Save a dozen typical drawing files out as both Inventor DWG and IDW, and compare the sizes yourself to determine which is right for you.

For Inventor users, there is essentially no difference between using .dwg or the traditional .idw file format. The native .dwg file includes a Layer 0 in the layer list and an AutoCAD Blocks folder in Drawing Resources. These are the only noticeable differences between the two file formats. An .idw file can always be saved as an Inventor DWG, and vice versa, without any loss of fidelity or data. If there's a good chance of someone wanting to see a DWG version of your Inventor file, you might consider choosing .dwg as your default file format. Inventor's Task Scheduler enables you to batch convert a set of IDW files into DWG files.

Utilizing Drawing Resources

You should customize three areas of the template to conform to your chosen drafting standards and personal preferences: *Drawing Resources, Document Settings,* and document *Styles and Standards.*

Drawing resources are simply a collection of reusable sketches that are stored in a drawing file. There are four types of drawing resources: sheet formats, borders, title blocks, and sketched symbols. If you've decided to use .dwg as your template format, you'll notice AutoCAD blocks are also managed as Inventor drawing resources.

Drawing resources are accessed from your drawing browser under the Drawing Resources folder, as shown in Figure 12.4. If you expand the Drawing Resources node, you'll see a folder for each of the drawing resource types listed, and contained in each of the subfolders are drawing resource definitions. Double-click any drawing resource to place an instance in your drawing.

You can employ several document management techniques with respect to templates, sheet sizes, borders, and title blocks. Although you could create and maintain separate drawing templates for each sheet size and title block you might need, it's generally recommended that a single drawing template be used to maintain each of these different configurations. In the following sections, you'll take a look at the various drawing resources.

FIGURE 12.4
The Drawing
Resources node
in the drawing
browser

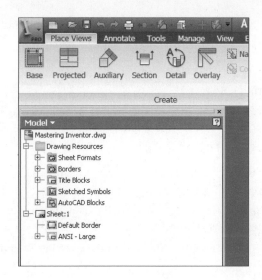

SHEET SIZE

When you start a new drawing from one of the templates installed with Inventor, a border and title block are already present on the sheet, and the sheet is set to a default size. You can change the default sheet size by right-clicking on the sheet in the browser and choosing Edit Sheet from the right-click. For example, if you are using the ANSI (in) template, the default sheet size is C. If you change the sheet size to D, the border on the sheet updates automatically to accommodate the change in sheet size.

To have your templates default to a different size of sheet, follow these steps:

1. On the Get Started tab, click the Open button.

2. Browse to your template location, and open a drawing file (such as Standard.idw)(see the Understanding Template Locations section earlier in this chapter).

3. Right-click the sheet in the browser, and choose Edit Sheet.

4. Click the arrow in the drop-down box, and choose the size or sheet format from the list.

5. Click the Inventor button ![Inventor button] and choose Save (or press Ctrl+S on the keyboard).

Now when you start a new file from the template, this new sheet size will be active.

MULTIPLE SHEETS

If needed, you can add sheets to your template, which is recommended if most of your design documents require more than one sheet. It is recommended that you use caution when creating multiple sheet sets of a sizable number, because performance may suffer, depending upon the size and complexity of the models you are detailing. Be aware too of "putting all of your eggs into one basket" should a file become corrupt or lost. To insert a new sheet into your document, follow these steps:

1. Right-click any blank area on the page, and choose New Sheet (or click the New Sheet button on the Place Views tab).

2. Note that this adds the border and title block and the same size sheet as the active sheet.

3. To switch between sheets, double-click the sheet node in the browser.

CREATING A BORDER

The default border used on the Inventor templates may not meet your needs. To create a new border, follow these steps:

1. Expand the sheet node in the browser.

2. Right-click the border instance, and choose Delete.

Recall that this removes the instance of the border from the sheet. The border definition is still stored in the Borders folder of the Drawing Resources node. To create a new, custom border in your template, follow these steps:

1. In your template file, expand the Drawing Resources node in the browser.

2. Right-click the Borders folder, and choose Define New Border. (You might have the option to choose Define New Zone Border, but you'll use a simple border here to explore the steps required.)

Zone Border   Brings up an input dialog box into which you can specify the number of horizontal and vertical zones, alpha or numeric zone labels, font and font size, as well as margins spacing. A sketch is created from your input automatically.

Border   Creates a sketch with the four corners of the sheet projected in. You can sketch a rectangle to create a simple custom border and use dimensions to specify the margins off the sheet corners. Dimensioning to the sheet corners allows your border to automatically resize to any sheet size, holding the specified margins. Borders can be as simple or complex as required, but the sketch should always be fully constrained.

3. On the Sketch tab, select the Two Point Rectangle tool.

4. Sketch a small rectangle on the screen; ensure that you do not sketch it on the sheet corners.

5. On the Sketch tab, select the Dimension tool.

6. Place dimensions from the corners of your rectangle to the projected corner points of the sheet so that the edges of the rectangle will be **10 mm**.

FORMATTING COLOR AND LINE-WEIGHT IN A BORDER SKETCH

By default, all geometry created in a border is set on a layer named Border. You can change the color and line weight of that layer to modify all the entities of your border, or you can override the properties of individual entities as required. To do the latter, right-click the object you want to modify and select Properties.

---

7. When your border sketch is complete, right-click, and choose Save Border (or use the Finish Sketch button on the Sketch tab).

8. Enter the name of your border definition.

9. Click Save.

10. Look in the border folder of the Drawing Resources node in the browser for your new border definition.

11. Right-click your border, and choose Insert to place an instance of it on the current sheet.

12. If you need to modify the border definition, right-click your border instance or the definition in Drawing Resources, and choose Edit Definition or Edit.

CREATING A TITLE BLOCK

Customizing title blocks is done in much the same way as borders. Title blocks typically contain more text-based information than the border, so the concentration here will be on creating sketch text in this section. There are three common ways of creating a custom title block:

◆ You can use an existing title block originally drawn in AutoCAD.

◆ You can modify a default Inventor title block.

◆ You can create one completely from scratch in Inventor, drawing the line work and inserting the text fields.

In this next section, you will bring in an existing AutoCAD title block and make it intelligent to Inventor. In doing so, you will explore the tools used to create a title block used in the other methods mentioned. Although not required, you should probably first delete the default title block from your sheet before creating a new title block. To do this, follow these steps:

1. From your template file (or any standard Inventor drawing file), expand the sheet node in the browser.

2. Right-click the title block instance, and choose Delete.

3. On the Get Started tab, click the Open button.

4. Browse for the file named mi_12a_033.dwg located in the Chapter 12 directory of the Mastering Inventor 2011 folder. You may need to change the Files Of Type drop-down to see All Files or AutoCAD Drawings (*.dwg) to locate the file.

5. Click the Options button in the Open dialog box.

6. Ensure that Open is selected; otherwise, Inventor will take you to the import options.

7. Click OK.

8. Click Open.

Notice that when you open an AutoCAD drawing in Inventor, you can view and measure the file. You should see a black background, and if you check the browser, you will see that you are viewing the model space of the file.

9. Right-click the title block, and choose Copy.

10. Use the Open Documents tabs at the bottom of the screen to switch back to your template file (or press Ctrl+Tab on the keyboard).

11. On the Drawing Resources Folder in the browser, right-click the Title Blocks folder, and choose Define New Title Block.

12. Right-click in the graphics area, and choose Paste.

13. Click in the middle of the sheet to place the title block.

You'll note the line work is under-constrained and not dimensioned at all. You can take the time to dimension it if you'd like, but because this will become a block, and therefore a static entity, you most likely will not need to do so.

Continue adding intelligence to the text now.

14. Right-click the text field containing CDW, and choose Edit Text.

15. In the Format Text dialog box, select the text, and press Delete on the keyboard.

16. Locate the Type drop-down, and choose Properties – Drawing, as shown in Figure 12.5.

17. Set the Property drop-down to Designer.

18. Click the Add Text Parameter button 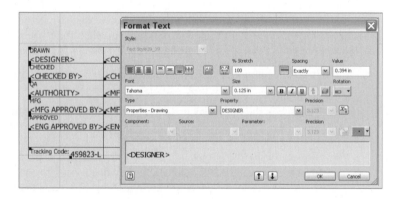 to set the Designer property to the text field.

19. Click OK.

FIGURE 12.5
Customizing the title block

20. Repeat steps 14 through 19 for the date field directly to the right of the field you just edited. Use the Creation Date property instead of the Designer.

21. Right-click and choose Save Title Block (or click the Finish Sketch button on the Sketch tab).

22. Enter a name for the new title block.

23. Look in the Title Block folder of the Drawing Resources node in the browser for your new title block definition.

24. Right-click your title block and choose Insert to place an instance of it on the current sheet.

25. If you need to modify the title block definition, right-click your title block instance or the definition in Drawing Resources, and choose Edit Definition or Edit.

Obviously, you have not configured the entire title block at this point, but before going any further, it is important to understand where the properties you linked to the title block text fields are coming from. You can find these properties in the file iProperties. Follow these steps to change an iProperty in the file and see that change show up in the title block:

1. Click the Inventor button and choose iProperties.

2. Go to the Project tab and change the Designer input to **Test Designer**.

3. Change the Creation Date input to **1/1/ 2011**.

4. Click OK.

Your title block will have updated the two fields automatically based on the iProperty changes you made, demonstrating that you have linked those fields to the iProperties of this particular drawing file. You would continue to configure your title block to retrieve the iProperties needed, until all of the fields are automatically filled out by updating the iProperties. For now, you can close the file you have open without saving changes and continue to the next section to learn more about iProperties.

iProperties

Each Inventor file has its own iProperties allowing you to pull that information into your title block. There are two distinct areas from which you can draw iProperties into your title block: from the drawing file or from the model file.

Table 12.1 lists the standard iProperties available. Each of these can be accessed from the Type drop-down in the Text Format dialog box as described in the previous steps. You'll learn more about iProperties in Chapter 13, "Inventor Tools Overview."

TABLE 12.1: Standard iProperties

FILE IPROPERTIES		
Author	Designer	Mfg Approved Date
Authority	Eng Approval Date	Part Number
Category	Eng Approved By	Project
Checked By	Engineer	Revision Number
Checked Date	Estimated Cost	Status
Comments	Filename	Stock Number
Company	Filename and Path	Subject
Cost Center	Keywords	Title
Creation Date	Manager	Vendor
Description	Mfg Approved By	Weblink
Design Date		

> ### Linking Your Model and Drawing iProperties
>
> Often you will want the iProperties for the model file and drawing file to match. You can use the Copy Model iProperty Settings to have this happen automatically.
>
> To do this, open your drawing template, go to the Tools tab, click Documents Settings, go to the Drawing tab in the dialog box that opens, and click the Copy Model iProperty Settings button at the bottom. You can have some or all of the model properties copied to the drawing.
>
> Note that once copied, the properties do not update automatically when they are changed in the model. To update them, select the Manage tab, and click Update Copied Model iProperties.

Follow these steps to modify a title block so it is pulling information from the model iProperties. You'll note that this title block is calling the model filename iProperty for the drawing title. Most of the other fields are being pulled from the drawing iProperties. The field you will be modifying is static and needs to be set to pull from the model iProperties.

1. On the Get Started tab, click the Open button.

2. Browse for the file named mi_12a_024.idw located in the Chapter 12 directory of the Mastering Inventor 2011 folder.

3. Expand the sheet node in the browser.

4. Right-click the title block instance (named MI_TB_04) in the browser, and choose Edit Definition.

5. Zoom up on the title block, and locate the Part Number area toward the bottom.

6. Right-click the text field showing ###, and choose Edit Text.

7. In the Format Text dialog box, select the text (###), and press Delete on the keyboard.

8. Locate the Type drop-down, and choose Properties – Model.

9. Set the Property drop-down to Part Number.

10. Click the Add Text Parameter button to set the property to the text field.

11. Click OK.

12. Right-click, and choose Save Title Block (or click the Finish Sketch button on the Sketch tab).

13. Click Yes at the Save Edits prompt.

To see the part number update in the title block, you will need to open the model file and change the iProperties of it.

14. Hover your cursor over either of the drawing views on the sheet and then right-click and choose Open (make certain you are not right-clicking on a line or part of the model).

15. In the browser, right-click on the top level node (Arbor_Frame.ipt) and choose iProperties.

16. Select the Project tab and then edit the Part Number field to read **98765**.

17. Click Apply and then OK.

18. Use the Open Documents tabs at the bottom of the screen to switch back to the drawing file.

19. You will see that the title block has read the model part number and displays the change.

Experiment with the title block to understand the way it works with iProperties from the model, and then you can close the file without saving changes.

ICHECK IT ADD-IN FOR INVENTOR

There are several add-ins available that check to ensure that users have not forgotten to fill out required iProperties. One such add-in is *iCheck It* from TaTa Technologies. iCheck It goes far beyond just checking iProperties, however, as it will also check to ensure the file naming convention has been followed, the first sketch of a model is constrained to the origin, that all sketches are fully constrained, that only approved dimension styles are used, and much more. There are over 100 checks that can be defined in all. Visit www.tatatechnologies.com/icheckitinventor to download a 30-day free trial version.

GENERAL FILE PROPERTIES

In addition to iProperties, you can use some other standard file properties to fill out your title block automatically. You can access them from the Type drop-down in the Text Format dialog box just as you did the iProperties. Table 12.2 lists several general properties that can be called into a text field.

TABLE 12.2: Available Properties

PHYSICAL PROPERTIES OF THE MODEL	GENERAL DRAWING PROPERTIES	DRAWING SHEET PROPERTIES	SHEET-METAL FLAT PATTERN PROPERTIES
Area	Number Of Sheets	Sheet Number	Flat Area
Density		Sheet Revision	Flat Length
Mass		Sheet Size	Flat Width
Volume			

Follow these steps to set up the sheet number area of the title block to call on general file properties of the drawing file to automatically fill out the title block:

1. On the Get Started tab, click the Open button.

2. Browse for the file named mi_12a_025.idw located in the Chapter 12 directory of the Mastering Inventor 2011 folder.

3. Expand the sheet node in the browser.

4. Right-click the title block instance (named MI_TB_05), and choose Edit Definition.

5. Zoom up on the title block, and locate the Sheet 1 Of 2 area at the bottom right.

6. Right-click the text field showing ?#?, and choose Edit Text.

7. In the Format Text dialog box, select the text (?#?), and press Delete on the keyboard.

8. Locate the Type drop-down, and choose Drawing Properties. (Note that there is one called Properties – Drawing also, so ensure that you have the correct one.)

9. Set the Property drop-down to Number Of Sheets.

10. Click the Add Text Parameter button to set the Number Of Sheets property to the text field.

11. Click OK.

12. Right-click the text field showing ??, and choose Edit Text.

13. In the Format Text dialog box, select the text (??), and press Delete on the keyboard.

14. Locate the Type drop-down, and choose Sheet Properties.

15. Set the Property drop-down to Sheet Number.

16. Click the Add Text Parameter button to set the Sheet Number property to the text field.

17. Click OK.

18. Right-click, and choose Save Title Block (or click the Finish Sketch button on the Sketch tab).

19. Click Yes at the Save Edits prompt.

Experiment with adding new sheets and reordering the sheets (just drag and drop in the browser) to see how the title block updates, and then you can close the file without saving changes.

PROMPTED ENTRY

You can also create fields in your title block to enter information manually using what is known as a *prompted entry*. However, experienced Inventor users will tell you that prompted entries should be used sparingly for two reasons.

First, information entered into a prompted entry field is stored in the title block and nowhere else. If you need to update the title block for your entire drawing library at some point in the future, you can do so easily with Inventor's Drawing Resource Transfer Wizard, which can swap out old title block definitions with a new one, en masse. (See Chapter 13 for more on this tool.) This works well when title blocks have been populated with iProperties, because the information resides in the file, not the title block. However, if a prompted entry was used, that information will not be carried over, because it exists only in the old title block instance.

Second, since iProperties are stored in the file, there are a couple of important tasks that can be performed on them:

◆ iProperties can be viewed, searched, and copied easily using a number of tools such as Find, Design Assistant, and Vault.

◆ Non-Inventor users can use iProperties to sign off on drawings without opening the file in Inventor.

Getting in the habit of using iProperties will pay large dividends in the future, once you have created many Inventor files. With these things in mind, you should use prompted entries in title blocks rarely. Here are the steps for creating a prompted entry in a title block if you determine that it is required:

1. On the Get Started tab, click the Open button.

2. Browse for the file named `mi_12a_026.idw` located in the Chapter 12 directory of the Mastering Inventor 2011 folder.

3. Expand the sheet node in the browser.

4. Right-click the title block instance (named MI_TB_06), and choose Edit Definition.

5. Zoom up on the title block, and locate the Tracking Code area at the bottom left.

6. Right-click the text field showing #####, and choose Edit Text.

7. Locate the Type drop-down, and choose Prompted Entry.

8. Replace ##### with **Enter Tracking Code**.

9. Click OK.

10. Right-click any empty space in the graphics area, and choose Save Title Block.

11. Click Yes at the Save Edits prompt.

12. Enter **12345** for the tracking code, when prompted.

13. Click OK.

You can edit a prompted entry in a title block by expanding the block instance in the browser and double-clicking the Field Text node. If no prompted entry is established, you will only be able to view the fields. When you've finished exploring prompted entries, you can close the file without saving changes.

Sketched Symbols

Sketched symbols are created, edited, placed, and managed much like other drawing resources, but there is no limit to the number of sketch symbol instances you can place on a sheet. Like other drawing resource definitions, sketched symbols are placed by double-clicking the definition node in the browser or using the User symbols button found on the Symbols panel of the Annotate tab.

Sketched symbols can optionally include a leader. Using a leader, you can associate a sketch symbol with a model so that model-specific properties can be displayed in the symbol. For example, you could create a sketch symbol that calls out a component's mass:

1. On the Get Started tab, click the Open button.

2. Browse for the file named `mi_12a_030.idw` located in the Chapter 12 directory of the Mastering Inventor 2011 folder.

3. Expand the Drawing Resources browser folder.

4. Right-click the Sketch Symbol folder, and select Define New Symbol.

5. In the Draw panel of the Sketch tab, click the Text button (or press T on the keyboard).

6. Click anywhere on the page to set the text location.

7. In the Format Text dialog box, type in a static text string that reads **MASS**.

8. Locate the Type drop-down, and choose Physical Properties – Model.

9. Set the Property drop-down to MASS.

10. Click the Add Text Parameter button to set the MASS property to the text field.

11. Click OK.

12. Right-click anywhere in the graphics area, and choose Done.

13. Choose Save Sketched Symbol from the right-click menu.

14. Enter **Mass** for the name, and click Save.

15. To insert the symbol into the drawing, right-click the Mass sketch symbol definition in the drawing browser, and select Symbols.

16. Ensure the Mass symbol is chosen from the list on the left side of the Symbols dialog box, and select the Leader option.

17. Click OK.

18. Click any model edge in the drawing view.

19. Click again for each leader vertex you'd like, and then choose Continue from the right-click menu.

20. Continue to place additional symbol instances, but be sure to point to a different Arbor Press component each time.

You'll notice that the symbol in Figure 12.6 has a bit more geometry than the simple symbol you just created. You can make a sketch symbol as elaborate as you like, but for the purposes of this exercise, the Mass property reference is all that is required. A finished symbol named Mass_2 has been created for you in this drawing file. If the Mass shows up as "N/A," it indicates that the model needs to be updated. You can open the assembly model and go to the Manage tab and click the Update Mass button to do this. Then return to the drawing to see the update.

FORMATTING YOUR TEXT TO CENTER YOUR SYMBOLS

Generally, text objects are created with a justification setting other than middle center. However, a middle-center justification will allow you to center your text in the symbol geometry by using sketch constraints.

FIGURE 12.6
Applying sketched
symbols to a
drawing view

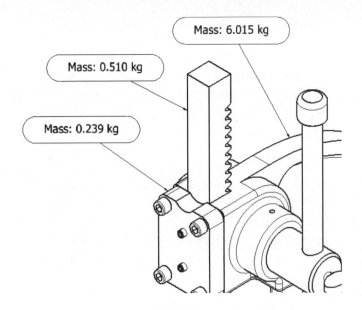

Here are some more sketch symbol points to remember:

◆ Sketched symbols can be placed as needed on new documents or placed on the template itself, which can be useful for standard drawing notes that will be placed in every drawing.

◆ If there is field text in the sketch symbol, it becomes populated just like title block field text when you create a new drawing.

◆ If you need to establish a symbol reference to a model but do not want to see the leader, you can edit the symbol and then select (double-click or select Edit Symbol from the symbol's right-click menu) and uncheck the leader Visibility option.

◆ Static sketched symbols cannot be graphically rotated or scaled like symbols that are not static can.

◆ Sketched symbols placed by double-clicking the definition are set to static by default; you can set this option prior to placement if you use the User button on the Symbols panel of the Annotate tab.

◆ Sketched symbols placed by right-clicking on the definition and choosing Symbols or by using the User button on the Symbols panel of the Annotate tab are set to have more controls than static symbols initially.

◆ You can switch a static symbol to be not static by right-clicking on it and choosing Edit Symbol.

◆ When you mouse over a sketch symbol that is not static, a single blue hot point is shown on the center top of the symbol, and four yellow hot points are displayed at the four corners of the symbol.

◆ Clicking and dragging the blue hot point causes the symbol to rotate, while clicking and dragging any of the yellow hot points enables dynamic scaling.

◆ You can change the insert point of a sketched symbol by adding a Point to the sketch and then using the Set Insertion Point Grip button to mark it as the insertion point. This button can be found next to the Driven Dimension button on the Format panel of the Sketch tab.

◆ Sketched Symbols can be patterned by right-clicking on an instance of a symbol and choosing Pattern Symbol.

AutoCAD Blocks

Blocks created in AutoCAD can be used in Inventor in the same way sketched symbols are used. However, there are some differences between the way they are created and used. AutoCAD blocks are only available for use when using an Inventor `.dwg` file and cannot be used in an Inventor `.idw` file. Also understand, you cannot create or edit AutoCAD blocks in Inventor. To bring blocks into an Inventor `.dwg` file you can:

◆ Copy and paste from AutoCAD.

◆ Right-click on the AutoCAD blocks folder found in the Drawing Resources folder, and choose Import AutoCAD.

Other points to remember about blocks:

◆ Once blocks are imported, you can scale, rotate, and pattern blocks by right-clicking on the block instance.

◆ Blocks containing attributes can be modified by right-clicking on the block instance and choosing Edit Attributes.

◆ Color and layer properties can be modified by right-clicking on the block instance and choosing Properties.

Sheet Formats

Sheet formats are a preset collection of a drawing sheet, border, title block, sketched symbols, and/or base and projected views. They essentially give you the ability to quickly generate multiview drawings just by referencing a single model file. To create a multiview drawing, follow these steps:

1. On the Get Started tab, click the Open button.

2. Browse for the file named `mi_12a_037.idw` located in the Chapter 12 directory of the Mastering Inventor 2011 folder.

3. Expand the Drawing Resources browser folder.

4. Expand the Sheet Formats folder.

5. Right-click the C Size, 4 Views, 1 To 1 Scale format, and choose New Sheet.

6. Browse for the file named `mi_12a_038.ipt` located in the Chapter 12 directory of the Mastering Inventor 2011 folder, and click Open.

7. Click OK in the Select Component dialog box.

You will note that a new sheet has been created to the specifications of the sheet format and set active. This technique is ideal if you find yourself detailing similar designs of common size and complexity. You can close the file without saving changes.

To save your own sheet format, set up your sheet the way you like it, select Create Sheet Format from the active sheet's right-click menu in the browser, and name the sheet format as you'd like.

Here are some more sheet format points to remember:

◆ Only base and projected views are saved in a sheet format. Section, detail, and other such views will not be included.

◆ Placed drawing resources such as standard notes (in the form of sketched symbols) can be included in a sheet format.

◆ You can preload your drawing template as a sheet format as well. Simply open a template, create base and projected views of any model, and then save and close them. When you next use your template for a new drawing, you'll be immediately prompted to reference a model file, and the drawing views are automatically created.

TRANSFER DRAWING RESOURCES

You can copy drawing resource definitions from drawing to drawing by following these steps:

1. Right-click on the definition of the title block, sketched symbol, or other drawing resource you want to copy, and select Copy from the right-click menu.

2. Right-click the appropriate drawing resource node (or the Drawing Resources folder itself in the target document).

3. Select Paste.

You can use this technique to add new drawing resources and update existing resources. You can also select the entire Drawing Recourses folder in one drawing and paste it into the Drawing Recourses folder of another drawing. You will be prompted to replace or make a new instance of any duplicate resources.

AREA CODE CHANGES

In 2002, the phone number area code for Rochester, New York, and the surrounding areas changed from 716 to 585. This meant that every manufacturing, engineering, and architectural group in the area suddenly had hundreds and thousands of drawings with the wrong phone number in the title block of working drawings. Many companies that wanted or needed to update their title blocks had to manually copy and paste title blocks on each drawing in their archives (the savvier groups wrote custom application scripts to perform this task). Unfortunately, the Drawing Resource Transfer Wizard was not released until some years later. It would have likely saved thousands of hours of work.

The copy-and-paste technique is efficient for single changes or transfers between two drawings, but to push one or more new or updated design resource definitions to multiple drawings, use the Drawing Resources Transfer Wizard discussed in Chapter 13.

Editing Styles and Standards

Like color, material, lighting, and sheet-metal styles in the modeling environment, the Drawing Manager makes heavy use of XML-based styles. The basic framework of drawing styles is no different from those in the modeling environment. Drawing style settings are viewed and edited using the Style and Standard Editor dialog box. They can be shared among a workgroup via the same XML style library as the modeling styles, and they can be imported and exported as stand-alone XML files.

Drawing styles differentiate themselves from modeling styles more in concept than in practice, however, and the drawing styles themselves are a collection of drafting rules that include the following:

◆ Dimension styles

◆ Text styles

◆ Balloon styles

◆ And many more

To explore the use of styles, study the following real world scenario and refer to it in the example to come.

OBJECT DEFAULTS

CERT OBJECTIVE

The true key to understanding how styles are used to determine the formatting of everything you can create on a drawing sheet is the notion of object defaults.

In the previous example, it was clear that the majority of a designer's day-to-day drawing work is focused on creating prints for manufacturing. Therefore, the styles used for that type of drawing would be the styles set up as the object defaults. Object defaults are automatically set as the current styles in the template drawings. For Mastering Inventor, Inc., the object defaults would likely be configured as shown in Table 12.3.

TABLE 12.3:   Object Defaults Styles

STYLE TYPE	OBJECT DEFAULT
Dimension style	Dim_Shop
Text style	Text_125
Balloon style	Balloon_Item_Count

STYLES IN USE, A CASE STUDY

A standard is a collection of styles. A company called Mastering Inventor, Inc., has created a basic company standard using dimension styles, text styles, and balloon styles. The various styles' names are listed here, followed by the style category:

Dim_Shop: Dimension style

Dim_Client: Dimension style

Dim_Marketing: Dimension style

Text_125: Text style

Text_250: Text style

Text_Script: Text style

Text_Partslist: Text style

Balloon_Item_Count: Balloon style

Balloon_Partnumber: Balloon style

Balloon_Partname: Balloon style

Having these styles set up allows Mastering Inventor, Inc., to create three types of standard drawings:

◆ The majority of the drawings are created for use by the shop floor to make parts. These drawings are required to be clear, concise, and detailed with tolerances.

◆ Also required are client approval drawings, showing some design specifics but also purposely limited in detail so that a competitor cannot manufacture from them.

◆ Occasionally, stylized drawings for use on the company web page or trade shows are created.

To facilitate this, Mastering Inventor, Inc., has created a separate dimension style for each of these three drawing types. The company also created several different text styles, which are called into the dimension styles and used independently as notes, and so on. Also created were balloon styles, each set up to call different iProperties from the models. This works great, because Inventor users can quickly switch to the style needed without having to stop and define a style, override another style, or worry about not maintaining consistency and/or corrupting the company standard.

The question then becomes this: if this company has three sets of styles in the company standard, how does Inventor know which one to use by default? The answer is *object defaults*.

Now that you understand the overall concept of object defaults, follow these steps to see how they are managed:

1. On the Get Started tab, click the Open button.

2. Browse for the file named `mi_12a_041.idw` located in the Chapter 12 directory of the Mastering Inventor 2011 folder.

3. Zoom to the top of the drawing, and note the three balloons.

Each balloon on the sheet is using a different balloon style. Each balloon style is calling a different set of iProperties, as you will see by comparing the balloons to the parts list. To see how object defaults work, you'll now create more balloons on the ram part, which is the square-shaped bar with teeth cut into it.

4. Select the Annotate tab and then click the Balloon button (on the right-hand side).

5. Note the two style drop-downs all the way to the right of the Annotate tab. The top one controls layers, and the second controls styles.

6. Click the Style drop-down to show the available balloon styles. You should see one line denoted as By Standard and three listed below that, one of which is the one called out in the By Standard line.

7. Select the Balloon_Partname style from the list, and then select any edge of the ram.

8. Drag out and place the balloon on the page by clicking.

9. Right-click, and choose Continue (or press Enter on the keyboard).

10. Repeat steps 11 through 13 for the other two balloon styles, until you have three balloons on the ram part, each using a different balloon style.

11. Right-click, and choose Done when complete.

This demonstrates the use of different styles and shows that one of these styles is set as the company standard default style. You'll now go into the Style And Standard Editor and change the object default for the balloon style.

12. Select the Manage tab, and then click the Styles Editor button. You will be presented with the Style And Standard Editor. (It may take a few seconds to index the styles initially.)

13. Use the plus sign to expand the Balloon, Dimension, Object Defaults, and Text style categories, as shown in Figure 12.7. Note the style names listed under each style category. Look at the following items:

    ◆ Company Standard (Mastering Inventor, Inc.)

    ◆ Balloon styles

    ◆ Dimension styles

    ◆ Object Defaults (MI, Inc.)

    ◆ Text styles

14. Click Object Defaults (MI, Inc.).

15. Locate the Balloon row in the Object Type column.

16. Click the Object Style cell for the Balloon row, and set the drop-down to Balloon_Item_Count.

17. Click the Layer cell for the Balloon row, and set the drop-down to Balloons.

18. Click the Save button at the top of the editor.

19. Click Done to exit the editor.

20. Select the Balloon button from the right of the Annotate tab.

21. Then select any edge of the Ram and place another balloon just as you did before.

22. Note that the Balloon tool now defaults to the Balloon_Item_Count style and is placed on the Balloon layer.

FIGURE 12.7

Standards, styles, and object defaults

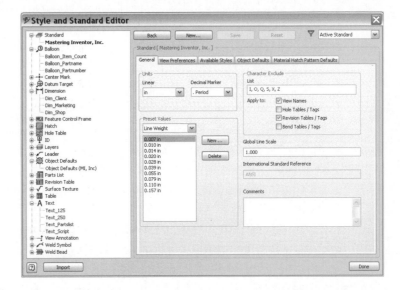

When setting object defaults, you typically want to use the most common style. Of course, you can always use another style by manually selecting the style from the Style drop-down as you place the object. You'll note that when you select an existing object, the Style and Layer drop-downs display that object's style and layer, allowing you to change layer and style assignment to existing objects as needed.

Objects that have been set to a specific style, rather than following the By Standard, will not update if you make any modifications to the object defaults. However, the objects will update if the specific style is updated. A quick way to get a set of objects (like your balloons, for example) to return to their object default is to window or Ctrl-select the objects on the screen and then select By Standard from the style drop-down. All the objects will update to use the newly selected standard.

SET THE STYLE DROP-DOWN TO LAST USED

You can set the Style drop-down to remember the last used object style by going to the Tools tab, clicking the Application Options tab, and then selecting the Drawing tab. On the right-side of the Drawing tab, you will find a Default Object Style setting. If you set the drop-down to Last Used, the last used object and dimension style is the default. As an example, if you are placing dimensions on a drawing using a fractional style, but the decimal style is the default, you can set the application option to Last Used so you do not need to keep changing the style back to fractional every time you access the dimension style. The Last Used setting is for the current editing session for the drawing, so if you close the file and reopen it, the Object Default will list again, until changed.

CREATING STYLES

As evident in the balloon example, you can have multiple styles for the same object type. Or you can have a single style that you always use. It's up to you to choose how many styles you have for each type, and this will be dictated largely by need. Although this section will not go through all the settings for all the styles, you will explore how to create and configure a new style as a foundation to creating all style types.

1. On the Get Started tab, click the Open button.

2. Browse for the file named mi_12a_046.idw located in the Chapter 12 directory of the Mastering Inventor 2011 folder.

3. Select the Manage tab, and click the Style Editor button.

4. In the left pane, expand the Text node to see the list of text styles.

5. Next expand the Balloon node to see the list of balloon styles. (In this case, there is just one.)

6. Click the balloon style named Balloon_Partnumber to display the style settings in the right pane.

7. Click the New button at the top of the editor dialog box, and enter **Balloon_Item_Qty** for the style name.

8. Ensure that the Add To Standard check box is selected, and click OK.

9. In the Balloon Style settings, under the Sub-styles section, use the drop-down to set the text style to use the style called Text_125.

10. Click the Shape button, and select the second shape (Circular – 2 Entries) from the list.

11. Below that, in the Property Display area, click the Property Chooser button.

12. Click the Part Number property in the right pane, and click the Remove button to take it out of the property list for this balloon style.

13. In the Left pane, locate the ITEM and ITEM QTY properties, and use the Add button to pull them into the right pane. Do this one at a time.

14. Use the Move Down and Move Up buttons to set ITEM as the top property.

15. Click OK.

16. Click the Save button.

17. Click the Help button in the lower-left corner of the Style And Standard Editor, and notice that this takes you to a listing and description of each setting in the balloon style. This is true of all of the style types.

18. Close the Help dialog box, and click Done in the Style Editor.

19. Select the Annotate tab, and click the Balloon button.

20. Select Balloon_Item_Qty from the styles drop-down on the far right of the Annotate tab, and choose your new Balloon style from the list.

21. Click the edges of parts to place balloons on the drawing.

Although the settings for each style type vary, the concepts for creating them remain consistent throughout all styles. These concepts are as follows:

◆ Create a new style based off of an existing style.

◆ Specify substyles (if applicable).

◆ Configure the style settings as desired.

◆ Save the new style.

Working with Substyles

A basic example of a substyle in the modeling environment is the color style, which is a substyle of the material style. Once you apply a new material to a part, not only are you changing its physical parameters but you're potentially changing its color so that it shows the material's color substyle.

The use of substyles in the Drawing Manager is extensive. Almost every kind of annotation you create in a drawing contains some kind of text (dimensions, weld symbols, and parts lists), and many make use of leaders. The text style and leader style, therefore, are frequently used as substyles of other styles. This basically provides one-stop shopping if you wanted to quickly change all the text on your document. If you wanted to change the font for all text, for example, you wouldn't have to go to the parts list style and change the font, then to the dimension style and change the font, and so on; instead, you would simply change just one or two text styles that are being called into those other styles.

Substyles are coupled with their parent styles, which means a substyle cannot be purged if it's in use by another style. If you cache a high-level style into your document from the library or if you save a high-level style into the library from your file, all substyles participate in those operations.

Styles are an extremely powerful formatting tool that enables you to quickly change the entire face of a document. This also serves as a warning that modifying styles without understanding how they work can quickly generate unexpected results.

TAKE THE TIME TO UNDERSTAND STYLES

Although there's probably never been a single person who decided to use Inventor just for the "exciting" styles and standards tools, these tools are extremely powerful, and you'd be doing yourself a disservice if you don't spend some time getting to know them. They may seem complex at first, but once you understand them, they will become a very powerful tool. Play around with changing styles in a scratch drawing and see how the annotations change.

Another good resource for learning more about Styles can be found by inserting the installation disk and clicking the *Read The Documentation* link on the first screen of the setup; then click the *Fundamentals For The Autodesk Inventor CAD Manager* under the installation guides category. This will open the *CAD Manager Fundamentals* PDF file. If you do not have the installation disks, you can likely find this PDF file by searching your Inventor Install directory for ADMCADMgr_15_0.pdf.

Once you have a good understanding of Styles, sit down with your design group and come up with a set of standards with which everyone is happy. Apply these styles to your documents and use them for a while. One of the great aspects of the style library is that if you want to make a change, you can make it to the library, and everyone will have access to this new/changed style each time they open a file.

Drawing Style Administration

Each drawing template that comes with Inventor has a full set of styles saved (cached) in the drawing document. Although you can use the style library as a sharing and update tool, there is no direct link between objects on your sheet and styles in your library. Any in-use style is loaded into your document either automatically or manually.

If your project is set to use the style library (the Use Style Library setting is Yes or Read Only), then it's important to keep your style definitions in sync between your template file and the library. If your project is using the style library and you have a style in the library that has the same name as a style in your template and those styles have different settings, the definition in the library automatically overwrites the definition in the template each time it's used to start a new drawing (a warning dialog box is shown when this condition is detected).

The best way to ensure synchronization is to open your template file and run either the Update Styles tool (which pulls updates from the library) or the Save Styles To Style Library tool, depending on which way you want to transfer the styles. You can find both of these options and the Purge tool on the Manage tab.

Creating Drawing Views

You will explore the various view creation and editing tools in the following sections as you cover documenting different types of 3D models: part, assembly, sheet metal, weldment, and iPart/iAssembly.

Drawing views reference part, assembly, or presentation files. The workflows involved in creating and editing views from these different sources are similar, but with some notable exceptions are detailed in the following sections.

Creating a Base View

Creating views in an Inventor drawing is a very intuitive process. You'll start by creating some basic views of a part file, while exploring the procedure and options along the way. Before you create any views, first open the part to become familiar with it.

1. On the Get Started tab, click the Open button.

2. Browse for the file named mi_12a_048.ipt located in the Chapter 12 directory of the Mastering Inventor 2011 folder, and click Open.

3. Spin the part around, and take a look at it using the ViewCube or the Orbit tool. Do not close the part.

4. On the Get Started tab, click the New button.

5. On the Metric tab, choose the ANSI(mm).idw template.

6. On the Place Views tab, click the Base button to create a base view.

7. With the Drawing View dialog box open, move your mouse pointer around on the drawing, and you will see a dynamic preview of the part file. Do not click screen just yet, or you will inadvertently place the drawing view.

8. Note that all open model files are listed in the File drop-down. You can select any open model file from the list or click the Browse button to select another file.

9. In the Scale input box, enter **2**, or use the drop-down to select 2:1. You can specify scales in fractional or decimal formats (1/2 or 0.5 both work for half scale).

10. Click the lightbulb button to turn on the View/Scale label.

11. In the View Identifier input, type **Front**.

12. In the Orientation pane on the right, click through the available options, and watch the preview at your mouse pointer change. Select Top when you're finished. You'll note that although the orientation is called *top*, you have entered Front in the view identifier box. The orientation name can be considered a suggestion, and the word *top* will not show up anywhere but here.

CUSTOM VIEW ORIENTATIONS

If the view you need to show does not exist in the Orientation pane, you can use the Change View Orientation button to step into the model and create any view orientation possible.

---

13. In the Style area, click just the middle button to create an unshaded view with no hidden lines. Note that the shaded button (blue) can be toggled on and off independently of the other two, but the hidden lines and no hidden lines buttons are mutually exclusive to one another.

14. Uncheck the *Create Projected Views Immediately After Base View Creation* check box, found in the lower left-hand corner.

15. Click anywhere on the page to create the view (or click the OK button). Here are some tips for working with base views:

- Right-click any view and choose Open to open the model in a new window.

- Most of the options you see in the Drawing View dialog box can be altered later by editing the view, but it's important to set the orientation correctly originally because it cannot be changed once placed.

- To delete a view, simply hover over a view and then select the dotted view boundary, right-click, and choose Delete.

CERT OBJECTIVE

- Views can be edited by right-clicking or double-clicking the view.

- Tangent edges and thread features that are not showing up in the view can be turned on by editing the view, going to the Display tab, and selecting the respective boxes.

- Views can be moved by selecting the dotted view boundary that appears when hovering over them and dragging into place.

- Clicking a line or lines in a view gives you control options for just those lines.

- Right-click lines, arcs, or circles and uncheck Visibility to hide those entities.

◆ Right-click the view and choose Show Hidden Lines to bring back lines that were hidden.

◆ Each base view created is listed in the browser; note the base view button.

◆ Expanding the view node in the browser shows the model tree for that view, where you can select all the edges of features at once. You can then right-click the selected objects on the page and toggle off the visibility, change the layer, and so on.

◆ To rotate a view, right-click the view, and choose Rotate; then select an edge to make horizontal or vertical, or use the drop-down to specify by angle.

◆ You can have as many base views as you need on a drawing, but the iProperties will be pulled from the first view placed.

◆ Views can be renamed in the browser or by editing the view.

◆ To display the view name without the scale for a single view, right-click View Label, and choose Edit View Label; then remove *<Scale>* from the text box.

◆ You can suppress a view by right-clicking on it and choosing Suppress.

Once you've explored the settings and edit options for the base view, you can close the file without saving changes and continue.

SET VIEW PREFERENCES IN THE STANDARD

You can set up view preferences for your company standard by accessing the Styles Editor, selecting the Standard, and then selecting the View Preferences tab. This allows you to choose which properties to display or not display in the View Label, set the First or Third Angle projection and much more.

CREATING PROJECTED VIEWS

Once a base view is created, you can quickly create other views based on it without having to specify the model again:

1. On the Get Started tab, click the Open button.

2. Browse for the file named mi_12a_049.idw located in the Chapter 12 directory of the Mastering Inventor 2011 folder, and click Open.

3. Select the Projected button on the Place View tab.

4. Click the base view.

5. As you drag your mouse pointer around the base view, notice the view previews that are being generated.

6. Drag straight to the right and click. You will see a rectangular bounding box indicating a view will be placed there.

7. Drag straight up from the base view and click, again noting the preview.

8. Finally, drag diagonally up and to the right from the base view and click.

9. Then right-click and choose Create to generate the projected views.

10. Expand the plus sign next to the Front view in the browser to see that the projected views are listed, as shown in Figure 12.8.

FIGURE 12.8
Drawing views in
the browser

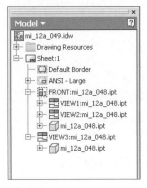

Here are some tips for working with projected views:

◆ Orthographic projected views are linked to the parent view in style and alignment and stacked below them in the browser tree.

◆ To break the style link between a projected view and its parent view, double-click to edit the projected view and deselect the Style From Base button in the lower right of the Drawing View dialog box. Then change the shading and hidden line options as you like.

◆ Isometric views are not linked to the parent view in style and alignment and are listed separately in the browser tree.

◆ To break the alignment between a projected view and its parent view, right-click the projected view, and choose Alignment ➢ Break. A view arrow will be placed next to the parent view, and the projected view is labeled to match.

◆ To break the alignment without getting a view arrow, right-click the projected view, and choose Rotate. You can set an already horizontal edge horizontal and still break the alignment.

◆ To reset the alignment, right-click the projected view, and choose Alignment and then Horizontal or Vertical as appropriate. The projected view will move back into place. Choose In Position to link the projected view to the parent in its current position.

◆ By default, deleting a parent view or a base view will remove all projected views as well.

◆ To delete a parent view without removing the projected views, click the >> button in the Delete View dialog box, click Yes next to the views you want to keep, and set them to No.

- ◆ Projected views can be created from views other than base views, such as detail views, section views, and even other projected views.

- ◆ You can select the parent view first and then issue the projected view tool, or you can issue the tool and then select the view. Either order is acceptable. If you have a view preselected accidentally and click the projected view button, that will be the view you are projecting.

- ◆ If you select the *Create Projected Views Immediately After Base View Creation* check box, found in the lower left-hand corner of the Base View creation dialog box, you can create base views and projected views at the same time.

- ◆ You can suppress a view by right-clicking on it and choosing Suppress.

You can close the current file without saving changes and continue.

MOVING AND COPYING VIEWS

You can move drawing views between sheets by dragging and dropping the browser nodes. When a projected view is moved to a different sheet than its parent, a view arrow is generated automatically on the parent view.

To move a view, follow these steps:

1. On the Get Started tab, click the Open button.

2. Browse for the file named mi_12a_050.idw located in the Chapter 12 directory of the Mastering Inventor 2011 folder, and click Open.

3. Expand the Front view node in the browser to show projected views 1 and 2.

4. Click the browser node of View2, and drag it down to the Sheet2 browser node.

5. Rest your mouse pointer over the top of the Sheet2 browser node icon, and release the mouse button.

6. Sheet2 becomes active to show you where View2 has been moved. Notice there is a browser icon for the Front view with an arrow and the sheet name in parentheses. This indicates it is linked to the parent view on Sheet1. Notice too the moved view has been renamed.

7. Right-click the Front view icon in the Sheet2 browser, and choose Go To to be returned to Sheet1.

8. Notice that a view arrow has been created next to the Front view.

To copy a view, follow these steps:

1. With mi_12a_050.idw still open, ensure you are on Sheet1.

2. Right-click View3, and choose Copy.

3. Right-click the browser node for Sheet2, and choose Paste.

4. Sheet2 becomes active to show you where the view has been copied to. Notice the new view has been named the next available view number.

You can close the current file without saving changes and continue.

CREATING SECTIONS VIEWS

CERT
OBJECTIVE

Section views are created by "sketching" a line across an existing view to define the section cut. The sketch is created automatically for you as you define the section line.

To create a section view, follow these steps:

1. On the Get Started tab, click the Open button.

2. Browse for the file named mi_12a_051.idw located in the Chapter 12 directory of the Mastering Inventor 2011 folder, and click Open.

3. On the Place View tab, click the Section button.

4. Click the Front view to choose it as the view to be sectioned.

5. Hold down the Ctrl key, and click to the left of the view. This ensures that you do not accidentally constrain the start point of your section line to any midpoints, centerpoints, or endpoints.

6. Let up on the Ctrl key, drag the line across the part, and click to the right of the part, ensuring that you see either a perpendicular or horizontal constraint to indicate you are getting a straight line.

7. Right-click, and choose Continue.

8. In the Section View dialog box, note you can change the section identifier, scale, style, and section depth. You can also create a zero depth section called a *slice*. Leave all these options at the defaults.

9. Drag your cursor above the original view, and notice how the placement is constrained perpendicularly to the section line.

10. Hold down the Ctrl key, and click the screen to create and place the section view anywhere you like.

11. Click the section arrow, and drag it up or down to see the section update automatically.

12. To align the section view with the base view, right-click on the section view and choose Alignment and then Vertical.

13. Click on the base view to specify it as the view to align the section to.

14. Click on the section view boundary to see how the alignment works.

Look at the browser to see how the section view was added as a child view of the base. Also, notice the sketch that was created on the base view listed just above the section view node (Figure 12.9). This sketch is the section line itself and can be edited like any other sketch. You can add or remove constraints (including sketch dimensions) as needed to precisely position the section line around your base view. You do this by right-clicking the sketch in the browser and choosing Edit Sketch, just as you would any other sketch.

Here are some tips for working with section views:

◆ Section line appearance is controlled by a layer and a style just like most other annotation objects. To determine which layer and style are used, switch to the Annotate tab, and then click the section line. Note the Layer and View Annotation style in the Layer and Style drop-downs on the far right of the Annotate tab.

- Project a section view to create an isometric section.

- Orthographic section views are hatched automatically, but isometric sections are not.

- Edit or hide a hatch by right-clicking it.

- Display a hidden hatch or turn a hatch on for isometric section views by editing the view (right-click and select Edit View), going to the Display Options tab, and selecting Hatching.

- You can hatch by material if you have mapped the materials and hatch patterns in your standard.

- Flip the section arrow direction by right-clicking the section line and choosing Reverse Direction.

- Show just the arrows of the section line by right-clicking the section line and choosing Show Entire Line.

- Edit the section depth by right-clicking the section line and choosing Edit Section Properties.

- To constrain a section line to the center of a hole, run your mouse over the hole to project the center point when you are creating the sketch line.

FIGURE 12.9
Part section view

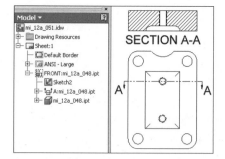

You can close the current file without saving changes and continue.

You defined the section line on the fly during the previous exercise. Now you will bring in a sketch created in the part model and use it to create a section view. Figure 12.10 shows the sketched line in the model.

MAPPING MATERIALS TO HATCH PATTERNS

You can set up your template to use a predefined hatch pattern per the material of the sectioned part so that copper parts are hatched with one hatch pattern, mild steel parts are hatched with another, and so on:

1. Select the Styles And Standards panel of the Manage tab, and click Styles Editor to open the Styles And Standard Editor.

2. In the left pane, expand Standard, and then click your standard.

3. In the right pane, click the Material Hatch Pattern Defaults tab.

4. Set the Default Hatch Style for new materials added in the mapping.

5. Click the From File button to select a part file that contains all the material styles you want to import (set this up ahead of time), or use the From Style Library button.

6. For each imported material, click the Hatch Pattern field, and select a new hatch pattern from the list. Use Ctrl or Shift to change several materials at the same time.

7. Click Save to save the changes to the current document, and then click Done to close the dialog box.

FIGURE 12.10
Section line sketch on model

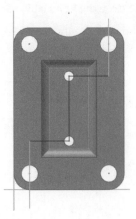

To create a section from a model sketch, proceed with these steps. If you still have mi_12a_052.idw open, you can skip to step 3.

1. On the Get Started tab, click the Open button.

2. Browse for the file named mi_12a_052.idw located in the Chapter 12 directory of the Mastering Inventor 2011 folder, and click Open.

3. Locate the sheet node in the browser, and then click the plus symbol to expand it.

4. Then expand the view node called Front to reveal the model.

5. Finally, expand the model node to reveal the part features.

6. On the part node (mi_12a_048.ipt), right-click and choose Get Model Sketches.

7. You will now see that a model sketch called Section Sketch is present; right-click it, and choose Include.

8. This will reveal a zigzag line on the part view.

9. On the Place View tab, click the Section button.

10. Click any part of the included sketch, or click the sketch in the browser to use as the section line.

11. In the Section View dialog box, click the Include Slice check box to create a zero-depth section. Leave the other options at the defaults.

12. Drag your cursor to the right of the original view and click on-screen to create the section.

13. To change the section properties, right-click the section line, and choose Edit Section Properties.

14. Deselect the Include Slice box to change the section to a full-depth section; then click OK.

15. Right-click the hatch, and choose Edit; then click the Double check box.

16. Click OK to close the Edit Hatch Pattern dialog box.

Your section should look similar to Figure 12.11.

FIGURE 12.11
Section using
model sketch

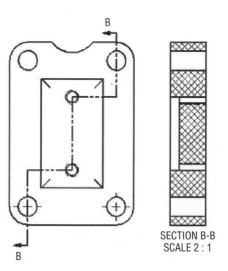

SECTION B-B
SCALE 2 : 1

You can close the current file without saving changes and continue.

IMPORT HATCH PATTERNS

You can load hatch patterns from an external PAT file to add custom hatch patterns to your drawings. You can do this by editing a hatch and selecting Other from the Pattern list and then clicking Load. You can also do this in the Styles and Standards editor to add custom hatches to your company standard.

SLICE VIEWS

Slice views are simply zero-depth section views. Slice views are often used to create cut profiles of complex surfaced parts such as automobile bodies, aircraft wings, boat hulls, and so on. A Slice view is generated by creating a sketch associated to a view and then using that sketch as the slice profile. The Slice is then executed on the selected target view.

For a quick reference of how to slice views, go to the Get Started tab and click the Show Me Animations button. On the Show Me Animations screen, select the Drawing - Drawing Views link, and then click the Slice View Animation link on the resulting screen.

USING BREAKOUT VIEWS

You can also use a breakout to show a cutaway. Unlike the Section View tool that creates a new view, a breakout is a cut operation you perform on an existing view. Breakouts start with a closed loop profile drawn on a view sketch, so you'll begin there as well. It is important to note that in order to use a sketch for a breakout, it must be associated to the drawing view. To create an associated sketch, first select the view, and then click the Create Sketch button. Clicking the Create Sketch button without selecting the view first will result in a sketch that is not associated with any view.

To create a breakout view, follow these steps:

1. On the Get Started tab, click the Open button.

2. Browse for the file named mi_12a_067.idw located in the Chapter 12 directory of the Mastering Inventor 2011 folder, and click Open.

3. Select the view named Front View. You can determine that the view is selected by looking at the browser; it should be highlighted.

4. On the Place Views tab, click the Create Sketch button.

5. Sketch a shape similar to Figure 12.12. The results don't need to be exact, but you do need to ensure that the sketch is a closed loop.

6. Click the Finish Sketch button on the Sketch tab, when your sketch is complete.

FIGURE 12.12
Creating a
breakout sketch

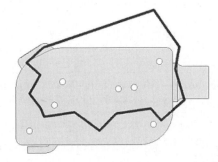

7. To ensure that the sketch has been created correctly, you can select the view on the sheet and drag it around a bit. If the sketch travels with the view, then it is associated to the view. If it stays put, it is not. You can also look at the browser and ensure that the sketch node is stacked under Front View. If you see it above Front View, it is not associated and will not work for the breakout.

8. On the Place Views tab, click the Break Out button.

9. Select the Front View.

10. Your sketch should automatically be selected as the Profile, provided you have only one unconsumed sketch. Otherwise, you will select the sketch for the profile. If you cannot select the sketch, review step 3.

11. Ensure the Depth area is set to From Point, and then click the center of the upper-rightmost hole.

12. Enter a depth value of **25 mm**, and click OK.

Your result should look similar to Figure 12.13. Note the Break Out view node in the browser. You may be able to see some portions of the internal parts, because they have been cut away as well. You'll explore how to control this in the coming pages, for now you can close the file without saving changes.

FIGURE 12.13
Break Out
view node

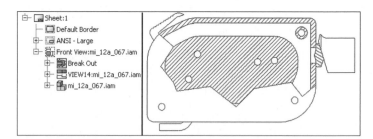

Next you'll open a file and modify a breakout view to explore the other depth options:

1. On the Get Started tab, click the Open button.

2. Browse for the file named mi_12a_072.idw located in the Chapter 12 directory of the Mastering Inventor 2011 folder, and click Open.

3. In the browser, right-click the Break Out node, and choose Edit Break Out. You may have to expand the sheet node and the Front View node to locate it.

4. In the Depth area, set the drop-down to To Sketch.

5. Select the zigzag sketch line in the top view. This sketch has been created associated to the top view by selecting the view first and then creating the view. This is required to use it as a To Sketch.

6. Click OK.

Examine the isometric view, and you will see the breakout used the zigzag line as the depth extents and cut the internal and external parts. You can adjust this by going to the model tree and removing the file from the section participation as explained in the following steps.

7. Select the model node for the Front View. Hover your mouse pointer over model nodes in the browser, and watch the views on the sheet to ensure you are selecting the one for the Front View.

8. Expand the model node to reveal all the part files, and select the parts ending in 04 through 07, as shown in Figure 12.14.

9. Right-click the selected parts, choose Section Participation, and then select None.

FIGURE 12.14
Removing parts from the breakout

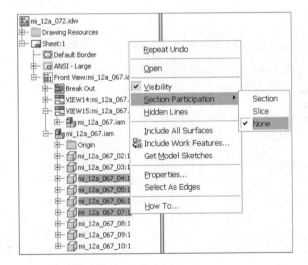

10. The views will update on the sheet to show these parts un-sectioned.

11. In the browser, right-click the Break Out node, and choose Edit Break Out. Click the Section All Parts check box. This will override the Section Participation settings.

12. Change the Depth option to To Hole, and click the hole/circular edge in the Top View.

13. Click OK.

14. Notice that the zigzag sketch line reappears because it is no longer used by the breakout. Also notice that the breakout depth has adjusted to stop at the center of the hole.

15. Edit the breakout once again, and set the Depth drop-down to Through Part.

16. In the browser select the parts ending in 02, 03, 08, and 09 to ensure they are sectioned through.

17. Click OK; your results should be similar to Figure 12.15.

FIGURE 12.15
Break out through
part option

SECTION PARTICIPATION

Section participation can be controlled per the part file or per the part instance. If the part is a standard part such as a fastener, you might want to set the section participation per file, so the part is never sectioned. If you just want to exclude a part from a particular section or break out view for clarity, then you can do so per instance.

Per file: Open the part file you want to change the section participation for, go to Tools tab, and select Document Settings and then choose the Modeling tab. Uncheck the *Participate in Assembly and Drawing Sections* check box. The part will now default to None in the section participation of any new section and break out views, but can be set to participate on a per instance basis.

Per instance: Place the section or break out view of the assembly, expand the view node in the browser and then locate the browser node for the parts you want to adjust the section participation for, right-click on them and choose Section Participation and set it to None as needed.

If the part was set to section in the Document Settings before a view was created and then you change the Document Settings to not section, the drawing view will stay at section and will need to be changed per instance.

It should be pointed out that the preceding steps have created a situation that may yield inconsistent results by excluding some of the parts from the section participation settings and then setting the depth of the breakout to Through Part. Typically, you would use the section participation settings only with the first three depth options and not with the Through Part option.

You will have noticed that, as you modified the breakout, the isometric view was linked to those changes. This is because isometric projected views created for views already having a breakout inherit the breakout by default. Orthographic projected views, such as the top view, do not inherit the breakout.

To switch the inheritance setting of the isometric view, right-click it and select Edit View. Go to the Display Options in the Drawing View dialog box, and deselect the Break Out check box in the Cut Inheritance area, as shown in Figure 12.16. You can also turn on hatching from this tab. You can use the current file to explore these hatch settings, and then you can close the file without saving changes.

FIGURE 12.16

Cut inheritance for isometric views

USING DETAIL VIEWS

You can use the detail view to enlarge and segregate a particular portion of a drawing view as a new view. Follow these steps to explore the options of detail views:

1. On the Get Started tab, click the Open button.

2. Browse for the file named mi_12a_077.idw located in the Chapter 12 directory of the Mastering Inventor 2011 folder, and click Open.

3. On the Place Views tab, click the Detail button.

4. Next click anywhere on the Front view to use it as the basis of the new detail view.

5. In the Detail View dialog box, you can modify the View/Scale Label And Style settings just as you can in other view creation dialog boxes. You can also set a fence and cutout shape. The Full Boundary and Connection Line options are available only if using the Smooth cutout option. Figure 12.17 shows examples of these options.

FIGURE 12.17

Detail view options

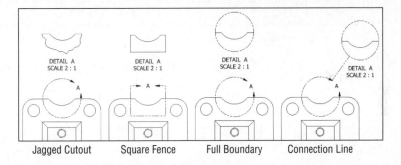

6. Leave the dialog options set at the defaults, and then click the Front View, approximately in the center of the crescent-shaped feature, as shown in Figure 12.17.

7. Drag the boundary out to a size close to that shown in Figure 12.17 as well.

8. Click the screen where you would like to place the detail view, and the detail is created.

9. Click the detail boundary on the Front View, and note the six green grips. Click and drag on any of the outer grips to resize the boundary, and use the center one to control the location.

10. You can also double-click the two grips near the arrowhead and change the head style.

Here are more options for detail views:

◆ Right-click the detail boundary and choose Attach to anchor the detail to a specific point on the base view.

◆ Right-click the detail boundary and choose Options to change the detail from rough to smooth and then to add a full detail and then to add a connection line.

◆ Click and drag on the detail label character (the letter *A* in Figure 12.17) in the boundary fence to reposition it.

◆ To move the detail label character out away from the boundary, right-click the detail boundary, click Leader, and then click the detail label character and drag it; it will be attached with a leader.

◆ Right-click or double-click the detail view to edit the view and change scale, style, detail name, and so on, as you would any other view.

Use the current file to explore these detail options and then close the file without saving changes.

USING DETAIL VIEW ANNOTATION

Although detail views are created at a scale larger than the base view, Inventor takes this into account when creating dimensions for the detail view. Therefore, all your dimensions will be to the correct scale.

CREATING BREAK VIEWS

Often when detailing components that are much longer proportionally than they are tall, such as frame components, it is a good idea to use the Break tool to remove portions of the model. This allows the detail of the end treatments to be the focus of the drawing. Follow these steps to explore the Break tool:

1. On the Get Started tab, click the Open button.

2. Browse for the file named mi_12a_078.idw located in the Chapter 12 directory of the Mastering Inventor 2011 folder, and click Open.

3. On the Place Views tab, locate the Break button on the Modify panel and click it.

4. Click on the Front view.

5. In the Break dialog box, set the gap to **10 mm**.

6. Click the view just to the left of where it extends past the drawing border on the left side.

7. Drag the break symbol over and click just to the right of where the view extends past the drawing border on the right side, and then click on-screen.

8. Notice the break is carried through to both views.

9. Zoom in on the break symbol and then click on it.

10. Click and drag the green grip point to the left to reposition it.

11. Select the right half of the break symbol and drag it to the right, and then let up. This will remove more material from the view.

12. Select the right half of the break symbol and drag it to the left, and then let up. This will add more material from the view.

13. Adjust the view until your view fits on the drawing sheet.

14. Next click on the view named Top View and choose Edit View.

15. Click the Display Options tab and uncheck the Break check box in the Cut Inheritance area. Then click OK. You'll notice the view no longer inherits the break from the parent view (in this case the Front View).

16. Click on the Break symbol on the Front View and choose delete.

17. Right-click on Sheet 2 in the browser and choose Activate.

18. Click the Break button and select the view named Top View to place the break on.

19. Notice the *Propagate to Parent View* check box. Uncheck this option to break only the view named Top View and leave the parent view from which it was created without a break.

20. Click the start and endpoints on the view to create the break, and you'll see the parent view is left as is.

You can continue to experiment with the Break tool, and then close this file without saving changes. Here are some more points to know about break views:

◆ To edit an existing break, right-click on the break symbol and choose Edit Break.

◆ The distance value entered in the Break dialog box refers to the space on the paper between the break symbols.

◆ You can break views vertically and horizontally using the options in the dialog box, but there is not a way to break a view at an angle when a component is not vertical or horizontal.

◆ There is no "pipe break" symbol for round components.

◆ By default, a dimension placed on the view will be broken as well, providing the break intersects it.

◆ You can slide the dimension break view under the dimension text to hide it on a per instance case.

◆ You can edit the dimension style and turn off the dimension break symbol option if you like. The setting is found on the Display tab of the dimension style settings.

BREAK SYMBOLS FOR STRUCTURAL DETAILING

If you detail plate girders and built-up members with vertical stiffeners, gussets, clip plates, and so on, you might find the break symbol on the drawing view causes confusion. To break a view without showing the break view symbol, you can configure it so that it does not show, as described here:

◆ Use the slider bar in the Break dialog box to set the break symbol to the smallest scale (slide it to the far left).

◆ Set the break gap to 0.0001 or some number nearing zero (Inventor will not allow a zero value).

◆ Select the break symbol (it will now display as vertical line) and then switch to the Annotate tab, and then use the Layer drop-down box to place the break symbol on a non-plotting layer (you will likely need to create such a layer in your drawings).

You can try this with the file named mi_12a_078.idw, as there is a layer called No Plot already created in this drawing.

CROPPING VIEWS

You can use the Crop tool found on the Modify panel of the Place Views panel to crop unneeded areas of a drawing view, in much the same way a photograph is cropped. You can specify the crop boundary as part of the crop operation or create a sketch on the view first and then use it as the crop boundary. When you create a sketch to be used as a crop boundary, you must first select the view and then create the sketch, thereby associating the sketch to the view. Unassociated sketches cannot be used as a crop boundary.

The following view types cannot be cropped:

◆ Views containing a view break

◆ Views with overlays

◆ Views that have been suppressed

◆ Views that have already been cropped

For a quick reference of how to crop views, go to the Get Started tab and click the Show Me Animations button. On the Show Me Animations screen, select the Drawing - Drawing Views link, and then click the Crop View Animation link on the resulting screen.

USING DRAFT VIEWS

Draft Views are essentially just 2D sketches created in a drawing and packaged in view "container," allowing them to be scaled and handled like other drawing views. For instance, if you have standard details drawn in AutoCAD, you might copy them into a Draft view and then place and scale them as needed.

To create standard details from Inventor views, you can use Save Copy As to create an AutoCAD .DWG file, and then paste the detail back into Inventor as a draft view. However, Draft views have limited capabilities as far as being shared between drawings, so you might consider Sketched Symbols for standard details you plan to use over and over.

To create a Draft View, follow these general steps:

1. From the Place Views tab, click the Draft button found on the Create panel.

2. In the Draft View dialog box, set the label and scale, and then click the Label Visibility button (looks like a lightbulb) to display the view name and scale on the drawing.

3. Click OK to close the Draft View dialog box.

4. An empty view and sketch are created. Use the Sketch tools to add geometry, text, and dimensions as needed, or paste in copied geometry from AutoCAD.

5. Click the Finish Sketch button to create the sketch and draft view.

CREATING OVERLAY VIEWS

You can create Overlay views to show positional representations overlaid on top of one another, thereby communicating the change in position exiting between the positional representations. This allows you to effectively show an assembly motion of multiple positions using a single view. To create an Overlay view, the assembly must first have positional representations set up to be used. Follow these steps to explore Overlay views:

1. On the Get Started tab, click the Open button.

2. Browse for the file named mi_12a_080.idw located in the Chapter 12 directory of the Mastering Inventor 2011 folder, and click Open.

3. On the Place Views tab, click the Overlay button, and select the existing view on the sheet.

4. In the Overlay View dialog box, choose Closed from the Positional Representation drop-down, and then click OK.

The result is a view of the alternative position shown in a phantom line—type overlaid on the original. You can dimension to the overlay lines as you would any others, in order to capture a mechanism's extension length, rotation angle, and so on. The key to overlay views is really in setting up the positional representations in the assembly beforehand.

When you create the overlay, you are given the opportunity to specify a view representation for the overlay view. It's recommended that before you create an overlay view, you create a view representation that visibly isolates only the components that move as a result of the positional representation. Otherwise (as is the case in this example), all the nonmoving components are redrawn over the same components in the base view.

To change positional representations used in an overlay view, simply delete the existing overlay view and specify a different positional representation when placing a new overlay view. Also be aware that because weldments are not allowed to use positional representations, overlays are not allowed for weldment drawing and will be removed if they exist when an assembly is converted to a weldment.

You can close the file without saving changes.

Annotating Part Drawings

Once you've created the appropriate views to document the model, you can add annotations. You can find the Annotation tools on the Annotate tab. The Annotate tab is divided into several groups of tools, including Dimension, Feature Notes, Text, Symbols, Sketch, Table, and Format tools. In the following sections you'll explore the Annotation tools.

USING CENTERLINE AND CENTER MARKS

There are four standard centerline and center mark tools as well as an automated centerline tool. These tools are called Centerline, Centerline Bisector, Center Mark, and Centered Pattern, and you can access them from the Symbols panel of the Annotate tab (look for the four buttons next to the Create Sketch button). Recall that hovering your mouse pointer over the tool buttons provides a tool tip with the button name and that hovering a moment longer allows a dynamic tool tip to appear showing an illustrated example of each. The automated centerline tool is accessed differently than the other centerline and center mark tools, as explained in the coming pages.

Centerline

Use Centerline to draw a centerline style line, arc, or circle by specifying points. When centerline arcs are created using circles or arcs as the selection points, a center mark is drawn on the arc along with the centerline.

1. On the Get Started tab, click the Open button.

2. Browse for the file named `mi_12a_082.idw` located in the Chapter 12 directory of the Mastering Inventor 2011 folder, and click Open.

3. From the Annotate tab, select the Centerline tool.

4. On VIEW 1, click the hole at the 12 o'clock position and then the hole at 2 o'clock. Notice the tool is drawing a straight line at this point.

5. Click the hole at 4 o'clock, and notice the centerline becomes an arc.

6. Continue on around clicking each hole and then close the centerline by clicking 12 o'clock once again; then right-click and choose Create.

7. You should still be in the Centerline tool at this point. On VIEW 4, click the center of hole A1, then B1, then B2, and finally A4.

8. Right-click and choose Create; then right-click and choose Done. Your centerline should resemble the one on the left of Figure 12.18.

FIGURE 12.18
Centerlines

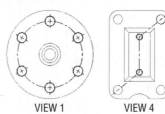

VIEW 1   VIEW 4

As you can see, the Centerline tool will triangulate the first three points and attempt to establish a centered pattern. In this way, you can use it to draw centerline arcs, circles, and lines. However, if you just need to draw a series of lines, this functionality can get in the way.

To draw just centerlines, click the first two points, then click any blank space on the sheet, then click the next two points and click a blank area again, and so on. The blank clicks are the same as right-clicking and choosing Create. Try this on VIEW 5 to draw centerlines between each of the corner holes.

WATCH YOUR MOUSE CLICKS DURING CENTERLINE CREATION

The Centerline tool is a bit specific in the order it wants to see mouse clicks. After you have selected the final features on which to place the center mark, right-click and select Create. If you do not select Create and continue to select the next hole, you may end up with undesirable results. Also, do not be confused by the Done option. This exits you from the Centerline tool without creating any of the centerlines that have not yet been created. It takes a little getting used to, but you'll quickly figure it out.

Centerline Bisector

Use Centerline Bisector to create a centerline halfway between two edges or two points. Note that the edges do not have to be parallel or the same length. You can even select two circles, and you will get a centerline halfway between them.

1. Still in mi_12a_082.idw, select the Centerline Bisector tool on the Annotate tab.

2. Zoom in on the center shaft area of view Section A-A.

3. Click the top and bottom lines on the shaft to create a centerline running down the middle of the section view. Notice the distance between the two lines is bisected with a centerline.

4. Place bisector centerlines in two holes in Section A-A by clicking the opposing lines for each.

5. Right-click, and choose Done.

6. Click the centerline you placed in the center shaft and drag out the left end so it extends past the shaft. Bisector centerlines are created based on the size of the lines you choose and may need to be adjusted. Your section view should resemble Figure 12.19.

Center Mark

Use the Center Mark tool to annotate hole centers, circular edges, cylindrical geometry, and arcs such as filleted corners. Center marks, as well as centerlines, are primarily formatted by the Center Mark style, but there is a distinct difference between how ANSI and non-ANSI center marks are drawn, so be sure your active standard is set properly for your needs.

1. Continuing with mi_12a_082.idw, select the Center Mark tool on the Annotate tab.

2. Zoom in to VIEW 2.

3. Click the edge or the centers of each hole.

4. Click the outermost circle as well.

5. Right-click, and choose Done.

6. Select the large center mark you just created and then click the Style drop-down box (found on the Format panel of the Annotate tab).

7. Select the style called Center Mark (ISO) from the list, in order to set the existing center mark to the ISO style. You'll notice the change in style.

FIGURE 12.19
Bisecting
centerlines

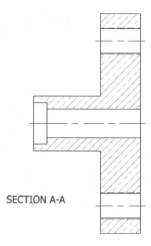

SECTION A-A

Here are some Center Mark options to be aware of:

◆ For large center marks that are mostly solid lines, you can right-click them, choose Edit ➤ Add/Remove Dashes, and then click the lines to place the dashes. Do the same to remove extra dashes once placed.

◆ Once extra dashes have been added, click them to slide them into place.

◆ To lock extra dashes down, right-click, and choose Edit ➤ Uniform Spacing.

◆ You can align center marks with an angled edge by right-clicking them, choosing Edit ➤ Align To Edge, and then selecting a diagonal edge in the view.

◆ You can adjust center mark overshoots by clicking the ends and dragging in or out as required.

◆ To reset overshoots, right-click the center mark, and choose Edit ➤ Fit Center Mark.

◆ To simplify center marks to just a center cross, right-click them, and choose Edit ➤ Extension Lines.

◆ You can right-click a center mark and choose Edit Center Mark Style to adjust the way center marks are drawn by default.

Centered Pattern

Use Centered Pattern to create a centerline on parts or features that have a consistent pattern. If the pattern is circular, a center mark is automatically placed:

1. Continuing with mi_12a_082.idw, select the Centered Pattern tool on the Annotate tab.

2. Zoom in to VIEW 3.

3. Click the center hole first to establish the pattern axis.

4. Then click all the holes in the pattern, and click the starting hole again to close the pattern.

5. Right-click and choose Create, and then right-click and choose Done.

There are many options for creating centerlines and center marks manually, but in the next section you'll create them in a more automatic fashion. You can close the current file without saving changes and continue.

Automated Centerlines

Rather than placing centerlines and center marks manually, you can use the Automated Centerlines tool. This tool is in the right-click menu of each view, and you can run this on multiple views on the same sheet at one time (multiselect views while holding your Ctrl key down before executing the tool).

1. On the Get Started tab, click the Open button.

2. Browse for the file named mi_12a_084.idw located in the Chapter 12 directory of the Mastering Inventor 2011 folder, and click Open.

3. Hold the Ctrl key, and select all four views.

4. Right-click, and choose Automated Centerlines. If you do not see this option in the right-click menu, you have most likely selected something other than a view.

5. In the Automated Centerlines dialog box, use the Apply To buttons to select the type of objects you want to apply center marks and centerlines to. In this case, choose all of the following:

   - Hole features

   - Cylindrical features

   - Revolved features

   - Circular patterned features

6. In the Projection area, ensure that both the Normal and Parallel projection buttons are selected; otherwise, the sections' views will be ignored.

7. In the Radius Threshold area, enter **3** in the Maximum box for Circular Edges. This will ensure that no center mark is placed for the outer edge of the revolved part or for the 3.94 radius circle in the hub.

8. Click OK, and notice the centerlines and marks that have been created.

You can set the defaults for automated centerlines by going to the Tools tab, clicking Document Settings, and going to the Drawing tab in the dialog box that appears. Do this in your template, and you will not have to go through the process of selecting the Apply To buttons or specifying minimum and maximum threshold values each time.

Use the Undo button to reset the drawing and then experiment with the options to gain more understanding of the different features. When you are finished, you can close the file without saving changes.

CREATING DIMENSIONS

A significant portion of any detailing job is placing and modifying dimensions; therefore, it is important to become familiar with the various Dimension tools and formatting options available in Inventor's Drawing Manager. Here is a quick reference of the dimension types available:

- ♦ Linear dimension from one element. For instance, select a line and drag and drop the dimension.

- ♦ Linear dimension between two elements. Select two endpoints, and drag and drop the dimension.

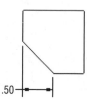

- ♦ Aligned dimension between two elements. For instance, select two endpoints of an angled line, right-click, and select Aligned to force an aligned solution.

◆ Angular dimension between three points. Select three points; they can be endpoints, mid-points, center points, and so on.

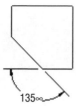

◆ Angular dimension of an interior angle. Select two angular lines, and drag to the minor angle.

◆ Angular dimension of an exterior angle. Select two angular lines, and drag to the major angle.

◆ Angular dimension from a reference line, such as a line from an object line and a centerline or a projected work axis.

◆ Radial dimension. Select any circle or arc, and right-click to choose either a radius or a dimension. Radius is the default for arcs.

◆ Diameter dimension. Select any circle or arc, and right-click to choose either a radius or a dimension. Diameter is the default for circles.

◆ Baseline dimensions. Select objects, and then set the direction and base dimensions.

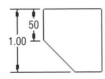

◆ Ordinate dimensions. Select objects, and then set the direction and origin dimensions.

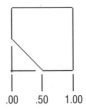

◆ Chain dimensions. Select objects, and then set the direction and chain dimensions.

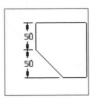

◆ Implied intersection dimension. Select the first intersecting object, then right-click and choose Intersection, and finally select the second intersecting object. Next, select an object to dimension the intersection point to.

◆ Apply General, Ordinate, and Baseline dimensions to spline endpoints.

◆ Apply General and Ordinate dimensions to the X and Y Min/Max points of a spline.

Most of these dimensions can be created with just one tool, the General Dimension tool.

General Dimensions

You can find the General Dimension tool by clicking the Dimension button on the Annotate tab. This will be your primary dimensioning tool. It works very much like the Sketch Dimension tool discussed earlier in this book, in that this single tool can generate several different types of dimensions depending on the geometry you select.

Once geometry is selected, you can right-click to choose the applicable options for placing the type of geometry you've selected. You can also control snap options, arrowhead options, and leader options specific to each dimension type from the right-click menu.

A few more types of dimensions are available in drawings than can be generated in sketches using the General Dimension tool. For instance, once an arc is selected (not a full circle), a radius dimension is created by default, but prior to placement, you can right-click and choose Diameter, Angle, Arc Length, or Chord Length from the Dimension Type flyout, as shown in Figure 12.20.

FIGURE 12.20
Arc dimension options

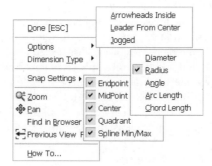

Prior to placing a linear dimension between two points or two parallel lines, you can create Linear Diameter or Linear Symmetric dimensions by choosing from the dimension's right-click Dimension Type flyout. These types of dimensions are used commonly with symmetrical parts, especially turned cylindrical parts. Figure 12.21 shows the Linear dimension options available when two points or two parallel lines have been selected.

FIGURE 12.21
Linear dimension
options

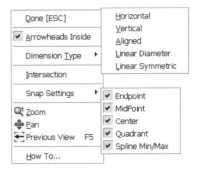

Prior to placing diameter dimensions, you can right-click and switch to a radius or change the leader options, as shown in Figure 12.22.

FIGURE 12.22
Diameter dimen-
sion options

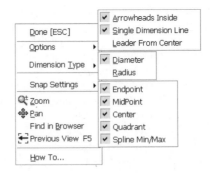

Dimension Filters

You can create and access selection filters by holding your Shift key down and right-clicking or by clicking the selection drop-down from the Quick Access tool bar at the top of the screen. Selection filters specify the elements that can be selected when working in a drawing. For instance, if you choose the Detail selection filter, only common objects common to detailing tasks are selectable, and items such as view boundaries, view labels, section view lines, and so on, are filtered out and cannot be selected. If you choose the Select All Inventor Dimensions, you can quickly select all of the draw-ing dimensions and then use the Style drop-down menu to change them all to a different dimen-sion style. You can create a custom filter also by Shift+right-clicking and choosing Edit Select Filters.

Recovering Model Dimensions

Another way to quickly add dimensions to your model views is using the Retrieve Dimensions tool. You can access this tool from the view's right-click menu or from the Annotate tab. This tool allows you to recover sketch and feature dimensions that were used to model your part and bring them into the drawing view. To recover model dimensions, follow these steps:

1. On the Annotate tab, click the Retrieve button.

2. Select the view you want to retrieve dimensions for.

3. You can choose to retrieve dimensions per feature or per part, depending upon what makes sense. You might choose per part when working with an assembly view, for instance. Set the radio button as you require.

4. Next select the feature(s) or part(s) in the graphics window. You can select multiple objects by holding down Shift or Ctrl key as you select them. Or you can window-select the whole view.

5. When selected, the part or feature will display all of the dimensions normal to the view. Click the Select Dimensions button to choose which dimensions to keep. Again, you can use a window selection to select them all.

6. Click the Apply button, and then select another view to retrieve or click OK.

BE WARNED ABOUT MODEL DIMENSIONS

You should be aware there are often dimensions required to model features that are not necessarily required or desired for use on a drawing. For example, if you were to recover model dimensions for View 7 in the file named mi_12a_084.idw, you would see the pocket is dimensioned from one end of the part and the holes are dimensioned from the other end. Not only is this poor practice, since it requires the machinist to rezero the mill, but it can also cause a tolerance stack-up.

Recovered model dimensions behave similarly to regular, placed dimensions with respect to editing and formatting. Recovered model dimensions cannot be detached or reattached from the geometry they're referencing.

Model dimension values can be directly edited from the drawing view, thus changing the model parameter value and affecting the size and shape of your model feature. Access the dimension value by selecting Edit Model Dimension from the dimension's right-click menu.

The ability to change model dimension values is set during Inventor installation; the default setting is to have the ability enabled. If you would prefer that users can retrieve model dimensions but not be allowed to edit them from the drawing, go through the installation configuration settings to disable this.

EXERCISE CAUTION WHEN EDITING MODEL DIMENSIONS

The option to enable edits of model dimension values from the drawing can be *very* powerful and very dangerous. Editing a model dimension from a drawing is a quick way to edit the size and shape of a model, but it is often blind to other issues it may create. For example, if a part is used in an assembly and another part references holes adaptively in that assembly, changing the model dimension may affect this second part without your knowledge. It is suggested that you always open the assembly to see what else your changes will affect.

Once a particular model dimension is recovered in one view, it cannot be recovered again in any other view in the same file. You can move recovered model dimensions between views, however, provided appropriate attachment points exist in the target view. To do this, right-click the dimension, and choose Move Dimension.

Baseline Dimensions and Baseline Sets

Baseline dimensions are a series of linear dimensions that terminate to a common point (or baseline). The Baseline Dimension and Baseline Dimension Set tools offer a mechanism to quickly add dimensions to a drawing view in an orderly way.

When you execute the Baseline Dimension tool, you're left with a series of conventional linear dimensions. This tool simply automates what you could do on your own with the General Dimension tool. The Baseline Dimension Set tool, however, generates a collected group of linear dimensions that are edited and moved (through dragging and editing) as a single group.

To understand this more fully, open the file named mi_12a_085.idw located in the Chapter 12 directory of the Mastering Inventor 2011 folder, and compare the two dimensioned views. The one on the left was done with the Baseline Dimension tool, and the one on the right was done with the Baseline Dimension Set tool.

Use the views on the bottom to create baseline dimensions. Start either tool, click the left vertical part edge (this will be the baseline), and then manually or multiselect additional features (these can be model edges or hole centers). When you've selected all the geometry you want to dimension, right-click and click to place the dimensions (shown in Figure 12.23). After you place the dimensions, you can continue to select points on the view (points on geometry rather than explicit geometry), or you can right-click and select Create.

FIGURE 12.23
Baseline
dimensions

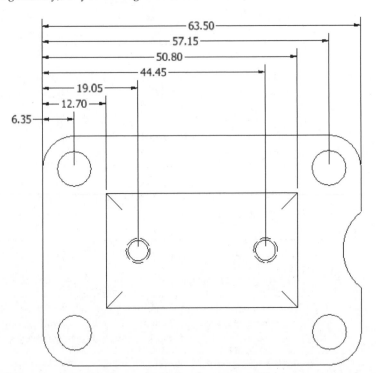

Once a baseline set is created, you can right-click on any of the dimensions and choose from the options to Add a Member, Delete a Member, Detach a Member, and Arrange the entire set. You can also choose Make Origin to reset the base of the set.

Chain Dimensions and Chain Sets

CERT OBJECTIVE

Chain Dimensions and Chain Dimension sets enable you to quickly select objects and then place a chain of dimensions from point to point along the selected direction. To understand Chain Dimensions more fully, open the file named mi_12a_092.idw located in the Chapter 12 directory of the Mastering Inventor 2011 folder, and compare the two dimensioned views. The one on the top left was done with the Chain Dimension tool, and the one on the top right was done with the Chain Dimension Set tool.

Use the view on the bottom left to create chain dimensions.

1. From the Dimension panel of the Annotate tab, select Chain.

2. On the drawing, select the geometry to dimension by clicking to select individual edges or by clicking and dragging a window from right to left to select multiple edges.

3. Next, right-click and select Continue.

4. Move your cursor to preview the placement and then click to set the direction.

5. When finished, right-click and select Done.

Use the Chain dimension tool to select the baseline dimensions in the bottom center view to convert them to chain dimensions.

1. From the Dimension panel of the Annotate tab, select Chain.

2. On the drawing, select all of the baseline dimensions by clicking and dragging a window from right to left.

3. Next, right-click and select Continue.

4. Select the center marks for the two smaller holes to add additional dimensions.

5. Then right-click and select Create.

Note: there appears to be a bit of a bug in the way the dimensioned are arranged. To remedy this, use the Arrange button, as described here.

6. From the Dimension panel of the Annotate tab, select Arrange.

7. On the drawing, select all of the chain dimensions you just created by clicking and dragging a window from right to left.

8. Right-click and choose Contour Entity.

9. Select the edge of the part (or optionally click anywhere to the right of the part).

Use the view on the bottom right to create a chain dimension set.

1. From the Dimension panel of the Annotate tab, select Chain Set from the Chain drop-down list.

2. On the drawing, select just the top and bottom edge of the part and any one of the holes.

3. Next, right-click and select Continue.

4. Move your cursor to preview the placement and then click to set the direction.

5. Select an additional hole to add to the set.

6. Next, right-click and select Create.

7. Now, add more members to the set by right-clicking on the set and choosing Add Member.

8. Select all of the geometry needed to complete the set so that it matches the top right view and then right-click and choose Done.

9. Right-click on any of the dimensions in the set and choose Delete Member.

Once you've experimented with the chain dimension options, you can close the file without saving changes.

Ordinate Dimensions and Ordinate Sets

CERT OBJECTIVE

Ordinate dimensions and ordinate dimension sets are created much the same way as baseline and chain dimensions and dimension sets. Again, a dimension set is managed and formatted as a single, selectable object (with some exceptions), while the Ordinate Dimension tool results in independently controlled dimensions.

Another key difference between ordinate dimensions and an ordinate dimension set is that you can have multiple ordinate sets on a single view with different origin points. However, once you specify an origin for ordinate dimensions on a view, all ordinate dimensions placed on that view will reference that origin as well as any hole tables referencing that view. The reverse is true as well: once an origin is specified for a hole table, ordinate dimensions on that view share the origin.

CHANGING ORIGINS

You can set the origin for an ordinate dimension set after you have selected the geometry. The default origin is the first selected geometry, but you can change it. This is very powerful for updating a drawing. For ordinate dimensions, you can click on the origin indicator and drag it to a different endpoint, midpoint, or center point to change the geometry reference. You can also hide the origin indicator by right-clicking on it and then show it again by right-clicking on any of the origin dimensions.

To understand this more fully, open the file named mi_12a_099.idw located in the Chapter 12 directory of the Mastering Inventor 2011 folder, and compare the two dimensioned views. The one on the left was done with the Ordinate Dimension tool, and the one on the right was done with the Ordinate Dimension Set tool. Use the views on the bottom to create ordinate dimensions and ordinate dimensions sets matching the views at the top. Once created, explore the right-click options for the dimensions and the dimension set.

Dimensions in Isometric Views

Although you may have been taught at some point that dimensions should never be placed on isometric views because traditional detailing techniques do not allow an accurate dimension to be pulled from an isometric, Inventor can overcome this by pulling the intelligence from the physical model. When you use the General Dimension tool to add dimensions to an isometric view, the resulting dimensions are fundamentally different from those you place in orthographic views.

This is immediately noticeable when you see how the resulting dimensions are drawn on the sheet: all of the dimension geometry (text, arrowheads, extension lines, and dimension lines) are drawn in 3D space and not in sheet space. Dimensions generated on isometric views are called *true* (meaning they reflect the true model space dimensional value). Dimensions added to orthographic views are known as *projected* because the dimension value represents the calculated distance or angle between endpoints or geometry projected onto the sheet.

When placing an isometric dimension, Inventor tries to determine an appropriate annotation plane based on your geometry selection. In many cases, particularly with linear dimensions, multiple inferred annotation planes are available. Prior to placing the dimension, you can toggle through these inferred annotation planes by pressing the spacebar.

If none of the inferred work planes meets your needs, you can project the dimension either onto the sheet plane or onto a model work plane. For instance, oftentimes you will find that hole notes and leader dimensions such as radii and diameters look better placed on the sheet plane rather than in the isometric plane; therefore, you can right-click and choose Use Sheet Plane when placing them.

The change in dimension behavior (true versus projected) happens automatically depending on the view orientation. Any projected isometric or base isometric view results in True dimensions. As a rule, newly added dimensions to a view are treated as true if none of the model's origin planes is parallel to the sheet (with the exception of auxiliary views). You can override this rule on a view-by-view basis by right-clicking a view and changing the dimension type (True or Projected).

RETRIEVE DIMENSIONS FROM ISOMETRIC VIEWS

A quick way to place dimensions on an isometric view is to right-click the view and choose Retrieve Dimensions.

Isometric dimensions are functionally identical to orthographic dimensions; however, they cannot be "moved." That is, they cannot be detached and reattached to different geometry, and they can't be moved using the dimension Move option on the dimension's right-click menu. All formatting options and behavior are otherwise identical.

Although placing isometric dimensions may seem unconventional, you can, in fact, oftentimes eliminate the number of views required to concisely communicate the design by placing dimensions on an isometric view. Try adding dimensions to the isometric view in mi_12a_105.idw, as shown in Figure 12.24.

FIGURE 12.24
Isometric view
dimensions

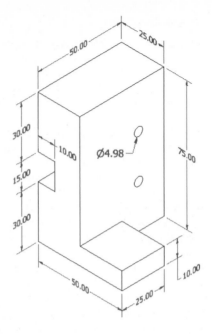

Formatting and Editing Dimensions

All the different types of dimensions discussed in this section are initially formatted by an associative dimension style. Indeed, each different type of dimension can be set to use a different dimension style if needed. Almost every formatting option available for dimensions is set through the dimension style. There are literally dozens of individual style settings—too many to list here. To illustrate how to change dimension formatting through styles, you'll walk through setting up a new dimension style to apply a symmetrical tolerance.

1. On the Get Started tab, click the Open button.

2. Browse for the file named mi_12a_107.idw located in the Chapter 12 directory of the Mastering Inventor 2011 folder, and click Open.

3. On the Manage tab, click the Style Editor button.

4. In the Style And Standard Editor, expand the Dimension node on the left side, and click the Default – mm (ANSI) dimension style.

5. Click the New button along the top, thus creating a new style based upon the Default – mm (ANSI) style. You can also right-click the dimension style you want to start from and choose New Style.

6. Enter **PM1** for the dimension name, and click OK.

7. Click the Tolerance tab, and set the Method drop-down to Symmetric.

8. Enter **0.100** for the Upper value field, and then set the Linear Precision to three places, as shown in Figure 12.25.

9. Go to the Units tab, and change the Linear Precision setting to three places (3.123).

10. Click the Save button along the top, and close the Style Editor dialog box.

FIGURE 12.25
Dimension style
tolerance settings

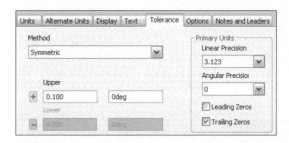

11. Apply this dimension style to the existing dimensions on the sheet by first selecting them and then going to the Annotate tab and selecting PM1 from the Style drop-down (found just under the Layer drop-down to the top right of the screen). The selected dimensions will immediately update to reflect the new style assignment.

CREATING DIMENSION STYLES

It is a good idea to create all your standard dimension styles before rolling out your style library. By creating standards for all users to use, you eliminate any discrepancy that comes from multiple users all trying to create drawings that look the same. You can create all your decimal place dimensions (one place, two place, three place, and so on), toleranced dimensions, and even dowel pinhole–toleranced dimension styles that users need only select.

---

12. Next, double-click the 25 mm dimension to edit it, and click the Precision And Tolerance tab. The ±0.100 tolerance setting is reflected here in the Edit dialog box. Change the tolerance value to ±0.200, and then click OK.

You've now created two formatting overrides for the 25 mm dimension. You have overridden the standard dimension style assignment by setting it to a dimension style other than the By Standard style, and you then set a tolerance override. In addition to making style-level formatting changes to dimensions, you can copy and paste dimension formatting between dimension objects on your sheet.

13. Right-click the 25 mm dimension you just edited, and select Copy Properties.

14. Then click the 30 mm dimension. It will adopt both the style formatting and the local tolerance value override from your source dimension.

You can configure which properties are copied before selecting the target dimension by right-clicking and selecting Settings after invoking the Copy Properties tool. To edit a dimension's style, right-click the object and choose Edit Dimension Style, which will take you right into the Style Editor and highlight the dimension style. You can do this with just about any annotation object.

Hole and Thread Notes

A hole note differentiates itself from a traditional diameter dimension by calling out feature information beyond just the hole diameter. The Hole/Thread Note command (in the View Annotation panel) generates a leadered note that displays all pertinent hole feature information derived from the hole edge that is selected.

For example, a hole note pointing to a simple blind hole might appear as 10 × 20. A hole note pointing to a through partial-tapped hole might appear as 10-32 UNF-2B × 20.00. Inventor provides you with the ability to tailor the exact contents of the hole note through your dimension style.

Use the Hole/Thread Note tool to add a single note for the mounting hole and tapped hole in the faceplate front view. You can configure hole notes to display whatever string of description text you prefer as well as set the various hole parameter values' Precision and Tolerance settings. These preferences are set and stored in the dimension style.

You can configure more than 50 types of holes in this interface; they generally correspond to the different kinds of holes you can create using the Hole feature tool in part and assembly modeling (holes as a result of circular-extruded cuts, voids, or circular sheet-metal cut features are also supported by hole notes).

You can configure hole notes to display the hole quantity as part of the note. You can add a quantity note either directly on an individual note through the Edit Hole Note dialog box (right-click a hole note and choose Edit Hole Note) or at the style level (right-click a hole note and choose Edit Dimension style) so they appear for all holes of the same type. You can use the hole note in `mi_12a_109.idw` to explore this.

To add a quantity note at the style level, make sure you're editing the dimension style associated with the hole notes on your drawing (the best way to ensure this is to right-click on the hole note and choose Edit Dimension Style). Select Thru – Full Thread in the Note Format drop-down, and then click in the text field so that the cursor is in front of the note text; finally, click the button with the # sign on it. This inserts the <QTYNOTE> variable token in front of the note, as shown in Figure 12.26.

FIGURE 12.26
Hole note settings
in dimension style

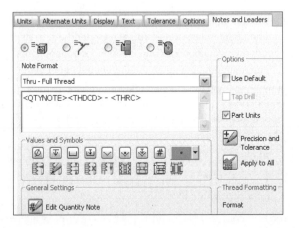

You can customize the quantity note by clicking the Edit Quantity Note button on the dimension style's Notes And Leaders tab, as shown at the bottom left of Figure 12.26. By default, the quantity note is set up as a prefix to the full hole note (2 ×). This dialog box also lets you determine how the hole quantity is determined (either the number of holes in a feature or pattern or a complete evaluation of identical holes in a view where all the hole axes are normal to the view).

As soon as you save the changes to your dimension style, you should see the hole note for the tapped holes update to include the quantity of holes (2 ×).

The Notes And Leaders tab on the Dimension style also enables you to pre-configure other kinds of feature notes including chamfer notes (which are actually calculated notes and not feature-dependent), punch notes, and bend notes (both of which are available only for views of sheet-metal parts).

Leadered Symbols

Many of the annotations you can apply to a drawing belong to a common class of annotations we'll refer to as *leadered symbols*. These are all grouped together in the Drawing Annotation panel: Surface Texture Symbol, Welding Symbol, Feature Control Frame, Feature ID Symbol, Datum ID Symbol, and five different Datum Target tools. Each of these are created the same way, and each is formatted by replace with its own dedicated style.

In the following steps, you will walk through an exercise that involves adding geometric dimensioning and tolerancing symbols to a drawing of a faceplate:

1. On the Get Started tab, click the Open button.

2. Browse for the file named mi_12a_109.idw located in the Chapter 12 directory of the Mastering Inventor 2011 folder, and click Open.

3. On the Annotate tab, use the drop-down on the Symbols panel, and choose the Datum Identifier Symbol button.

4. Click the far-right edge of the part, and drag the leader to the desired length.

5. Click the screen to set the leader, and then right-click and choose Continue.

6. Accept the default A value in the text editor, and hit OK.

7. Click the bottom edge to add a second datum ID (B), but rather than placing a leader, right-click, and choose Continue immediately after clicking the initial part edge point. You can do this with most Inventor leader features.

8. Next, on the Annotate tab, use the drop-down on the Symbols panel, and choose the Feature Control Frame button.

PROBLEMS WITH ATTACHING THE SYMBOL TO THE LEADER

At the time of the writing, attaching the symbol to the leader, as described in steps 9 through 12, is not working. This is a known bug that occurred during a service pack of Inventor 2010 and persists into first release build of Inventor 2011. This is scheduled to be fixed in a service pack or hotfix for Inventor 2011. Depending on the update level you are running at the time you are reading this, attaching a symbol to a dimension may not work as described. You can search online for *Autodesk Inventor Updates and Service Packs* to find any released updates.

9. Rather than attaching the frame to the part, instead hover your mouse pointer near the bottom middle of the hole note, until you see a green dot indicating the snap point (just below the N in UNF), and then click it.

10. Then right-click and choose Continue to place the frame without a leader. This will attach the frame to the dimension text.

11. Fill out the appropriate fields for a positional tolerance relative to the A datum and the B datum, as shown in Figure 12.27; then hit OK.

12. To see that the frame is attached, select the hole note, and then drag the leader landing to move the note. Notice how the frame remains constrained to the hole note.

FIGURE 12.27
Feature control frame attached to hole note

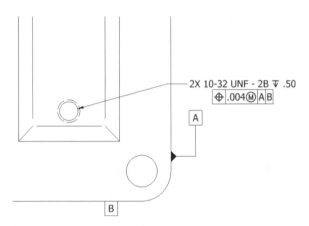

Drawing Text

You can add text to your drawing in multiple ways. The Text tool (found on the Annotate tab) is used to create general drawing notes. This kind of text is limited because it can't be associated (constrained) to a drawing view and because it offers no control over which component iProperties and parameters are being accessed when you have multiple components detailed on the same sheet.

In addition to the Text tool, you can also use the Leader Text tool (also found on the Annotate tab), which can be associated to a view or a component, allowing you to extract and display iProperty and model parameter values from the component to which the leader is attached. If view associativity is required but you don't want a leader, you can right-click the leader text and choose Delete Leader.

Each of these tools utilizes the generic Format Text dialog box. This dialog box is used to edit any text-specific annotations as well as other annotations such as hole tags and datum and feature IDs. The general text formatting for any drawing annotation containing text ultimately comes from a text style. Text style formatting (size, font, color, and so on) can be overwritten in the Format Text dialog box.

General Tables

You can create a table on a drawing sheet by using the General Table tool found on the Annotation tab (the button is located on the Table panel and is called General). When you click the General button, you are presented with the Table dialog. You can create and empty table and then add information, or you can choose a data source from which to populate the table.

iParts and iAssemblies   These can be used to create tabulated configuration tables. For instance, you might have an iPart bracket in six different lengths. You could select the iPart file to use as the table data source and then place a table with a row for each of the six lengths listed by their part numbers. You would choose the Length parameter to use as the column, and each row would be populated with the appropriate length value, as defined in the iPart. You can then place a view of one of the brackets and edit the dimension to read Length, rather than the numeric value.

Sheet metal parts   These parts can be used to create bend tables. Selecting an existing flat pattern view as the data source allows you to choose the parameters you want to use in the bend table, and then place a table indexing the bends on the flat pattern. Bend ID numbers are automatically placed on the flat pattern view. Editing the Bend ID in the table updates the ID number on the flat pattern. Editing the table overrides the bend order annotation of the part file; therefore, it is typically best to use the Bend Order Annotation tool in the sheet metal part to set the order.

XLS files   These files can be used to link an Excel spreadsheet file to a general table. Use the General Table tool and select the XLS file to place the table on the drawing sheet and link to the original file. To update the table, right-click it in the browser and choose Edit to Open the XLS file. If the XLS file is linked, you can edit it outside of Inventor and right-click to choose Update to bring in the changes. To point the table to a different XLS file, expand the 3rd Party folder and right-click on the table link and choose Change Source. Be aware there are limitations to the number of rows you can have using this method. Also note blank rows in the XLS file will be read as the end of the table.

Hole Tables

You can document hole descriptions, quantities, and locations on a view by using a hole table rather than using hole notes. Indeed, you can use the hole table to document not only hole features but sheet-metal punches as well. You can even use a hole table to call out locations of recovered work points in your model. This technique can be used to detail specialized features such as slots and bosses.

Hole tables, like most types of annotation in Inventor, are initially formatted by an associative style—a Hole Table style in this case. The Hole Table style enables you to select which columns you want displayed in your table, format precision and units for the X and Y location columns, change line formatting, filter on different hole types, and configure various grouping mechanisms depending on your needs.

Everything about the hole table is formatted by the Hole Table style except for the description string for the hole. The description string uses the same configuration as your hole notes and receives this particular formatting by the hole tag's dimension style (hole tags are created with the hole table and are formatted by a dimension style).

In the following steps, you'll walk through setting up a Hole Table style and creating a hole table for the faceplate:

1. On the Get Started tab, click the Open button.

2. Browse for the file named mi_12a_111.idw located in the Chapter 12 directory of the Mastering Inventor 2011 folder, and click Open.

3. On the Manage tab, click the Styles Editor button.

4. In the left pane of the Styles Editor, expand the hole table node, and click the style named Hole Table – mm (ANSI). The right pane will update to show the settings for this style, as shown in Figure 12.28.

FIGURE 12.28
Hole Table Style interface

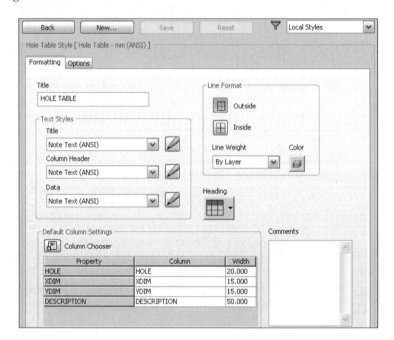

5. At the top of the right pane, click the New button, and set the name of the new hole table style to **HT_02**.

6. Click the Column Chooser button, and select the Quantity property on the left of the resulting property list.

7. Click the Add button to add it to the included list of columns on the right.

8. Use the Move Up button to move the Quantity column up in the list as you like; then click OK.

9. Right-click the XDIM Property in the Default Column Settings frame, and select Format Column.

10. In the Format Column dialog box, change the precision to three places, and change the column heading to X LOCATION. Note that you can format columns in this manner in almost all of Inventor's annotation tables, such as parts lists and so on.

11. Click OK, and repeat for the YDIM column.

12. Click the Save button to save the changes, and exit the Style Editor dialog box by clicking the Done button.

You will now need to place a hole table on the drawing. Three hole table variations are available on the Table panel of the Annotate tab:

Selection   This allows you to select the holes you want to include in the table, and then only those holes are included.

View   This documents all holes in a view, although you can use filters to exclude certain hole types. As holes are added to the part, the hole table updates to include them.

Features   This allows you to select an instance of the types of holes you want to include in the table, and then all holes of that type are included.

To continue this exercise, you'll choose to place a hole table using the View method.

1. On the Annotate tab, select the Hole drop-down on the Table panel, and choose Hole View.

2. Select the view on the sheet.

3. Next, you need to place the origin on the view. You can click any edge or vertex of the part, or you can project the edges to find the apparent intersection of the lower-left corner.

4. To place a table using the table style you created, go to the Style drop-down at the top right of the screen, and choose HT_02 from the list.

FINDING A CORNER INTERSECTION

To find an apparent intersection for placement of an origin marker, zoom into the lower-left corner of the part. Then scrub your mouse pointer over the vertical and horizontal edges of the part, and bring your mouse pointer to the apparent intersection; you should see the edge projected down and over and a yellow dot at the intersection. When you do, click it to set the origin at that point. Be sure you run over the edges (lines) and not just the endpoints of the edges.

---

5. Next, click the screen to set the hole table on the sheet.

For each individual hole in the view, a hole tag is placed next to the hole edge, and a corresponding row is generated in the hole table. Also notice that because each hole is called out individually in this table, each row has a quantity of 1 (shown in Figure 12.29). You can edit the hole table by right-clicking it and choosing Edit Hole table. From there, you can set the table to roll up all A-type holes and all B-type holes from the Options tab by selecting the Rollup radio button.

FIGURE 12.29
Hole table

HOLE TABLE				
HOLE	QUANTITY	X LOCATION	Y LOCATION	DESCRIPTION
A1	1	6.35	6.35	⌀.27 ▽ .75
A2	1	38.10	6.35	⌀.27 ▽ .75
A3	1	6.35	57.15	⌀.27 ▽ .75
A4	1	38.10	57.15	⌀.27 ▽ .75
B1	1	22.23	19.05	10-32 UNF - 2B ▽ .50
B2	1	22.23	44.45	10-32 UNF - 2B ▽ .50

You can also edit the Tag, Note, or Description text by right-clicking the text in the table. You can make direct overrides to hole descriptions by double-clicking the description text, and you can override X and Y location precision by right-clicking an individual cell. You can access several other options by right-clicking the text in the table as well, so be certain to explore them all. When finished, you can close the file without saving changes.

HOLE TABLES SAVE TIME ON LARGE PARTS

For large plates with many different holes, hole tables are wonderful. A large plate could take a half hour or more to fully dimension. Furthermore, it's often difficult for a machinist to tell where all five of the same holes are located if they are not all called out individually. The hole table gives the machinist X and Y locations of the holes that they can use to program their CNC milling machine extraordinarily quickly. Don't be surprised if the machinist asks you to dimension all your parts using hole tables.

Annotating Assembly Drawings

Creating/annotating drawing views of assemblies is similar to doing so for parts. All the same views and annotation tools discussed in the previous sections can be executed when working with assembly and presentation models. When creating views of assemblies, you will typically create parts lists and balloons and may need to control reference parts, interference edges, and assembly representations. These subjects and others dealing specifically with assembly files are covered in the following sections.

ASSEMBLY REPRESENTATIONS

One of the most significant differences between part and assembly model views are the view options available for assembly views. When an assembly file is referenced in the Base View, representation options become available on the Component tab of the Drawing View dialog box. These controls allow you to specify which assembly view, positional, or LOD representation is displayed in the resulting drawing view.

View representations can optionally be made associative to the view (using the check box at the top of the View Representation control). Specifically, an associative view representation means that as a component's visibility is changed in the assembly, the change is witnessed in the drawing view as well. If the associative option is deselected, you can toggle component visibility from the drawing itself by expanding the view node in the browser and then expanding the model tree on the view node and then right-clicking on a components and choosing Visibility. If the visibility option is grayed out, the view is associative and the component visibility is being controlled in the assembly.

MAKING YOUR VIEWS ASSOCIATIVE

Most of the time you are going to want to make your views associative. If you do not, you'll be scratching your head trying to figure out why the drawing view is not matching your view representation.

Recall the general definitions of each assembly representation type:

View representations   These control component visibility, color overrides, and parts list filters.

Positional representations   These show an assembly in different physical positions.

Level-of-detail (LOD) representations   These control visibility and manage memory consumption by suppressing components.

In the next several steps, you will edit a view of an assembly to see how to use assembly representations in drawing views:

1. On the Get Started tab, click the Open button.

2. Browse for the file named mi_12a_115.idw located in the Chapter 12 directory of the Mastering Inventor 2011 folder, and click Open.

3. In the browser, expand the Sheet1 node to reveal the node for each existing view.

4. Expand the Main View node to reveal the assembly node, and then expand the assembly node to reveal the parts tree.

5. Right-click the Main View and choose Edit View to examine the view options dealing with representations. Notice the different presentations, as shown in Figure 12.30.

FIGURE 12.30
Assembly base
view creation

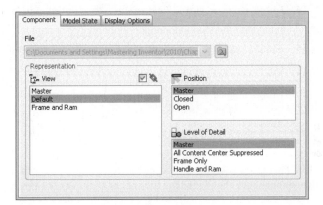

6. In the View area, choose the view representation named Frame And Ram, and then click OK.

You'll notice all of the parts are gone now except the frame and ram. This was set up in the assembly by toggling the visibility state off for all the other parts and then saving the view configuration as a view representation. Examining the browser, you'll see it shows the parts set to not be visible are gray.

7. Right-click the Main View, and choose Edit View again.

8. In the Level Of Detail area, choose the representation named Handle And Ram, and then click OK.

You'll note that only the ram remains on-screen. This is because you have the view set to use two different representations at once. The view representation has the visibility turned off for everything but the frame and ram, but the frame was suppressed in the level of detail. Examining the browser you'll see suppressed parts are not listed.

Typically, it's best not to use these two representations together because it can be confusing as to what is being controlled where. However, there are times when this is the best way to achieve the desired results.

9. Right-click the Main View, and choose Edit View once again.

10. Set the view representation to Master, and set the positional representation to Closed (leave the LOD as is); then click OK.

You'll see that now just the handle, shaft, and ram parts are shown (because of the LOD representation), and the positional representation is controlling the positions of these parts.

11. Right-click the Main View, and choose Edit View once more.

12. Set the view representation to Default, and click the Associative check box button (looks like a chain link).

13. Set the LOD representation to Master, and then click OK.

14. In the browser, right-click on the Arbor Frame node and notice the visibility option is grayed out.

14. Right-click the Main View, and choose Edit View one more time.

15. Uncheck the Associative check box button, and then click OK.

16. In the browser, right-click on the Arbor Frame node and notice the visibility option is now available.

17. Click Visibility to toggle it off, and notice the frame is removed from the view.

You are now controlling component visibility at the drawing level rather than using the assembly view representation's visibility controls. You can continue experimenting with the representation options and then close the file without saving changes.

REFERENCE DATA IN DRAWING VIEWS

Assembly components can be designated as Reference. You can apply this attribute as a document setting on the part or assembly file itself or on a per-instance basis when placed in a higher-level assembly. In addition to being omitted from the assembly mass property calculations, BOM, and subsequent drawing parts lists, reference components are drawn and calculated differently in assembly drawing views.

By default, all reference component edges are mapped to a unique layer with a broken line style (double-dash chain). Hidden line calculation, by default, is run separately for reference components and nonreference components. Finally, reference components do not affect the calculation of the drawing boundary. This means that if you have a reference component well apart from nonreference parts in an assembly, it may not be visible in a drawing view until you increase the reference margin.

To explore these settings, you can open the file named `mi_12a_117.idw` located in the Chapter 12 directory of the Mastering Inventor 2011 folder and compare the two views. The view on the left shows the reference part at the default settings. The view on the right has been adjusted to show the reference part as a standard part. Right-click the view and choose Edit to adjust all the reference data view behaviors on the Model State tab of the Drawing View dialog box. Figure 12.31 shows the default settings.

FIGURE 12.31
Reference
data settings

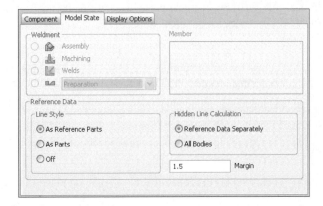

INTERFERENCE AND TANGENT EDGE DISPLAY

As you place and constrain components in an assembly file, it may be necessary to create an interference condition between parts. This is common for press-fit conditions such as pins in undersized holes. This condition is common in Inventor even when you have a threaded fastener being inserted into an equal-diameter threaded hole. These edges are designated as interference edges and can be turned on or off as needed.

Although not specific to assemblies, you can also control the display of tangent edges for cylindrical faces, fillet edges, and so on in your drawing views. Both tangent and interference edges can be enabled by editing the view and selecting the Interference Edge check box on the Display Options tab.

Figure 12.32 shows the difference between two views with these edges turned off and turned on. The interference edge in this case is the small set screw in the middle of the plate. All other differences are tangent edges.

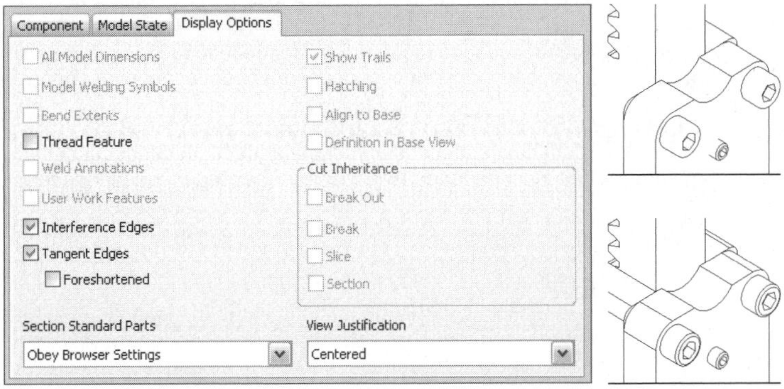

FIGURE 12.32
Tangent and Inter-
ference edges

PARTS LISTS

Parts lists are a formatted report of the assembly bill of materials placed on the drawing in a table. Most of the data you see in a parts list comes ultimately from the assembly BOM, but the BOM and the parts list are managed separately inside Inventor, providing control and flexibility for managing both.

Parts lists have a dedicated formatting style that provides dozens of formatting variations. You'll walk through a typical parts list editing and creation workflow to demonstrate what kind of capabilities can be leveraged in the parts lists.

1. On the Get Started tab, click the Open button.

2. Browse for the file named mi_12a_119.idw located in the Chapter 12 directory of the Mastering Inventor 2011 folder, and click Open.

3. On the Manage tab, click the Styles Editor button, expand the Parts List node, and click the style named MI_PL_02.

4. Click the Column Chooser button, and add the Material property from the list on the left. Then click OK.

5. Click the Heading button, and change the placement to Bottom.

6. Save your changes, and exit the Style dialog box using the Done button.

7. On the Annotate tab, click the Parts List button.

The Parts List dialog box allows you to either click an assembly or presentation drawing view or browse directly to an assembly or presentation file (you can create a parts list on a drawing with no drawing views). You can choose either a structured (first or all levels) or parts-only parts list. If the parts list is too long for the sheet size you're placing it on, you can also enable the option to wrap the parts lists based on a specified number or rows.

8. Click the view on the sheet, and ensure Structured is selected for the BOM view type. Click OK, and then snap the parts lists to the lower-left corner of the drawing border.

Although you can specify the default column width at the style level, you may need to adjust the width based on the length of the text strings read in from the component iProperties. You can adjust column width by clicking and dragging the vertical column lines on the parts list on your sheet.

9. Resize the Material column on the parts list to better accommodate the long description text.

The initial item numbering for the components and the row order come from the last save state of the assembly BOM but can be changed by editing the parts list.

10. Double-click the parts list to launch Parts List dialog box (or right-click and choose Edit).

11. Click the Sort button, and sort by Part Number in descending order, and then click OK.

12. Next, click the Renumber Items button, and notice how new item numbers are assigned based on the sort order.

The new item numbers appear blue and bold in the Parts List dialog box to indicate that they do not match the BOM. Any change you make to any of the cells in the Parts List dialog box (except for custom rows or custom columns) are treated as overrides to the BOM data. However, only Item number overrides can be written back to the BOM. All other overrides are preserved at the parts list level, allowing for greater flexibility of parts list edits at the drawing level without worries that they will be discarded if updated in the BOM. Item number changes can be saved to the assembly BOM cell by cell from the right-click menu or for the entire parts list in one of three ways:

- ◆ While editing the parts list, click the Save Item Overrides To BOM button along the top.

- ◆ Right-click the parts list itself on the sheet, and choose Save Item Overrides To BOM.

- ◆ Right-click Parts List browser node, and choose Save Item Overrides To BOM.

If you intend for the overrides of properties other than the item numbers to match in both the BOM and parts list, you should make those edits in the BOM, where they will push through to the parts list. You can access the BOM quickly by right-clicking the parts list and choosing Bill Of Materials. Edits made in the BOM editor are written back to component iProperties and, therefore, push through to the parts list, provided no parts list overrides have already been made.

13. Click OK to apply the changes and exit the Parts List edit dialog box.

14. Right-click the drawing view and choose Edit View.

15. Set the view representation to Frame and Ram, and then click OK.

Notice the parts list still displays the full assembly even though the view now only shows the frame and ram parts. To set the two to coincide, you will apply a parts list filter.

16. Edit the parts list and click the Filter button, found along the top of the Parts List edit dialog box.

17. From the Define Filter Item drop-down box, select Assembly View Representation.

18. Choose Frame and Ram from the drop-down box, and then click the green check mark. Then click OK to apply the filter.

19. Click OK in the Parts List edit dialog box.

You'll see the parts list update to show only the parts corresponding to the view representation. The parts list is not directly associated with any drawing view (if you choose a view when you create the parts list, it acts only as a pointer to the assembly file itself). You can close the file without saving changes and explore balloons in the next section.

Balloons

Assembly drawing views are related to parts lists by ballooning the components in the assembly drawing view. Balloons are perhaps the only type of annotation relevant for assembly views only. By default, balloons are set to display just a component's assigned item number, but through changes to the balloon style, a balloon can be configured to display any component iProperty or BOM property. Review the creation and editing of balloon styles in "Editing Styles and Standards" section earlier in this chapter.

You should know that only items visible in a view can be selected for placing a balloon; however, you can string multiple balloons together on a single leader, including parts that are not visible, virtual parts, and even line items added to the parts list that do not exist in the assembly BOM. This is also a common technique when ballooning a collection of hardware such as a screw, lock washer, and split washer.

Follow these steps to explore methods and options for balloon placement:

1. On the Get Started tab, click the Open button.

2. Browse for the file named mi_12a_120.idw located in the Chapter 12 directory of the Mastering Inventor 2011 folder, and click Open.

3. On the Annotate tab, click the Balloon button. Select the cap on the end of the handle, drag out and place the balloon on the sheet, right-click and choose Continue, and then right-click again and choose Done.

4. Right-click the balloon, and select Attach Balloon.

5. Then click the lever arm. The balloon for the lever arm is shown attached to the handle cap's balloon (Figure 12.33). Drag your mouse pointer around the balloon to set the position of the attached balloon, and then click to place it.

6. Right-click the balloon, and select Attach Balloon From List.

7. Select the box next to Spare Cap, and click OK. The Spare Cap is a virtual component created in the assembly BOM.

FIGURE 12.33
Attached balloons

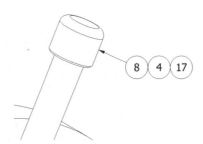

4	Lever Arm
5	Thumb Screw
6	Table Plate
7	Ram
8	Handle Cap
9	Collar
10	Gib Plate
11	Groove Pin
14	Cap Screw
15	Socket Screw
16	Set Screw
17	Spare Cap

Balloons can be added one at a time, or you can use the Auto Balloon tool (under the Balloon flyout) to quickly add multiple balloons to a drawing view.

8. Click the drop-down on the Balloon button, and select Auto Balloon.

9. Select the view on the sheet, and then window-select all the components in the view.

10. Click the Select Placement button, and change the placement options. Move your mouse pointer around the sheet to see how the preview graphics update.

11. Set the placement option to Horizontal, place the balloons above the assembly, and then click OK.

Here are some tips for working with balloons:

◆ Click a balloon to reposition it on-screen.

◆ Click the leader and drag it off the part edge and onto a part face if the edge is not clear as to what part is being specified.

◆ Be aware that balloon contents do not update items when not attached to an edge, so if you pull a balloon from the edge of item 1 and place it on the face of item 2, the balloon will still read *item 1*.

◆ You can re-associate balloons from one part to another part by dragging the arrowhead from one part edge to the edge of a different part.

◆ Balloons not attached to an edge use an alternative leader style (most often a dot). You can specify a different alternative leader style in the balloon style.

◆ If you right-click a balloon and choose Edit Balloon, you can change the item number and have it update the part list, or you can type in an override, and it will not update the parts list.

◆ If you right-click a balloon leader, you can choose Attach Text To Leader and add text along the leader line.

Explore the balloon options and then close the file without saving changes.

Center of Gravity Display

You can display the center of gravity (COG) of a part or assembly in a drawing view as a center mark. Only one COG can be shown per view with the exception of overlay views. Using a drawing containing an overlay view, you will take a look at displaying the COG marker in a drawing to show the change in the COG between the two overlaid positional representations.

1. On the Get Started tab, click the Open button.

2. Browse for the file named mi_12a_123.idw located in the Chapter 12 directory of the Mastering Inventor 2011 folder, and click Open.

3. Expand the sheet node in the browser, and locate the base view node and expand it.

3. Right-click the mi_12a_115 assembly icon, and select Center Of Gravity.

Doing this recalculates the model's center of gravity (it does not read the value in from the model's physical properties) and draws a center mark at the calculated location.

4. Locate the overlay node in the browser, and expand it.

5. Right-click the mi_12a_115 assembly icon listed in the overlay tree, and select Center Of Gravity.

6. Finally, dimension the location of these center marks relative to the bottom-right corner of the Arbor Press frame.

7. Double-click to edit one of these dimensions, and add **(COG)** as a suffix to the dimension value on the Text tab of the Edit Dimension dialog box.

8. Right-click on the dimension and use the Copy Properties option to copy this appended text to the other COG dimensions, as shown in Figure 12.34.

FIGURE 12.34
Overlay view with
recovered COG

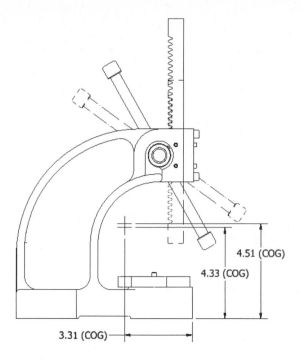

4.51 (COG)

4.33 (COG)

3.31 (COG)

Working with Sheet-Metal Drawings

Drawing views of sheet-metal parts offer some unique options beyond what are normally available for conventional part files. Among these are the inclusion of bend notes, bend lines, punch notes, and tables, and the creation of flat pattern views.

FLAT PATTERN VIEWS

CERT OBJECTIVE

When a sheet-metal part file has a flat pattern definition, you can create a drawing view of the folded model or the flat pattern. You can include both as well but need to separate base views to do so. To take a look at these options, follow these steps to create a flat pattern drawing view to start off:

1. On the Get Started tab, click the Open button.

2. Browse for the file named mi_12a_130.idw located in the Chapter 12 directory of the Mastering Inventor 2011 folder, and click Open.

3. Right-click the existing isometric view, and choose Open to open the model file.

4. Take a look at the model, and note that this file has been created using the Sheet-Metal tools discussed in Chapter 6, "Sheet Metal," and that a flat pattern has been generated in the model.

5. Use the file tabs at the bottom of the screen to switch back to the drawing file (or press Ctrl+Tab).

6. On the Place Views tab, click the Base View button.

7. Ensure the component listed in the File drop-down is `mi_12a_130.ipt`.

8. On the Component tab in the Drawing View dialog box, select the Flat Pattern option as well as the Recover Punch Center option, and then place the view of the flat pattern on the sheet.

Leave this file open because you will use it in the following pages.

Bend Centerlines and Extents

Bend centerlines are drawn on sheet-metal flat pattern views where the center of the bend is located on the material face. Inventor tracks negative and positive bend centerlines independently of one another to enable users to apply different line formatting for these two conditions. This has already been done in file `mi_12a_130.idw`, but it should be noted that the default behavior is to have both positive and negative bend lines placed on the same layer. If you want to separate them, simply create a new layer called Bend Centerline (negative), and then go to the Object Defaults in the Styles And Standards Editor and assign the Sheet Metal Bend Centerline (+) and (-) to the appropriate layers.

Lines representing bend extents can be enabled by right-clicking the flat pattern view, choosing Edit View, going to the Display Options tab, and selecting the Bend Extents option.

Bend and Punch Notes

You'll find two sheet-metal-specific annotation tools on the Annotate tab: Bend Notes and Punch Notes.

Bend notes are placed on bend centerlines in sheet-metal flat pattern views and can convey information about the bending operation including the bend radius, direction, angle, and K-factor. To place bend and punch notes, continue working with file `mi_12a_130.idw`, or open this file and activate Sheet2 to pick up from this point.

1. Click the Bend button on the Feature Notes panel of the Annotate tab.

2. Click one of the bend centerlines in the drawing view to place a single note.

3. To place the rest of the bend notes, window-select the entire view. This tool looks only for bend centerlines, so you needn't be concerned about unintentionally selecting regular model edges.

By default, the bend notes are drawn adjacent to the bend centerlines, but where the note may be obscured in the view, you can drag individual bend notes to flip them to the opposite side of the bend centerline, or you can drag away from the bend centerline, and a leader is generated back to the bend centerline. Try this with the two outermost bend notes on the electrical box flat pattern view (shown in Figure 12.35).

The style formatting and direct editing of bend notes is identical to hole notes. You can preconfigure the contents of the note with the note's dimension style by adding one or more variable tokens for the bend note attributes. Punch notes are used to convey information about sheet-metal punch features (a special kind of iFeature). Punch notes can be applied only to flat pattern views of sheet-metal parts. They can be attached to recovered punch centers (shown as center marks in the flat pattern drawing) or on any model edge generated by the punch.

FIGURE 12.35
Bend notes in flat
pattern view

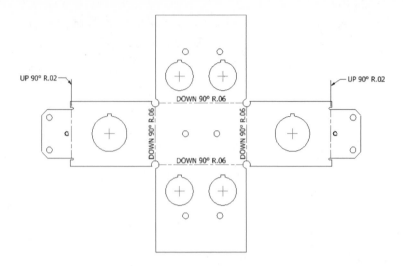

Punch notes can be configured to display the punch identifier (defined as part of the iFeature definition), the punch angle, the depth, and the direction. Punch notes are likewise formatted through dimension styles and have a similar editing interface to hole notes.

BEND TABLES

Bend information can alternatively be displayed in a table rather than a note. A bend table is generated using the General button on the Table panel on the Annotate tab. The Table tool basically morphs into several different kinds of tables depending on what you specify as a data source. If a flat pattern view is selected, then a bend table will be generated.

GENERAL TABLES

If no data source is selected in the Table dialog box, you'll end up with an empty table that you can populate manually. You can also browse and import data from a .csv or .xls file into the table.

To create a bend table for file mi_12a_130.idw, activate Sheet3, and then follow these steps:

1. Click the General button on the Table panel of the Annotate tab.

2. Select the flat pattern view.

3. Click the Column Chooser button, and select Bend Radius from the list on the right.

4. Click the Remove button, and then click OK.

5. For Bend ID, select the Alpha option, and then click OK.

6. Place the table on the sheet, and adjust the Bend ID tags as required by clicking them and dragging.

A bend table is edited and maintained like a parts list. The Table dialog box is essentially identical, and any changes to the cell data are treated as overrides to the data source (in this case, the bend data stored in the sheet-metal file). You can close the file without saving changes. Figure 12.36 shows a simple bend table and bend ID tags.

FIGURE 12.36
Bend table

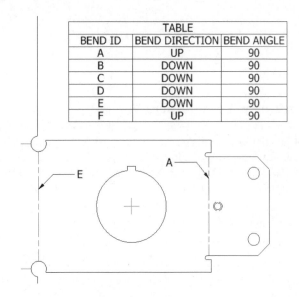

TABLE		
BEND ID	BEND DIRECTION	BEND ANGLE
A	UP	90
B	DOWN	90
C	DOWN	90
D	DOWN	90
E	DOWN	90
F	UP	90

PUNCH TABLES

Punch information can likewise be displayed in a table, but because punches closely resemble holes with respect to the kind of information required to be displayed, a hole table is used to generate tabulated punch data. The only difference in creating a hole table and creating a punch table is that you use a predefined hole table style that is set to pick up only sheet-metal punch features. Here are the general steps used to create a Punch table:

1. Ensure your flat pattern view has been set to collect punch centers. (Select Edit View ➤ Recover Punch Centers.)

2. Start the Hole Table View tool.

3. Select the flat pattern view.

4. Select an origin point.

5. Prior to placing the table, change the table's style to a Punch Table style. If you forget this step, you can always select the existing hole table and change it to the Punch table style using the Style drop-down (top right of the screen).

Figure 12.37 shows a simple Punch table.

FIGURE 12.37
Punch table

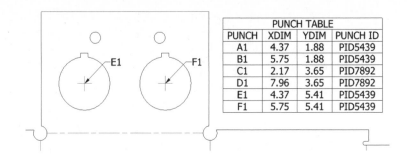

Working with Weldment Views

Weldments are a special kind of assembly model and offer unique drawing view and annotation options in the Drawing Manager. Here you'll take a quick look at the way drawing views handle weldment stages for detailing. For more information on working with weldments and weldment annotation, refer to Chapter 10, "Weldment Design." A drawing view of a weldment assembly can display any of the weldment states, which are as follows:

Assembly   Displays the base assembly prior to the preparation, welding, and machining stages.

Machining   Displays assembly features that represent the post-weld machining and finishing.

Welds   Displays the assembly as it exists during the weld stage, before machining but after preparations have been made. Weld beads are also shown.

Preparations   Displays assembly features such as chamfers, extrude cuts, and holes used to remove material to prepare the assembly for welding. You can set the view to display the entire assembly during the preparation stage or set the view to look at a single component as it exists at the preparation stage.

Follow the steps to explore the way that weldments are handled in drawings and drawing views:

1. On the Get Started tab, click the Open button.

2. Browse for the file named mi_12a_139.idw located in the Chapter 12 directory of the Mastering Inventor 2011 folder, and click Open.

3. Notice the following about the views on this drawing sheet:

    ◆ Views 1 through 4 show the assembly with no preparations, welds, or machining.

    ◆ Views P1 through P3 show each part at the preparation stage.

    ◆ View W1 shows the weldment with welds but no machining done after the weld stage.

4. Right-click View-1, and choose Edit View; then click the Model State tab in the Drawing View dialog box.

5. Currently, this view and the views projected from it are set to the assembly state. Select the Machining option, as shown in Figure 12.38, so the view displays the completed weldment. Click OK.

FIGURE 12.38
Weldment state
settings

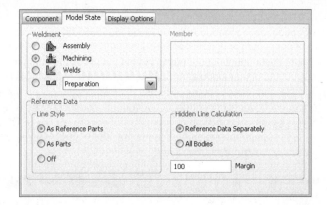

6. Notice that views 1 through 4 now show the weldment at its completion, including the machined holes that run through the weld on one side.

7. Edit View-W1 and check the Model State tab to see that it is set to the Welds option.

8. Click the Display Options tab, and select the options to recover Weld Annotations and Model Weld Symbols. Then click OK.

9. Because the weldment included the weld symbols, they can be pulled into the drawing. Click each symbol, and use the grip snaps to arrange them as you like.

You'll also notice a series of arcs indicating the weld bead brought in via the Weld Annotations option. You can right-click those and choose Edit Caterpillar to adjust the appearance of each, or you can turn the visibility off as required. Figure 12.39 shows the view with recovered weld annotation and symbols.

FIGURE 12.39
Weldment drawing with recovered annotation and weld symbols

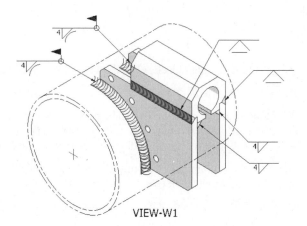

VIEW-W1

10. Edit View-P1 through P3 to check the Model State tab settings for these views. Notice that each of these views is actually created from the assembly file but is set to look at the individual parts at their preparations stage.

You might also note the balloons on View-P1 through P3 are calling out the filenames and that both of the side plates are the same file but have opposing chamfers. This is because a common plate was used for both sides and then prepared as required in the weldment assembly. If you were to make views of the parts themselves as opposed to each part at the weldment preparation stage, the chamfers would not be present. You can close this file without saving changes.

If you don't have the need to use the Weldment tools in assembly modeling but still need to convey welding information in a drawing, you can create weld symbols and weld annotations (end fills and caterpillars) manually on the drawing view. Each is available in the Symbols panel of the Annotate tab (as shown in Figure 12.40) and is formatted by a dedicated style (the Weld Symbol style and Weld Bead style, respectively).

FIGURE 12.40
Weldment annota-
tion and weld sym-
bols can be created
in the drawing.

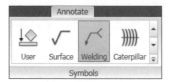

Working with iParts and iAssembly Drawings

When your drawing view references an iPart or iAssembly, you can choose, from the Drawing View Model State tab, which member file you want to document.

Annotations (particularly dimensions) attached to drawing views of iParts and iAssemblies generally remain attached if you edit the base view and change the iPart member on the Model State tab. This means you can fully annotate just one iPart or iAssembly member and select Save Copy As for each unique member after changing the member referenced in the base view. Or you can create a tabulated drawing detailing all of the iPart/iAssembly members on a single sheet. To look at this workflow, follow these steps:

1. On the Get Started tab, click the Open button.

2. Browse for the file named mi_12a_148.idw located in the Chapter 12 directory of the Mastering Inventor 2011 folder, and click Open.

3. On the Annotate tab, click the General button found on the Table panel.

4. Next select the flat pattern view on the sheet to set the focus of the table.

5. Because this part file is both a sheet-metal part and an iPart, you are given the choice to create either a bend table or an iPart table (you can create both but need to do so in successive steps). Set the table data source to iPart/iAssembly Table.

6. Click the Column Chooser button, and use the Add button to include the Length Parameter; then click OK.

7. Click OK in the Table dialog box, and place the table on the sheet.

8. Next, right-click the 100 mm dimension at the top of the flat pattern, and choose Edit. Select the Hide Dimension Value box, and then type **Length** into the text box below. Then click OK.

9. Finally, right-click the table and choose Edit, and then right-click the Member header in the table and select Format Column.

10. Deselect the Name From Data Source box, enter **Mark #**, click OK, and then click OK again to return to the sheet. Your table should resemble Figure 12.41.

FIGURE 12.41
A tabulated
iPart drawing

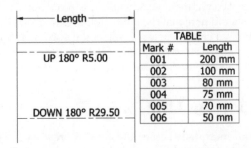

TABLE	
Mark #	Length
001	200 mm
002	100 mm
003	80 mm
004	75 mm
005	70 mm
006	50 mm

If you create a tabulated drawing in this manner and then add rows to the iPart/iAssembly table, your drawing table will automatically add the new row(s) as well. Rows can then be hidden in the table if needed simply by editing the table on the sheet and then right-clicking the row in the Table editor and unselecting Visibility. You can close the file without saving changes.

Sharing Your Drawing Outside Your Workgroup

Once your design is fully annotated, you can share the design documents with others in numerous ways. Of course, the traditional hard-copy route is available from the Print tool, but there are other electronic means to share your Inventor drawings with people who do not have Inventor. The native file formats offer several possibilities. Inventor IPT, IAM, IPN, and IDW files can be viewed using the freely distributed Inventor View application. A version of this is already installed with Inventor but can be downloaded for free from the Autodesk website.

As mentioned earlier, if you use DWG as your drawing file format, anyone with a copy of AutoCAD or AutoCAD LT 2007 or newer can view, plot, and measure the Inventor drawing. There are object enablers on the Autodesk website that even allow older versions of AutoCAD to open Inventor DWG files.

Using the Publish tool (click the Inventor button and select Export ➤ Export to DWF), you generate a neutral .dwf or .dwfx file. The .dwf or .dwfx file can store both your 2D drawing and the 3D models referenced in the drawing. DWF files are viewed using Autodesk Design Review, which is available for download from the Autodesk website.

You can find any of the products mentioned earlier by going to www.autodesk.com or www.google.com and searching for one of these terms:

◆ *Autodesk Inventor View*

◆ *Autodesk Object Enabler*

◆ *Autodesk Design Review*

PDF is a popular publishing format that can be read by Adobe Acrobat Reader. You can save a PDF from Inventor using the Save Copy As option and changing the file type to PDF or by using Export ➤ Export to PDF. You can also download a number of PDF printer drivers that will allow you to print to PDF. Acrobat Reader is available for download from Adobe's website: www.adobe.com.

There are some options for creating PDFs found by clicking the Options button in the Save Copy As dialog box, when the file type is set to PDF. For instance, you might want to include all sheets in the PDF and create it in black and white. You can do so using the Options button. Unfortunately, you cannot configure these options to be the defaults.

You should note that the option to have the PDF viewer automatically open the PDF when it is created is a bit hidden and is set by the Publish options used when creating a DWF. To disable the automatic view of PDFs, click the Inventor button and select Export ➤ Export to DWF. Then uncheck the *Display Published File in Viewer* option.

The Bottom Line

Create an exploded assembly view by creating a presentation   Presentation files are used to virtually disassemble an assembly so downstream consumers can better visualize the design. The explosion created in the presentation file can be referenced in an assembly drawing to complement nonexploded assembly views.

> **Master It**   Your assembly design is complex and contains many internal components that can't be visualized in traditional assembly drawing views.

Create and maintain drawing templates, standards, and styles   Inventor provides numerous methods to create, store, and use drawing templates and styles. Careful planning should be considered for how and where to manage these resources. Consideration must be given to how templates are deployed on your network and whether to use the style library.

> **Master It**   Rather than using one of Inventor's out-of-the-box drawing settings, you need to set up a drawing template, a drafting standard, and annotation styles to conform to a particular international, industry, or company drafting standard.

Generate 2D drawing views of parts, assemblies, and presentations   The Drawing Manager environment in Inventor enables you to generate traditional 2D drafting views from your 3D solid models.

> **Master It**   You've used Inventor's modeling tools to generate parts and assemblies to meet your design criteria. Now you need to generate drawing views of this design so that it can be communicated to machinists, fabricators, and inspectors.

Annotate drawing views of your model   Drawing Manager provides a rich set of Dimensioning tools, special symbols, and tables that enable you to fully annotate part and assembly drawings conforming to several international drawing standards.

> **Master It**   Now that you've generated drawing views of your design, the views must be fully annotated in accordance with your company's or your customer's required drafting standard.

Chapter 13

Inventor Tools Overview

Using tools effectively helps you improve your productivity and get the most out of Autodesk Inventor. Initially, tools require a certain amount of familiarity to be productive; however, they pay off in the long run.

This chapter assumes you have a good understanding of parts, assemblies, and drawings. In this chapter, you will learn the various aspects of Inventor tools and some of the add-ins that are helpful. We will cover the key aspects of the tools and add-ins that come with Autodesk Inventor and some relevant workflows. Many other tools that are built using the Autodesk Inventor application programming interface (which is not covered in this book) are available on myriad websites. We will cover various topics in this chapter, including the AEC Exchange, AutoLimits, Design Assistant, Drawing Resource Transfer Wizard, style tools, Supplier Content Center, Task Scheduler, the iProperties tool, the Measure tool, the CIP, CER, and more.

In this chapter, you'll learn to:

- ◆ Take your models from Inventor to Autodesk Building Systems

- ◆ Create AutoLimits (design sensors)

- ◆ Manage design data efficiently using Inventor tools

- ◆ Manage styles

- ◆ Create expressions with iProperties

- ◆ Measure in assemblies

- ◆ Give feedback to Autodesk

Exploring the AEC Exchange

The Architecture, Engineering, and Construction (AEC) Exchange is an add-in environment for parts and assemblies. Using the AEC Exchange, you can import Inventor models into Autodesk AutoCAD MEP and Revit MEP, which are also Autodesk products used for building design and construction systems. The MEP products are used to document the building mechanical, electrical, and plumbing information of the designs. To access the AEC Exchange environment, select the Environments tab and click AEC Exchange while in a part or an assembly.

Model Simplification

Typically, when you author an Inventor model for use with an ABS application, you will want to reduce the amount of detail in that model so that the file size is smaller and so that you are not giving away too much intellectual property. You start with a part or assembly file and use either a simplified or shrink-wrap level of detail (LOD) representation to remove unneeded detail from your model.

You can do this by following these steps:

1. Go to the Component panel of the Assemble tab, and click the Shrinkwrap Substitute tool.

2. In the Create Shrinkwrap Part dialog box, specify the part name, template file, file location, and BOM structure, and then click OK.

3. Configure the settings as required, and then click OK.

The shrink-wrap part file is created, and you are returned to the source assembly. In the assembly, the shrink-wrap will be the active LOD. Now you are ready to author the model for the AEC Exchange. See Chapters 808 and 909 for more detailed information on LOD representations.

Model Authoring

The AEC Exchange environment allows you to create connector objects such as cables, conduits, ducts, and pipes on the simplified model. These connector objects define the interfaces, which are the connection points between Inventor and the AEC model. Autodesk Inventor allows you to create, edit, and delete connector objects. Here are the steps to create a conduit connector:

1. On the Get Started tab, click Open.

2. Browse for the file named mi_13a_444.ipt located in the Chapter 13 directory of the Mastering Inventor 2011 folder, and click Open.

3. Select the Environments tab, and click AEC Exchange.

4. On the Exchange tab, click the Conduit Connector icon.

5. In the Conduit Connector dialog box, select Circle as the shape for the connector (using Undefined allows the selection of any oval, circular, or rectangular face).

6. Select the yellow circular face to place the connector. The location of the connector appears as a cylindrical arrow. Click the direction button to reverse the connector direction.

7. Clear the check box next to the size field, and enter a value. Or leave the box selected to have the value linked to the model.

8. In the Connection Type drop-down menu, select Threaded.

9. Click Apply to continue to add connectors, or click OK to create the connector and close the dialog box.

10. Add a pipe connector to the blue circular face and a duct connector to the top red rectangular face. Explore the options, and author these connectors with values of your choosing.

11. Save the file.

Model Publishing

A part in the AEC Exchange is the basic unit, that is, a specific size of the component placed within a part family. The part has instance-specific properties associated with it, for example, a name and geometric representation. Use the Export Building Components tool to save model geometry, properties, and connectors to an Autodesk Exchange File (*.adsk) file. An *.adsk file can be read by programs such as Revit MEP and AutoCAD MEP (note that earlier versions of Revit and AutoCAD MEP may not support the *.adsk file format).

For programs that do not currently read the *.adsk file format, such as standard AutoCAD, use the Save AS DWG Solids tool on the AEC's Ribbon to save an active Inventor model as a base solid *.dwg file. You can open this solid in any AutoCAD or Revit program that will read a 3D *.dwg and then use it to ensure fit and placement. Note that there is no connector or property data attached to it. It may be important to know that the resulting solid is initially contained in a block definition. Follow these steps to publish a model in the AEC Exchange tools:

1. On the Get Started tab, click Open.

2. Browse for the file named mi_13a_445.ipt located in the Chapter 13 directory of the Mastering Inventor 2011 folder, and click Open.

3. Choose the Environments tab, and then click AEC Exchange. Note the connectors have been authored already. Do not be too concerned that this exercise model is not realistic in its configuration, because its purpose is merely to demonstrate the available tools.

4. Click the UCS tool in the AEC Exchange tab to define a new user coordinate system.

5. Specify the origin by choosing the vertex at the corner indicated with the black arrow.

6. Specify the x- and y-axes by choosing the vertices on the edges indicated with the black X and Y.

7. Notice the new UCS node in the browser. You can rename it by clicking it twice slowly.

8. Next click the Check Design icon, and notice that there are some yellow warning icons indicating missing information.

9. Click OK.

10. Click the Export Building Components icon.

11. To set the component type, click the Browse button.

12. Choose the following from the drop-down menu:

    ◆ 23.75.00.00 Climate Control (HVAC)

    ◆ 23.75.70.00 HVAC Distribution Devices

    ◆ 23.75.70.17 Water Heated and Cooled

    ◆ 23.75.70.17.37 Unit Heaters

13. Click OK.

14. Enter the following information in the Component Properties area. Notice that the Cost field text turns blue to indicate that it does not match the iProperty. This allows you to enter property overrides and still be aware of which are overrides and which are pulled from the model. All iProperty fields have a cyan colored background.

    ◆ Model: 12345-6T

    ◆ Cost: 990.01

15. Choose a user UCS from the Named UCS drop-down.

16. Click the Check Design button, and note that all the yellow warning icons are now gone.

17. Click OK.

18. Click OK in the Export Building Components dialog box to save an `*.adsk` file (you can click Cancel and choose not to save this file if you'd like).

 Real World Scenario

A TYPICAL SCENARIO FOR THE AEC EXCHANGE

Say your company uses Inventor and specializes in electrical and mechanical designs and that you supply the air conditioner for a building being designed by an architectural firm. To minimize the risk in losing information and future rework, you meet with the architectural and construction firms to ensure the interfaces between your product and the building are all agreed upon. The architects and contractors do not care about any internal details of the air conditioner unit and actually prefer having a lightweight model that will not add extra overhead to the Revit model, but they are extremely sensitive to any changes in the interfaces between your product and their work.

The plan is to author your model and interfaces in Inventor and send the design to the architectural firm so that they can use your model to know exactly the dimensions and locations to tie into. Although you can output the files from the AEC Exchange tools to Revit users "as is," it becomes apparent that having your products authored in Revit format will allow Revit designers to specify your products in their designs more quickly and accurately.

Depending upon the relationship you have with the architectural firm, you may be able to trade them the simplified models that you output from the AEC Exchange tools in return for the Revit family files to be placed on your company's website for download by other firms that would like to specify your product line in their designs. If the architectural firm does not have the time to do this for you, it may be determined that hiring outside help to create these Revit files is the way to go.

Using AutoLimits

The AutoLimits tool allows you to monitor model changes so that you can reduce errors and engineering changes. You can think of it as a sensor. For example, say you are a plastics manufacturer and want to analyze the situation when the wall thickness of the components becomes too thin, or perhaps you are a machinist and want to know when two holes come too close to one another. You want to define this "check" and ensure that such a situation is caught early in the design. With AutoLimits, you can set up these limits and let the system warn you. The AutoLimits that you create with the tool are passive and hence do not drive geometry or stop a feature from violating a limit. They simply notify you when it does. Another way to look at the AutoLimits tool is as a persistent measure tool. The standard Measure tool performs the measurement and the result does not persist, while with the AutoLimits tool the measurement persists. When you open a file, the AutoLimits you have created are not shown unless you activate the AutoLimits panel bar.

The AutoLimits tool monitors the following limits:

Dimensional   Length, Distance, Angle, Diameter, Minimum Distance

Area-Perimeter   Area, Perimeter

Physical Property   Volume, Mass

Figure 13.1 shows the AutoLimits tool icons as accessed from the AutoLimits panel of the Analysis tab.

FIGURE 13.1
AutoLimits access

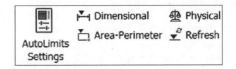

Feedback is given to the user in terms of shape and color. For example:

◆ A green circle means it is within the boundary limit.

◆ A yellow inverted triangle means it is near the boundary limit.

◆ A red square means it is beyond the limit.

Figure 13.2 shows the different types of AutoLimits and their settings. (Click the AutoLimits Settings icon shown in Figure 13.1 to access this dialog box.) You can control the visibility of each AutoLimit type by using the On and Off radio buttons shown. In an assembly, only the edited document's AutoLimits are visible in the browser; in other words, AutoLimits at subassembly levels are not visible or available unless that subassembly is edited.

FIGURE 13.2
AutoLimits Settings dialog box

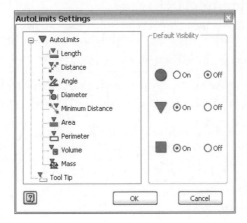

To see AutoLimits in action, follow these steps:

1. On the Get Started tab, click Open.

2. Browse for the file named mi_13a_002.ipt located in the Chapter 13 directory of the Mastering Inventor 2011 folder, and click Open.

3. On the Inspect tab, click AutoLimits Settings button and ensure that all three Default Visibility options are set to on, and then click OK.

This part has a layout sketch upon which the solid was based. The length has been left underdefined by creating the visible driven dimension. Two AutoLimits have been added. The first alerts you if the distance from the front edge to the rectangular cut becomes too thin, and the second alerts you if the mass of the part becomes too heavy. To adjust the model, follow these steps:

A. Click the sketched point or construction line, and drag it in or out.

B. Then use the Update button ![Update] (select it from the Quick Access toolbar) to see the edit take place.

4. Drag the sketch point out so that the visible dimension is around 470, and click the Update button. Note the red square in the middle of the part. This is the Mass AutoLimit, indicating that current length causes the part to be too heavy.

5. Drag the sketch point in so that the visible dimension is less than 300, and click the Update button. Note the red square on the edge of the part; this is a lower limit, Length AutoLimit, indicating that current overall length causes the width between the rectangular cut and the edge of the part to become too thin.

LOADING AUTOLIMIT TOOLS

When you load a file that contains existing AutoLimits, the AutoLimits tools are not loaded or displayed in that file until you use an AutoLimit tool. A quick way of doing this is to use the Refresh button found on the AutoLimits panel.

Creating AutoLimits

AutoLimits come in three types: Dimensional, Area-Perimeter, and Physical Properties. In the following steps, you'll create a Minimum Distance limit and then define the limit boundaries:

1. On the Get Started tab, click Open.

2. Browse for the file named mi_13a_003.ipt located in the Chapter 13 directory of the Mastering Inventor 2011 folder, and click Open.

3. On the Inspect tab, click the AutoLimits Settings icon.

4. Set all three default settings to On, and click OK.

5. Click the Dimensional icon in the AutoLimits panel.

6. On the left of the dialog box, click the Minimum Distance AutoLimit icon (the last one on the bottom).

7. For the selections, you can click the edges with work axes running through them, or you can click the axes (the axes are not required and have been placed just to help identify the correct edges).

8. Click the Boundary tab.

9. Click the Click To Add bar to place the green "okay" AutoLimit.

10. Set the Lower value to 50 mm.

11. Rather than setting an Upper value, you will change the Usign column so that the Upper limit is open ended. Click the < under Usign, and choose the blank or empty entry from the drop-down.

12. Next you want to add another row to define the lower limits. To do this, hold down the Ctrl key, and click the Click To Add bar. The new row should appear above the previous row in the table.

SETTING AUTOLIMIT BOUNDARIES

Hold down Alt and click the Click To Add bar before you add any boundaries. This will place all five boundary levels at once, allowing you to define the green "target" boundary as well as a yellow "warning" and a red "danger" boundary on each side of the target.

Clicking the Click To Add bar always adds an upper boundary unless the green "target" boundary has been set to have no upper value. Clicking the Click To Add bar while holding down the Ctrl key always adds a lower boundary unless the green "target" boundary has been set to have no lower value.

You can add as many ranges as are required when using the standard Click To Add or Ctrl-click methods; however, you can have only one range (five boundaries) when using the Alt-click method.

---

13. Click the yellow triangle twice slowly in the Level column, and change it to the red square in the drop-down.

14. Set the Upper value to 49.999 mm.

15. Change the Lsign column so that the lower limit is open ended. Click the < under Usign, and choose the blank or empty entry from the drop-down. Your boundary should resemble Figure 13.3.

FIGURE 13.3
Dimensional
AutoLimits
dialog box

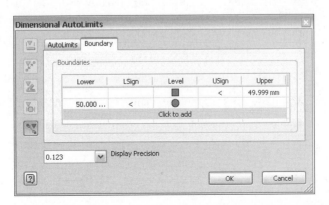

16. Click OK, and then click OK in the message dialog box.

17. You should see a green dot appear on your model; this is your AutoLimit.

18. Double-click the Length dimension, and change the value to 299 mm.

19. Click the Update button (select it from the Quick Access toolbar) to see the edit take place. Note the AutoLimit displays the red square indicating that the distance is now below the value set as acceptable.

20. Change the Length Dimension to 300 mm, and click Update. Note the AutoLimit displays a gray X. This indicates that there is a gap in the AutoLimit.

21. Hover your mouse pointer over the gray X until it changes color; then right-click and choose Edit AutoLimits.

22. Click the Boundary tab.

23. Select the Lower limit for the green row, change 50 mm to 49.9999 mm, and then click any other cell. Note that it sets the value back to 50.000 mm.

24. Click OK to return to the model, and note that the AutoLimit is now green, as shown in Figure 13.4.

FIGURE 13.4
Length AutoLimits

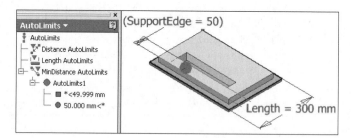

Editing AutoLimits

You can view all the existing AutoLimits in your model by clicking the white arrow on the browser bar and changing from the Model browser to the AutoLimits browser. You can edit AutoLimits in the AutoLimits browser by selecting each AutoLimits entry and right-clicking it. It is recommended you set the selection filter to Feature Priority, because it will be easier to select the AutoLimits glyphs. You can copy or delete AutoLimits by right-clicking them in the browser. You can also create a group of AutoLimits to control the visibility of related AutoLimits. To do this, follow these steps:

1. Right-click the top node in the AutoLimits browser, and select Create Group.

2. Right-click any AutoLimit, and choose Copy AutoLimit.

3. Right-click the group, and choose Paste AutoLimit.

4. Now you can right-click the group to toggle visibility.

> ### DON'T GO CRAZY WITH AUTOLIMITS
>
> Use only the minimum number of AutoLimits in an assembly required to monitor just the critical design information of interest. Using more than 10 AutoLimits can begin to impact the processing speed of your model. You can use AutoLimits in all environments except Autodesk Inventor Studio, the AEC Exchange, Dynamic Simulation, the construction environment, Solid Edit, the Flat pattern environment, and Engineer's Notebook.

Introduction to iLogic

For many people in engineering the constant need to verify combinations of features on a part or parts in an assembly is a huge consumer of time. This validation is critical but low productivity work.

The concept of establishing rules by which an assembly could be configured or a part constructed is not new. There are systems such as Autodesk Intent that will allow a company to construct highly detailed and deeply structured rules systems, but many people just need a basic system that they can create and maintain themselves. This is where the iLogic tools come in.

In a part file, parameters controlled by the iLogic process can change feature size, count, and suppression, similar in fashion to an iPart but programmatically. By constructing the options using a program, you can more easily modify the component options by changing rules or adding additional information, versus editing an iPart table.

The modification and control of components can also be done from the assembly with the additional benefits of controlling constraints and even patterns of components within the assembly taking the iAssembly concept to new limits with the continued benefit of ease of modification.

Creating the rules does not require programming expertise either, though you should gain experience and familiarity with the workflows and architecture of Inventor to prepare to create an efficient rule set. There are two excellent tutorials on constructing iLogic parts and assemblies included with Inventor to help get you started.

Using the Design Assistant

The Design Assistant helps you find, manage, and maintain Autodesk Inventor files and related documents, spreadsheets, and text files. Imagine your company is evaluating a new design that involves doing minor changes to an existing design. You would like to reuse the parts, assemblies, drawings, and presentations as much as possible. Once you make the required changes and finish the new design work, you need to send the existing and modified designs to another department for their input on the overall design. The Design Assistant (DA) and Pack And Go tools can help in this situation. Based on file relationships, you can perform searches, create file reports, and work with links across Inventor files. In addition, you can preview and view the iProperties.

You can launch the DA in three ways:

- Within Inventor, click the Inventor button and choose Manage ➤ Design Assistant while a file is open.

- Right-click a file in Windows Explorer, and select the Design Assistant tool.

- Select Start ➤ All Programs ➤ Autodesk ➤ Autodesk Inventor 2011 ➤ Design Assistant.

MANAGING FILES IN THE DESIGN ASSISTANT

Note that the Manage button will not be visible if you open the DA from an actively open file in Inventor. To manage the links, you must open the file from the Design Assistant directly or via Windows Explorer, and they cannot be open in Inventor while you do this.

The Design Assistant dialog box, as shown in Figure 13.5, contains three buttons in the left column: Properties, Preview, and Manage. You can open files using the File ➢ Open menu. Figure 13.5 shows the result of selecting File ➢ Open in an assembly named `Demote Stapler.iam`. The assembly is listed in the left pane, and all parts related to the assembly are listed in the right pane.

FIGURE 13.5
Design Assistant
dialog box

You can right-click any file in the DA and select View in Inventor View 1.0, which launches the Inventor View dialog box, as shown in Figure 13.6. In the Inventor View dialog box, you can use the view functions such as Zoom, Pan, and Rotate.

FIGURE 13.6
Inventor View
dialog box

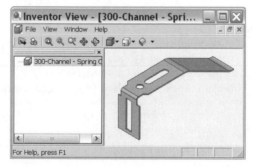

USING THE INVENTOR VIEW DIALOG BOX

Inventor View is a lightweight version of Autodesk Inventor that can be used to view models and drawings. You can access it from the Design Assistant or from the Windows Start menu, or you can simply right-click a file in Windows Explorer and select View With Inventor View. This application is especially useful for nonengineering users who might need to view and print models and drawings but do not have the authority to edit or create models. It can be installed on a computer without installing Inventor.

To view the preview in the DA, you can click the Preview button in the Design Assistant dialog box too, as shown in Figure 13.6. The DA shows the preview for all the files. Figure 13.7 shows the preview of the top-level assembly and one of the parts contained in the assembly. You can choose any listed file to display its preview.

FIGURE 13.7
Preview button

Using the Find Files Tool

You can use the Find Files tool to locate all references to a specified file. This can be very useful when trying to determine how an edit, revision, or change order will affect existing designs. To use the Find Files tool, follow these steps:

1. Click the Manage button in the left column, as shown in Figure 13.8.

2. Click the Drawings, Assemblies, and Parts check boxes. These check boxes are located next to the text Include Files Of Type in the Design Assistant dialog box.

3. You can check Search Subfolders shown next to the Parts check box in the Design Assistant dialog box to include subfolders.

4. Find Files will find the files that use the selected file. In Figure 13.8, 300-Channel - Spring Clip.ipt has been selected, and the referencing files found are listed in the bottom pane.

FIGURE 13.8
Using the Find
Files function

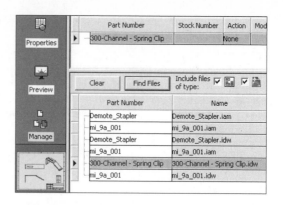

Right-clicking a file and selecting iProperties gives you the properties for the selected part or assembly without opening the part or assembly in Inventor, as shown in Figure 13.9. Note that you do this after clicking the Properties or Preview button; the iProperty option is not available from Manage view.

FIGURE 13.9
iProperties in the
Design Assistant

Using the Where Used Tool

Selecting Tools ➤ Find ➤ Where Used shows all the files that use the current file. For example, to find out the files that use Assembly1.iam, you can do the following:

1. Select Tools ➤ Find ➤ Where Used (in the Design Assistant dialog box). You will see the dialog box shown in Figure 13.10.

2. Select the options in the Where Used dialog box such as Parts, Drawings, Include Subfolders, and so on.

3. Click Search Now.

In the Path area under Look In, you can add paths that you want to search. The Where Used tool will list all the files where the specified file is used in some way. File relationships can include but are not limited to derived components and using a part or assembly in an assembly, drawing, presentation, and so on. Figure 13.11 shows a Where Used search run using the Design Assistant on a file in the local Vault workspace. However, the Design Assistant is often used without Vault.

FIGURE 13.10
Where Used
dialog box

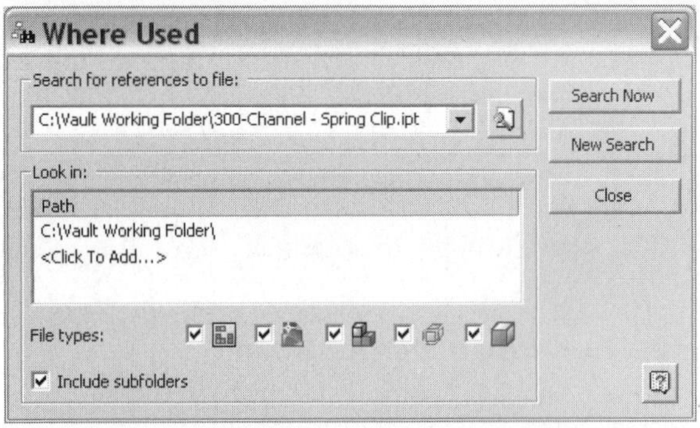

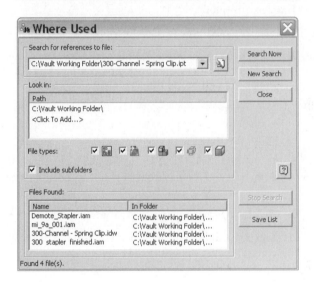

FIGURE 13.11
Results of clicking
Search Now in
the Where Used
dialog box

Renaming, Copying, and Replacing Files

You can use the DA to perform management tasks such as renaming, copying, and replacing Inventor files without breaking the links to the files that reference them. This is because DA not only performs the management task on the files but also "cracks" the referencing files and updates the link to the file at the same time. This is the fundamental difference in doing these operations in Windows Explorer (not recommended) and doing them in the DA.

RENAMING FILES WITH DESIGN ASSISTANT

To rename a file that is in an assembly, drawing, or presentation, follow these steps:

1. Close Inventor.

2. Open the assembly, drawing, or presentation file in the Design Assistant.

3. Click the Manage button. In the Manage browser, click to select the component to be renamed. Right-click in the Action column, and select Rename. All occurrences of the component are highlighted.

4. Right-click the Name column, and select Change Name. In the Open dialog box, change the name, and select Open (you're not really opening anything; you are just setting the name).

5. Click Save to apply the changes.

COPYING FILES WITH DESIGN ASSISTANT

To copy a file that is in an assembly, drawing, or presentation, follow these steps:

1. Close Inventor.

2. Open the file in the Design Assistant.

3. Click the Manage button. In the Manage browser, click to select the component to be renamed. Right-click in the Action column, and select Copy. All occurrences of the component are highlighted.

4. Right-click the Name column, and select Change Name. In the Open dialog box, enter the name of the new copy, and select Open (you're not really opening anything; you are just setting the name).

5. Repeat steps 3 and 4 for all the files you want to copy. For instance, if you are copying a drawing and the part that this drawing details, you would complete steps 3 and 4 for both the drawing and the part.

6. Click Save to create the copies. Your copies will be created right next to the original files.

This can be incredibly useful when you want to create a copy of an existing detailed design so that you can make changes to the copy. Create the copy of the drawing(s) and the components and then make the changes.

REPLACING FILES WITH DESIGN ASSISTANT

If you want to replace a part or assembly file with an assembly, you can right-click the Action cell and then select Replace. Right-click the Name cell for the component, and then click Change Name. In the dialog box, select the replacement file. After a file is replaced, renamed, or copied, other files that reference the original file need an update. The Update option will be useful, as shown here:

1. Open the assembly file in the Design Assistant.

2. Click Manage, and select files that are being modified from the upper browser.

3. In the lower browser, select the file types you want to include in the update.

4. Click Find Files. The referencing files are displayed in the lower browser.

5. In the lower browser, select the file types you want to include in the update.

6. Click the Save button to apply the changes.

The Design Assistant cannot make changes in certain circumstances. Examples are when the active project is set to semi-isolated, when the design state of a file is set to released, when read-only permissions are set, when trying to change the workgroup copy of the file, and so on.

THE DESIGN ASSISTANT VS. VAULT

Although the Design Assistant can make many of the changes discussed here, if you find yourself copying designs, changing filenames, and relinking projects often, you owe it to yourself to investigate Autodesk Vault. Vault can do all of these operations and much, much more.

Using Pack And Go

You can use the Pack And Go tool to package an Autodesk Inventor file and the set of referenced Inventor files in a project or folder to a single location. This is a useful feature to typically archive a design and all the files related to the design into a single ZIP file. For example, if you had the following assembly:

◆ `Assembly1.iam`

◆ `Part1.ipt`

◆ `Part2.ipt`

◆ `Part3.ipt`

the problem is you are not sure what directories the part files are in. Pack And Go can find all the parts for `Assembly1.iam` and copy them into a new directory. You can then zip the files in that new directory to be archived or sent to other users. You can access the Pack And Go tool by right-clicking in Microsoft Windows Explorer or from a Design Assistant session started outside Inventor. Click the Properties or Preview tab, and right-click the Assembly to access the Pack And Go tool.

To use Pack And Go on an assembly, follow these steps:

1. Click the Application button and choose Save As ➢ Save As Pack And Go. This will open the Pack And Go dialog box.

2. Set the destination directory to the folder where you want to copy the files.

3. If you have multiple project files, use the Browse button to ensure you are looking at the proper one.

4. Click the More button to expand more Pack And Go options, as shown in Figure 13.12.

5. Click Search Now to find the IPT and IAM files that are referenced by the assembly file. They will appear in the Files Found section at the bottom of the dialog box.

6. This finds all the files referenced by the assembly file, but what if you know that the assembly and part files had drawings detailing them? To search for referencing files, click the Search Now button in the Search For Referencing Files area.

7. If files are found, you can select which ones to add and then click the Add button. Note that there is no progress bar in this dialog box, so you have to watch the top of the dialog box and wait for "Found # file(s)" to appear to know that it is done, as shown in Figure 13.13.

8. Click the Start button to start the copying process. Once the files are copied, the Cancel button turns into a Done button to let you know.

FIGURE 13.12
Pack And Go
dialog box

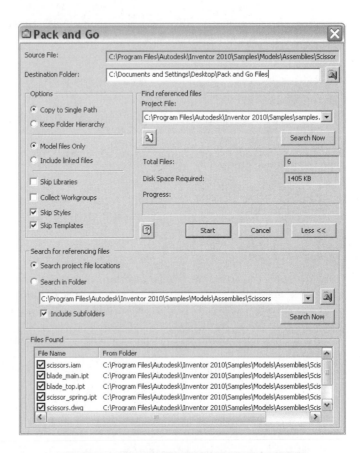

FIGURE 13.13
Pack And Go refer-
encing files found

Typically you will want to configure some of the options because these will yield different Pack And Go results. Here is a description of each:

Copy To Single Path   Copies the referenced files to a single folder, reducing folder hierarchies. If any files have the same filename, only one of the files can be placed at the destination folder.

Keep Folder Hierarchy   Preserves the folder hierarchy under the destination folder. Use this option for round-trip file transfers such as sending files to a contract worker or customer or when you are packing files to work on a laptop while offsite. Maintaining the folder hierarchy will allow you to move the files back to the original destination smoothly when they return.

Model Files Only   Copies only Inventor files (`.iam`, `.ipt`, `.idw`, `.dwg`, and `.ipn`) to the destination folder. Referenced files such as spreadsheets, embedded pictures, and text files are not copied.

Include Linked Files   Includes referenced files such as spreadsheets, embedded pictures, and text files.

Skip Libraries   When selected, all files found in a library path such as Content Center files and user-defined library files are excluded from the Pack And Go tool.

Collect workgroups   If selected, workgroups and the workspace are collected into a single folder. This is typically relevant only when working with a legacy project type.

Skip Styles   If selected, style XML files are not copied with the packaged file.

Skip Templates   Templates are not copied with the Pack And Go files, when this option is selected. You can generally use this option and deselect it only for special circumstances.

It is important to note that Pack And Go does not modify the source files. When you package Inventor files, they are copied to the new destination. A log file and a copy of the original project file with a `.txt` suffix are also copied to the destination folder. Changes made to the packaged files do not affect source files.

Uses of Pack And Go include the following:

◆   Archiving so that you can package files on a CD-ROM.

◆   Sending files to another user.

◆   Separating the referenced files from other files in the same source folders.

◆   Copying an assembly to a new location and then creating a design variant by making changes to the copy. The original is unaffected.

USING PACK AND GO AS A CLEANUP TOOL

Pack And Go can be useful as a project cleanup tool. Often a project folder will become clogged with numerous unused files. Use Pack And Go on the top-level assembly and all the drawings in a secondary location.

Pack And Go uses the active project file. You can change the active project file. If you have files in multiple locations, the project file must specify all those locations.

Using the Drawing Resource Transfer Wizard

The Drawing Resource Transfer Wizard helps copy drawing resources such as borders, title blocks, and sketched symbols from one source drawing to one or more destination drawings. To use the tool, you have to close Autodesk Inventor just to avoid a situation where you are in the middle of modifying a drawing and you want to use that drawing as part of the process for transferring resources.

For example, imagine your company has hundreds of drawings in Inventor. However, there has been a change in the standard note that is on every drawing. If the standard note was created as a sketched symbol, then this update can be batched. The transfer wizard is an ideal solution to solve this kind of problem.

Follow these steps to use the wizard:

1. Select Start ➤ All Programs ➤ Autodesk ➤ Autodesk Inventor 2011 ➤ Tools ➤ Drawing Resource Transfer Wizard.

2. On the welcome screen, click Next.

3. On the Select Source Drawing And Resources screen, select the drawing template, and then click OK.

4. This loads the preview (if available) under Preview and shows the available drawing resources hierarchy in the source under Source Resources. You can deselect the resources you don't want to transfer to destination, as shown in Figure 13.14.

5. Click Next to go to the Select Target Drawings screen. On this page, select one or more drawings (with Shift-select), and click Open. You can click the file or path column name to sort files.

6. Click Next, and select Yes or No for replacing resources in the target file with the same name as in the source. Selecting Yes means using the same name as the source for the target file. Selecting No means give a unique name to target drawing resources that have the same name as those in the source file. For instance, instead of writing over a title block definition named TB_100, you would end up with TB_100 and Copy of TB_100 in your files.

7. Click Start, which shows the progress bar and a Pause button to temporarily halt the process.

8. When done, click Exit to complete the process.

If you have a number of old drawings that you need to bring up-to-date with a new standard, this tool is very useful.

USING THE WIZARD FOR NEW TITLE BLOCKS

A problem that pops up quite often in manufacturing is changing title blocks. Companies change addresses, change logos, and get bought or merged; any number of things can happen to require you to have to change your title block. This is where the Drawing Resource Transfer Wizard can come in handy. Simply edit the title block as required in your template file and then transfer it to all your old drawings.

USING STYLE TOOLS | **603**

FIGURE 13.14
Selecting source
drawing resources

Using Style Tools

Two helpful Style tools that are external to Autodesk Inventor are the Style Library Manager and the Style Management Wizard. Both can be used to manage style libraries in your template files. You should consider using these tools when attempting to remove unwanted styles from templates. You can access them both by selecting Start ➤ All Programs ➤ Autodesk ➤ Autodesk Inventor 2011 ➤ Tools.

Using the Style Library Manager

You can use this tool to copy, rename, and delete style libraries. For example, imagine you are a CAD administrator who rolls out all the standards for your company, and you want to ensure that a good library of styles exists for others to use. The Style Library Manager comes to the rescue in this situation. You can create a new style library using the Create New Style Library button, as shown in Figure 13.15 under the Style Library 2 column. Figure 13.15 shows the dialog box for the Style Library Manager. Any changes in the style library are not available in other documents until Autodesk Inventor closes and a new session is reopened.

FIGURE 13.15
Style Library
Manager

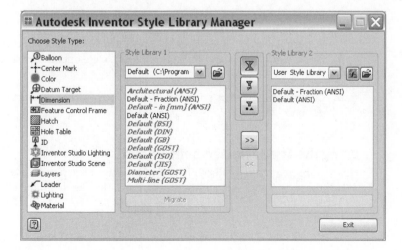

You can reuse your styles by copying them from one style library to another by following these steps:

1. Click the Style Library Manager tool.

2. In Style Library 1, click the drop-down arrow to select the source library styles you want to copy, or use the Browse button.

3. In Style Library 2, you have three options:

   ◆ Choose an existing library.

   ◆ Copy an existing style library.

   ◆ Create an empty style library.

Use the Create New Style Library button to select the last two options, and use the Browse button to use the first. Figure 13.16 shows a new empty library being created.

FIGURE 13.16
Creating a new
style library

4. Click one or more styles in Style Library 1, and then click the >> button to add them to Style Library 2. Click the arrow buttons to add or remove styles to the destination as desired.

Creating a new empty library and then bringing in approved styles one at a time is the best way to ensure that you a get a clean styles library with only the styles that you want and nothing else.

5. In Style Library 1 or 2, you can right-click a style name and select Rename or Delete. A warning will appear that all document links to that style will be broken or the style will be permanently deleted from the style library. Click Yes to continue, and enter a new name. Click No to cancel the Rename or Delete operation. Note that you cannot undo or reverse a deletion.

6. Changes are saved as you make them. Once all changes have been made, click the Exit button.

Using the Style Management Wizard

This wizard helps you go through a set of Inventor files (parts, assemblies, and drawings), collect all the style definitions within those files, and write them into a new library or append them to an existing style library. Prior to Autodesk Inventor 9, all styles were stored locally in documents. The key point is that this tool helps you collect the scattered styles into one central repository. Your Inventor files need to be migrated to the current release before using this tool. You can harvest dimensions and text styles directly from your AutoCAD DWG files too. This helps you roll the changes to multiple files in one operation.

HARVESTING STYLES

The source is a group of Inventor files such as parts, assemblies, and drawings, and the destination is a style library. Harvesting styles means you can collect all the styles from these source files and add them to the target style library.

To harvest styles, follow these steps:

1. Select Start ➤ All Programs ➤ Autodesk ➤ Autodesk Inventor 2011 ➤ Tools ➤ Style Management Wizard.

2. On the welcome screen, click Next.

3. Specify the project to use, and click Next.

4. Add files using one these methods:

   ◆ Select a project and add all its files (by clicking the Add All Files In Active Project button).

   ◆ Select and add individual files (by clicking the Add Specific Files button).

   ◆ Drag and drop files from Windows Explorer into the Style Management Wizard.

   ◆ Add a top-level assembly or drawing, and then right-click it in the Style Management Wizard and select Get Referenced Files.

   ◆ Add a top-level assembly or drawing, and then right-click it in the Style Management Wizard and select which files to get, as shown in Figure 13.17.

Once files are added, you can click the column headings to sort like you do in Windows Explorer. Click Next once all files have been added.

FIGURE 13.17
Selecting files
to process

5. In the Management Options area, click Harvest Styles Into Target Style Library. You can then select the target library by one of these methods, as shown in Figure 13.18:

◆ Use Source Project Style Library, if applicable, automatically selects the style library specified in the project.

◆ Create a new style library by clicking the Create A New Style Library radio button and then clicking the Create New Style Library button to specify the name and location.

◆ Select an existing style library by selecting the Select An Existing Style Library radio button and then choosing the library from the drop-down or by using the Browse button.

FIGURE 13.18
Autodesk Inventor
Style Management
Wizard

6. Once you've set the management options, click Next.

7. Review the selections you have made, and then click Start to begin the process.

8. A log file is generated during processing, and you can halt the process by clicking Pause. You can also click Cancel to stop.

PURGING STYLES

In large files (assemblies), it becomes imperative to keep only the styles that are used. Oftentimes because you have used template files to house your styles originally, you might have an abundance of unnecessary styles in every file. Having extra material and color styles in each part may not be an issue for small assemblies, but when you think about all the extra overhead that these styles add for assemblies with part counts of 1,000 or more, you can begin to realize that it is significant. For drawing files, extra styles can contribute to slow load times, as well as mistakes created by accidentally selecting the wrong dimension style, and so on.

To remove unused styles, you can specify a group of files such as parts, assemblies, and drawings and remove every unused style in all the documents. This technique is used to remove styles from legacy documents that now use a style library. It is recommended that you back up the styles before you do this operation since the involved styles are permanently deleted. You can use similar steps as in harvest styles to process the files. The major difference for Purge Styles From Harvest Styles is that in step 5 of the previous section, you select Purge All Unused Styles From Files.

Exploring the Supplier Content Center

You can access the Supplier Content Center in the following ways:

◆ Go to www.autodesk.com/suppliercontent.

◆ From within Inventor, with no files open, click the Supplier Content icon on the Tools tab.

◆ Select Start ➢ All Programs ➢ Autodesk ➢ Autodesk Inventor 2011 ➢ Tools ➢ Supplier Content Center.

Figure 13.19 shows the Supplier Content Center web page.

FIGURE 13.19
Content from suppliers

The main advantages of using the Supplier Content Center are the following:

◆ The Supplier Content Center promotes design reuse.

◆ The Supplier Content Center supplies Autodesk Inventor native data: parts or 2D views. Also available are Mechanical Desktop and AutoCAD parts and assemblies from commercial suppliers.

◆ The Supplier Content Center ensures that part numbers and metadata are accurate, and it makes ordering easy and accurate.

◆ The Supplier Content Center provides reconfigurable parts and assemblies to meet your custom needs.

◆ The Supplier Content Center keeps parts up-to-date.

These parts are available in native Autodesk Inventor format from more than 100 suppliers. Some supplier contents are listed here:

◆ Part solutions

◆ 3D model space

◆ Traceparts

On the Supplier Content Center website, you can browse the information by category such as Bearings, Fasteners, Hydraulics, and so on. You have to log in to download parts and reuse them. You can also do a keyword search and select the category.

To use parts and assemblies from the Autodesk Supplier Content Center, follow these steps:

1. Go to the Supplier Content Center website, and create an account.

2. Log in with a username and password.

3. Under Settings, click the CAD format you need; it will show parts in this format.

4. Search and navigate the catalogs for the desired part. Configure the part or assembly. You can click the eye icon to preview a part.

5. Add the part to My Documents by clicking the shopping cart icon.

6. Download the part by clicking the disk icon.

7. Click the download icon after the generation of the part is finished to save it.

Once the content has been downloaded through the Supplier Content Center sites you can include these components in your assemblies. You should move the content to a folder included in the path defined in your Project File before including it an assembly.

Using the Task Scheduler

A large design repository needs to have a way to manage tasks for efficiency and repeatability. Nonproductive and mundane tasks tend to be expensive and tedious. The purpose of the Task Scheduler is to precisely automate such tasks. To access the Task Scheduler, select Start ➢ Programs ➢ Autodesk ➢ Autodesk Inventor 2011 ➢ Tools ➢ Task Scheduler.

Imagine you are working for a service company that handles outsourcing work for auto suppliers. The supplier works with hundreds of files. The supplier is trying to decide whether to move to Inventor 2011. You have been asked to evaluate this for the supplier. You want to do testing and present quantitative data on the results of migration or some other custom tasks the supplier normally performs on legacy files. The main purpose of the Task Scheduler is to automate the tasks and quickly give you results. The Task Scheduler has the ability to create various tasks such as the following:

- Migrating a set of files from AutoCAD, Autodesk Mechanical Desktop, and Autodesk Inventor software

- Converting Inventor IDWs to Inventor DWGs

- Publishing DWF files

- Importing files and exporting files

- Updating parts, assemblies, and drawings

- Checking out and checking in from Vault

- Retrieving files from Vault

- Printing sheet sets

- Refreshing Content Center components used in assemblies

- Running a custom macro (such as a Visual Basic routine)

- Creating single part from an assembly using the Shrinkwrap tool

Creating a Task for Migrating Files

To create a task to migrate files in Task Scheduler, follow these steps:

1. Open the Task Scheduler by selecting Start ➤ Programs ➤ Autodesk ➤ Autodesk Inventor 2011 ➤ Tools ➤ Task Scheduler.

2. Select Create Task ➤ Migrate Files, as shown in Figure 13.20.

FIGURE 13.20
Create Task menu

3. In the Migrate Files dialog box (see Figure 13.21), enter the task name, frequency, start time, and start date. If Immediately is checked, the task will start immediately after you click OK. The log file helps to see the output of the task.

FIGURE 13.21
Migrating files

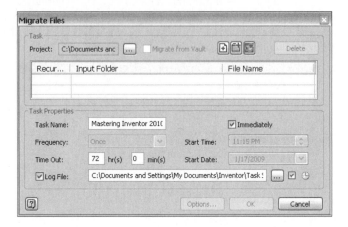

4. Use one of the three buttons along the top to add files in one of the following ways:

Add Files   Select files from the active project to add to the task.

Add Folder   Browse to a folder or folders to add to the task. Use the File Name drop-down to select which file type to process. Ensure the Recursive check box is selected to include subfolders.

Add Project   Select a project to include all files in that project's search paths.

5. Click the Options button to open the Migration Options dialog box like the one shown in Figure 13.22. The options are also listed here:

Total Rebuild   Rebuilds all the parts and assemblies.

Skip Migrated Files   Ignores files created in the current version or files already migrated.

Skip Files with Unresolved References   Ignores files with broken links and references.

Set Defer Updates (Drawings Only)   Toggles on the setting that allows drawings to be made static so that they do not update as the part or assembly they detail updates. This can be toggled off manually from the drawing later.

Purge Old Versions   Deletes former versions after the migration task finishes keeping file size to a minimum.

Compact Model History   Purges file history used for fast feature editing. This is intended for working with large assemblies when you experience capacity limitations. Do not select this option when migrating files to a new release.

6. Click OK to run the task. When the task is done, you will see the status shown as completed.

FIGURE 13.22

Migration Options
dialog box

Users can run, edit, delete, or disable tasks once they are created, as shown in Figure 13.23. Tasks are also saved so they can be run again. By clicking Task ID and Name columns, you can sort the data by that column.

FIGURE 13.23

Editing a task

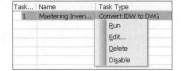

Performing Sequential Tasks

You can create several subtasks to set up multiple tasks and schedule them to run in a specified sequence at a specified time. Custom subtasks can be used also in a sequential task. One subtask can depend on the output of the previous subtask. Examples of multiple subtasks are as follows:

- Importing files

- Updating designs

- Publishing DWF files

- Printing files

- Generating a cost report (custom task)

Performing Custom Tasks

A form of a COM object that implements the COM interface could be a custom task. For instance, you can use a custom task to open a batch of text files. A type library file called `ServiceModuleInterfaceDef.tlb` is shipped with the Task Scheduler. To access the COM interface, reference this file within your project. You can create custom tasks in any programming language that supports COM.

Tweaking Multi-Process Settings

In the Multi-Process Settings dialog box, as shown in Figure 13.24, you can tweak parameters to complete batch jobs in less time by leveraging the multi-process support in the Inventor Task Scheduler. Up to 16 processes can be run at the same time. You can set the number of processes and the amount of memory to be used. You can find this setting in Task Scheduler by selecting Settings ➢ Multiple Process.

FIGURE 13.24

Multi-Process Settings dialog box

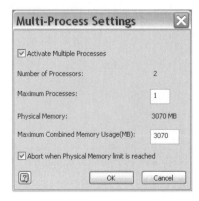

FIGURE 13.24

Multi-Process Settings dialog box

BATCH PLOTTING WITH THE TASK MANAGER

One of the more powerful uses of the Task Manager is to batch plot a number of drawings. Simply select Print Files from the Create Task menu and then select the files to be printed. Click Options to set the paper size and other print parameters.

Publishing DWF Files and Filenames

If you were to use the Task Scheduler to publish a DWF file named MI777.ipt, then that would become the destination MI777.ipt.dwf. Some users find this difficult to accept. The motivation to rename it not as filename.dwf is as follows: if Inventor produces MI777.dwf, then it can be overwritten if you have two files with the same name but different extensions, that is, MI777.ipt and MI777.idw. Therefore, the Task Scheduler takes the current filename with the extension (such as .ipt or .idw) and appends .dwf at the end. There are programs available on the Internet or Windows scripting commands to rename files from MI777.ipt.dwf to MI777.ipt, which could be used to fix the filenames.

Using iProperties

Autodesk Inventor files have file-specific properties known as iProperties. The iProperties dialog box helps you specify and view them. You can enter custom data into iProperties, search by those fields, and update your title blocks and parts lists in drawings and BOMs. You can launch this dialog box by clicking the Inventor button 📄 ⁻ and then iProperties or by right-clicking the filename in the browser and selecting iProperties. Figure 13.25 shows the iProperties dialog box for a part. The iProperties dialog box in the parts and assemblies environments contains seven tabs, while the iProperties dialog box in the drawing environment contains only six tabs (it's missing the Physical properties tab).

FIGURE 13.25
Physical properties with aluminum as the material

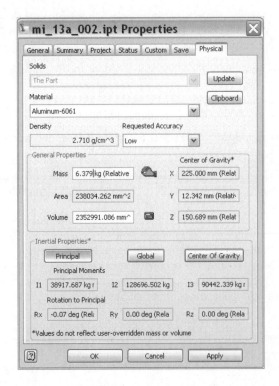

You can also right-click a file in Windows Explorer and choose Properties ➢ iProperties to add or edit iProperties outside of Inventor. Or from Windows Explorer, right-click a file and choose Design Assistant to work with files outside of Inventor. In the iProperties dialog box, you can modify data on the Summary, Project, Status, and Custom tabs. On unsaved files, changing the iProperties using the Design Assistant could lose unsaved changes. You can save any open Inventor files before using the Design Assistant to change iProperties.

The various tabs in the iProperties dialog box are as follows:

◆ The General tab contains fields that cannot be modified by the user.

◆ The Summary tab contains fields that can be modified by the user, such as Title, Subject, Author, and so on.

◆ The Project tab contains important fields such as Part Number, Revision Number, Project, and so on.

◆ The Status tab contains drop-down controls for Part Number, Status, Checked Date, and so on.

◆ The Custom tab helps define your own attributes. These attributes follow the Name, Type, and Value format. For example, you can have Name = Department, Type = Text, and Value = Design123.

◆ The Save tab helps you specify whether to save the preview picture of your files so that it can be used in most "browse for file" dialog boxes. You can also specify an image file to use for this preview picture.

◆ The Physical tab lets you calculate and display the physical properties (Area, Volume, Inertia, and so on) for a part or an assembly. The material selected is used to calculate the mass properties. The Update button on the Physical tab is useful to update the physical properties based on changes to your models.

◆ The Summary, Project, Status, and Custom tabs are used to search files to update the BOM and parts lists.

Figure 13.25 shows an example of iProperties on a simple part. If this were a multibody part, the mass properties of each individual property could be evaluated by setting the Solid drop-down to look at just that solid.

Also notice the hand icon next to the Mass input box. This indicates that the mass has been overridden or manually entered rather than being calculated from the part. The calculator icon shown next to the Volume input box indicates that the volume is being calculated from the part and will update as changes are made. The Density field cannot be changed in this dialog box. To change the density for this example, go to the Manage tab, click Styles Editor, and find Aluminum-6061 under Material. Then change the density.

OVERRIDING MASS AND VOLUME FOR A SIMPLIFIED REPRESENTATION

Sometimes you'll want to model a simplified representation of a part but still need to have an accurate measure of its mass or volume. In these cases, simply type over the mass or volume in the iProperties dialog box. The calculator icon will then change to the hand icon signifying that the mass and/or volume has been overridden. To allow Inventor to recalculate the mass or volume, simply delete all the text from the box and click the Update button. Inventor will then compute the mass and volume based on the size and density of the model.

Copying iProperties to Drawings

You can copy the model iProperties to the drawing iProperties so that they are the same. Copied model iProperties can be used in part lists, title block standard notes, or any annotation that accesses the iProperties. If the iProperties are set up in your drawing template, when you place views of the model on a new drawing, the selected iProperties are copied to the drawing from the source file.

Be aware that, once copied, the properties do not update automatically when changed in the model. To update the copied model iProperties in the drawing, go to the Manage tab (from the drawing file), and click Update Copied Model iProperties. Note also that a drawing will pull properties from only one source. So if you have views of two different models on a single drawing, the properties are pulled from the first model from which a view was created. If you remove all the views of the first model, then the drawing will pull from the second model, but you will need to use the Update button to make this happen.

You can copy iProperties from a model file to a drawing file by following these steps:

1. In the Drawing file, go to the Tools tab and click Document Settings; then go to the Drawing tab.

2. Click the Copy Model iProperty Settings button, which opens the dialog box shown in Figure 13.26.

3. Select the boxes for the properties you want to copy. You can select the All Properties check box at the bottom to copy all the properties.

FIGURE 13.26
Copy Model
iProperty Settings
dialog box

Creating Expressions with iProperties

If you have a need to create "stock size" of your parts to be used in your BOM with associativity to model parameters, you can create and manage expressions for iProperties by using the following steps:

1. Click the Inventor button and then iProperties, and go to the Summary, Project, Status, or Custom tab. Then click a field where an expression needs to be created.

2. Start with the = sign, and type the text. If you want to include parameters or iProperty names, then simply include them in brackets. A detected expression is denoted by *fx*. Figure 13.27 shows an expression that concatenates the thickness, width, and length parameters. This is the expression used:

    = <Thickness> x <Width> X <Length>

    The resulting Stock Number property is as follows:

    30.000mm x 25.000mm x 50.000mm

3. To edit an existing expression, you can right-click the expression and choose Edit Expression.

FIGURE 13.27
Concatenating text
and parameters in
iProperties

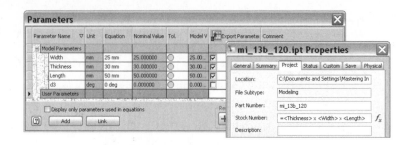

Before creating the expression from parameters, you should visit the Parameters dialog box
(go to the Manage tab and click the Parameters icon) and do the following:

- In the Export Parameter column, click the check box next to all parameters you want to use
  in expressions. If you forget this step, the expressions will not build.

- In the Equation column, right-click the parameter, and choose Custom Property Format.
  The Export parameter must be selected to get this option. Figure 13.28 shows the Custom
  Property Format options. Notice that you can click the option to apply the formatting to all
  comparable parameters. In other words, if it's a length parameter, then set this format for
  all length parameters; if it's a volume parameter, then set this format for all volume parameters; and so on.

FIGURE 13.28
Customizing an
exported param-
eter format

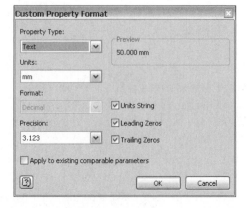

FIGURE 13.29
Expression Builder
in the Bill Of Mate-
rials Editor

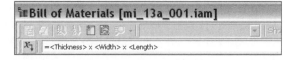

To promote reuse, create a template file with predefined expressions for iProperties that lets
you unify your parts list and other documentation. The Bill Of Materials dialog box provides
the Property Expression Builder, which helps you create expressions for iProperties as well. You

can then copy the expression to the parameter field of multiple parts in the Bill Of Materials Editor. Using the Bill Of Materials Editor allows you to "reach into" several parts at once and set an expression en masse.

Working with the DA and iProperties

You can use the Design Assistant to copy design properties from one Inventor file to another. To copy design properties from one source file to another, use the following procedure:

1. In Inventor, click the Inventor button ⊞ ▾ and choose Manage ➤ Design Assistant.

2. In the Design Assistant, select Tools ➤ Copy Design Properties to get the Copy Design Properties dialog box.

3. Set the source file in the Copy From box.

4. Select the properties to copy.

5. Select the destination files to receive the properties.

6. Click the Copy button.

7. If the properties exist in the destination file, you are prompted to overwrite them one by one or not; you can choose Yes To All or No To All as well.

8. Once copied, click Done.

9. You can then step into the files (from Inventor or DA) and change the values of the copied iProperties as required.

Figure 13.30 shows the custom iProperties of one file being copied to another file. You can refer to the "Using the Design Assistant" section earlier in the chapter to learn more about the DA and iProperties. If the active project is set to shared or semi-isolated, then you cannot copy properties to a file that is checked out to someone else or into the workgroup version of a file.

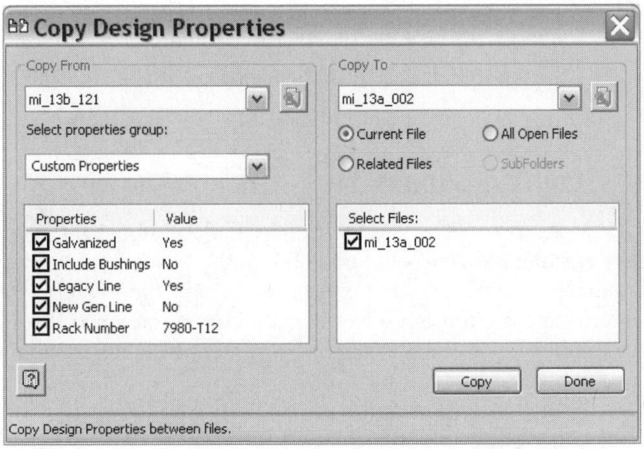

FIGURE 13.30
Copying custom iProperties from one file to another

Creating Design Property Reports

You can use the Design Assistant to create design property reports that show the iProperties selected by you. The report is written out to a `*.txt` file. In the Properties view browser in the Design Assistant, you can select the design properties to display for files.

1. While in the Properties view, select View ➢ Customize in the Design Assistant, and select the required property group.

2. Select the properties to display. Clicking the Add or Remove button helps you move a property from the Available Properties list to the Selected Property list. You could also double-click it. The Name property is a default property that is mandatory in all displays.

3. To include custom properties that you've created yourself, follow these steps:

   A. Set the Property Group drop-down to Custom Properties.

   B. Click the New button.

   C. Expand the Add New Property column using the >> button.

   D. Use Ctrl or Shift to select multiple properties.

   E. Click Apply. Note that only nine properties may be listed.

4. Click Done.

5. Notice that the properties you selected are now listed as columns.

6. Select Tools ➢ Reports, and choose the report type you want:

   Hierarchy Report   Shows the hierarchy within the selected folder or assembly. If a folder is selected, the report shows the subfolders it contains. If an assembly file is selected, the report shows the paths for the files in the assembly.

   Design Property Report   Shows values of the specified properties for the files in the selected file or group of files.

7. Choose the number of levels to display, and click Next.

8. Specify the report name and save location.

Using the Measure Tools

The Measure tools let you measure distances, angles, loops, and areas. These tools are available by selecting the Tools tab and going to the Measure panel, as shown in Figure 13.31. These are available in the assemblies, parts, sheet-metal, flat pattern, construction, and 2D and 3D sketch environments. You can select sketches, edges, faces, bodies, and work geometry to take measurements. In addition to the measurement tools mentioned, you can use measure regions while in a 2D sketch.

The Distance tool   Lets you measure length of a line, arc, distance between points, radius, diameter of a circle, distance between two components, two faces, or positions in relation to the active coordinate system.

The Angle tool Lets you measure the angle between points, edges, or two lines. To measure between points, click two points to define a line and then a third point to measure the angle.

The Loop tool Gives you the length of the loops. For 2D sketches, it measures open or closed loops. For 3D sketches, it measures only open loops.

The Area tool Gives you the area of closed regions.

The Region tool Calculates the area, perimeter, and the area moment of inertia properties of 2D sketch loops. Measurements are taken from the sketch coordinate system.

FIGURE 13.31
Measure tools

Using Measurement Helpers

Measurements can be accumulated, cleared, and displayed in different ways. Figure 13.32 shows some of the options that are useful while using the Measure tool. Here's a list:

The Add To Accumulate option The Add To Accumulate option adds the current measurement to the total sum.

The Clear Accumulate option The Clear Accumulate option resets the sum to zero.

The Display Accumulate option The Display Accumulate option displays the current sum.

The Dual Unit option The Dual Unit option lets you see the measurement in the desired units.

The Precision option The Precision option displays eight formatting values and the option to display all decimals.

FIGURE 13.32
Measurement
helpers

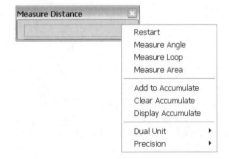

One of the advantages of the Measure tool is to enter feature parameters by measuring versus directly entering it. For example, in Figure 13.33, extrusion depth can be entered as a value of 30 mm. Alternatively, you can select the Measure tool from the Depth flyout and then select a model edge. The length of the edge will appear in the Depth control of the Extrude dialog box. This is a convenient way to input dimensions by measuring versus directly entering it into the dialog box. In the graphics window, click the geometry to measure. The measurement is transferred to the dialog box automatically. Note that this can be used with sketch dimensions as well.

FIGURE 13.33
Measure tool and
feature parameters

Also shown in Figure 13.33 is the Show Dimensions option. Choosing this option allows you to select an existing feature to temporarily see the consumed dimensions within that feature. You can then select the dimensions on-screen to link the value of that dimension to the dimension you are currently entering. This differs from the Measure method in that the value will update if the object changes, whereas the measured value will stay static.

Measuring in Assemblies

In assemblies, since you have faces and components, there is a need to differentiate measuring between them. In the context menu, you can change the selection priority.

When Component Priority is selected, the minimum distance is measured between subassemblies. Part priority signifies measurement between parts only. Faces And Edges Select Priority lets you select only faces and edges, which is the default when nothing is preselected. Changing the selection priority resets any existing selections. Figure 13.34 shows the priority type and the respective choices for the selection filter.

FIGURE 13.34
Selection priority
for measurements

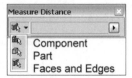

In Inventor 2011, you can measure preselected entities. If a selection set is valid for a measurement, the select filter in the Measure dialog box is updated, and the measurement is displayed. For example, if you select two points and then start Measure Distance, you will get the distance between the points. However, if you select three points and start Measure Angle, then the select set is cleared because the Measure tool doesn't know which point is the vertex of the angle.

Participating in the CIP and CER

The Customer Involvement Program (CIP) aids in collecting your specific use of the Autodesk Inventor software. Customer error reporting (CER) aids in sending information to Autodesk when the software program closes unexpectedly.

Participating in the CIP

To guide the direction of the Autodesk design software in the future, your specific use of the Autodesk Inventor software is forwarded to Autodesk if you participate in the CIP. You can access this feature by selecting Help ➤ Customer Involvement Program. In the Customer Involvement Program dialog box, you can select a level of participation and then click OK. Information collected includes the following:

- Autodesk product version and name

- Inventor commands and time spent

- Error conditions (catastrophic and nonfatal)

- Other information such as system configuration, IP address, and so on

The CIP is committed to privacy protection. It can collect neither drawing or design data nor personal information such as names, addresses, and phone numbers. It will not contact users by email or any other way. The Customer Involvement Program aids in letting Autodesk know about the most commonly used tools and features, the most common problem areas, and so on. You can stop participation at any time by accessing the controls from the Autodesk Help menu. Your system administrator can also choose to block the CIP.

Participating in CER

Customer error reporting is a process by which Autodesk Inventor users can report crashes to Autodesk. A software crash happens when the software program closes unexpectedly. When you have an unexpected error, Inventor shows a dialog box, and you can choose to send the error to Autodesk. CER records the subset of the code that was in use before the crash. The CER report collects a variety of information such as the following:

- Operating system and graphics driver name, version, and configuration

- Autodesk software name and version

- List of recently used Autodesk commands

- Lines in the code where the crash happened

You can enter the step-by-step process that led to the crash. In addition, you can include your email and contact information. The error data is sent to Autodesk using a secure Internet connection in an encrypted form. If you have concerns about security and personal confidential information being sent to Autodesk, please do not send the customer error report.

At Autodesk, an automated system sorts the report based on the code call stack so that the Autodesk development teams can analyze them. Each set of reports is prioritized based on the number of users having the same issue and how often the problem happens. If there is no current update, Autodesk will use that information for a future update or major release. When the issue is fixed, it is included in either a future maintenance update or a future release of the product. Customers who reported the error are notified. If there is a current update (immediate update notification), it is immediately sent to the customer. If not (delayed update notification), customers are notified when their error is addressed in a future software update.

Using Miscellaneous Tools

In the following sections, we will cover some miscellaneous tools such as the Inventor Multi-Sheet Plot, the Add-In Manager, and the Project Editor. The following tools are available by either going to Start ➢ All Programs ➢ Autodesk ➢ Autodesk Inventor 2011 or Start ➢ All Programs ➢ Autodesk ➢ Autodesk Inventor 2011 ➢ Tools. If you find that you are using these tools often, it may be helpful to create a desktop shortcut to them.

Using the Autodesk Multi-Sheet Plot Tool

The Autodesk Multi-Sheet Plot tool opens the dialog box shown in Figure 13.35. It allows you to print one or more drawing sheets of various sizes. Clicking Next takes you to another dialog box that allows you to select drawings. Once the drawings are selected, you can schedule to print the multi-sheet. This tool helps you reduce paper usage and reduce plot setup time. Besides, it optimizes sheet layout on a selected paper size that you can print directly or save as a batch file. You can access the Multi-Sheet Plot tool by going to Start ➢ All Programs ➢ Autodesk ➢ Autodesk Inventor 2011.

FIGURE 13.35
Autodesk
Multi-Sheet Plot
dialog box

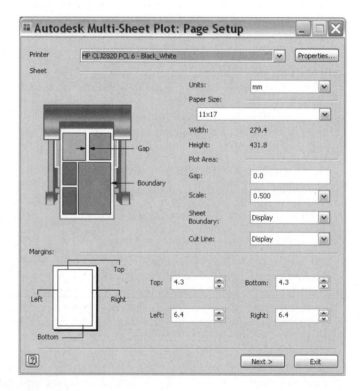

Using the Add-In Manager

The Add-Ins icon opens an Add-In Manager dialog box to make selections on which add-ins you want to load or unload when Inventor starts up. You can access this tool by going to Start ➢ All

Programs ➢ Autodesk ➢ Autodesk Inventor 2011 ➢ Tools, or when in Inventor by going to the Tools tab, clicking the Customize icon, and clicking Add-Ins, as shown in Figure 13.36. Once the Add-In Manager dialog box is open, click the add-in in the Available Add-Ins area, and at the bottom of the dialog box for Load Behavior, deselect the Loaded/Unloaded option to unload it.

FIGURE 13.36
Accessing the
Add-Ins Manager

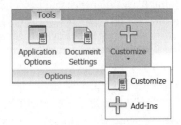

USING THE ADD-IN MANAGER TO SPEED INVENTOR LOAD TIME

If there are add-ins you know you do not use, then you can use the Add-in Manager to prevent these add-ins from loading when Inventor loads. This will slightly speed up the load time (and reduce the amount of RAM) Inventor uses. Be sure you understand what add-ins do because some are required for the proper operation of the software.

Using the Project Editor

Selecting the Project Editor tool opens a dialog box for Inventor's Project Editor. This is similar to the dialog box that opens after you select the Get Started tab and click Projects in Inventor. You can select each project, make changes to it, and save it without having to open Inventor. You can access this tool by going to Start ➢ All Programs ➢ Autodesk ➢ Autodesk Inventor 2011 ➢ Tools or by right-clicking on any *.ipj file from Windows Explorer and choosing Edit. Project files can also be edited from within Inventor by going to the Get Started tab and clicking the Projects button.

The Bottom Line

Take your models from Inventor to Autodesk Building Systems   If you frequently need to take your Inventor models to ABS, then AEC Exchange can help you in this process with three simple steps. Inventor provides a variety of ways to simplify the model and author it. Such models can be published in ABS.

Master It   You can do this with the following three steps: model simplifying, authoring, and publishing. You can also save a DWG as a solid.

Create AutoLimits (design sensors)   You use AutoLimits to monitor design parameters in which you are interested.

Master It   How many AutoLimits can you use in an assembly?

Manage design data efficiently using Inventor tools   There are different tools for managing design data, which is typically distributed across part, assembly, and drawing files. You can associate Excel spreadsheets, text files, Word documents, and so on, with these tools.

> **Master It**   The Design Assistant keeps the file relationships while copying, renaming, and moving files. Whenever you are sending Inventor files to others, use Pack And Go, which hunts the file relationships down for you and then you can package it into a single ZIP file. You can delegate many of the tasks in Inventor to the Task Scheduler. You can propagate source drawing template information to several destination drawings using the Drawing Resource Transfer Wizard.

Manage styles   You can use the Style Library Manager and the Style Management Wizard to organize your styles to keep them simple and clean.

> **Master It**   How do you manage your styles? Styles normally need to be copied, edited, and deleted. Use the Style Library Manager. How can you create a central repository of styles? How do you purge styles? Use the Style Management Wizard for these tasks.

Create expressions with iProperties   Property fields can be concatenated to produce desired customized information in BOM and parts lists.

> **Master It**   You can break down, for example, "stock size" of your parts to be used in your BOM with associativity to model parameters. You can create and manage expressions for iProperties.

Measure in assemblies   Click the right Measure tool and selection filters to make measurements.

> **Master It**   How do you measure in assemblies? Once you set the selection filter, you make the selections and use the measurement helpers to get complex measurements.

Give feedback to Autodesk   You can participate in the Customer Involvement Program (CIP). Customer error reporting (CER) helps Autodesk know about any issue you might experience.

> **Master It**   You have a repeatable crash that you suspect is related to a specific file, or a specific machine, and want to know if Autodesk can help you determine this.

Chapter 14

Exchanging Data with Other Systems

The need to bring files created by other CAD applications into Inventor is common to many Inventor users. For instance, if you design components that others use in their designs, you might need to output files to a standard format so that others can use them with a different software package. Or, if you are a manufacturing "job shop," you may receive many different file formats from customers that you need to bring into Inventor. The ability to open and translate files into Inventor 2011 has been improved with the inclusion of even more native file format translators as well as the ability to open and save neutral file formats.

In this chapter, you will learn how to:

◆ Import and export geometry

◆ Use Inventor file translators

◆ Work with imported data

◆ Work with Design Review markups

Importing and Exporting Geometry

Essentially, three data types make up a 3D model: curves or wires, surfaces, and solids. Wire frame models composed of only curves lack volume but have a size and shape. A surface model, on the other hand, is composed of curves that define the surfaces. A solid model is composed of curves, which define surfaces, which in turn define the solid. Understanding the hierarchy of geometry data will help you understand the translation issues that can occur when translating from one of these data types to another.

Within the category of curves and wires, there are different ways in which wires and curves are defined. If you are translating files that represent wires and curves as Non-Uniform Rational B-Splines (NURBS) to a format that represents wires and curves as simpler basis splines (B-splines), then there might be something lost in translation. Likewise, when you translate a surface model, if the surface normal were to get reversed (think positive vs. negative), then you will have translation issues. And so it is with translating solids; if a solid model is translated so that a gap is formed where two surfaces meet, then translation may not be complete.

Translation of curves, surfaces, and solids occur between different packages because software packages use different methods of geometric accuracy. Accuracy controls such things as how close two points in space are before being considered a single point or how close two edges can be before they are considered connected, and so on.

To help with translating from one software package that solves curves using method A to software that uses method B, you can create an intermediate or neutral file. Common neutral file formats include IGES (Initial Graphic Exchange Specification), STEP (Standard for the Exchange of Product), SAT (Standard ACIS Text), and others.

WORKING WITH NEUTRAL FILE FORMATS

Although using neutral formats will help avoid problems, keep two things in mind when translating files:

◆ Generally speaking, you should strive to keep the number of file formats between the source software and the destination software as low as possible.

◆ Not all neutral file formats are created equally.

DWG

When an AutoCAD DWG file is imported into Inventor, the file is translated into an Autodesk Inventor part, assembly, and/or drawing file, based on the import settings. The original AutoCAD file is not changed. When exported from Inventor to a DWG, a file is translated into AutoCAD objects. The translated DWG is not linked to the Inventor file from which it was created. Instead, the DWG data is fully editable within AutoCAD.

To import a DWG file, follow these steps:

1. Click Open on the Get Started tab.

2. Set the Files Of Type drop-down to AutoCAD Drawings (*.dwg).

3. Select the DWG file you are going to import.

4. Click the Options button and choose Import. (If you are translating a number of DWG files, you can set Import to be the default by clicking the Tools tab, then selecting the Application Options button, and choosing the Drawing tab.)

5. Once you've selected Import, as shown in Figure 14.1, click OK.

6. This returns you to the Open dialog box, where you will click the Open button to start the DWG/DXF File Wizard. Note the Configuration drop-down box.

7. If you have an import configuration already saved, you can specify it now and click Finish. If you have not yet created a configuration template, click Next to go to the Import Destination Options dialog box.

FIGURE 14.1
Importing a
DWG file

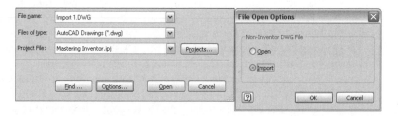

You need to consider a number of options when importing DWG files, depending on the DWG data input and the intended translation output. The following sections discuss these considerations in relation to the import options.

IMPORTING **3D SOLIDS**

If the AutoCAD DWG has 3D solids, you can check the 3D Solids check box to translate them into Inventor part files. Use the Solids To Single Part File check box if you want multibody solids to be translated into an Inventor part file. Leave this option unchecked if you want each solid body in the DWG to be created as an individual Inventor part file and automatically placed in an Inventor assembly. Figure 14.2 shows the import options for 3D solids.

FIGURE 14.2
3D Solids Options

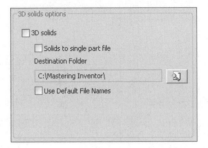

Set the destination folder to a path in which you want to have the part files created and choose Use Default File Names to allow Inventor to name the resulting part files automatically. If you choose this option, the new Inventor parts will be given a name based on the DWG name and be incremented by a value of 1. For instance, if the DWG is named Engine.dwg, then each solid in the DWG will be named Engine1.ipt, Engine2.ipt, Engine3.ipt, and so on. If left unchecked, each solid in the DWG will be named Part1.ipt, Part2.ipt, Part3.ipt, and so on.

IMPORTING **2D DATA**

If the DWG contains only 2D data, then you can leave the 3D Solids check box deselected and turn your attention to the Destination For 2D Data area of the dialog box, as shown in Figure 14.3. Selecting the New Drawing radio button translates the DWG data to a new Inventor DWG or IDW. If you check Promote Dimensions To Sketch, the 2D data is placed in a draft view that is created in the Inventor drawing.

FIGURE 14.3
2D data options

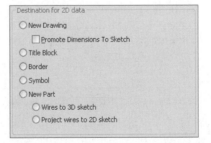

You can use the Title Block radio button to convert an AutoCAD title block DWG into an Inventor title block. When doing this, be sure to click the mapping options to set the layer and font mapping options, as shown in Figure 14.4. You can click the Symbols radio button to translate the 2D data into a sketched symbol for use in an Inventor DWG or IDW file. Click the New

Part radio button to translate AutoCAD 2D data into a new IPT sketch. Choose between creating a 3D or 2D sketch within the file.

FIGURE 14.4
Mapping options

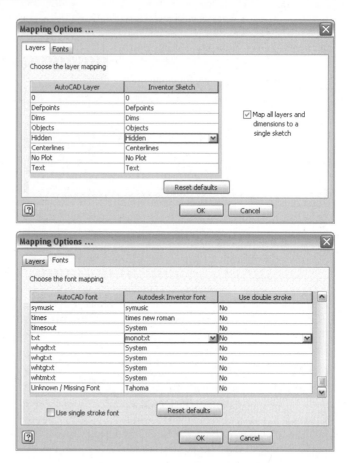

Inventor has both a decimal and a fractional unit style for dimensions. When dimensions are translated, if Inventor detects that the AutoCAD file employs a scientific, decimal, engineering, or Windows Desktop style, those styles are converted to decimal style. Fraction and architectural are mapped to fractional style.

THINK BEFORE IMPORTING AUTOCAD GEOMETRY

Although you might be tempted to import 2D AutoCAD geometry and start extruding away, you do need to keep a few things in mind. If this is a part that will never change or is a reference part, this approach is probably okay. However, if you are re-creating old AutoCAD data to be used in your Inventor models as part of a fully parametric design, you might consider modeling the parts from scratch. It *will* take longer, no doubt. However, modeling from scratch allows you to place the design intent into the parts that importing simply cannot do. You can create the model in a proper order and with the proper constraints that will allow you or others to easily modify it in the future.

UNITS, TEMPLATES, CONSTRAINTS, AND CONFIGURATIONS

Whether importing to 2D or 3D, you will use the templates area to specify which template to use for each of the file types to translate to. In the Import Files Units area, you can specify the units if they do not match the units that Inventor detects from the AutoCAD file. The detected unit is based on the INSUNITS system variable in the DWG file.

You can use the Constrain End Points and Apply Geometric Constraints check boxes to allow Inventor to place constraints on sketch entities when it can. Endpoints found to be coincident will be given a coincident constraint; lines found to be parallel will be given parallel constraints; and so on.

Once all these options are configured, you can click the Save Configurations button, as shown in Figure 14.5, to write out a file to use the next time you convert a DWG file. Doing this allows you to convert files more accurately and more quickly.

FIGURE 14.5
More import desti-
nation options

When all the configuration settings have been made and saved, click Finish to start the import process. Inventor will create the new files based on your configurations and leave the files open in the current Inventor session.

Mechanical Desktop (MDT) DWG

Mechanical Desktop (MDT) files can be imported into Inventor part and assembly files. If the source files contain geometry or features that are not recognized in Inventor, they are omitted, and the missing data is noted in the browser or the translation log file. No links are maintained to the existing MDT files. You must have MDT on your computer to import files into Inventor. Note that the AutoCAD Inventor suite does not ship with MDT. If you have a need to use MDT for translation, the 2009 version can be downloaded from the Autodesk website or you can purchase or request installation media. MDT 2009 is the last version that Autodesk will release.

You can import MDT DWG files using the Options button in the Open dialog box just as you would a regular DWG. However, if Inventor detects that the file is an MDT file, you are given the option to read the data as an MDT file or as an AutoCAD or AutoCAD mechanical file, as shown in Figure 14.6.

Although many of the options for template, units, and configuration settings are the same as previously described for regular DWG files, the assembly and part options are specific to MDT files, as shown in Figure 14.7.

FIGURE 14.6
Reading MDT
file contents

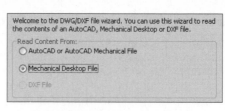

FIGURE 14.7
MDT assembly and
part options

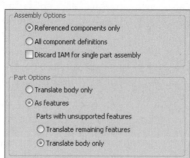

Consider the following items when migrating MDT files to Inventor:

◆ Broken views, base section views, and breakout section views from MDT will be turned into base views.

◆ Exploded views will become unexploded views (no tweaks applied).

◆ Importing discards (AMPARDIMS) from MDT automatically creates associative model dimensions in Inventor.

◆ If Move With Parent is selected in an MDT file, Inventor aligns all views according to the view type.

◆ If a parent view is missing in an MDT file, a child view is not created in Inventor.

◆ Inventor centerlines and center marks are automatically generated during translation; therefore, they might not be the same as in the MDT file.

◆ Radial section views have broken alignment in Inventor.

In addition to importing MDT files one at a time, you can use the Inventor Task Scheduler to batch the translation from MDT to Inventor. It is important to ensure that the MDT files are migrated to the latest version of MDT before attempting to translate them into Inventor files.

STEP and IGES

STEP (Standard for the Exchange of Product) and IGES (Initial Graphic Exchange Specification) are nonproprietary file formats to write data to, in order to exchange data among proprietary software. When opening a STEP or IGES file in Inventor, one part file will be created if the file contains only one part body; otherwise, you can create multiple Inventor part files placed within an assembly file.

Although no links are maintained between the original STEP or IGES file and the Inventor files created from them, when importing an updated STEP or IGES file, Inventor updates the geometry and maintains all modeling constraints and features applied to that STEP or IGES file.

To import a STEP or IGES file, follow these steps:

1. Click Open on the Get Started tab, and set the Files Of Type drop-down to STEP Files (`*.stp`, `*.ste`, `*.step`) or IGES Files (`*.igs`, `*.ige`, `*.iges`).

2. Select the file you intend to import.

3. Click the Options button, and you will be presented with the Import Options dialog.

In the Import Options dialog, you can choose from three save options:

Save In Workspace   Writes the files to the Workspace folder defined in your current project file (see Chapter 2, "Data and Projects," for more on projects and workspaces). The files are saved as Inventor files during the import process.

Select Save Location   Allows you to specify where the resulting Inventor files will be saved. If the translated file contains separate solid bodies, you can configure the import to save those files to one location and the top-level assembly file to another location.

Save At Import File Location   Writes the resulting Inventor file(s) to the same location as the original file. Figure 14.8 shows the Import Save options.

FIGURE 14.8
STEP or IGES
save options

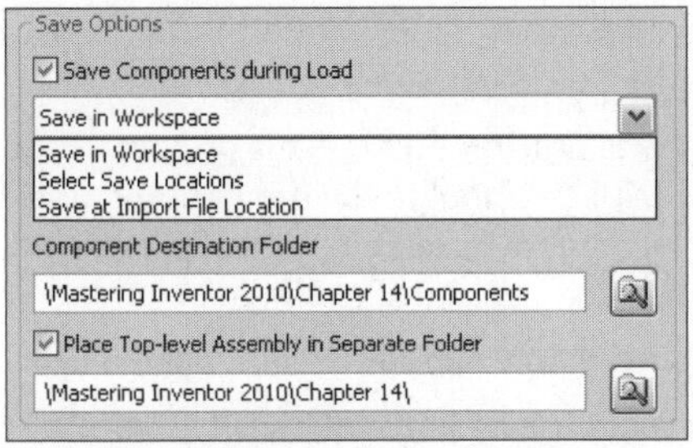

In the Entities To Import area, use the selection buttons to specify the inclusion of solids, surfaces, wires, and points in the import action. Click the Import Assembly As Single Part check box to turn a multibody STEP or IGES into a single-part file. Then choose from one of two options:

Single Composite Feature   This allows you to import the assembly as a single composite feature into a single-part file.

Multiple Solid Part   With this option, you can import the assembly as individual solid bodies into a single-part file.

Click the Import Multiple Solid Parts As Assembly check box to turn a multibody STEP or IGES into individual part files. When imported, the new Inventor parts will be given a name based on the filename and incremented by a value of 1. For instance, if an IGES were named 4278_T.igs, then the Inventor parts will be named 4278_T 1.ipt, 4278_T 2.ipt, 4278_T 3.ipt, and so on.

If you leave both of those check boxes deselected, you can specify how surface objects will be translated:

Individual Surface Bodies   Imports each surface as a single surface body all contained in a single-part file.

Single Composite Feature   Imports surfaces as a single composite all contained in a single-part file.

Multiple Composite Features   Imports surfaces as multiple composites all contained in a single-part file. Composites are created for each level, layer, or group, according to the Create From information specified.

Single Construction Group   Imports surfaces as a single group in the construction environment of a single-part file.

Multiple Construction Groups   Imports surfaces as multiple groups in the construction environment of a single-part file. Construction groups are created for each level, layer, or group, according to the Create From information specified.

A *composite* is a collection of surfaces, as opposed to a single quilt of surfaces. A composite can consist of any combination of single- or multiple-faced surfaces or closed volume surfaces. Often these surfaces will not be connected even if they appear to be. Composites can be used when many surfaces are imported as an expedient way of getting surface data into Inventor for reference or inspection.

You can also specify which units the imported geometry will be converted to, and the post-process options as listed here:

Check Parts During Load   This performs a quality check on the imported data. Bad data is marked with a symbol in the browser and any remaining data is not checked. If the parts are determined not to have any errors, they are marked with a green check mark in the browser. Checking parts can significantly increase the time required to translate a file.

Auto Stitch And Promote   This stitches surfaces into a quilt or solid, when possible. If the stitch results in a single body, it is promoted out of the construction environment; otherwise it remains in the construction environment.

Enable Advanced Healing   This allows small alterations in the surface geometry in order to stitch the surfaces.

Figure 14.9 shows the STEP and IGES options.

Figure 14.10 shows the same file imported in four different ways:

Far Left   Data is placed into Multiple Construction Groups.

Middle Left   Data is placed into Multiple Composite Features.

Middle Right   Data is placed into a Single Construction Group.

Far Right   Data is placed into a Single Composite Feature.

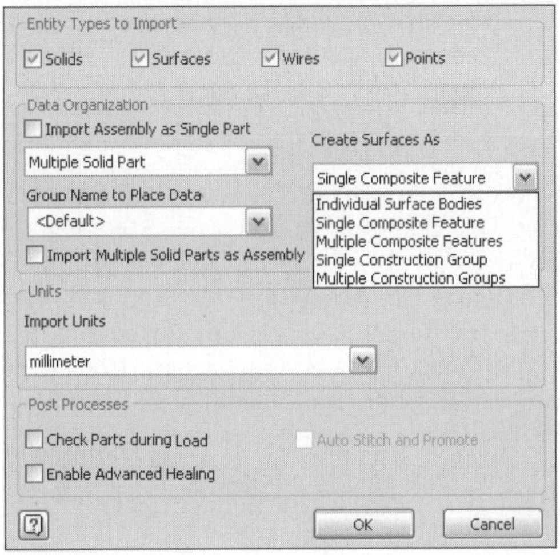

FIGURE 14.9
STEP or IGES
import options

FIGURE 14.10
Group mapping
comparisons

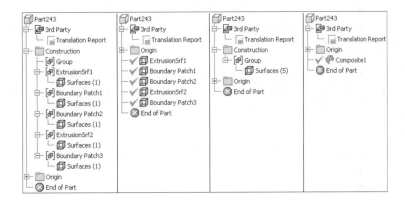

Many Inventor users prefer to send and receive STEP files to and from vendors or clients because they find STEP files import better than other file formats. Here is a list of attributes that make STEP a popular choice:

◆ STEP files can retain the original part names when importing to an assembly.

◆ STEP creates instances for duplicated parts. If you are sent a STEP of an assembly created in another software package and that assembly has 12 instances of a certain screw size, Inventor will typically create just one file for the screw and instance it 12 times, as opposed to creating 12 different files.

◆ STEP files can maintain assembly hierarchy, meaning that subassembly structure can be translated. In other formats, assemblies may be translated with all parts at the top-level assembly.

♦ STEP translates part colors, whereas other formats generally do not contain the information needed to carry part colors across different platforms.

♦ STEP format is governed independently and is not tied to a particular modeling kernel; as a result, it is often considered somewhat of a more standard format.

To export a file as a STEP, click the Inventor button ▌▾, then select Save Copy As. In the resulting dialog box, set Save As Type to STEP Files (*.stp, *.ste, *.step). Click the Options button to set the STEP version. You can also choose to include sketches. Included sketches are translated to the STEP file in named groups.

To export a file as an IGES, click the Inventor button ▌▾, select Save Copy As, and set Save As Type to IGES Files (*.igs, *.ige, *.iges). Click the Options button to set the IGES output to either surfaces or solids. You can choose to include sketches. Included sketches are translated to the IGES file in named layers.

To export a file as an IGES, click the Inventor button ▌▾, select Save Copy As, and set Save As Type to JT Files (*.jt). You can then apply options manually or select a configuration file through the dialog that appears.

The JT file is a lightweight representation used by PLM products that is similar to the Autodesk .DWF format.

If you are asked to give a JT file as a deliverable, be sure to ask if there is a JT configuration file that the recipient can offer to make sure that options for export match their needs.

SAT

SAT (Standard ACIS Text) files are written in the standard file exchange format for the ACIS solid modeling kernel. To import a SAT file, follow these steps:

1. Click Open on the Get Started tab.

2. Set the Files Of Type drop-down to SAT Files (*.sat).

3. Select the file you want to import.

4. Click the Options button, and you will be presented with the Import Options dialog box.

In the Import Options dialog box, you can choose from three save options:

Save In Workspace   Writes the files to the Workspace folder defined in your current project file (see Chapter 2 for more on projects and workspaces). The files are saved as Inventor files during the import process.

Select Save Location   Allows you to specify where the resulting Inventor files will be saved. If the translated file contains separate solid bodies, you can configure the import to save those files to one location and the top-level assembly file to another location.

Save At Import File Location   Writes the resulting Inventor file(s) to the same location as the original file.

In the Entities To Import area, use the selection buttons to specify the inclusion of solids, surfaces, and wires in the import action. Use the Import Assembly As Single Part check box option to turn a multibody SAT into a single-part file. Then choose from one of two options:

Single Composite Feature   Imports the assembly as a single composite feature into a single-part file.

Multiple Solid Part   Imports the assembly as individual solid bodies into a single-part file.

If you leave this check box deselected, you can specify how surface objects will be translated:

Individual Surface Bodies Imports surfaces as an individual surface all contained in a single-part file.

Single Composite Feature Imports surfaces as a single composite all contained in a single-part file.

Single Construction Group Imports surfaces as a single group in the construction environment of a single part file.

Some CAD software outputs SAT files in a default unit without regard for the units used to create the original file. You can specify which units the imported geometry will be converted to, as well as the post-process options listed here:

Check Parts During Load This option performs a quality check on the imported data. Bad data is marked with a symbol in the browser and any remaining data is not checked. If the parts are determined not to have any errors, they are marked with a green check mark in the browser. Checking parts can significantly increase the time required to translate files.

Auto Stitch And Promote This option stitches surfaces into a quilt or solid, when possible. If the stitch results in a single body it is promoted out of the construction environment; otherwise, it remains in the construction environment.

Enable Advanced Healing This option allows small alterations in the surface geometry in order to stitch the surfaces.

Figure 14.11 shows the SAT import options.

FIGURE 14.11
SAT import
options

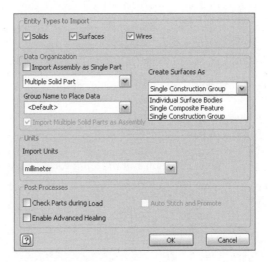

To export a file as a SAT, click the Inventor button ![button], choose Save Copy As, and set Save As Type to SAT Files (*.sat). Click the Options button to set the SAT version. The default is version 7.0. You can also choose to include sketches. Included sketches are translated to the SAT ungrouped.

WATCH FOR SAT FILE VERSIONS

As of Inventor release 5.3, Autodesk broke away from the ACIS SAT standard when it created its ShapeManager kernel. This means that Autodesk Inventor cannot read in any SAT file that is newer than version 6.0. Keep this in mind when requesting models from third parties or when downloading them from a vendor's website.

Using Inventor File Translators

With Inventor, you can access files from other CAD systems without downloading an add-in or translating the files to an intermediate format such as STEP, IGES, or SAT. Instead, you simply open the file, and Inventor will translate the file into an Inventor file on the fly. You can translate all of the file types in the following list by clicking Open on the Get Started tab and then setting the Files Of Type drop-down to the appropriate type. Once the file type is selected, click the Option button to configure the import options.

- CATIA V4

- CATIA V5

- Pro/ENGINEER

- Unigraphics

- Parasolids

- SolidWorks

- Autodesk Alias

In the Import Options dialog box, you can choose from three save options:

Save In Workspace Writes the files to the Workspace folder defined in your current project file (see Chapter 2 for more on projects and workspaces). The files are saved as Inventor files during the import process.

Select Save Location Allows you to specify where the resulting Inventor files will be saved. If the translated file contains separate solid bodies, you can configure the import to save those files to one location and the top-level assembly file to another location.

Save At Import File Location Writes the resulting Inventor file(s) to the same location as the original file.

Figure 14.12 shows the import save options.

FIGURE 14.12
Import save
options

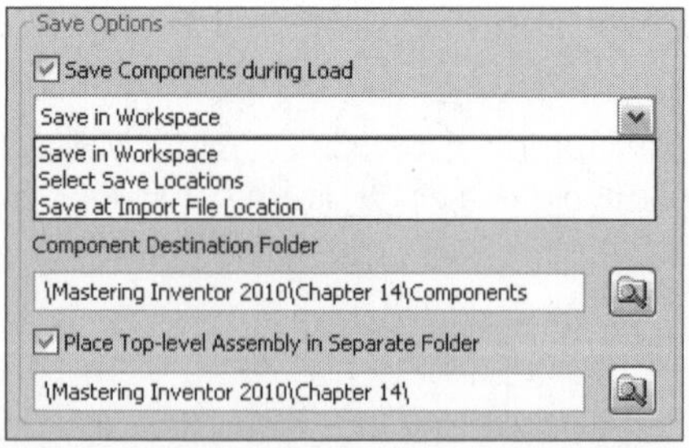

For each of these file types, you can specify which units the imported geometry will be converted to as well as the post-process options listed here:

Check Parts During Load   This option performs a quality check on the imported data. Bad data is marked with a symbol in the browser and any remaining data is not checked. If the parts are determined not to have any errors, they are marked with a green check mark in the browser. Checking parts can significantly increase the time required to translate files.

Auto Stitch And Promote   This option stitches surfaces into a quilt or solid, when possible. If the stitch results in a single body, it is promoted out of the construction environment; otherwise, it remains in the construction environment.

Enable Advanced Healing   This option allows small alterations in the surface geometry in order to stitch the surfaces.

CATIA

When importing CATIA V4 or V5 files, you can choose between solids, surfaces, meshes, wires, and points. To open CATIA files, follow these steps:

1. Click Open on the Get Started tab.

2. Set the Files Of Type drop-down to CATIA V5 Files (`*.CATPart; *.CATProduct`).

3. Select the CATIA file you want to open and click the Options button.

Figure 14.13 shows the import options for CATIA files.

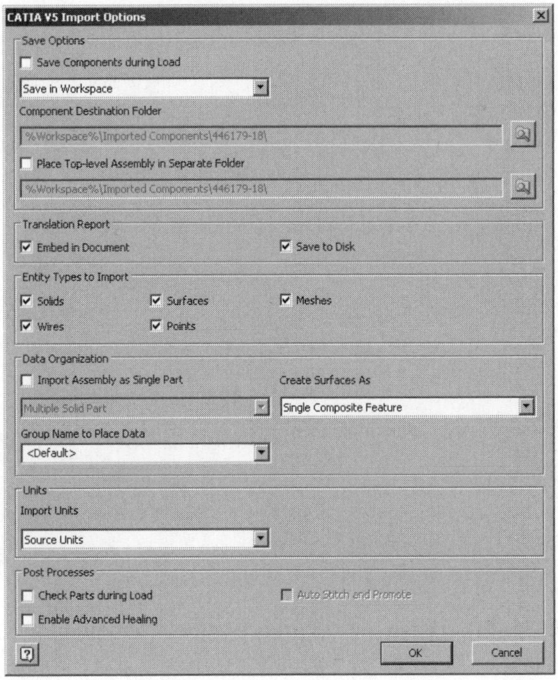

FIGURE 14.13
CATIA import options

In the Entities To Import area, use the selection buttons to specify the inclusion of solids, surfaces, wires, and points in the import action. Use the Import Assembly As Single Part check box to turn a multibody CATIA file into a single-part file. Then choose from one of two options:

Single Composite Feature   Imports the assembly as a single composite feature into a single-part file.

Multiple Solid Part   Imports the assembly as individual solid bodies into a single-part file.

If you leave this check box deselected, you can specify how surface objects will be translated:

Individual Surface Bodies   Imports surfaces as an individual surface all contained in a single-part file.

Single Composite Feature   Imports surfaces as a single composite all contained in a single-part file.

Single Construction Group   Imports surfaces as a single group in the construction environment of a single-part file.

Pro/ENGINEER

To open models created in Pro/ENGINEER, follow these steps:

1. Select Open from the Get Started tab.

2. Set the Files Of Type drop-down to Pro/ENGINEER (*.prt*; *.asm*) or (*.g) or (*.neu*).

3. Select the Pro/ENGINEER file you want to open, and click the Options button.

Figure 14.14 shows the import options for Pro/ENGINEER files.

FIGURE 14.14
Pro/ENGINEER
import options

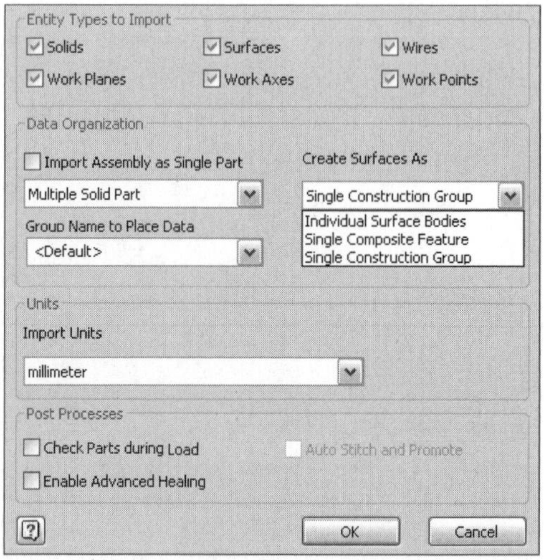

In the Entities To Import area, use the selection buttons to specify the inclusion of solids, surfaces, wires, work planes, work axes, and work points in the import action. Use the Import

Assembly As Single Part check box to turn a multibody Pro/ENGINEER file into a single-part file. Then choose from one of two options:

Single Composite Feature   Imports the assembly as a single composite feature into a single part file.

Multiple Solid Part   Imports the assembly as individual solid bodies into a single part file.

If you leave this check box deselected, you can specify how surface objects will be translated:

Individual Surface Bodies   Imports surfaces as an individual surface all contained in a single-part file.

Single Composite Feature   Imports surfaces as a single composite all contained in a single-part file.

Single Construction Group   Imports surfaces as a single group in the construction environment of a single-part file.

To import Pro/ENGINEER parts or assemblies that contain instances of family tables, the accelerator files (`*.xpr` or `*.xas`) must be saved independently of the Pro/ENGINEER part and assembly files.

When the files are opened in Inventor, they will consist of a base solid, work features, and a translation report. You can then add features to the base solid using standard Inventor part-modeling tools. Figure 14.15 shows an imported Pro/ENGINEER file with translated work features.

FIGURE 14.15
An imported Pro/
ENGINEER part

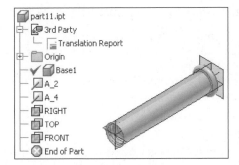

Unigraphics and Parasolids

You can access Unigraphics and Parasolids files in the same way you would Pro/ENGINEER files. To do so, follow these steps:

1. Click Open on the Get Started tab.

2. Set the Files Of Type drop-down to Parasolids Text Files (`*.x_t`), Parasolids Binary Files (`*.x_b`), or Unigraphics (`*.prt`).

3. Browse for the file you want to open and click the Options button.

Figure 14.16 shows the Parasolids import options.

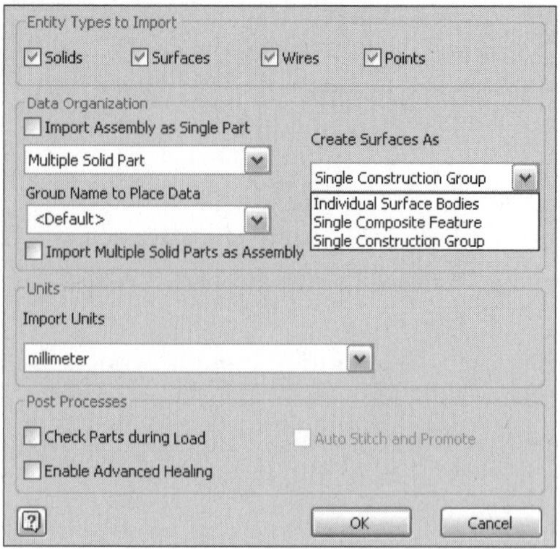

FIGURE 14.16
Parasolids import
options

In the Entities To Import area, use the selection buttons to specify the inclusion of solids, surfaces, and points in the import action. Use the Import Assembly As Single Part check box to turn a multibody Parasolid file into a single-part file. Then choose from one of two options:

Single Composite Feature Imports the assembly as a single composite feature into a single-part file.

Multiple Solid Part Imports the assembly as individual solid bodies into a single-part file.

Use the Import Multiple Solid Parts As Assembly check box to turn a multibody Parasolid file into individual part files. When imported, the new Inventor parts will be given a name based on the name of the original files.

If you leave both of those check boxes deselected, you can specify how surface objects will be translated. Here are the options:

Individual Surface Bodies Imports surfaces as individual surfaces all contained in a single-part file.

Single Composite Feature Imports surfaces as a single composite all contained in a single-part file.

Single Construction Group Imports surfaces as a single group in the construction environment of a single-part file.

SolidWorks

To open models created in SolidWorks, follow these steps:

1. Click Open on the Get Started tab, and set the Files Of Type drop-down to SolidWorks (*.prt, *.sldpart, *.asm, and *.sldasm).

2. Select the SolidWorks file you want to open, and click the Options button.

Figure 14.17 shows the import options.

FIGURE 14.17
SolidWorks import options

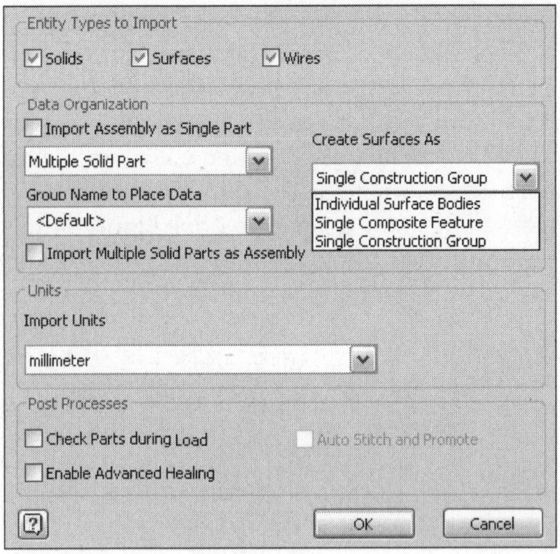

In the Entities To Import area, use the selection buttons to specify the inclusion of solids and surfaces in the import action. Use the Import Assembly As Single Part check box to turn a multibody SolidWorks file into a single-part file. Then choose from one of two options:

Single Composite Feature   Imports the assembly as a single composite feature into a single-part file.

Multiple Solid Part   Imports the assembly as individual solid bodies into a single-part file.

Use the Import Multiple Solid Parts As Assembly check box to turn a multibody SolidWorks file into individual part files. When imported, the new Inventor parts will be given a name based on the name of the original files.

If you leave both of those check boxes deselected, you can specify how surface objects will be translated. Here are the options:

Individual Surface Bodies   Imports surfaces as an individual surface all contained in a single-part file.

Single Composite Feature   Imports surfaces as a single composite all contained in a single-part file.

Single Construction Group   Imports surfaces as a single group in the construction environment of a single-part file.

IDF Board Files

Intermediate Data Format (IDF) is the standard data exchange format for transferring printed circuit assembly (PCA) files between printed circuit board (PCB) layouts and mechanical design programs. You can access IDF board files by clicking Open on the Get Started tab and setting the Files Of Type drop-down to IDF Board Files (*.brd, *.emn, *.bdf, and *.idb).

IDF board files can be imported into Inventor as assembly or part files. When brought in as an assembly, board components are translated into individual parts, contained in the new assembly. When imported as a part, the board components are translated into sketches and features. Inventor will translate IDF outlines, keepouts, group areas, drilled holes, and components.

Part files are automatically named based on the information in the existing board file. Once imported, the files can be placed into Inventor assemblies and detailed in Inventor drawings just as you would any other Inventor model. Figure 14.18 shows the IDF import options. You are presented with this dialog box automatically when you open an IDF board file.

FIGURE 14.18
Importing an IDF board file

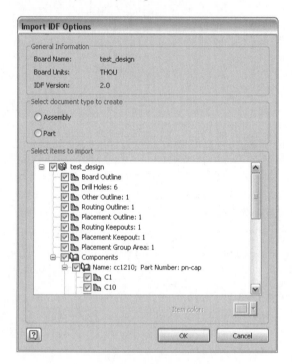

Placing Components from Other CAD Systems

So far you have learned about importing and translating files into Inventor using the Open dialog box to convert files into Inventor files. You can also access most of these file types in the assembly environment and place them straight into your Inventor assembly file just as you would any other model.

To place a non-Inventor component into an Inventor assembly, click the Place Components icon in the Assembly panel. In the Open dialog box, select the file type of the component you intend to place, or set the file type to All Files. Select the file, and then click the Options button. Configure the options as required, and click OK. Click Open to translate, and place the component into the assembly.

Working with Imported Data

In a perfect world, you would not need to import or export data at all. Instead, all files would exist in one perfect, universal file format. Of course, this perfect world does not exist, and you are probably required to import files created in another program from time to time. In a near-perfect world, imported data would always come in healthy and without any problems. Of course, that is rarely the case.

Instead, importing data can sometimes be a struggle. Typically the biggest struggles come with importing surface models. Inventor provides a construction environment for repairing poorly translated surfaces. Once repaired, imported surfaces must be promoted to the part environment for use in parametric modeling or so they can be seen in an assembly.

Working in the Construction Environment

If you choose Auto Stitch And Promote when importing a surface IGES or STEP, Inventor will attempt to automatically promote imported surfaces to the part environment. If surfaces cannot be promoted, they are left in the construction environment. With Auto Stitch And Promote turned off, the surfaces open directly in the construction environment.

If a construction folder exists in the browser, you can right-click it and choose Edit Construction to enter the construction environment. If no Construction folder is present, you must copy composite features to the Construction folder. You can do this by right-clicking the composite in the browser and choosing Copy To Construction.

To examine the construction tools in action, follow these steps:

1. On the Get Started tab, click the Open button.

2. Set the file type drop-down to IGES.

3. Browse for and select the file named mi_14a_001.igs located in the Chapter 14 directory of the Mastering Inventor 2011 folder.

4. Click the Options button, as shown in Figure 14.19.

FIGURE 14.19
Opening an
IGES file

5. In the Options dialog box, ensure that all the Entities To Import buttons are selected.

6. Set the Create Surfaces As drop-down to Multiple Construction Groups.

7. Ensure that the Auto Stitch And Promote check box is not selected. You can leave all the other settings at their defaults.

8. When the specified settings match Figure 14.20, click the OK button, and then click Open.

FIGURE 14.20
Import options

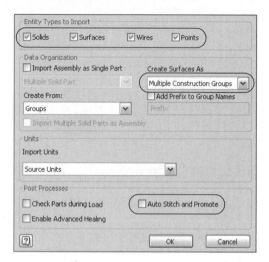

9. Once the file is open, examine the Model browser for the presence of the Construction folder. Expand this folder, and verify that there are 90 surfaces in one group within the folder. If you do not see this, check the import options shown in Figure 14.20 and ensure you have set them as shown. In particular, ensure the Autostitch And Promote option is not selected.

Notice you cannot select the surfaces in the graphics area. This is because all the surfaces reside in the construction environment. Note that had you selected the Auto Stitch And Promote option, the surfaces might have been promoted from the construction environment automatically. Depending on the quality of the surfaces, you might be required to stitch and promote surfaces manually, as you will here. Examine the model, and notice that there are some missing surfaces. You will need to repair these surfaces in order to promote them and turn this part into a solid. Figure 14.21 shows the location of the missing and errant surfaces.

FIGURE 14.21
Missing and errant surfaces

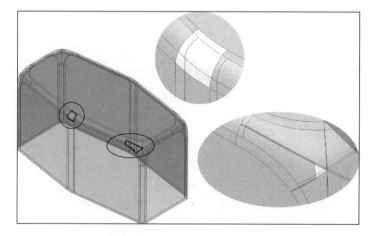

10. To activate the construction environment, right-click the Construction folder in the browser and choose Edit Construction. This opens the Construction tool panel.

11. Select the Stitch Surface tool from the Construction tab, and create a window selection of all of the surfaces on-screen.

12. Enter **0.001 in** in the Maximum Tolerance field, and click Apply.

You will see the 90 surfaces stitched into a single quilted surface. The gaps created by the missing and errant surfaces are also highlighted, and the remaining free edges are reported in the Stitch dialog box, as shown in Figure 14.22.

FIGURE 14.22
Stitching surfaces

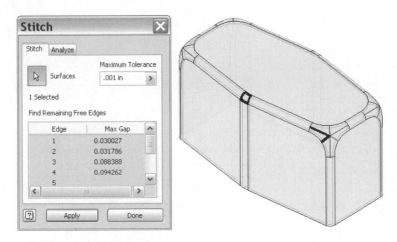

Next you will use the Boundary Patch tool to create a surface to fill in one of the gaps.

13. Click Done in the Stitch dialog box and zoom in to the area indicated with a circle in Figure 14.21. Notice the missing surface.

14. Choose Boundary Patch from the Construction tab. Select the four edges as indicated in Figure 14.23, and then click OK.

FIGURE 14.23
Boundary patch

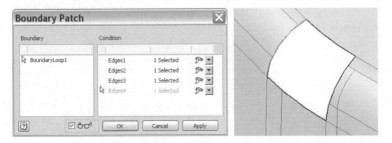

15. Notice in the browser there are now two surfaces in the Group folder. Using the Stitch tool, select the new surface and any face on the rest of the other surface to stitch the two together.

16. Zoom to the corner area that was indicated with an ellipse back in Figure 14.21, and notice the missing errant surface.

17. You'll notice two of the surfaces extend beyond the adjacent surfaces and the corner of the surface is cut short, leaving a gap. To resolve this, you will first select the surface and choose Unstitch, as shown in Figure 14.24.

FIGURE 14.24
Unstitching the
errant surface

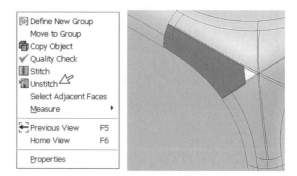

18. To fill the gap in the surface, select the Extend Faces tool from the Construction tab, and choose the edge, as shown in Figure 14.25. Enter **0.026 in** for the distance, and click Apply. This will extend the surface over the existing gap.

FIGURE 14.25
Extending a face

19. Now you need to trim the surface edges to the adjacent surfaces. To do this, select the Boundary Trim tool on the Construction tab, then select the edges of the adjacent faces, as shown in Figure 14.26. Finally, choose the unstitched surface, and click Apply.

FIGURE 14.26
Using the Bound-
ary Trim tool

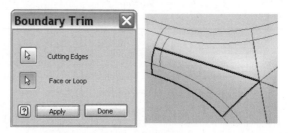

20. Once the surface is trimmed, click the Stitch tool and select the both the trimmed surface and the existing surface quilt (you can window-select the entire part to do this). Click Apply and then click Done.

When you do, you will see the group switch from Surfaces (2) to Solid (1), indicating that you have a surface set that is ready to be promoted to a solid.

21. Choose Copy Object from the Construction tab, and select Solids (1) from the model tree. Set the Output setting to be solids by clicking the icon, and then click OK, as shown in Figure 14.27.

FIGURE 14.27
Copying the object

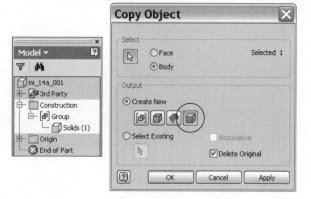

You will now have a base solid in the Model browser, as well as the Construction folder and the third-party translation report. Click the Finish Construction button to exit the construction group, and then you can remove the translation report (in the 3rd Party folder) and Construction folder by right-clicking them in the browser and choosing Delete.

Editing Imported Data Using Inventor Fusion

You can add features to the base solid by sketching any of the desired surfaces and using the standard Inventor part-modeling tools.

Autodesk Inventor Fusion is an application that installs with Inventor that will allow you to quickly manipulate data from all of the applications listed in the translation information.

To edit the imported body, follow these steps:

1. On the Get Started tab, click the Open button.

2. Browse for and select the file named mi_14a_003.ipt located in the Chapter 14 directory of the Mastering Inventor 2011 folder.

3. Right-click on the Base1 feature in the browser and choose Edit Solid.

This will open a dialog (Figure 14.28) informing you that Inventor will open the Inventor Fusion 2011 application to edit the base solid.

FIGURE 14.28
Editing a base solid is done with Inventor Fusion

4. Click OK to open Inventor Fusion.

5. Once the model is open in fusion, rotate it so that you can see the bottom edge as shown in Figure 14.29.

FIGURE 14.29
Editing the compo-
nent in Fusion

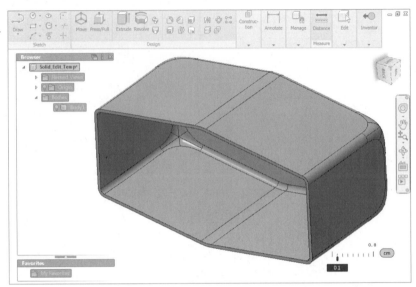

6. Select the narrow face of the bottom edge as shown in Figure 14.30.

FIGURE 14.30
Extending or
contracting a
solid body

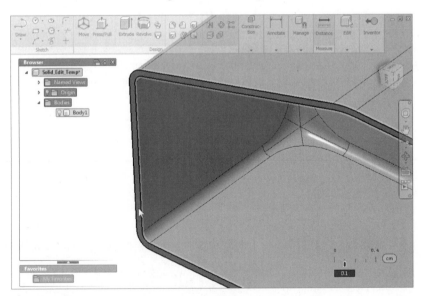

7. Once the face is selected, right-click on the screen. A circle of tools called a Marking Menu will appear. Select the move icon and a triad will appear to allow the face to be moved.

8. Drag the Yellow arrow of the Triad to the right until the Value frame reads -1 cm, as shown in Figure 14.31.

9. Right-click again and select the Finish button (green checkmark) to accept the edit.

FIGURE 14.31
Moving a face

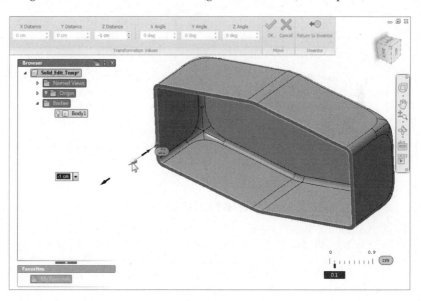

10. Select the Return to Inventor icon at the right end of the ribbon to transfer the changes back to Inventor.

Selecting the Return to Inventor icon will reopen Inventor and close Fusion. This is only a basic example of the potential interaction between Fusion and Inventor. See Figure 14.32 for the completed model.

FIGURE 14.32
The updated model in Inventor

USE EDIT SOLID TO MODIFY PURCHASED PARTS

When building custom machinery, we often run into a situation where we do not know what size air cylinder we might need for a design. Many times we will have downloaded a SAT file of, say, a 3˝-long cylinder, and we then discover that we really need a 4˝-long model. Rather than download and import a new model, you can take a shortcut by using these Edit Solid tools to make the body of the cylinder longer.

Viewing DWF Markup

Autodesk Design Review offers Inventor users a simple and effective way to view and mark up both 2D and 3D DWF files. Design Web Format (DWF) files are lightweight versions of your Inventor files you can publish from Inventor and email to a collaborator to be viewed and redlined with Autodesk Design Review (ADR). Non-Inventor users can download and install ADR free of charge from the Autodesk website.

The DWF markup process begins from within Inventor where you will publish a DWF from your Inventor files. Once the DWF is published, it is sent to the reviewer and marked up with ADR. You can then bring those markups into your Inventor file and change the status of a markup, add comments, or accept the markup. You have the additional choice of publishing to DWFx format, allowing reviewers to access the file directly through Internet Explorer 7.0 or Windows Vista.

A typical DWF markup process is as follows:

1. **Publish:** You write out the DWF file from Inventor 2D and/or 3D files.

2. **Receive:** The reviewer receives the DWF file from you and opens it with ADR to check for errors and omissions.

3. **Review:** The reviewer can comment on and mark up the DWF file using callouts, text blocks, shapes, dimensions, stamps, and custom symbols. Then they save those markups to the DWF file.

4. **Return:** The reviewer then sends the markups back to you for your review.

5. **Revise:** You load the marked-up DWF into Inventor and revise the Inventor files as required.

6. **Republish:** After revising, you write out the DWF file from Inventor 2D and/or 3D files again.

Publishing a DWF or DWFx File

With the file you intend to publish open in Inventor, click the Inventor button and select Export ➢ Export to DWF, which opens the Publish dialog box. There are three options for publishing the DWF or DWFx:

Express Publishes only the active sheet without the 3D model.

Complete Publishes all sheets and all 3D models except sheets excluded from printing.

Custom Chooses sheets and 3D models to publish, depending on the type of file you are publishing. Extra tabs appear in the Publish dialog box for each file type as required. Here's what's included for each file type when you are using the Custom option:

Drawing files The DWF or DWFx file includes all sheets and tables, as well as the complete referenced 3D models.

Assembly files The following assembly options are available:

- ◆ The DWF or DWFx file includes the assembly with view and positional representations, as well as enabled BOM views.

- ◆ The DWF or DWFx file includes all members and the iAssembly table with view and positional representations.

- ◆ The DWF or DWFx file includes the assembly with view and positional representations, as well as enabled BOM views.

- ◆ The DWF or DWFx file includes the assembly with view and positional representations, as well as enabled BOM views, weld beads, and weld symbols.

- ◆ The DWF or DWFx file includes the assembly with view and positional representations, as well as enabled BOM views.

- ◆ When an assembly is at any other LOD other than the master, only that LOD is published to the DWF or DWFx. All view and positional representations, as well as enabled BOM views, are also published.

Part files   The following part options are available:

- The DWF or DWFx file includes only the part model.

- The DWF or DWFx file includes the folded model and flat pattern (if one exists).

- The DWF or DWFx file includes all iPart members and the iPart table.

- The DWF or DWFx file includes only the iPart model.

- The DWF or DWFx file includes the model with stress/constraint indicators as well as a stress scale.

Presentation files   The DWF or DWFx file includes the presentation views, animations, and assembly instructions, as well as the complete assembly.

DWF or DWFx files can be published with the ability to measure, print, and enable and disable markups. They can be password protected for security also. Figure 14.33 shows the publish options for an iAssembly factory.

FIGURE 14.33
DWF or DWFx
publish options

Once you choose the appropriate options, click Publish to specify either the DWF or DWFx format, and specify a location to create the file. The resulting file can be opened in Design Review to create markups.

Reviewing and Marking Up DWF and DWFx Files

Once a DWF or DWFx file is open in Design Review, you can create markups in the form of callouts, text blocks, shapes, stamps, custom symbols, and measurements. Figure 14.34 shows the Markup and Measure tab.

FIGURE 14.34
Markup and
Measure tools

When markups are created, they are listed in the Markups palettes and organized by the sheet upon which they reside. Most markups contain the following collection of properties: Status, Notes, History, Created, Creator, Label, Modified, and Sheet. Drawn markups such as lines do not have properties.

Each markup can have its own status. The status can be <None>, For Review, Question, or Done. When you click a markup in the Markups palettes, the screen will zoom to the markup at the same zoom scale at which it was created. Once markups are complete, the DWF or DWFx file can be saved. Figure 14.35 shows a view marked up in Design Review.

FIGURE 14.35
Marked-up view in
Design Review

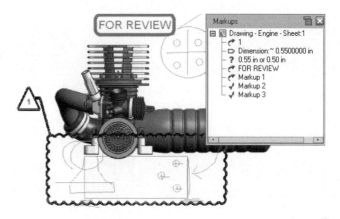

Accessing DWF or DWFx Markups in Inventor

To open a markup set in Inventor, select File ➢ Load Markup Set. The DWF markups will be overlaid onto the Inventor drawing, and the Markups browser displays the markup set in the tree view. You can then edit the status and properties of each markup by right-clicking the markup in the browser, as shown in Figure 14.36.

FIGURE 14.36
Markups loaded
into Inventor

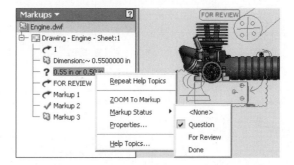

 Real World Scenario

DWF IN THE REAL WORLD

When communicating with vendors and clients who have never used Design Review and are accustomed to receiving PDF files, we recommend that you do not force DWF on them. Generally you will have much better luck getting the uninitiated to use and eventually request DWF files if you send them both a PDF and DWF file initially. Include a link to the Design Review download on the Autodesk website in your email and mention that the download is free and that the files can be viewed in 3D. This approach allows the person on the other end to make the choice at their convenience. Typically once they have used Design Review, this is the format they will request.

Once you've reviewed all markups, you can save the markups back to the DWF or DWFx file. You can choose to republish only the sheets that are marked up or republish all sheets. You can access these commands by right-clicking the DWF or DWFx filename in the Markups browser, as shown in Figure 14.37.

FIGURE 14.37
Saving and republishing markups

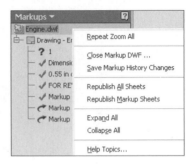

The Bottom Line

Import and export geometry   In the design world today, you most likely need to transfer files to or from a customer or vendor from time to time. Chances are, the files will need to be translated to or from a neutral file format to be read by different CAD packages.

> **Master It**   You are collaborating with another design office that does not use Inventor. You are asked which you would prefer, IGES or STEP files.

Use Inventor file translators   Inventor offers native file translators for CATIA, Pro/ENGINEER, SolidWorks, Unigraphics, and other CAD file types. This allows you to access these file formats with Inventor and translate the files into Inventor files directly.

> **Master It**   You are a "job shop" and in the past have been required to maintain a copy of SolidWorks in addition to your copy of Inventor in order to work with customers who send you SolidWorks files. You would like to eliminate the cost of maintaining two software packages.

Work with imported data   Using the construction environment in Inventor, you can repair poorly translated surface files. Often a file fails to translate into a solid because of just a few translation errors in the part. Repairing or patching the surfaces and promoting the file to a solid allows you to use the file more effectively.

> **Master It**   You download an IGES file from a vendor website, but when you attempt to use the component in your design, the surface data is found to have issues.

Work with Design Review markups   Design Review offers you and the people you collaborate with an easy-to-use electronic markup tool that can be round-tripped from Inventor. Design Review markups can be made on both 2D and 3D files.

> **Master It**   You want to use Design Review to communicate with vendors and clients in order to save time and resources, but you have found that others are unsure of what Design Review is and how to get it.

Chapter 15

Frame Generator

Frame Generator consists of several tools to automate frame modeling. You can select lines, edges, and points to specify the location of members. Frame Generator derives the selections into a part. This part is called a skeleton because it provides the framework for the members. The skeleton part automatically updates when a change is made to the original geometry, which updates the frame member size or position.

Frame Generator gets structural profiles from Content Center. In addition to the structural profiles included in the Inventor libraries, you can author and publish your own profiles. This is useful for adding profiles of extruded aluminum, plastic, and other materials, since the structural profiles in the Inventor libraries are standard steel shapes.

In this chapter, you will learn how to:

◆ Work with frame files

◆ Insert frame members onto a skeleton model

◆ Add end treatments to frame members

◆ Make changes to frames

◆ Author and publish structural profiles

◆ Create BOMs for Frame Generator assemblies

Accessing the Frame Generator Tools

The Frame Generator panel, shown in Figure 15.1, is on the Design tab of the assembly ribbon. It has tools specific to Frame Generator plus the Beam and Column Calculator from the Design Accelerators.

FIGURE 15.1
The Frame Generator tools on the Design tab of the Assembly Ribbon

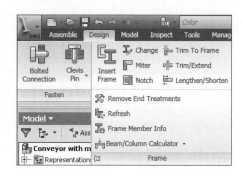

The tools fall into four categories:

Creating Frame Members Frame members can be created using the Insert Frame and Change tools.

Creating End Treatments End treatments can be created with these tools:

◆ Miter

◆ Trim To Frame

◆ Trim/Extend

◆ Notch

◆ Lengthen/Shorten

◆ Remove End Treatments

Performing Maintenance Maintenance can be performed with the Frame Member Info and Refresh tools.

Performing Calculations and Analysis Calculations and analysis can be performed with the Beam and Column tool.

ABOUT FRAME GENERATOR

The Frame Generator application is an add-in that uses the Inventor API (application programming interface). Since the API does not provide access to all the Inventor functionality, there are some user interface differences between add-ins and core Inventor tools. For example, the edit fields in core Inventor have an extensive flyout menu. The add-ins do not have access to this functionality, so their edit fields are more limited.

Exploring the Frame Generator File Structure

When you create the first members in a frame assembly, a dialog box prompts you for filenames. Frame Generator creates a subassembly and a skeleton file in the parent assembly. The subassembly does several things. It acts as a container for the skeleton and frame members, isolating them from the assembly solver, and it acts as a filter so Frame Generator tools, such as Frame Member Info, ignore other assembly components. The skeleton file is created in the subassembly and is made of all of the edges and points you select when placing frame members. Each frame member is created as a separate file, and saved into a subdirectory named after the frame assembly.

As an example, imagine you create a cube to use as the basis on which to model a frame. You name the cube file Cube_Frame, and then place this cube into an assembly called Cube_Frame_ Assembly. Both files are saved in a folder called My_Frames. You could then use the cube to create a basic frame, using each of its edges as a placement reference for the frame members. When you create the frame you will be prompted to supply:

◆ A New Frame File Name and Location; this is the name and location of the frame subassembly.

◆ A New Skeleton File Name and Location; this is the name and location of the frame skeleton reference.

If you just accept the defaults you would end up with a folder such as \My_Frames\Cube_Frame_Assembly\Frame\. In this folder (once you saved the top level assembly) you would find an assembly file named Frame0001.iam and a part file named Skeleton0001.ipt. Special attributes in the frame subassembly contain references to the parent assembly. This enables the frame skeleton to maintain references to the other assembly components. Figure 15.2 shows the default frame subassembly and skeleton file naming.

FIGURE 15.2
Creating a
new frame

MAKE SURE YOU SAVE

When you click OK to create the Frame Generator assembly and place the first members, a folder is created in the directory. However, like all Inventor files created in the context of an assembly, the parts are not written to disk until you save the assembly. This is true when you create frame members as well, and since it so easy to create members, it may not be obvious that you need to save them after the initial creation. Pay attention to the Save reminders, and limit the amount of data you risk losing between saves.

COPY FRAMES

You can find a limited-feature Copy Design utility that will copy Frame Generator assemblies and preserve the references to the other assembly components at C:\Program Files\Autodesk\Inventor 2011\SDK.

The User Tools are a collection of API sample programs with their own installer. When you run the MSI file, it unpacks the programs in the SDK directory. You can't install the tools if you have restricted user privileges. To install User Tools, follow these steps:

1. Double-click the UserTools.msi file to unpack those tools.

2. Locate the Copy Design folder in the unpacked UserTools directory.

3. Locate CopyDesign.exe in the Copy Design\Bin directory and double-click it.

This tool requires a drawing of the top-level assembly to work. It copies the drawing and all of the files referenced by the drawing to a folder of your choice, and allows you to specify a prefix name for each file. This tool is a "bonus" tool and may not work with some areas of Inventor. However, if you have the need to copy an existing Frame Generator assembly to be a standalone assembly, this tool is useful.

Note that there are a couple of limitations to be aware of. First, you cannot create more than one frame subassembly in the same assembly. Another limitation is that you can't use copies of the frame generated with the assembly Copy tool in other assemblies and maintain Frame Generator functionality.

Exploring the Anatomy of a Frame Member

Frame Generator initially creates frame members the same length as the selected geometry. When you add end treatments, the length is adjusted to make the member longer or shorter. To accomplish this, the structural profiles are created with a From-To extrusion between two work planes, as shown in Figure 15.3.

FIGURE 15.3
A typical frame member

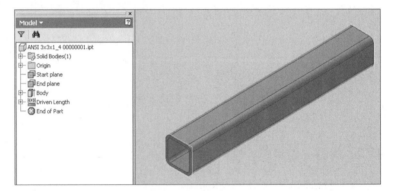

When the part is first created, the start plane is coincident with the XY plane, and the end plane is set to the initial length. When an end treatment is added, the start or end plane is moved to shorten or lengthen the member.

The parameter relationships that control the length are complex. Three parameters drive the length, two parameters are driven by those parameters to determine the length, a reference parameter reports the overall length, and a parameter is used in the BOM, as indicated in Figure 15.4.

Table 15.1 lists the length parameters.

TABLE 15.1: Frame Member Parameters

PARAMETER	DESCRIPTION
B_L	The initial length of the member.
G_OFFSET_START	The offset value of the start work plane.
G_OFFSET_END	The offset value of the end work plane.
d13	The parameter for the start work plane. It is driven by G_OFFSET_START.
d14	The parameter for the end work plane. It is driven by G_OFFSET_END.

TABLE 15.1:   Frame Member Parameters   *(CONTINUED)*

PARAMETER	DESCRIPTION
d19	A reference dimension that measures the overall length of the part.
G_L	The length parameter that is used in the BOM. It is equal to the reference dimension.

FIGURE 15.4
Frame member parameters

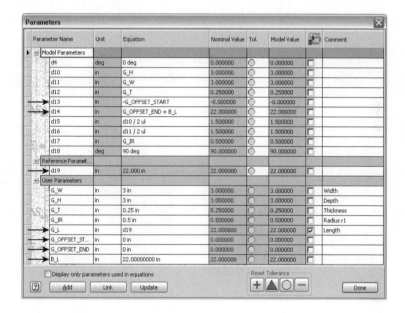

Inserting Frame Members

The process for inserting frame members can be broken down into three basic steps. You select the frame member profile (this comes from Content Center), select the placement geometry for placing the frame members, and then adjust the orientation of the frame members.

Specifying a Structural Shape

The left side of the Insert dialog box, shown in Figure 15.5, has a series of drop-down fields for specifying the structural shape.

You use the Standard, Family, and Size fields to select the member from Content Center. These fields are progressive, and the update behavior varies. If you select a new standard, the first family is automatically selected. If you select a new family, the size is not automatically selected.

FIGURE 15.5

Frame Member
Selection group

Changing the Orientation

After you have selected the placement geometry, you can change the position and orientation of the member. A thumbnail of the profile is displayed in a grid of radio buttons that control the position of the member, as shown in Figure 15.6. These positions are based on the rectangular bounds of the profile. As a result, the corner positions of a 1-inch by 1-inch square tube are the same as a 1-inch diameter pipe.

FIGURE 15.6

Orientation group

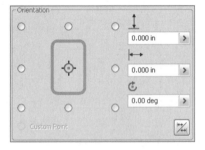

ADJUSTING ORIENTATION

You can fine-tune the placement position by entering values in the horizontal and vertical offset fields. You can also rotate the member. For example, food processing equipment frequently has horizontal members rotated 45 degrees so spilled food doesn't build up on top of square tubing.

The Mirror Frame Member button is used for profiles that don't have rotational symmetry, such as C-channel and angle iron. The orientation changes affect all the members of a select set. Depending on the geometry, it might be more efficient to use a batch select tool and change the orientation of a few members afterward, or you might want to select only those members that have a similar orientation.

Since structural shapes are extruded, Frame Generator needs a method for determining the extrude direction. When an edge is selected, Frame Generator uses the closest endpoint as the start of the extrusion. Depending on where you select an edge, the same radio button can cause the member to be in a different position. The thumbnail is the view of the profile looking at the XY plane. It takes some practice to get a good feel for the relationship between how an edge is selected and the behavior of the radio buttons. Once you understand this relationship, you will be able to predict the behavior and use it to increase your productivity.

> ### DO I NEED TO USE 3D SKETCHES WITH FRAME GENERATOR?
>
> Although you can use 3D sketches to base a frame on, you don't need to. You can create 3D solids or surfaces to create a frame base. Once you have a 3D shape you can then add 2D sketches to the various faces and use those sketches as selection edges as well. So you don't need to be well-versed in the 3D sketch tools to create 3D frames.

When using a custom profile with an alternate insertion point defined, the Custom Point control is enabled. This adds another insertion point to the nine standard ones. The custom point is not displayed in the thumbnail image, so you should confirm the preview is in the expected position relative to the selected edge. Figure 15.7 shows a profile with an alternate insertion point.

FIGURE 15.7
Profile with an alternate insertion point

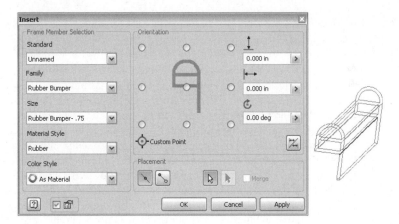

Selecting Placement Geometry

When selecting placement geometry, you can select edges of 3D models and visible sketch lines, or you can select two endpoints. For instance, if you had a cube-shaped base solid you would use the edges to place vertical and horizontal frame members. To place diagonal cross bracing, you would use the corner endpoints.

INSERT SELECTION METHODS

When you use the default *Insert Members On Edges* option, you can select edges and lines for placement references. Using edges for placement allows you to insert multiple members at once. When you use the *Insert Members Between Points* option, you select two vertices or endpoints. This method allows you to place only one member at a time. The most common placement method is by selecting lines and edges. This allows the most flexibility in geometry selection and the use of Batch Select tools.

There are two philosophies for placing frame members. Some people like to place frame members individually, making sure each one is in the correct position and orientation. Other people like to place as many members as possible and then edit them as necessary. The method you choose will depend on the type of models you work with, how much effort you put into setting up the skeleton models, and, most importantly, the way you like to work.

BATCH SELECTION TOOLS

Frame Generator has several tools for selecting geometry. *Multi Select* is the default selection mode. The standard methods for creating a multi-select selection allow you to select individual edges, use selection windows, and use the Shift and Ctrl keys to add and remove objects to or from the selection. In addition to Multi Select, two additional select modes are available in the context menu shown in Figure 15.8: Chain Select and Sketch Select.

FIGURE 15.8
Select mode
context menu

Chain Select automatically selects all lines and edges that are tangentially connected to the selection. Chain Select will not follow past a point that has multiple lines or edges, even if one of them is tangential. For instance, if you have a rectangular sketch profile with rounded corners, you can use Chain Select and select just one of the lines or arcs and all of the others will be added automatically. By contrast, if you have the same profile in a 3D shape, Chain Select will not automatically select the edges because each edge of the 3D shape has multiple edge intersections.

Sketch Select selects all the lines in a sketch. You can select the sketch in the browser or click a line in the graphics window. For instance, if you have a ladder-shaped sketch, you can use Sketch Select and automatically select the rungs and rails all at once.

The *Merge* option is enabled when there are connected lines or edges. Merge combines the selections into one member. Although Merge is useful when you want to have one continuous member, you cannot add end treatments to merged members.

Create a Basic Frame

To create an elementary frame, you'll use a prepared file that has been set up for you. This is an assembly file consisting of just two parts and the frame subassembly. One of the parts contains an unconsumed sketch that you will use to place frame members. The frame members will be automatically placed in the predefined frame subassembly. When creating your own frame designs from scratch, you'll be asked to supply the name and locations for the frame subassembly and skeleton files.

1. Click the Get Started tab, and choose Open.

2. Browse for the file named mi_15a_001.iam located in the Chapter 15 directory of the Mastering Inventor 2011 folder, and click Open.

3. From the Design tab, click the Insert Frame button.

4. Set the Standard drop-down box to use the standard of your choice.

5. Set the Family drop-down box to use a square tube or hollow section profile.

6. Set the Size drop-down box to use an 80 mm × 80 mm (or 3 inch × 3 inch) section, using a wall thickness of your choice.

7. Select the middle vertical sketch line on the back of the sign plate in the model.

8. Use the radio buttons in the Orientation area of the Insert dialog box to orient the frame member so it matches up with the square cutout.

9. Select the other four vertical sketch lines as well. Note the two on the ends are not centered.

10. Holding the Ctrl key, select the two end members to remove them from the selection.

11. Click OK to generate the frame members; then click OK in the Frame Member Naming dialog box to accept the defaults.

12. Next, click the Insert Frame button again and click the bottom half of one of the outside vertical sketch lines.

13. Use the radio buttons in the Orientation area to orient the frame member so it matches up with the square cutout.

14. Select the bottom half of the other outside vertical sketch line and notice the frame member preview does not match with the cutout.

15. Using the Orientation radio buttons, you'll notice none of the solutions allow both members to match the cutouts.

16. Holding the Ctrl key, click one of the frame members to remove it from the selection.

17. Select the sketch line again, this time towards the top, and you'll see this flips the orientation to provide the correct solution.

18. Uncheck the Prompt For File Name check box. This suppresses the file naming dialog box and automatically accepts the default naming for the frame members.

19. Click OK. Your assembly should resemble Figure 15.9.

In this simple example you explored the basics of placing frame members. You can close this file without saving changes and continue to the next section. In the next example you'll explore more selection and orientation options.

FIGURE 15.9
Frame members placed using Frame Generator

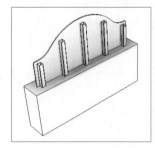

WHERE ARE THE OTHER COMMON SIZES?

You might note that there are several common sizes you use daily that are not listed in the size drop-down. This is because the sizes included are only the sizes listed in that particular standard. Of course, most mills produce other sizes commonly used in general design. You can add those sizes using the Structural Shape authoring tools.

In the following steps you will explore the offset, rotation, and merge options, as well as the right-click selection options:

1. Click the Get Started tab, and choose Open.

2. Browse for the file named mi_15a_002.iam located in the Chapter 15 directory of the Mastering Inventor 2011 folder, and click Open.

3. From the Design tab, click the Insert Frame button.

4. Set the Standard drop-down box to use the standard of your choice.

5. Set the Family drop-down box to use a flat bar section profile.

6. Set the Size drop-down box to use a 50 mm (or 2 inch) bar, using a thickness of your choice.

7. Right-click in the graphics area and set the selection method to Chain Select.

8. Click on any part of the C-shaped sketch and notice the entire sketch loop is selected without having to click each sketch segment.

9. Set the horizontal offset to **-100 mm**.

10. Set the rotation to **90** degrees.

11. Click the Merge check box to ensure the result is a continuous piece of rolled flat bar, rather than a piece for each segment of the loop.

12. Click Apply to create the frame member.

13. Right-click in the graphics area and set the selection method to Sketch Select.

14. Select any of the segments in the ladder sketch, and notice the entire sketch is selected.

15. Set the horizontal offset to **0 mm** and the rotation to **0 degree**.

16. Click Apply to create the frame members.

17. Right-click in the graphics area and set the selection method to Multi Select.

18. In the Placement area of the Insert dialog box, click the Insert Members Between Points button and then select end points of the gap in the C-shaped sketch.

19. Set the rotation to **90 degree**.

20. Click OK to create the short length of flat bar, and close the dialog box. Figure 15.10 shows the final result.

FIGURE 15.10
Flat bar frame
members

As you can see, the selection options along with the offset, rotation, and merge options allow you to create frame members using just a simple sketch and still get a varied result. You can close this file without saving changes and continue to the next section.

Aligning Frame Members

Frame Generator follows two rules to give a frame member its initial orientation. If you are creating the first member in a selection set, the member is aligned to adjacent geometry or the coordinate system. For the rest of the selection set, Frame Generator tries to align the members to the first selection. These rules work well for most rectangular machine frames. However, if part of the frame is at an angle and there isn't a good reference, Frame Generator might select an orientation that doesn't match your design intent.

The frame in Figure 15.11 has two sketch lines running down from the center point to be used for supports. The members for the base and back have already been inserted, and the two angled supports need to be inserted. When a member is inserted on angled lines, the orientation is skewed, as shown in the inset in Figure 15.11.

To resolve this, a reference line can be selected first to establish the orientation and then the angled line can be selected to add the support member and have it follow this orientation. Once the angled line is selected, the reference line can be deselected and the angled line will hold the proper orientation, as shown in Figure 15.12.

FIGURE 15.11
Skewed
orientation

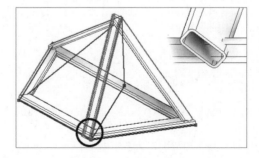

FIGURE 15.12
Using a helper
line to establish
orientation

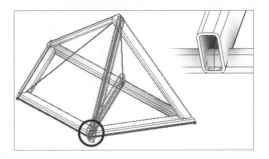

Using reference geometry for angled frame members is a bit of an art. If you regularly create these types of frames, you will develop a feeling for the ways that Frame Generator aligns members, and you will learn when and how you need to add references. To better understand the use of reference geometry for alignment, follow these steps:

1. Click the Get Started tab, and choose Open.

2. Browse for the file named mi_15a_003.iam located in the Chapter 15 directory of the Mastering Inventor 2011 folder, and click Open.

3. From the Design tab, click the Insert Frame button.

4. Set the Standard drop-down box to use the standard of your choice.

5. Set the Family drop-down box to use a rectangular tube or hollow section profile.

6. Set the Size drop-down box to use a 100 mm × 50 mm (or 4 inch × 2 inch) tube, using a thickness of your choice.

7. Ensure the placement option is set to Insert Members On Edges. Ensure the offsets and rotation fields are set to zero. Set the orientation to be centered, and then click the diagonal line that runs into the frame peak.

8. Click OK to create the member.

Notice how the frame member is coming in at a skewed orientation. To resolve this, you will first delete this member and then place another, but this time you'll use a helper edge to establish the orientation.

9. In the browser, expand Frame_MI_1503 so you can see the frame members.

10. Hover over each member until you see the one you just created highlighted in the graphics area (it should be at the bottom of the list).

11. Right-click on it and choose Delete with Frame Generator.

Using this option not only deletes the part, but also cleans up any end treatments involving other members related to the deleted one.

12. Click the Insert Frame button again. This time click the line in the horizontal base first, and then click the line for the diagonal peak support.

13. Next hold the Ctrl key and deselect the line in the horizontal base. (If both members highlight when you try deselecting just the one, check to ensure the Merge check box is not selected.)

14. Click OK to create the frame member in the correct orientation.

Keep this alignment trick in mind as you create frames, and you will likely find it to be very helpful. You can close the file without saving changes.

Using the Change Tool

You can use the Change tool to change the standard, family, size, material, color, and orientation of an existing frame member. You can use the check boxes to set the various options to allow or prevent changes. To see the Change tool in action, follow these steps:

1. Click the Get Started tab, and choose Open.

2. Browse for the file named mi_15a_004.iam located in the Chapter 15 directory of the Mastering Inventor 2011 folder, and click Open.

3. From the Design tab, click the Frame panel drop-down arrow.

4. Select the Frame Member Info button from the list.

5. Click one of the shorter uprights in the frame. The Frame Member Info dialog box displays the information about this part. Click Done to close the dialog box.

6. From the Design tab, click the Change button.

7. Click one of the shorter uprights in the frame again, and then select the other one. Notice the selection only allows one to be selected at a time.

8. Click the Multi Select check box in the Change dialog box, and then select the other short upright member.

9. Click the Change Orientation check box and then set the rotation to **45 degree**.

10. Change the Color Style to blue, and then click OK.

This simple exercise demonstrates the use of the Change tool to modify frame members. You can close this file without saving changes. Keep in mind that if you make a change that requires a new file to be generated, such as changing the size, the old part will be replaced with a new one, but the old file will remain in the folder in which it is saved.

Adding End Treatments

The end treatments are some of the most powerful Frame Generator tools. As you add end treatments, the frame member length automatically updates. The end treatments also carry over if you change the frame member to a different profile. End treatments are listed under the frame member node in the browser and can be accessed by expanding the browser node as shown in Figure 15.13.

FIGURE 15.13
End treatment in
the browser

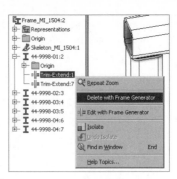

You can delete end treatments from the browser, or you can use the Remove End Treatments tool found on the Frame drop-down list of the Design tab. When you use the Remove End Treatments tool, all end treatments are stripped from the selected frame member.

If a member has end treatments on it already and you attempt to add another, you will need to select the Delete Existing End Treatment(s) check box in the dialog box, otherwise an error such as the one shown in Figure 15.14 may be created.

FIGURE 15.14
Conflicting end
treatment error

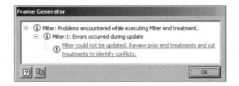

If you do encounter an error, simply undo the change and reapply the end treatment, this time using the Delete Existing End Treatment(s) option.

Miter

The Miter end treatment makes angle cuts on two members. Figure 15.15 shows the Miter dialog box. You can miter multiple members by applying the end treatment to each pair of members.

FIGURE 15.15
Miter dialog box

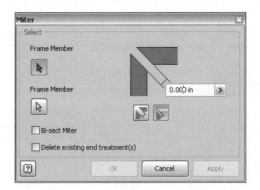

The default selections cut along an angle resulting in full-face contact between the members as shown in Figure 15.16. Bi-sect Miter splits the angle between the members. Figure 15.17 shows the cut is located where the centers of the two members intersect.

FIGURE 15.16
The standard miter joint has full-face contact.

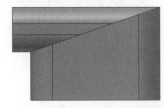

FIGURE 15.17
The optional bi-sect miter cuts both members at the same angle.

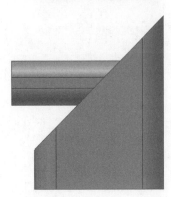

You can add a gap between the members. The default gap is split between the two members. If you want the gap to be taken from just one member, you can use the Miter Cut At One Side option, and the gap will be taken from the first member you selected. Figure 15.18 shows a one-sided gap where the vertical member was selected first.

FIGURE 15.18
Miter gap on one member

Figure 15.19 has a miter end treatment between the two angled members and a vertical member running through them. The vertical member needs to be mitered to fit. Figure 15.19 shows the left member and the vertical member being selected for the first step to create the miter.

The vertical member still needs a miter to trim the other side, so the miter is repeated with the same settings, this time choosing member on the right and the vertical member, as shown in Figure 15.20.

The resulting miter, shown in Figure 15.21, requires two cuts on each member. An alternate method that produces a more cost-effective joint can be made using the Trim/Extend to Face tool.

FIGURE 15.19
First miter cut

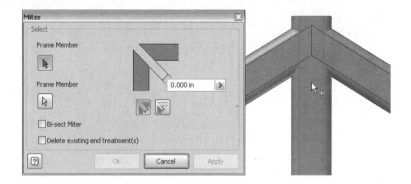

FIGURE 15.20
Second miter cut

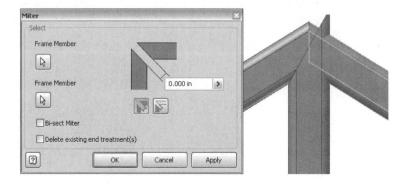

FIGURE 15.21
Resulting miter
joint between the
three members

You can open the file called `mi_15a_006.iam` to explore the Miter tool. Practice creating miter gaps and two- and three-member miters to understand the process.

Trim/Extend to Face

This end treatment is the only one that can trim multiple members at once. When trimming or extending to a face, you select the members you want to trim and then select the cutting face. A separate end treatment feature is created for each frame member. If you edit or delete the end treatment for a particular member, it does not affect the other members. Figure 15.22 shows a typical trim to face situation. You would select the vertical member for the member to trim, and the top face of the horizontal member as the face to trim to.

FIGURE 15.22
A trim to face
scenario

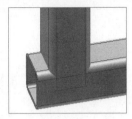

This end treatment can also be used to create miters. Applying miter end treatments to already mitered frame members results in a costly complex joint cut for all three members. Trimming the third member to fit the first two angled members using the Trim/Extend to Face tool, results in the less expensive detail shown in Figure 15.23.

FIGURE 15.23
Creating a miter
using Trim

You can open the file called mi_15a_007.iam to explore the Trim/Extend tool. Remember you can select multiple frame members to trim to the same face. Experiment with this file as you like—there is no set solution to the final frame outcome.

Trim to Frame Member

This end treatment trims or extends both members so they are flush. The first selection is made flush to the second selection, and the second selection butts up to the first. Figure 15.24 shows the selections, and Figure 15.25 shows the results.

FIGURE 15.24
Trim To Frame
selections

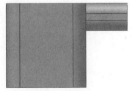

You can open the file called mi_15a_008.iam to explore the Trim to Frame tool. Experiment with this file as you like—there is no set solution to the final frame outcome. If you cannot get the result you want from the Trim to Frame tool alone, consider the Trim/Extend to Face tool as well. These tools are often used together to achieve a specific result.

FIGURE 15.25
Trim To
Frame results

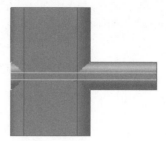

Notch Frame Members

The Notch tool cuts one frame member to match the other. It uses the profile to create a cutting surface. By default you can't create an offset, so the cut is an exact match. This is simply a cut operation, so the frame member is not shortened or extended before the cut. If you have authored a notch into a custom frame member library file, you can select the Apply Notch Profile check box, however if the member does not contain a notch profile definition, the check box is grayed out.

If you were to notch the short I-beam shown in Figure 15.26, which extends past the tall I-beam, the extra lump would remain on the right as shown in Figure 15.27. If the members don't intersect, the notch will have no effect.

FIGURE 15.26
Frame members
before notch

FIGURE 15.27
The result of
removing the
intersecting
material

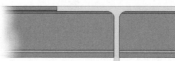

A notch is frequently a secondary end treatment. For example, if you add a Trim/Extend To Face end treatment first, the notch will remove any intersecting material. To explore the Notch tool, open the file called mi_15a_009.iam. Use the flanged beams to create notches in the T-shaped members.

CREATING ACCURATE NOTCHES

Notch shapes are driven by manufacturing requirements. Typically, the shape is simplified to reduce cost and there may be a gap between the members to allow for tolerances. The easiest way to create these shapes is to add a Trim/Extend To Face to make the member the correct length, and then add an iFeature to trim the end of the member to the correct shape. You can also define notch profiles in custom frame member definitions.

Lengthen/Shorten Frame Member

You can use the Lengthen/Shorten tool to change the length of a frame member. By default, frame members are initially assigned the length of the reference edge or the distance between selected points. However, you will often have the need to change the length. Much of the time you will simply use another frame member and one of the Extend or Trim tools. Sometimes, though, there isn't another frame member you can use as a reference, so in those cases you would use the Lengthen/Shorten tool.

When using the Lengthen/Shorten At One End option, the Extension value is applied to the end closest to the pick point, meaning that if you select a vertical frame member toward the top end and specify an extension length of 100 mm, that value will be applied to the top end. When using the Lengthen/Shorten At Both Ends option, the Extension value is applied to both ends. So if you applied a 100 mm extension value, the frame member would grow 100 mm on both ends for a total of 200 mm. If you enter a negative value the frame member will be shortened.

FRAME END TREATMENTS ARE NOT EXEMPT FROM DESIGN INTENT

You should spend time planning your frame design to minimize the number of end treatments required, because each end treatment is an opportunity for the model to fail if a change is made. For example, if you create a skeleton to the inside dimensions of a frame, you can offset members during placement so the members butt against one another without adding end treatments.

Maintaining Frames

Maintaining existing assemblies can be time-consuming. Frame Generator provides several tools that help streamline the process of modifying end treatments and determining how frames were originally designed.

Remove End Treatments

The Remove End Treatments tool removes all end treatments from a selected frame member. You can also select multiple members for the batch removal of end treatments. This is handy if you need to change the end treatments on a few members or if you have to rebuild a frame. You can find the Remove End Treatments tool in the Frame drop-down list indicated by the small black arrow found on the Frame panel of the Design tab.

Frame Member Information

The Frame Member Information tool is used to query frame members. It displays the family and size information, mass properties, and material. This is a useful tool because it quickly gives you information about a member. For example, it can help you quickly determine the difference in the wall thickness of two similar sized hollow tubes. Since the tool filters for only frame members, you can use it at any level of the assembly. You can find the Frame Member Information tool in the Frame drop-down list indicated by the small black arrow found on the Frame panel of the Design tab.

Refresh

The Refresh tool is a Content Center tool. It checks Content Center for the latest revision of the members in the frame. If a newer version is available, it will prompt you to replace it. End treatments are retained during refresh, but other features, such as holes, are not carried over to the new member. You can find the Refresh tool in the Frame drop-down list indicated by the small black arrow found on the Frame panel of the Design tab.

 Real World Scenario

MANAGING FRAME GENERATOR FILES

Frame Generator uses an algorithm to create default file names. You can rename the files as you create them, when prompted by the Frame Member Naming dialog. But often this slows the design process and requires you to enter information you may not currently know.

Another approach is to let Inventor apply the file names automatically. To do so, you can uncheck the file naming prompt check box in the Insert Frame dialog box and Inventor will create the file names and save the files to the location specified when the frame subassembly and skeleton files were initially created. It is a good idea to set the frame subassembly and skeleton filenames and locations to use a well planned naming scheme, whether you specify the frame member names or whether you let Inventor do so.

If you decide to accept the default file names, it is a good idea to use the BOM Editor to set the part number iProperty for each file to match your standard. In this way, you have a unique identifier for each part member. You can set two identical frame members to have the same part number, so they are rolled up together in the BOM. Using part numbers (you can think of them as mark numbers) to manage the frame members rather than the file names, provides a more flexible and real world work flow for the typical frame design.

Once part numbers have been defined, you can also set the assembly browser to use the part number rather than the file names. This allows you to quickly index individual frame parts more easily. Do this by going to the Assembly tab, clicking the drop-down list on the Productivity panel, and choosing the Rename Browser Nodes tool.

Although Frame Generator can create frames (and therefore a lot of part files) very quickly, once the frame is modeled you should slow down and take the time to manage part numbers. This allows your design to be managed properly in the detailing and revision stages.

Performing Calculations and Analysis

Included in the standard Frame Generator tools are two calculator tools: the Beam and Column Calculator and the Plate Calculator. These calculators are Design Accelerator tools that can do a simple stress analysis. The Beam and Column Calculator, for instance, can analyze a single beam or column, but it assumes a uniform cross section, so it does not take into account holes or end treatments.

If you have Inventor Professional or Inventor Simulation, you can use the Frame Analysis tools that are part of those packages. You can learn more about the Frame Analysis tools in Chapter 17, "Stress Analysis and Dynamic Simulation."

The Beam and Column Calculator

You can find the Beam and Column Calculator tool in the Frame drop-down list indicated by the small black arrow found on the Frame panel of the Design tab. Like other Design Accelerator dialog boxes, the message pane at the bottom and the calculation results pane on the right side can be opened and closed by clicking the small >> symbols. You can drag the splitter bar (double gray lines) to resize the panes or you can double-click the splitter bar to open or close the panes.

CALCULATING SECTION PROPERTIES

As you cover the subjects in the following pages you can refer to the conveyor assembly in the file called mi_15a_014.iam. Take a moment to open this file from the Chapter 15 directory to become familiar with it. You will use this file to complete the exercise steps covered later.

Select an Object

In this assembly, the Beam and Column Calculator might be used to calculate the loading on the power roller supports. When one of the gold tubes is selected, the calculator automatically loads the section properties from Content Center, as shown in Figure 15.28. Although Content Center has most of the section properties, be aware that some data is missing. You can use several methods for determining the properties.

FIGURE 15.28
The section properties for a selected object are loaded from Content Center.

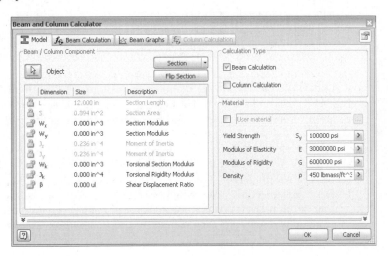

Use the Region Properties Tool

Inventor has a tool to calculate the properties of a closed sketch profile. If you want to use this tool for the section properties of a frame member, you can open the frame member, place a sketch on one end, and project the face. Once you have the profile, select the Tools tab, and click the Region Properties tool found on the drop-down list of the Measure panel. Select the profile you want to analyze and click Calculate. The basic region properties for any closed loop are calculated. You can then calculate the rest of the properties based on those results.

The region properties are calculated with respect to the sketch origin. Depending on the profile, you may have to edit the sketch coordinate system to locate the sketch origin at the center of the profile.

Use the Section Button

Another option for calculating section properties is to use the Section button in the Beam and Column Calculator. When you click the button, a list of geometric shapes displays. When you select a shape, a dialog box like Figure 15.29 displays, and allows you to enter dimensions. The calculated properties assume sharp corners and constant thickness, so the results won't be accurate for profiles with tapered flanges, but may be good enough for many applications.

FIGURE 15.29
Rectangle section properties calculation dialog box

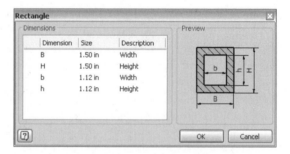

The Flip Section button is used to change the orientation of the x- and y-axes. The z-axis is always in the direction of the extrusion. Gravity is always in the negative y-axis direction, so it is important to make sure the calculation coordinates match the assembly coordinates. If the beam is at an angle, you have a couple of options for handling gravity. You can place a copy of the beam horizontally in the assembly. If you want to ignore the effect of gravity, there is an option on the Beam Calculation tab to turn the gravity load off.

Both beam and column calculations are available. The beam calculations focus on deflection based on loads and supports. The Column calculation checks for buckling. You can select Beam, Column, or both calculation types. The Calculation tabs are turned on and off based on the selections.

The default material properties do not correspond to a material style, and are not linked to the style library in any way. Instead, these materials provide you with a starting point and an example of the required properties. You can enter properties for a particular material, or you can select one of the generic materials listed. When you check the box, a dialog box displays with materials such as gray cast iron, steel, and aluminum. These properties can be used for initial calculations, but for more accurate results, you should enter the properties for the particular alloy you are using.

The following steps use the power roller supports found in the conveyor assembly `mi_15a_014.iam`. Follow these steps to enter the member data into the dialog box:

1. Click the Beam/Column button to start the calculator. Recall this button can be found in the drop-down list indicated by the small black arrow found on the Frame panel of the Design tab.

2. Select one of the lower (gold colored) supports for the power roller.

3. If necessary, click the padlock icon for the Section Length row in the table, thereby unlocking it for editing. Change the value to **12 inch**.

4. Click the Section button, and select Rectangle from the drop-down list.

5. In the Rectangle dialog box, enter the tubing dimensions. Enter **1.5 inch** for the outside dimensions (B and H) and **1.12 inch** for the inside dimensions (b and h). Then click OK.

6. Select both the beam and column calculation check boxes in the Calculation Type area.

7. Click the check box next to the Material field to launch the Material Types dialog box. Select Steel, and click OK.

8. Leave this dialog open, as you will use it in the next set of steps concerning loads and supports.

The coordinate system alignment is correct for this example. So in this case, gravity could be ignored, but having the correct orientation simplifies adding the loads and interpreting the results.

The dialog box should look like Figure 15.30. Note that all the section properties except Shear Displacement Ratio are calculated. This property is optional for the calculations. Comparing the calculated values with the original ones, Section Area and Moments Of Inertia are close but higher.

FIGURE 15.30
Model data entered into the Beam and Column Calculator

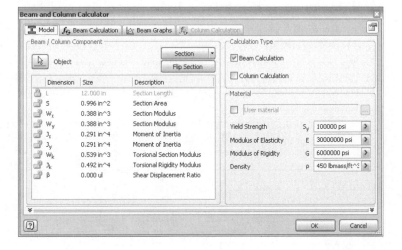

Beam Calculation Tab

The Beam Calculation tab, shown in Figure 15.31, has the controls for defining the loads and supports for beams and columns, as well as calculation options. The Engineer's Handbook (hidden
away in the Power Transmission panel drop-down list, called Handbook) contains the equations
used in the calculations. You might want to review those equations before using the calculator.

FIGURE 15.31

The Beam
Calculation tab

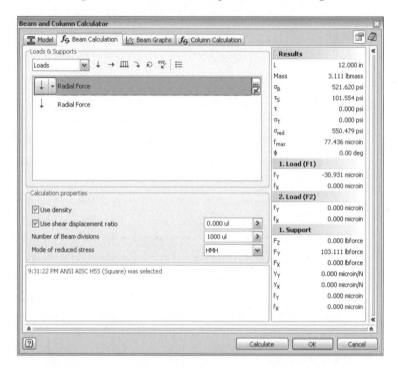

Loads & Supports

The Loads & Supports area contains controls along the top and a browser pane for adding and
removing loads and supports for the frame member. All of the controls can be accessed using
the buttons at the top or by right-clicking and choosing them from the context menu in the
browser pane area.

The drop-down menu switches the browser between Loads and Supports view. The controls, as
shown in Tables 15.2 and 15.3, change depending upon whether Loads or Supports is set current.

TABLE 15.2: Loads Buttons

BUTTON	DESCRIPTION
↓	Adds a force.
→	Adds an axial force.

TABLE 15.2   Loads Buttons *(CONTINUED)*

BUTTON	DESCRIPTION
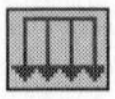	Adds a distributed force.
	Adds a bending moment—a single twisting force perpendicular to the z-axis.
	Adds a torque load—a twisting force around the z-axis. Two equal and opposite torque loads are required.
	Adds a combined load—any of the forces added at the same point on the beam.

TABLE 15.3:   Supports Buttons

BUTTON	DESCRIPTION
	Displays the Options dialog box.
	Adds a fixed support.
	Adds a free support.
	Fixes one end of the beam.

The Options dialog box, shown in Figure 15.32, gives access to visibility controls for the 2D and 3D previews. By default, the size of the loads and supports dynamically update to maintain the same size as the view scale changes. You can turn off the automatic update and set a static scale value. The Options dialog box is the same whether it is launched from the loads or supports controls.

FIGURE 15.32
Loads & Supports
Options dialog box

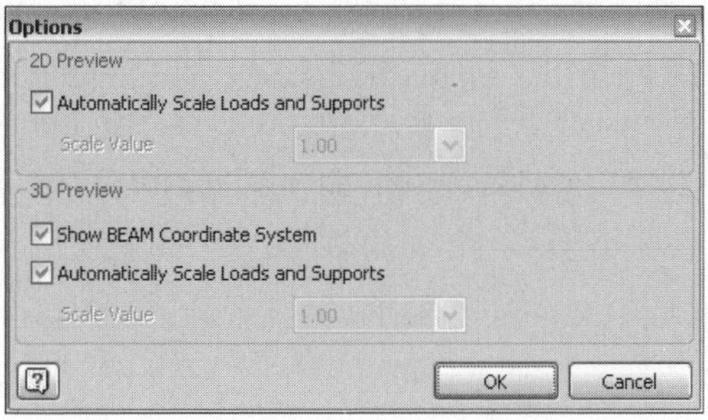

Each load or support can be edited in the browser by double-clicking or by clicking the ... button. A Properties dialog box displays controls for specifying the location, size, and direction of the force.

Calculation Properties

The Calculation Properties group, as shown in Figure 15.33, has four controls. The controls adjust how the calculations are made.

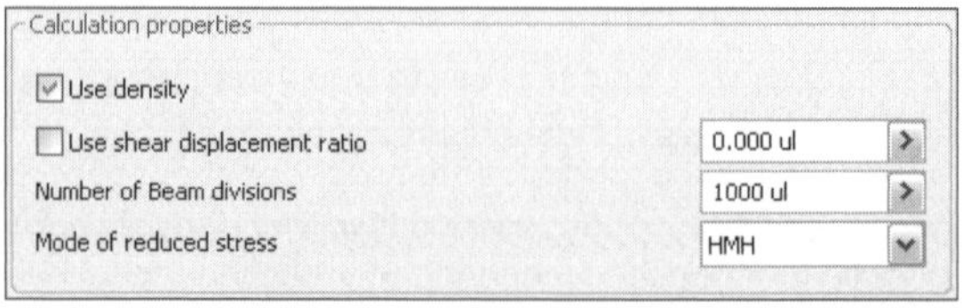

FIGURE 15.33

The Calculation Properties group

The *Use Density* check box adds gravity as a load. This is selected by default. The *Shear Displacement Ratio* check box is used when calculating the twist angle caused by torsional loads. The value is determined by the profile shape. It is also called the *form factor of shear*. This check box is selected by default.

The default setting for *Number Of Beam Divisions* is 1,000. Increasing the number of divisions can result in improved accuracy for longer beams. You should experiment with different values to see whether the number of divisions causes a significant change in the results.

Mode Of Reduced Stress has two options for modeling the stress distribution. The Huber-Mises-Hencky (HMH) method is based on the maximum-energy-distortion criterion, and the Tresca-Guest method is based on the maximum-shearing-stress criterion. The HMH method is the default selection.

Results

The result pane on the right side updates when you click the Calculate button. Warnings will display in the lower pane if the calculation indicates that stresses are too high.

For the conveyor example, the support will be welded to the frame at one end and unsupported at the other. The power roller weighs 150 pounds, and the torque is 40 pound-feet. The torque causes the power roller to twist between the supports. The edge of the flat is 1.5 inch from the center of the power roller. This means the reaction force at that point is 320 pounds. Both the weight and the reaction force are split between the two sides.

1. Ensure the first load type is set to Radial Force.

2. Click the ... button to add a force for the power roller weight.

3. Enter **10** (inches) for the distance, and **75** (pounds-force) for the force. This is the maximum distance for the power roller. Click OK to close the Radial Force dialog box.

4. Click the Add Force button to add a torque reaction force.

5. Enter **11.12** (inches) for the distance, and **160** (pounds-force) for the force, and then click OK.

6. Click the drop-down list to switch from Loads to the Supports browser.

7. Delete the Free support by selecting it and then clicking the red X button.

8. Click the drop-down arrow for the Fixed support and select Restraint.

9. Leave the Use Density option checked.

10. Deselect Use Shear Displacement Ratio since you don't have a value for that property.

11. Click Calculate; the reduced stress is 4,146 psi, which is 9.4 percent of the 44,000 psi yield strength of the specified material.

12. Leave this dialog open, and use it to explore the next topics.

The dialog box should look like Figure 15.34. Note that the forces are displayed in the graphics window. If you hover over a force arrow on the model, a tool tip displays the information. You can drag the force to a different position, or you can double-click the force to display the properties dialog box.

FIGURE 15.34
Loads & Supports data entered into the calculator

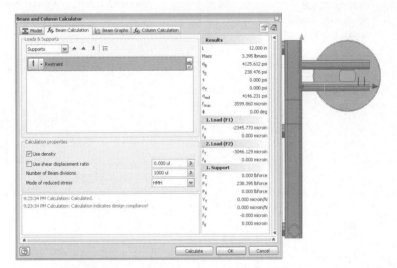

BEAM GRAPHS TAB

On the Beam Graphs tab, the Graph Selection pane allows you to select the results you want to display. The selected graph displays in the bottom of the Graph area. At the top of the Graph area is a schematic of the beam, supports, and loads. You can drag the supports and loads to different positions to update them. If you double-click a support or load, the properties dialog box displays so you can directly edit the data. The Calculate button is not available on the Beam Graphs tab, so you need to switch back to the Beam Calculation tab to update the results.

The Beam Graphs tab is primarily intended for reviewing results. Twenty-two graphs are available on the tab. This example is a pretty simple analysis. You should experiment with other loads (torques and bending moments) and support types and then view the results on the graphs.

COLUMN CALCULATOR TAB

The Column Calculator tab checks for column buckling. In the Loads area, you enter the axial load and the safety factor, and select a coefficient for the end loading conditions. When you click the … button, a dialog box displays with four end conditions. If you have different end conditions, you should enter the proper coefficient from a reference book.

You shouldn't need to enter any data in the Column area. The length, section area, and least moment of inertia are carried over from the Model tab. The reduced length value is calculated by multiplying the length by the end coefficient.

For example, imagine that during transport, the frame shifts and the power roller supports slam into the trailer wall. The power roller was removed during shipping, so the supports take all the force from the impact, estimated at 4,000 pounds evenly distributed across the four supports. Set the axial load to 1,000-pound force, and click Calculate to determine whether the supports will buckle. Figure 15.35 shows the results.

FIGURE 15.35
Column calculator
results

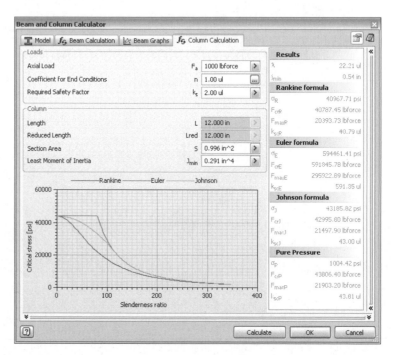

HTML RESULTS

When you click the Results button in the upper-right corner of the dialog box, an HTML page displays with all the data, calculation results, and graphs. You can save or print this file for your records.

FILE NAMING

The File Naming button, found next to the Results button in the upper-right corner of the dialog box, allows you to specify the calculations filename. When you click OK to exit the Beam and

Calculations dialog box, a subassembly file is created in the assembly file. This subassembly file is just a container for the calculations, allowing you to access them again at any point. A browser node is created for the calculations. To edit the results, simply right-click on the browser node and choose Edit Using Design Accelerator.

Publishing Frame Members

Frame Generator's frame member library is integrated with Content Center. The authoring and publishing process is similar to that used to create any custom Content Center files. Since Frame Generator requires specific modeling techniques, the authoring process will make some changes to the model and the parameters to ensure all of the required parameters are included.

Authoring a Part

The authoring process for a frame member is similar to component authoring. The Structural Shape Authoring tool, located on the Part-Modeling panel bar, is used to prepare the part for publishing. The tool identifies the geometry used for placement, sets the parameters, and modifies the part so Frame Generator can use it.

CREATING A RUBBER BUMPER

This example uses a rubber bumper iPart file, as might be attached to frames to guard against impact. In the iPart table there are parameters to control the dimensions, and three sizes defined. If this were a true frame member profile, the engineering properties (moments of inertia and so on) might need to be calculated, and therefore that information would be set up as well. Since this isn't a load-bearing part, these properties aren't required. To explore the authoring process, follow these steps:

1. Click the Get Started tab, and choose Open.

2. Browse for the file named mi_15a_020.ipt located in the Chapter 15 directory of the Mastering Inventor 2011 folder, and click Open.

3. From the Manage tab, locate the drop-down list on the Author panel, and then click the Structural Shape button.

4. When the authoring tool starts, everything is blank. Once a category is selected, the dialog box will update with the appropriate controls. Since this is an unusual part, select the Other category, as shown in Figure 15.36.

Frame Generator looks in the Structural Shapes category only, so you have to select one of the standard categories or create a new one in the Content Center editor. You can't add a category through the authoring tool, so you have to add the category to Content Center before authoring. See Chapter 7, "Part and Feature Reuse," for more information on Content Center.

Since there is only one extrusion in the part, the base feature is automatically selected. The default base point is indicated at the center of the profile. For this part, the inside corner of the flanges is the natural insertion point.

5. Click the drop-down list and choose Select Geometry, and then select that point in the model, as shown in Figure 15.37. Note you may need to use the ViewCube to look at the end view of the part to see the insert point selection.

FIGURE 15.36
Selecting the category

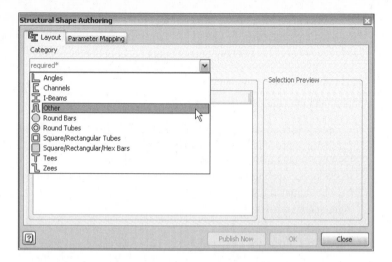

FIGURE 15.37
Selecting the default base point

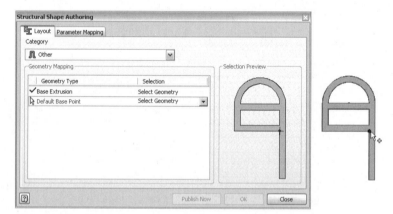

The Notch Profile option is used when authoring frame members where you want to include a predefined notch profile to be used with the Notch tool. In this case there is no notch profile.

6. Click the Parameter Mapping tab.

7. Set the Base Length row to use the Length parameter by clicking the Please Select cell in the table and then choosing Length from the list.

The Parameter Mapping tab has one required field: Base Length. This is the parameter for the extrusion distance. Since this is an iPart, when you click in the field, the iPart properties are listed as shown in Figure 15.38. If this were a regular part, the Part Template Parameters dialog box would display a browser tree, as shown in Figure 15.39. The rest of the parameters are optional. They are mechanical properties of the profile necessary for calculating loads with the Beam and Column Calculator.

FIGURE 15.38
Specifying the
length parameter
for an iPart

FIGURE 15.38
Specifying the
length parameter
for an iPart

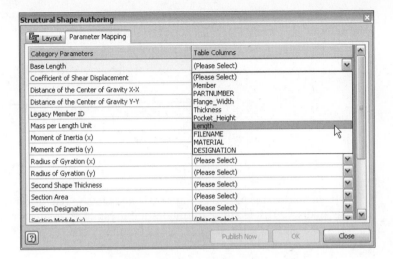

FIGURE 15.39
Specifying
parameters for
a regular part

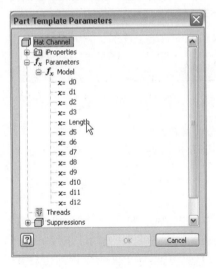

When the geometry and Base Length parameter are mapped, the Publish Now and OK buttons are enabled.

8. Click the OK button to update the part with the authoring changes.

Clicking either the Publish Now or the OK button will update the part and close the dialog box. Publish Now will also launch the Content Center publishing wizard. Once the part is updated, a dialog box displays with information about the changes. A log file, as shown in Figure 15.40, is created in the project directory that lists the changes to the part.

9. Click OK in the Structural Shape Authoring notice dialog box.

10. You can close the file without saving changes, or use this file to explore the publishing options.

FIGURE 15.40
Log file for an
authored part

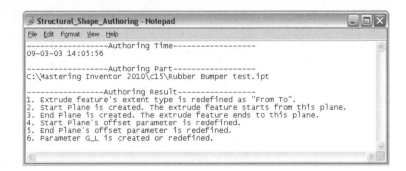

If you inspect the part after authoring, you will see that the browser and parameters have been updated. The details of the model and parameters are discussed in the section "Exploring the Anatomy of a Frame Member," earlier in this chapter.

TEST BEFORE YOU PUBLISH

Before you publish the member for use by all your team members, be sure to test it in every conceivable situation. Even a seemingly well-constructed frame member can cause issues after applying end treatments.

Publishing a Part

The publishing process uses the Publish Guide wizard. Since the part was authored, most of the publishing information has already been added to the file. If you aren't familiar with publishing to Content Center, review the end of Chapter 7.

These publishing steps are important for Frame Generator:

◆ When you define the family key columns, the Length parameter must be set as a key column.

◆ In the Family Properties pane, the standard organization is used to categorize the member during insertion. If you leave this field blank, the category selection will be Unknown.

◆ In the thumbnail image pane, a special thumbnail is displayed. Since the thumbnail is used as the orientation image in the dialog boxes, it is important to use the thumbnail Frame Generator creates.

Frame Assemblies and BOMs

By default, Frame Generator parts are set to calculate their base quantity from the length of the part. This differs from standard parts that calculate their base quantity from the number of parts in the assembly. When parts are authored for use in the Frame Generator, the Base

Quantity setting is automatically set to the length. To get a part count in the parts list for your assemblies, you will want to configure them to read the item quantity rather than the base quantity. You can use both columns if that fits your needs, or have the BOM display one quantity and the parts list display the other.

You can also use the BOM expression builder to create a description built off the Stock Number property and GL parameter (Length). You can use the CUTDETAIL parameters in expressions to show the end treatment information for each member. Note that you can copy the expression in one cell of the BOM, multi-select the rest of the column, and then right-click and choose Paste to set the expression to all of the parts in the BOM. Figure 15.41 shows the BOM editor listing the base quantity and the item quantity along with an expression being built to fill out the description.

FIGURE 15.41

BOM expression

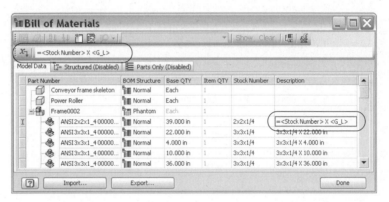

It is a good idea to let Frame Generator name the frame members for you and use the Part Number property to manage the parts, rather than the part name. Once you've set an expression as just described, you can sort the BOM by that column to group the like items, then set one of the part numbers, multi-select the items, and choose Paste from the context menu to set them all the same. If you want the items to be merged, leave the Part Number Merge Settings selected. The Part Number Merge Settings button is in the top right of the BOM editor dialog box.

In the drawing environment, use a Parts List style similar to the default Material List style found in the standard templates. This parts list is already configured to group by Stock Number and Material, as well as sum the values of each unique stock number type. Figure 15.42 shows a parts list placed using the Material List style to roll up the lengths.

FIGURE 15.42

Material List style

MATERIAL LIST		
TOTAL QTY	STOCK NUMBER	MATERIAL
548.64 cm	3x3x1/4	Steel, Mild
2194.34 cm	2x2x1/4	Steel, Mild
121.92 cm	1-1/2x1-1/2x3/16	Steel, Mild

The Bottom Line

Work with frame files   Frame Generator puts all the members at the same level in the assembly.

Master It   You have a frame that is built up in sections that are welded together. You need to document the manufacturing process.

Insert frame members onto a skeleton model   Frame Generator builds a skeleton model for the frame from the selected lines and edges.

Master It   Since Frame Generator builds its own skeleton model, you don't have to build a master model before you start creating the frame. What would you reference in your assembly to use as a frame skeleton?.

Add end treatments to frame members   Frame Generator does not support end treatments on merged members.

Master It   Let's assume you are building a stairway and the handrail has curved sections. How would you approach the curved handrail so that its ends can be treated?

Make changes to frames   Inventor provides detailed frame member information.

Master It   You need to determine the size and wall thickness of the tubing and make it either thicker or larger.

Author and publish structural profiles   Frame Generator uses structural shapes from Content Center.

Master It   You need to add custom aluminum extrusions to Content Center so Frame Generator can access them.

Create BOMs for Frame Generator assemblies   Frame Generator has special parameters for frame members.

Master It   You need to add the profile dimensions and the length to the Description field.

Chapter 16

Inventor Studio

The means to communicate your design, in order to sell your concept or product, is valuable whether your customer is internal or external to your company. Visualization, through static imagery or animation, has the potential to improve that communication by providing your customers with a conceptual or practical demonstration of your design. Inventor Studio, a rendering and animation environment, is a visualization tool built into Inventor's assembly and part environments.

With Inventor Studio, you can create and apply surface styles that enhance the realism of your components and create lighting styles that draw attention to specific aspects of your design. Inventor Studio comes with many surface styles and a modest set of lighting and scene styles to use. You can modify the delivered styles or make as many new ones as you need. The goal is to make your image as true to your concept as you want.

Inventor Studio uses assembly constraints and positional representations for animation purposes. You can animate a single part or an assembly. This chapter will discuss how to use Inventor Studio to create the images and animations that communicate your design to the targeted audience.

In this chapter, you will learn how to:

- ◆ Create and manage surface, lighting, and scene styles

- ◆ Create and animate cameras

- ◆ Start new animations, modify animations, and use the various animation tools

- ◆ Use multiple cameras to create a video production of your animation

- ◆ Use props to enhance your scene

- ◆ Render realistic and illustrative images

- ◆ Render animations and video productions

Exploring the Inventor Studio Environment

The Studio environment contains the tools required for creating realistic imagery and animations of mechanistic movement. This section will discuss the various tools, environment settings, and browser in the Studio environment.

Before entering Inventor Studio, you may want to consider what you will be using as resources (diffuse maps, bump maps, decals, and so on) for your images. Inventor comes with a collection of diffuse and bump maps, but if you have any images for textures or bump maps, you should include the directories where these files reside in your project file. Doing so ensures those resources will be available when you work in Inventor Studio. Then, plan ahead by storyboarding your animation, giving thought to camera positions and settings, lighting, and animation.

To enter the Studio environment from either a part file or an assembly file, select the Environments tab, and click the Inventor Studio icon, as shown in Figure 16.1.

FIGURE 16.1
Accessing Inventor Studio

This will set the Render tab active along the top of the graphics area, and it opens the Studio Scene browser in place of the Model browser. The Render tab is divided into four panels organized by task—Render, Scene, Animate, and Manage—each containing tools for those tasks. Figure 16.2 shows the Render tab.

FIGURE 16.2
Studio's Render tab

Studio's Scene browser is a custom browser that contains folder nodes specific to Inventor Studio. Right-clicking a folder node allows you to create one or more productions, animations, cameras, and local lights within the same file. The instances are maintained in the corresponding folder.

Creating and Managing Studio Styles

Three types of styles are used in Studio: surface, lighting, and scene styles. Each has a different purpose and contributes to the final image you produce. In the style dialog boxes, covered in the following sections, you'll see a set of four common tools and, where applicable, a set of tools for the particular style's dialog box.

Figure 16.3 shows the style categories on the Render tab and the common style tools in the each style dialog box.

FIGURE 16.3
Common style tools

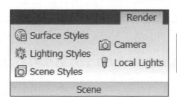

From left to right, the style tools are as follows:

◆ Clicking New Style creates a new local style based on the Inventor defaults. Local styles are available in the current document but are not available globally to all documents.

◆ Clicking Purge Style removes the selected local style from the list.

◆ Clicking Update Style updates the selected style from the style library.

◆ Clicking Save To Style Library saves the selected local style to the style library. The style becomes global, available to all components, when saved to the style library.

Keep in mind that style modifications are applied to the selected style. A style does not have to be active or in use to be modified. We'll cover surface styles first by looking at the Surface Styles dialog box. Then we'll look at the Lighting Styles and Scene Styles dialog boxes.

Exploring the Surface Styles Dialog Box

Surface styles are the means by which you create color and texture for your components. Many surface styles are combined in collections called *categories*, which are containers for styles. The Surface Styles dialog box has a variety of controls to assign color, reflection, opacity, and diffuse and bump maps, as shown in Figure 16.4.

FIGURE 16.4

Surface Styles dialog box

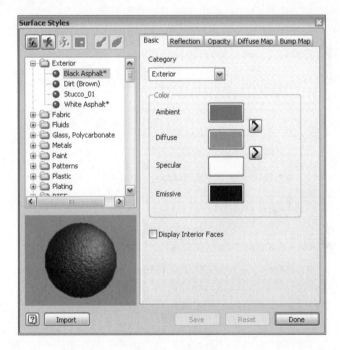

The Surface Styles dialog box consists of the following tabs and sections:

◆ The tool section at the top left of the dialog box is divided into two areas, one for creating and editing the surface style and the other for dealing with the component or face.

◆ The group of four icons along the top left provides tools for creating styles, purging styles, updating styles from the library, and saving styles to the library.

◆ The group of two icons along the top are the Get Surface Style tool, which is used to interrogate faces for their surface styles, and the Assign Surface Style tool (aka the paintbrush), which assigns the current style to a component or face.

- The surface style list on the left shows categories, their styles, and the general styles.

- The preview pane displays the selected surface style, including diffuse and bump maps.

The rest of the controls are on the other tabs.

To better show how these controls work, we will walk you through the process of taking an existing surface style, creating a new one based on it, altering its appearance, and placing it in a category.

Here are the steps:

1. Click the Surface Styles icon on the Render tab.

2. From the general list of colors, select Blue (Sky).

3. To create a new surface style from an existing style, right-click the existing style, and then select Copy Surface Style. This creates a local copy of the surface style and presents a dialog box so you can name the new style.

4. Specify a new name by typing **Blue Sky (Gloss)**.

5. Next, on the Basic tab, assign a category for the new surface style. In the Category drop-down, enter **Paint**. In this one step, you've created a new category and assigned the surface style to it.

6. Set the colors accordingly (these values are RGB):

   - Ambient: 0, 20, 129

   - Diffuse: 0, 20, 129

   - Specular: 255, 255, 128

   - Emissive: 0, 47, 0

7. On the Reflection tab, set Shininess to 61.

8. Click Save to retain this local style.

All three style types—surface, lighting, and scene—have corresponding new and copy tools.

CREATING A SURFACE STYLE

You can produce a new surface style in two ways, in the context menu:

- Clicking New Surface Style starts a new style from a default set of values. The style is named Default.

- Clicking Copy Surface Style makes a copy of the selected style and names it Copy Of [selected style]. The name is presented in a naming dialog box so you can provide the desired name. You cannot have two styles with the same name. When the displayed value is red, the value is invalid, and you must change it before continuing.

LOOKING AT THE BASIC TAB

On the Basic tab of the Surface Styles dialog box, you specify the category, the color parameters, and the display of interior faces.

Category

As you just experienced, categories either exist or are created at the same time as surface styles. To populate a new category, simply assign a surface style to that named category. In a like manner, by reassigning or deleting all surface styles in a category, you delete the category.

If you create a new surface style that is designed to give a metal appearance, for example, you can set the category for the style to Metals, and the surface style appears in and is accessed through that category folder.

Categories provide a useful means of organizing your surface styles for easy access. To add a new category, simply type the category name, and press the Enter key. The current surface style is assigned to that category, and the category is added to the list in the Surface Styles dialog box.

To remove a surface style from a category, empty it of all surface styles, and it will be removed.

Color

You can use the four color adjustment buttons to set up and control the color properties for a given surface material:

Ambient   This is the color the component reflects in areas covered by shadow. You can make interesting colors by altering this setting. You can set the ambient color to match the diffuse color, using the button between the two inputs.

Diffuse   This is the color the object reflects in direct daylight or artificial lighting. When referring to an object's color, diffuse color is what is meant.

Specular   This is the color of the reflections in the object. You can set the specular color to match the diffuse color using the button between the two inputs. Matching the specular color to the diffuse color will reduce the shininess of the object. Specular color changes can provide interesting variations. After you create a diffuse color, experiment with it, adding small amounts of another color using the Specular setting. To clearly see the difference, you should render the scene.

Emissive   This is the color given off by an object as if it contained a light source that is projecting light through the color. This color does not interact with lighting styles.

Display Interior Faces

As you define transparent surface styles, determine whether the interior faces will be seen. Consider the simple drinking glasses shown in Figure 16.5; their faces are transparent, so the interior faces are seen. To display interior faces, select the Display Interior Faces option on the Basic tab.

FIGURE 16.5
Displaying interior
faces

LOOKING AT THE REFLECTION TAB

The Reflection tab is where you define the style reflectivity or shininess. For objects that have a matte finish or low reflectivity, you'll use numbers less than 50. The lower the number, the more dispersed the lighting is across the surface. If you are creating a shiny style such as paint, chrome, and so on, then you will use a setting greater than 50.

To give you an idea of where to set the value, Studio's Chrome styles use a Shininess setting of 88.

For any surface style, you can define a reflection map. Inventor surface styles use the default map that is installed with Inventor. However, if you want the surface style to use a specific reflection map, you must specify the map for that style.

To globally change the reflection map, you can replace the delivered image with one of your choice. If you're overwriting the existing map, you must use the same name as the delivered map, `Car3.bmp`.

Inventor specifies a default reflection map and keeps that map in the Textures directory. For a standard XP install, this is `C:\Program Files\Autodesk\Inventor 2011\Textures`. If you've installed on Windows Vista, the location will differ because of the permission requirements of Windows Vista.

LOOKING AT THE OPACITY TAB

The Opacity tab has two controls, Opacity and Refraction.

Opacity

Opacity defines how impenetrable the surface style is for lighting. An easy way to think of it is as the opposite of transparent. The control reflects that notion as well; 100 percent opaque means light will not shine through an object. As you can see in Figure 16.6, the block's opacity setting is increased from one block to the next, starting on the left: 30 percent, 60 percent, and 100 percent. The amount of light that passes through the object decreases, and the shadow darkness increases as less light makes it through the object.

FIGURE 16.6
Opacity
comparison

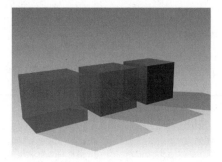

Refraction

Refraction settings manage the degree to which the light direction is changed when passing through the object. This implies surface style transparency or low opacity. There are preset refractive index values to get you close to where you want to be when using this option. In the dialog box, click the Refraction Presets button above the refraction value to display the list.

The name of common items that have that index of refraction helps you relate to the value and quickly choose one that is closest to what you need. You are able to provide your own value up to an index of 3.0.

LOOKING AT THE DIFFUSE MAP TAB

A diffuse map gives the appearance of surface texture without bumpiness. You might liken it to a bowling ball that has multiple colors in patterns around it. The surface is smooth but has an interesting surface appearance.

When specifying a diffuse map, the directory where the map resides should be included in the project file libraries or frequently used folders. If not, you will get a warning message.

You are able to scale the image from 1 percent to 1000 percent. If that amount of scaling is insufficient for your map, you will have to do some extra work in an image editor to change the pixels-per-inch/mm ratio. To increase the relative size of the image—for example, if you are working on a building or ship—lower the pixels-per-inch ratio. To map the image to a very small object, you need to increase the pixels-per-inch ratio.

Let's say you have an image that is 120 pixels per inch and you want to cover a large object with that image. Then you would do the following:

1. Make a copy of the image.

2. Edit the image by changing the pixels per inch (ppi) to 30 ppi, and create another copy at 12 ppi. The net effect is that the 30 ppi image will be four times as large on the model, as shown in Figure 16.7, and the 12 ppi image will be 10 times larger.

FIGURE 16.7
Increasing the size of a diffuse map

By using this method, you can enlarge diffuse images. At some point, though, the image will not have enough resolution and can begin to look stretched or out of focus. You may have to create or resample an image to use in such a case.

LOOKING AT THE BUMP MAP TAB

Now that you have a diffuse map, you will want to use a bump map to provide the notion of a textured surface. Inventor Studio has bump maps that match some of the diffuse maps. Figure 16.8 shows the dramatic difference a bump map makes, where the only difference is that the part on the right has a bump map.

FIGURE 16.8
Comparison without and with bump map

To use a bump map, click the Bump Map tab, and select the Use Bump Image check box. If you want the bump map pattern to match the diffuse map, you can select the Same As Texture option. However, that option may not provide optimal results because displacement is based on the color's lightness (or whiteness, to be more exact). As Figure 16.9 shows, white areas are raised. You can reverse the effect by selecting the Invert option just below the percentage of bump to apply, as shown in Figure 16.9.

FIGURE 16.9
Inverting the white areas

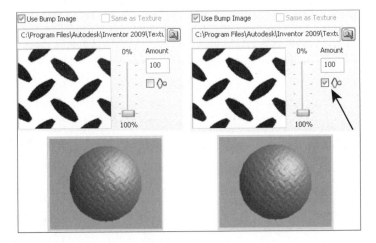

The bump map colors do not affect the diffuse map color, but using a colored bump map does affect the degree of bump you can apply. The more black and white you can define on the map, the greater your control over the overall appearance. Therefore, the amount of contrast between the bump map colors plays a part. In Figure 16.10, the middle component is what the component looks like without a bump map. The left component uses a black and white map, which yields the greatest bump contrast. The right component uses a similar but gray and white map. The bump contrast is less visible.

FIGURE 16.10
Map contrast

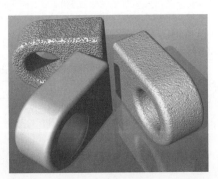

The control beneath the percentage input field inverts the bump effect. This control is very useful when you specify that the bump map is the same as the diffuse map.

Getting and Assigning Surface Styles

As mentioned earlier in the chapter, the Surface Styles dialog box contains the tools Get Surface Style and Assign Surface Style. After selecting the part or face, use Get Surface Style to find out what style is assigned. The dialog box displays the surface style for editing. Use the Assign Surface Style tool to apply the selected style to the selected face or component.

If you are working on applying surface styles to specific faces or features, you must be working in the part document. To assign a style to an assembly, sublevel or top-level, you must be working in the assembly document.

 Real World Scenario

Creating a Real-World Surface Style

Although you might find the surface styles that load with Inventor to be adequate for general rendering needs, you might also want to create new surface styles in order to match a material you use in the real world. Many of the default materials have an emissive color that is too bright and therefore renders out as too reflective. By creating new surface styles and tweaking the settings, you can gain material surface styles that mimic the real world very closely. This can often be the difference between a rendering that looks "close" and one that looks right. Follow these steps to create a brushed stainless steel style:

1. Activate the Surface Style tool. The Surface Styles dialog box appears.

2. In the Metal category, right-click Metal-Steel (Stainless, Brushed), and then select Copy Surface Style.

3. Give the style a new name by typing **Stainless Steel – Brushed**.

4. On the Reflection tab, set Shininess to 15.

5. On the Diffuse Map tab, click the Browse button, and select Metal_15.bmp.

6. On the Bump Map tab, deselect the Use Bump Image check box. Since this is a finished surface treatment, there should be very little, if any, bump visible.

7. Click Save.

8. If you have an assembly open, click a component to which you want to assign the style. Then right-click the component and choose Assign Surface Style, or click the Assign Surface Style button in the dialog box, to assign the style to the component.

Now you have a new surface style for brushed stainless steel. If you want, continue modifying settings until you get the appearance you want.

Exploring Lighting and Lighting Styles

Several lighting styles are provided with Inventor, and you can use them as is or modify them to meet your needs. You can also create new lighting styles to suit your needs. Lighting styles differ from surface and scene styles. Lighting styles have settings that affect all lights in the style, and individual lights have settings for only the selected light. However, individual lights have the option of being set to use the style settings to allow consistent control across multiple lights.

On the Render tab, next to the Surface Styles tool is the Lighting Styles tool. Click to activate it and display the Lighting Styles dialog box. The New Light button (the lightbulb along the top of the dialog box) adds a new light to the selected lighting style. The new light dialog box displays, where you specify the settings.

Next you'll explore the light styles and what they control.

LIGHTING STYLES

In this section, we'll discuss the lighting style settings. The settings affect all lights in the style. In the Lighting Styles dialog box, a list of lighting styles is presented on the left. Each style has a set of controls:

◆ Brightness   ◆ Shadows

◆ Skylight   ◆ Orientation

◆ Ambience   ◆ Scale

◆ Bounced Light   ◆ Position

Note that the active style, currently displayed in the scene and used for rendering, is listed with bold letters, and the selected style, the one whose settings are exposed for editing, has background fill, as shown in Figure 16.11. You can double-click a style in the list to edit it. The style does not have to be the active one.

FIGURE 16.11
Active and
selected styles

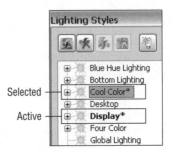

Besides the common style tools, you'll also see a New Light tool in the tools area of the Lighting Styles dialog box. This adds a new light to the lighting style you have selected in the list. The new light then is made the active edit target so you can complete the definition.

General Tab

Brightness controls the overall style brightness. This tool affects all lights in the style.

Skylight is the tool that provides uniform, directionless illumination in the scene. When enabled, you are able to specify light intensity and color, or you can use an image for lighting the scene. The image supplies colors for the lighting but should not be confused with high dynamic range image (HDRI) illumination.

Using the Skylight and Bounced Light tools is computationally intensive, and therefore they should be used sparingly, usually for final renders only.

Indirect Tab

The Ambience setting controls the amount of ambient light used in the scene. Setting the value higher increases the amount of light in the scene, so if you have a scene that is lit but is too dark and needs a minor adjustment to get more light, try increasing the Ambience setting.

The Bounced Light setting is a component of global lighting and is included when the Skylight option is selected. However, you can use Bounced Light without the Skylight option. Bounced Light provides the lighting that comes from objects as light encounters them and then reflects off the surfaces. With Bounced Light, you have the option of using preset values for the number of rays that are sampled for bounced lighting. There is also a custom setting should you decide you need a value other than those provided.

Shadows Tab

The Shadows tab provides access to the following:

Type   You can specify None, Sharp, and Soft.

Quality   You can specify Low, Medium, and High.

Density   You can specify 0 to 100 percent.

Light Parameter   Here you specify the spherical diameter for a soft shadow effect.

If the light casts no shadow, then the type should be set to None, and all other controls on the page are disabled and not used.

Sharp shadows provide a well-defined shadow, where the boundaries of an object define a sharp contrast between shadow and nonshadow areas.

Soft shadows blur the area between shadow and nonshadow areas. The Light Parameter setting, available only for soft shadows, defines the spherical diameter of influence for soft shadows.

Figure 16.12 shows a comparison of the three shadow types: None, Sharp, and Soft shadows.

FIGURE 16.12
Shadow types:
None, Sharp,
and Soft

Note that the Light Parameter setting controls the *penumbra* (dispersing shadow around the darkest part of the shadow) and that it is a diameter dimension.

Shadow density provides an additional level of control because you can set the density on a per-light basis. As Figure 16.13 shows, the shadow density increases with the value of the parameter.

FIGURE 16.13
Shadow density
at 15 percent,
45 percent, and
75 percent

It is easy to see how working with these settings you can greatly affect the results of your rendered image or animation.

As mentioned earlier, the Light Parameter setting is a spherical diameter value that controls the influence of soft shadows. If you want soft shadows around the whole scene, then the sphere must be set to be somewhat larger than the scene. If the influence is to be limited, you can use a lower setting. A good rule of thumb is to estimate the extents of your assembly and add 10–15 percent for a reasonable penumbra.

Position Tab

The Position tab gives you access to the orientation, scale, and location of the lighting style. Orientation is derived from one of the following:

Canonical origin planes   XY plane, XZ plane, YZ plane.

Scene style ground planes   Available in the drop-down list.

Any model face or work plane   Use the select button.

If you want to reverse the lighting style orientation, you can use the Flip button next to the drop-down list and invert the direction of the lighting style.

Scale affects all lights in the style. This allows you to quickly modify your lighting style to fit the model conditions. You can specify any scale factor from 1 percent to 1000 percent.

Lighting style position is expressed in model units and is based on the center of the top-level assembly. If you want to relocate the entire style, the position settings allow you to easily reposition the lighting style.

Adding a New Light

To add a new light to an existing style, use the New Light tool in the dialog box or context menu in the light style list. Then follow these steps to produce a new light:

1. Specify a face to act as the light target and normal. The face selection determines the light target location and beam direction.

2. After selecting a face, you'll see a straight line proceeding from the target or face; drag your mouse pointer along that line to define the light position.

3. In the dialog box, modify the light parameters to fit your needs.

If you adjust the settings before defining the position, return to the General tab, and select the Target or Position tool to begin specifying the light position interactively.

Creating a New Lighting Style

You can create new lighting styles in three ways:

◆ Use the New Lighting Style tool, which is also available from the list context menu. The new lighting style contains one each of the three light types with default values.

◆ Copy an existing lighting style. Then edit it to suit your needs.

◆ Import a lighting style from a file.

When you create a new lighting style, you are provided with each of the three types of discrete lights. You can change the light types, add more lights, and modify parameters to achieve the lighting effect you want.

If you copy an existing lighting style, you are able to rename it, modify the parameters, add new lights, or change the light types for the existing lights.

If you have an exported lighting style that you want to import and use, you can use the Import tool, which is the button at the bottom of the dialog box; navigate to the appropriate file, and then import it. Be advised, though, that if you import a lighting style with the same name as an existing lighting style, the imported style will overwrite the current same-named style.

DISCRETE LIGHTS

In the lighting styles dialog box you can create and edit individual discrete lights for each light style by using the New Light button. When you create a new light, the tabs in the Lighting Style dialog box reflect the settings for that light, rather than the style. Discrete lights can be one of three types: directional, point, or spotlight. Certain controls for the discrete light types differ from the style controls, but shadow parameters can be linked to the style and managed globally for the style from there.

Discrete lights, though three different types, all have only one set of parameters. Based on the light type, access to invalid parameters is blocked. This provides a distinct ease-of-use feature, switching between light types without having to delete and re-create new ones. You can experiment with different light types quickly and determine which is best for your circumstances.

Figure 16.14 demonstrates the difference between a spotlight (left) and a point light (right). The light type is the only difference. The spotlight was set up for the scene, rendered, and then changed to a point light; then no other changes were made, and it was rendered again.

FIGURE 16.14
Spotlight and point
light compared

As you can see, the difference can be dramatic. The point light sends light in every direction, whereas the spotlight can be pointed and focused on an area of interest. As you work with lights, experiment so that you learn their characteristics and are able to easily add the type of light you want to a scene.

General Tab

When you create a new light or select an existing light to edit, you'll see the options on the General tab become specific to that light. On the General tab, you're able to do the following:

- You can define the light type; you can choose Directional, Point, or Spot.

- You can set the on/off condition. This condition can be animated.

- You can redefine the position and, for the Directional and Spot types, the target.

- You can flip the light, reversing the target and position locations.

You can copy and paste lights, so once you've set one up, you can quickly duplicate it. You cannot create arrays of lights.

Illumination Tab

The Illumination tab contains controls for light color and intensity. Intensity is a percentage value from 0 to 100 percent.

Light color, as most people realize, helps inject emotion into a scene. Warm colors (yellows, oranges, reds, and so on) evoke a different response than do cool colors (blues, greens, and so on). Let's say you want light in the scene but would like to give the impression it is turned off at a certain point. However, you want enough light to see the scene clearly. How can you achieve this? Instead of actually turning the light off, you could change the color and intensity of the light from yellow at 80 percent to light blue at 30 percent, giving the impression the light is off while still illuminating the scene.

Shadows Tab

The Shadow tab duplicates the style Shadows tab. Thus, the shadows of any discrete light can be linked to the style shadows and derived from there. If you choose to have the selected light use different settings, deselect the Use Style Settings check box. Then, specify the settings for the selected light.

Directional Tab

Directional lights provide parallel beams of light from a single direction. The light source is considered as being an infinite distance away. Thus, you could use directional light to simulate sunshine. To add to that metaphor, the positional information for a directional light is defined by longitude and latitude values.

The latitude and longitude controls easily relate to seasonal positioning for lighting. You need to be familiar with where the seasonal lighting is for your geography.

Directional lights do not participate in soft shadow lighting. The control is disabled for any directional light.

Point Tab

Point lights cast light in all direction and therefore have only position parameters for locating the light. The light target is ignored and for all intents and purposes is considered as traveling with the light position. Position values are listed in absolute X, Y, Z values based on the top-level assembly origin.

The light decay controls apply to point lights and spotlights only. These controls have an impact on how real the lighting looks. There are three decay types:

None   This specifies that light energy will not decay over distance. If you want indirect light to remain constant throughout the scene, regardless of the distance between objects, use this setting.

Inverse   Light energy decays at a rate proportional to the distance traveled. Photon energy is $1/r$, where r is the distance from the light source.

Inverse Squared   Light energy decays at an inverse square rate. Photon energy is the inverse of the square of the distance from the light source, that is, $1/r^2$.

In the real world, light decays at an inverse square rate. However, for lighting to be realistic, the light values must also be real-world accurate. You'll find that it takes more lights to amply light a scene when you use Inverse Squared for decay.

The rendering cost, in time, increases as you move from no decay to Inverse and again from Inverse to Inverse Squared. For most renders, you can use None or Inverse and get good results based on how you set up your lighting style. When using light decay, you are able to specify the distance from the light source when the decay begins to occur. The greater the decay start distance, the brighter the light will appear to be. This means that if you have a lighting style you prefer but want to make it less bright in some areas, you can change specific lights to use Inverse decay and have a considerable effect on the output. Light decay is a setting that takes experimentation to get a feel for when and how to use it.

Spot Tab

Spotlights provide light in a more focused manner, at a specific location. For spotlights, there are more controls for adjusting the light parameters. You can do the following:

- You can explicitly position the light target or light source.

- You can specify the light hotspot and falloff.

- You can specify the light decay type and start distance.

As discussed thus far, you can modify lighting styles giving explicit values for input. You can also interactively modify lighting styles. For example, you can edit position, target, hotspot, and falloff interactively.

To interactively modify any of these settings, you must first edit the light you intend to change. Place your mouse pointer over the light graphic, which is the light node in the Scene browser, and right-click; then select Edit from the context menu. At this point, place your mouse pointer over the graphical representation of the element you want to edit, and do one of the following:

- Click the light source to display the 3D Move/Rotate tool for modifying the position or target.

- Click and drag the graphic representing the hotspot or falloff to change its size.

- Click the line representing the light beam; it connects the position graphic to the target graphic. The 3D Move/Rotate triad is placed over the center of the line, enabling a reposition of the entire light. Click and drag the arrow to move the light in that direction.

LOCAL LIGHTS

Local lights are discrete lights that belong to the scene but not the lighting style. They are useful for control panel lights, and so on, that you may want to animate individually. Thus, local lights come only in the Spot or Point light type. Local lights travel with components, so if you create a lightbulb component, you can specify a local light for use with the bulb object. The advantage is when you animate a component with a local light, the light travels with the component.

Local lights use the same controls as discrete style lights. In fact, you can easily create a local light by right-clicking any style-based discrete light and selecting the tool in the context menu.

Local light settings and position can be animated only when the light is at the top level of the assembly or part model.

Exploring the Scene Styles Dialog Box

Scene styles provide a backdrop for your scene. You can use a single solid color, a gradient color, an image, or a spherical image. What you use depends on how you want to compose your scene.

Scene styles provide a built-in ground plane that eliminates the need for you to add geometry in the model to provide the illusion of ground or a surface on which your assembly is sitting. However, if you have specific needs or use props that replace the ground plane, then it is not necessary to show shadows or reflection. The Scene Styles tool is located in the tool panel next to the Lighting Styles tool.

LOOKING AT THE BACKGROUND TAB

The Background tab provides access to the various controls for specifying the type of background and location of images to use. You can forego specifying any of this information by selecting the Use Application Options check box. The current Inventor background will be used. You can choose from four background types, covered next.

Solid Color

If you want a single solid color background, click the Solid Color button, and specify the color to use in the Colors section.

You could use the Solid Color option to produce an image so that the background could be removed or specified as a transparent color. However, there is a much easier method that we'll discuss when it comes time to render images; see the "Composing and Rendering Images" section for more information.

Color Gradient

Color Gradient is a popular choice because it has the potential to look more like a presentation. Both color controls become enabled, and you specify the top and bottom gradient colors, respectively. With the environment controls, you can further tune the background, using shadows and reflection, to make the scene style complement your model.

Experiment with different solutions. You'll find some really nice sets of colors that work well together. For example, the use of dark blue (top) and black (bottom) with reflections on and set to 80 percent looks very elegant with the proper lighting.

Image

The Image setting enables the image controls at the bottom section of the dialog box. When you activate this choice, the Open dialog box is automatically displayed so you can select the desired image. The default location for the image choices is the Textures directory that is created and populated during the Inventor installation. If you plan to use images other than those supplied, you should do one of two things:

◆ Edit the project file to include the directory where the images are located as a library. (This is recommended.)

◆ Place any image you will use in the installed Textures directory.

Figure 16.15 demonstrates the use of the `forest 2.bmp` background. The proper placement of the assembly relative to the background enhances the end product. Be sure to take the time to analyze your background to see what may need to be adjusted to optimize your output. In this instance, we arranged a lower camera angle and turned on shadows in the scene style. The lighting style was set to produce soft shadows.

FIGURE 16.15
Scene style with
image background

When the image section is enabled, you have three choices of how to use the image in the scene. You can center, tile, or stretch the image. If you choose to tile the image, the Repeat controls are enabled for your use. A little later in the "Matching Your Camera to an Image" section we'll discuss how to match the model view to your image.

Image Sphere

If you use the Image Sphere option, the selected image is mapped to an environment sphere. The image is stretched to map to the sphere.

LOOKING AT THE ENVIRONMENT TAB

The Environment tab manages the ground plane orientation, shadows, reflection, and environment mapping.

Direction & Offset

The scene style ground plane orientation is based on one of the three canonical assembly work planes. Select the orientation you desire, and specify an offset, if any is required, to position the plane at the proper height for your model. Negative values position the ground plane below the assembly plane to which it is parallel.

Show Shadows

The option to show shadows is useful when the scene style is acting like a ground plane for the assembly, in other words, not using any prop models or other model to serve as a floor. The Show Shadows setting specifies whether shadows are cast on the scene style ground plane.

Show Reflections

If your scene style is serving the purpose of a model ground plane and you want to reflect the model in the ground plane, select the Show Reflections option, and adjust the percentage of reflection you want in the rendered image. The higher the numbers, the more reflection you see in the ground plane. If set to 100 percent, it will reflect the assembly as if it were sitting on a mirror.

Reflection Image

The Use Reflection Image setting is there for you to specify an environment image map. This is the image you will see reflected in those parts having reflectance in their surface style when rendered. Depending on the image, it can have minor to major influence on the rendered outcome. Here again, experimentation is the best teacher.

Collect or produce a set of widely different images, and make new scene styles using the images for reflection mapping. Render the same model with the different styles to see what sort of influence the image produces.

MATCHING YOUR CAMERA TO AN IMAGE

If you want to match your model up to a photograph, use the Image Background type for the scene style. Analyze the photo you will use for the background. Determine where the light is coming from and how much shadow is being cast. Then, set your view to use a perspective camera. Orient the model so that its horizon and vanishing point are similar to the image. Next, create or modify a lighting style so that it produces light and shadows similar to those in the photo. Do a few test renders, and refine the camera position and lights until you're able to get something that looks like what you want.

Here's an example of the workflow you can use:

1. On the Get Started tab, click the Open button.

2. Browse for the file named `mi_16a_001.ipt` located in the Chapter 16 directory of the Mastering Inventor 2011 folder, and click Open.

3. Select an image, and make a scene style using the Image background type. You can use the mountain background image named `mi_16a_001.tif` in the Chapter 16 directory.

4. Orient the model, as shown in Figure 16.16, to look like it fits into the scene.

5. Use the Outdoor lighting style, and scale it to fit the scene. To make sure the shadows are close, modify the style orientation to match the shadow angles on the mountains. Do a test render, make a couple of tweaks to the style position, and then render the image, as shown in Figure 16.17.

FIGURE 16.16
Model orientation

FIGURE 16.17
Platform with
background

In the next example, Figure 16.18, we used an existing Inventor background, centered in the scene. We used a previous release Inventor sample model—an engine assembly. This time, we wanted to produce an image more for marketing purposes. So, to help make the product (the sample assembly) emerge from the image, we oriented the assembly and made it large enough to extend beyond the background image, giving the illusion of it protruding from the image. We then rendered the image.

FIGURE 16.18
Scene style
example

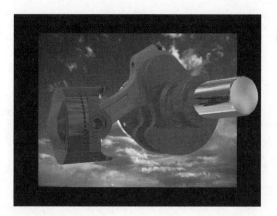

Composing and Rendering Images

Although it is good to know how to use the tools to produce styles, it is also important to know the purpose of the image you are composing and rendering. What is its use? Who is the target audience? The type of image you compose and render will be different based on the answers to those questions. For example, if you are producing imagery for an assembly or repair manual, as used by technicians, you may elect to use an illustration style of output as opposed to a realistic style. The noncritical content may be simplified to a degree. However, if you are presenting a product to a group of investors or potential customers, you may want to compose an image showing the product in its anticipated environment. The use of props can add context to your image or animation and possibly add more realism.

Since you are using an engineering assembly to create an image, it is likely you do not want to alter the engineering models for the sake of the image—not adding prop content to an engineering model. So, the recommended step is to place the product model into a *wrapper* assembly. Wrapper assemblies are simply a level higher assembly that include the engineering assembly and can contain nonengineering content that serves as props for composing the final rendered images or animations. Let's say you are producing a product that is used in a machine shop. You place the product's final assembly in a wrapper assembly and add shop content, such as walls, tables, tools, and so on, to set the stage for the rendered image or animation, as shown in Figure 16.19.

FIGURE 16.19
Wrapper assembly
with props

As you can see, there is nonessential content in the scene, but when combined, those items contribute to communicating a purpose for the items in the image. Even the surface style on the tabletop evokes a sense of a well-used workbench. It is small touches such as these that enhance your images.

CREATING AND USING CAMERAS

Although you might conclude that cameras would be best used for animations, they are also very useful for working with images. Cameras make it easy to recall view orientation, and they can be animated. There are two methods for creating cameras: the Camera tool and the view context menu.

Camera Tool

To use the Camera tool, located on the Render tab, do the following:

1. Click the Camera tool.

2. Select the target, a component face. The camera direction line is presented normal to the face preview and selection. Click to select the target. The tool then cycles to the camera position input.

3. Specify the camera position by moving the mouse pointer over the camera direction line and moving it along the line. When the preview is satisfactory, click to select the camera position.

4. If you select the Link Camera To View check box, the camera graphics are hidden, and the view is changed to what the camera sees. When the check box is deselected, the camera graphics are restored. This gives you an easy way to check your settings.

5. Set the Camera Zoom value to fit your requirements.

6. Depth Of Field provides two methods of setting the range of focus: Focus Limits and f-Stop.

The Focus Limits setting provides you with near and far values, in model units. Content between the near and far values will be in focus. Content outside those values will be proportionally out of focus. f-Stop, the other method, uses an f-Stop value and a Focus Plane setting.

To make setting up the camera a little easier, you can link the focus plane to the camera target. Then, whenever the target is moved, the depth of field adjusts to fit with the camera. That makes less work when it comes to updates.

7. Click OK, and the camera is created. You can rename the camera with the browser node slow-click method.

Current View

The graphic region context menu method is useful for rapidly creating a camera using the current view. To access the other camera settings, you must edit the camera after creating it. To use the graphic region context menu method, simply orient the view so it displays what you want the camera to show, right-click, and click Create Camera From View. A camera is added for this position. You can edit the other camera parameters via the Camera dialog box.

It is not unusual to have 8 to 10 cameras defined when you consider the various vantage points from which you might look at a product.

RENDERING IMAGES

Now that the stage is set, the lighting selected, and the model positioned, you're probably anxious to render something to see how it's coming. You can always render using the current view. So, whatever position you set the view to, you can render and get results. It is not required that you have a camera defined in order to render. However, repeatedly getting back to that same camera location, settings, and so on, really requires that you define a camera. So, before discussing rendering, we'll talk briefly about setting up a camera.

The easiest method, by far, is to orient your model, choose orthographic or perspective viewing, and then in the graphic region right-click and select Create Camera From View. That's it! You have defined a camera. Now, you can easily recall that camera if you change the view orientation. As with any Inventor browser, you can click the node twice and rename it. We recommend naming your cameras for ease in selecting, recalling, or animating them.

The Render Image tool presents the Render Image dialog box with three tabs: General, Output, and Style. The following sections will briefly discuss the controls and use of the Render Image tool.

General Tab

The General tab contains controls for sizing the image and for specifying the camera, lighting style, scene style, and render type to use in producing the image. Active styles prepopulate the style choice fields.

The size controls, Width and Height, provide you with explicit image size control. Directly to the right is a drop-down list of predefined image sizes that are typical in the industry. Beneath the drop-down list is a check box for locking the image aspect ratio. If you determine that a specific image size is consistently used, you can enter the values, lock the aspect ratio, and then create images at that ratio or at any size within the permitted limits. This makes scaling an image, post-rendering, easy.

As mentioned earlier, the camera choices include those you have defined and Current View. If you are doing test renders at a low resolution by moving the camera around to see where the best shot will be taken from, use Current View. It's simple and straightforward. Once you determine the camera locations, you can then define and refine those positions and camera settings.

The Lighting Style drop-down list shows all the available lighting styles, local (document) styles, and global styles (the style library), including those you have made and maintained locally or in the style library. If you have activated a lighting style, it is preselected. Specify the desired lighting style.

As with the lighting style, the same is true of the scene style. Make your selection based on available local and global styles.

As you were composing the scene, likely you determined whether the end result would be rendered as a realistic or illustration image. Here is where you set that choice. The choice dictates what controls are available on the Style tab.

Output Tab

The Output tab contains controls for where the image is saved and whether to use antialiasing and to what extent to use it.

If you want to save the image, select the Save Rendered Image box. When you do so, the Save dialog box displays. You specify the location and name for the image. If you don't specify this in advance, you are still able to save the image from the render window.

The antialiasing tools include the following choices, from left to right:

None   Antialiasing is not used. This selection requires the least render time and provides the coarsest results.

Low   This specifies a low antialias setting. This eliminates the major coarseness seen in the None selection but still displays a degree of coarseness.

High   This specifies a high antialias setting. This setting virtually eliminates all signs of coarseness in the image. For final renders, in scenes without soft shadows, this selection performs very well.

Highest   This specifies the highest antialiasing setting. This setting is provided particularly for use with refining the image's soft shadows.

With each selection there is an increase in quality accompanied by an increase in render time. Thus, when you select the Highest setting, recommended for soft shadow use only, the quality is increased, as is rendering time. It is up to you to determine what meets your need.

Style Tab

When using the Realistic style, there is only one control on the Style tab, True Reflections. When selected, this option ensures that the objects in the scene are seen in reflective surfaces. If not selected, the image map specified in the surface style or scene style is used.

When using the Illustration style, several settings yield a variety of results. We'll cover some of these next.

To render a line art illustration like you might see in a technical or assembly manual, do the following:

1. Set the graphics display to use the Presentation color scheme with the background set to 1 Color. Color scheme selection can be set by going to the Tools tab, clicking Applications Options, and going to the Colors tab in the dialog box that opens.

2. In Studio, set up the model conditions to fit your requirements. If you want to show something in the state of moving, then use an animation, and select a time position that illustrates the condition.

3. Activate the Render Image tool, and specify the Render Type setting as Illustration.

4. On the Style tab, set Color Fill Source to No Color, as shown in Figure 16.20. Since there is no color, you likely want the exterior and interior edges to show. Select both options in the Edges section.

FIGURE 16.20
Illustration render type settings

5. Render the scene. The results will be something like Figure 16.21.

FIGURE 16.21
Render Type set to Illustration with no color

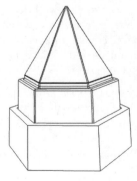

Take some time to experiment with these settings, and you will be able to come up with some very interesting imagery. For example, make the following changes to the Illustration rendering type settings:

1. On the Style tab, set Color Fill Source to Surface Style.

2. Set Levels to 5 (midway across the slider).

3. Select the Show Shiny Highlights option.

4. On the General tab, set the lighting style to Table Top.

5. Render the scene. The results will look something like Figure 16.22.

FIGURE 16.22
Render Type set to Illustration with the Surface Style option

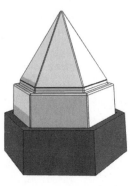

As you can see, with just a few changes, you can get dramatic differences. Using the same settings, render the scene with a different scene style. The results really start to get interesting.

Animating with Studio

Inventor Studio was designed to use assembly constraints to produce the mechanistic movement within your assemblies. You should consider the following basic concepts when it comes to animating with Inventor Studio:

◆ When you enter the Inventor Studio environment, the model is considered to be in model state, that is, whatever the condition the model was in when you left the part or assembly environment. This means when you exit Inventor Studio, modify the assembly, and then reenter Inventor Studio, the assembly changes are reflected in the model state. That includes view representations, positional representations, component visibility, position, color, and so on. For animations, the model state represents frame 0. Therefore, all modifications affecting the model state also affect all animations in that document because frame 0 has changed.

◆ Modifications made in frame 0 of the animation become the starting point for that animation. For example, component 1 in animation 1 is flush with component 2. In animation 2, the flush constraint for component 1 is offset by 1.5 inches. By changing the constraint in frame 0 for animation 2, you don't cause a change in animation 1. Had you changed the flush offset in the assembly or Studio model state, animation 1 would also be affected.

◆ Because Inventor Studio animates constraints, the free-form movement of a component, part, or assembly may require suppressing constraints that limit movement or the component's degrees of freedom.

◆ Animation actions are a result of modifying constraints; thus, any component that is constrained to a moving object will also move.

◆ The Animation Favorites folder contains all the constraints that have been animated in the active animation. It also contains any parameters you have nominated to appear there. This makes it easier to locate any parameters intended for animation and those constraints that have been animated.

◆ Animation dialog boxes have a common workflow through the dialog box—specify the animation parameters, and specify the time parameters. Based on the animation action target (component, light, camera), the dialog box presents controls relative to the target.

◆ Editing an animation action uses the same dialog box and therefore has virtually the same workflow.

Using Animation Tools

All animation tools are applicable to assemblies. However, in part models only cameras, lights, and parameters can be animated. The Render tab is divided into panels. Animation tools are grouped on the Animation panel.

Using Animation Timeline

You can find the Animation Timeline tool on the Animation panel of the Render tab. The animation timeline is where animation actions for any object are maintained and managed. Any time you use an animate tool, it results in an animation action that is placed in the timeline. Animation actions can be interactively changed using the start or end handle, as well as action's location along the timeline by using the middle section of the action graphic or by editing the animation action.

To edit an animation action, use the action's context menu, or double-click the action graphic in the timeline.

The playback tools are along the top left of the window. These are similar to other timeline or video playback controls you have used. Figure 16.23 shows these and the other timeline controls.

FIGURE 16.23
Animation
timeline

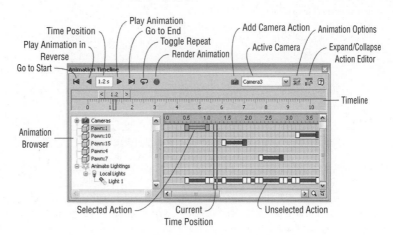

The tools provided are as follows:

Go To Start Moves the timeline slider to frame 0 and updates the graphics region to show frame 0.

Play Animation In Reverse Is just as the name implies. You move slider to a point in time, you click the tool, and the animation plays in reverse.

Current Time Mark Specifies the current time position. You may type into the field to explicitly change to another time position. The graphics region updates content to show what the animation looks like at that time.

Play Animation Does what the name implies; plays the animation forward from its current position.

Go To End Puts the time slider at the end of the animation. The graphics region updates content to show what the animation looks like at that time.

Toggle Repeat Turns on the repeat tool. When you play the animation, it will automatically repeat until you click Stop.

Record Animation Activates the Render Animation tool and displays the dialog box.

You can edit selected actions with the dialog box by double-clicking the action in the track section, where the action bars appear, or by right-clicking the context menu and selecting Edit.

You can edit action duration without going to the dialog box; just hover the mouse pointer over the start or end handle, and then click and drag the handle to change the position. Hovering over the center of the action and then clicking and dragging moves the entire action in the timeline.

USING ANIMATION FAVORITES

Animation Favorites is a list that contains any animated constraint or parameter that you have nominated for animation. The purpose is to make it easy to find those animation targets when you need to see or use them.

To populate the folder with a parameter, the parameter must be nominated by you. To do this, activate the Parameters Favorites tool. The Parameters Favorites dialog box, shown in Figure 16.24, displays, and you select the box in the row of any parameters that you plan to animate.

FIGURE 16.24
Parameters Favorites dialog box

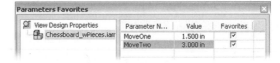

This causes the parameter to populate the Favorites list. From there you can use the Animate Parameters tool however you'd like.

POPULATING THE PARAMETER FAVORITES LIST

For parameters to show up in the list, you might need to set them to be exported in the general model parameter settings. To do this, exit the Studio environment, and click the Parameters button on the Assemble tab. Then select the check box for the Export Parameter column for each parameter to be exported. When you return to the Studio environment, the exported parameters will be listed in the Parameter Favorites list.

USING COMMON ANIMATION CONTROLS

In each animation tool dialog box is a section entitled Time.

The Time section contains all the controls to manage an animation action's time allocation. You specify whether the action starts from the end of a previous action, is a specified time range, or is instantaneous.

Based on the time method, you are able to specify a start time and duration, duration and end time, start time and end time, or simply an end (instantaneous only). The default method is From Previous, which starts the action at frame 0 if there is no previous action defined; otherwise, the new action begins at the end of the previous action.

The other common tools are those on the Acceleration tab.

The Velocity Profile setting defines how rapidly an action starts, proceeds, and ends. You can specify an action to occur at a constant speed. The default option specifies that the action starts with zero velocity and then takes 20 percent of the action duration to achieve complete acceleration. The next 60 percent of the duration is at full acceleration. The last 20 percent of the duration decelerates until it reaches zero at the end of the action. The longer the action, the more observable this becomes.

Think in terms of an electric motor; when it powers up, acceleration is not immediate but occurs over a period of time, however long or short. When the power is turned off, the armature decelerates and eventually comes to a halt. This is essentially what occurs with the animation action based on the Velocity Profile setting.

The values presented in the dialog boxes are in the document's units.

You can access the appropriate animation tool from the context menu of the item that is to be animated. For example, you can right-click a constraint and select Animate Constraints to animate the selected constraint. The same is true of the other animation tools and their corresponding browser nodes.

As we discuss the individual animation tools, we won't include the common sections.

USING ANIMATE COMPONENT

You can find the Animate Component tool on the Render tab. Animate Component is used for the unconstrained animation of parts or assemblies. Think of it as animating a component's degree of freedom. Note that if a component does not move when you create an animation action for it using Animate Component, it likely has a conflicting constraint.

The Animate Component controls are as follows:

Select Components This is active (default) when initiated; select the component, part, or assembly that will be animated.

Position This displays the 3D Move/Rotate triad to allow you to implicitly move or rotate the component as desired. Selecting the arrowhead indicates a move vector. Selecting an axis, between the arrowhead and intersection, indicates a rotation axis.

Distance This is where you enter the distance value. Specify this value after selecting the vector on the Position triad.

Rotation This is explicit input in degrees for a rotation action. Select the axis to be used for rotation.

Revolution   This is explicit input for the number of revolutions the animated component will make. This is an alternate way to input rotation.

Path   This has two options, Sharp and Smooth. Sharp uses no smoothing between the start, duration, and end values. Smooth uses a continuous motion curve between the start, duration, and end values.

USING ANIMATE FADE

You can find the Animate Fade tool on the Render tab. The Animate Fade setting changes the opacity of a component over time. The parameters allow for this to happen over any defined period of time or instantly if you desire. You can animate to any level of opacity, from 100 to 0 percent.

This tool is useful for fading components to reveal interior components while still giving a sense of the overall envelope, as shown in Figure 16.25.

FIGURE 16.25
Faded exterior

Animate Fade is not associated with a component's visibility state; rather, it is a separate control for animating component opacity. This means you must create an instantaneous action in frame 0 for the component to start out with less than 100 percent opacity.

For example, if you were to start an animation of a transmission with the housing at 10 percent opaque, you must create the action at frame 0 for the opaque value. Then, during the animation, you could create a different action to increase the Opacity value in order to make the housing 100 percent opaque.

The Animate Fade controls are as follows:

Select Components   Active (default) to allow selection of the objects to fade

Start   The component's percent Opacity value at the start of the action

End   The component's percent Opacity value at the end of the action

USING ANIMATE CONSTRAINTS

You can find the Animate Constraints tool on the Render tab. Assemblies are built using constraints that remove degrees of freedom and cause components to remain in place with relation to one another. They also work as engines to cause mechanistic movement. Thus, constraints make it easy to animate objects.

The Animate Constraints tool is used to modify a constraint over time. The component's orientation changes as constraints are modified.

The constraint's current value is the starting value, and the value you give the end parameter determines the degree to which the object, and those constrained to it, responds.

When animating with constraints, there will be times when something does or does not respond. This is most often caused by other constraints causing a conflict with the animated constraint. One way to overcome this condition is to suppress the conflicting constraint if that doesn't cause a radical change in the animation or its purpose.

USING ANIMATE PARAMETERS

You can find the Animate Parameters tool on the Render tab. If you have used parameters in your assembly and want to animate the parameters, this is the tool you will use. The parameter must first be added to the Animation Favorites folder, as discussed earlier.

You can also use Animate Parameters with part parameters. As a result, you can morph the physical shape of a part given the right set of parameters and animation actions. For example, let's say you are designing a vascular stent. As part of the product presentation, you want to show the degree to which the stent can expand and perform its function. How would you do this?

1. Create a stent diameter parameter in the part model.

2. In Studio, use the Parameter Favorites tool to nominate the parameter for animation use.

3. Set the timeline to two seconds.

4. Use Animate Parameters and change the stent diameter, thereby demonstrating the expansion the product undergoes.

If you've created user parameters on a part or assembly, you can access the parameters and animate them with these basic steps.

USING ANIMATE POSITIONAL REPRESENTATIONS

You can find the Animate Positional Representations tool on the Render tab. Positional representations (aka PosReps) use constraints to locate components while respecting the other constraints. You could conclude they work almost like keyframes for a Studio animation. And, in fact, Inventor Studio treats them almost like that. Studio allows you to animate between positional representations.

All that is required is specifying the two PosReps and time over which the transition is made. Studio does the rest. To animate a positional representation that is "deep," meaning it is deeper within the assembly hierarchy, you will need to set the subassemblies, between the top level and the component owning the positional representation, to Flexible. You do this using the component's context menu. The top-level PosRep must cause the "deep" PosRep to be activated.

You can also activate a "deep" PosRep by creating PosReps in each of the subsequent subassemblies. Each higher-level assembly has a PosRep that calls the child subassemblies' PosRep. This is repeated for each subsequent subassembly.

Editing a PosRep animation action is like any other action, but there is a bonus. If you select the PosRep and expand the node in the Animation browser, you will see the participating members of the PosRep. Each of the members has an action bar, and you can edit the duration and position of the members interactively. The values must stay within the bounds of the defined PosRep. Initially, all members occupy the full span of the action, but you can change that by editing the PosRep. When you edit the PosRep, the members enable so you can adjust them. For an example of what this looks like, see Figure 16.26.

FIGURE 16.26

Editing a positional representation

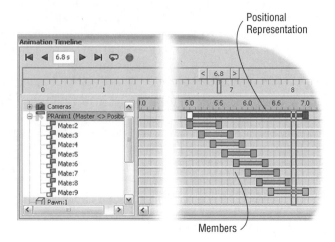

USING ANIMATE CAMERA

You can find the Animate Camera tool on the Render tab. When animating a camera, the current camera parameters are used as the "from" parameters of the animation action. Using the Animate Camera controls, you define the "to" parameters for the animation action. With these controls, you can do the following:

◆ You can change the Camera Definition interactively or through a dialog box.

◆ You can use the view tools to position the camera and snapshot it as a keyframe using the Add Camera Action tool in the Animation Timeline window.

◆ You can use the turntable functionality.

◆ You can define a path and have the camera and/or target follow the path.

In the Animate Camera dialog box, you select the camera to animate from the drop-down list. Then, using one of two methods, you define the end position of the camera for that animation action.

The first method is to use the Definition tool. To access the dialog box, just click the Definition button in the Camera section. The steps are the similar to when you define a camera using the dialog box, such as setting the target and position selection, as well as additional animation options.

When you click the Definition button, the Camera dialog box displays, and you are able to specify the following:

◆ Target Placement sets the line of sight the camera uses.

  ◆ Fixed: The target does not change positions.

  ◆ Floating: The target maintains positional relationship to camera.

  ◆ Path: The target follows a path made of 2D or 3D sketch geometry.

- Camera Position sets the camera position relative to the target.
    - Fixed: The camera does not change positions.
    - Floating: The camera maintains positional relationship to target.
    - Path: The camera follows a path made of 2D or 3D sketch geometry.
- Roll Angle defines rotation around the camera to the target axis, displayed as a line between the camera components.
- Zoom defines a horizontal field of view.

The second method for defining camera animation is to use the current view. The steps to do this are as follows:

1. In the Timeline Active Camera list, select the camera you want to animate.

2. Position the timeline slider at the time position representing the end of the action you are defining.

3. In the Scene browser, right-click the camera you specified in the list, and click Animate Camera in the context menu. Alternatively, you can select the camera in the graphics region.

4. Use the view tools to orient the graphics region to the view you want to see at that time position.

5. Click the Add Camera Action (camera button) next to the Timeline Active Camera list. You will see the view briefly revert to the last known position and then update to the current position.

Repeat steps 2, 4, and 5 as much as is needed for as many cameras as you want.

If you simply want a camera to travel around your part or assembly in a circle, the turntable function makes this very easy.

To use the Turntable functionality, do the following:

1. Right-click the camera you want to use as a turntable camera, and click Animate Camera. Alternatively, use the view tools to set the camera to its initial position, right-click, and click Create Camera From View.

2. In the Animate Camera dialog box, select the Turntable tab.

3. Select the Turntable check box to enable the turntable controls. A graphic preview of the current axis is displayed in the graphics region. In the Axis list, select from any of the canonical axes or the current camera horizontal (Camera-H) or vertical (Camera-V) handles.

4. Specify the direction of rotation around the selected axis.

5. Specify the number of revolutions.

6. Qualify the number of revolutions by selecting the literal (+/−), per minute, or per second option. For partial turntable effects, use a value less than 1.

7. In the Time section, select whether to loop the camera, or use a time period to define the length of the action.

As mentioned earlier, when you select the camera definition method, you have the option to specify that the target or camera follows a path.

If you are planning on animating a camera along a path, you must define the path geometry in advance. You do this in a separate part file using 2D or 3D sketch objects. The part file is added to the assembly and positioned where you want it before ever entering Studio. You can, of course, add the path file later and then animate the camera, associating it to the path.

Note that in order for the path part file to be hidden from the bill of materials, the part should be designated as a reference part.

When you select the Path option, move your mouse pointer into the graphic region, and select the path you want to use. The tool searches for sketch geometry, so there are no conflicting inputs when you are in the graphics region.

After you select the path geometry, two handle glyphs appear on the path (Figure 16.27): a green triangle at the beginning of the path and a red square at the end of the path. The glyphs perform two functions:

◆ They tell you the direction the camera is traveling along the path.

◆ Also, the glyph can be moved along the path serving as a limit setting for how much of the path is used. To adjust the glyph position, place the mouse pointer over the glyph, and click and drag along the path. Release the mouse button to accept the location.

FIGURE 16.27
Path edit handles

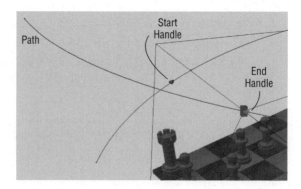

USING ANIMATE LIGHT

You can find the Animate Light tool on the Render tab. You can approach animating lights in a few ways. You can animate the lighting style, lights within a style, or local lights. When animating lights, the Animate Light dialog box has the same controls that were used to create or edit the lights. When defining an animation action for a light, you specify the light parameters as they will be at the end of the action. Studio tools use the previous parameter values as the starting point of the animation action and the new parameter values as the ending point of the animation action. You specify the time period over which the action occurs.

The first steps for animating a light are the same regardless of the object to be animated:

1. Activate the Animate Light tool. Alternatively, select the object to be animated, and use the context menu entry, Animate Light. The Animate Light dialog box displays.

2. If nothing was selected to start, specify the lighting style, style light, or local light to be animated. The Select tool is active by default.

3. Click the Definition button.

4. The corresponding dialog box displays, and only parameters capable of being animated are enabled.

5. If a style is selected for Lighting Style, you are able to animate the style brightness and ambience parameters.

6. For a local light or a light in a style, a variety of parameters are enabled for animating. Specify the values you want represented in the animation at the selected time position.

7. Click OK to commit to the values for the animation. An action is added to the timeline.

Local lights, when defined in components deeper in the assembly, are not accessible at the top-level assembly for animation. Local lights are meant to be light sources that travel with components. Thus, if you define a local light to be in a part used in the top-level assembly, that light will be lit and be a source of light in any renders or animations. The local light is part of the component, and wherever the component goes, the light goes also. Examples where local lights might be used are lighted gauges, switches, headlights, and so on.

Figure 16.28 shows a sequence of frames at time positions 2.3, 2.6, and 2.8. The local light has both intensity and position animated.

FIGURE 16.28
Animated local
light

Time: 2.3   Time: 2.6   Time: 2.8

Lights within lighting styles can provide animated scene lighting. Examples of uses are gallery lights, showroom lighting, and so on. Exploring the various ways to animate lights is worth the effort, not only for gaining experience but also for getting an idea of how much light affects everything in the scene.

DYNAMIC SIMULATION TO STUDIO

If you use Dynamic Simulation, part of Inventor Professional and Inventor Simulation, you will see the Create Studio Animation tool in that environment's tool panel, which allows you to render your simulation in Inventor Studio. The tool is used after you have run a simulation but before you leave run mode. You *must* run the simulation before using the tool.

The tool initiates the studio environment, creates a new animation called Dynamic_ Simulation, and adds a new parameter called Simulation_timeline. The parameter is placed in the Animation Favorites folder and is ready to animate. The parameter represents the time steps used in the simulation. For this reason, it is recommended that you use the same number for the parameter value that is used for the images in the simulation. This way, you will be able to relate the animation to the simulation.

Animate the parameter, using the Animate Parameters tool, to see your simulation. Then use the other Studio tools, such as lighting and scene styles, to help enhance the animated result. When you're ready, render the animation.

Using Video Producer

Video Producer provides the ability to compose a single animation from one or more animations. You are able to select from all cameras that you have set up, whether animated or not. Reasonably, to provide content for a production, you must create one or more cameras and usually at least one animation.

Video Producer supports the following:

◆ Multiple cameras in the same animation

◆ Camera transitions

◆ Multiple productions in the same assembly document

◆ Interactive modification of camera shots and transitions

It is also possible to create a production of still shots using a variety of cameras.

Video Producer is presented in a window similar to the Animation Timeline window, but with different controls.

The playback controls are the same as those in the Animation Timeline window and most other playback or player software.

The composing timeline and tabbed browser on the left are where you will find the shots and transitions. *Shots* are the cameras that have been defined in Studio, whether animated or not. *Transitions* are available to use between shots. Transitions are overlays over the shots, not segments between shots. Therefore, transitions extend into the shot in one or two directions. This means that when you plan to use transitions, you will need to specify enough shot time to allow for the transitions.

When you activate Video Producer, all cameras are collected, and all image representations are made and listed in the Shot browser. This action is session-based. Thereafter, only the cameras that change will be updated when you return to Video Producer during that Inventor session.

Four transition types are available, but five possibilities exist when you consider "no transition" as an option. The transitions are as follows:

◆ Fade: From color to shot, shot to shot, shot to color

◆ Gradient Wipe: From left to right

◆ Swipe Left: Moves from left to right

◆ Swipe Right: Moves from right to left

You can compose with Video Producer in two ways: via a dialog box or by dragging and dropping. Each has its own advantage. First we'll discuss dragging and dropping, or the interactive means of creating and editing. This method's advantage is fast production layout. Note that the composition is an additive process, starting from the beginning of the production.

Using the interactive method, you simply determine the camera shot you want to use and then drag and drop it onto the production track. You change the length of the shot by positioning the mouse pointer over either end, horizontally, and then clicking and dragging. Figure 16.29 shows an example of each of these techniques.

FIGURE 16.29
Interactive edit
handles

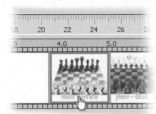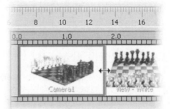

You can also drag and drop to reorder the shots in the timeline. For more precise control over the time used and shot segment, double-click the shot, and edit the parameters. Alternatively, use the Edit tool in the context menu.

Transitions behave in a similar manner. You simply drag and drop one onto the track and then adjust them as needed. Double-clicking or using the context menu to select Edit will give you explicit control over parameter values through dialog boxes.

To make it easier to edit contiguous production timeline members, you can select one and then move your mouse pointer over the neighboring member that is to be edited. The selected member displays a cyan highlight, and the new select target gets a red highlight, as shown in Figure 16.30. When both are highlighted, click and drag the boundary between them; they edit and update simultaneously.

FIGURE 16.30
Multimember edit

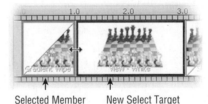

Selected Member   New Select Target

In the Shot dialog box there are two sections: Animation Footage and Shot Footage. Animation Footage refers to what the camera records in the animation. Shot Footage is the portion of animation footage that is used in the active production.

In the production timeline, the shot footage displayed is the amount of time in the production that footage is displayed. Any portion of the selected camera, from the designated animation footage, can be displayed during that shot duration.

In the Transition dialog box, you can edit the type of transition and its parameters.

Transitions that start or finish a production use color as the secondary member for the transition. Use the color selection to change the selection.

After placing a shot or transition into the Video Producer timeline, right-click and select Edit to display the Shot or Transition dialog box. In the Shot dialog box, you can edit the following:

◆ You can specify the animation from which the footage came.

◆ You can specify the point in time in the footage to begin using it.

◆ You can specify the particular camera to get footage from.

◆ You can specify the time frame of the camera footage to use.

In the Transition dialog box, you can edit the following:

◆ You can specify the transition type.

◆ You can specify the transition color.

◆ You can specify the start, duration, and end timeline positions.

These are the same parameters that are being edited when you do so interactively.

Rendering Video or Animations

It is important to note that if a production is active when you use the Render Animation tool, the active production, and *not* the animation, will render. If you want to render a single animation and you have productions, be sure to deactivate the production before rendering.

The available animation formats are WMV and AVI, which will be discussed in more detail in a moment.

The Render Animation dialog box is used whether rendering an animation or production. With productions, you have already selected the camera(s), so that field is disabled. If you are rendering an animation, the camera input is enabled.

The General and Style tabs of the Render Animation dialog box use the same controls as the Render Image dialog box.

The Output tab, shown in Figure 16.31, has controls that specify the various parameters for the rendering the animation.

FIGURE 16.31
Animation output

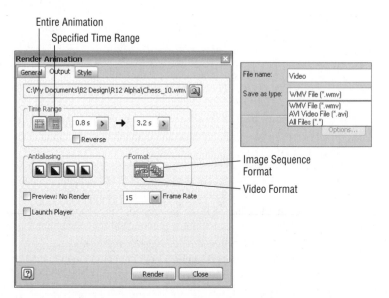

On the Output tab you specify the name for the file(s) that is created. If you use a video format, you can choose from Windows Media Video (WMV) or Audio Video Interleave (AVI).

Based on the file type selection and after the OK button has been clicked, you are asked to specify the final parameters before rendering:

WMV Format You are asked to specify Advanced Systems Format (ASF) Export properties, in particular, the network bandwidth. If you use one of the default choices and the output is not to your liking, use the custom setting; start with 700, Kbps and increase from there.

AVI Format You are asked to specify the video codec of choice. One or more codecs may have been delivered with the computer software. However, these at times may not produce the desired results.

Over the past few years, two video codecs have emerged as ones that routinely give good-quality results with small to medium AVI file sizes. Although this is not an endorsement, it is good to know that the TechSmith (`www.techsmith.com`) and DivX (`www.divx.com`) codecs provide very good results.

In the Time Range section, specify whether the entire animation or a time range will be rendered. If time range is selected, the timeline fields enable so you can specify the start and end times. If you want to reverse the rendered animation, select the Reverse check box.

Note that the controls on the right side of the input fields give access to the most recent values specified for the tool.

The Antialias settings are the same as those used in the Render Image dialog box; from left to right they are None, Low, High, and Highest.

The Format section is where you specify whether the animation is output in video format or as a list of frame sequences. If frame sequence is specified, the name provided has incremented numbers appended as images are created. If you plan on adding comments within the video or if you do not have enough disk space, you can output as images and then composite them later. This allows you to move the images to another location and continue rendering.

Then, specify the number of frames per second the video will output with. You will find that 24 and 30 frames per second (fps) are commonly used in broadcast and film media. A 15 fps animation may look good to you. Try it at 24 or 30 fps; you will notice the improvement.

A major concern of anyone rendering is the amount of time it takes to generate an image or animation. Rendering an animation without some idea of what it will look like is a potentially expensive proposition at best. To enable better decision-making processes, you are able to create a preview render; just select the box. Preview renders do not use lighting styles and render quickly. This gives you a means of determining whether any adjustments are needed before committing to rendering over a lengthy period of time.

These are the tools and concepts to accomplish rendering and animation in Inventor Studio. The creative part is up to you. Spend time experimenting, and you'll find you can create compelling imagery.

Additional Resources

In addition to the step by step information and exercises in this chapter there are also three tutorials that can be found by going to Get Started ➤ Learn about Inventor ➤ Tutorials. Once the Tutorials window is open you can find tutorials in the Experienced Users tab on Renderings, Animations, and Positional Representations.

The Bottom Line

Create and manage surface, lighting, and scene styles   Creating your own more realistic styles is often the difference between a rendering that looks kind of real and one that is photorealistic.

> **Master It**   You need to create a surface style that portrays black, bumped plastic.

Create and animate cameras   Although static camera animations are a common part of any animation, creating and animating cameras give your renderings a much more professional feel. You need to create a camera and animate it.

> **Master It**   You decide to use the most expedient means to capture camera keyframe positions.

Start new animations, modify animations, and use the various animation tools   Animating your assemblies so that the function of the mechanism is showcased is often the purpose of an assembly animation.

> **Master It**   You have an existing animation but want to do a variation on it. You want to copy and edit an existing animation.

Use multiple cameras to create a video production of your animation   Video Producer provides the means to combine camera shots into a single video output.

> **Master It**   You have created several cameras, animated and static, and want to make a composite animation.

Use props to enhance your scene   Inventor assemblies can be combined with other components to create a more realistic scene for rendering.

> **Master It**   You have completed a design and want to render a realistic image of it in its working environment.

Render realistic and illustrative images   Inventor provides the means to render both realistic and illustrative images.

> **Master It**   With your new product nearing completion, the marketing department has asked for rendered images for marketing collateral and technical documents such as white papers.

Render animations and video productions   Inventor provides the means to render animations and video productions.

> **Master It**   You've created a wrapper assembly and set up the scene with cameras, lighting, and a scene style. Now you want to render an animation for design review and a video production for a multidiscipline review or marketing use.

Chapter 17

Stress Analysis and Dynamic Simulation

This chapter will cover the tools of the Stress Analysis and Dynamic Simulation environments found in the Inventor Professional suite and the Inventor Simulation suite. The Stress Analysis environment allows you to perform static and modal analysis on parts and assemblies by defining component materials, loads, constraints, and contact conditions. A second type of Stress Analysis (referred to as Frame Analysis in this chapter) uses beam elements represented with a line segment that is centered in a Frame Generator member and interpolates the effects of loads on the geometry of the frame. This greatly improves the speed of the analysis.

The Dynamic Simulation environment allows you to analyze an assembly in motion by specifying loads, constraints, motion joints velocities, acceleration, and environmental factors such as gravity and friction. These environments can be used together to determine motion loads enacted upon one component by another component at a given point in time.

In this chapter, you will learn how to:

◆ Set up and run stress analysis simulations

◆ Set up and run dynamic simulation simulations

◆ Export results from the Dynamic Simulation environment to the Stress Analysis environment

Introduction to Analysis

Although the terms *stress analysis* and *finite element analysis* (FEA) are often used interchangeably in conversation, it may be helpful to understand these terms as they relate to the tools available to you in the Inventor Stress Analysis environment. FEA is an analysis of a complex object solved by dividing that object into a mesh of smaller elements upon which manageable calculations can be run. The *stress analysis* done by Inventor uses this method to allow you to analyze your design under a given set of conditions specified by you in order to determine basic trends in regard to the specifics of your design.

Deriving an exact answer from the analysis of a model is generally reserved for an analyst with specific training, often for a more powerful set of analysis tools. With that said, you can use the Inventor simulation tools to run basic analyses to confirm design validity. This can be useful to determine design basics before going down a wrong path. Or you can use these tools to help find out, for example, whether a component or assembly is being over- or underdesigned for a given set of loads and/or vibrations. Inventor's stress analysis tools are also useful when determining how feature size and locations will affect the integrity of the part. For instance, how close to the edge of a bracket can you move a hole? Is another brace required to prevent a sheet-metal face from "pillow casing" because of a pressure load? Questions of this nature are ideal uses for these tools and can significantly reduce the number of physical prototypes required to prove a final design.

Dynamic simulation allows you to set the components of your model in motion to verify how those parts interact with one another and to determine the force enacted on one component (or group of components) by another component (or group of components). The Dynamic Simulation environment allows you to define the way parts relate to one another and how the forces present create motion in the context of a timeline. From the simulation, you can determine how and when parts interact as well as the amount of force present for any point in time. For example you might use these tools to simulate a force applied to a shaft used to turn a lever, which in turn contacts a catch stop, where the goal is to determine the maximum force present throughout the entire sequence. Once this maximum force is determined it can be applied to the shaft as loads in a stress analysis study.

Conducting Stress Analysis Simulations

You can simulate a stress situation on your design to determine the effects of various load and constraint scenarios to determine areas of weakness, better design alternatives, how much a part is over- or underbuilt, to what extent a design change will impact a design, and so on. Using parametric studies, you can determine a combination of these elements to see how multiple changes impact a design at the same time. For more information on this, refer to the "Conducting Parameter Studies" section in this chapter. This is an important task because understanding the basic tools and workflow is the first step to setting up effective simulations.

The basic stress analysis workflow is as follows:

1. Enter the Stress Analysis environment (go to the Environment tab, and select Stress Analysis).

2. Create a simulation.

3. Specify the type of Simulation you want to conduct (for assemblies you may want to use an alternate view, positional or level of detail representation).

4. Specify the materials for the components.

5. Specify the load types, locations, and amounts.

6. Specify the support types and locations.

7. For assemblies, gather and refine contact between components.

8. Generate a mesh.

9. Run the simulation.

10. Interpret the results.

To aid you in the process of learning how to conduct a stress analysis study, Autodesk has built in the Simulation Guide.

Simulation Guide

The Simulation Guide can be found near the right end of the Stress Analysis tab when you have begun to construct a simulation. Accessing this tool will be covered later in this chapter.

This tool was built with two types of user in mind: the novice who is looking for an understanding of the process of conducting a simulation, and the intermediate user who has been using an FEA tool in the past and is looking for additional advice on using the Inventor toolset or seeking to improve their knowledge.

The tools can be launched before you begin the steps listed above, or if you've already begun setting up a simulation it will open to the next appropriate step to offer guidance. The guide contains a series of hyperlinks that when selected will step you through various options on how the component or assembly is constructed and how it moves or is supported, to help in selecting load and constraint types. It will even check with you to see if there are features that may not influence the result of the analysis but may add unnecessary time to the process.

Static Stress vs. Modal Analysis

You can perform static and modal stress analysis on parts and assemblies in the Stress Analysis environment. To enter this environment, click the Stress Analysis button on the Environments tab. Once in the Stress Analysis environment, you use the Create Simulation button, and specify either Static Analysis or Modal Analysis. It's important to understand the difference between static and modal analysis:

Static analysis   This attempts to determine the stress placed on a component by a particular set of loads and constraints. The stress is considered static because it does not vary due to time or temperature. You can import motion loads determined from the Dynamic Simulation environment to analyze the stress at any given time step for moving parts.

Modal analysis   This attempts to determine the dynamic behavior of a model in terms of its modes of vibration. An example would be trying to determine whether the vibration generated by a running motor would create significant disturbance to a sensitive mechanism within the design.

Simplifying Your Model

When working with assemblies, you should exclude parts that are not affected by or do not add to the results of the simulation in order to simplify the simulation and reduce the time required to run it. Excluding small parts such as fasteners, whose functionality is replicated by simulation constraints or forces, is also recommended. You can do this by expanding the assembly browser node, right-clicking the part to be excluded, and then selecting Exclude From Simulation.

When working with a part file in the simulation environment, you can suppress small features that are irrelevant to stress concentrations, such as outer fillets and chamfers. These "finish" features typically only complicate the mesh needed for the simulation and add overhead to the analysis. Other features that are typically excluded from simulations are small holes with diameters of less than 1/100 of the length of the part, embossed or engraved text, and other aesthetic features. Excluding features of these types can have a significant impact on the meshing process and the simulation's run time. Figure 17.1 shows the exclusion of features on the left and parts on the right. Using the appropriate selection filter, you can select features and parts to exclude in the design window using typical right-click context menu behavior while in the assembly.

FIGURE 17.1
The Exclude features for a simulation

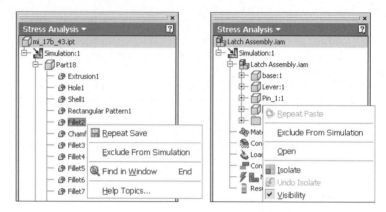

Specifying Materials

To specify the material of each part in a simulation, use the Assign button on the Material panel of the Stress Analysis tab. Material properties must be fully defined in order for the material to be used for the simulation. Materials with incomplete information are marked with an icon. Figure 17.2 shows the Assign button used to access the Assign Materials dialog box, as well as the icon indicating incomplete materials have been specified.

FIGURE 17.2
Assigning materials

You can specify the original material for each component or specify an override (per simulation) from the Material Library. To change the original material of the part file while in the Stress Analysis environment, click the Inventor button 【▾】, select iProperties, and go to the Physical tab. You can use the Styles Editor button in the Assign Materials dialog box to step into the Style And Standard Editor to edit, add, or just review the properties of any material style. You can find the physical characteristics of a given material from a number of resources on the Internet, such as www.matweb.com.

It is assumed that materials are constant, meaning there is no change because of time or temperature to the structural properties of the material. All materials are assumed to be homogenous, with no change in properties throughout the volume of the part. And it is also assumed that stress is directly proportional to strain for all materials.

By default the browser will display any material that has been overridden with the components using that material beneath. You can also display all materials assigned to components with a right-click on the Material category in the Browser and then selecting All Materials from the context menu.

Applying Simulation Constraints

Constraints added in the simulation limit the movement or displacement of the model for the purposes of the simulation. To constrain a model for static simulations, you should remove all free translational and rotational movements. You should also strive to neither over- nor under-constrain your model because both can impact the simulation results.

You can create all the constraint types by clicking the constraint tool buttons on the Constraints panel of the Stress Analysis tab, as shown in Figure 17.3.

FIGURE 17.3
The simulation
constraint tools

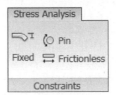

These are the types of simulation constraints available:

Fixed constraints   These remove all translational degrees of freedom and can be applied to faces, edges, or vertices, typically to simulate a part that is bonded or welded to another component. You can click the >> button to specify the Use Vector Components option and free the component in a given vector plane. Fixed constraints can also be used to specify a known displacement of a component in order to determine the force required to create the displacement.

Frictionless constraints   Use these constraints to prevent the selected surface from deforming or moving in a direction normal to the selected surface. You can also use frictionless constraints to simulate linear bearings and slides. Because most surface-to-surface situations are not entirely frictionless, you can expect the simulation to return more moderate results. If friction is considerable, it can be compensated for in the Dynamic Simulation environment, and the results can be imported into the Stress Analysis environment.

Pin constraints   These are used to apply rotational constraints on a selected cylindrical face or faces, such as where holes are or where parts are supported by pins or bearings. Use the >> button to set the direction options. A pin that rotates in a hole would have only the tangential direction free, one that slides in a hole but does not rotate would have only the axial direction free, one that slides and rotates would have both the axial and tangential directions free, and so on.

Figure 17.4 shows the simulation constraint dialog boxes.

FIGURE 17.4
The simulation constraint dialog boxes

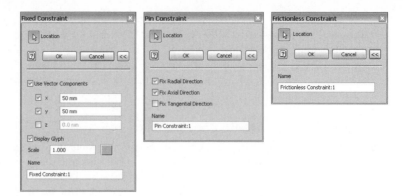

Applying Loads

Loads are forces applied to a part or assembly resulting in stress, deformation, and displacement in components. A key to applying loads is being able to predict or visualize how parts will respond to loads. For simple static simulations, this is generally fairly straightforward, but for more complex designs where one component exerts a force on another, which exerts a force on yet another, loads will likely need to be determined through the use of the Dynamic Simulation tools, as discussed later in this chapter.

You can access all the load types from the Loads panel of the Stress Analysis tab, as shown in Figure 17.5.

FIGURE 17.5
The load tools

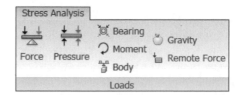

These are the types of load available:

Force This is specified in newtons (N) or pounds-force (lbf or lbforce). Forces can be applied by selecting a single or set of faces, edges, or vertices for the location. Selection sets must be of the same type, meaning that once you select a face, you can add faces to the selection set but not edges or vertices. The force direction can be specified by selecting an edge or face and then changed using the Flip Direction button. Direction is automatically set to the normal of the face (with the force directed at that face) when a face is selected for either a location or a direction. You can avoid stress singularities by selecting faces or the location rather than edges or vertices.

Pressure This is specified in megapascals (MPa) or pounds per square inch (psi). Pressure can be applied only to a face or set of faces. Pressure is uniform and is applied normal to the surface at all locations. When applying loads to faces that are involved in contacts, you should use pressure instead of force.

Bearing These are specified in newtons (N) or pounds-force (lbf or lbforce). Bearing loads are applied only to cylindrical faces. By default, the load is along the axis of the cylinder, and the direction is radial. You can specify the direction by selecting a face or edge. These are generally used to simulate a radial load such as roller bearing or a moment when specified perpendicular to the axis.

LOADS AND CONSTRAINTS

Loads and constraints can be applied to the same entity as long as they are compatible. When incompatible loads and constraints exist on the same entity, such as a face fixed in the X direction while a load is applied in the same direction to the same face, the constraints will override the forces.

Moment   These are specified in units of torque such as newton meters (N m or N*m) or pounds-force inch (lbforce in or lbf*in). Moment locations can be applied to faces only. Direction can be defined by selecting faces, straight edges, axes, and two vertices.

Remote Force   These can be used as an alternative to applying a force load directly to a part, by specifying the location in space from which the force originates. Apply Remote Force by selecting faces and specifying in N or lb.

Gravity   These are specified in units of acceleration such as millimeter per second squared (mm/s^2) or inch per second squared (in/s^2). Apply gravity to a face or parallel to a selected edge. The default gravity value is set to 386.220 in/s^2 or 9810.0 mm/s^2.

Motion   Unlike the other forces, there is no tool to apply Motion loads in the Stress Analysis environment; instead these are created from reaction forces determined from the Dynamic Simulation environment using the Export to FEA tool for a component per specified time step(s). Once done, you can consider motion loads by one of the following methods:

- For a new simulation, click Create Simulation button on the Stress Analysis tab.

- For an existing simulation, right-click the existing simulation in the browser node, and select Edit Simulation Properties.

- In either case, once the Simulation Properties dialog box is open, you follow these steps:

  1. In the Simulation Properties dialog box, select the Motion Loads Analysis check box.

  2. Select the part from the enabled list.

  3. Select the time step from the list.

  4. Click OK.

Body   These are specified in units of acceleration such as millimeter per second squared (mm/s^2) or inch per second squared (in/s^2). Body loads are the forces acting on the entire volume or mass of a component, such as gravity, linear acceleration, centripetal force, and centrifugal force. Select a planar face for linear acceleration or a cylindrical face for an axial direction. Use a body force to simulate the effect of outside forces. Only one body force per simulation is allowed.

Use the Linear tab to specify linear acceleration and the Angular tab to specify angular velocity or angular acceleration. The Angular tab has three possible results depending upon what is specified and how:

◆ Velocity and acceleration have the same rotation axis, with an unspecified location. The solver determines the location along the axis.

◆ Velocity and acceleration have different rotation axes, with an unspecified location. The solver determines the location along the axis. A point is selected along the velocity rotation axis for the acceleration location.

◆ Velocity and acceleration have different rotation axes, with a specified location.

USING SPLIT TO APPLY LOADS ACCURATELY

When you assign bearing loads to components, you may need to split the face first in order to select just a portion of a continuous face. For instance, consider applying a load to a shaft. If you select the cylindrical face, the load might be distributed along the entire face rather than concentrated on just the area intended to be loaded. You can use a work plane to split the face. This can be useful when placing loads on flat surfaces as well. Use a sketch to divide the surface into a face appropriate to the load. You can access the Split tool in the modeling environment from the Modify panel of the Model tab.

Specifying Contact Conditions

Contacts between components are detected when the simulation is run and automatically listed in the browser under the contact node. However, you can run the Automatic Contact tool to see them before running the simulation and then modify any of the automatic contacts listed or manually add other contacts. To add contacts, click either the Automatic or Manual button on the Contacts tab, as shown in Figure 17.6.

FIGURE 17.6
Contact tools

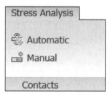

In order for contacts to be added, the faces must meet the following criteria:

◆ The selected faces must be within 15 degrees of parallel. This 15-degree limit is a system setting and cannot be changed.

◆ The distance between the selected faces cannot exceed the Tolerance setting specified in the simulation's properties. You can access the simulation's properties by right-clicking the simulation node in the browser for existing simulations, or you can specify them when you create the simulation.

Contacts are listed in the contact node in the browser and categorized per contact type. The type and components involved are set in the contact node name. Contacts are also listed under the browser node of each involved component. Modal analysis lists only the Bonded and Spring contact types, whereas all types are available for static analysis. You can change the contact type of automatic contacts by right-clicking a contact and choosing Edit Contact or by using the Ctrl or Shift key to multiselect contacts and then right-clicking and choosing Edit Contact. You can suppress contacts as well. Figure 17.7 shows the edit options.

FIGURE 17.7
Contact edit options

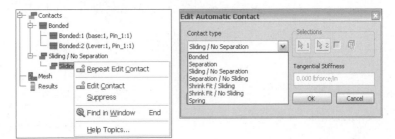

These are the available contact types:

Bonded   This creates a rigid bond between selected faces.

Separation   This partially or fully separates selected faces while sliding.

Sliding/No Separation   This creates a normal to face direction bond between selected faces while sliding under deformation.

Separation/No Sliding   This partially or fully separates selected faces without them sliding against one another.

Shrink Fit/Sliding   This creates conditions similar to Separation but with a negative distance between contact faces, resulting in overlapping parts at the start.

Shrink Fit /No Sliding   This creates conditions of Separation/No Sliding but with a negative distance between contact faces, resulting in overlapping parts at the start.

Spring   This creates equivalent springs between the two faces. You define total Normal Stiffness and/or Tangential Stiffness. The Normal Stiffness and Tangential Stiffness options are available for the Spring contact only.

You can change the contacts between two components to see how the simulation results change. Figure 17.8 shows the same simple assembly simulation with a different contact applied between the two plates. On the left, a bonded contact is used, and the results show that the vertical plate is deformed by the load and that stress is concentrated at, and distributed out from, the contact joint. On the right, a Sliding/No Separation joint is used, and the results show that the vertical plate is essentially pushed along the horizontal plate, with the stress being spread over the vertical plate, with little or no concentration and no stress being distributed to the horizontal plate.

Generating a Mesh

Although you can accept the default mesh settings and run the simulation, often you will want to adjust the mesh settings to compensate for areas where a finer mesh is required. You can adjust the global mesh settings or use a local mesh control when needed. Figure 17.9 shows the Mesh tools found on the Prepare panel.

FIGURE 17.8
Contact comparison

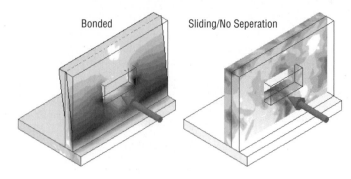

Bonded

Sliding/No Seperation

FIGURE 17.9
Mesh tools

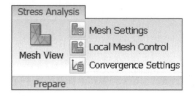

MESH SETTINGS

Use the Mesh Settings tool to change these mesh properties:

Average Size   Controls the mean distance between mesh nodes. Setting the average size to a smaller value results in a finer mesh. This setting is relative to the overall size of the model. A value between 0.100 and 0.050 is generally recommended.

Minimum Size   Controls the minimum distance between mesh nodes as a fraction of the Average Size value. Increasing this will decrease the mesh element density. Decreasing this value will increase the mesh element density. This setting is sensitive, and changes typically result in dramatic changes to the mesh quality. A value between 0.100 and 0.200 is generally recommended.

Grading Factor   Controls the ratio of adjacent mesh edges where fine and coarse mesh areas come together. The smaller the factor used, the more uniform the mesh will be. A value of 1 to 10 can be used, but a value between 1.5 and 3.0 is typically recommended.

Maximum Turn Angle   Controls the maximum angle for meshes applied to arcs. Specifying a smaller angle results in a finer mesh on curved areas. A value between 30 and 60 degrees is typically recommended.

Create Curved Mesh Elements   Controls the creation of meshes with curved edges and faces. If unselected, a less accurate mesh is created, but performance may be better.

Ignore Small Geometry   This should be deselected for models with thin and/or long profiles that contain small detailed cross sections.

Use Part Based Measure For Assembly Mesh   This sets part mesh sizes relative to the overall dimensions of the part models. Deselecting this option sets the mesh size relative to the overall assembly dimensions. Use this option for assemblies composed of several parts of varying sizes. This setting is available only in an assembly.

Once the mesh settings have been adjusted, you can click the Mesh View button to generate the mesh initially and then toggle on the visibility of the mesh afterward. It is not required that you generate the mesh manually because it will be done during the simulation, but this may allow you to identify areas of importance on the model that are not meshed to your liking and then apply a local mesh.

LOCAL MESH CONTROL

You can use the Local Mesh Control button to select faces and edges that require a finer meshing than what is required for the rest of the model. This allows you to manually improve the mesh quality for small or complex faces. A browser node is created in the Mesh node for each local mesh you create. You can right-click the local mesh and select Edit Local Mesh Control to change the mesh size or change the faces or edges selected.

When mesh settings or local mesh controls have been updated, a lightning bolt icon will display in the browser to indicate that the mesh is out-of-date. You can right-click the Mesh browser node and choose Update Mesh, as shown in Figure 17.10. This figure shows a simple cube with a local mesh applied to the top face; the other faces are meshed according to the mesh settings.

FIGURE 17.10

Updating a mesh

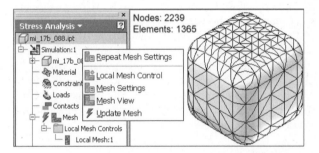

UNDERSTANDING MESH SETTINGS

To understand the way these settings affect the mesh generated, you can use the file named mi_17b_88.ipt in the Chapter 17 directory of the Mastering Inventor 2011 folder and apply a mesh to it. This file is a simple cube with rounded edges. Experiment with the options using the Mesh Settings tools. Then apply a local mesh. Exit the Stress Analysis environment, edit the model, and change the value for Extrusion1 to 30 mm (all of the dimensions of the cube are set to be the same and will update to match).

Return to the Stress Analysis environment, and update the mesh. Note that the mesh adjusts as the cube size increases, whereas the local mesh holds an absolute size. Use the Mesh Settings tool to take a look at the other settings as well. Understanding the impact of each setting on a simple part model will allow you to determine the effect of each setting on your more complex models.

MESH ERRORS

When model errors prevent a mesh from being created, a mesh failure warning is displayed. Errors are reported in the Mesh progress dialog box, in the mesh browser node, and with an error label and leader on the model in the graphics area.

AN INTERFACE OPTION WORTH NOTING

The previous sections discuss the selection of Materials, application of Loads and generating Meshes. These things are categorized in the Browser.

An alternative to using the tools in the Stress Analysis tab is to right-click on these categories in the Browser and select the same tools from the context menu presented.

Running the Simulation

Once you have set the material, loads, constraints, and contacts, you are ready to run the simulation. To run a simulation, click the Simulate button on the Solve panel, or right-click the simulation node in the browser and select Simulate. The Simulate dialog box displays information about the simulation to be run and will display warning and stop errors when not all criteria is available to run. For instance, if you have forgotten to set a material type, the Simulate dialog box will stop you and tell you this. If you need to cancel a simulation in process, click the Cancel button, or press the Esc key.

When a simulation becomes out-of-date because of changes to mesh settings, loads, constraints, or other design parameters, you will see a red lightning bolt next to the Results browser node. To update the simulation, simply right-click the browser node and click Simulate, or just click the Simulate button on the Solve panel again.

When working with parametric studies, it is possible to run simulations for more than one configuration at a time. You can run an Exhaustive Set or Smart Set of configurations or just run the current configuration. You can find more information on simulating configurations in the "Conducting Parameter Studies" section.

Interpreting the Results

Once a simulation is run, the Results node of the browser is populated, and the graphics area updates to show the shaded distribution of stresses. You can switch between available results types by double-clicking each type in the Results browser folder. Figure 17.11 shows a typical simulation result. Note the Results folder in the browser.

The Results node of the browser will display the subcategories of results, each displayed on the model by the use of color contours. The colors displayed on the model correspond to the value ranges shown in the color bar legend. Typically areas of interest are displayed in warm colors such as red, orange, and yellow. These colors represent areas of high stress, high deformation, or a low safety factor. You can adjust the number of colors used in the color bar as well as the position and size of it by clicking the Color Bar button on the Display panel. Listed here are the results subcategories:

Von Mises Stress   Maximum stress theory states that failure will occur when the maximum principal stress in a component reaches the value of the maximum stress at the elastic limit. This theory works to predict failure for brittle materials. However, in elastic bodies subject to three-dimensional loads, complex stresses are developed, meaning that at any point within the body there are stresses acting in various directions. The Von Mises criterion calculates whether the combining stress at a given point will cause failure. This is represented in the results node as the Von Mises Stress, also commonly known as *equivalent stress*.

1st Principal Stress   Principal stresses are calculated by converting the model coordinates so that no shear stresses exist. The 1st principal stress is the maximum principal stress and is the value of stress that is normal to the plane in which shear stress is zero. This allows you to interpret maximum tensile stress present because of the specified load conditions.

3rd Principal Stress   The 3rd principal is the minimum principal stress, and it acts normal to the plane in which shear stress is zero. It helps you to interpret the maximum compressive stress present in the part because of the specified load conditions.

Displacement   The displacement results show you the deformed shape of your model in a scaled representation, based on the specified load conditions. Use the displacement results to determine the location and extent to which a part will bend and how much force is needed to bend it a given distance.

Safety Factor   The safety factor is calculated as the yield strength of the material divided by 1st principal stress. This shows you the areas of the model that are likely to fail under the specified load conditions. The calculated safety factor is shown on the color bar legend as the value followed by *min*. A safety factor of less than 1 indicates a permanent yield or failure.

Frequency Modes   Modal results appear under the Results node in the browser as frequency modes only when running a modal analysis. You can view the mode plots for the number of specified natural frequencies. In an unconstrained simulation, the first six modes will occur at 0Hz corresponding to the six standard rigid body movements.

FIGURE 17.11
Simulation results

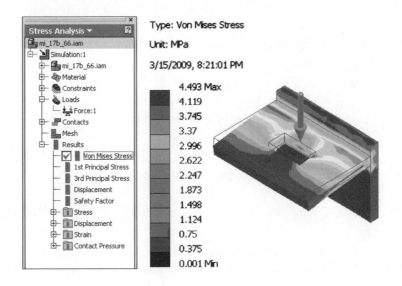

Using the Result, Scaling, Display, and Report Tools

You can use several display tools to adjust the results display in order to clearly interpret the calculated results. You can access these tools on the Display panel, as shown in Figure 17.12.

FIGURE 17.12
Result, scaling, display, and report tools

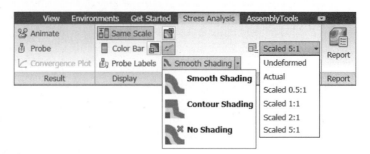

The following list describes the result, display, and report tools shown in the previous figure:

Same Scale   Maintains the same scale while viewing different results.

Color Bar   Opens the Color bar dialog box so you can adjust the color bar display settings.

Probe   Allows you to select on the model and display results information per the selection. Right-click a label to edit or delete it.

Probe Labels Display   Toggles the visibility of probe labels.

Shading   Displays color changes using a blended transition when set to Smooth Shading, striated shading when using Contour Shading, and no color shading when set to No Shading.

Maximum   Turns on and off the display of the point of maximum result, which allows you to quickly identify the maximum result on the model.

Minimum   Turns on and off the display of the point of minimum result, which allows you to quickly identify the minimum result on the model.

Boundary Condition   Turns on or off the display of load symbols on the part.

Displacement Scale   Allows you to select from a preset list of displacement exaggeration scales.

Element Visibility   Displays the mesh over the top of the result contours.

Animate Displacement   Animates the displacement for the current result type and displacement scale.

Report   Generates reports of analysis simulations in HTML format with PNG graphics.

Conducting Parameter Studies

Often the purpose of a stress analysis simulation is to determine how a change to a design feature will impact the part or assembly's strength. The parametric study tools allow you to make comparative evaluations based on different parameter values at the feature, part, and assembly levels. To create a parametric study, you nominate certain parameters for evaluation in the study, define the range for each parameter, specify the design constraints that you are interested in seeing for those parameters, and finally analyze the results of each variation.

To create a parametric study, use these steps as a guideline:

1. Set the simulation's design objective to Parametric Dimensions. How you do this depends on whether you are creating a new simulation or editing an existing one. You can set the design objective to Parametric Dimensions by using the Create Simulation button when creating a new simulation or by right-clicking an existing simulation in the browser and choosing Edit Simulation Properties, as shown in Figure 17.13.

FIGURE 17.13
Setting a simulation to the Parametric Dimension design objective

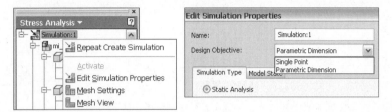

2. Nominate selected parameters for use in the study by expanding the browser node for the model and then right-clicking the assembly, part, or feature node you want to use in the study and selecting Show Parameters. Figure 17.14 shows a parameter called Side_Offset being nominated.

FIGURE 17.14
Nominating a parameter

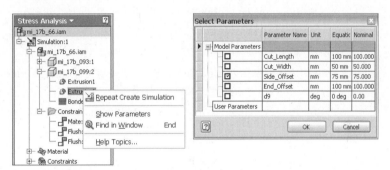

3. Define the range for the selected parameters by following these steps:

   A. Click the Parametric Table button on the Manage panel of the Stress Analysis tab.

   B. Enter a parameter range in the Value column; values must be in ascending order.

   C. Create a simple range by separating the minimum and maximum values with a hyphen; for instance, you can enter **70-85**.

   D. Specify specific values in a range by separating each value with a comma, colon, hyphen, or slash; for instance, you can enter **70, 75, 80, 85**.

   E. Add a colon to a range to specify the number of points included; for instance, you can enter **70-85 : 4**.

   F. Use the slider to set the current value.

G. Right-click the parameter row, and choose from the options to generate the geometry configurations. For instance, if you were to set the range of a hole position to 70, 75, 80, 85, four model configurations would be created with the hole positioned at each of those values. Figure 17.15 shows a Parametric Table configuration for the Side_Offset parameter.

FIGURE 17.15
Defining a parameter range

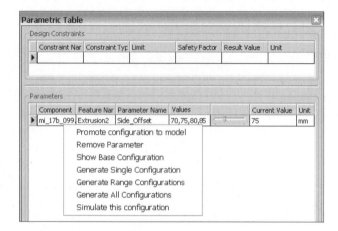

4. Add design constraints to the parametric table by following these steps:

A. In the Design Constraints area of the Parametric Table, right-click a row, and select Add Design Constraint.

B. In the Select Design Constraint dialog box, specify a results component, such as Von Mises Stress, Displacement, Safety Factor, and so on.

C. Specify the value of interest such as Minimum or Maximum (this applies to all geometry).

D. You can modify the selection set by selecting Include or Exclude and then selecting bodies, faces, or edges on-screen. Doing so focuses the results to a specific area of interest. Figure 17.16 shows the Safety Factor design constraint being added.

FIGURE 17.16
Adding a design constraint

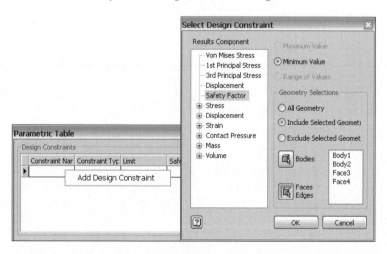

5. Specify the constraint type, set limits, enter a safety factor, and review the results using the following steps:

A. In the Parametric Table dialog box, click the Constraint Type drop-down, and select from the list.

B. Enter a value in the Limit column to filter the results to the set that meets the bounding limit when optimizing other design constraints.

C. Enter a safety factor to specify at what extent a variable can be exceeded before causing the design constraint to fail. A comparison to the limit factored by the Safety Factor setting determines whether it meets the limit or range.

D. The Result Value column displays the value of the design constraint for the simulation. When the value is within the limit, it displays green. When the limit is exceeded, it displays red. When out of range, it displays gray, and the closest value display is displayed. Figure 17.17 shows the Mass design constraint being configured.

FIGURE 17.17
Configuring a
design constraint

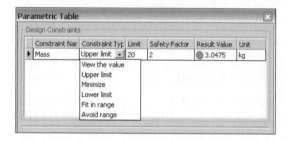

6. When multiple parameters are added to the table, configurations can be created. These configurations can then be generated and simulated by following a few simple steps:

A. In the Parametric Table dialog box, set the parameter values to the combination you want to simulate, right-click any parameter row, and choose Simulate This Configuration.

B. To simulate all configurations, exit the Parametric Table dialog box, and click the Simulate button on the Solve panel. You can choose to run an exhaustive set, a smart set, or the current configuration.

C. Once the simulations have been run, you can use the slider bar in the Parametric Table dialog box for each parameter to set the combinations and observe the results.

D. The Exhaustive Set Of Configurations setting runs all possible combinations of parameter settings, whereas the Smart Set Of Configurations setting runs only those combinations of parameter settings that Inventor determines have not yet been run. Figure 17.18 shows the choices for running simulation configurations.

Once you determine that a given configuration satisfies your design needs using the Parametric Table dialog box, you can right-click any of the parameter rows in the table and choose Promote Configuration To Model. This will write the parameter values of the configuration to the source files where you select Yes in the prompt dialog box.

FIGURE 17.18
Simulation
configurations

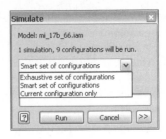

Conducting a Frame Analysis

As you learned in Chapter 15, "Frame Generator," having a library of predefined metal shapes can save a tremendous amount of work by not having to recreate standardized geometry. Frame Analysis allows you to further leverage those predefined shapes by using the known behavior of the shape under load and calculating what the loads would be along the center of a length of material rather than the surface.

The process of conducting a frame analysis is similar to performing an assembly analysis but frames add some additional tools that allow for an even more efficient solving process. Here is the process including some optional steps:

1. Enter the Frame Analysis environment through the Environments tab or using the icon on the Design tab.

2. Create a simulation.

3. Specify the support types and locations.

4. Specify the load types, locations and amounts.

5. Specify Connections between beams, additional nodes or releases (optional).

6. Run the simulation.

7. Interpret the results.

Frame Constraints

The concept of the constraint is the same for frame analysis but the realities of how a frame is constructed can be different. Portions of the frame may be built with the ability to have one end move freely or slide along another member. This opens up the need to be able to approach things differently to assure accuracy.

You can access all the constraints types from the Constraints panel of the Frame Analysis tab, as shown in Figure 17.19.

FIGURE 17.19
The frame
constraints

These are the types of constraints available:

Fixed constraints   Like the Fixed constraint in FEA, it restricts all movement of the beam or node that it is applied to.

Pinned constraints   Applying the Pinned constraint to a beam or node will allow rotation about the selected element, but it cannot move in space.

Floating constraints   This constraint allows free rotation of the beam or node, but it also allows movement in one plane.

Custom constraints   If you need a node or beam to be able to move or rotate within a boundary or with an amount of elasticity the Custom constraint can establish those conditions in any or all directions, including the ability for that movement to be unidirectional for one value and free in another direction.

Frame Loads

By removing the need to apply a mesh to a frame model it may become necessary to define the loads in a different manner. This means that there are more options for loads in frame analysis.

The three primary loads are shown in the Loads panel of the Frame Analysis tab as shown in Figure 17.20.

FIGURE 17.20
The frame loads

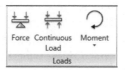

Force   This is specified in newtons (N) or pounds-force (lbf or lbforce). The value of the force can be applied to a node along the length of a beam. Once an approximate position has been selected a dialog will appear and will prompt you for the position along the beam element. The icon that appears has a series of handles that allow you to change the angle of the plane the force is applied in, the angle to the plane of the force and by clicking the arrow that represents the direction of the force the dialog will prompt you for the magnitude of force.

Continuous Load   This is specified in newtons (N) or pounds-force (lbf or lbforce). This force applies evenly to the entire beam segment. The input dialog is the same allowing for directing the load.

Moment   This is specified in units of torque such as newton meters (N m or N*m) or pounds-force per inch (lbforce in or lbf*in). A moment can be applied to a point at the end or along the beam segment with a graphical input very similar to the onscreen feedback for applying a Force.

There are also two types of load that are under the Moment in a pull down menu.

Axial Moment   This is specified in units of torque such as newton meters (N m or N*m) or pounds-force per inch (lbforce in or lbf*in). This is a moment that can be applied along the axis of the selected beam. You can control the position of the moment along the axis but it is automatically normal to the axis.

Bending Moment This is specified in units of torque such as newton meters (N m or N*m) or pounds-force per inch (lbforce in or lbf*in). A bending moment can be applied to a point at the end or along the beam segment. It is applied in the plane of the axis. You can change the angle about the axis that it is applied.

Connections

Due to the nature of working with the Frame Generator, there are situations where additional information needs to be added to the model for a proper simulation: conditions where there are gaps or flexibility in the model or you want to add additional nodes.

These tools are located in the Connections panel of the Frame Analysis tab as shown in Figure 17.21.

FIGURE 17.21
The frame
constraints

Release This connection can be applied to a beam adjacent to another loaded beam. You can control the flexibility between the beams. The resistance to the movement can be controlled in the primary planes and about the axes using either a specific force or a partial stiffness coefficient.

Custom Node You can add additional nodes along the beam to represent where contact will be made or to shortcut the loading process.

Rigid Link If you have a machined or cast part built into your design, the frame analysis tool may not properly account for a rigid element between two points that appear to be free in the frame generator model. The rigid link tool allows you to select a Parent Node and have a Child Node maintain its position to it through the simulation.

Results

People doing frame analysis need to understand what is happening to the model along the length of a beam. In an FEA model this is easy to visualize and the coloration of the beam element also helps. Over time, methods for diagramming a beam have been developed, and to offer a familiar way to understand the results of the simulation diagramming tools have been added to the frame analysis environment.

These tools are located in the Result panel of the Frame Analysis tab as shown in Figure 17.22.

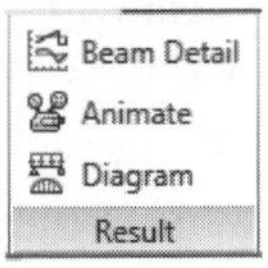

FIGURE 17.22
Diagramming tools

Beam Detail This tool launches a dialog that allows you to see the basic results on the right and diagrams of the specific results for the selected beam on the left.

Diagram Selecting this tool opens a dialog where you can request various results to be displayed on the model.

Additional tools in the Display panel will place Beam and Node Labels in the design window to more easily understand where these elements are rather than highlighting them using by hovering in the browser.

For static stress analysis the tools offered for parts, assemblies, and frames will offer you a great opportunity to better understand the effects of changes to your designs.

 Real World Scenario

CONSIDERING EVERY LOAD SCENARIO

An engineer was involved in a redesign of an equipment accessory that had unfortunately failed in the field. The problem originated from two sources: one was the use of an incorrect material that offered too much flexibility when under a particular load condition.

However, the second dynamic of this failure stemmed from the way the design was actually used in the field. During the design process, the considerations were mostly focused on how the mechanism would be operated during installation and how it would hold up under its highest load during use. Both were valid design considerations, but neither predicted the ultimate failure of the design.

As it turned out, it was the way these accessories were uninstalled that led to their high rate of failure. Not having anticipated this part of the way the product was used, the design team had no means to understand the unique torque loads that would ultimately make a good design fail. In the end, a slight modification to the design and the use of a different material type resolved the issue, but not before many dollars were wasted purchasing components that ultimately could not be used.

Keep this in mind as you create simulations, and remember that the results you generate can only be as good as the assumptions you make. Simulating every loading situation your design might encounter will expose these things before the first part is made or purchased.

Conducting Dynamic Simulations

Dynamic simulation is useful during the prototyping stages of design to test the function of interacting parts and for use in failure analysis where interacting parts enact stresses upon one another. When creating a dynamic simulation, you should follow the basic workflow listed here:

1. Define joints to establish component relationships.

2. Define environmental constraints such as gravity, forces, imposed motions, joint friction, and joint torque.

3. Run the simulation.

4. Analyze the output grapher to determine maximum or minimum stress at a given time step, maximum or minimum velocities, and so on.

5. Export the results to the Stress Analysis environment for motion stress analysis simulation.

To access the Dynamic Simulation tools, you first open the assembly you want to create the simulation in, and then you click the Dynamic Simulation button on the Environments tab.

Working with Joints

In the Dynamic Simulation environment, joints are used to define the way that components relate to one another concerning motion. Although you might at first associate joints with assembly constraints, joints and constraints are actually two separate concepts. In the assembly environment, all components are assumed to have six degrees of free motion until grounded or constrained in such a way that some or all of these degrees of freedom (DOF) are removed. Standard joints approach the issue of DOF from the opposite end. In the Dynamic Simulation environment, all components are assumed to have zero DOF until joints are applied to add free motion. You can then add special joint types manually to restrict degrees of freedom.

Understanding the difference between assembly constraints and joints is important when working with joints. However, if you have a properly constrained model, much of the joint creation can be automated by setting the Simulation Settings option to Automatically Convert Constraints To Standard Joints. You can do this by clicking the Simulation Settings button on the Dynamic Simulation tab. Figure 17.23 shows the Automatically Convert Constraints To Standard Joints option.

FIGURE 17.23
Automatic constraint to joint conversion

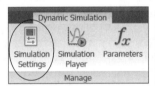
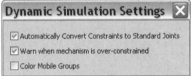

When the convert constraints option is on, any assembly constraints that are changed will automatically update and be converted to a standard joint when possible. You can apply constraints while in the Dynamic Simulation environment by switching to the Assembly tab or pressing C on the keyboard. When the convert constraints option is off, you can use the Convert Constraints button to manually convert assembly constraints.

To convert constraints manually, you must have the automatic convert constraints option turned off and the Convert Assembly Constraint button enabled. Using the Convert Assembly Constraint tool, you simply select the parts you want to apply a joint to, and the assembly constraints that exist between the two will appear in the dialog box. You can deselect one or more of the constraints to apply a less restrictive joint solution. Figure 17.24 shows the different results achieved by selecting or deselecting the constraints that exist on a shaft and handle.

FIGURE 17.24
Manual constraint to joint conversion

In addition to the automatic joint creation, you can (and most often need to) apply joints to your model manually. You can access the joint tool by clicking the Insert Joint tool. When you do so, the Insert Joint dialog box offers a drop-down with all the joint types listed. Alternatively, you can click the Display Joint Table next to the drop-down to display the five joint categories as buttons in the top of the table. Clicking a category button shows the available joint types for that category. Figure 17.25 shows the joint categories.

FIGURE 17.25
Joint categories

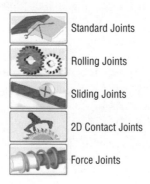

Standard Joints

Rolling Joints

Sliding Joints

2D Contact Joints

Force Joints

STANDARD JOINTS

Standard joints are created by converting assembly constraints to joints, either automatically or manually. Only one type of standard joint, called Spatial, is listed in the Display Joints table when the option to automatically create constraints is on. Here is a list of all the standard joints:

Revolution joints   Used to create a rotational relationship between cylindrical faces and axes of two components.

Prismatic joints   Used to constrain the edge of one component to the edge of another.

Cylindrical joints   Used to constrain the axis of one cylindrical component to the axis of another, thereby allowing the second component to slide along the axis of the first.

Spherical joints   Used to create ball and socket joints between two components.

Planar joints   Used to constrain the planar face of one component to the planar face of another. The first component is the motionless component, and the second is allowed to move along the face of the first.

Point-Line joints   Used to constrain the center point of a sphere to the axis of a cylinder or a point on another component.

Line-Plane joints   Used to constrain a planar face of one component to a point on another.

Point-Plane joints   Used to constrain the point of one component to the planar face of another.

Spatial joints   Used to create a relationship between two components where all six degrees of freedom are allowed to be free, without causing errors of redundancy in the simulation.

Welding joints   Used to create a relationship between two components so that there are no degrees of freedom between them so that they are considered as a single body in the simulation.

ROLLING JOINTS

Ten types of rolling joints are available. Rolling joints are used to restrict degrees of freedom. Here is a list of the rolling joint types:

Rolling Cylinder On Plane joints   Used to constrain a rotating cylindrical face to a 2D planar face. The relative motion between the two selected components is required to be 2D. A basic, continuous, cylindrical face is required for this joint type.

Rolling Cylinder On Cylinder joints   Used to constrain one rotating cylindrical face to another rotating cylindrical face. The relative motion between the two selected components is required to be 2D. A basic, continuous, cylindrical face is required for this joint type.

Rolling Cylinder In Cylinder joints   Used to constrain one rotating cylindrical face to the inside of another rotating cylindrical face. The relative motion between the two selected components is required to be 2D. A basic, continuous, cylindrical face is required for this joint type.

GEARS AND ROLLING JOINTS

If you have created a gear using the Design Accelerator, you will find a basic surface cylinder present in the part model. To make the surface available for use in the creation of rolling joints, you can edit the part and set the surface to be visible.

Rolling Cylinder Curve joints   Used to constrain a rotating cylindrical face to maintain contact with a curved face such as a cam. The relative motion between the two selected components is required to be 2D.

Belt joints   Used to constrain a belt component to two cylindrical components that rotate. Faces, edges, and sketches can be selected.

Rolling Cone On Plane joints   Used to constrain a rotating conical face to a 2D planar face. Faces, edges, and sketches can be selected.

Rolling Cone On Cone joints   Used to constrain a rotating conical face to another rotating conical face. Faces, edges, and sketches can be selected.

Rolling Cone In Cone joints   Used to constrain a rotating conical face to the inside face of a component that is not rotating. Faces, edges, and sketches can be selected.

Screw joints   Used to constrain components that screw together by specifying a thread pitch to define the travel per rotation. Faces, edges, and sketches can be selected.

Worm Gear joints   Used to constrain a component to a helical gear by specifying a thread pitch to define the travel per rotation. Faces, edges, and sketches can be selected.

SLIDING JOINTS

The five joint types in the sliding category are used to restrict degrees of freedom between the two components selected. In all five, the relative motion between the two selected components is required to be 2D. Here are the five types of sliding joints:

Sliding Cylinder On Plane joints   Used to constrain a cylindrical face to a 2D planar face so that it will slide along the plane without rotating.

Sliding Cylinder On Cylinder joints   Used to constrain a cylindrical face to slide on another cylindrical face.

Sliding Cylinder In Cylinder joints   Used to constrain a cylindrical face to slide inside another cylindrical face.

Sliding Cylinder Curve joints   Used to constrain a cylindrical face to slide on a curved face such as a cam.

Sliding Point Curve joints   Used to constrain a point on the second component to slide along a curve defined by the selected face, edge, or sketch on the first component.

2D CONTACT JOINTS

There is only one joint type in this category, and it is used to restrict degrees of freedom:

2D Contact joints   Creates contact between curves on two selected components. Curves can be faces, edges, or sketches, but the relative motion between the selections must be planar. The contact is not required to be permanent for this joint type.

3D CONTACT JOINTS

3D Contact Joints create an action or reaction force when applied. This category consists of just two joint types:

Spring/Damper/Jack joints   These create joints for resisting forces, shock absorption, and lift jacking forces.

3D Contact joints   These detect the contact and interference between all the surfaces of two selected parts. Subassemblies are not considered in this joint type.

More on Working with Joints

When components are assigned joints, either manually or automatically, they are grouped according to the results of the joints in the browser. For instance, if components are fully constrained to one another in the assembly, then they will be assigned a weld joint and listed in the browser as a welded group. If one of those components is grounded, then the welded group will be listed in the Grounded folder in the browser. If one of them is used in a motion joint, then it will listed as in the Mobile Groups folder. Figure 17.26 shows an assembly with two welded groups present. One is listed under Grounded, and the other is listed under Mobile Groups. You'll notice that both are used in the joint called Revolution: 2.

FIGURE 17.26
Browser grouping

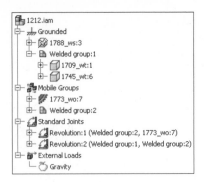

Here are some points to remember when creating joints:

◆ The Joint Table displays a pictorial representation for each joint type to assist you with determining which to use.

◆ Assembly constraints are not converted to joints in a one to one fashion, but instead joints are often created by combining assembly constraints. For instance, a mate and two flush constraints between two parts might be converted to a weld joint.

◆ Dynamic simulation performance is affected by the number of joints present. If you are simulating a particular set of components in a large assembly, it might be beneficial to manually weld most of the components and consider motion only for the set you need.

◆ When placing joints, you are often required to align the z-axis of the joint on both components. Failing to do so will prompt a warning.

◆ If you have the option to automatically convert assembly constraints selected, any assembly constraint you place in the Dynamic Simulation environment will automatically be converted to a standard joint.

When placing joints, you should keep an eye on the coordinate triad and ensure that the arrows align when required. Figure 17.27 shows the use of the flip arrow to align the z-axis.

To more easily review the joints that you've placed you can select components in the browser or the design window and joints associated with them will highlight in the browser.

FIGURE 17.27
Aligning component axes

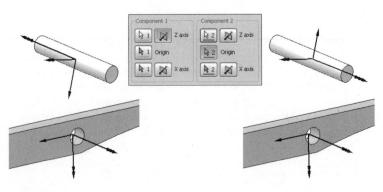

Working with Redundancy

In the Dynamic Simulation environment, joints are said to contain redundancy when they are over-constrained or have too many unknowns to solve. When redundancy occurs, Inventor prompts you to use the Repair Redundancy tool to repair the joint. In most cases, one or more solutions are suggested in the Repair Redundancy tool. Figure 17.28 shows a link assembly that has a redundancy in joint 4, the Cylindrical joint. To resolve this, the Mechanism Status tool is selected.

FIGURE 17.28
Using the Mechanism Status tool to resolve redundant joints

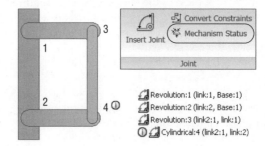

In the Mechanism Status And Redundancies dialog box, you can use the >> button to expand the options for resolving a redundancy. Typically a new joint type is suggested for the redundant joint. Often you can expand the drop-down and select from a list of possible alternatives, as shown in Figure 17.29. This dialog can also be shown while the simulation is running.

FIGURE 17.29
Resolving a redundant joint

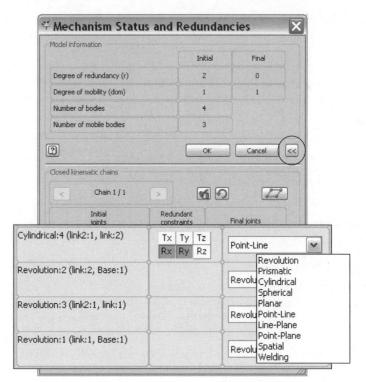

Also listed in the Mechanism Status And Redundancies dialog box are the redundant constraints. Tx, Ty, and Tz are the translational (linear) constraints, and Rx, Ry, and Rz are the rotational constraints. In Figure 17.25, the Cylindrical joint shows the Rotational X (Rx) and Rotational Y (Ry) are redundant.

Working with Environmental Constraints

Once joints are applied to the model, it is often required to apply environmental constraints to make the joints perform more realistically or to set the simulation up more efficiently. For example, if you apply a prismatic joint between a rail and a linear bearing pad, a certain amount of friction would be anticipated, so you would modify the joint and apply a dry friction coefficient value. You might also want to create an imposed spring to emulate a spring cushion in the slide channel or set the start position of the slide for the simulation. And then you might want to apply an imposed motion on the joint so that it moves during the simulation as expected. All of this can be done by right-clicking the joint and choosing Properties. When an environmental constraint for a particular joint is added, the constraint is marked with a green pound sign next to it in the browser, as shown in Figure 17.30.

FIGURE 17.30
A joint with an environmental constraint set

MODIFYING THE INITIAL POSITION

Often you will want to change the initial position of a component involved in a joint so that the simulation will run differently to how it is constrained. For instance, the rail and bearing pad example might be constrained so that the bearing is in the start position, but for the purposes of reducing the time of the simulation, it needs to run only from the middle of the cycle to the end. Setting the initial position allows this. To adjust the initial position of a joint, follow these general steps:

1. Right-click the joint in the browser, and select Properties.

2. Select the appropriate DOF tab. Depending upon the joint, there may be multiples.

3. Click the Edit Initial Conditions button.

4. Enter a new position value in the input box.

Here are some additional options that may apply depending upon the simulation and results you are trying to achieve:

- Select Locked so that the joint cannot be modified in the simulation.

- Deselect the Velocity check box to manually set the initial velocity of this degree of freedom, or leave it selected to allow the software to automatically compute the initial velocity. It's recommended that you leave this set at Computed and impose a velocity, using the Impose motion option (covered in the coming pages).

- Set the initial minimum or maximum bounds values for the degree of freedom if desired. Value sets the boundary for the force or torque of this DOF, Stiffness sets the stiffness of this DOF, and Damping sets the damping boundary for this DOF.

JOINT TORQUES

Joint torques can be set to control damping and friction and also to impose a spring cushion. Depending upon the simulation, you can often apply these things to a few key joints and have other dependent joints react off of them. Of course, this depends on the mechanism and the simulation. To adjust a joint for these things, follow these general steps:

1. Right-click the joint in the browser, and select Properties.

2. Select the appropriate DOF tab (depending upon the joint, there may be multiples).

3. Click the Edit Joint Torque button (the appearance of this button varies between rotational and translational joints).

4. Select the Enable Joint Torque check box.

5. Right-click an input box, and choose the input type required. Use Constant Value if the value does not change over time, or use the input grapher to enter a graduated input.

Figure 17.31 shows the Joint Torque properties for a prismatic joint.

FIGURE 17.31
Adding friction and damping to a joint

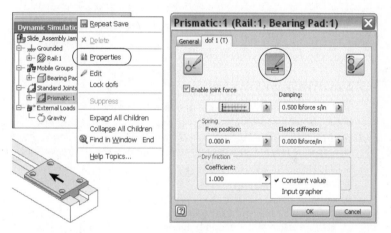

The range of inputs for Damping, Elastic Stiffness, and Friction are listed here:

◆ Damping is proportional to the velocity of the DOF.

◆ Free Position sets the position at which an imposed spring exerts no force.

◆ Elastic Stiffness sets the imposed spring stiffness.

◆ Friction is added as a coefficient between 0 and 2.

IMPOSED MOTION

Although motion can be created by applying external forces where that is important, often an imposed motion on a joint is desired to allow control of the timing and position of components not involved in an external force. For instance, in the rail and bearing pad example, the bearing might need to slide out of the way of another component that is being driven by an external force. Setting the imposed motion in the joint properties allows this to happen without the need to apply an external force on the bearing pad. To adjust a joint to include an imposed motion, follow these general steps:

1. Right-click the joint in the browser, and select Properties.

2. Select the appropriate DOF tab (depending upon the joint, there may be multiples).

3. Click the Edit Imposed Motion button.

4. Select the Enable Imposed Motion check box.

5. Select a Driving motion parameter type, and enter a value. The parameter types are as follows:

   ◆ Position imposes a motion to a specified position, typically specified using the input grapher to set the position relative to a time step (in other words, move 100 cm over 10 seconds).

   ◆ Velocity imposes a motion at a specified velocity. Use constant input or use the input grapher to enter a variable velocity to account for startup times and so on.

   ◆ Acceleration imposes a motion as a specified acceleration. Use constant input or use the input grapher to enter a variable acceleration.

USING THE INPUT GRAPHER

The input grapher is available in a number of input boxes used throughout the Dynamic Simulation environment. When an input is set to use the input grapher, a graph button is present in the input box. If no graph button is present, you can right-click in the input box and select input grapher from the context menu. To open the input grapher, simply click the graph button.

Typically the input grapher is used to specify a value that varies over time. In Figure 17.32, a velocity is being imposed on a joint starting at 0 in/s and coming up to 100 in/s in the first 10 seconds, at which time it levels off for the next 10 seconds before returning to 0 in/s at 30 seconds. The user has right-clicked in the graph to add a control point.

Each portion of the graph between points is selectable as a sector by clicking the graph. In Figure 17.32, the first sector is selected and is shaded. When a sector is selected, the inputs in the bottom half of the Input Grapher dialog box are specific to that sector. You can edit the sector's start and endpoints as well as the law applied to that specific sector.

You can modify the input graph by changing the x-axis variable, the laws applied, the freeing sector condition, and more. Here is a brief description of these graph input variables.

Input References

By default, Time is the x-axis variable for the curve graph in the input grapher. In many inputs, you can specify a different x-axis reference. Clicking the Reference button displays all variables available to be used as x-axis variables in the curve graph. Imposed motions cannot use x-axis references other than Time. Figure 17.33 shows a curve graph being set to call Velocity as the x-axis of the curve.

FIGURE 17.32
Adding a velocity
curve with the
input grapher

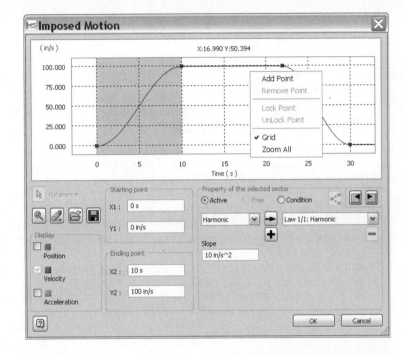

FIGURE 17.33
Setting the input
grapher to use
Velocity rather
than Time

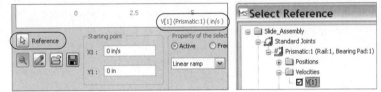

Laws

Laws can be applied individually or in combination to define the sector curve. To assign a sector a specific law, select the law from the list in the drop-down, and then use the arrow button to apply the law. Use the plus button to add laws to the sector, and use the minus button to remove laws from the sector. Here is a list of the available laws:

- Linear ramp
- Cubic ramp
- Cycloid
- Sine
- Polynomial
- Harmonic

◆ Modified sine

◆ Modified trapezoid

◆ Spline

◆ Formula

Freeing and Application Conditions

Each sector can be set to Active, Free, or Condition. Active indicates the sector has no conditions. Free indicates the sector has no values defined. Condition indicates one or more conditions have been assigned to the sector.

To create a condition, click the Condition radio button. By default, the Freeing Conditions dialog box appears. To edit or add a condition, click the Define Conditions button, and then click the Variable, Equal, or Value hyperlinks to set those options. Use the plus and minus signs to add or remove conditions. Figure 17.34 shows a condition being added.

FIGURE 17.34
Adding conditions

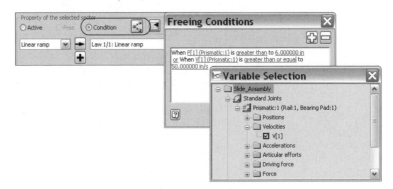

More Functions

The input grapher has a few functions that might not be apparent but are useful to know about when setting up and using the input grapher:

◆ The bottom display is dependent upon what is selected in the graph. Selecting a point gives inputs for just that point, selecting a sector gives sector options, and clicking in the graph outside all sectors gives Out Of Definition options that are used to describe the part of the curve on the left or right of the first and last points.

◆ Using the wheel button on your mouse, you can pan and zoom in the graph. This can be helpful when dealing with sectors that are dramatically different in scale. You can also use the Zoom button in the grapher dialog box.

◆ Curve definitions can be saved and loaded using the Save Curve and Load Curve buttons.

EXTERNAL FORCES

In order to set a component in motion, you can apply an imposed motion on the joint or apply an external force on the component itself. External forces consist of Loads and Gravity. External forces can be used to initiate, complement, or resist movement. For instance, in the rail and bearing pad example, if the bearing traveled past a catch stop mechanism designed to prevent back travel, you might apply an external force on the bearing pad at that position to ensure it can overcome a maximum resistance. External forces are often used just to set the simulation in motion, as well. Loads and Gravity are further defined here.

Loads

You can apply as many force and torque loads as required and manage them from the External Loads browser node, where all force and torque loads are listed once created. To apply external load forces, click the Force or Torque buttons on the Load panel, and set the location, direction, magnitude, and so on, as described here:

Location   For the Location setting, a vertex must be selected. You can select a vertex, circular edge, sketch point, work point, and so on.

Direction   For the Direction setting, select an edge or face, and then use the Flip button to change it if needed.

Magnitude   Enter the Magnitude setting as a constant, or select Input Grapher.

Fixed and Associative load buttons   Use the Fixed and Associative load buttons to designate the load direction method. Fixed sets the load to be constant to the direction it is defined. Associative sets the direction to follow the component as it moves during the simulation. For instance, if an associative direction is established using the edge of a hinge, the direction will stay aligned to that edge as the hinge swings.

The >> button   Use the >> button to set the Vector Components as required.

Display check box   Set the Display check box to see the Force or Torque arrow, and then set the scale and color of the arrow.

Gravity

You can define the gravity for the entire simulation by expanding the External Load node in the browser, right-clicking the Gravity button, and choosing Define Gravity. A default value of 386.220 in/s2 or 9810,0 mm/s2 is supplied, but you can edit this to any value required. To define gravity, you simply select an object face or edge and then use the Flip button to set the direction. You should choose static components to define gravity.

Running a Simulation

Once the model is defined with joints, loads, and environmental constraints, you are ready to run the simulation. Running the simulation entails two primary controls: the Simulation Player and the output grapher. The tools are generally used together.

SIMULATION PLAYER

You use the Simulation Player to run and stop the simulation. The Simulation Player is displayed by default but can be toggled on and off using the Simulation Player button on the Manage panel of the Dynamic Simulation tab. Figure 17.35 shows the Simulation Player options, and Table 17.1 provides a description for each.

FIGURE 17.35
The Simulation Player

TABLE 17.1: Simulation Player Options

ITEM NUMBER	TITLE	DEFINITION
1	Construction Mode	Once the simulation is run, use this button to return to the construction mode to make changes.
2	Final Time	Enter the simulation's run time.
3	Simulation Time	Displays the current time step in the running simulation.
4	Percentage of Completed Simulation	Displays the percent complete value for the running simulation.
5	Images	This value is set in construction mode to control the number of image frames displayed during the simulation. A higher number results in a higher-quality simulation display (smoother motion) but comes at the expense of performance.
6	Real Time Of Computation	Displays the amount of time it has taken to run the simulation.
7	Filter	Sets the number of images displayed during the simulation playback. If set to 10, for instance, image 1 is displayed and then image 10, skipping 2 through 9. This can be used to gain performance for large or complex simulations.
8	Player controls	These include the standard play, stop, rewind to the beginning, fast-forward to the end, and continuous loop controls, as well as a Deactivate Screen Refresh During Simulation. Deactivating the screen refresh speeds up the simulation.

OUTPUT GRAPHER

You can access the output grapher during or after running a simulation to view and use the data collected during the simulation. Data can be exported to Microsoft Excel or marked for use in the Stress Analysis environment. You can also export the results as an *.iaa file and import the file into another simulation for comparison of the graph results.

Once the curve type is selected, you can examine the time steps to see the value for each step. Figure 17.36 shows an acceleration curve displayed in the output grapher. The time step for 6 seconds is selected (1) and is marked in the graph area with a vertical line (2). You can click in the graph area to select a time stamp or select it from the top pane. You can also use the arrow keys on the keyboard to advance through each step.

FIGURE 17.36

Acceleration curve

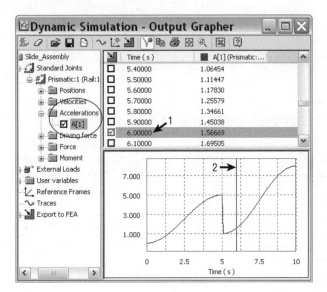

You can use the Save Simulation button to save a simulation result before making changes and then use the Import Simulation button to bring it back in once the modified simulation has been run. This allows both simulation curves to be overlaid for comparison. Figure 17.37 shows the location of the Save and Import simulations buttons in the Output Grapher dialog box. In this illustration, the original acceleration curve has been imported and overlaid on to a modified simulation. You can see that the changes made just after six seconds has slowed the extended lag time and has reduced the end acceleration from 8 in/s in the original to just over 6 in/s in the modified version. Both simulations are marked in the browser.

Also shown in Figure 17.37, the context menu is obtained by right-clicking either of the curve columns. From this menu you can search for the minimum and maximum values as well as zero values. You can also select Curve Properties and change the curve colors and well as analyze the average, minimum, maximum, median, standard deviation, and amplitude of the curve.

FIGURE 17.37
An imported acceleration curve

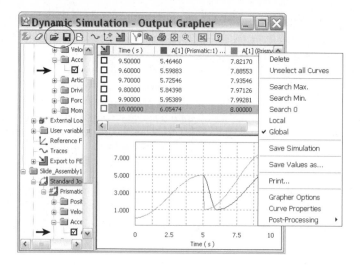

Exporting to FEA

You can use the output grapher to identify maximum forces and then export those forces for use in the Stress Analysis environment. Although the maximum stress is likely the most common value to be exported, you can export the force for any time step in the simulation. This can be useful when trying to focus on a particular event in the simulation. Here are the general steps for exporting a maximum force:

1. Select that force in the left pane of the output grapher.

2. Right-click and choose Search Max.

3. Select the check box for the time step identified as the maximum value.

4. Click the Export To FEA button in the output grapher or on the Dynamic Simulation tab.

5. Select the part or parts to export the load information to.

6. Select the load bearing faces on the part or parts.

Figure 17.38 shows the steps involved in exporting the time step to FEA. Notice that once the time step is exported, it is listed in the Export To FEA node in the output grapher browser. You should also note that you can export multiple time steps at once by selecting them all before clicking the Export To FEA button.

Using the Dynamic Simulation Information in Stress Analysis

Once you've exported the information from the Dynamic Simulation environment, you can go to the Environments tab and select the Stress Analysis button to enter that environment. Follow these general steps:

1. Click the Create Simulation button, or right-click an existing simulation and choose Edit Simulation Properties.

2. In the Simulation Properties dialog box, select the Motion Loads Analysis check box, and then select the part and time step you intend to run the simulation analysis on. Then click OK.

3. Make modifications to the simulation parameters if needed, and then run the simulation.

FIGURE 17.38
Exporting a maximum load time step to FEA

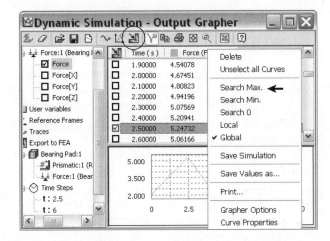

You should note that motion load analysis is limited to a single part occurrence and a single time step, per simulation. You can create multiple simulations to consider other time stamps or parts. All other components are automatically excluded from the simulation for motion loads. Figure 17.39 shows the Motion Loads option in the Simulation Properties dialog box.

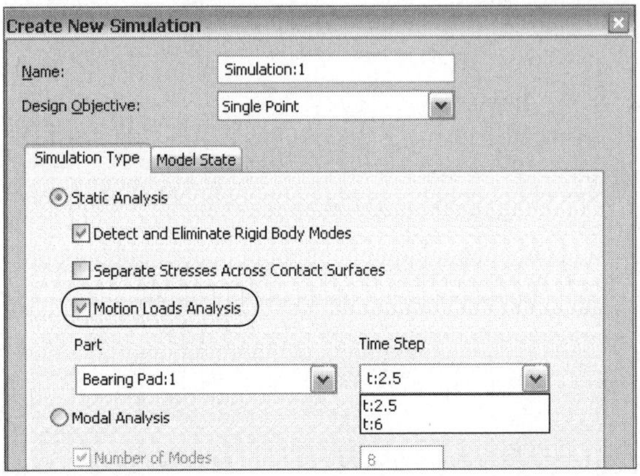

FIGURE 17.39
Enabling motion loads from dynamic simulation

Additional Resources

In addition to the step by step information and exercises in this chapter there are also fourteen tutorials that can be found by going to Get Started ≻ Learn about Inventor ≻ Tutorials. Once the Tutorials window is open you can find three tutorials in the Simulation tab.

The Bottom Line

Set up and run Stress Analysis simulations   Oftentimes you may find yourself guessing at what impact a change to your design might have on the strength and overall integrity of your part. Questions such as "Can I make this part a bit lighter?" or "Can I move this cutout closer to the edge?" become key to the success of your design.

> **Master It**   Set up a parameter study in your model to explore the consequences of editing features and their locations. Nominate all the crucial parameters to the table, and then create the configuration simulations for all of the combinations.

Set up and run Dynamic Simulation simulations   When you find yourself working out the details of a design with many moving parts, consider using the Dynamic Simulation tools early in the process to prove what will or will not work before going forward.

> **Master It**   Even before the assembly is complete, switch over to the Dynamic Simulation environment, and create assembly constraints in the simulation. Test the motion as you build the parts, and attempt to understand how contact will occur from the beginning.

Export results from the Dynamic Simulation environment to the Stress Analysis environment   Often when setting up a stress analysis simulation you are guessing at what the loads might be based on rough calculations. As you make changes to the design, those calculations become out-of-date and therefore invalid.

> **Master It**   Use the Dynamic Simulation tools to determine the force exerted on one part by another. When the parts are modified, the load calculations will automatically update based on the mass properties.

Chapter 18

Routed Systems

This chapter will cover the tools of the routed systems environments found in the Inventor Professional suite and the Inventor routed systems suite. Two primary tool sets comprise Inventor routed systems: tube and pipe and cable and harness. The tube and pipe tools are used in routing pipe and hosing through mechanical assembly designs. The cable and harness tools are used for electrical design where routing wires and cables around obstacles and checking for fit are important.

In this chapter, you will learn how to:

- ◆ Create routes and runs

- ◆ Author a tube and pipe component

- ◆ Author an electrical component

- ◆ Create and document cable and harness assemblies

Tube and Pipe

The tube and pipe tools are based on Inventor fundamental concepts such as sweeps, 3D sketch paths, adaptive parts, subassembly structure, and more. The tube and pipe tools automate many of these fundamentals, making the design of tube and pipe routes faster, more intuitive, and less tedious. However, it is best to have an understanding of these fundamental concepts before jumping into the tube and pipe tools so you can understand how Inventor does things and, therefore, how to proceed when required to manually adjust or repair your designs. A lack of understanding of these fundamentals can often bring inexperienced Inventor users to a screeching halt in their tube and pipe endeavors and may leave them with a perception that the tools just don't work. Therefore, in the following sections, you will explore how to create routes, runs, and general tube and pipe assembly structure, as well as tube and pipe styles.

Understanding Routes, Runs, and Assembly Structure

Understanding the way that tube and pipe assembly structure is created is an important part of successfully creating and managing your tube and pipe designs. There are three primary levels to any tube and pipe assembly:

- ◆ A top-level assembly

- ◆ A tube and pipe runs assembly

- ◆ A run assembly

All tube and pipe designs are comprised of runs. A *run* is a subassembly that contains one or more route paths, pipe or hose segments, and fittings. For instance, a standard hot-water supply line is a run.

When you begin a tube and pipe design, you start with a new assembly template and click the Tube And Pipe button on the Assemble tab. Doing so opens the Create Tube & Pipe Run dialog box, prompting you to set a name and location for the tube and pipe runs assembly file and the first run assembly file. Figure 18.1 shows the Create Tube & Pipe Run dialog box for a top-level assembly named mi_18a_051 being created. You can also add a new Tube and Pipe assembly to an existing assembly.

FIGURE 18.1
Create Tube & Pipe
Run dialog box

Notice that the default paths are created based on where the top-level assembly is stored. In this case, mi_18a_051.iam is stored in a directory called Workspace. The tube and pipe runs assembly is simply a container assembly created to contain the multiple runs you might create in the design. It is prefixed with the top-level assembly name and defaulted to a folder under it named the same as the top-level assembly and then AIP\Tube and Pipe.

The run assembly is prefixed with the top-level assembly name, given an incremental suffix (in this case 01), and defaulted to the same directory structure plus a subfolder named Run plus the increment number. Although you can change this file structure per tube and pipe assembly, accepting the default does maintain a certain standardization of structure. Figure 18.2 shows the assembly browser structure and file structure of a tube and pipe design set to the default paths.

Once a run is created, you can create a route within it. *Routes* are 3D paths created to define the path for pipes, tubes, or hoses to follow. In Figure 18.2, there are two elbow fittings (DIN 2605 90 Deg Elbow) that were placed outside of the run and in the tube and pipe runs assembly. Route01 was then created as a component of Run01, starting from one of the DIN elbows and running to the other. Run01 consists of Route01, three Pipe Segments, and two 90 Deg Elbows.

Although the pipe segments and the route path files were saved under the Run01 folder, you'll notice that the elbow files were saved to the Content Center Files path. Because fittings such as elbows, tees, and couplings are generated from Content Center, these part files are automatically saved to the Content Center Files path defined in either your project file or your Application Options settings.

Here are a few things to note when working with tube and pipe runs:

◆ A unique part file is created for each pipe, tube, and hose segment in the run, even if more than one segment is the same length. Although this may seem a departure from what you'd expect, this is key to allowing runs to be edited downstream.

◆ Enter meaningful names for the runs and routes as you create them. As you create more complex designs, the abundance or multiple Route01s scattered throughout the assembly may create confusion during edits.

FIGURE 18.2
Assembly and file structure of tube and pipe design

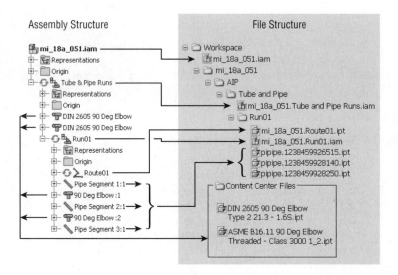

Exploring the Tube and Pipe Styles

Runs and routes are determined by tube and pipe styles. Properties such as material, diameter, and fitting types are set in the tube and pipe style. Rules such as minimum and maximum segment length can also be set in the style. The Inventor tube and pipe tools load with several default styles based upon the ANSI, DIN, ISO, and JIS tube and pipe standards and the Parker hose and fittings. Styles fall into three primary categories:

Flexible hoses   These are single hose segments connected by a start point and endpoint selection. The hose style can include, but is not required to have, fittings for the start and stop points.

Rigid tubing   This does not contain elbows and follows a default bend radius. The radius can be set per bend as needed. Minimum and maximum segment lengths are set in the style, and couplings are placed where segments connect.

Rigid piping   These styles are required to include 90-degree elbow fittings and can include 45-degree elbows, flanges, and couplings. There are three subcategories for rigid piping styles:

Self-draining   These styles require a pipe, a coupling, a 45-degree elbow, a 90-degree elbow, and a custom elbow or tee to match the desired slope angle.

Welded   These styles require a pipe and a 90-degree elbow. Butt welded styles require a weld gap size.

Flanged   These styles require a pipe, an elbow, a flange, and optionally a gasket.

Figure 18.3 shows a flexible hose run, a rigid tubing run, and a rigid piping run, from top to bottom.

FIGURE 18.3
Hose, tube, and
pipe runs

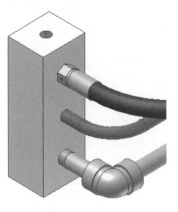

THE TUBE & PIPE STYLES DIALOG BOX

You can access the Tube & Pipe Styles dialog box from the master tube and pipe runs assembly, the run assembly, or the route by clicking the Tube And Pipe Styles button on the Ribbon or by using the default right-click context menu. The dialog box is divided into a pane on the left listing the styles and two tabs on the right controlling the general settings and the style rules. Figure 18.4 shows the Tube & Pipe Styles dialog box with a Hydraulic Hose style set active, denoted in bold. A second style is selected and has been right-clicked, showing the options that correspond with the buttons along the top of the dialog box.

FIGURE 18.4
Tube & Pipe Styles
dialog box

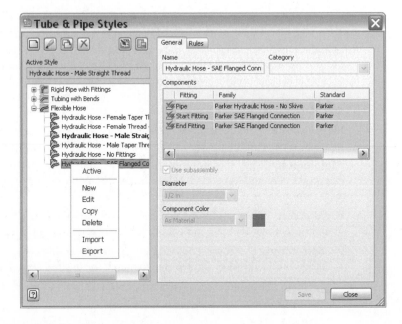

When editing, copying, or creating a new style, some components may be either required or optional, depending upon the style type. If the component is not specified and it is required, it will be marked with a red arrow next to it in the General tab. If it is empty and shows a gray arrow, it is optional. When the component is selected, the arrow will be green. Figure 18.5 shows two style types being created from scratch.

FIGURE 18.5
Creating
pipe styles

On the left side, a Butt Welded style required a pipe and a 90-degree elbow. The pipe has been selected, but the elbow is still required, as indicated by the red (dark) arrow. The 45-degree elbow is not required, and its optional status is indicated by the gray (light) arrow. On the right side of Figure 18.5, a Flanged pipe style is being created; note that more components are listed. Pipe, Elbow 90, and Flange are the component categories required for this style, with Pipe having already been selected. In both images, the user has right-clicked in the Elbow 90 row and selected Browse in order to specify the required elbow type. You can also double-click a row to open the style library browser.

In the style library browser, you can select from the list of available styles based upon the size, schedule, and material settings made in the General tab and the availability from the Content Center library. You can set additional filtering in the style library browser. When you set the filter to a particular standard, the materials available for that particular standard are listed. If an asterisk is displayed, all the content for that setting is displayed.

Back in the Tube & Pipe Styles dialog box, you can specify a minimum and maximum size range for creating route segments on the Rules tab. It is recommended that you set the minimum segment length to at least 1.5 times the nominal diameter value to avoid minimum segment length violations that occur when pipe segments are too small in relation to the nominal diameter.

Each style type has different rule criteria:

♦ For Rigid Tubes, you can set the default bend radius for the bends.

♦ For Flexible Hoses, you can set a minimum bend radius and hose length round-up value.

♦ For Butt Welded pipe styles, you can set the gap size for the groove welds and control the display of the gaps in the graphics display and in drawings.

♦ For Butt Welded Flanged pipes, you can specify the coupling style.

♦ Fitting connections are determined by the end treatment set for the particular fitting.

♦ All other end treatments use a gap at segments and fitting joints.

Generally, it is best practice to set the style before creating routes and placing fittings. However, you can create and apply styles at any time. Setting styles can be done in a number of ways. You can change the active style for the tube and pipe assembly so that all new runs follow the style; you do this by selecting a style from the Style drop-down. Or you can change the style for the active route by setting that route active and using the Style drop-down to select a different style. You cannot change a rigid pipe route to a flexible hose style or vice versa. To make such a change, you must delete the route and re-create it.

AUTHORING TUBE AND PIPE COMPONENTS

Tube and pipe components, like components for other applications, require authoring before they can be published into Content Center. The tube and pipe authoring process is more complex because the router uses the component geometry. For example, the router needs to know the difference between a tee and an elbow, and it needs to know how much the connector overlaps the pipe.

In this example, we will show how to author a PVC pipe to an NPT adaptor:

1. On the Get Started tab, click Open, and browse to the Chapter 18 directory in the Mastering Inventor 2011 folder.

2. Open file `mi_18a_010.ipt`.

3. Switch to the Manage tab, and select Tube And Pipe from the Authoring drop-down list. The Tube & Pipe Authoring dialog box displays, and the part changes to shaded wireframe display.

4. Select Adapters from the Type drop-down, as shown in Figure 18.6.

5. Change the number of connections, and observe that the connection buttons update to match. Confirm that Connections is set to 2.

FIGURE 18.6
Setting the fitting type

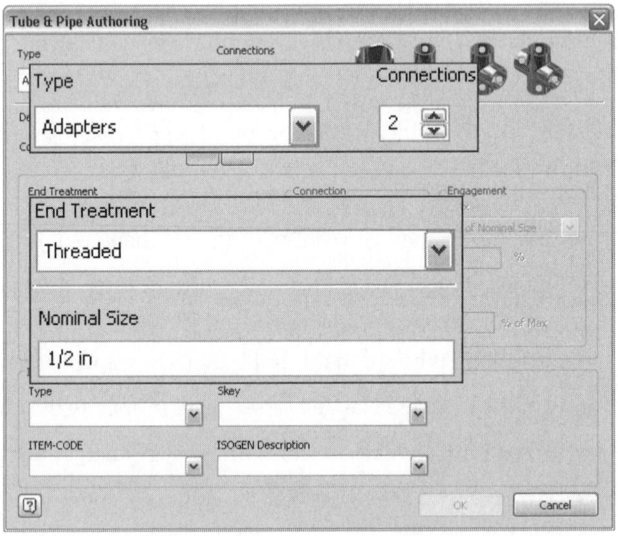

6. Confirm that the End Treatment is set to Threaded, and enter **1/2 in** for the Nominal Size setting.

7. By default, the button for connection 1 is active. Select one of the circular edges to define the connection point. Click the Axis button, and select the z-axis from the Origin folder in the browser. An arrow displays, showing the connection direction, as shown in Figure 18.7. The default connection type is Female, but you can set it to Male or Neutral (for flanged or butt welded fittings).

FIGURE 18.7
Defining the connection and engagement

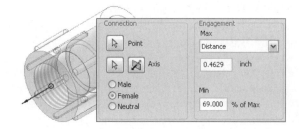

8. The Engagement defines the maximum and minimum overlap between the connector and pipe. The router needs a range because the pipe usually has a minimum length increment. The engagement range allows the router to adjust the position of the pipe in the fittings.

9. To determine the Engagement, go to the Design Data folder (the default location is `C:\Program Files\Autodesk\Inventor 2011\Design Data`), and open `Threads.xls`. Select the NPT For PVC Pipe And Fitting tab. For tapered threads, the engagement value depends on how tightly the fitting is screwed onto the pipe. You need the maximum engagement value, so add the Handtight Engagement value, which is 0.32, and the Wrench Makeup, Internal value, which is 0.1429. Set Max to Distance, and enter **0.4629** for the total value. For Min, divide the handtight engagement, 0.32, by the total engagement, 0.4629, which comes to **69%**.

10. Click the 2 button to define the other connection.

11. In this example, Socket Welded was chosen as the End Treatment setting, since that seemed to be the best description. You should choose an end treatment that is consistent with your other parts.

12. Select a circle at the opposite end of the part for the connection point, and select the z-axis again. You will see that the arrow points into the adapter, and the orange line representing the engagement is outside of the part. Using the flip/arrow button next to the Axis button, change the direction so that the arrow is to the outside, and then engagement is to the inside, as shown in Figure 18.8.

FIGURE 18.8
Connection direction and engagement

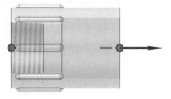

13. The depth of the socket is 0.84 inch. You don't want to design to full depth engagement because of tolerances, so set Max to Distance and specify **0.75** as the depth. For Min, accept the default value of 50%.

14. The ISOGEN data is optional. For this exercise, this information will be left blank. Click OK to complete authoring the adapter.

Now that the part has been authored as a tube and pipe adaptor, it is ready to be published to a read/write Content Center library. You can find more information on publishing parts to Content Center in Chapter 7, "Part and Feature Reuse."

Placing Fittings

Fittings can be placed from Content Center or from a user-created directory of authored fittings. As a rule, you should use the place tools found on the tube and pipe tabs rather than placing fittings as you would normal assembly parts. The place options on the tube and pipe tabs ensure that the authored connections are used as intended. Figure 18.9 shows the place options available on the Pipe Run tab.

FIGURE 18.9

Place options

When fittings are placed, either from Content Center or from a user-defined library of authored fittings, you can drag the fitting over the route segments or nodes, and you will see the placement point appear. Use the spacebar to toggle through available orientations if more than one exists. When you click to place the fitting, the Select Orientation tools appears, allowing you to rotate the orientation to the desired position.

You can edit connections by right-clicking them while the route is active for edits and choosing Edit Fitting Connections. In the Edit Connections dialog box, you can select a segment and then use the X button to remove the connection. You can also select Change Fitting Diameter and Edit Fitting Orientation, as shown in Figure 18.10.

FIGURE 18.10

Editing fitting options

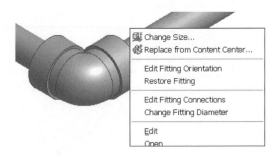

Creating Routes

Routes define the path for pipe and hose segments and the corresponding fittings. Route paths can have a simple start point and endpoint or can include as many intermediate points as are required. Several tools and options are used to start and create route paths:

Authored connection points   You can use any the predefined connection points for any library fitting or custom-authored part. When you move your mouse pointer over the library fitting, the connection point(s) will highlight.

Circular edges   You can use any circular edge in the assembly to set the route point at the center of it with the exception of authored parts such as fittings. For those parts, only the authored connection points can be used.

Precise and offset start points   You can hover your mouse pointer over an edge to display a direction arrow. Running your mouse pointer along that arrow allows you to select the arrow to set the offset at that distance, or you can right-click and choose Enter Distance. If the arrow points the wrong direction, you can use the spacebar to toggle it or right-click and choose Select Other Direction. Figure 18.11 shows the offset start point options.

FIGURE 18.11
Offsetting a
start point

3D Orthogonal Route tool   Once a start point is selected, run your mouse pointer along the projected axis and click or use the right-click menu's Enter Distance option to set a value for the second point. You will then be presented with the 3D Orthogonal Route tool. You can use the control handles to change the angle or rotate the control. The cross arrow toggles between 90-degree and 45-degree solutions, and the arc arrows allow you to rotate the route tool. You can also right-click and choose Custom Bend to enter an angle other than 90 or 45. When you enter a Custom Bend angle that cannot be accommodated with an elbow fitting, Inventor will place a bend in the tube or pipe segment. When the 3D Orthogonal Route tool is displayed, you can use the + and - keys to change the size of it onscreen. Figure 18.12 shows the 3D Orthogonal Route tool used to rotate the route at 60 degrees.

FIGURE 18.12
3D Orthogonal
Route tool

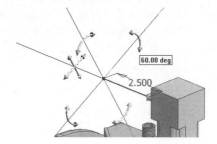

Route nodes   When placing a point along a route or setting an offset start point, you will see a colored dot tracking along the Route tool. If it is a yellow *X*, the offset is not enough to create a minimum segment as set in the style rules, and the point cannot be selected. If it is a blue dot, the segment might be too short to accommodate an elbow, but you are allowed to select it. If it is a green dot, the location is satisfactory to all of the style rules. In Figure 18.13, the node showing 5.537 appears in is green and indicates the location will produce no issues.

FIGURE 18.13
Route nodes

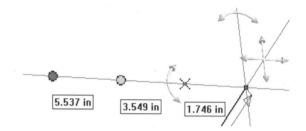

Autoroute options   You can select the start point and endpoint of a route and use the Autoroute tool to flip through the available Autoroute solutions. You can also use this to close two parts of an already created route. Use the Select Other tool to toggle through all the Autoroute variations. Once an Autoroute is created, use the Move Segment button to adjust the segments and create new solutions. Figure 18.14 shows a variation with five segments at 29.268 inches on the left and an adjustment being made later using the Move Segment tool on the right.

FIGURE 18.14
Autoroute and
move segment
options

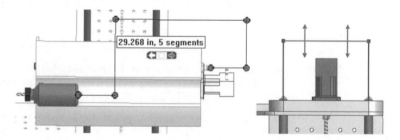

Sketched routes   Route paths can also be based on an existing 3D sketch. These 3D sketches are used as the route by deriving the geometry into the route. Changes to the 3D sketch update the route automatically. You can use the Include Geometry tool to include any existing part edges in the route. You can also switch to the 3D Sketch tab while creating a route and use the standard 3D sketch tools to create route geometry as required. Whether routing in the tool or using a Derived route, watch the visual cues offered by the sketch. Now you will use a combination of tools to create two types of pipe and tubing routes.

1. On the Get Started tab, click Open, and browse to the Chapter 18 directory in the Mastering Inventor 2011 folder.

2. Open file mi_18a_015.iam.

3. Select the Tube and Pipe tool in the Begin panel of the Assemble tab.

4. Accept the defaults offered by the Create Tube & Pipe Run dialog by clicking OK

In the browser you will see a Run has been created and it is active. There is also a specialized tab added to the ribbon named Pipe Run.

5. In the Manage panel of the Pipe Run tab, use the pull down to select the *ASME B36.10M-ASME B11 - Steel Threaded Pipe* style.

6. Pick the New Route icon in the Route panel.

7. Click OK to approve the default values for the Create Route dialog.

8. Another new tab will appear named Route. Pick the Derived Route button in the Create panel.

9. Select the path that was already present in the assembly, as shown in Figure 18.15.

FIGURE 18.15
Selecting an existing 3D sketch as a Piping Route

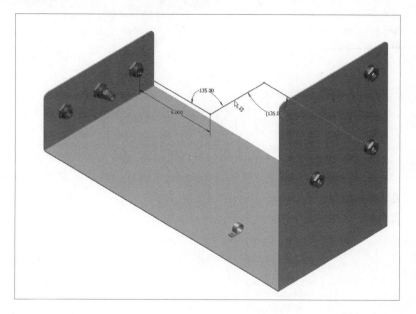

10. Right-click and select Done from the context menu to use the selected sketch as part of your pipe route.

This will add four route points to the route in the browser. Rather than focusing on all of the geometry, the reuse of the points improves performance.

11. Pick the Finish Route tool from the Route tab to return to the Pipe Run tools.

12. In the Route panel, select the Populate Route tool to check that the route displays properly.

13. Once the route has properly previewed, you can select the Finish Tube and Pipe Run tool. See Figure 18.16.

FIGURE 18.16
The Piping run created from the 3D sketch

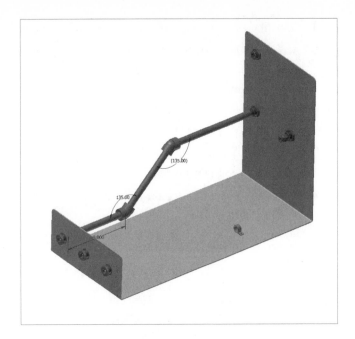

14. Pick the Finish Tube and Pipe tool on the Tube and Pipe tab to exit the Tube and Pipe environment and return to the assembly.

15. In the browser expand the mi_18a_012 part in the browser and double-click the 3D Sketch to edit it.

16. Change the 9 inch dimension in the sketch to 11.

17. Change the 135 degree dimension that does not have parentheses around it to 90 and see Figure 18.17

FIGURE 18.17
The updated 3D sketch

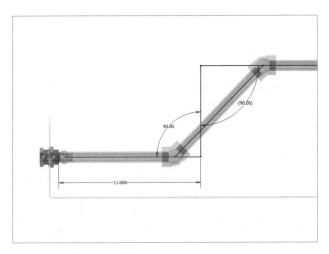

18. Click Finish Sketch and then Return to update the assembly and the pipe route that you created based upon it.

19. Turn off the visibility of the 3D sketch and save your work.

The use of a 3D sketch is not necessary to place a run like this, but it can be easier for some users to visualize the route before starting the routing tools. It is also a great tool for people who've used 3D sketches and Sweep features to replicate piping runs in the past.

Now let's look at using the 3D Orthogonal Route tool to create a tubing section.

1. Select the Tube and Pipe tool again and accept the dialog to create a new run, noting that the run name has been incremented from the first run.

2. In the Manage panel, set the style to *ASTM B 88-ASME B16.22 - Soldered Copper Tubing*.

3. Select the New Route tool accepting the default naming.

4. Now pick the Route tool from the Create panel.

5. Rotate the assembly so you can see the fitting in the center of three fittings in a row.

6. As you near the fitting points for engagement, arrows indicating the initial direction of a run will appear. Select the option that will set the direction toward the other fittings, as shown in Figure 18.18, and click the mouse when it is highlighted.

FIGURE 18.18
Setting the direction towards the other fittings

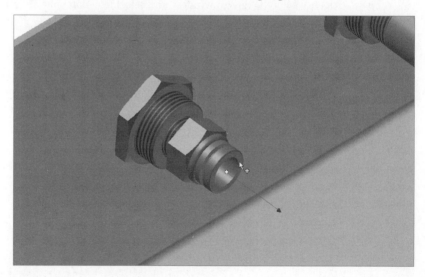

After the selection is made, a centerline will be displayed. Move your mouse along the line and a dimension will display your distance from the selected point. See Figure 18.19. You can increase the length the of the line by pressing the + key, or you can enter a value that will ignore the length of the preview.

FIGURE 18.19
The preview allows
you to visually
place the end of the
first segment.

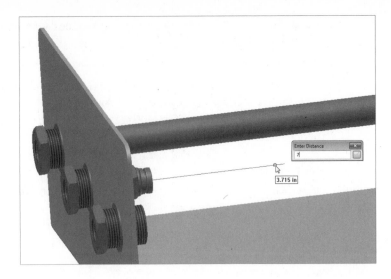

7. Press the 7 key to set the length and press Enter to create the first segment to 7 inches.

8. After creating the first segment appears and the route nodes appear, right-click in an open area of the design window and select Rotation Snap from the context menu.

9. Click and drag the curved arrow on the green axis and move your mouse to the opposite fitting, as shown in Figure 18.20, and pick that fitting.

FIGURE 18.20
Rotation and Point
snaps aid in build-
ing between
fittings.

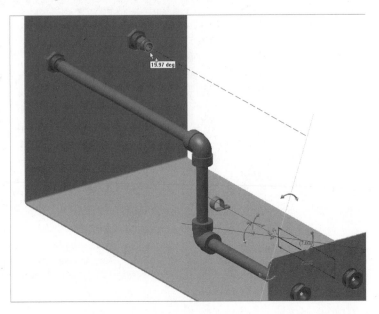

This will align the route nodes to the second fitting and allow a great deal of flexibility in building a complex route.

10. Now select the engagement node on the second fitting.

11. This will present a preview of a route. The preview will include the number of segments and the Select Other icon so you can cycle between options.

12. Select the option that will create 2 segments by picking the green icon in the Select Other icon.

13. Finish and then populate the route.

14. Now select Finish Tube and Pipe Run.

Flexible hose routes are similar to rigid pipe routes with a few exceptions. Whereas rigid pipe paths are a series of line segments connected with arcs or points, the flexible hose paths consist of a single spline segment. Flexible routes offer a couple of tools and options specific to this type of route, such as the ability to right-click a surface, select Enter Offset, and then adjust the hose length. You can use these options in the general steps to create flexible hose routes listed here:

1. Select the Create Pipe Run tool and accept the defaults.

2. Set the style to *Hydraulic Hose - Male Taper Thread*.

3. Create the new route and accept its default name.

4. Click the Route tool.

With this style of hose, rather than selecting an existing fitting for the hose to begin on, you'll be asked to select the location for two fittings that will be placed before any routing options are offered.

5. Place the first fitting on the remaining anchor fitting that is in line.

6. Place the second fitting on the last remaining fitting on the opposite side.

Placing the second fitting will generate the spline centerline of the hose. At this point you can create additional points offset from faces on the part or even use natural centers on curved faces to pass the hose through.

7. Select the curved edge of the Hose Retainer, as shown in Figure 18.21, to route the hose through the retainer.

8. Once the hose center is displayed use the Hose Length tool in the Manage panel and use the slide bar to set the hose length to 44 inches.

9. Click OK to complete the path for the hose.

10. Finish and populate the route and Finish the Tube and Pipe Run and compare to Figure 18.22.

There are a number of options that can go along with creating these routes that should be explored. There is also the ability to add fittings inline. These added fittings will break the segments of pipes and tubes to create room for the fittings and set their engagement with the fittings automatically. If you later remove the fitting, the pipe will be "healed" and restored to a single segment.

FIGURE 18.21
Routing the hose
through a retainer

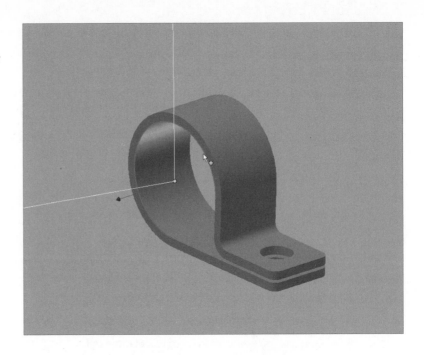

FIGURE 18.22
The completed
routes

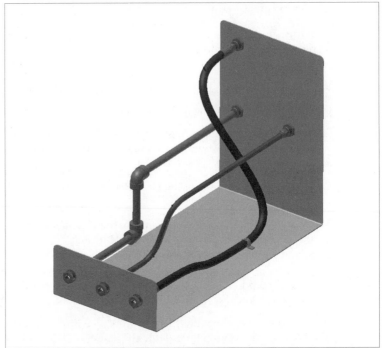

Exporting ISOGEN Files

Often isometric centerline drawings are required for straight pipe fittings documentation of tube and pipe designs. The ISOGEN Output tool is available on both the Tube And Pipe tab and the Pipe Run tab. You can save all your tube and pipe runs as an ISOGEN (`*.pcf`) file directly from the master run assembly; just click the ISOGEN Output button on the Tube And Pipe tab. Or you can use the ISOGEN Output button while at the individual run level to save just that run. When flanged routes are created, gaskets are required for flanged connections if ISOGEN files are to be created from them.

Cable and Harness

The cable and harness tools in Inventor are based on the fundamental tools of part and assembly creation; however, the parts and assemblies created with the cable and harness tools are structured differently than standard part and assembly models. Understanding these differences requires a solid understanding of the way that standard part and assemblies are created and structured. In the following sections, you will explore the creation and placement of electrical parts, harnesses, wires, cables, and segments, as well as how to copy and document cable and harness designs.

Creating and Placing Electrical Parts

You can use any Inventor model as an electrical connector by adding cable and harness–specific pin features to them. Parts can be created from scratch using standard modeling techniques or downloaded from supplier websites, as well as a number of 3D content websites such as `http://mfgcommunity.autodesk.com/content/`. When downloading content from the Internet, you will often find models in other formats such as STEP, IGES, Solidworks, and so on. These files can be translated into Inventor files using the methods described in Chapter 14, "Exchanging Data with Other Systems."

AUTHORING ELECTRICAL COMPONENTS

The basic steps to turn a standard Inventor part into an electrical component are as follows:

1. Open the part file in Inventor.

2. Click the Place Pin tool in the Harness panel of the Model tab.

3. Select one of the following to place the pin:

    ◆ Center point of any circular edge, face, or hole

    ◆ Visible sketch points

    ◆ Work points

    ◆ Model vertex points

    ◆ Any model face

4. Enter a unique pin name/number.

5. Click the Harness Properties button in the pin naming input box to enter additional pin properties if required.

6. Repeat steps 3 through 4 for each pin.

7. Click the Harness Properties tool in the Harness panel of the Model tab.

8. Enter a reference designator (RefDes) placeholder. The RefDes property is intended to be used at the assembly level where each instance of the connector will have a unique RefDes.

9. Select a Gender option (Male, Female, or None).

10. Set a wire offset point if required.

CREATING A CONNECTOR

In the following steps, you will open an existing Inventor part file and create pins as just described. Figure 18.23 shows the Harness tools available in the parts environment.

1. On the Get Started tab, click Open.

2. Browse for the file named mi_18a_007.ipt in the Chapter 18 directory of the Mastering Inventor 2011 folder, and open it.

3. Click the Place Pin button in the Harness panel of the Model tab.

4. Select the visible sketch point.

5. Enter **A1** in the Place Pin input box, and click the Harness Properties button.

6. Select the Custom tab, click the Name drop-down, and select Embedded Length.

7. Enter 5 mm in the Value input box, and then click OK. Then click the green check mark, or press Enter on the keyboard to set the pin.

8. To place the next pin, click the rounded edge on one of the top cutouts, enter **A2** for the pin name, and then set the pin without entering any harness properties.

9. Click roughly in the center of the blue square face to set the third pin, and enter **B1** for the name.

10. Right-click and click Done to exit the Place Pin tool.

11. In the Work Features panel of the Model tab, click the Point button to create a work point.

12. Right-click and select Loop Select, and then click the square profile edge for the remaining cutout. Be certain you are selecting the outer edge loop and not the inner loop. Right-click and click Done.

13. Select the Place Pin tool again, and select the work point you just created. Set the name to **B2**, right-click, and choose Done.

14. Next edit Extrusion1, and change the Distance from 10 mm to 15 mm.

FIGURE 18.23
Harness part tools

Notice which work points hold their positions relative to the geometry and which ones remain at the position they were created in. You can right-click the pins that didn't update as expected and choose Redefine Feature. Note that when redefining a pin, you can right-click and choose Loop Select; this option is available when redefining a pin but not when placing the pin originally. Understanding how pin locations will update is important when defining a connector part intended for use in iPart creation where you will want the pin location to update as different pin sizes are created. For static pins not likely to change, nonassociative pins work just fine.

In addition to redefining the pin location, you can right-click any pin in the browser and choose Harness Properties to change the name or add/edit properties. Keep in mind that pin names must be unique.

PLACE PIN GROUPS

Although the Place Pin tool works well for defining pins not arranged in a pattern or for small numbers of pattered pins, you can use the Place Pin Group tool to place larger numbers of patterned pins. The following steps explore the Pin Group tool:

1. On the Get Started tab, click Open.

2. Browse for the file named mi_18a_009.ipt in the Chapter 18 directory of the Mastering Inventor 2011 folder, and open it.

3. Click the Place Pin Group button in the Harness panel of the Model tab.

4. For Start Location, select WorkPoint1.

5. Enter **8** for the number of pins per row.

6. Enter 4.5 mm for the pin pitch (spacing), and then select an edge to establish the pin direction. Use the flip arrow if required.

7. Enter **2** for the number of rows.

8. Enter 4.5 mm for the row pitch, and then select an edge to establish the pin direction. Use the flip arrow if required.

9. Enter **A** for the prefix letter and **101** for the start number.

10. Switch the radio button for the numbering scheme options to Sequential Column, Circumventing, and then back to Sequential Row to see differences in each.

11. Click OK to set the pins. Figure 18.24 shows the Place Pin Group dialog box settings and pin group.

FIGURE 18.24
Creating a
pin group

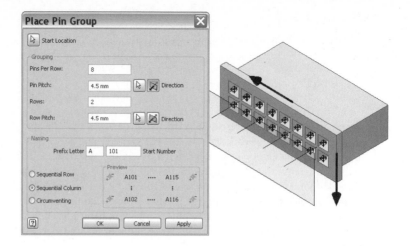

Notice the 16 pins created and listed in the Model browser. You can right-click any of the pins and choose Edit Pin Group to change the start point, spacing, and direction if required. You can also right-click and select Delete Pin Group to start over, or you can select Delete to remove an individual pin. Note too that you can right-click any of the pins and choose Redefine Feature to set an individual pin to a nonpatterned location.

As a final step, you will create four work points in front of the connector for use later as a stop point for the wire or cable segment.

12. Click the Point button on the Work Features panel of the Model tab.

13. Right-click and ensure that Loop Select is not selected.

14. Click the edge of the visible work plane and then one of the work axes. You'll see a work point created at the intersection. Do the same for the remaining three axes, and then right-click each axis and the plane and turn off their visibility.

The work points allow you to place the end of wire segments appropriately off the connector. Figure 18.25 shows a connector utilizing a segment-end work point.

FIGURE 18.25
Work points for
segment ends

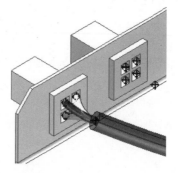

Creating a Harness

Electrical components including connectors, wires, and cables are assembled and constructed within a harness subassembly. Although you can place connectors at any structure level within the assembly and route wires to them, as a rule you typically place connectors within the harness assembly when the harness and connectors are purchased together so that your BOM will reflect the harness as an item. The general steps for creating and routing a wire harness are as follows:

1. In an assembly file, place and constrain connector parts that will not be part of the harness assembly into the assembly either at the top level or within a subassembly.

2. Click the Cable And Harness button in the Begin panel of the Assemble tab.

3. Enter a name and location for the harness subassembly file to be created.

4. Place and constrain connectors to be part of the harness.

5. Use the Create Wire, Create Cable, or Create Ribbon Cable tools to connect the pins of the connectors.

6. Use the Create Segment tool to create wire bundles, routing them around geometry obstacles of other parts in the assembly.

7. Use the Route or Automatic Route tool to route the wires or cables through the segments (wire bundles).

8. Use the Create Splice tool to create wire or segment splices as required.

When a harness is created, it is composed of a harness assembly file and a harness part file of the same name. The part file is the container in which the wires, cables, and segments will be built as they are added. Both files comprise the overall harness and are required for the harness to work. Inventor will warn you if you try to edit these files directly rather than through a top-level assembly using the wire harness tools.

In the following steps, you will open an existing Inventor assembly file, create a simple harness assembly, and then place connectors.

1. On the Get Started tab, click Open.

2. Browse for the file named mi_18a_018.iam in the Chapter 18 directory of the Mastering Inventor 2011 folder, and open it.

3. On the Assemble tab, click the Cable And Harness button in the Begin panel.

4. Accept the default name and location for new harness assembly, and click OK. Note the harness subassembly and part nodes listed in the browser.

5. Click the Assemble tab, and then click the Place Component button.

6. Browse for and locate the connector file named mi_18a_004.ipt, and click Open.

7. Click twice in the graphics area to place two instances of the connector; then right-click and select Done.

To assemble the connectors (residing in the subassembly) to the base part (residing in the top-level assembly), you'll need to return to the top-level assembly and place the constraints.

Parts within the harness can constrain to the parts in the top-level assembly because the harness subassembly is adaptive.

8. Click the Finish Cable And Harness button to return to the top-level assembly.

9. Place an Insert constraint on the connectors and the holes on the outside flanges. Ensure that the connector pins face the inside of the base part.

10. Click the Finish Cable And Harness button to return to the top-level assembly. You can close this file when done.

This simple exercise illustrates the steps required to create a harness subassembly and place connectors within it. You can also place connectors in the top-level assembly before creating the harness assembly and then demote components from the top-level assembly into the harness subassembly. To do so, follow these steps:

1. Place the connectors in the top-level assembly.

2. Create the harness assembly.

3. Next while the harness subassembly is active, expand it in the browser.

4. Click the connector components in the browser, and drag them down into the harness assembly.

SETTING GLOBAL HARNESS SETTINGS

You can access the settings for the entire harness by right-clicking the top-level node of the harness in the browser while it is active for edits.

Placing Wires

Once the harness assembly is created and the electrical connector parts are added and constrained, you can add wires and/or cables. When wires are created, you enter a unique wire ID name, select a wire category, and set the wire name (type). Then you select the two pins you want to run a wire from and to. To see how the Create Wire tool works, open the file named mi_18a_020.iam in the Chapter 18 directory of the Mastering Inventor 2011 folder, and follow these steps:

1. Double-click the Harness subassembly to set it active for edits (or right-click it and choose Edit).

2. On the Cable And Harness tab, click the Create Wire button.

3. Set Wire ID to **Wire101**.

4. Select Generic from the Category drop-down.

5. Set the Name drop-down to 14AWG-BLK.

6. Select the Pin 1 (work point) on one of the red connectors for the Pin 1 selection. You'll see the pin number when you pause your mouse pointer over the pin. Figure 18.26 shows the pin selection and wire settings.

FIGURE 18.26
Placing a wire
on pin 1

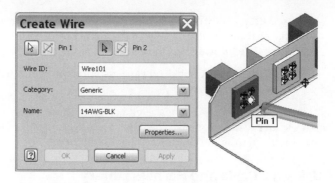

7. Select the Pin 1 (work point) on the other red connector for the Pin 2 selection.

8. Click Apply to set the wire. It should run in a straight line between the two connectors.

9. Set the remaining three pins for the red connectors as listed here:

   ◆ Pin 2 = Wire102, Generic 14AWG-RED

   ◆ Pin 3 = Wire103, Generic 14AWG-WHT

   ◆ Pin 4 = Wire104, Generic 14AWG-GRN

10. Once you set all four wires, click Cancel to exit the Create Wire dialog box.

11. In this assembly, a segment (blue wire bundle) has already been created. Click the Route button to route a wire through the segment.

12. Click just one of the wires for the Wires selection, and then click the segment for the First Segment selection.

13. Select the Single Segment check box, and then click Apply. Note that the segment will shrink to size based on the wire.

14. Click Cancel to exit the Route dialog box, and then click the Automatic Route button.

15. In the Auto Route dialog box, select the All Unrouted Wires check box, and click OK.

16. Expand the Harness1 part node in the browser, and you'll notice a Wires folder containing all of the wires you created. Right-click Wire101, and choose Harness Properties. Browse the tab to examine the read/write and read-only properties available for this wire. When finished, return to the Occurrence tab, set the Bend Radius to 2× diameter, and then click OK.

17. Right-click the Wires folder in the browser, and select Bend Radius ➢ Check All Bend Radii.

18. Note that you will receive a warning stating that one or more objects contain an empty bend radius. Click OK, and note that wires 102 through 104 are marked with a warning icon in the browser. In this case, the warning indicates the bend radius has not been set. You can edit the wire property, set the bend radius, and then repeat the bend radii check. If the bend radius for each wire in the model is in compliance with the setting for that wire, then the check will clear. Editing segments will be covered more in the "Placing

and Editing Segments" section. Now that the problem area is identified, you could make the decision to either change the general layout of the assembly or edit the segment route to change the fit so that the bend isn't so sharp.

19. Click the Finish Cable And Harness button to return to the top-level assembly. You can close this file when done.

This simple exercise demonstrated how to create wires in a harness and the routing of these wires in an existing segment. The wire categories and names listed in the Create Wires dialog box are drawn from the Cable And Harness library.

Using the Cable And Harness Library

The Cable And Harness library is located in the Design Data folder but can be set per harness. In most cases, you will want to configure it per the Inventor Design Data folder. You can set this option by right-clicking a harness assembly while it is active for edits, selecting Harness Settings, and then going to the File Locations tab.

The library file name that installs by default is `Cable&HarnessDefaultLibrary.iwl`. You can locate this file by checking the Design Data path in your Inventor project file (`*.ipj`) or by going to the File tab of the Application Options dialog box. Recall that the project Design Data path trumps the application's Options path if set.

To add objects to the Cable And Harness Library, click the Library button on the Manage panel of the Cable And Harness tab. You can add new wire, cable, and segment objects, just to name a few, and you can create your own custom object type. Figure 18.27 shows the library being edited.

FIGURE 18.27
Cable and harness library

Placing Cables

Adding cables is much like adding wires. To explore the cable tools, open the file called `mi_18a_022.iam` in the Chapter 18 directory of the Mastering Inventor 2011 folder.

1. Double-click the Harness subassembly to set it active for edits, or right-click it and select Edit.

2. Click the Create Cable button on the Cable And Harness tab.

3. Set Cable ID to **C201**, and set Category to **Alpha**.

4. Select **2254/4** from the Name drop-down.

5. Note that Conductor ID 1 is set active. Select the Pin 1 (work point) on one of the gray connectors for the Pin 1 selection. You'll see the pin number when you pause your mouse pointer over the pin.

6. Select the Pin 1 (work point) on the other gray connector for the Pin 2 selection. Note that the conductor ID advances automatically to the next line.

7. Set the remaining three pins for the gray connectors as listed here:

   ◆ Pin 2 = C201:2, Red

   ◆ Pin 3 = C201:3, White

   ◆ Pin 4 = C201:4, Green

8. Click OK to set the cable.

9. Click the Automatic Route button, select the All Unrouted Wires check box, and click OK.

10. Expand the Cables folder in the browser and then right-click the listed cable and choose Harness Properties. Note the Bend radius is set to 10 × diameter. If you click in the input box, you will see that the value is being pulled from the Cable And Harness Library. Click OK to exit the dialog box.

11. Right-click the cable, and choose Bend Radius ➢ Check. Click OK in the warning dialog box.

12. Note that the cable browser node has turned red to indicate a problem. Right-click it in the browser, and select Bend Radius ➢ Show Violations. You will see a red marker on the segment in the graphics area along with a dialog box. Click OK.

13. Click the Finish Cable And Harness button to return to the top-level assembly. You can close this file when done.

The check bend radius function allows you to locate problem areas with the design. You could remedy the violation either by adjusting the segment points in an attempt to modify the fit of the cable route or by moving components and/or features in the assembly. Often a design might require adjusting both the assembly arrangement and the cable routing. But it's important to be able to check for bend radius violations so that you can determine what needs adjustment. In the next section, you will explore segment creation and editing.

Placing and Editing Segments

Segments are used to define the route path in which wires and cables will be run though a design so as to avoid interference and identify possible problem areas where bend radii may be too tight. A segment is created by selecting geometry on-screen, either outright or as an offset base. For each selection or offset point, a work point is created.

Once segments are created, you can refine them by adding points or redefining existing points. To explore the cable tools, open the file called mi_18a_024.iam in the Chapter 18 directory of the Mastering Inventor 2011 folder.

1. Double-click the Harness subassembly to set it active for edits, or right-click it and select Edit.

2. Click the Create Segment button on the Cable And Harness tab.

3. You will first run a route segment from the red to green connectors. Select the work point in front of the red connector for the start point of the segment.

4. Next click any circular edge on the black grommet hole; this will select the center. Repeat this for the green grommet hole.

5. For the third point, you will specify an offset value and then select the flange with the two square-shaped notches along the top.

   ◆ First right-click and choose Edit Offset.

   ◆ Enter 10 mm in the Edit Offset box, and then click OK.

   ◆ Rub your mouse pointer around on different faces to observe the way the offset behaves. Then select roughly in the center of the face of the notched flange in front of the green connector.

6. Next select the work point in front of the green connector.

7. Right-click and choose Continue.

8. Next you'll create another short segment from the orange connector and tie it into the first segment. Select the work point in front of the orange connector.

9. Then click the work point at the center of the green grommet hole, and click Finish. Figure 18.28 shows the segments.

FIGURE 18.28
The created
segments

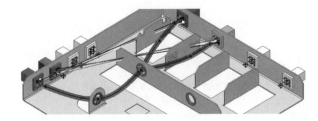

Use the Automatic Route tool and select the All Unrouted Wires option to route the wires through the segments. Upon doing so, you'll notice two things:

◆ The segments adjust to compensate for the wire diameters.

◆ The cable coming off the blue connector has routed in an undesirable way.

Use the Unroute tool, and select any of the wires at the blue connector. Because they all belong to a cable, you need to select only one, and then they all highlight. Once they are unrouted, you can use the Create Segment tool to create a new segment from the blue connector to the black grommet hole and then use Route or Automatic Route to reroute the cable.

You'll notice that the middle section of the segment needs to be adjusted. To do so, follow these steps:

1. Run your mouse pointer over the centerline of the segment, right-click, and choose Add Points.

2. Select roughly in the middle of the segment, and then click Finish.

3. Right-click the new work point, and select Redefine Point.

4. Right-click, select Edit Offset, enter 10 mm for the offset value, and click OK.

5. Click roughly in the center of the square emboss on the base part.

6. Next you'll make an adjustment using the 3D triad. Right-click the same work point, and select 3D Move/Rotate.

7. Click the blue cone (z-axis) of the triad, enter 4 mm, and then click Apply.

8. Select the small plane between the blue arrow and the green arrow (YZ plane), enter -6 mm in both the Y and Z inputs, and then click OK.

9. Next you'll edit the segment type. Select Assign Virtual Parts on the Cable And Harness tab, and select the centerline of all the segments. From the Type drop-down, select Loom, set the Category drop-down to Sample, set the Name drop-down to Wire Sleeve, click the Add button, and then click OK. Note that the selections in this dialog box are interdependent. For instance, you might need to set the category first in order to get the option selections for the name.

SEGMENT DEFAULTS

You set the default Edit Offset, Color Style, and Diameter settings, and more per harness by right-clicking the harness browser node, selecting Harness Settings, and then going to the Segments tab.

Because the middle segment routes all the wires and the cable, it is larger in diameter. This is based on a setting in the harness properties. To determine its evaluated size, right-click the segment centerline, and choose Harness Properties. You can determine the diameter at the bottom of the Occurrence tab. Because the grommet holes have an inside diameter of 10 mm, you can make a judgment as to whether a larger hole size is required.

On the Wire/Cables tab of the Segment Properties dialog box, you can review the wire and cable information. Double-clicking a line item will open the properties of that wire or cable. Figure 18.29 shows the wire properties of a wire contained in a segment.

FIGURE 18.29
Wire properties

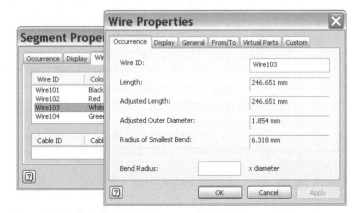

Copying Cable and Harness Designs

Because of the adaptive relationships between assemblies and the harness assemblies and their containing harness part file, copying existing harness and assembly designs must be done in a particular way so as not to break the adaptive relationship between the original files when working on the new files. Before looking at the steps to copy a harness, take a look at Figure 18.30 to understand the files involved. Each harness is comprised of an assembly file, where you can place connectors and other components, and a part file, where the wires, cables, segments, and other harness components are created.

FIGURE 18.30

Harness assembly structure

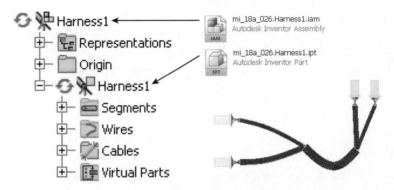

To copy a harness design, open the file called mi_18a_028.iam in the Chapter 18 directory of the Mastering Inventor 2011 folder. Then follow these steps:

1. Expand the assembly browser so that you can identify the harness assembly and part nodes.

Notice the harness used in the assembly is called mi_18a_26.Harness2 and the part within is named the same. This is because this top-level assembly file was created by using the Save Copy As tool and, therefore, still references the original harness. Although it may seem logical to use the assembly Replace tool or some other method to swap out the harness, such methods can't be used because the adaptive relationships must be updated throughout the file references.

2. Right-click the mi_18a_26.Harness2 file in the browser, and choose Delete.

3. Click No in the prompt box so that adaptively is not cleared in the original assembly.

4. On the Assemble tab, click the Place button.

5. Browse for the Harness_Files folder in the Chapter 18 directory, select the file named mi_18a_26.Harness1.iam, and click Open.

6. Click anywhere in the graphics screen to place the harness; then right-click and select Done.

7. Typically, you would constrain the harness using assembly constraints at this point. For the purpose of this exercise, though, you don't have to do so. Instead, right-click the harness assembly in the browser, and choose Make Adaptive. If prompted to save, click Yes.

8. In the Make Adaptive dialog box, you can set the new names for harness files or accept the default name.

9. In the Location area at the bottom of the dialog box, click the Browse button, browse for the Harness_Files folder in the Chapter 18 directory, and then click OK. Note that by default a subdirectory of the same name as the top assembly is created along with sub-folders for the component organization. You can accept this path and just make that part of your standard file management if you'd like.

10. Click OK and the new files are created, are made adaptive, and are ready for your design edits.

To make copies of a harness within the same assembly, you can simply copy and paste an existing harness, or you click an existing harness node and drag and drop it into the graphics area. Then right-click and choose Make Adaptive, and follow the renaming and location options detailed in the earlier steps.

Creating Nailboard Drawings

Documenting harnesses is a pretty straightforward process with purposely built tools for detailing harnesses as traditional nailboard drawings. To explore these options, open the file called mi_18a_026.iam in the Chapter 18 directory of the Mastering Inventor 2011 folder, and follow these steps:

1. Double-click the Harness subassembly to set it active for edits, or right-click it and select Edit.

2. Click the Nailboard button on Cable And Harness tab.

3. Select a drawing template of your choice from the Open Template dialog box, and click OK.

4. You will be taken into an active sketch within the drawing. Click the Nailboard tab to switch to the nailboard sketch tools.

SWITCHING TO THE NAILBOARD TAB

To use detailing tools specific to nailboard drawings, the user is required to manually switch from the Sketch tab to the Nailboard tab once the nailboard view is created or edited. Using the Dimension tool on the Sketch tab will not give you the same results as using the Harness Dimension tool on the Nailboard tab.

---

5. Use the Harness Dimension tool to place dimensions from the points on the harness. These will display as driven sketch dimensions for now but will show as drawing style dimensions once out of sketch mode.

6. Click the Pivot button on the Nailboard tab, and then select the sketch point at one of the 90-degree intersections. Then click a sketch endpoint of the harness leg, and drag to pivot the angle. Then right-click and choose Finish.

7. Zoom to any end on the harness, and select all of the wires (you can use a selection window to do this quickly).

8. Once the wires are selected, the Fan In and Fan Out buttons are available on the Nailboard tab. Click the Fan Out button, enter **180**, and then click OK. Note the change in the wire fan angle. You window the entire harness and use the Fan In/Out tools to set all the fans to the same angle as well. You can also manually click and drag each wire if needed.

9. Click the Finish Sketch button when you are satisfied with the dimensions, leg pivots, and fan angles.

10. Click the Place Connector Views button on the Nailboard tab.

11. Accept the defaults, and click OK.

12. Note that a drawing view of each connector is placed near each wire fan. Right-click one of these views, and select Edit View Orientation. Notice that you can change the styling, scale, and so on, as you would with any Inventor view, but you can also change the view orientation.

13. Feel free to experiment with view settings, and then click OK.

14. Next click the Edit button on the Nailboard tab. If the Sketch tab becomes active, switch to the Nailboard tab.

15. On the Nailboard tab, click the Property display button.

16. Set Selection Filter to All Wires.

17. Choose Wire ID from the Property Name list, and then click Apply.

18. Click onscreen to establish the position of the ID label to the wire, and you will see all the wire ID labels placed. Click OK. Click and drag labels to adjust them.

19. Expand the Segment browser node, select all the listed segments, and then right-click and deselect the Display As Actual Diameter option.

20. Expand the Wires node, right-click one of the wires, and choose View Path. Notice how the wire path is highlighted.

21. Click the Finish Sketch button.

Here are a few more settings and options to use when working with Nailboard drawings:

◆ Right-click the top-level harness node in the browser, and choose Nailboard Settings to adjust the global settings of the Nailboard view.

◆ You can open a drawing template first and use the Nailboard button on the Place Views tab to create a nailboard view and set the display settings, rotation, and other view options as you place the view.

◆ You can use the Table tool to place wire/pin tables from existing `*.xls` files.

◆ You can use the Broken Sketch Entity tool in the drawing view sketch environment to break long harness runs so they will fit on the drawing sheet.

The Bottom Line

Create routes and runs Using routed systems tools allows you to quickly define many different route types in order to check for clearance and fits within a design, all while creating a bill of materials that can be used downstream in the manufacturing process.

Master It How can you extract a bill of materials from a routed systems assembly?

Author a tube and pipe component   To create your own fittings, coupling, and so on, to be used within tube and pipe design, you need to first author it for use with the tube and pipe tools.

> **Master It**   How can you set the depth at which pipe, tube, or hose segments are inserted into a fitting?

Author an electrical component   To create your own electrical connector components to be used within cable and harness designs, you need to first define pins within the parts.

> **Master It**   How can you create a family of electrical connectors with varying numbers of pins?

Create and document cable and harness assemblies   Cable and harness assemblies are created using a specific subassembly and part structure. Each harness is contained in a harness subassembly, and the parts such as wires, cables, and segments are created within a harness part file.

> **Master It**   You have a complex design that includes many harness assemblies and would like to turn some of them off while you work on others and/or create new ones. What is the best way to do this?

Chapter 19

Plastics Design Features

When creating thin wall plastic parts, there are two popular approaches to getting started. One approach is to start with a solid and shell it out; the other is to start with a surface and thicken it. Although these methods approach thin wall features from different start points, the end result can be the same. You can also mix and match the two methods as required in order to achieve your design.

Typically, once you've established the base feature, you can add other plastic part features. Inventor has several specialized tools for creating plastic part features when working in the parts modeling environment. You'll find these tools on the Plastic Features panel of the Model tab. Although many of the other tools covered in this chapter, such as Shell and Thicken/Offset, are used to design all types of parts, they are commonly used along with the plastic-specific tools and, therefore, are covered in this chapter.

In this chapter, you will learn how to:

- ◆ Set up plastic part templates
- ◆ Create thicken/offset features
- ◆ Create shell features
- ◆ Create split features
- ◆ Create grill features
- ◆ Create rule fillet features
- ◆ Create rest features
- ◆ Create boss features
- ◆ Create lip and groove features
- ◆ Create snap fit features
- ◆ Create rib and web features
- ◆ Create draft features
- ◆ Create an injection mold

Using Plastic Part Templates

When working with plastic thin wall parts, it is helpful to follow certain design parameters throughout the features of the part in order to avoid issues with shrinkage and voids caused by uneven cooling once the part comes out of the mold. To help with this, you may want to create a plastic part template with your design parameters already set up. Figure 19.1 shows an example of the parameters in such a template with the design rules already set up and ready for use.

FIGURE 19.1

Example of plastic design parameters

User Parameters						
WL	mm	2 mm	2.000... ○	2.0...	☑	Wall Thickness
OR	mm	WL + IR	2.500... ○	2.5...	☑	Radius - Outside
IR	mm	WL * 0.25 ul	0.500... ○	0.5...	☑	Radius - Inside
DA_MIN	deg	0.5 deg	0.500... ○	0.5...	☑	Draft Angle - Minimum
DA_MAX	deg	2 deg	2.000... ○	2.0...	☑	Draft Angle - Maximum
BST_A	mm	WL * 0.6 ul	1.200... ○	1.2...	☑	Boss_Thickness under 3mm
BST_B	mm	WL * 0.4 ul	0.800... ○	0.8...	☑	Boss Thickness over 3mm
RIB	mm	0.7 ul * WL	1.400... ○	1.4...	☑	Rib Thickness

Creating Thicken/Offset Features

You can use the Thicken/Offset feature to add thickness to a surface feature in order to create a thin wall solid. Although you can use this tool to create output surfaces and remove solid material, typically when using Thicken/Offset to create plastic thin wall features, you'll select an existing surface feature to thicken and then set the output type to produce a solid.

To create a thin wall part using the thicken method, follow these steps:

1. Click Open on the Get Started tab, and browse for the file named mi_19a_022.ipt in the Chapter 19 directory of the Mastering Inventor 2011 folder and open it.

2. On the Model tab, select the Revolve tool, and notice that Output defaults to Surface because the sketch is an open profile.

3. For the Profile selection, click any solid line in the sketch.

4. For the axis, select the dashed centerline.

5. Leave the extents solution set to Full, and click OK.

6. Next select the Thicken/Offset tool on the Surface panel of the Model tab.

7. Switch the select mode from Face to Quilt, and then select any face on the revolved surface.

8. Set the distance input to 2 mm, and change the direction arrow so that the thickened material is placed to the inside of the part.

9. Ensure the output is set to Solid, and then click OK.

Notice the sharp edges. Although you could use the Fillet tool to select all the outside edges of the solid and then attempt to set fillets to all the inside edges of the solid, there is an easier way. If you place the fillets on the surface, then the thickened solid feature will follow the shape and include the fillets. To do this, continue with these steps:

10. From the browser, select the end-of-part (EOP) marker, and drag it above the thicken feature.

11. Select the Fillet tool on the Modify panel, and set the radius to 8 mm.

12. Set Select Mode to Feature, and then select the revolved surface.

13. When you see a preview of three fillet edges, click OK.

14. Next drag the EOP marker down below the fillet feature in the browser, and you'll note the thickened solid now includes the filleted edges.

15. Lastly, right-click the revolution feature in the browser, and toggle the visibility off. Figure 19.2 shows the revolved and thickened part.

FIGURE 19.2
A revolved and thickened part

Creating Shell Features

Another approach to creating thin wall features and parts is to create a solid and then use the Shell tool to hollow it out. When creating a shell feature, you set the wall thickness and select the faces you want to remove. Material from the interior of the part is removed, resulting in a cavity. To create a thin wall part using the shell method, open the file named mi_19a_024.ipt in the Chapter 19 directory of the Mastering Inventor 2011 folder, and then follow these steps:

1. On the Model tab, select the Revolve tool, and notice that Output defaults to Solid because the sketch is closed. The profile and axis selections will automatically select, because there is only one possible solution for each.

2. Leave the extents solution set to Full, and click OK.

3. Next click the Shell button on the Modify panel of the Model tab.

4. Select the circular face on the top of the revolution feature as the Remove Faces selection.

5. Ensure the direction is set to Inside, set the thickness to 2 mm, and then click OK.

Notice the odd result at the opening of the part. You will fix this by creating a boundary patch surface and then using the Thicken/Offset tool to recut the hole. You'll also place some fillets on the sharp outside edges.

6. Select the Boundary Patch tool on the Surface panel.

7. Click the larger diameter edge of the center hole for the BoundaryLoop selection, and click OK. This creates a surface feature you'll use to recut the hole.

8. Select the Thicken/Offset tool on the Surface panel, and click the boundary patch's surface.

9. Set Solution to Cut, set Distance to 2 mm, and set the direction to go down into the part.

10. Ensure the output is set to Solid, and then click OK.

11. Select the Fillet tool on the Modify panel, and set the radius to 8 mm.

12. Select the three outside edges—two along the bottom and one along the top. Be certain these are the outside edges and not the inside edges; then click OK.

13. Next drag the fillet feature above the shell feature in the browser. This will allow the shell to follow the outside fillets and translate them to the inside edges. If you cannot drag the fillet above the shell feature, mostly likely you have inadvertently selected an inside edge. If so, the fillet cannot exist before the shell because it is dependent upon the edge created by the shell.

14. Lastly, right-click the boundary patch feature in the browser, and toggle the visibility off. Figure 19.3 shows the revolved and shelled part.

FIGURE 19.3
A revolved and shelled part

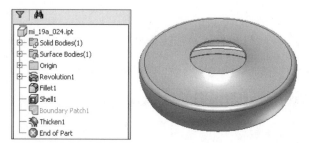

If you were to compare the parts created by the Thicken/Offset method and the Shell method, you would find that the two are not quite identical. The difference is in the opening cutout. In the shelled version, a boundary patch was used to recut the opening down into the part (along the y-axis). In the thickened version, the opening was left in its natural condition. You could use the Boundary Patch tool to clean up the opening in that case as well.

Using either method, it is also important to consider a draft angle for the walls of the component that are in the direction that a mold would be separated in. Not including this early on can lead to a lot of difficult cleanup work in the long run before a mold can be created.

Creating Split Features

Often when designing plastic parts, it is useful to create mating parts within the same file. To do this, you can use the Split tool to divide a single body into two mating bodies. You can also use the Split tool to split the surfaces on a solid so that they can be manipulated individually. To see how the Split tool is used, open the file named mi_19a_026.ipt in the Chapter 19 directory of the Mastering Inventor 2011 folder, and then follow these steps:

1. Expand the Solid Bodies folder in the browser, and notice there is currently only a single solid listed in the folder. You will use the Split tool to divide this into two separate solids.

2. On the Model tab's Modify panel, select the Split tool.

3. For the Split Tool selection, click the sketch profile running through the part.

4. For the method, click the Split Solid button (third from the top), which will split the existing part into two separate solids.

5. Click OK, and notice Solid1 has been replaced with two new solids in the Solid Bodies folder.

6. To work with just the top solid, select it in the Solid Bodies folder of the browser, right-click, and choose Hide Others.

7. Next you'll create a 3D sketch to split the surface of the solid. Use the Sketch drop-down on the Model tab, and select 3D Sketch.

8. On the 3D Sketch tab, select the Silhouette Curve tool, choose the solid as the Body selection and the visible y-axis as the Direction selection, and then click OK.

9. This creates a sketch curve along the face where a beam of light shining down from above would create a shadow. Click Finish Sketch to exit the 3D sketch.

10. Select the Split tool again, and choose the 3D Sketch curve for the Split tool selection.

11. For the Face selection, choose the face that the 3D Sketch curve is encircling. Ensure the Faces option is set to Select and not All. This will split just the outside face of the part, whereas All would split both the outside and inside faces. Click OK.

12. Now select the Thicken/Offset tool, choose the bottom half of the face you just split, and set the Distance to 1 mm.

13. Ensure Output is set to Solid, Solution is set to Join, and Direction is thickening out from the part; then click OK.

14. Next right-click the thickened part you just created in the browser, and choose Properties.

15. Set Feature Color Style to Blue, and click OK.

16. Right-click the solid in the Solid Bodies folder, and choose Properties. Enter **Cover** for the name. Click the Update button to set the general properties of this solid. You'll notice also that you can set the color for the entire solid body here. Selecting the Strip Overrides check box would reset the blue thicken feature to abide by the color of the entire solid. Feel free to choose a color of your liking, and then click OK.

17. Finally, right-click the solid in the Solid Bodies folder, and choose Show All to turn the visibility of the other solid back on.

There are a number of uses for a multibody part, but for this type of product they are invaluable.

Creating Grill Features

You can use the Grill tool to create vents and openings on the thin wall parts to provide access and airflow to parts housed within an exterior part. To create grill features, use the Grill tool to project 2D sketches on the surface of the part to create various raised or recessed features. Although the boundary sketch is the only required grill element, you can create islands, ribs, and spars and then give them all a draft angle. You can also check the flow area of the opening to ensure it meets the required area. Open the file called mi_19a_028.ipt in the Chapter 19 directory of the Mastering Inventor 2011 folder, and then follow these steps to create a grill feature:

1. Select the Grill tool from the Plastic Part panel of the Model tab. You'll see a sketch with all the various elements of what will become the grill within it. Figure 19.4 shows the sketch elements separated out into the grill elements.

FIGURE 19.4

Grill elements

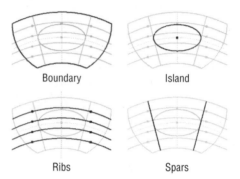

2. For the Boundary profile, select the outer profile of the sketch, as identified in Figure 19.4. Set Thickness to 2 mm, Height to 6 mm, and Outside Height to 2 mm, as shown in Figure 19.5.

FIGURE 19.5

Grill boundary settings

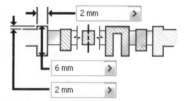

3. Next click the Island tab, and select the elliptical profile of the sketch, as identified in Figure 19.4. Leave Thickness set to 0 mm so that the island is a solid fill.

4. Next click the Rib tab, and select the four arcs identified as the ribs in Figure 19.4. Set Thickness to 2 mm, Height to 4 mm, and Top Offset to 2 mm, as shown in Figure 19.6.

FIGURE 19.6

Grill rib settings

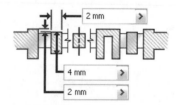

5. Next click the Spar tab, and select the two lines identified as the spars in Figure 19.4. Set Top Offset to 2 mm, Thickness to 6 mm, and Bottom Offset to 0 mm, as shown in Figure 19.7.

FIGURE 19.7
Spar rib settings

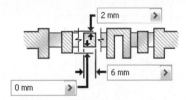

6. Click the >> button at the bottom of the dialog box, and note the Flow Area setting; then click OK to create the grill feature.

7. Next you'll pattern the grill feature around the parts. Click the Circular Pattern tool (located next to the Work Features tools).

8. Select the grill feature for the Features selection, and then click the visible y-axis for the Rotation Axis selection.

9. Enter **3** for Occurrence Count and **90deg** for Occurrence Angle.

10. Click the Midplane button to set an occurrence on each side of the original, and then click the >> button.

11. In the Positioning Method area, select Incremental to set the spacing of the grills at 90 degrees each, and then click OK. Figure 19.8 shows the patterned grill features.

FIGURE 19.8
Grill features patterned

Creating Rule Fillet Features

With rule fillets, you can create fillets based on a list of rules you've set up in order to determine which edges to fillet. This approach can be a powerful time-saver when working with plastic parts, because it allows you to create many fillets all at once without having to select each and every edge. When a part feature is changed with significance to the rule-based fillets, the rule is evaluated to determine whether it still applies. If so, then the fillets are regenerated for new edges that fit the rule and discarded for edges that do not. Although the Rule Fillet tool is categorized as a plastic feature tool, you can use rule-based fillets for any part you design.

Open the file called mi_19a_030.ipt in the Chapter 19 directory of the Mastering Inventor 2011 folder, and then follow these steps to create a rule fillet feature:

1. Expand the Solid Bodies folder in the browser, right-click the solid named Cover, and choose Hide Others.

2. Select the Rule Fillet tool on the Plastic Part panel.

3. Click the drop-down under the Source column, and select Face.

4. Rotate the part around, and select the underside face of the grill features (they've each been colored yellow for easy identification).

5. Set the radius to 2 mm, and then set the drop-down in the Rule column to Incident Edges.

6. In the Options area, deselect the All Rounds check box, leaving All Fillets selected.

7. In the Incident Edges area, select the visible y-axis as the Direction selection, and then click OK to create all the previewed fillets. Figure 19.9 shows the results of the rule fillet on one of the grill faces.

FIGURE 19.9
An example of
Rule fillets

You'll notice the edges where one of the spars that meets the grill boundary along the top did not receive fillets. This is because they do not qualify according to the rule of incident edges. Although it might seem as if the rule fillet has malfunctioned, close inspection of the grill feature will show there is a gap between the spar and the boundary face. To resolve this, the lines in the grill sketch used for the spars would need to be extended past the boundary edge.

Here is a brief description of the results of the Rule Fillet tool when Faces is selected:

Incident Edges   Only edges contacting the source faces that are parallel to a selected axis (within a specified tolerance) are filleted.

All Edges   Edges generated by the selected faces and other faces of the part body are filleted.

Against Features   Two selection sets are created: a "source" selection and a "scope" selection. Only edges formed by the intersection of the faces in the source with features in the scope selections are filleted.

Here is a brief description of the results of the Rule Fillet tool when Features is selected:

All Edges   Edges generated by the selected features and the part body are filleted.

Against Part   Only edges formed by the intersection of the faces of the feature(s) and the faces of the part body are filleted.

Against Features   Two selection sets are created: a "source" selection and a "scope" selection. Only edges formed by the intersection of the features in the source with features in the scope selections are filleted.

Free Edges   Only edges formed by faces of the selected feature are filleted.

Creating Rest Features

A rest feature is a shelf or landing area applied to a curved or slanted face of a plastic part, often used as a surface on which to mount other components. The results of the rest feature are largely dependent upon the orientation of the rest sketch in relation to the target body and the combination of settings and selections you choose. The Through All option will extend the rest profile through the extents of the target body. The direction arrow will change the results, as shown in the comparison of Figure 19.10 and Figure 19.11.

FIGURE 19.10
Through All termination with the direction set downward

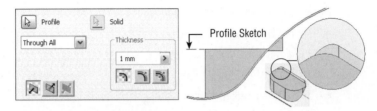

FIGURE 19.11
Through All termination with the direction set upward

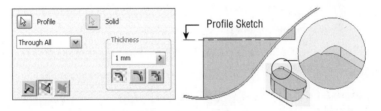

Additionally, you can set a Distance extent. Figure 19.12 shows a rest created 25 mm off the profile sketch in both directions.

FIGURE 19.12
Using Distance extents for a rest

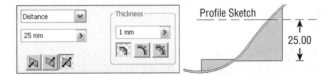

You can also set the rest to terminate using a selected surface. Figure 19.13 shows a rest set to use the target body surface as a termination, with the direction set to go up from the sketch. Notice the result adds material but does not create a pocket.

FIGURE 19.13
A rest using a surface termination

You can use the More tab in the Rest dialog box to set the Landing options such as taper angles and termination settings. Open the file named mi_19a_032.ipt in the Chapter 19 directory of the Mastering Inventor 2011 folder, and then follow these steps to create a rest feature:

1. Expand the Solid Bodies folder in the browser, right-click the solid named Cover, and choose Hide Others.

2. On the Plastic Part panel, select the Rest tool. Because only one profile is available in the visible sketch, it is selected automatically.

3. Set the direction arrow to point up (use the flip arrow on the left).

4. Set the thickness to 2 mm, and set the thickness direction to Outside.

5. Click the More tab, set the Landing Options drop-down to To Surface, and then select the visible surface. Set the landing taper to **12 deg**, and then click OK.

6. Turn the visibility of the landing surface off, and inspect the results. You'll notice that the surface contours are translated to the tapered faces. If this is not the result you want, you can use the Delete Face option to clean up the contours.

7. On the Surface panel, select the Delete Face tool.

8. Select the Heal check box. Then select the four contoured faces, as shown in Figure 19.14, and click OK.

FIGURE 19.14
Deleting and
healing faces

 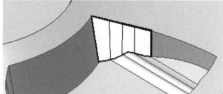

Delete Face Tool

The Delete Face tool is a good way to clean up geometry when needed, but it should not be used indiscriminately because it may create unpredictable results during feature edits. If you have the option to edit an existing sketch or feature in order to get the same result as using the Delete Face tool, then that is typically the best practice. There are also times when cleaning up geometry can be bypassed by using a different technique. Rather that cleaning up an interior corner to apply an edge fillet, you may be able to apply a two-face fillet and have the fillet feature "absorb" the inconsistent faces that would be patched over. Also, it is a good idea to create small selection sets to delete multiple faces rather than trying to delete them all at once. For example, in this design you would need to delete the contours on the sides of the rest feature on all the inside and outside faces in order to remove the contours completely. This would be best to do as several different features created with the Delete Face tool.

Creating Boss Features

CERT OBJECTIVE

To hold plastic parts together without risking damage to the thin wall features, Boss features are often used to provide a more rigid connection point than just a simple hole. You can use the Boss tool in Inventor to create matched pairs of bosses on mating parts. The half accepting the fastener is the *head,* and the other half is the *thread.* You can create both types of bosses using the Boss tool. When required, you can add strength ribs so that the boss features will not be snapped off under load. As a rule, you should consider adding ribs any time the length of the boss exceeds the diameter by more than three times.

Open the file called mi_19a_034.ipt in the Chapter 19 directory of the Mastering Inventor 2011 folder, and then follow these steps to create boss features:

1. Expand the Solid Bodies folder in the browser, right-click the solid named Base, and choose Hide Others.

2. Because the Base part has an uneven edge, the boss features to be created will be different heights. To locate the bosses, you will first create work points. Select the Point tool on the Work Features panel.

3. To create the work point, select the edge of Work Plane4, and then select the inside edge of the base near the intersection of the work plane and the edge.

4. Repeat this for Work Plane5 and the inside edge of the part. You'll note the work points are placed at different heights from the bottom of the base part. Figure 19.15 shows the resulting work point.

FIGURE 19.15
Work point
locations

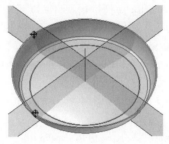

5. Next you will create grounded work points to establish the inset location for the boss features. Use the drop-down on the Work Features panel to select the Grounded Point tool.

6. Select the first work point you created at the intersection of the part edge and Work Plane4. You will see the 3D Move/Rotate dialog box, and the triad will appear at the work point location.

7. Click the Redefine Alignment or Position button in the dialog box.

8. Next select the small plane on the triad running between the green y-axis and the red x-axis. Then select the edge of Work Plane4. The triad will realign to the work plane.

9. Now you are ready to place the grounded work point. To do so, first click the red cone shape (arrowhead) of the triad for the x-axis. This will isolate x-axis input in the dialog box. Enter 15 mm, and click Apply. This will create a grounded work point.

10. Next click the Redefine Alignment or Position button in order to redefine the triad location. Click the black ball at the center of the triad first, and then select the work point at the intersection of the Work Plane5 and the inside edge of the part.

11. Click the blue cone shape (arrowhead) of the triad for the z-axis. This will isolate the z-axis input in the dialog box. Enter -15 mm, and click Apply. This will create a second grounded work point.

12. Now you are ready to create the boss features. Select the Boss tool on the Plastic Part panel.

13. Ensure the Placement drop-down is set to On Point, and then select the two grounded work points for the Centers selection. Click the visible y-axis for the Direction selection, and ensure the preview shows the bosses extending down toward the part base. If they do not, use the Flip arrow to change the direction.

14. Next click the Head tab. Note the buttons on the left of the dialog box. If you click the lower one, the Head tab becomes the Thread tab, allowing you to place a different boss type. Click the (+) plus button next to the Draft Options area to view the draft inputs available. You can leave the inputs at the defaults.

15. Next click the Ribs tab, and select the Stiffening Ribs check box to set these options active. Enter **4** in the Number Of Stiffening Ribs input box.

16. Enter 6 mm for the Shoulder Radius input, and then click the (+) plus button next to the Fillet Options area to view the fillet inputs available. Leave the inputs at the defaults.

17. Click the Start Direction button at the bottom of the dialog box, and then select either Work Plane4 or Work Plane5 to establish the direction. (You can also just enter **45 degrees** into the angle input in this particular case.)

18. Next, click OK to create the boss features. You'll notice each is created at a different height.

19. Finally, use the Mirror tool to mirror the boss feature, using the YZ origin plane as the mirror plane. Figure 19.16 shows the completed bosses.

FIGURE 19.16
Plastic boss
features

Now that the Base half of this design has the head boss features completed, you can create the sketch or work points at the centers of each boss and then use those points to create the thread bosses in the cover.

> **TURNING OFF WORK FEATURE VISIBILITY**
>
> Recall that it is best practice to right-click and toggle off the visibility of each work feature you create, once you are finished using it. Leaving the visibility on or using the Object Visibility display override at the part level can make managing work features difficult at the assembly level.

Creating Lip and Groove Features

Lip and groove features are used to mate two parts together so that they fit together precisely. You can use the Lip tool in Inventor to create either the lip or the groove of the part by specifying a path consisting of a set of tangent, continuous boundary edges. You can also use work planes to establish a path extents where a lip is not needed around an entire edge. Open the file called mi_19a_036.ipt in the Chapter 19 folder of the Mastering Inventor 2011 directory, and then follow these steps to create lip features:

1. Expand the Solid Bodies folder in the browser, right-click the solid named Base, and choose Hide Others.

2. Select the Lip tool on the Plastic Part panel, and set the type to Lip by clicking the Lip button on the left side of the dialog box.

3. Select the inside edge of the part for the Path Edges selection, and then select the top face for the Guide Face setting.

4. Next click the Lip tab, set the outside angle to **10 degrees** and the clearance to 0.5 mm, and then click OK. Figure 19.17 shows the Lip selections.

FIGURE 19.17
Creating a lip feature

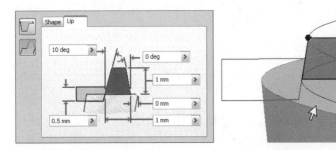

5. Next you'll create the groove on the Cover solid. Expand the Solid Bodies folder in the browser, right-click the solid named Cover, and choose Hide Others.

6. Select the Lip tool, and set the type to Groove by clicking the Groove button on the left side of the dialog box.

7. Select the inside edge of the part for the Path Edges selection, and then select the center of one of the bosses to establish a pull direction.

8. Next click the Groove tab, set the outside angle to **10 degrees** and the clearance to 0.5 mm, and then click OK.

Note that if you did not set a clearance value, you would likely get an error. The Clearance value is useful for creating a planar surface along the path where needed.

Creating Snap Fit Features

Snap fit features are used to secure a plastic part to another part. Although you can model any number of snap fit connections using Inventor's standard modeling tools, Inventor includes a tool to create the common hook-and-loop cantilever snap fit. Figure 19.18 shows a few common snap fits you might create with the Snap Fit tool.

FIGURE 19.18
From left to right: a permanent locking snap, non-locking snap, and U-shaped removable locking snap

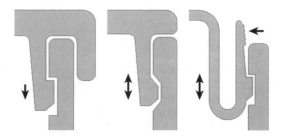

To insert a snap fit, select an insert point made of either a sketch point or a work point. Open the file called mi_19a_038.ipt in the Chapter 19 directory of the Mastering Inventor 2011 folder, and then follow these steps to create snap fit features:

1. The first step in creating the snap fit for this part is to bring an existing part into the design using the Derive tool. On the Manage tab, click the Derive button.

2. Locate and select the file named mi_19a_099.ipt in the Chapter 19 folder, and then click Open.

3. In the Derived Part dialog box, select the first button for the Derive Style to create a single solid-body part with merged seams between planar faces.

4. Next expand the Solid Bodies folder, and ensure Solid1 is colored yellow, denoting that it is set to be derived into your current design. Expand the Work Geometry folder, set Work Axis1 to be derived as well, and then click OK. You can use the ViewCube to return to the home view.

5. You'll now use the derived part to subtract material from the Cover part so that it will fit into the opening. Click the Model tab, and then select the Combine tool on the Modify panel.

6. For the Base selection, select Cover. For the tool body, select the derived part. Set the solution to Cut, click the Keep Toolbody check box, and click OK.

7. When the tool body component (in this case the derived part) is combined with the base part, its visibility is automatically toggled off. Expand the Solid Bodies folder, and you'll see the derived part listed as a solid with its visibility turned off.

8. Next you'll create a work point to set the location of the snap fit feature. Select the Point tool on the Work Features panel, and zoom into the yellow face located on the cutout of the cover. Select the midpoint along the top edge of the yellow face to set the work point.

9. Now you're ready to create the snap fit. Select the Snap Fit tool on the Plastic Part panel.

10. Ensure the Placement drop-down is set to On Point and the Cantilever Snap Fit Hook button is selected (on the left of the dialog box).

11. For the Centers selection, click the work point you created.

12. For the Direction selection, click the visible y-axis.

13. For the Hook Direction selection, click the derived work axis running through the yellow face.

14. Use the Flip button to set the direction correctly if the preview shows it facing down.

PREVIEWING THE SNAP FIT

The Extend check box might make the preview of the snap fit feature look as if the feature is going to build incorrectly. We've created a short video showing this feature being built for your reference. To play the video, you can expand the browser named 3rd Party, located in the Model browser, and double-click the Snap Fit Video node. You can also access the video from the Chapter 19 folder. It is named mi_19a_038.wmv.

---

15. Ensure the Extend check box is selected so that the snap will match the contour of the curved face on which it is being created.

16. Click the Beam tab, set the beam length to 7 mm, the Beam Width At The Hook setting to 9 mm, and the Beam Width At The Wall setting to 10 mm.

17. Click the Hook tab, and take a look at the settings; leave these settings at the defaults, and then click OK.

18. Use the Circular Pattern tool to pattern the hook around the opening for a total of three.

19. On the Solid bodies tab, right-click all of the solids, and choose Show All. Investigate the snap fit, and note the derived part has the mating half of the hook built in. Figure 19.19 shows the completed snap fit feature.

You can open the file named mi_19a_040.ipt in the Chapter 19 folder to experiment with the various snap fit settings. Use the work points to place hook and loop features to your liking. You can also open mi_19a_042.ipt for comparison. This file contains two halves of a simple plastic box. Interrogate the model features to see how the hook and loops were created in combination with extrude features to get a precise placement.

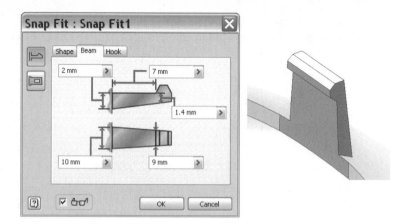

FIGURE 19.19
Snap fit feature

WORKING WITH MULTIBODIES

At any point during your design, you can save the solids within a multibody part as individual parts and even have them automatically placed into an assembly. Creating multiple solid bodies in a single-part file offers some unique advantages compared to the traditional methods of creating parts in the context of an assembly file. You can explore the steps for doing this in Chapter 5, "Advanced Modeling Techniques."

Creating Rib and Web Features

Ribs and webs are often used in plastic parts to prevent warping and add stiffness to thin wall parts. To create a rib feature, first create an open profile sketch to define the cross section. Then define the direction and thickness. If the rib feature runs perpendicular to the sketch plane, you can add a draft taper. By default, the profile extends to intersect the next face. To create a rib network, you can select multiple sketch profiles at once. Alternatively, you can create a single rib feature and then pattern and/or mirror it.

Open the file called mi_19a_044.ipt in the Chapter 19 directory of the Mastering Inventor 2011 folder, and then follow these steps to create rib features:

1. You'll notice there is a small diagonal line sketched in the corner of the part. This will be the sketch profile of the first rib feature. Select the Rib tool on the Create panel, and the sketch profile will be selected automatically.

2. Move your mouse pointer around the screen, and you will see the direction arrow adjust. It may be difficult to get the arrow to point in toward the rounded edge unless you rotate the view. Use the ViewCube to change the view, and then click the screen when you see the arrow point in toward the rounded edge. If you make a mistake, simply click the Direction button in the dialog box, and reset the direction.

3. Set the thickness to 0.5 mm, and use the arrows to adjust the direction in which the thickness is applied. In this case, you want to use the Midplane option.

4. Click OK, and notice how the rib extends to the profile.

5. Next right-click Sketch3 in the browser, and choose Visibility to make it available for use.

6. Select the Rib tool again, and select the four lines and the ellipse as profiles.

7. Click the Direction button, drag your mouse pointer down to set the direction arrow and preview to extend toward the base of the part, and then click to set the direction.

8. Toggle the Extend Profile check box off and on to notice the difference in the preview. Ensure that this check box is selected so that the profiles do extend.

9. Set the thickness to 0.5 mm, and use the arrows to adjust the direction in which the thickness is applied. In this case, you want to use the Midplane option.

10. To explore the Finite option, toggle the Extents solution to Finite, and type 5 mm. This holds the depth of the ribs to 5 mm rather than allowing them to extend to the base. Set Extents back to the To Next option.

11. Enter **5deg** in the Taper input, and then click OK to create the rib feature.

You can use the Mirror and Rectangular Pattern tools to copy the first rib around the part as you see fit. Figure 19.20 shows the finished example.

FIGURE 19.20
Complete rib
features

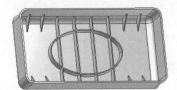

Creating Draft Features

Taper or draft often needs to be applied to part faces so the part can be extracted from the mold in which it is manufactured. You can create draft features by selecting a pull direction and then selecting the faces/edges upon which to apply the draft, or you can select a fixed face and apply drafts to the faces intersecting it. To explore both options, open the file called mi_19a_046.ipt in the Chapter 19 directory of the Mastering Inventor 2011 folder, and then follow these steps to create draft features:

1. Select the Draft tool on the Modify tab.

2. For the Pull Direction selection, click the yellow base face.

3. To select the faces, you will click the green faces near the edge that contacts the yellow base face. If you move your mouse pointer over the faces before selecting them, you will see that the edge closest to your mouse pointer will be selected. If you accidentally select an extra or errant edge, you can press the Ctrl key and deselect it.

4. Enter **5deg** for the taper, and then click OK. You'll notice the top faces of the thin walls have been reduced because of the draft taper. To remedy this, you'll place a draft on the outside faces also.

5. Rotate the part around so you can see the red and blue faces, and then click the Draft tool again.

6. This time, click the Fixed Plane button on the left of the dialog box.

7. Select the red face for the Fixed Pane selection, and ensure the arrow is pointing out.

8. Select the blue faces for the Faces selection, enter **5deg** for the taper, and then click OK.

You can open the file named mi_19a_048.ipt in the Chapter 19 folder to compare how creating the same tapers is made easier by the inclusion of the corner filet. Also note that you can use a combination of split faces and work planes to create draft features that will separate faces, as shown in Figure 19.21 and demonstrated in the file mi_19a_050.ipt.

PLASTIC PARTS AND COOLING SHRINKAGE

Designing plastic parts of uniform wall thickness is typically a fairly easy task when the part consists of a simple shell. However, when bosses and ribs are introduced, the resulting tees and feature intersections can create cross section thicknesses that are significantly thicker than the wall thickness average. As is often the case when modeling 3D parts, there is nothing to tell you that the model will not work in the real world, other than knowledge and experience. For Inventor Professional users, the Tooling functions that allow Mold design include calculations for material shrinkage based on the material properties.

The issue with adding bosses and ribs arises when the part is cooling after the molding process. Uneven part thickness will often result in sinking and deformation where the thicker walls cool slower than the rest of the part. The result can be a very disappointing resemblance to the eye-catching design you intended to create.

To deal with these problem areas, you can do one or more of the following:

◆ You can use a textured surface to disguise uneven cooling.

◆ You can create cores, corner reliefs, and tee inset features to eliminate thick areas.

◆ You can use foam- or gas-assisted molding processes.

◆ You can redesign the problem areas to avoid thickened walls.

Although it will certainly vary depending upon the materials and process, a rule of thumb is to keep tee walls at 60 percent of the standard part wall thickness. As shown here, the feature on the left has some obvious problems with areas that exceed a consistent thickness. The feature on the right has been designed to perform the same function and yet maintain a desirable wall thickness throughout.

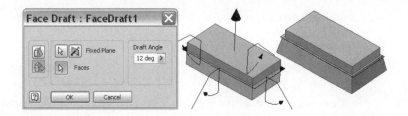

FIGURE 19.21
Draft applied to
a split face, using a
work plane as the
fixed plane

Mold Design Overview

The Process of Mold Design is a complex combination of advanced science, knowledge of an individual producer's equipment and processes, and for the highest quality it often requires a great deal of experience. Too often it isn't possible to access that experience, and with many companies having their plastic parts injection molded outside of their own walls, it isn't reasonable to expect to have the thorough understanding of the equipment available. Securing the time and expertise of a plastics engineer helps to overcome these issues, but their time is expensive and in very high demand. As with the stress analysis tools, Inventor includes tools to help an engineer with a lower degree of expertise do a lot of the fundamental analysis to make the best use of an expert's time.

INVENTOR TOOLING

The Inventor Professional Suite and the Inventor Tooling Suite include the Inventor Tooling functions. This is a plastic part analysis and injection mold design environment that allows you to predict how the mold will fill and what defects may occur in the part. Defects such as weld lines or air pockets can be reviewed to decide if you want to change gate placement or modify the part being manufactured.

The software includes over seven thousand types of resin so you can select the appropriate material for the part. This material information affects the quality and fill analysis settings. The process is fairly straight forward, and the interface allows you to move from step to step easily and walks through most of the tools in order.

The process of creating the mold is similar to a combination of a Design Accelerator and a Weldment. Design Accelerators guide you toward a standard component that will accomplish your unique design requirement. The Weldment is a hybrid to the standard assembly and acts as a specialized environment. Each type of component is listed in the Browser as an element of the design rather than just a component in the assembly; placing an element may affect several others. The power is in the fact that the user doesn't have to specify these interactions.

Take a look at some of the tools used in the workflow to create a mold using the Tooling features. These will be the first tools you will use in the exercises to explore designing a mold. In these exercises we will not complete every step of the process, and Inventor has several great tutorials to augment this chapter if you want to look at some of the advanced features. The intent here is to get you started and introduce the possibilities.

Plastic Part   To create a new mold, this is the starting point. This tool will convert an existing part into a mold design element. Around this part everything else will be built.

Place Core And Cavity   If you have an existing Core and Cavity set, you can import them and use them as the basis for the mold design.

Adjust Orientation In order to properly align the mold components, an opening direction must be established. This orientation can be altered by setting axis directions or rotating the part.

Select Material To properly adjust for shrinkage and to load temperature properties for simulation, you must select the material the component will be made of.

There are a few tools that you can select in different stages depending on your preference. For example, you can place a sketch to define you runner before or after the core and cavity have been calculated.

Manual Sketch This tools is a flyout option under the Auto Runner Sketch tool. It can also be used to create a runner sketch, but it is also used to sketch complex cooling line routes.

Runner Many of the standard runner shapes can be applied to the core, cavity, or both sides of the mold. These shapes have additional options such as applying a cold slug to the end of the runner.

Gate Like the Runner, the Gate has a selection of the common gate types. You can enter values to modify their size to suit.

You will now start the process of defining the plastic part and the material that will drop out of the mold with it in the context of the mold design.

1. In the New File dialog box in the English tab, begin creating a new file using the Mold Design (in).iam template.

2. Give the new design the name Mastering Inventor Tooling and click OK to create the file.

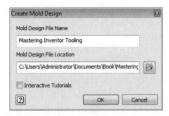

Two new tabs have been added to the ribbon: Mold Layout and Mold Assembly. Similar to annotation in Inventor, you may need to manually switch tabs to access certain tools at different times. Other tabs will be created during the Mold design process as well.

3. Click the Plastic Part icon in the Mold Layout tab and select the `mi_19a_044_Mold.ipt` file as the component you want to import. Click Open to import the file.

4. Pick the Adjust Orientation tool from the Mold Layout panel. The preview of the Opening Direction will appear. Using the icon in the dialog box, flip the Z direction of the part so your preview looks like Figure 19.22.

5. Select Done when the direction has been properly set.

6. Start the Select Material tool and change the manufacturer to BASF and the Tradename to Terluran GP-22. Click OK to complete the selection.

7. Rotate the model so you can see the bottom of the part.

8. Under the Auto Runner Sketch flyout, select the Manual Sketch tool.

9. Check to make sure that Runner Sketch is the type of sketch you are creating and select bottom most face on the part, as shown in Figure 19.23. Click OK to create the sketch

10. Draw a line segment .5 inches long that is .2 inches from the left edge of the part and is coincident with the origin of the part. See Figure 19.24

FIGURE 19.22
Setting the Opening Direction

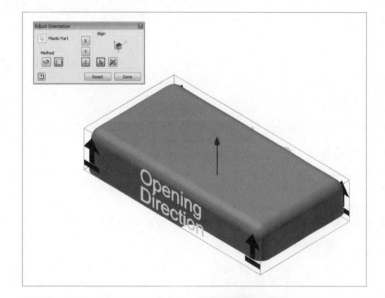

FIGURE 19.23
Creating a Runner sketch

FIGURE 19.24
Dimensioning
the Runner

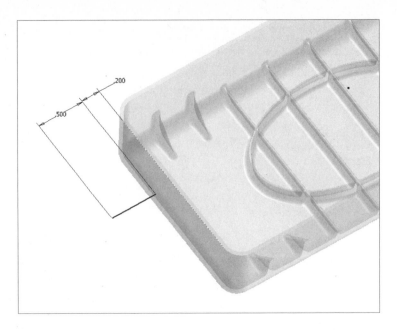

11. Finish the sketch when the line is complete to return to the Mold Layout tools.

12. Save your work.

The process of creating a runner sketch can be done after the core and cavity have been calculated. For some it is easier to visualize how the runner and gate material will appear attached to the part when it drops from the mold. This is the approach you will take for the next exercise. Now you will place the runner, the gate, and create the core and cavity.

1. Start the Create Runner tool.

2. Set the Section Type to U Shape. Set the Runner to be created on the Cavity side and set its diameter to .1.

3. Have the runner create a Cold Slug at the end position with a length of .125 as the dialog box shows in Figure 19.25.

4. Click OK to create the Runner.

5. Start the Gate Location tool.

6. Select the bottom left edge of the part. A ratio will appear in the dialog box. Set this to be .5, meaning that the gate will be placed half way along the length of the edge.

7. Click Apply to create the gate location and then Done to close the dialog box.

Now you will add the gate. There are a lot of options so you will take them in several steps.

8. Click on the Gate tool to open the dialog box.

9. Set the Placement to Cavity side.

FIGURE 19.25

Placing the Runner

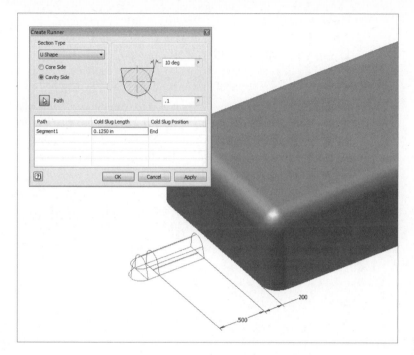

10. Set the Placement to Two Points; this will start Inventor looking for the Gate location.

11. Pick the work point that displays the gate location you just placed.

12. Once selected, Inventor will want the endpoint. Pick the end of the runner sketch nearest to the part.

13. In the dialog box, set the value of W1 to .35.

14. Set H1 to .25l.

15. Set W2 to .15.

16. Set H2 to .05 and compare your screen and dialog box to Figure 19.26.

17. Click OK to create the gate if everything appears correct.

18. Save your work.

Now you have defined our part's material and how we want the plastic to flow into the mold. The next step is to begin defining the mold itself. Keep in mind that all of the geometry you've been working on will become a void in the components you are about to create.

The tools needed to discover if the part will fill properly and to establish the geometry of the core and cavity are more automated than tools that you would typically use in Inventor. These tools will also inform you if you have missed a step in the process. Let's take a look at some of these tools.

Part Process Settings Optimal values for the mold temperature and pressures are loaded from the material information. This dialog box allows you to make modifications to accommodate for your equipment if need be.

Part Fill Analysis   Inventor Tooling has the ability to analyze the fill time, quality, and other important considerations as where weld lines may appear or air traps may occur.

Define Workpiece setting   Establishing the size of the tool your core and cavity will be cut from is an important step. You must accommodate the Runner and eventually the components of the assembly that move the material to the cavity.

Create Runoff Surface   A Runoff surface can be seen as an extension of the parting line. It is the surface that will be used to divide the workpiece so the parts of the mold can separate.

Generate Core and Cavity   This tool launches you into another environment that is focused on the how the workpiece will be modified to create the void for the plastic to fill.

FIGURE 19.26
Placing the Gate between the part and runner

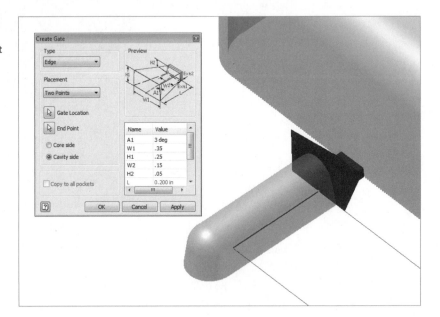

To create the core, cavity, and other components, you will need to change the environment that you are working in.

1. Click the Core and Cavity tool in the Mold Layout panel. This will add the Core/Cavity tab to the interface and give you access to the tools needed to create the workpiece that will be added to the mold base to complete the design.

2. Pick the Gate Location tool and replace the gate location as you did before.

3. Click the Process Settings tool. You will not be making any changes so click OK to close the dialog box.

4. Click the Part Fill Analysis tool.

5. When the Part Fill Analysis dialog box appears, pick the Start button; you will also need to pick the OK button in the dialog box letting you know that the analysis is running.

6. When the analysis is complete, a Summary will be displayed showing the results. In Figure 19.27, you can see that your part can be filled, but the quality is a concern to the system.

FIGURE 19.27
Part Fill Analysis summary

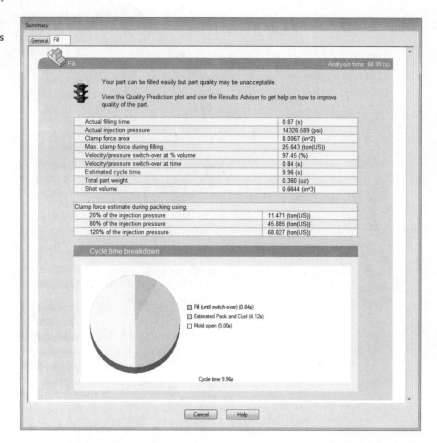

7. In the Browser, expand the mi_19a_044_Mold component and then expand the Results node and then the Fill node.

8. Double-click Fill time to display the graphic in the design window. See Figure 19.28

9. Start the Define Workpiece Setting tool and set the X_total value to 6.5, the Y_total value to 3.5, and the Z_total value to 2, as shown in Figure 19.29.

10. Click OK to preview the workpiece in the design window.

11. Pick the Create Runoff surface tool from the Parting Design panel.

12. In the upper left corner of the dialog box, select the Auto Detect button to allow Inventor to search for the best parting line and create the runoff surface. The result should appear like Figure 19.30.

FIGURE 19.28
Fill time analysis
results

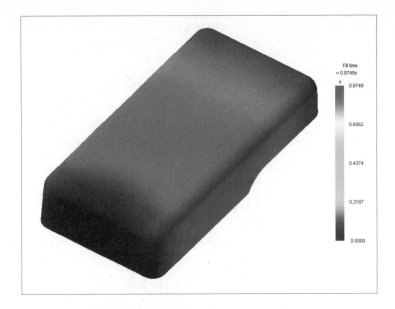

FIGURE 19.29
Setting the work-
piece size values

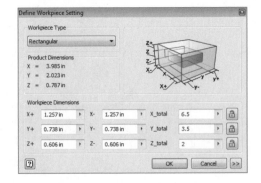

FIGURE 19.30
Generating the
runoff surface for
splitting the mold

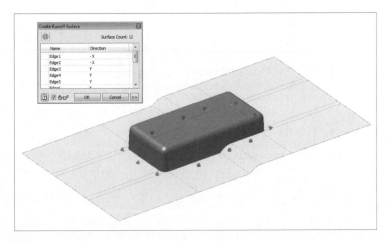

13. Click Ok to create the parting surface that will divide the core and cavity.

14. Start the Generate Core and Cavity tool.

15. On the dialog box that appears, pick the Preview/Diagnose button. This will preview the core in blue and the Cavity in green.

16. Drag the Body Separation slide to the right and back to show how the parts will separate.

17. Click OK to generate the two parts.

On occasion, the runner and gate information created beforehand does not update with the generation of the core and cavity. Select the Mold Update tool from the Quick Access toolbar to bring this data up into the cavity side of the workpiece.

18. Click the Finish Core/Cavity tool at the end of the ribbon to return to the Mold Layout tools.

19. Save your work and compare it to Figure 19.31.

FIGURE 19.31
The completed
workpiece

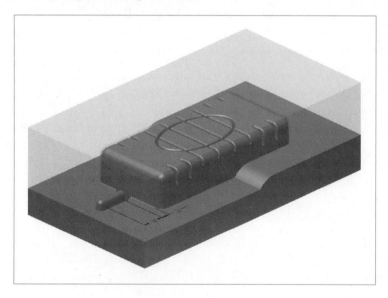

Now that the workpiece is complete, we can focus on generating the rest of the mold. These tools are located on the Mold Assembly tab. The tools in this tab are focused on the tools needed by manufacturing to generate the part efficiently.

Mold Base Inventor Tooling contains tens of thousands of parts for mold bases, as defined by the manufacturers. This works like a design accelerator to keep you from specifying something that will be a custom order or an inaccurate component.

Ejector Accessing the library of standard Ejector pins is only part of this tool. It will make it easy for you to properly align the pins based on the center of the component, using a coordinate system that is used by the tool makers.

Sprue Bushing This tool places the standard Sprue Bushing based on the location of the Runner, simplifying the process of placement and improving the quality.

You will now build out the entire mold base in amazingly few steps with very minimal input or effort. This is a great example of how the Functional Design approach can work for you.

1. Switch to the Mold Assembly tab on the ribbon.

2. Pick the Mold Base tool in the Mold Assembly panel

The Mold Base dialog box will not only allow you to select from a huge library of standard mold base designs, it will allow you to pick options within those base designs.

3. From the Vendor and Type pull-down, select the DME type E base.

4. Set the size to 346 mm x 346 mm.

5. Expand the dialog box by picking the double arrow icons on the top or bottom right of the dialog box.

Expanding the dialog box will show the list of components included in the mold base.

6. Pick on part labeled E 400 346X346X76.

7. Once selected, a few icons appear. Pick the icon with the ellipsis. The tool tip will say Property Settings.

8. Once picked, this will launch a dialog box for changing what if any options exist. Pick on the H_ value and change it from the pull-down list from 76 mm to 56 mm, as shown in Figure 19.32

9. Click OK to close the dialog box. This will update the E400 plate's description and the preview in the dialog box.

10. Reactivate the Placement Ref point indicator and select the bottom point in the front left corner of the workpiece.

FIGURE 19.32
Changing the mold
base components

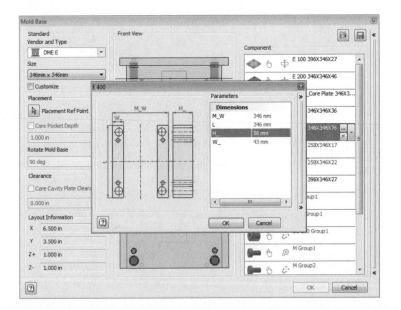

A preview outline of where the mold base will be position around the workpiece will appear. Make sure the workpiece appears inside the rectangle.

11. Once you've verified this, click OK in the dialog box to generate the mold base.

12. If the Mold Update icon becomes visible, pick it and then save your work and compare it to Figure 19.33.

FIGURE 19.33
The mold base
after placement

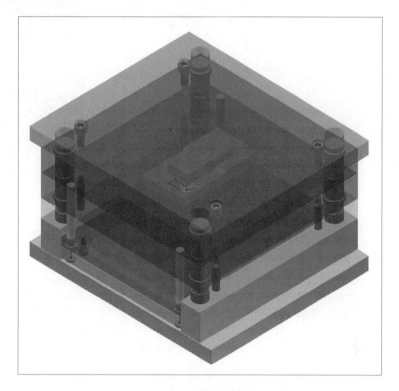

You may not have been expecting the entire mold base to be generated, but since the components are purchased, it makes sense to place them as a unit as they would be assembled.

Now you will do one last series of steps to see the final critical details of placing Ejectors and the Sprue Bushing.

1. Start the Ejector tool.

This will clear the screen of everything but the original part and runoff surface. It will also bring up a dialog box containing standard ejector pins and their optional sizes.

2. Leaving the options to their default, pick four placements for the ejectors between the pairs of ribs that you created.

3. Click the More button in the dialog box and enter precise values, as shown in Figure 19.34.

FIGURE 19.34
Placing the
ejectors

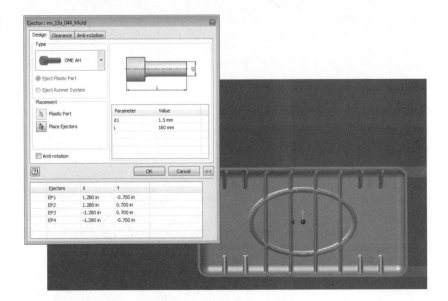

The order you picked your ejector placements in will give different positive or negative values, but filling out the table as shown will give you the correct result.

4. Click OK to place the Ejectors in the mold.

Placing the ejectors will cause Inventor to make clearance cuts in other plates and cut the length or even the contour of the ejector to prepare all of the components in the mold base. Picking on any of the pins in the browser will show how they terminate at the core face of the mold.

Now let's place our sprue bushing and a locking ring using an even easier technique.

5. Start the Sprue Bushing tool. It will be looking for a point to locate from.

6. Pick the end of the runner sketch farthest from the part.

7. Set the Type to DME R 79.

8. Set the length (L value) in the dialog box to 76 mm from the pull down.

9. For an offset, value enter -14 mm.

10. Click OK to place the bushing and cut the clearance geometry in the relevant parts.

11. Select the Sprue Bushing in the Design window.

12. Right-click and select open from the context menu.

13. Rotate the part to see how the runner geometry has been cut from the bushing, as show in Figure 19.35

14. Close the Sprue Bushing part and do not save changes to return to the assembly.

15. Select the Locating Ring tool from the Mold Assembly panel.

16. Set the type to DME R DME - Standard(R 60 12 SIERIE).

FIGURE 19.35
The Runner geometry is cut into the Sprue Bushing.

17. Click OK to place the ring into the assembly.

18. Save your work.

The finished base should look like Figure 19.36.

Through use of functional design techniques, the steps of designing a mold that are the most tedious are eliminated or greatly simplified. Explore the Inventor Tooling tools and enjoy just how easy it is to create a complex mold design.

FIGURE 19.36
The finished base

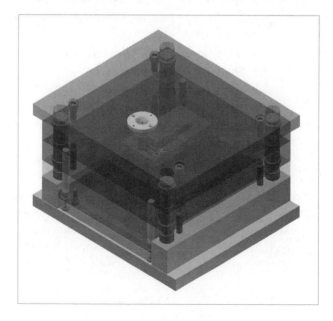

The Bottom Line

Set up plastic part templates   Creating templates that are specific to your design work saves time, reduces the tedium of initial part creation, and is an efficient way to create consistency from one design to another.

Master It   How do you create a template with design information focused on plastic part design?

Create thicken/offset features   When creating plastic parts, you will often find that working with surfaces allows you to achieve more free-form shapes than working with solids. Once the surfaces are created, you'll need to give them a thin wall thickness.

Master It   How would you create a plastic part file with many curved, free-form elements?

Create shell features   Shelling solids parts and features is a common way to create base features for plastic parts. Once the shell feature is created, other features can be added to it.

Master It   You want to create a shell feature but need to have the thickness of some faces be thicker than the rest. How would you accomplish this?

Create split features   Many times you may want to establish the overall shape of the feature and then divide the shape into separate parts of the overall design. You can use the Split tool to do just that and more.

Master It   You have a plastic part that needs to have a raised face for a rubber grip applied during the manufacturing process. How would this be done?

Create grill features   Grill features allow the inflow or outflow of air through a plastic thin wall part. Grills can be created with a number of subfeatures such as islands, ribs, and spars, but only the outer profile of the grill is required.

Master It   How would you determine the area of a grill opening to determine the airflow that it can handle?

Create rule fillet features   Rule fillets can be an extremely efficient way to apply fillets to many edges throughout the design that meet the same rule criteria.

Master It   How would you apply fillets to all the edges that are generated by extruding a shape down to an existing set of base features?

Create rest features   Rest features can be used to create level platform faces for mounting other parts to an irregular plastic part face.

Master It   You want to create a rectangular pocket on the inside of a plastic housing to hold an electronic component. How would you do this?

Create boss features   Boss features are ideal for creating fastener-mounting standoffs for thin wall plastic parts. You can use the Boss tool to create both halves of the fastener boss.

Master It   You want to create multiple boss features around the perimeter of a flat, pan-type, base part, but you know this base part is likely to change size. How would you set up the boss features to adjust to the anticipated edits?

Create lip and groove features   When designing plastic parts, it is often required that one half of a design fit into the other half. The Lip tool allows you to create both lip and groove features for these situations.

> **Master It**   You want to create a groove around the edge of an irregular, curved edge. How would you ensure the lip on the corresponding part would match?

Create snap fit features   Snap features are a common way to join plastic parts together so that they can be disassembled as needed. You can use the Snap Fit tool in Inventor to quickly create these features.

> **Master It**   How would you create a U-shaped snap fit with the Snap Fit tool?

Create rib and web features   Ribs and webs are often used to add rigidity and prevent warping during the design of plastic parts. You can add ribs based on open profile sketches in Inventor.

> **Master It**   How would you create a network of ribs that are evenly spaced, where some of them contain different cutouts than others?

Create draft features   Because plastic parts must be extracted from a mold during the manufacturing process, drafted faces must be included to ensure the parts can indeed be extracted from the mold.

> **Master It**   You want to create drafted faces on a complex part containing various shapes within it. How would you do this?

Create an injection mold   To generate the components you have designed with the plastic part features, you need to properly define the cavity to create the part and define how the material will flow into the cavity

> **Master It**   You want to create a mold base design in an efficient manner using parts that can be purchased. How would you do this?

Appendix A

The Bottom Line

Each of The Bottom Line sections in the chapters suggest exercises to deepen skills understanding. Sometimes there is only one possible solution, but often you are encouraged to use your skills and creativity to create something that builds on what you know and lets you explore one of many possible solutions.

Chapter 1: Inventor Design Philosophy

Create Parametric Designs   The power of parameter-based design comes from the quick and easy edits, where changing a parameter value drives a change through the design. In order to make changes easily, though, you need follow certain general rules, so that the changes update predictably.

> **Master It**   You want to create a model of a base plate, a rectangular-shaped part with a series of holes, and rectangular cutouts. What would your initial sketch look like in Inventor?
>
> **Solution**   To start a model for the part above, your initial sketch would most likely be just a rectangle defining the width and length of the part. This rectangle would be extruded to give it a thickness, and then you would create secondary sketches for the other features and cut them from the plate. This approach follows the best practice of creating simple sketches, to create simple features, to build a complex part.

Get the "Feel" of Inventor   Inventor's interface contains many elements that change and update to give you the tools you need to perform the task at hand. Getting comfortable with these automatic changes and learning to anticipate them will help you get the "feel" of Inventor.

> **Master It**   You create an extrude feature using the Extrude button, but cannot seem to find an Edit Extrude button. How can you edit the extruded feature to change the height?
>
> **Solution**   In order to edit an extrude feature (or any feature) you can simply right click on it in the browser and choose Edit Feature. This makes feature edits universal and does not require a separate edit tool for each feature type. Keep in mind that for most features, you can double-click the feature icon in the browser to edit it as well.

Use the Inventor Graphical Interface   Inventor 2011 uses the Ribbon Menu interface first introduced in Inventor 2010. This Ribbon consists of grouped tools that make finding tools intuitive once you become familiar with the basic layout.

> **Master It**   You are trying to draw a line on the face of a part, but you cannot seem to find the sketch tab in the Ribbon. How do you get it back?

Solution   The sketch tab is only present when you have created a new sketch or are editing an existing sketch. To access the Line tool then, you must first use the New Sketch tool to create a sketch, then you will see the sketch tab, and on it the Line tool.

Use the Inventor File Types   Inventor supports many different file types in its native environment, separating tasks and files to improve performance and increase stability.

Master It   You have trouble keeping the various file types straight because all of the file icons look rather similar to you. Is there a way you can see which file is what type?

Solution   You may want turn on the view of file extensions on your system, so that you can read the file extensions (`.ipt`, `.iam`, `.idw`, and so on) as you open and save files. You can find a tip in the previous pages of this chapter on how to do so depending upon your operating system.

Move from AutoCAD to Inventor   If you are making the move from AutoCAD to Inventor, you are not alone; most Inventor users have made that transition as well. You may find that over time you use AutoCAD less and less, or you might find that Inventor and AutoCAD both have a place in your design work. It is largely dependent upon the industry you work in.

Master It   You find Inventor to be a bit foreign and wish it worked more like AutoCAD. How can this be overcome?

Solution   One of the often repeated phrases of experienced Inventor users (who started out using AutoCAD themselves) is: Inventor is not AutoCAD. Typically this is repeated three times for good measure. The point is really that although the two applications can both be used for mechanical design, they are separate tools that approach design tasks differently. After all, you would never expect Excel to work like AutoCAD. So understand that it largely a matter of perception and after a while you will use Inventor in one way and AutoCAD the way you always have.

Create 3D Virtual Prototypes   It is important to understand that the full power of Inventor is realized when your models become more than just 3D, and become true prototypes of the object of your design.

Master It   You want to make your models as intelligent and as close to real life as possible, so how do you get started?

Solution   Start with the basics and as you master the creation of part, assemblies and detail drawings, you will soon see many opportunities to improve upon your Inventor knowledge and skill set. As design challenges arise, you will likely find ways of solving them in your model, whereas in the past you would have built test parts and prototypes.

Use Functional Design   Functional design includes a number of tools in Inventor. Most often, though, the design accelerators are what come to mind when one hears the term Functional Design.

Master It.   You need to fasten two assemblies together, but are not certain what size bolt to use; is there anything in Inventor that will assist with that?

Solution   You can use the Bolted Connection tool to create a fastener stack containing a bolt, washers, nuts, and so on, but you can also use the calculator built into the Bolted Connection tool to help you calculate the size requirement for your design. This is functional design.

Chapter 2: Data And Projects

Understand how project search paths work   Knowing how Inventor resolves file paths when it opens linked files, such as assembly and drawings, goes a long way toward helping prevent broken links and repair links that do get broken.

Master It   What type of file does Inventor use to point the assembly file to the parts that it contains?

Solution   Inventor uses the project file (*.ipj) to hold workspace and library search paths. If files are outside of these search paths then Inventor will not find the files and you will be required to point the assembly to them each and every time.

Set up library and Content Center paths   Library and Content Center paths are read-only library configurations set up in the project file.

Master It   When you set up a library or Content Center path to a folder that does not exist, what happens?

Solution   When you create a path to a nonexistent folder, Inventor will create that folder for you. Keep this in mind when you create paths in the project file and watch out for spelling and syntax errors, as Inventor will create a new folder according to typos as well.

Create and configure a project file   Project files are a key component to working successfully in Inventor; however, for many people this is a one-time setup. Once the project is created for the most part you just use it as is.

Master It   After creating a project file initially, you want to make one or more changes to the configuration, but you can't seem to do so. What could be the problem?

Solution   Keep in mind that while you are working with a project file it is held in a read-only status by Inventor. In order to make changes you need to first close all of the files you have open that are included in the project path. If you close all the files and the project is still held in the read-only state, switch to a different project in Inventor, and then browse out the .ipj file in Windows Explorer, and then right-click and check the read-only attribute of the .ipj file. Windows often seems to leave the read-only attribute set on .ipj files, and then it needs to be manually taken off. Once it is off you can switch back to that project in Inventor and make changes.

Determine the best project type for you   Although the Autodesk solution to a multiuse environment is Autodesk Vault, many people may not be able to use Vault. For instance, if you use another CAD application that links files together like Inventor, Vault will likely not know how to manage the internal links for those files.

Master It   Because you generally do not work concurrently on the same files as your co-workers you think you might be best to set up a single-user project for now, while you continue to investigate the Vault solution, but you are not sure if that will work.

Solution   Set up a single-user project and then point everyone's computer to that file. Keep a close eye on how well it works in the first several days and watch for signs that people are making changes to the file at the same time. If your workflow is fairly linear, with one department handing file off to the next, this may not be an issue. However, if you see that people are reaching for the same files at the same time, you probably need to make Vault a priority.

Chapter 3: Sketch Techniques

Set up options and settings for the sketch environment   Understanding the settings and options that apply to the sketch environment is an essential first step in working with Inventor.

Master It   You want to configure your own set of options and settings for your sketch environment and then back them up and/or distribute them to other workstations. How would you do this?

Solution   There are primarily two sets of options you can configure in Inventor. The Application Options configure Inventor itself, and the Document Settings configure the settings on a per file basis. You access both options and settings by going to the Get Started tab and selecting either the Application Options or the Document Settings button. In the Application Options you will go to the Sketch tab to configure the sketch environment. Once the changes are made you can click the Export button to save the settings as an .xml file for redistribution.

Create a sketch from a part file template   Creating a sketch in a blank template file is the fundamental step in creating 3D parametric models. You will use this basic step to start most of your part designs.

Master It   How would you capture the intent of your design when creating a base sketch for a new part?

Solution   Use a combination of lines, arcs, and geometry as well as sketch constraints and dimensions to properly constrain your sketch. You can then use this sketch to create a base feature for your part. Keep in mind the importance of keeping sketches simple and fully constrained.

Use sketch constraints to control sketch geometry   Understanding what each sketch constraint does when applied will allow you to determine when to use each type. Recall that often more than one constraint will work in any given situation.

Master It   How would you create a sketch that allows you to test "what if?" scenarios concerning the general shape and size of your part?

Solution   First ensure that your sketches are properly constrained. Sketches that are properly constrained are needed to allow you to experiment with your dimensional parameters by changing values and testing "what if?" scenarios. If the sketch geometry is not properly constrained, then changes to dimensions may create unpredictable results.

Master general sketch tools   Learning the features and tricks of the sketch tools will allow you to master Inventor sketching.

Master It   You are given a print of mixed units to work from and need to enter dimensions exactly as they are on the print. You understand that you can enter any dimensions in any unit simply by adding the correct suffix. But how would you create a radius dimension on a circle or a dimension from the tangents of a slot?

Solution   Recall that you switch between variant dimension solutions such as diameter to radius simply by right-clicking after having selected the geometry. You can also get alternate dimension solutions by selecting different parts of the same geometry. For instance, selecting a line and then almost anywhere on a circle will give you a dimension from the center point of the circle to the line, whereas selecting a line and the tangent quadrant point of the circle will give you a dimension from the tangent point of the circle and the line.

Create sketches from AutoCAD geometry   You can use existing AutoCAD files to create a base sketch for an Inventor model of the same part.

Master It   You have many existing 2D AutoCAD drawings detailing legacy parts. You want to reuse these designs as you convert to 3D modeling. How would you proceed?

Solution   You can copy and paste selected geometry from AutoCAD directly into an Inventor sketch and then turn it into a solid model. Keep in mind that the results are dependent on the accuracy of the original AutoCAD data. Once you become proficient with Inventor it is often just as quick to model a part from scratch rather than by copying it.

Use 3D sketch tools   Much of working with a 3D parametric modeler can be done by sketching in a two-dimensional plane and then giving depth to the sketch to create 3D features. However, sometimes you need to create paths or curves that are not planar. In those cases, you use the 3D sketch tools.

Master It   You know the profile of a complex curve as viewed from the top and side views. How would you create a 3D sketch from this data?

Solution   Start by creating a separate 2D sketch for both the top and side views of the curve. Then create a 3D sketch and use the 3D Intersection Curve tool to find the intersecting curve.

Chapter 4: Basic Modeling Techniques

Set application options and settings for part modeling   Understanding the settings and options that apply to the modeling environment is essential for getting the results you want from Inventor.

Master It   You want to configure your options and settings for your sketch environment and then back them up and/or distribute them to other workstations. How would you go about doing this?

Solution   You will first configure the options and settings by clicking Application Options on the Get Started tab, and then selecting the Sketch tab in the Application Options dialog box. Then use the Export button to save the settings as an .xml file.

Create basic part features   In this chapter, you learned how to plan a workflow that allows you to create stable, editable parts that preserve the design intent.

Master It   You need to create a fairly complex part consisting of many extrusions, revolves, sweeps, or lofts. In addition, you will need to create holes, fillets, chamfers, and other part modifiers. This part may need significant modification in the future by you or by other designers.

Solution   Determine how this part will be manufactured. Think about how the part might be designed to minimize production costs, while still fulfilling the intent of the design, by determining how many machining operations will be required. Determine the design intent of this part and how your approach will affect stability and any future edits or modifications.

Use the Extrude tool   The Extrude tool is one of the most common feature tools in the Inventor modeling tool set. Understanding the options and solutions available in this tool will prove useful throughout your designs.

Master It   Imagine you need to create an extruded feature but don't know the exact length; instead, you know the extrude will always terminate based on another feature. However, the location of that feature has not been fully determined just yet.

Solution   Use the Extrude To option and extrude the feature profile to a face or work plane of the other feature. Then as you determine the location of the other feature and make adjustments, your extrusion will update as well.

Create revolved parts and thread features   Creating revolved features and parts in Inventor can often resemble the creation of turned part and features in the real world. Applying thread features to a cylindrical face allows you to specify threads without having to actually model them.

Master It   Let's say you have a part that you intend to fabricate on a lathe. Although you could create the part with a series of stepped circular extrusions, it occurs to you that the Revolve tool might work also.

Solution   Oftentimes it may make sense to create a base extrusion from an extruded circle and then use the Revolve tool to create revolved cuts. This allows you to design both the stock material and the cut features with the intent of the design in mind, anticipating changes that might occur. You can then use the Thread tool to apply threads to any features requiring them.

Create work features   Using work features, work planes, work axes, and work points enable you to create virtually any part or feature. Work features are the building blocks for sketch creation and use.

Master It   Your design will require creating features on spherical and cylindrical faces. You need to precisely control the location and angle of these features.

Solution   Using existing origin features, created model features and edges, sketch objects, and other existing geometry within the file will permit you to create parametric work features as the basis for additional geometry creation.

Use the Fillet tool   The Fillet tool has a great deal of functionality packed into it. Taking the time to explore all the options on a simple test model may be the best way to understand all the options.

Master It   You are trying to create a series of fillets on a part. You create four sets of edge selections to have four different fillet sizes, but when you attempt to apply them, you receive an error stating that the feature cannot be built.

Solution   Sometimes the creation of multiple fillet sizes combined into one feature is not the way to go. Instead, identify the edges that will "compete" for a common corner, particularly where they differ in radius size, and create these fillets as individual fillet features. This allows Inventor to solve the corner in steps and makes the results more robust and less ambiguous.

Create intelligent hole features Although you can create a hole in a part by sketching a circle and extrude cutting it, this is typically not the recommended approach.

Master It You need to create a part with a series of various-sized holes on a plate. You would like to lay out the hole pattern in a single sketch and then use the Hole tool to cut the holes to the sizes required. However, when you select the From Sketch option in the Hole tool, it selects all of the holes, so you're thinking you must need to sketch out the hole pattern as circles and then use the Extrude tool to cut them out.

Solution Using the Extrude tool is not the way to go. Instead, create a sketch on the face of the plate, and use center points to mark the hole centers. Dimension each center point in place, and then start the Hole tool. Hold down Ctrl to deselect the center points for holes of a different size, and then create the hole feature for the first set of holes. Locate your sketch in the browser, right-click it, and choose Share Sketch. Then use the Hole tool to place the next size holes.

Bend parts You can bend a portion of a part after you define a bend line using a 2D Sketch line. You can specify the side of the part to bend, the direction of the bend, and its angle, radius, or arc length.

Master It You need to create a model of a piece of rolled tube and would like to specify the bend direction, but when you use the direction arrow, you get a preview in only one direction.

Solution Use a work plane to create a sketch in the middle of the part and then sketch the bend line on that work plane. This will allow you to specify either direction for the bend.

Chapter 5: Advanced Modeling Techniques

Create complex sweeps and lofts Complex geometry is created by using multiple work planes, sketches, and 3D sketch geometry. Honing your experience in creating work planes and 3D sketches is paramount to success in creating complex models.

Master It How would you create a piece of twisted flat bar in Inventor?

Solution Create the flat bar profile in a base sketch. Then create a work plane offset from the original sketch the length of the bar. Create the profile sketch on this work plane at a rotated orientation to match the degree of twist needed. Create a 3D sketch, and connect the corners of the first profile to the appropriate corners of the second profile. Use the Loft tool to loft from one profile to the other, using the 3D sketch lines as rails, to produce the twisted part.

Work with multi-body and derived parts Multi-body parts can be used to create part files with features that require precise matching between two or more parts. Once the solid bodies are created, you can create a separate part file for each component.

Master It What would be the best way to create an assembly of four parts that require features to mate together in different positions?

Solution Create the parts in a multi-body part file, and subtract material from one part based on the profile of the other. Consider creating the first two parts in one multi-body part file and the other two in another multi-body part file in order to keep the files as simple as possible. You can also derive the first multi-body part into the second for better control.

Utilize part tolerances   Dimensional tolerancing of sketches allows the checking of stack-up variations within assemblies. By adding tolerances to critical dimensions within sketches, parts may be adjusted to maximum, minimum, and nominal conditions.

Master It   You want to create a model feature with a deviation so that you can test the assembly fit at the extreme ends of the tolerances. How would this be done?

Solution   Use the Parameters dialog box to set up and adjust tolerances for individual dimensions. In the Parameters dialog box, set the tolerance to the upper or lower limits for the part, and then update the model using the Update button. Check the fit of the feature against its mating part or parts in the assembly environment, and then edit the part to set it back to the nominal once done.

Understand and use parameters and iProperties   Using parameters within files assists in the creation of title blocks, parts lists, and annotation within 2D drawings. Using parameters in an assembly file allows the control of constraints and objects within the assembly. Exporting parameters allows the creation of custom properties. Proper usage of iProperties facilitates the creation of accurate 2D drawings that always reflect the current state of included parts and assemblies.

Master It   You want to create a formula to determine the spacing of a hole pattern based upon the length of the part. What tools would you use?

Solution   Set up a user parameter that calls the part length and divides by the number of holes or the spacing, and then reference this user parameter in the hole pattern feature.

Troubleshoot modeling failures   Modeling failures are often caused by poor design practices. Poor sketching techniques, bad design workflow, and other factors can lead to the elimination of design intent within a model.

Master It   You want to modify a rather complex existing part file, but when you change the feature, errors cascade down through the entire part. How can this be done?

Solution   Position the end-of-part marker just under the feature you intend to modify, and then make the change. Then move the end-of-part back down the feature tree one feature at a time, addressing each error as it occurs. Use the Rebuild All tool from time to time, to see if re-computing the tree will force a "fix" to cascade down the tree. Continue until all features have been fixed.

Chapter 6: Sheet Metal

Take advantage of the specific sheet-metal features available in Inventor   Knowing what features are available to help realize your design can make more efficient and productive use of your time.

Master It   Of the sheet-metal features discussed, how many require a sketch to produce their result?

Solution   Five sheet-metal features consume a sketch: Contour Flange, Face, Cut, Punch, and Fold. Since Inventor has well-established paradigms for how sketches can be manipulated, knowing which features consume sketches may allow you to develop designs that are flexible and parametrically configurable.

Understand sheet-metal templates and rules   Templates can help get your design started on the right path, and sheet-metal rules and associated styles allow you to drive powerful and intelligent manufacturing variations into your design; combining the two can be very productive as long as you understand some basic principles.

Master It   Name two methods that can be used to publish a sheet-metal rule from a sheet-metal part file to the style library.

Solution   Rules and styles can be published or written to the style library either from Inventor or by using the Style Management Wizard (the harvester). Using the native Inventor method, right-clicking a given rule/style produces an option called Save To Style Library. Using the harvester, you can select a specific file and add its style information to your existing style library or create a new one.

Author and insert punch tooling   Creating and managing Punch tools can streamline your design process and standardize tooling in your manufacturing environment.

Master It   Name two methods that can be utilized to produce irregular (nonsymmetric) patterns of punch features.

Solution   Sketch center marks can be patterned within the insertion sketch as a symmetric array. During Punch tool insertion, the Centers control on the Geometry tab can be used to deselect center marks where you want a tool to be placed. The feature-patterning tools can also be used to create irregular patterns after a punch feature has been created. You can do this by first creating a symmetric pattern of punch features, then expanding the child pattern occurrences in the feature browser, and finally individually suppressing them. Both methods prevent the feature from being displayed in the folded and flat pattern as well as omit the Punch tool information in the flat pattern punch metadata.

Utilize the flat pattern information and options   The sheet-metal folded model captures your manufacturing intent during the design process; understanding how to leverage this information and customize it for your needs can make you extremely productive.

Master It   How can you change the reported angle of all your Punch tools by 90 degrees?

Solution   The flat pattern's orientation infers a virtual x-axis for punch angle calculation, so rotating the flat pattern by 90 degrees will change all the punch angles by the same amount. The flat pattern can also affect the bend and punch direction (up or down) by flipping the base face, and reported bend angles can be changed from Bending Angle to Open Angle by changing options in the Bend Angle tab of the Flat Pattern Definition dialog box.

Understand the nuances of sheet-metal iPart factories   Sheet-metal iPart factories enable you to create true manufacturing configurations with the inclusion of folded and flat pattern models in each member file.

Master It   If you created sheet-metal iPart factories prior to Inventor 2009, any instantiated files contain only a folded model. Name two methods that you could use to drive the flat pattern model into the instantiated file.

Solution Once you have opened, migrated, and saved a legacy sheet-metal iPart factory, you can decide between two methodologies for obtaining the flat pattern model within your instantiated files: push or pull. The *push method* is accomplished from within the iPart factory by using the context menu option, Generate Files, which is associated with the member filename. This method pushes out a new definition of the member file including the flat pattern model. The *pull method* requires you to be using the Inventor Rebuild All tool, followed by saving the factory file. Now that the factory has been rebuilt, any time you open one of the instantiated files associated with the factory, it will see that it's out-of-date and will trip the update flag. Selecting Update will pull the flat pattern model into the instantiated member file.

Model sheet-metal components with non-sheet-metal features Inventor doesn't always allow you to restrict yourself to sheet-specific design tools; understanding how to utilize non-sheet-metal features will ensure that your creativity is limitless.

Master It Name two non-sheet-metal features that can lead to unfolding problems if used to create your design.

Solution As discussed in the chapter, Loft and Shell can lead to numerous problems during unfolding because of nondevelopable curvature introduced by Loft and non-uniform thickness introduced by Shell.

Work with imported sheet-metal parts Understanding the way in which Inventor accomplishes unfolding as well as how to associate an appropriate sheet-metal rule are keys to successfully working with imported parts.

Master It Name the one measured value that is critical if you want to unfold an imported part.

Solution The measured sheet thickness is the most important geometric measurement in an imported sheet-metal part. Ensuring that the thickness of your imported part matches the active Thickness parameter means the difference between success and frustration. Although you can change the active rule (or create a new one) to match all the geometric conditions of your imported part, these will affect only new features or topology that you introduce. Thickness is the key.

Understand the tools available to annotate your sheet-metal design Designing your component is essential, but it's equally important to understand the tools that are available to efficiently document your design and extract your embedded manufacturing intent.

Master It What process is required to recover flat pattern width and height extents within your Drawing Manager parts list?

Solution By creating custom iProperties within your sheet-metal part file set equal to <FLAT PATTERN LENGTH> cm and <FLAT PATTERN WIDTH> cm, flat pattern extents can be referenced by your parts list by adding these new properties using the Column Chooser tool. To make this process more efficient, you can predefine the custom iProperties in your sheet-metal template file, and the custom properties can be authored into a custom Drawing Manager parts list template for quick application.

Harvest your legacy sheet-metal styles into sheet-metal rules Using the harvesting utilities provided, you can extract your legacy sheet-metal styles and publish them into style library sheet-metal rules, pre-associated to material styles, sheet thickness values, and sheet-metal Unfold Rules.

Master It   How can you extract sheet-metal style information from legacy part files or template files for the purpose of publishing it with a Sheet-Metal Rule?

Solution   By launching the Style Management Wizard application (also known as the *harvester*) from Program Files ➢ Autodesk ➢ Autodesk Inventor 2011 ➢ Tools ➢ Style Library Manager, you can process individual files or entire project directories to extract sheet-metal styles information and automatically publish it to a new or existing Sheet Metal Rule and Sheet Metal Unfold Rule XML files for use by your style library. As a reminder, although it is possible to harvest sheet-metal rules that contain references to model parameters and linked external files, this is simply a result of the harvester's inability to detect these conditions. The extracted rule information will be broken, and the rule will not be usable. By default, the sheet-metal document will leverage some programmatic values to keep your model from being corrupted, but once you open the Style And Standard Editor dialog box, you will see errors that must be resolved. To avoid this situation, it is recommended that you preview the contents of files before utilizing them for harvesting. If you need to be able to reference model parameters or external files to drive your sheet-metal rule, define these rules within your template file.

Chapter 7: Part and Feature Reuse

Create and modify iParts   iParts are the solution to creating parts that allow for an infinite number of variations without affecting other members of the same part family already used within your designs.

Master It   You use a purchased specialty part in your designs and would like to create the many size configurations this part comes in ahead of time for use within assembly design. How would this be done?

Solution   Create or use an existing model, and edit the parameter list to name specific parameters to logical names. Add the configuration table by creating an iPart from this model. Configure the parameters in the table and add rows according to variations needed. And finally, test the newly created iPart by inserting all variations of the part into a blank assembly.

Create and use iFeatures and punches   Creating a library of often-used features is essential to standardization and improved productivity within your design workflow.

Master It   You want to be able to place common punches, slots, and milled features quickly, rather than having to generate the feature every time. What is the best way to approach this?

Solution   Extract iFeatures from existing standard and sheet-metal part features, and place them in user-defined folders within the `Catalog` subfolder. Using your custom-created iFeatures as well as standard iFeatures, practice placing them into your designs to see how they behave and how they can be modified. Finally, once the iFeatures or punches have been proven to work as expected, use them to quickly place common features in your production designs.

Copy and clone features You do not have to create iFeatures in order to reuse various part features in your designs. If a part feature will have limited use in other designs, it is often better to simply copy it from part to part or from face to face on the same part.

Master It You need to reuse features within a part or among parts. You consider iFeatures, but realize that this feature is not used often enough to justify setting up an iFeature. How would you proceed?

Solution Right-click the existing feature, and choose Copy. Determine whether dependent and independent features such as fillets and chamfers need to be copied as well, and then paste the feature onto another face in the same part. Or open a different part file and paste onto a selected face. Copying between two parts is called *cloning*.

Link parameters between two files Linking design parameters between two or more files allows you to control design changes from a single source, making it easy to update an entire design from one file.

Master It You want to specify the overall length and width of a layout design in a base part and then have other components update as changes are made to this part. What are the methods to do this?

Solution From the other component files, open the parameter editor, use the Link button to specify the source file, and then choose which parameters to link. You can then call those linked parameters into the sketch and feature dimensions of the other components in your design.

Configure, create, and access Content Center parts Content Center provides a great opportunity to reuse database-created geometry within assemblies and within functional design modules. The Content Center Editor provides the means to add custom content into Content Center. You can create and add custom libraries to your current project file.

Master It You would like to change the part numbers in some Content Center components to match the part numbers your company uses. You would also like to add proprietary components to Content Center. How do you customize the Content Center?

Solution Create a custom Content Center library. Configure your project file to include your newly created read/write Content Center library. Utilize the Content Center Editor to create new categories within your custom Content Center library. Convert a part or an iPart to a Content Center component using the Publish option.

Chapter 8: Assembly Design Workflows

Assemble components using assembly constraints Assembly constraints are an important part of working with Inventor assembly files. Assembly constraints determine how assembly components fit together. As constraints are applied between components, degrees of freedom are removed.

Master It You are new to 3D and find the concept of assembly constraints a bit challenging. Where can you find a simple overview of constraints?

Solution You can find a good overview of constraints by going to the Get Started tab, and clicking the Show Me Animations button. From there select Assembly - Constraints from the list. You can then click any of the assembly constraint topics listed to watch a short animation detailing how to create each constraint type.

Organize designs using structured subassemblies.   Subassemblies add organization, facilitate the bill of materials, and reduce assembly constraints; all this results in better performance and easier edits. One of the habits of all Inventor experts is their effective use and understanding of subassemblies.

Master It   You need to hand off an accurate BOM for finished designs to the purchasing department at the end of each design project.

Solution   Organize parts in subassemblies in a real-world manner matching the way that components are assembled on the shop floor. Use Phantom assemblies when structuring parts merely for the purpose of reducing assembly constraints. Set assemblies as Purchased or Inseparable when you want multiple components to appear as a single item in the BOM. Export the BOM from the assembly to an Excel spreadsheet or other intermediate format to give to purchasing.

Work with adaptive components   Geometry can be set to be adaptive so that it can be sized and positioned in the context of where it is used in the assembly. You can set underconstrained geometry to be adaptive by specifying the elements allowed to adapt.

Master It   You want to set a feature of a part to be adaptive so that it can adapt to another part in an assembly. However, the feature is based on a fully constrained sketch. How would this be done?

Solution   To set a fully constrained sketch to be adaptive you would edit the sketch and then set the dimensions that are intended to adapt, to be driven dimensions. Doing so will leave the sketch in an underconstrained state, opening it up for adaptively.

Create assembly level features   An assembly feature is a feature created and utilized within the active assembly file. Because the feature is created within the assembly file, it does not exist at the single part or subassembly level.

Master It   You want to make a notch in a standard part that will not affect its use in every other assembly it is used in. Can this be done?

Solution   Create the notch in the assembly it is used in rather than the part file itself, and then the notch will only exist for that instance of the part, and not in other instances of it.

Manage Bills of Materials   Managing a bill of materials can be a large part of any assembly design task. Understanding the BOM structure goes a long way toward successfully configuring your bill of materials.

Master It   You need to mark a component as a reference component in just one assembly file. However, when you attempt to do so using the BOM editor, it is designated as reference in every assembly. How can you set just a single instance of a component to be a reference component?

Solution   When components are set to reference in the BOM editor, the BOM structure for that file is being changed globally. In order to override a component's BOM structure per instance, right-click on it in the browser and choose BOM structure from the right-click context menu and then select reference.

Use positional reps and flexible assemblies together.   Often you may need to show a design in various stages of motion to test interference and/or proof of concept. Copying assemblies so that you can change the assembly constraints to show different assembly positions can become a file management nightmare. Instead, use flexible subassemblies and positional representations.

Master It   You need to show your assembly in variations dependent upon the position of the moving parts and the task the machine is accomplishing at given stages of its operation.

Solution   Leave subassemblies underconstrained if they have parts that determine their position based on the relationships with parts within another subassembly. Set them to Flexible to allow them to be mated to other parts and used in different positions within the same top-level assembly. Create positional representations to show the design in known kinematic states, such as fully opened, closed, opened at a given angle, and so on. As an added benefit, animating assemblies in Inventor Studio is very simple when positional representations have been set up in the model.

Copy assembly designs for reuse and configuration   Because of the live linked data that exists in Inventor assemblies, using Windows Explorer to copy designs and rename parts is difficult and often delivers poor results. Using the tool provided in Inventor will allow you to copy designs and maintain the links between files.

Master It   You need to duplicate an existing design in order to create a similar design.

Solution   Use the Copy Components feature in the assembly environment to copy designs and choose which parts to copy and rename, reuse, or omit from the new design. Use Autodesk Vault to take it to the next level and include all the 2D drawings in the copied design.

Substitute a single part for entire subassemblies   Working with large assemblies, particularly where large, complex assemblies are used over and over as subassemblies within a top-level design, can tax almost any workstation if not approached in the correct manner.

Master It   You would like to swap out a complex assembly for a simplified version for use in layout designs or to use in large assemblies in an attempt to improve performance.

Solution   Create LOD representations to suppress components when not in use during the design cycle. Create single substitute parts from large complex assemblies to be used as subassemblies within the design. Enjoy the benefits of referencing fewer files while maintaining an accurate bill of materials.

Chapter 9: Large Assembly Strategies

Select a workstation   Having the right tool for the job is the key to success in anything you do. This is true of selecting a large assembly workstation. You have learned that for optimal performance you should strive to keep your system working in physical memory (RAM).

Master It   You notice that your computer runs slowly when working with large assemblies and want to know whether you should consider a 64-bit system.

Solution   Evaluate the amount of time you spend working on large assemblies and the amount of that time you spend waiting on your workstation in order to decide whether your system is adequate. Monitor your RAM usage, and decide whether upgrading to

64-bit system is a good solution for your needs. You should plan for hardware upgrades in your budget to make them more manageable. Remember that if you have a system that was built in the last year or two it may already be capable of running a 64-bit operating system so you may only need to upgrade the OS rather than replace the hardware.

Adjust your performance settings   You have learned that there are many settings in Inventor and in Windows that you can use to configure the application to work more efficiently with large assemblies.

Master It   You want to make your current workstation run as efficiently as possible for large assembly design.

Solution   Disable the unneeded Windows visual effects and discontinue the use of screen savers, large resolution screen sizes, and desktop wallpapers. Learn the location of the Application Options settings within Inventor that will provide performance gains.

Use best practices for large assembly   Knowing the tools for general assembly design is only half of the battle when it comes to conquering large assemblies. Understanding the methods of large assembly design and how they differ from a general assembly design is a key to success.

Master It   You want to create adaptive parts so that you can make changes during the initial design stage and have several parts update automatically as you work through the details. But you are concerned about how this will adversely affect your assembly performance.

Solution   Create adaptive relationships between parts as you normally would, but ensure that the adaptivity is turned off once the initial design is done. If the parts require an update, turn adaptivity back on, make the edits, and then turn adaptivity back off.

Manage assembly detail   Inventor includes several tools to help manage assembly detail so that you can accomplish your large assembly design goals.

Master It   You want to reduce the number of files your large assembly is required to reference while you are working on it and yet maintain an accurate bill of materials.

Solution   Use substitute LOD representations to derive a subassembly into a single part file. Place multiple instances of the subassembly into the top-level assembly at the substitute level-of-detail.

Simplify parts   Creating highly detailed parts may be required for generating production drawings or Inventor Studio renderings, but using those high-detail parts in large assemblies may have an adverse affect.

Master It   You want to create a lower level-of-detail part file for common parts to be reused many times over in your large assemblies but are concerned about managing two versions of a part.

Solution   Create an embedded link between the two versions so that you can easily locate and access the other version if the first version requires an edit.

Chapter 10: Weldment Design

Select and use the right weldment design methodology   We have shown you three weldment design methodologies. Before starting on any weldment design, it is imperative to keep the documentation, interference analysis, mass properties, and other design criteria in perspective and select the right design methodology.

Master It   What is the right weldment strategy for you? If you don't need to document the weldment design stages, you could consider the part files and part features methodology or the weldment assembly and derived methodology. With the weldment assembly methodology, you get to document the different stages of weldment design and reap the benefits of any new enhancements.

Solution   Talk to your machine shop, and then choose the one that best suits you. Use the weldment assembly design methodology if you can't decide.

Create and edit weld preparations and machining features   Following the weldment methodology, you need to plan on creating the gaps needed (weld preparations) to deposit the weld beads. You need to create post weldment machining features that go through the weld beads.

Master It   Where can you find preparation and machining features, and when do you use them? Weld preparations and machining features are similar to part modeling features. Based on the weld bead shape needed, you need to plan for creating the preparations in advance. Once the welds are done, you need to create the features for the machining processes.

Solution   Double-click the Preparations or Machining tool in the assembly Model browser to go into those environments. Chamfer and Move Face are most commonly used. Most groove welds require some kind of weld preparations.

Create and edit different kinds of weld beads such as cosmetic, fillet, and groove   We have described the relative advantages and disadvantages of cosmetic and solid weld beads. Weldment design involves the optimal mix of these weld beads based on needs and requirements.

Master It   You need to create the weld annotations only in drawings, without any need to create them in the model. You have weld subassemblies that need only lightweight representation in both the model and drawings. In situations involving accurate interference and mass properties, you need accurate weld beads. The question is: What type of weld beads should you use?

Solution   Double-click Welds in the assembly Model browser, and choose the desired weld bead type. For a lightweight representation with no interference and accurate mass properties, use cosmetic welds. For interference and accurate mass properties, use the solid representation. Use a combination of fillet and groove welds as needed to generate the desired weld bead shape. Use the split technique in cases where you need precise control. Observe that you can use a single weld symbol to call out multiple weld beads.

Document weldment stages in drawings   Welds need to be documented in assemblies or drawings. It is important to show the different stages of weldment design in drawings to get a good idea of how to manufacture the weldment. You can use the drawing tools effectively to annotate the welds in drawings. This will help the welder understand the design intent better.

Master It   What are the different tools used for weld documentation? You can annotate the welds in assemblies. If you prefer to document the welds in drawings, you could document the four stages of weldment design: as-assembled, as-prepped, as-welded, and as-machined stages in drawings. Besides, you could use other drawing manager tools to customize weld documentation.

Solution   While creating a drawing view on the Model State tab of the Drawing View dialog box, select Assembly, Machining, Welds, or Preparation. Use the End Fill tool to customize the weld bead process shape. The Weld Caterpillars is another useful tool to show welds in a drawing.

Generate and maintain a consistent BOM across welded assemblies, drawings, and presentations   You have been shown how to generate and maintain a consistent bill of materials for weldment assemblies and a parts list in drawings. Mark parts or assemblies as inseparable to designate them as weldments.

Master It   How do you generate the BOM and parts list for your weldment? You can generate the bill of materials and mark the components as Inseparable. In the drawing, you generate the parts list for the weldment assembly.

Solution   Click the BOM tool in a weldment assembly. In the Structure column, you can set each part to be inseparable. Use the Parts List tool and appropriate table wrapping options to generate the parts list.

Chapter 11: Functional Design

Use Inventor's Design Accelerators   Design Accelerators and Design Generators allow you to rapidly create complex geometry and the associated calculations that verify the viability of your design.

Master It   Your design needs a bolted connection, but you are not certain about the number of bolts to use to ensure a proper connection.

Solution   Use the Bolted Connection Generator to determine the optimum number of bolts for a given material and loading conditions.

Use Inventor's Design Calculators   Design Calculators do not create any geometry, but they permit you to store the calculations in the assembly and repeat the calculation with different input values at a later time.

Master It   You need to calculate the size of a weld between two plates to withstand a certain lateral force.

Solution   Use the Fillet Weld Calculator to determine the size, type, and material of the weld bead.

Understand the interaction of these tools with Content Center   Some of the generators use content center, while others create custom geometry.

Master It   You receive an error when you try to specify fasteners for a Bolted Connection.

Solution   The Bolted Connection Generator requires Content Center. If you use Desktop Content, check your project file to make sure you have Content Center Libraries configured. If you use shared content, confirm that you are logged into the Content Center server.

Develop best practices for using these tools   In this chapter, you learned how to use Design Accelerators in the best possible way by providing best practices and tips and tricks concerning the use of templates, exploring the benefits of using a particular type of calculation or connection method for a given scenario, and showing how to select the right material to do the job.

Master It   You need to design a camshaft to activate an inlet valve that needs to respect a specific lift-over-time graph. You also want to reuse the design and slightly modify it for other similar cams like the exhaust valve.

Solution   Use the Disc Cam Generator to design the shape of the cam; then use a template to export the design, import it, and reuse it for a new design.

Master It   You want to design a compression spring that operates within very strict dimensional limitations and find a spring material that also satisfies the load requirements.

Solution   Use the Spring Generator to select the combination of pitch, wire diameter, and material that withstands the applied force without becoming fully compressed.

Master It   Your design needs a gear transmission between two shafts with a predefined position, and you want the gears to be separate components that need to be connected to the shaft.

Solution   Use the Spur Gear Generator to construct the gears. Use the Key Connection Generator to connect the gears to the shafts.

Chapter 12: Documentation

Create an exploded assembly view by creating a presentation   Presentation files are used to virtually disassemble an assembly so downstream consumers can better visualize the design. The explosion created in the presentation file can be referenced in an assembly drawing to complement nonexploded assembly views.

Master It   Your assembly design is complex and contains many internal components that can't be visualized in traditional assembly drawing views.

Solution   Create a new presentation file, reference an assembly, and tweak parts and subassemblies away from their constrained positions. Add as many tweaks as necessary to communicate the design effectively. You may choose to create several explosions in one presentation file to achieve this goal.

Create and maintain drawing templates, standards, and styles   Inventor provides numerous methods to create, store, and use drawing templates and styles. Careful planning should be considered for how and where to manage these resources. Consideration must be given to how templates are deployed on your network and whether to use the style library.

Master It   Rather than using one of Inventor's out-of-the-box drawing settings, you need to set up a drawing template, a drafting standard, and annotation styles to conform to a particular international, industry, or company drafting standard.

Solution   Use one of the drawing templates that are installed with Inventor, and reconfigure it to meet your or your company's requirements. Edit the drawing resources to customize your title block, border, and sketched symbols. Define annotation styles such as dimension and parts list styles, and determine how best to share them across your workgroup.

Generate 2D drawing views of parts, assemblies, and presentations   The Drawing Manager environment in Inventor enables you to generate traditional 2D drafting views from your 3D solid models.

Master It   You've used Inventor's modeling tools to generate parts and assemblies to meet your design criteria. Now you need to generate drawing views of this design so that it can be communicated to machinists, fabricators, and inspectors.

Solution   Generate drawing views of your model using the Drawing Views panel in Inventor's Drawing Manager. Generate as many projected and cut views as necessary to fully communicate your design.

Annotate drawing views of your model   Drawing Manager provides a rich set of Dimensioning tools, special symbols, and tables that enable you to fully annotate part and assembly drawings conforming to several international drawing standards.

Master It   Now that you've generated drawing views of your design, the views must be fully annotated in accordance with your company's or your customer's required drafting standard.

Solution   Use the Drawing Annotation panel to place dimensions, tables, and symbols on your part or assembly views to fully communicate the design. Use styles to help create consistent drafting techniques and conformity to drafting standards.

Chapter 13: Inventor Tools Overview

Take your models from Inventor to Autodesk Building Systems   If you frequently need to take your Inventor models to ABS, then AEC Exchange can help you in this process with three simple steps. Inventor provides a variety of ways to simplify the model and author it. Such models can be published in ABS.

Master It   You can do this with the following three steps: model simplifying, authoring, and publishing. You can also save a DWG as a solid.

Solution   Simplify the model using derived technology. Author the model with cables, conduit, ducts, or pipe. Create part families and catalogs.

Create AutoLimits (design sensors)   You use AutoLimits to monitor design parameters in which you are interested.

Master It   How many AutoLimits can you use in an assembly?

Solution   Create the AutoLimits and set up their boundaries. Although technically the number of AutoLimits you can use in your model is unlimited, you should consider limiting the number of AutoLimits to around 10, in order to avoid impacting the performance of your model.

Manage design data efficiently using Inventor tools   There are different tools for managing design data, which is typically distributed across part, assembly, and drawing files. You can associate Excel spreadsheets, text files, Word documents, and so on, with these tools.

Master It   The Design Assistant keeps the file relationships while copying, renaming, and moving files. Whenever you are sending Inventor files to others, use Pack And Go, which hunts the file relationships down for you and then you can package it into a single ZIP file. You can delegate many of the tasks in Inventor to the Task Scheduler. You can propagate source drawing template information to several destination drawings using the Drawing Resource Transfer Wizard.

Solution   In the Design Assistant, click the Manage button. Right-click the file in the Action column, and select Action. Right-click the file in the Name column, and select Change Name. Click Save Changes. Right-click the file in Windows Explorer to use Pack And Go. In the Task Scheduler, use the Create Task menu to create your task. In the Drawing Resource Transfer Wizard, select source resources, deselect any unwanted resources, and propagate the template information to destination drawings.

Manage styles   You can use the Style Library Manager and the Style Management Wizard to organize your styles to keep them simple and clean.

Master It   How do you manage your styles? Styles normally need to be copied, edited, and deleted. Use the Style Library Manager. How can you create a central repository of styles? How do you purge styles? Use the Style Management Wizard for these tasks.

Solution   You can create a new style library using the Create New Style Library button in the Style Library Manager. You can copy styles by clicking Style Library 1 and then clicking Style Library 2. To delete styles, right-click the style in the Style Library Manager, and then rename or delete the style. You can harvest styles by adding files and then clicking Harvest Styles Into Target Style Library. You can select an existing style library or create a new library by clicking Start. You could also purge styles in a library by clicking Purge All Unused Styles From Files in the Style Management Wizard.

Create expressions with iProperties   Property fields can be concatenated to produce desired customized information in BOM and parts lists.

Master It   You can break down, for example, "stock size" of your parts to be used in your BOM with associativity to model parameters. You can create and manage expressions for iProperties.

Solution   You can create expressions on the Summary, Project, Status, or Custom tab. Start with the = sign, and type in the text. To include parameters or iProperty names, include them in brackets. A detected expression is denoted by *fx*. You can create a template file with predefined expressions for iProperties to unify your parts list and other documentation.

Measure in assemblies   Click the right Measure tool and selection filters to make measurements.

Master It   How do you measure in assemblies? Once you set the selection filter, you make the selections and use the measurement helpers to get complex measurements.

Solution   Use the measurement helpers to accumulate measurements. Click the correct selection filter in the assembly's environment to get the measurement between components, parts, or faces and edges.

Give feedback to Autodesk   You can participate in the Customer Involvement Program (CIP). Customer error reporting (CER) helps Autodesk know about any issue you might experience.

Master It   You have a repeatable crash that you suspect is related to a specific file, or a specific machine, and want to know if Autodesk can help you determine this.

Solution   You can use the CER form to supply step by step information about repeatable issues and contact information, and then call reseller support or log a case with Autodesk through the subscription website. Autodesk can look up your CER based on the submittal time and contact information you entered.

Chapter 14: Exchanging Data with Other Systems

Import and export geometry   In the design world today, you most likely need to transfer files to or from a customer or vendor from time to time. Chances are, the files will need to be translated to or from a neutral file format to be read by different CAD packages.

Master It   You are collaborating with another design office that does not use Inventor. You are asked which you would prefer, IGES or STEP files.

Solution   Request a STEP file over IGES when you have the choice. Take advantage of the extra intelligence related to assembly structure and filenames that can be retained in the STEP file format.

Use Inventor file translators   Inventor offers native file translators for CATIA, Pro/ENGINEER, SolidWorks, Unigraphics, and other CAD file types. This allows you to access these file formats with Inventor and translate the files into Inventor files directly.

Master It   You are a "job shop" and in the past have been required to maintain a copy of SolidWorks in addition to your copy of Inventor in order to work with customers who send you SolidWorks files. You would like to eliminate the cost of maintaining two software packages.

Solution   Use Inventor to access the customer's files directly and convert them to Inventor files for your in-house use. Use Save Copy As to export the file back out as a SolidWorks file to send to the client for review. In this way you may be able to eliminate the need to maintain two software packages.

Work with imported data   Using the construction environment in Inventor, you can repair poorly translated surface files. Often a file fails to translate into a solid because of just a few translation errors in the part. Repairing or patching the surfaces and promoting the file to a solid allows you to use the file more effectively.

Master It   You download an IGES file from a vendor website, but when you attempt to use the component in your design, the surface data is found to have issues.

Solution   Open the file and copy the surfaces to the construction environment. Use Stitch Surface to create composite surfaces, and identify the gaps in the surface data. Use the construction tools to delete, patch, and extend surfaces in order to close the gaps and promote the data to a solid. Before getting started on this, evaluate the amount of time required to repair the surface data. You may find that you can model the vendor component, by using catalog specs or by measuring an actual part, faster than you can repair some surface models.

Work with Design Review markups   Design Review offers you and the people you collaborate with an easy-to-use electronic markup tool that can be round-tripped from Inventor. Design Review markups can be made on both 2D and 3D files.

Master It   You want to use Design Review to communicate with vendors and clients in order to save time and resources, but you have found that others are unsure of what Design Review is and how to get it.

Solution   Suggest using Design Review to the people you collaborate with and mention to them that this application is a free download. Send them the link to download the application and the online demonstration found in Design Review's Help menu. Continue to offer your collaborators the review material in PDF, DWG, or any other traditional file type in case they end up in a time crunch, but send them DWF files as well. If they use Internet Explorer 7, consider sending them DWFx files, and mention to them that they can open those files directly in their web browser.

Chapter 15: Frame Generator

Work with frame files   Frame Generator puts all the members at the same level in the assembly.

Master It   You have a frame that is built up in sections that are welded together. You need to document the manufacturing process.

Solution   Use Demote to create subassemblies of frame members. Select the frame members in the browser. From the context menu, select Component ➤ Demote Frame Generator Components. This preserves the Frame Generator relationships.

Insert frame members onto a skeleton model   Frame Generator builds a skeleton model for the frame from the selected lines and edges.

Master It   Since Frame Generator builds its own skeleton model, you don't have to build a master model before you start creating the frame. What would you reference in your assembly to use as a frame skeleton?

Solution   Use layout sketches and surfaces to design the basic frame shape. Position the components that will be mounted to the frame in the assembly, and reference edges on the parts. As you make changes to the assembly, such as the overall size or the position of components, the frame will automatically update.

Add end treatments to frame members   Frame Generator does not support end treatments on merged members.

Master It   Let's assume you are building a stairway and the handrail has curved sections. How would you approach the curved handrail so that its ends can be treated?

Solution   You can handle this situation in several ways:

◆   When you create the frame member, don't select the Merge option. This creates individual files for each segment. You can add end treatments to the end segments and document the details in the assembly drawing.

◆ Create the sketches so the ends of the curved member terminate at the face of another member. If the mating member has a flat face, you don't need an end treatment.

◆ Add short linear segments that aren't merged with the rest of the curved member. You can document that the length of the curved member does not include end treatments.

◆ Manually create end treatments using part-modeling commands. Frame members are created as custom parts that can be edited.

Make changes to frames   Inventor provides detailed frame member information.

Master It   You need to determine the size and wall thickness of the tubing and make it either thicker or larger.

Solution   Use the Frame Member Info tool to get the properties for the frame members. Then, you can use the Change tool to increase the wall thickness, increase the size, or select a different structural profile.

Author and publish structural profiles   Frame Generator uses structural shapes from Content Center.

Master It   You need to add custom aluminum extrusions to Content Center so Frame Generator can access them.

Solution   Use the Structural Shape Authoring tool to prepare the parts for publishing. Use the Publish Part tool to add the parts to the Content Center.

Create BOMs for Frame Generator assemblies   Frame Generator has special parameters for frame members.

Master It   You need to add the profile dimensions and the length to the Description field.

Solution   Use the BOM expression builder to add the Stock Number and G_L parameters to the Description field.

Chapter 16: Inventor Studio

Create and manage surface, lighting, and scene styles   Creating your own more realistic styles is often the difference between a rendering that looks kind of real and one that is photorealistic.

Master It   You need to create a surface style that portrays black, bumped plastic.

Solution   Here is the preferred way to create a new surface style:

1. Copy the Black surface style, giving the new style an appropriate name, such as Plastic (Black – textured).

2. On the Diffuse tab, click Use Texture Image.

3. In the list of images, select one of the Plastic image textures.

4. On the Bump tab, click Same As Texture, and set the percent value to 50 percent.

5. Save and apply the texture to the component.

Here is the preferred way to create a new lighting style:

1. Copy the lighting style containing most of what your new style needs, giving the new style an appropriate name.

2. On the various tabs, modify the lighting parameters.

3. Click OK.

Here is the preferred way to create a new scene style:

1. Copy the scene style that has similarities to the new style, giving the new style an appropriate name.

2. On the various tabs, modify the scene parameters.

3. Click OK.

Create and animate cameras   Although static camera animations are a common part of any animation, creating and animating cameras give your renderings a much more professional feel. You need to create a camera and animate it.

Master It   You decide to use the most expedient means to capture camera keyframe positions.

Solution   To create a new camera, do the following:

1. Use the view orientation tools to position the view to show what the camera would see in the first frame.

2. Right-click, and select Create Camera From View.

To animate the camera, do the following:

1. In the Animation Timeline window, in the drop-down list, select the new camera by name.

2. In the Animation Timeline window, set the time slider to the time position representing when you want the camera to be in another location.

3. In the Scene browser, right-click the new camera node, and click Animate Camera.

4. In the graphics region, use the view orientation tools to position the view to show what you want at that time position.

5. In the Animation Timeline window, click Add Camera Action.

Repeat as needed.

Start new animations, modify animations, and use the various animation tools
Animating your assemblies so that the function of the mechanism is showcased is often the purpose of an assembly animation.

Master It   You have an existing animation but want to do a variation on it. You want to copy and edit an existing animation.

Solution   Copy the animation:

1. In the Scene browser, expand the Animations node.

2. Right-click the animation for which you want to make a variation, and click Copy Animation.

3. Right-click the Animations folder, and click Paste Animation.

4. The Animations folder populates a new animation based on the selected animation.

Modify the animation:

1. Right-click the new animation, and click Activate.

2. In the Animation Timeline window, make modifications to actions as needed.

3. Add new actions as needed using the animation commands.

Use multiple cameras to create a video production of your animation   Video Producer provides the means to combine camera shots into a single video output.

Master It   You have created several cameras, animated and static, and want to make a composite animation.

Solution   Do the following:

1. In the Scene browser, expand the Productions node.

2. If no production exists, right-click the Productions node, and click New Production.

3. The cameras are loaded into the Video Producer window and ready for use.

4. Drag and drop shots into the timeline, and set their parameters.

5. Drag and drop the desired transitions between the shots.

Use props to enhance your scene   Inventor assemblies can be combined with other components to create a more realistic scene for rendering.

Master It   You have completed a design and want to render a realistic image of it in its working environment.

Solution   Do the following:

1. Create a new assembly that will be used as a wrapper assembly.

2. Place your product assembly in the new assembly.

3. Add any props, other parts, and other assemblies that make the scene more realistic.

Render realistic and illustrative images   Inventor provides the means to render both realistic and illustrative images.

Master It   With your new product nearing completion, the marketing department has asked for rendered images for marketing collateral and technical documents such as white papers.

Solution   To create a realistic rendering, do the following:

1. Prepare the scene with what you want to render.

2. Click the Render Image command.

3. In the Render Image dialog box, select Realistic as the render type.

4. Specify the camera, lighting, and scene styles to use.

5. Click Render.

To create an illustration rendering, do the following:

1. Prepare the scene with what you want to render.

2. Click the Render Image command.

3. In the Render Image dialog box, select Illustration as the render type.

4. Specify the camera, lighting, and scene styles to use.

5. On the Style tab, specify the appropriate settings for your rendering.

6. Click Render.

Render animations and video productions   Inventor provides the means to render animations and video productions.

Master It   You've created a wrapper assembly and set up the scene with cameras, lighting, and a scene style. Now you want to render an animation for design review and a video production for a multidiscipline review or marketing use.

Solution   To render the animation, do the following:

1. In the Scene browser, select and activate the animation you want to render.

2. Deactivate any active production. **Remember**: When a production is active, it is the render target. To render a single animation, you must deactivate any active production.

3. In the Studio tool panel, click Render Animation.

4. Specify the various styles to use and the render type.

5. Specify the output file type and other parameters.

6. Render the animation.

To render a production, do the following:

1. In the Scene browser, select and activate the production you want to render.

2. If you have not completed composing the production, you should do so.

3. In the Studio tool panel, click Render Animation.

4. Specify the various styles to use and the render type.

5. Specify the output file type and other parameters.

6. Render the animation.

Chapter 17: Stress Analysis and Dynamic Simulation

Set up and run Stress Analysis simulations   Oftentimes you may find yourself guessing at what impact a change to your design might have on the strength and overall integrity of your part. Questions such as "Can I make this part a bit lighter?" or "Can I move this cutout closer to the edge?" become key to the success of your design.

Master It   Set up a parameter study in your model to explore the consequences of editing features and their locations. Nominate all the crucial parameters to the table, and then create the configuration simulations for all of the combinations.

Solution   Interpret the results of the parameter study, looking for the configuration that promises to exhibit the results that come closest to your goals such as a target safety factor. Interrogate the various configurations to see which ones would be considered underbuilt and overbuilt, and then determine why. Understanding what works and doesn't work will allow you to get closer to the target from the beginning of the design process next time.

Set up and run Dynamic Simulation simulations   When you find yourself working out the details of a design with many moving parts, consider using the Dynamic Simulation tools early in the process to prove what will or will not work before going forward.

Master It   Even before the assembly is complete, switch over to the Dynamic Simulation environment, and create assembly constraints in the simulation. Test the motion as you build the parts, and attempt to understand how contact will occur from the beginning.

Solution   Enable the automatic assembly constraint option so that as you create constraints, standard joints are automatically created. Use the input grapher to design in the fourth dimension (time), understanding how a mechanism will or will not work as you go through the stages of its operation.

Export results from the Dynamic Simulation environment to the Stress Analysis environment   Often when setting up a stress analysis simulation you are guessing at what the loads might be based on rough calculations. As you make changes to the design, those calculations become out-of-date and therefore invalid.

Master It   Use the Dynamic Simulation tools to determine the force exerted on one part by another. When the parts are modified, the load calculations will automatically update based on the mass properties.

Solution   Export the FEA information for the crucial time steps from the Dynamic Simulation environment into the Stress Analysis environment, and run the simulation. This helps keep your calculations both accurate and up-to-date.

Chapter 18: Routed Systems

Create routes and runs   Using routed systems tools allows you to quickly define many different route types in order to check for clearance and fits within a design, all while creating a bill of materials that can be used downstream in the manufacturing process.

Master It   How can you extract a bill of materials from a routed systems assembly?

Solution   BOM data can be extracted from a routed systems assembly in the same way that it is in a standard assembly file, by using the Bill Of Materials button on the Assemble tab. Keep in mind that routed systems designs, by default, consist of subassemblies, which allows for greater control over the BOM data you extract.

Author a tube and pipe component   To create your own fittings, coupling, and so on, to be used within tube and pipe design, you need to first author it for use with the tube and pipe tools.

Master It   How can you set the depth at which pipe, tube, or hose segments are inserted into a fitting?

Solution   The pipe engagement is set during the tube and pipe component authoring process to determine how deep the segment will fit into the fitting. For butt weld–style components, the engagement is set to 0, since there is no insertion. Content Center components have the engagement positioning already set.

Author an electrical component   To create your own electrical connector components to be used within cable and harness designs, you need to first define pins within the parts.

Master It   How can you create a family of electrical connectors with varying numbers of pins?

Solution   First use the Place Pin or Place Pin Group tools to add the maximum number of pins to the connector part. Then convert the part to an iPart. In the iPart Author dialog box, use the Work Features tab to include only the pins required for each pin variation.

Create and document cable and harness assemblies   Cable and harness assemblies are created using a specific subassembly and part structure. Each harness is contained in a harness subassembly, and the parts such as wires, cables, and segments are created within a harness part file.

Master It   You have a complex design that includes many harness assemblies and would like to turn some of them off while you work on others and/or create new ones. What is the best way to do this?

Solution   You can create level-of-detail representations in cable and harness assemblies in much the same way that you would in a standard assembly. You can suppress an entire harness assembly and the harness part. But you cannot suppress other harness objects within the harness. Harness objects do not include connectors that are within the harness assembly. These can be suppressed.

Chapter 19: Plastics Design Features

Set up plastic part templates   Creating templates that are specific to your design work saves time, reduces the tedium of initial part creation, and is an efficient way to create consistency from one design to another.

> **Master It**   How do you create a template with design information focused on plastic part design?

> **Solution**   Start a new part file. Set up predefined user parameters according to the standard thickness, radii, draft angles, and so on. Then save the part to your template directory as a special plastics template.

Create thicken/offset features   When creating plastic parts, you will often find that working with surfaces allows you to achieve more free-form shapes than working with solids. Once the surfaces are created, you'll need to give them a thin wall thickness.

> **Master It**   How would you create a plastic part file with many curved, free-form elements?

> **Solution**   You can use the extrude and revolve features, among others, to create surface shapes that are much more free-form than what you can generally create with solid features. Once the surfaces are created, use the Thicken/Offset tool to give them a wall thickness.

Create shell features   Shelling solids parts and features is a common way to create base features for plastic parts. Once the shell feature is created, other features can be added to it.

> **Master It**   You want to create a shell feature but need to have the thickness of some faces be thicker than the rest. How would you accomplish this?

> **Solution**   You can use the >> button to expand the Unique Thickness option in the Shell tool dialog box to specify faces that require unique face thicknesses. Or you can use the Thicken/Offset tool to change the thickness of faces after a shell is created.

Create split features   Many times you may want to establish the overall shape of the feature and then divide the shape into separate parts of the overall design. You can use the Split tool to do just that and more.

> **Master It**   You have a plastic part that needs to have a raised face for a rubber grip applied during the manufacturing process. How would this be done?

> **Solution**   Use the Split tool to create a surface that is unique to the rubber grip area, and then use the Thicken/Offset tool to build up the rubber face.

Create grill features   Grill features allow the inflow or outflow of air through a plastic thin wall part. Grills can be created with a number of subfeatures such as islands, ribs, and spars, but only the outer profile of the grill is required.

> **Master It**   How would you determine the area of a grill opening to determine the airflow that it can handle?

> **Solution**   Edit the sketch that the grill feature was created from, and then use the Measure Region tool to determine the general area of the opening. Or create a sketch on the grill and project all of the islands, ribs, and spars into the sketch, and then use the Measure Region tool on it to determine the exact area of the opening.

Create rule fillet features   Rule fillets can be an extremely efficient way to apply fillets to many edges throughout the design that meet the same rule criteria.

> **Master It**   How would you apply fillets to all the edges that are generated by extruding a shape down to an existing set of base features?
>
> **Solution**   Use the Rule Fillet tool with the source set to the new extruded shape, the rule set to Against Features, and the scope set to include all the base features to include intersecting fillets. If this feature changes to create new edges or remove existing edges that fit the rule, the fillets are added or removed automatically.

Create rest features   Rest features can be used to create level platform faces for mounting other parts to an irregular plastic part face.

> **Master It**   You want to create a rectangular pocket on the inside of a plastic housing to hold an electronic component. How would you do this?
>
> **Solution**   Create a sketch on a work plane that defines the shape of the pocket. The work plane location will define the orientation. Use the Rest tool to create the pocket, using the options in the Rest tool to achieve the exact result you require.

Create boss features   Boss features are ideal for creating fastener-mounting standoffs for thin wall plastic parts. You can use the Boss tool to create both halves of the fastener boss.

> **Master It**   You want to create multiple boss features around the perimeter of a flat, pan-type, base part, but you know this base part is likely to change size. How would you set up the boss features to adjust to the anticipated edits?
>
> **Solution**   You can create a 2D sketch on a work plane that defines the height of the bosses. Use the Offset tool in the sketch environment to create an offset loop based on the perimeter of the part. Add sketch center points at all the required locations. Ensure that the offset loop and the sketch center points are fully constrained and dimensioned, and then use these points when creating the boss feature.

Create lip and groove features   When designing plastic parts, it is often required that one half of a design fit into the other half. The Lip tool allows you to create both lip and groove features for these situations.

> **Master It**   You want to create a groove around the edge of an irregular, curved edge. How would you ensure the lip on the corresponding part would match?
>
> **Solution**   Use the clearance height to remove uneven mating surfaces during the lip and groove creation, ensuring a proper fit.

Create snap fit features   Snap features are a common way to join plastic parts together so that they can be disassembled as needed. You can use the Snap Fit tool in Inventor to quickly create these features.

> **Master It**   How would you create a U-shaped snap fit with the Snap Fit tool?
>
> **Solution**   Use the standard sketch and extrude methods to create the base of the U-shape. Then use the Snap Fit tool to add the snap and loop as needed.

Create rib and web features   Ribs and webs are often used to add rigidity and prevent warping during the design of plastic parts. You can add ribs based on open profile sketches in Inventor.

> **Master It**   How would you create a network of ribs that are evenly spaced, where some of them contain different cutouts than others?

> **Solution**   Create an open profile sketch for the first single rib. Then use the Rib tool to create it. Use the Rectangular Pattern tool to pattern the rib as needed, and then create the cutout profile and use the Extrude tool to cut the shape from the first rib. Then pattern the cutout to match the rib pattern. Finally, suppress the cutouts you do not need.

Create draft features   Because plastic parts must be extracted from a mold during the manufacturing process, drafted faces must be included to ensure the parts can indeed be extracted from the mold.

> **Master It**   You want to create drafted faces on a complex part containing various shapes within it. How would you do this?

> **Solution**   Start the Draft tool, and then click the Help button in the lower-left corner; or just press F1 on the keyboard. This will open the help page specifically for the Draft tool. Expand the nodes on the Concept tab to explore the examples of the different results achieved by the different inputs. Use the various methods throughout the part where they will provide the correct result. Set up work planes to help establish fixed-plane faces.

Create an injection mold   To generate the components you have designed with the plastic part features, you need to properly define the cavity to create the part and define how the material will flow into the cavity

> **Master It**   You want to create a mold base design in an efficient manner using parts that can be purchased.

> **Solution**   Use the many steps of the Inventor Tooling package to properly define the core and cavity. Then use the analysis tools to ensures that the part will be made correctly. Finally use the library of features included with Inventor to construct the mold base assembly.

Appendix B

The Autodesk Certification Exams

Mastering Inventor 2011 and Inventor LT 2011 has been selected by Autodesk to be an official training guide for its Inventor 2011 professional certification exams. There are two levels of certification: the Certified Associate level and the Certified Professional level. The exam for the Certified Associate level consists of 30 computer-administered questions that include multiple choice, matching, and point-and-click. The exam for the Certified Professional level is a performance-based test that requires you to perform tasks in Inventor in addition to answering questions.

To help you focus your studies on the skills you'll need for these exams, we've included two tables: Table F.1 lists the sections and objectives for the Certified Associate exam, and Table F.2 lists them for the Certified Professional exam. The Section and Exam Objectives list in the tables are from the Autodesk Certification Exam Guide. These tables can direct you to the chapters in this book that will help you master the objectives for each exam.

Inventor 2011 Exam Preparation Roadmap

Autodesk certifications are industry-recognized credentials that can help you succeed in your design career—providing benefits to both you and your employer. Autodesk certifications are a reliable validation of skills and knowledge, and can lead to accelerated professional development, improved productivity, and enhanced credibility.

Autodesk highly recommends that you structure your examination preparation for success. This means scheduling regular time to prepare, reviewing this exam preparation roadmap, using Autodesk Official Training Guides, taking an Assessment test, and using a variety of resources to prepare for your certification. Equally as important, actual hands-on experience is recommended.

The Inventor 2011 Certified Associate exam consists of 30 questions that assess your knowledge of the tools, features, and common tasks of Autodesk Inventor. Question types include multiple choice, matching, and point and click (hotspot). The exam has a one-hour time limit (in some countries the time limit may be extended).

The Autodesk Inventor 2011 Certified Professional exam is a performance-based test. The exam is comprised of 20 questions. Each question requires you to use Inventor 2011 to create or modify a data file, and then type your answer into an input box. The answer you enter will be either a text entry or a numeric value. The exam has a 90-minute time limit (in some countries the time limit may be extended).

To earn the credential of Inventor 2011 Certified Professional, you must also pass the Inventor 2011 Certified Associate exam. You can pass the exams in any order.

To recertify from Inventor 2011 Professional to Inventor 2011 Professional, you need only pass the Inventor 2011 Certified Associate exam.

ASSESSMENT TESTS

Autodesk assessment tests will help identify areas of knowledge that you should develop in order to prepare for the certification exam. At the completion you will be able to review the items you missed and their correct answers. Contact an Autodesk Certification Center for more information at http://autodesk.starttest.com.

ATC® INSTRUCTOR-LED COURSES

The Autodesk Authorized Training Center (ATC®) program is a global network of professional training providers offering a broad range of learning resources. Visit the online ATC locator at www.autodesk.com/atc.

RECOMMENDED EXPERIENCE LEVELS FOR INVENTOR 2011 CERTIFICATION EXAMS

Actual hands-on experience is a critical component in preparing for the exam. You must spend time using the product and applying the skills you have learned.

2011 Certified Associate Exam

Mastering Inventor 2011 course (or equivalent) plus 100 hours of hands-on application

2011 Certified Professional Exam

Mastering Inventor 2011 course (or equivalent) plus 400 hours of hands-on application

---

TABLE F.1:   Certified Associate exam sections and objectives

TOPIC	OBJECTIVE	CHAPTER
User Interface	Describe how to use the heads up display (HUD) to create and edit features	3
	Identify how to use visual styles to control the appearance of a model	2
Project Files	Describe the options for controlling a project file	2
Sketching	Recall the function of each sketch constraint	3
	Demonstrate how to create dynamic input dimensions	3
Part Modeling	Create extrude features	4
	Create fillet features	4
	Create hole features	4
	Create a pattern of features	5

TABLE F.1:   Certified Associate exam sections and objectives *(CONTINUED)*

TOPIC	OBJECTIVE	CHAPTER
	Describe how to use the Project Geometry and Project Cut Edges commands	3
	Create revolve features	4
	Create a shell feature	5
	Create work features and a UCS	4 & 13
Drawing	Explain how to edit a base and projected views	12
	Describe how to create a slice view in a drawing	12
	Demonstrate how to create and edit dimensions in a drawing	12
	Describe how to edit a hole table	12
	Describe how to modify a parts list	12
	Demonstrate how to edit a section view	12
Assembly Modeling	Describe the process of finding the minimum distance between parts and components	8
	Describe the function of the different assembly constraints	8
	Describe how to modify a bill of materials	8
	Explain the method of creating a frame using the frame generator command	15
	Identify uses for surfaces in the modeling process	5, 6, & 19
Presentation Files	Describe how to animate a presentation file	12
Advanced Modeling	Describe the process to emboss text and a profile	4
	Create and constrain sketch blocks	8
	Describe the process of creating an iAssembly	8
	Describe the process to create an iPart	7
Sheet Metal	Demonstrate how to create and edit a sheet-metal flat pattern	6
	Describe the different types of sheet-metal flanges that Inventor can create	6
	Demonstrate how to annotate a sheet-metal part in a drawing	6

TABLE F.2:   Certified Professional exam sections and objectives

TOPIC	OBJECTIVE	CHAPTER
Part Modeling	Create extrude features	4
	Create hole features	4
Drawing	Demonstrate how to edit a section view	12
	Create a slice view in a drawing	12
	Demonstrate how to modify a style in a drawing	12
Assembly Modeling	Apply assembly constraints	8
	Create a part in the context of an assembly	8
	Create components using the Design Accelerator commands	11
	Create and edit a frame using the Frame Generator command	15
	Create a level of detail	8 & 9
	Create a positional representation	8
Advanced Modeling	Create a 3D path using the Intersection Curve and the Project to Surface commands	3
	Create a multi-body part	4 & 5
	Create a part using surfaces	4 & 5
	Create an iPart	7
	Create a loft feature	5
	Create plastic part features	19
	Create a sweep feature	5
Sheet Metal	Create flanges using the Flange, Contour Flange, and Lofted Flange commands	6
Weldments	Create a weldment	10

Index

Note to the Reader: Throughout this index **boldfaced** page numbers indicate primary discussions of a topic. *Italicized* page numbers indicate illustrations.